HANDBOOKS

W9-BEL-191

MONTANA
& WYOMING

CARTER G. WALKER

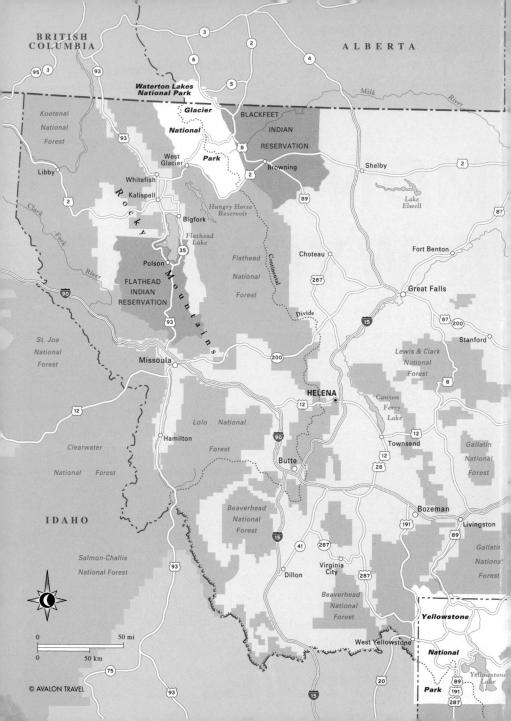

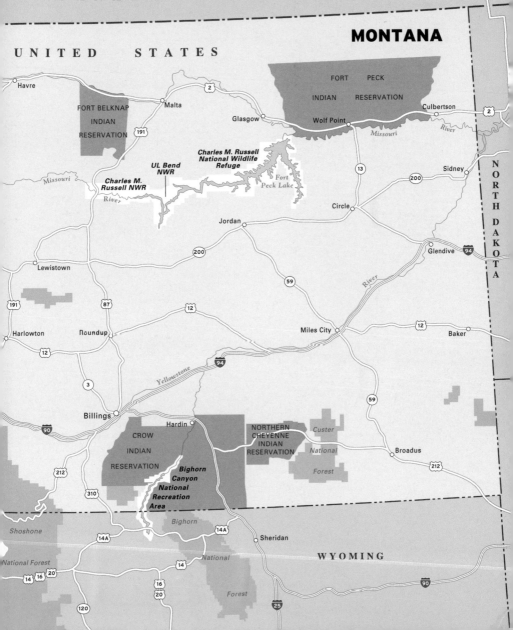

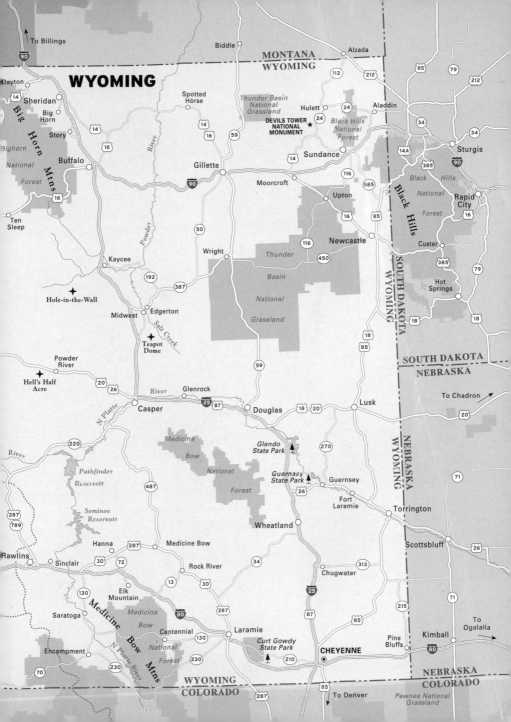

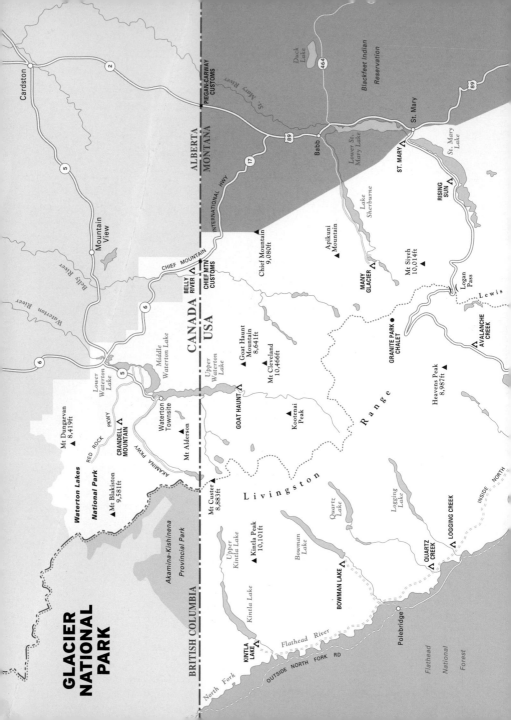

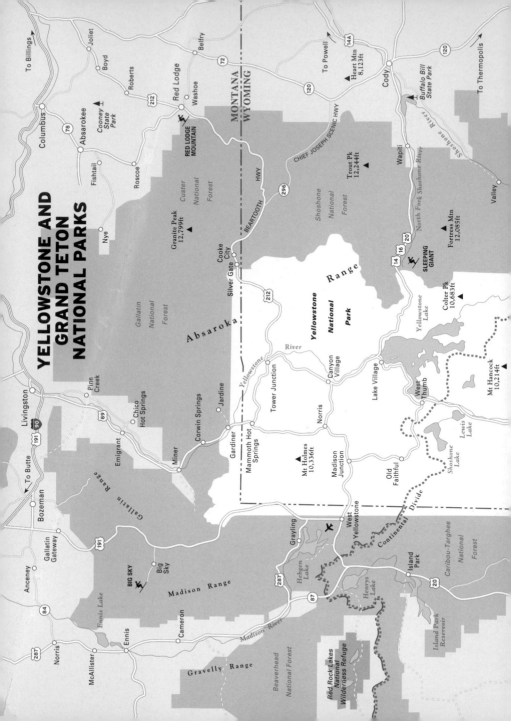

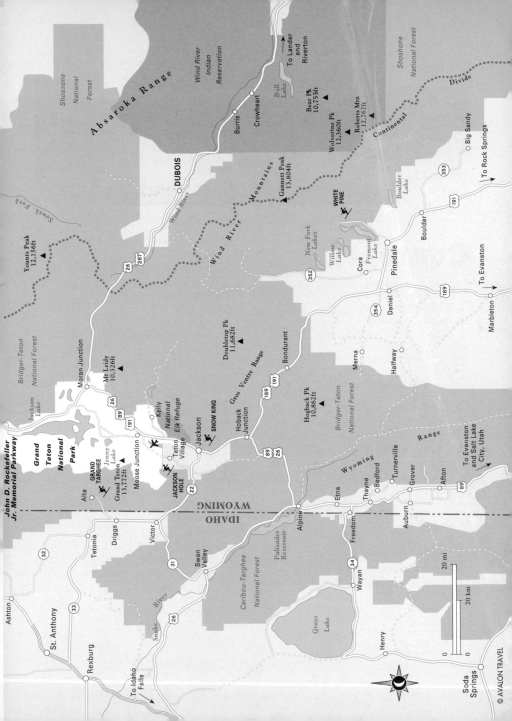

Contents

Discover
Montana & Wyoming

The rocky landscapes of Montana and Wyoming – from soaring mountains to narrow valleys and sweeping plains – were carved over eons by water, wind, fire, and ice. The culture was also shaped by conflict: between those who were from here and those who were not; those who valued the land itself and those who sought only its riches. Although their distinct histories, both natural and cultural, are evident everywhere, not just tucked away in dusty museums, these states continue to define themselves. Wyoming's Tetons thrust skyward at the rate of an inch or so each year. Montana's blue-ribbon trout streams, tumbling and falling, etch themselves deeper into valleys. The populations are perpetually shifting too, bringing new ideas, new conflicts, and an evolving culture.

Montana is as vast as the big sky that blankets it; rich with natural resources – fertile soil, coal, gold, forests, wind – and overflowing with beauty. From Glacier National Park to the Little Bighorn, its sites are enchanting, and sometimes haunting. Its communities are diverse too, with pioneer traditions embraced by new generations of transplants in cities like Bozeman, where ski bums and artists mingle with fifth-generation farmers. Then there are tiny towns like Loma, at the confluence of the Milk and Marias Rivers, where the headline is still that Lewis and Clark camped just south of town in 1805. Montana's cities make us aware of

the constant growth in the American West, while little dots on the map like Loma remind us of its almost magical timelessness.

Embodied by the bucking bronc on its license plates, Wyoming is a child's cowboy fantasy come to life, with rodeos aplenty and dude ranches where even city slickers try their hand at riding and roping. But what strikes people most about Wyoming is its authenticity. The harsh climate and isolation that make Wyoming the least populated state in the union result in an uncommon grace in its residents. It's expressed not just in the weathered creases on their faces but in the way they do business and welcome visitors. There is glitz here too, in places like Jackson Hole, but it doesn't detract from the essence of Wyoming. Those towns are simply a flash of silver, the shiny buckle on a well-worn belt.

Separated by history, culture, and even politics, Montana and Wyoming are still ideal neighbors, bound together by the forces of nature that make them so captivating.

Planning Your Trip

▶ WHERE TO GO

Billings and the Big Open

Beyond Billings, the state's largest and most industrial city, much of eastern Montana is made up of small but tightly knit communities separated by vast swaths of wide open country. It's also where four of the state's seven Indian reservations can be found. The landscapes are varied and dramatic—from the rimrocks in Billings and the rolling hills around the Little Bighorn Battlefield to the badlands of Makoshika State Park outside Glendive.

Great Falls and the Rocky Mountain Front

The vast plains erupt into soaring peaks along the Rocky Mountain Front—perhaps Montana's most under-appreciated region. The Bob Marshall Wilderness is one of the most spectacular and isolated mountainous areas in the Lower 48. Tiny towns like Choteau and Fort Benton offer a charming sense of community, along with fascinating sites like dinosaur mecca Egg Mountain and lovely historic hotels. Straddling the division between mountains and plains, Great Falls boasts two of the state's best museums: The C. M. Russell Art Museum and the Lewis and Clark National Historic Trail Interpretive Center.

Glacier National Park

"Crown of the Continent," Glacier National Park embodies the Montana you've always imagined: rugged mountains piercing the sky, crystalline lakes and plunging waterfalls, abundant wildlife, gravity-defying roads, and miles upon miles of trails. The park still lays

the Rocky Mountain Front, Montana

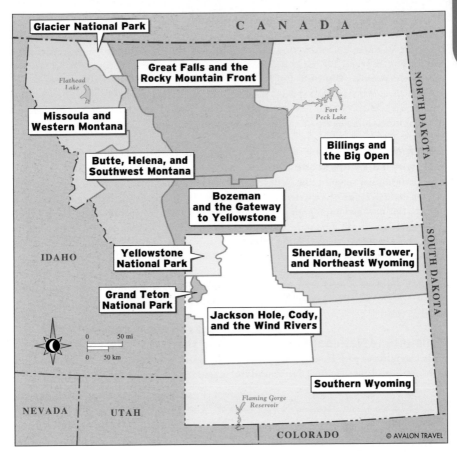

Glacier National Park

Great Falls and the Rocky Mountain Front

Missoula and Western Montana

Butte, Helena, and Southwest Montana

Billings and the Big Open

Bozeman and the Gateway to Yellowstone

Yellowstone National Park

Sheridan, Devils Tower, and Northeast Wyoming

Grand Teton National Park

Jackson Hole, Cody, and the Wind Rivers

Southern Wyoming

CANADA

NORTH DAKOTA

SOUTH DAKOTA

IDAHO

NEVADA

UTAH

COLORADO

Flathead Lake

Fort Peck Lake

Flaming Gorge Reservoir

0   50 mi

0   50 km

© AVALON TRAVEL

claim to 50 glaciers, which sadly are rapidly melting. You need little more than a sense of adventure, a few layers of clothes, some GORP, and some pepper spray to enjoy it all.

Missoula and Western Montana

Western Montana shows off with lush green mountain ranges and towering forests. In the far north, Whitefish is the ultimate mountain town, a skier's paradise. Just south, glittering Flathead Lake is Montana's Riviera, with glamorous mansions and luxe lodges at the water's edge. The town of Big Fork serves up

the finest in culture and cuisine. The scenic National Bison Range in Moiese can be visited en route to cultural hub Missoula, home of the University of Montana, great restaurants, and better bars. In the southwest corner of the state, the Bitterroot Valley combines a rich history with world-class fly fishing.

Butte, Helena, and Southwest Montana

This corner of the state wears its history like a badge of honor in mining towns like Bannack, Virginia City, and Nevada

City. Some of the other towns that survived the dramatic boom and bust cycles include charming Victorian Philipsburg and Butte, and Helena, the venerable state capital. Then there is the sweeping Big Hole Valley, with picturesque ranches and hot springs resorts, and the Big Hole National Battlefield, one of the most haunting battle sites in the state.

Bozeman and the Gateway to Yellowstone

The communities surrounding Yellowstone offer a diverse range of experiences. From skiing, fishing, and an abundance of outdoor adventures in the mountain and college town of Bozeman to the art and culinary scenes just over the pass in Livingston, the area's culture is as rich as its landscape. Big Sky and Red Lodge offer resorts with skiable terrain as well as some terrific places to stay.

Yellowstone National Park

This magnificent park is constantly in motion; nothing here is static. See abundant wildlife, including bison, bears, and wolves, marvel at geothermal features like the legendary Old Faithful, and stay in marvelous historic lodges like the Old Faithful Inn and the rambling Lake Hotel. Perimeter communities, including West Yellowstone, Gardiner, and remote Cooke City should not be missed.

Grand Teton National Park

Grand Teton packs some serious punch, particularly when it comes to mountain splendor. Twelve peaks in the Teton Range soar above 12,000 feet. While there are only 100 miles of roads in the park, there are twice as many miles of trails, leaving hikers endless options for adventure. Favorite landmarks include picturesque Jenny Lake, vast Jackson Lake, drive-to-the-summit Signal Mountain, and serene Oxbow Bend.

Jackson Hole, Cody, and the Wind Rivers

Wyoming's northwest corner is far more than a gateway to Yellowstone and Grand Teton

horse-drawn sleigh rides at the National Elk Refuge near Jackson, Wyoming

National Parks. Jackson Hole is a destination in and of itself, with glitzy galleries and boutiques, gourmet eateries, luxe accommodations, and a sensational art scene in immediate proximity to world-class ski resorts and white-water rafting. The National Museum of Wildlife Art and the National Elk Refuge are major draws for animal enthusiasts. In Cody the cowboy is still king, and the sun rises and sets on the Buffalo Bill Historical Center and its five museums. Farther south, outdoor enthusiasts will find hot springs and mountain meccas.

Sheridan, Devils Tower, and Northeast Wyoming

Where the prairies meet the mountains, cowboy culture comes alive. This is where you'll find dude ranches and Sheridan, one of the most charming and authentic Western towns in the state. The spectacular Cloud Peak Scenic Byway climbs into the mountains toward the pictograph-rich Medicine Lodge and the more mysterious Medicine Wheel. The isolated and enigmatic Devils Tower draws climbers, geologists, and Native Americans who consider it a sacred site.

Southern Wyoming

Southern Wyoming contains everything from sweeping deserts, sand dunes, and wild mustang herds to lush river valleys and green mountains. The southwest corner is noted for fabulous recreational opportunities along the Green River and in the Flaming Gorge National Recreation Area. It's also home to three of the state's largest cities: capital Cheyenne, synonymous with its legendary Frontier Days rodeo, college town Laramie, and onetime frontier town Casper.

▶ WHEN TO GO

Summer is the easiest (and busiest) time to travel the roads, both front- and backcountry, in Montana and Wyoming. Thoughtful planning and advance reservations, particularly for hotels and campgrounds, are essential. Hotel rooms are particularly hard to find during local events such as Frontier Days in Cheyenne or the Fourth of July celebration in Livingston, so check your calendar. Rates for accommodations are generally lower and rooms more available when snow is on the ground, except around ski areas, but winter road travel can be challenging because of the inevitable storms and possible closures. The shoulder seasons can be a delightful time to travel in both states. The national parks are heavenly and much less crowded in autumn, but keep in mind that winter comes very early at high elevations. There are also little-known ways to enjoy the parks by bicycle in the spring, before they open to cars.

Don't try to see too much in too short a time. This cannot be overstated. Consider that the drive from Montana's eastern border to its western border is 550 miles, about the same distance as from Chicago to New York. Don't spend so much time on the road that you miss the small details—idyllic hikes, roadside burger joints, the local people who give small towns their true character—that make Montana and Wyoming what they are. Trust me on this: In Montana and Wyoming, less is more.

Explore Montana & Wyoming

► THE 14-DAY GREATER YELLOWSTONE LOOP

With Yellowstone National Park at its heart, this generous two-week itinerary starts and ends in Bozeman, Montana, never exceeding 200 miles of travel in a single day. See and experience this breathtaking region without getting stuck behind the wheel.

Day 1: Bozeman

Start your trip in Bozeman, equal parts college town and mountain town. Fit in a trip to the Museum of the Rockies to see where dinosaur guru Jack Horner does much of his work. Throw in a hike up the M or Drinking Horse Mountain, just northeast of town, and end with a shopping stroll on historic

The roads go on forever in eastern Montana.

Main Street. Enjoy a game of pool, a local brew, and an excellent meal at the popular Montana Ale Works. Bed down for the night practically across the street at the Magpie Guest House.

Day 2: Bozeman to Red Lodge (About 174 Miles)

Start your morning with a quick jaunt up Peet's Hill, then walk a few blocks for breakfast at the Western Café. Head east toward Red Lodge, a much smaller but equally historic ski town. Along the way, stop in Livingston to peruse art galleries, look for celebrities, or even fish or raft the Yellowstone. Continue on to Big Timber for a late lunch at the Grand Hotel. Arrive in Red Lodge in time for a quick meal at the Red Box Car and a downy bed at historic Pollard Hotel.

Day 3: Red Lodge

After a leisurely breakfast, stroll by the shops up and down Broadway, and check out the critters at the Beartooth Nature Center. Later, grab some picnic supplies at Café Regis and head out on a scenic hike in the Beartooths, perhaps the Nichols Creek Trail. Back in town, enjoy a sumptuous meal at Bridge Creek Backcountry Kitchen and Wine Bar.

Day 4: Red Lodge to Cody (About 114 Miles)

Experience two of the most breathtaking drives in the region. Pack a picnic lunch and head up and over the Beartooth Highway

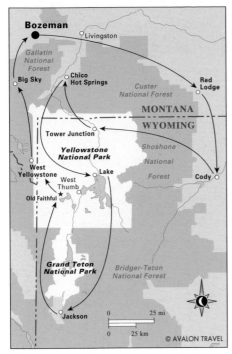

grab a cocktail and step outside to watch the Cody Gunfighters. After dinner, head over to the Cody Nite Rodeo for a two-hour action-packed show with local cowboys and cowgirls.

Day 6: Cody to Tower Junction (About 111 Miles)

On your way out of town, stop by Old Trail Town and the Museum of the West. Then head farther west on the Buffalo Bill Scenic Byway toward Yellowstone's east entrance. Stop for a bite at Buffalo Bill Cody's historic Pahaska Tepee resort. Once inside the park, check out the phenomenal Grand Canyon of the Yellowstone and the wildlife-rich Hayden Valley on your way to Tower Junction and the classic Roosevelt Lodge. Arrive in time to ride horseback (or travel by covered wagon) to the Old West Cookout Dinner. Then retire to your rustic cabin under the stars.

Day 7: Tower Junction to Paradise Valley (About 59 Miles)

Early birds will delight in a sunrise drive through the famed Lamar Valley for amazing opportunities to spot wildlife, including wolves and bears. Consider a hike up to Trout Lake or maybe meander along the trout waters of Slough Creek. Turn around and head back north to Mammoth Hot Springs, where you can amble around the colorful geothermal features. For lunch, try the mini trout tacos at the Mammoth Hotel Dining Room and Terrace Grill, just below the geothermal terraces. On your way out of the park, perhaps you'll want to soak in the Boiling River between Mammoth and Gardiner, or just wait until you arrive at Chico Hot Springs to enjoy the naturally heated waters. After a gourmet dinner, settle in to Chico for the night and listen for Percy, the resident ghost.

(Hwy. 212), and be sure to make plenty of stops along the way. Look for mountain goats at the summit. Consider an alpine hike: The Clay Butte Fire Lookout Tower, only a mile from the highway, puts you above 11,000 feet; the eight-mile scenic loop around Beartooth Lake offers level terrain with spectacular scenery. Stop in Cooke City if you need for a shot of civilization, or continue to the Chief Joseph Scenic Highway (Hwy. 296) south to Cody. Arrive in time for a fantastic dinner at Geysers on the Terrace and a cozy room at the Chamberlin Inn.

Day 5: Cody

After breakfast, head out on the hour-long Cody Trolley Tour, which includes tickets to the Buffalo Bill Historical Center. Spend most of the day exploring its five museums. Before dinner at the celebrated Irma Hotel,

NATIVE AMERICAN ROOTS

The culture and lives of indigenous people have powerfully defined the identities of both Montana and Wyoming. Both states offer tremendous opportunities for those interested in learning about and experiencing Native American history, traditions, and contemporary life.

Blackfeet Cultural History Tours
Step-on guided trips of the Blackfeet Reservation take guests to buffalo jumps, tipi rings, and medicine lodges. Tours often include visits to the **Museum of the Plains Indian.**

Big Hole National Battlefield
This moving historical sites site bears witness to the battle between Chief Joseph's band of Nez Perce and the U.S. Army.

Little Bighorn Battlefield National Monument
This is where thousands of Cheyenne, Sioux, and Arapaho warriors fought under such legendary figures as Sitting Bull and Crazy Horse. Lieutenant Colonel George Armstrong Custer and more than 200 men from his 7th Cavalry died in the brief battle. A wonderful way to explore the monument is by hiring a Native American guide through **Apsalooke Tours.**

Crow Fair
Held the third week in August every year since 1904, Crow Fair is considered the largest outdoor powwow in the world. More than 12,000 people camp out in more than 1,500 tipis erected on the banks of the Little Bighorn River.

Medicine Wheel National Historic Landmark
This mysterious carved stone wheel has spiritual but unexplained significance to many Native American tribes. Interpretive tours are offered by local Native American guides.

Devils Tower
This iconic rocky sentinel, the first national monument in the country, is considered sacred by numerous tribes, all of whom have unique origin stories for it. A voluntary climbing closure is in effect each June out of respect for various Native American ceremonies.

Colter Bay Indian Arts Museum
This museum in Grand Teton National Park is packed with important Native American artifacts that belonged to tribes from across the country. In summer, various Native American artisans practice their crafts, and prominent lecturers and daily educational events are scheduled on-site.

Wind River Reservation
Wyoming's only reservation is home to about 5,000 Northern Arapaho and some 2,500 Eastern Shoshone Indians. Sights of interest include the **Shoshone Tribal Cultural Center** and the grave sites of the two most prominent Shoshone Indians, **Chief Washakie** and Lewis and Clark's guide, **Sacagawea.**

The best time to visit is during the annual three-day powwows. The largest Shoshone powwow is the **Eastern Shoshone Indian Days Powwow and Rodeo,** held the fourth weekend in June. The largest Arapaho powwow is the **Ethete Powwow** in late July.

Day 8: Paradise Valley to Lake, Wyoming (About 91 Miles)

Backtrack through the park's northern entrance. River rats should take a morning raft trip on the Yellowstone River through Yankee Jim Canyon. Inside the park, head to Norris for another education in geology and supervolcanology. Then head to Canyon—check out the canyon or the falls from another angle, or even on a trail like Uncle Tom's Trail, which will take you to the spectacular Lower Falls. Wind up your day with a cocktail on the porch and a relaxing dinner at the idyllic Lake Hotel.

barn set against the backdrop of the Tetons

Day 9: Lake to Jackson (About 95 Miles)

After a morning stroll at water's edge, head down to West Thumb Geyser Basin, an incredible selection of geothermal features. From there, continue south to Grand Teton National Park. You'll pass this way again in two days, so don't feel pressured to stop at every scenic turnout. Grab lunch along the way and stop by the Colter Bay Indian Arts Museum. Try a hike along the gentle Lakeshore Trail, then continue down to Jackson and settle in at the Anvil Motel. Walk just a few blocks for dinner at the Snake River Grill, and perhaps a nightcap at the famous Million Dollar Cowboy Bar.

Day 10: Jackson Hole

Hit the local favorite—The Bunnery—for a hearty breakfast. White-water enthusiasts will have no shortage of options on the Snake River; mountain bikers and hikers can hit the alpine slopes at either Snow King in town or off the fabulous gondola at Jackson Hole Mountain Resort, or consider horseback riding. If you have the energy in the afternoon, visit the National Museum of Wildlife Art before grabbing a bite at Pica's. Wednesday and Saturday nights you can catch the Jackson Rodeo.

Day 11: Jackson to Old Faithful (About 98 Miles)

After breakfast, head north toward Grand Teton and Yellowstone. Stop at Jenny Lake for a hike to Hidden Falls or Inspiration Point, a boat ride, or just a picnic. Continue north through Grand Teton, checking out the sights you missed on the way down. Once

A wily coyote scampers through Yellowstone National Park.

sharing the road

in Yellowstone, drive north and west to Old Faithful and stay at the Old Faithful Inn for the night. There are great trails along the way, including an easy jaunt to Lone Star Geyser. Explore the area before settling in for dinner and a bed at the inn. If you can keep your eyes open, Old Faithful eruptions in the moonlight are pretty unforgettable.

Day 12: Old Faithful to West Yellowstone (About 32 Miles)

After a leisurely morning, head north and then west to the town of West Yellowstone. Enjoy this small but dense section of the park on your way out. Don't miss the opportunity to swim in the thermally heated waters of the Firehole River. In West Yellowstone, check out the Grizzly and Wolf Discovery Center and the adjacent Yellowstone IMAX Theater. Grab a bison burger at Buckaroo Bill's Ice Cream before calling it a night at the Three Bear Lodge.

Day 13: West Yellowstone to Big Sky (About 51 Miles)

Head over to the Freeheel & Wheel to rent a bike and then hit the famous Rendezvous Trails, where Olympic Nordic skiers have trained. After lunch, continue north through the scenic Gallatin Canyon toward Big Sky Resort. There are countless hiking trails and fishing spots along the way. Plan on spending the night at the Big Sky Resort; head to dinner in the nearby Timbers Restaurant at Moonlight Basin.

Day 14: Big Sky to Bozeman (About 44 Miles)

Start your day with a short hike to scenic Ousel Falls and then jump in a Geyser Whitewater raft to white-knuckle it down the canyon. Then head back to Bozeman to enjoy the mountain vistas and toast your trip over a bison steak or burger at Ted's Montana Grill.

▶ SEVEN-DAY GLACIER ROAD TRIP

Start your tour of Montana's magnificent northwest corner in Missoula, the hometown of *A River Runs Through It* author Norman Maclean and dozens of the state's literary heroes. Although the city is surrounded by wilderness, the University of Montana community gives the town something of an urban vibe…for Montana, anyway. Those who want to spend less time on the road could start and finish the journey in Kalispell. Because of the mountain terrain, the driving time is often much longer than the mileage suggests.

Day 1: Missoula to Big Fork (About 100 Miles)

Arrive in Missoula; check out the shops on Higgins Avenue, the hip Missoula Art Museum, and walk along the lovely riverfront trails. Next, head north toward Glacier country. At Ravalli, choose your direction—northwest toward the National Bison Range at Moiese or northeast to the historic mission at St. Ignatius. The forks come together again just south of Ronan, where you'll continue north along the east shore of Flathead Lake to the waterfront village of Big Fork. Stop along the way to gorge yourself on Flathead cherries, or just to stretch your legs and wet your toes in the lake. In Big Fork, settle in at the Mountain Lake Lodge for two restful nights.

Day 2: Big Fork

Try white-water rafting on the Flathead River or sea kayaking on the lake with the Flathead Raft Company, or rent your own craft at Bigfork Water Sports. Take an incredible hike—maybe to Black Lake or Twin Lakes—in the nearby Jewel Basin. Leave some time for browsing the cute shops around town, and reward yourself with a gourmet dinner at Coyote Roadhouse.

Day 3: Big Fork to Whitefish (About 34 Miles)

Start your day at the Echo Lake Café before heading north toward Kalispell, where you can check out the contemporary art scene at the Hockaday Museum of Art. Consider a hike or bike ride at Whitefish Mountain Resort. Consider hiking the Danny On Trail, just 3.8 miles to the summit, and then a gondola ride down. For dinner, try the Wasabi Sushi Bar, then wander the art galleries and boutiques. Settle in for the night at the Duck Inn.

Day 4: Whitefish to Many Glacier (About 94 Miles)

Get a hearty breakfast at Buffalo Café & Nightly Grill before heading into Glacier

WHERE THE WILD THINGS ARE

Appreciating wildlife is as much a part of the culture as mountains are part of the landscape. The most obvious choice for prime wildlife viewing is Yellowstone National Park, where animals have the right of way; just try telling a herd of rutting bison that you have to be somewhere. Grand Teton and Glacier National Parks are also great bets, although the restricted roads and dense forests can limit visibility. Both states are packed with public lands and refuges (Wyoming has seven national wildlife refuges, and Montana has 15) that offer prime habitat to any number of species.

Montana

- **Medicine Lake National Wildlife Refuge** is in fact two wildlife refuges and a wetland management district that host more birds than you could ever imagine.

- Located in **Moiese** between the Flathead and Missoula, **National Bison Range** is home to around 400 bison, along with white-tailed and mule deer, bighorn sheep, pronghorn antelope, and elk.

- About 30 miles south of Missoula in **Stevensville**, the **Lee Metcalf National Wildlife Refuge** provides habitat for migratory birds including ospreys, eagles, and hawks as well

as larger animals including wolves, coyotes, black bears, and badgers.

- Near **Lima,** the **Red Rock Lake National Wildlife Refuge** hosts more than 230 species of birds – including the once-endangered trumpeter swan – and other wildlife including bears, wolves, and moose.

Wyoming

- Just outside **Jackson,** the **National Elk Refuge** is home to more than 7,000 elk throughout the winter months.

- In **Dubois,** the **National Bighorn Sheep Interpretive Center** offers winter tours of the nearby **Whiskey Mountain Habitat Area.** Self-guided tours take visitors into prime sheep country, where waterfowl, raptors, and moose can often be seen as well.

- North of **Green River,** the wetland habitat of the **Seedskadee National Wildlife Refuge** hosts some 200 bird species, including Canada geese, great blue herons, and swans.

- Just north of **Rock Springs,** the **White Mountains** are home to 800-1,000 wild mustangs. Pronghorn, sage grouse, coyotes, and eagles also frequent the region.

National Park. Stop at Lake McDonald to soak in the majestic beauty, and prepare yourself for the vistas still ahead on the Going-to-the-Sun Road. Stop for a hike; the Hidden Lake Overlook from Logan Pass is a stunner. Continue east out of the park through St. Mary and Babb, where you can treat yourself to dinner at Two Sisters Café before heading back into the phenomenal Many Glacier valley to camp or stay at the historic Many Glacier Hotel.

Day 5: Many Glacier

Plan to spend the day adventuring around

Many Glacier. Possible activities include an endless number of hiking trails and canoeing, kayaking, or cruising on Swiftcurrent Lake. One option is to combine a scenic cruise with a hike to Grinnell Glacier. Other options include ranger-led hikes and Red Bus Tours. For dinner, try the fondue in the Ptarmigan Dining Room at the Many Glacier Hotel.

Day 6: Many Glacier to East Glacier (About 46 Miles)

After a morning hike, head south toward East Glacier. Stop for recreation in St. Mary or continue farther south into the isolated

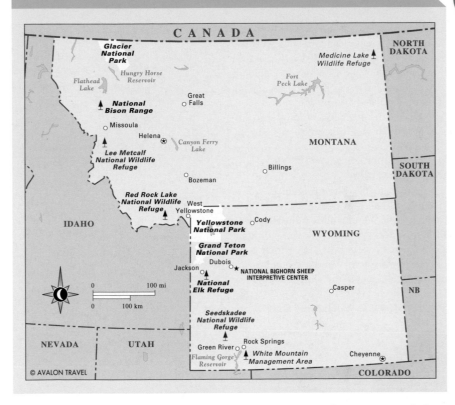

Two Medicine Valley. Consider combining a 45-minute cruise on Two Medicine Lake, cutting six miles off the hike to Twin Falls. Another option is to cruise and then hike to No Name Lake. Finish the day in East Glacier with a hearty meal at the Glacier Village Café and room at the historic Glacier Park Lodge.

Day 7: East Glacier to Missoula (About 222 Miles)

This is the longest day by far in the car, but there is some magnificent scenery and plenty of places to stop along the way. From East Glacier, drive southwest on Highway 2 over Marias Pass. As you enter Columbia Falls, turn south on Highway 206 and continue on Highway 35 toward Creston. Take Highway 83, the Swan Highway, south through the scenic Swan Valley. You'll pass Swan and Seeley Lakes, among others. At Highway 200, continue west back to Missoula, where you can recall the highlights of your trip over a delightful meal at Red Bird Restaurant.

▶ COWBOYS, HOT SPRINGS, AND WIDE OPEN SPACES

Though it is not as large as Montana, Wyoming feels remarkably spacious. This 10-day road trip includes two tried-and-true cowboy towns, a geological wonder, an outdoors mecca, four days at a working ranch, and all of the beautiful and historic sights in between. As is true of the other itineraries, the goal is to minimize driving time while maximizing the destinations.

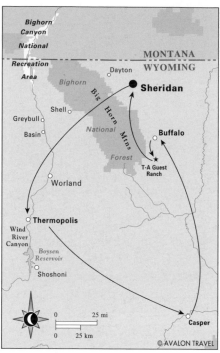

Day 1: Sheridan

Ease into your cowboy experience with a visit to the Trail End State Historic Site. Check out the Western duds at the legendary King's Saddlery, and don't leave without a King Ropes baseball cap, which is de rigueur in the West. Wander around town, nosing into some of the shops and galleries along Main Street. Enjoy dinner at the Sheridan Palace. Wind things down at the

Wyoming nightlife

classic Mint Bar. Find a comfy bed at the Sheridan Mill Inn.

Day 2: Sheridan to Thermopolis (160-205 miles)

To get from Sheridan to Thermopolis, there are a couple of starkly beautiful drives, both offering access to interesting sights and countless trails in the Bighorn National Forest.

The Big Horn Scenic Byway (about 205 miles) climbs up and over the mountains past such sights as the Connor Battlefield near Ranchester, the Medicine Wheel National Historic Landmark, and the Bighorn Canyon National Recreation Area, where mustangs

HISTORY, ROMANCE, AND A BED FOR THE NIGHT

There are dozens of historic accommodations that combine elegant lodging with a taste of Western history.

MONTANA

Izaak Walton Inn
Just outside Glacier National Park in the tiny town of **Essex,** this charming old railroad hotel is on the National Register of Historic Places.

Grand Union Hotel
Built in 1882 at the height of **Fort Benton's** steamboat era, the Grand Union was entirely and magnificently renovated before reopening in 1999.

Chico Hot Springs
Built around a natural hot spring that was discovered in the late 1800s by the miners who put it to good use, Chico Hot Springs Resort is 23 miles south of **Livingston** in Emigrant.

The Grand Hotel Bed and Breakfast
Located in **Big Timber,** this stately Victorian-styled railroad hotel features rich dark mahogany and 1890s furnishings.

WYOMING

Old Faithful Inn
The inspiration for modern-day "parkitecture," this soaring log structure was built in 1904 just feet away from its namesake geyser.

Occidental Hotel
This hotel in **Buffalo** retains its original 1880s splendor with everything from tin ceilings and stained glass to bullet holes. Its famous guest registry has included Butch Cassidy, the Sundance Kid, Calamity Jane, Teddy Roosevelt, and author Owen Wister — who is thought to have written much of *The Virginian* while in residence.

Irma Hotel
Named for Buffalo Bill's youngest daughter and built in 1902 in his chosen home of **Cody,** the stately Irma Hotel once accommodated royalty.

The Wort
In the heart of **Jackson,** the luxurious Wort Hotel was built in 1941, nearly burned to the ground in 1980, and was opened again the following year. Its famed **Silver Dollar Saloon** is worth a visit.

The Plains Hotel
Built in 1911, **Cheyenne's** handsome Plains Hotel once accommodated oil tycoons and cattle barons.

Nagle Warren Mansion
Also in **Cheyenne,** this 1888 mansion is an exquisite tribute to the Victorian West, with 19th-century artwork and period furnishings.

---

can be spotted. This route follows Highway 14 to Lovell and then south toward Thermopolis.

The shorter route (about 160 miles) is higher but no less scenic. It heads south to Buffalo past the impressive Fort Phil Kearney, then over the Cloud Peak Scenic Byway through Ten Sleep to Worland and eventually south to Thermopolis.

As you pull into Thermopolis, head to the colorful and otherworldly Hot Springs State Park. Stroll along the Spirit Trail or stop into the historic State Bath House for a swim before checking into the Best Western

Plaza Hotel. For dinner, try the schnitzel at Stones Throw Restaurant.

Day 3: Thermopolis to Casper (About 134 Miles)

Spend the day in Thermopolis, exploring the park and soaking in the medicinal waters. Arrange for a tour of the Wyoming Dinosaur Center and Dig Sites; You can even participate in their archeological digs. Fill your belly with crepes from Pumpernicks Family Restaurant before heading south through some of the oldest rock formations on the planet. Consider planning a white-water excursion with the Wind River Canyon Whitewater & Flyfishing Outfitter, the only outfit licensed to operate on the Wind River Reservation. Keep your eyes peeled for bighorn sheep. At Shoshoni, head east toward Casper. After a Mexican meal at La Costa, settle in for two nights at the Sunburst Lodge on Casper Mountain.

Day 4: Casper

Wake up to wilderness on Casper Mountain. There are endless options for ways to enjoy it: Hike or bike the trails, or fish on the well-recovered North Platte River. For a more cultural experience, head to the Nicolaysen Art Museum & Discovery Center and the wonderful National Historic Trails Interpretive Center. Lunch at the Cottage Café and plan for dinner at Bosco's. Baseball fans can get tickets to watch the minor league Casper Ghosts. Back on the mountain, if the Crimson Dawn Museum is open, stop in to drink in the lore of the mountain.

Day 5: Casper to Buffalo (About 115 Miles)

Head north on I-87, which runs parallel to the old Bozeman Trail. This is stark open country, with the Thunder Basin National Grassland sweeping out east of the highway. In Buffalo, belly up to the bar in the historic Occidental Hotel for a meal and a cozy room for the night. For a little exercise, hit the 13-mile Clear Creek Trail System. If you're lucky, you'll be able to catch the weekly Cowgirl Rodeo (Tuesday) or the Lion's Club Rodeo (Wednesday).

Day 6: Buffalo to T-A Guest Ranch (About 23 Miles)

Rise early and hightail it to the T-A Guest Ranch, south of Buffalo off Highway 196,

Hot-air balloons soar over Heart Mountain near Cody, Wyoming.

where you'll spend the next four days. This is where cowboy culture comes to life.

Days 7-9: T-A Guest Ranch

Spend the next three nights enjoying an authentic ranch experience. Activities range from riding twice daily to fly fishing, hiking, biking, and golf. You'll visit tipi rings and Bozeman trail sites on the property, plus important battlefields nearby. Expect to work and play hard.

Day 10: T-A Guest Ranch to Sheridan (About 59 Miles)

Trade your saddle for a bucket seat and head north to Sheridan. Consider a stop at Fort Phil Kearney State Historic Site and the tiny town of Big Horn to see the Bradford Brinton Memorial & Museum. Enjoy a last meal—Wyoming gourmet—at Oliver's Bar & Grill on Main Street.

BILLINGS AND THE BIG OPEN

Eastern Montana is an amalgam of landscapes and cultures. From Billings's rimrocks and urban vibe to the rolling hills of the Little Bighorn Battlefield and the stark yet startlingly beautiful terrain along the Missouri River Breaks, eastern Montana is a vibrant and colorful blend of past and present. Home to four of the state's seven Indian reservations, the region is rich with history and culture.

Sometimes referred to as Montana east of the mountains, rather than eastern Montana (in truth, the region occupies more than a third of the state's land mass), this region may not have the mountainous grandeur that most people expect when they visit Montana, but it has a sense of authenticity, a grittiness, that is not often duplicated elsewhere in the state. There are plenty of towns in eastern Montana that were founded by accident, when someone's wagon broke down and options were limited. A day's drive in this region gives visitors a true sense of the hardscrabble life in these parts, the unavoidable isolation and yet the incredible value placed on community. And there is beauty here that should not be overlooked. The often crumbling architecture of agriculture—leaning barns, lonely grain elevators, and rusted equipment—is as much a part of the landscape here as mountains are farther west. The tones of golden light are subtle but too plentiful to count. The clouds change their moods often and play tricks with the shadows.

Though few and far between, the northern communities in this region—Malta, Scobey, Plentywood, and Wolf Point, to name a few—are strong and tightly knit. The Fort Peck

HIGHLIGHTS

◖ Yellowstone Art Museum: Housed in an impressively expanded old jail, the Yellowstone Art Museum is probably the most important art museum in the state – renowned for its permanent collection of Montana artists, both historical and cutting-edge contemporary (page 34).

◖ Pictograph Cave State Monument: Just six miles south of Billings, the caves in this state park contain evidence of human habitation dating back more than 4,500 years. The highlights are the pictographs of people, animals, and even weapons (page 36).

◖ Little Bighorn Battlefield National Monument: The historical site is a moving tribute to one of the last armed battles in which Native Americans fought to preserve their land and way of life. An annual reenactment each June brings to life the terror and tragic meaning of the event (page 43).

◖ Crow Fair: Considered the largest modern-day Indian encampment in the country, this five-day celebration on the Crow Indian Reservation is a festive blur of color and Crow culture, with an all-Indian rodeo, daily parades, and horse racing (page 47).

◖ Custer County Art & Heritage Center: Housed in a century-old waterworks building that has been ingeniously renovated, this is a gem of a Western art museum (page 52).

◖ Miles City Bucking Horse Sale: Held annually the third full weekend in May, the Miles City Bucking Horse Sale is packed with rodeo action and cowboy swagger (page 52).

◖ Makoshika State Park: At the edge of Glendive in the heart of the rugged badlands, this is Montana's largest state park and one of the most fascinating. The colorful rock layers make for dramatic scenery and a fascinating lesson in geological time travel (page 56).

◖ Medicine Lake National Wildlife Refuge: An absolute paradise for bird lovers, the refuge is a stunning blend of glacial drift-prairie and shallow wetland depressions. Earth, water, sky – visitors can walk or drive through this beautiful landscape and will likely see hundreds or thousands of migrating birds (page 57).

◖ Pioneer Town in Scobey: At the edge of town is something of a graveyard for some of the coolest old structures from Scobey's history. More than 35 buildings have been restored to their early-20th-century glory; the best time to visit is during June's Pioneer Days (page 61).

◖ Fort Peck Dam: A triumph of Roosevelt's New Deal, the Fort Peck Dam was built between 1933 and 1940 and employed 11,000 people at its peak. The Interpretive Center and Museum chronicle not only the remarkable structure itself but the staggering number of fossils unearthed during its construction, local dinosaur finds, and Sioux and Assiniboine culture (page 64).

LOOK FOR ◖ TO FIND RECOMMENDED SIGHTS, ACTIVITIES, DINING, AND LODGING.

Indian Reservation is a hopeful study in relations between Native Americans and white settlers. In this part of Montana, the hunting ethos is as deeply rooted as the agricultural way of life. Farther south, bigger towns like Glendive and Miles City boast a strong cowboy culture and some surprisingly important art, and the Crow Indian Reservation is a carefully preserved piece of Western history. Billings, Montana's largest city and frankly not known for its beauty, is not unpleasant in its size, modernity, and ease of access. Though decidedly industrial, the city is populated by fiercely loyal and proud residents, many of whom have been in the area for generations. Strong art, theater, and sports scenes are part of the city's pulse.

Whether you see this region as the Big Sky, the Big Open, or just an obvious and easy access point, this is a part of the state that will enchant you with historical and geographic context for everything else Montana has to offer.

HISTORY

For thousands of years the area along the Yellowstone River and its vicinity were hunting and gathering sites for prehistoric and modern Indians. At various times, the territory around modern-day Billings was sought after by the Sioux, Blackfeet, Cheyenne, and Crow Indians. The area up and down eastern Montana was critical in the conflicts between the U.S. Army and Native Americans. Perhaps no battlefield in the country is better known than the Battle of the Little Bighorn, where Custer made his infamous last stand. The Crow and Sioux tribes continue to have a strong presence in the region on both the Crow Reservation near Hardin and the Fort Peck Reservation in the northeast corner of the state.

Lewis and Clark traveled through eastern Montana on their journey back from the West Coast in 1806. They left the only physical sign of their entire journey—Clark's signature and the date—on a 200-foot rocky outcropping that Clark named Pompey's Pillar, not far from Billings.

Coulson was the first town established in the area by white settlers, in 1877. When the Northern Pacific Railway was looking to extend its tracks, landowners in Coulson saw a quick way to make a lot of money and demanded exorbitant prices of the railroad. Rather than acquiesce to the requests, the railroad established a new town as the railhead for their western line, two miles southeast of Coulson, and named it after the Northern Pacific Railway's president, Frederick Billings. Within six months the city was bustling with a population of 2,000. Its rapid growth gave rise to the city's moniker, "the Magic City," which stands today. The open prairie around the city continued to attract many homesteaders and their families. When the Yellowstone Valley was irrigated in 1879, hundreds of sugar beet fields popped up, and by 1906 a sugar refinery was built in Billings. Soon migrant labor (including Japanese, Russo-Germans, and Mexicans) arrived to work in the fields. During the 20th century Billings grew and thrived as an industrial center with a diverse economy in agriculture (grains, sugar beets, beef, and dairy cattle), energy (coal, natural gas, and oil) and transportation (air, rail, and trucking). Today, Montana's largest city is a major health care hub for eastern Montana, Wyoming, and the Dakotas and is home to the state's busiest airport.

The vast open stretches of eastern Montana, interrupted by small agricultural or railroad towns, were long home to massive herds of bison and the Native Americans who lived in pursuit of the animal. Miles City, which grew into a town in 1876 thanks to a handful of wayward civilians fired by Commander Nelson Miles from his nearby military encampment along the Tongue River, became one of the largest shipping points for bison hides. Other towns in the region—Glendive, Fort Peck, Plentywood, and Scobey, among others—sprang up as the result of the railroads, the Great Northern and the Northern Pacific, as well as the various homestead acts that lured settlers with the promise of plentiful land.

BILLINGS AND THE BIG OPEN

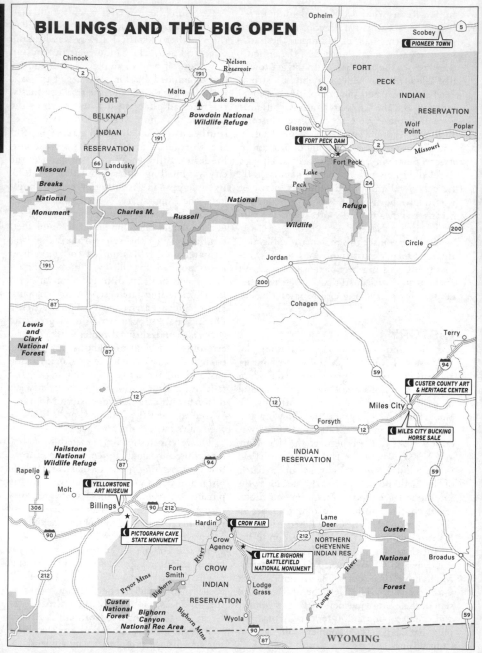

Opheim

Scobey   5
PIONEER TOWN

Chinook
2

Nelson
Reservoir

FORT

191

PECK

Malta
INDIAN

Lake Bowdoin

24

RESERVATION

FORT
Bowdoin National
Wildlife Refuge

Glasgow

Wolf
Point

Poplar

BELKNAP

INDIAN
191

FORT PECK DAM

2

Missouri

RESERVATION

Fort Peck

Missouri
66   Landusky

Lake

Breaks

Peck

24

National
National

Monument
Charles M.
Russell

Refuge

Circle   200

Wildlife

Jordan

191

200

87
Cohagen

Terry

Lewis
and
Clark
National
Forest

94

87

59

CUSTER COUNTY ART
& HERITAGE CENTER

12

Miles City

12

Forsyth

12

MILES CITY BUCKING
HORSE SALE

Hailstone
National
Wildlife Refuge

INDIAN
RESERVATION

59

Rapelje
87

94

YELLOWSTONE
ART MUSEUM

Molt

306

Billings

90   212

Lame
Deer

Custer

PICTOGRAPH CAVE
STATE MONUMENT

Hardin   CROW FAIR

212

NORTHERN
CHEYENNE
INDIAN RES

National

Broadus

90

Crow
Agency

LITTLE BIGHORN
BATTLEFIELD
NATIONAL MONUMENT

212

Fort
Smith

CROW

Forest

59

INDIAN

Lodge
Grass

Pryor Mtns

Custer
National
Forest

RESERVATION

Bighorn

Wyola

Bighorn Mtns

Bighorn

Tongue River

River

Bighorn
Canyon
National Rec Area

90
87

WYOMING

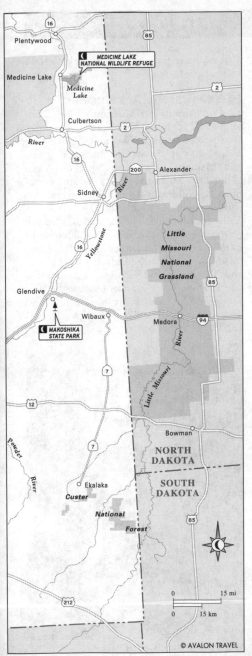

PLANNING YOUR TIME

For travelers who are willing to take their time and let the state unfold slowly as opposed to the drama of the one-two mountain-sky knockout punch, Eastern Montana is an ideal place to start a Montana road trip. There is subtlety here in the landscape and the light as well as a feeling of timelessness. When you drive on the prairie, it is not such a stretch to imagine the first travelers to this region. In fact, some Lewis and Clark buffs suggest that the only landscape the explorers would recognize today is Montana, simply because it hasn't changed much. Even a stroll down Main Street can feel like a step back in time, with still-bustling and vital local hardware stores in every town, and instead of fast-food or chain restaurants there are real bakeries, doughnut shops, and cafés. Take your time in Eastern Montana: Stop for pie, stop to chat, and just slow down and enjoy.

Most visitors traveling by car from the east will arrive in Montana via either I-94 at Wibaux or I-90 near Wyola, just south of the **Little Bighorn Battlefield.**

Although "the Magic City" is the largest in Montana, and one of the easiest and least expensive to get to by air, **Billings** is not what its moniker suggests. (For further evidence of this trend, visit nearby Laurel, "City of Lights.") Still, Billings has an authenticity and vitality that makes a visit worthwhile. It is also an excellent place to launch explorations of eastern and central Montana.

Driving in this region, and throughout Montana and Wyoming, can eat up entire days, but the journey itself can be incredibly worthwhile. In 2009 the state introduced a controversial advertising campaign with the slogan "Montana: There's nothing here." In eastern Montana that "nothing"—wide open spaces, vast wilderness refuges, and friendly little towns—is absolutely enchanting.

Billings and Vicinity

Though not a tourist attraction per se, Billings (population 101,876, elevation 3,124 feet) is the largest city in the state and the hub for much of eastern Montana. The city is a center for industry, including oil refineries and stockyards, and serves much of eastern and central Montana with two major hospitals, three colleges, and significant shopping options. Billings used to be *the* place to buy a car, see a specialist doctor, or stock up at Costco. That has changed with growth across the state, but Billings still attracts a good number of visitors from around the state for both practical and decidedly more entertaining purposes.

The MetraPark is popular as a venue for concerts, trade shows, and rodeos and serves as the fairgrounds and horse racing track. The Alberta Bair Theater for the Performing Arts is the largest of its kind between Minneapolis and Spokane. The Yellowstone Art Museum boasts an impressive collection of contemporary Montana art, in addition to past masters, and is well worth a visit. The rimrocks around the city offer wonderful perspectives—you can see five mountain ranges—and there is a great network of hiking and biking trails.

SIGHTS
Guided Tours

Billings is not as easily navigated on foot as Montana's significantly smaller cities, but a number of tour companies offer opportunities to see the city's high points. The **Fun Express Bus** (406/254-7180 or 888/618-4386, www.montanafunadventures.com, 10:30 A.M., 11:30 A.M., and 12:30 P.M. Mon.–Sat. June–Sept., 1 P.M. and 2 P.M. Mon.–Sat. Oct.–May, $25 adults, $20 students and military, free for children under 6) offers two-hour historic tours that feature underground tunnels, creepy cemeteries, haunted hotels, and the venerable Moss Mansion. The **Billings Trolley and Bus Company** (406/252-1778 or 800/698-1778, www.mttotaltransportation.com) offers customized and lighthearted tours of Billings's historic district; the Christmas Light Tour is a winner.

◖ Yellowstone Art Museum

The Yellowstone Art Museum (401 N. 27th St., 406/256-6804, www.artmuseum.org, 10 A.M.–5 P.M. Mon.–Wed., 10 A.M.–8 P.M. Thurs., 10 A.M.–5 P.M. Fri.–Sat., noon–5 P.M. Sun. Memorial Day–Labor Day, closed Mon. Labor Day–Memorial Day, $5 adults, $4 seniors, $3 children 6–18 and students, free for children under 6) is an important visual arts center for Montana. The Montana Collection is an impressive array of more than 3,000 works by the state's most lauded contemporary artists, including Rudy Autio, Deborah Butterfield, and Theodore Waddell. The museum also houses a significant number of works by Will James and an assortment of paintings and drawings by masters like Charles M. Russell and Joseph Henry Sharp.

Western Heritage Center

© DONNIE SEXTON

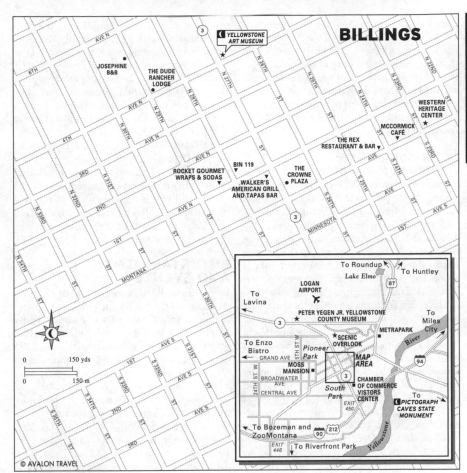

Moss Mansion

For 87 years the family of fabulously successful entrepreneur Preston Boyd Moss lived happily in Billings's Moss Mansion (914 Division St., 406/256-5100, www.mossmansion.com, tours on the hour 10 A.M.–3 P.M. Tues.–Sat., 1–3 P.M. Sun. summer, call for hours fall–spring, $7 adults, $5 seniors, $5 students with ID, $3 children 6–12). The 1903 home, designed by New York architect Henry Janeway Hardenbergh, who also designed New York City's original Waldorf Astoria and Plaza Hotels, was lovingly maintained by the family and turned into a museum. It can only be seen on the one-hour tours, which offer a fascinating glimpse into the Moss family's elegant lifestyle. Much of the original furnishings and art decorate the mansion today. Winter holiday tours are a special treat, when the mansion is decorated for Christmas.

Western Heritage Center

Beautifully housed downtown in the former Parmly Billings Memorial Library, the Western Heritage Center (2282 Montana Ave., 406/256-6809, www.ywhc.org, 10 A.M.–5 P.M.

Tues.–Sat., $5 adults, $3 students and seniors, $1 children) is an affiliate of the Smithsonian Institution and has an extensive collection that documents the history of the Yellowstone River Valley. There is also a sizeable collection of works by artist J. K. Ralston. The museum is one of the few dedicated to recording and collecting oral histories of various regional Native American groups.

◖ Pictograph Cave State Monument

Located southeast of Billings among the sandstone cliffs that form the rimrocks, Pictograph Cave State Monument (2300 Lake Elmo Dr., 406/247-2940, www.pictographcave.org, May 1–Sept. 30, $5 per vehicle nonresidents, free for Montana residents) contains three caves with evidence of human habitation that is more than 4,500 years old. Pictographs that date back 2,200 years can also be seen in one of the caves. Binoculars are helpful since visitors are kept some distance back in order to protect the ancient artwork. Just before World War II a significant archeological survey uncovered more than 30,000 artifacts from the site, including barbed harpoon points made from caribou horn, likely evidence of Eskimo culture. The park was vandalized in the 1950s and 1960s, when much of the artwork was covered with graffiti. Today it has been carefully restored, and in places, tracings from the initial archeological study have been overlaid on the originals in order to make the vivid images more visible. A nice trail system also winds through the park.

Pompey's Pillar

Twenty-five miles east of Billings is Pompey's Pillar (I-94 exit 23 to 2nd St. S., 406/875-2400, www.pompeyspillar.org, 8 A.M.–8 P.M. daily late May–Labor Day, call for off-season hours, pedestrians permitted off-season, $7 per vehicle per day), an age-old landmark that bears the signature of Captain William Clark of the Lewis and Clark expedition. Named by Clark for Sacagawea's son, Jean Baptiste Charbonneau, nicknamed "Pomp," the

sandstone pillar has a storied history both before and after Clark signed it on July 25, 1806: There were Indian pictographs on the 200-foot-tall rock when he first laid eyes on it. In 1873, Custer's troops were camped opposite the pillar along the banks of the Yellowstone River when they were fired on by Sioux warriors.

Every year on the last weekend in July, the Pompey's Pillar Historical Association host **Clark Days** (406/967-3281), a celebration of the pillar's past with lively history lectures and presentations, nature walks, hot meals, and plenty of fun interaction geared toward the whole family. It is the only night of the year that camping is allowed on the grounds of the pillar, and no admission fee is charged during the two-day festivities.

ENTERTAINMENT AND EVENTS

Few artificial objects enhance a skyline as spectacularly as a flock of hot-air balloons. Billings's annual **Magic City Hot Air Balloon Rally** (Amend Park off King Ave. E., 406/671-3104, www.magiccityhotairballoonrally.com, $175 for a ride), held on a weekend in late July, lights up the sky with early-morning flights, dusk Balloon Glows, and plenty of camaraderie.

Sponsored by the Yellowstone Art Museum, **Summerfair** (Veteran's Park, corner of Poly Dr. and 13th St. W., 406/256-6804, ext. 239, www.yellowstone.artmuseum.org, 10 A.M.–5 P.M. Sat.–Sun., $2 adults, $1 students, $5 family) is the largest juried arts and crafts festival in the region. Typically held on a weekend in mid–late July, the fair includes more than 100 artist booths, loads of activities for kids, live entertainment, and a food court.

The state's largest annual event, **MontanaFair** (MetraPark, 308 6th Ave. N., 406/256-2400 or 800/366-8538, www.montanafair.com, $8 adults, $5 seniors, $5 children 6–12, free for children 5 and under, call ahead for special deals and concert tickets), running for nine days starting the second week of August, is an agricultural fair in the classic tradition. In addition to arts and crafts competitions and displays in everything from pigs and tomato-growing to pickles and crochet, MontanaFair events include major concerts, motorsports, bull riding, rodeo, and a good old-fashioned carnival.

For beer lovers, the **Ales for Trails** event (Billings Depot, 2310 Montana Ave., 406/247-8637, www.bikenet.org) in late September offers 40 microbrews, local food vendors, and great local music. The event benefits the Heritage Trail System's 20-plus miles of pedestrian-friendly bike trails throughout Billings, which have earned Billings the "Green City" title in *Organic Gardening* magazine.

For visitors looking to add a little Old West experience to their Billings stay, **Pappy's Cowboy Cookout** (I-90 east to exit 462, south on Pryor Creek to the first gate on the right, 406/348-2048 or 406/672-5941, www.westernromance-company.com, dawn–dusk May 1–Sept. 30, call for prices), 15 minutes southeast of downtown, offers a gourmet cowboy dinner under the big sky. Guests arrive at the chuckwagon camp in a covered wagon. Games like horseshoes and calf roping are available at the camp, and live country music rounds out the evening. Trail rides can be arranged separately.

Billings also offers a host of more urban culture. There are numerous theatrical performances and concerts at the **Alberta Bair Theater** (2801 3rd Ave. N., 406/256-6052, www.albertabairtheater.org), including the **Billings Symphony Orchestra and Chorale** (406/256-3610, www.billingssymphony.org, Nov.–Apr.) and the **Rimrock Opera** (406/671-2214, www.rimrockopera.org), known for their One Act Festival each summer and popular performances throughout the year. The **Billings Studio Theatre** (1500 Rimrock Rd., 406/248-1141, www.billingsstudiotheatre.com) also offers excellent theater with tremendous community support.

SHOPPING

While Billings is more often thought of as a place for supplies rather than boutique shopping, there are a number of interesting shops worth visiting. The **Meadowlark Gallery** (118 N. 29th St., 406/294-8575, www.meadowlarkgallery.com, 10 A.M.–5 P.M. Tues.–Fri., Sat. by appointment), specializing in Western and sporting fine art, is like a museum, with more than 500 works decorating the walls. The gallery includes a sporting and firearms room, a library with several of the owners' books on Western artists, and an impressive collection of works by Bob Meyers, Richard E. Bishop, Bill Gollings, and German-born Wyoming artist Hans Klieber.

Oxford Antiques (2411 Montana Ave., 406/248-2094 or 406/656-2616, 10:30 A.M.–4:30 P.M. Mon.–Sat.) is Billings's oldest single-owner antiques shop. The building is a 1908 Victorian Italianate and suits the inventory perfectly. In addition to two floors of furniture, the store has an endless assortment of Montana-related items and other collectibles.

A unique piece of Montana can be ordered at **Reliable Tent & Tipi** (501 N. 23rd St., 406/252-4689 or 800/544-1039, www.reliabletent.com), which has been family-owned since 1945. Their tents are designed for the often rugged hunting conditions in Montana, and their specialty Crow and Sioux tipis are designed by Native Americans according to family and tribal traditions. They also make a wonderful Backyard Tipi for kids.

RECREATION

Under the shadow of the rimrocks, **Dehler Park** (2611 9th Ave. N., 406/252-1241, www.billings.mustangs.milb.com), built in 2008 to accommodate 6,000 baseball fans in stadium seats, bleachers, and grassy picnic areas, is home to the **Billings Mustangs**. The stadium's predecessor, Cobb Field, was built in 1948 and was home to the Pioneer League rookie affiliates for the Brooklyn Dodgers, the Pittsburgh Pirates, and the St. Louis Cardinals. Since 1974 the Mustangs have been affiliated with the Cincinnati Reds. George Brett is among the most well-known alumni of Cobb Field.

Horse racing fans can get their share of action with **Yellowstone Downs** (308 6th Ave. N., 406/869-5251, www.yellowstonedowns.com) at MetraPark mid-August–mid-September.

THE 24-HOUR BIKE RACE

Located 25 miles north of Columbus on Highway 306, Rapelje, Montana, has one post office, one church, one café, and a population of less than 100. So why would this diminutive farming and ranching community have its own sidebar? Because Rapelje hosts the state's only 24-hour bike race, and in the process demonstrates the remarkable spirit of community that keeps small towns like this from disappearing.

The history of this race is inextricably tied to a café and the goodwill of the town residents. As the story goes, Rapelje's local bar was unable to turn a profit, finally forced to close in 1997. Realizing that it was essential the town have a place to gather, in 1998 a handful of individuals decided to buy the bar and reopen it as a community-owned nonprofit café. Only the chefs at the newly named Stockman Café received a salary; the rest of the staff worked as volunteers. When it became evident that even with these measures, the restaurant could not subsist solely on revenue from local patrons, the residents devised another means to keep the café afloat. The Rapelje 24-hour Race began in 2001 with about 30 participants and now draws some 200 riders with their friends and families in tow. For one weekend in late June, the town's population practically quintuples.

A USA Cycling-sanctioned cross-country mountain bike race, the event takes place on the weekend closest to the summer solstice. The 12-15-mile course runs through wheat fields, cow paths, and rolling farmland. Participants can compete as individual riders or relay teams, and whoever completes the most laps in 24 hours walks away with the trophy. The Stockman Café serves as the hub of activity for the race, with a crew of volunteers feeding racers throughout the day. As the organizer of the event, Jason Frank, explained to the *New York Times*, "Here you have a café, a band, a pancake feed, and a pig feast after the race. Nobody else does that. It's the town of Rapelje and the people who live here that make this race so unique."

There are a number of golf courses in Billings, perhaps because the winters here are milder than much of western Montana and the summers are longer. **Briarwood Country Club's** 18-hole course (3429 Briarwood Blvd., 406/248-2702) is open to members and anyone who lives more than 100 miles from Billings. **Circle Inn Links** (1029 Main St., 406/248-4202) is a bargain of a nine-hole course. Eagle Rock Golf Course (5624 Larimer Lane, 406/655-4445, www.eaglerockgolfcourse.com) is an 18-hole public course, as are the challenging par-3 **Exchange City Golf Course** (19th St. W., 406/652-2553) and the Lake Hills Golf Club (1930 Clubhouse Way, 406/252-9244, www.lakehillsgolf.com). The newer Yegen Golf Club (1390 Zimmerman Tr., 406/656-8099, www.yegengolfclub.com) is a beautiful course.

Also known as Diamond X Disc Golf Course, **Phipps Park** (Molt Rd., 4 miles west of Billings) is ranked among the top five golf courses in Montana. The 350-acre city park offers 27 holes for disc golfers, panoramic views, and a network of rugged, challenging trails for both runners and mountain bikers. Right in town, **Riverfront Park** (S. Billings Ave.) has a nice pond with hungry ducks and geese, some nice walking trails, and undeveloped areas.

Hikers can find plenty of trails winding around the rimrocks, but there are some phenomenal mountain trails less than an hour from town. The **Island Lake Trail** (trailhead at Mystic Dam Power Station, end of W. Rosebud Rd.), 40 miles southwest of Billings in the Custer National Forest Beartooth Ranger District (406/446-2103, www.fs.fed.us/r1/custer), is a 12-mile out-and-back round-trip in the West Rosebud Valley. There are numerous trout-laden mountain lakes in the region, but the climb is significant, so allow ample time. Thirty-five miles southwest of Billings, **Sylvan Lake** is one of a few easily accessible golden trout lakes in the Beartooth Mountains. It is accessed by Trail 13 (trailhead at East Rosebud Campground, off E. Rosebud Rd., 406/446-2103, www.fs.fed.us/r1/custer). It's a challenging 10-mile out-and-back round-trip hike, but the views—and the fish—are phenomenal.

ACCOMMODATIONS

The Crowne Plaza (27 N. 27th St., 406/252-7400 or 800/588-7666, www.crowneplaza.com/billings, about $150 d) in downtown Billings is difficult to miss: It is a towering brick building that dwarfs its neighbors. The hotel was recently renovated, and the guest rooms are comfortable and plush. They offer a large assortment of amenities, including complimentary high-speed Internet. The Montana Sky restaurant is situated on the 20th floor with terrific views of the city.

Located in a 1912 historic home at the edge of downtown, **The Josephine Bed and Breakfast** (514 N. 29th St., 406/248-5898 or 800/552-5898, www.thejosephine.com, $95–115 d) offers a quiet stay in an intimate yet convenient setting. The inn provides airport pickup, free wireless Internet, passes to a 24-hour fitness center, and a gourmet breakfast.

The Dude Rancher Lodge (415 N. 29th St., 406/259-5561 or 800/221-3302, www.duderancherlodge.com, $60–80 d, depending on the season) is a unique independently owned frontier hotel. It is within walking distance of the shops, restaurants, and nightlife of downtown and prides itself on offering Western hospitality. Each guest room is individually furnished, and some come with refrigerators and microwaves.

Other hotels you may want to consider are the **Cherry Tree Inn** (823 N. Broadway, 406/252-5603 or 800/237-5882, $50–75) and the 1904 **Historic Northern Hotel** (19 N. 28th St., 406/245-5121 or 800/542-5121), Billings's oldest and currently being renovated. Scheduled to reopen in late 2011, it will be a modern Western chic hotel with 160 guest rooms and two restaurants.

CAMPING

Native Ways Primitive Campground (4055 High Trail Rd., 406/690-4046, Mar. 15–Nov. 1, call for amenities and rates), four miles southeast of Billings, offers a unique take on camping: They have four tipis, both Crow and Sioux style, on 25 wooded acres. Each site has its own tipi, fully supplied with sleeping bags and other necessities, if you need them, plus a washbasin, water, a picnic table, a lantern, and a garbage can.

The **Billings Metro KOA** (547 Garden Ave., 406/252-3104 or 800/562-8546, www.koa.com/where/mt/26104, Apr. 15–Oct.15, from $32 tents, from $40 RVs) offers 40 tent sites, many of them on the banks of the Yellowstone River, along with 135 RV sites and 11 cabins. There is a swimming pool and a spa for campers to use, a barbecue, miniature golf, a playground, and broadband Wi-Fi. The campground is conveniently close to town and offers pancake breakfasts and barbecue dinners mid-June–mid-August.

FOOD

As Montana's largest city, Billings has a lively dining scene and is a good place to splurge. **Bin 119** (119 N. Broadway, 406/294-9119, 11 A.M.–10 P.M. daily, bar until 2 A.M.) is a fairly new, European-influenced bistro and wine bar with 180 labels and more than 30 wines sold by the glass. Started by local students, it's stylish but not at all pretentious. The food, primarily inspired by Spanish tapas, is geared toward appetizer-size dishes that average $10–12.

Walker's American Grill and Tapas Bar (2700 1st Ave. N., 406/245-9291 or 406/245-1534, www.walkersgrill.com, lounge from 4 P.M. daily, dining room from 5 P.M. daily, tapas $8, entrées $25) is big-city chic with excellent food and award-winning wine. The menu is cosmopolitan (salami and Stilton pizza) and entirely Montana (buffalo osso buco), and the ambience elegant but vibrant; Sunday evenings May–September are enhanced by live jazz.

Enzo Bistro (1502 Rehberg Lane, 406/651-0999, from 5 P.M. daily, entrées $12–30) serves up hearty Mediterranean fare in a comfortable farmhouse. They import fresh fish from both coasts daily and cook many of the entrées on

THE PRAIRIE WINDS CAFÉ

Places like the Prairie Winds Café (110 Wolfskill Ave., Molt, 406/699-3857, 7 A.M.-3 P.M. Tues.-Sat.), in Molt, about 25 minutes outside of Billings, are small-town Montana at its best. It is as old as it is welcoming, and you'll see weathered ranchers sharing tables with Spandex-clad road bikers, eating mouthwatering cinnamon rolls as well as a case of fresh-baked pies, including their signature oatmeal pie. The building was built in 1915 as the town's hardware and lumber store, and it still retains much of its original character. People travel from miles around for the hearty home-style meals, but the Prairie Winds also serves as something of an impromptu community center – one of Montana's senators has been known to meet with the locals here to talk about agriculture and other important issues, and there are fund-raisers and celebrations from time to time. And 9 A.M.-noon Saturday mornings, the place is bursting at the seams with a live country or bluegrass band and hungry music lovers willing to stand in line to share a table. If you want to be sure you get a seat, arrive well before 9 A.M., when the band starts up. You'll be sure to leave contented, body and soul.

a wood-fired grill; the eclectic menu is a local favorite.

The **Rex Restaurant & Bar** (2401 Montana Ave., 406/245-7477, www.therexbillings.com, 11 A.M.-2 P.M. Mon.–Fri., 4 P.M.-2 A.M. Sat.–Sun., dinner from 5 P.M. daily, $10–15 on the patio, dining room entrées $30) was founded in 1919 by Alfred Heimer, the chef from Buffalo Bill Cody's Wild West Show, and was originally known for its "cold beer and good German lunches." Its storied past and award-winning preservation make the Rex one of the better-known establishments in town. The turn-of-the-20th-century interior suits the classic steak and seafood menu, and an outdoor patio is a splendid option on Billings's warm summer evenings.

For breakfast and lunch, **McCormick Café** (2419 Montana Ave., 406/255-9555, www. mccormickcafe.com, 7 A.M.-3 P.M. Mon.–Fri., 8 A.M.-3 P.M. Sat., 8 A.M.-1 P.M. Sun., breakfast $6, lunch $7.50) is another local favorite, offering everything from French crepes and wonderful pastries to savory sandwiches, wraps, and healthy salads.

Rocket Gourmet Wraps & Sodas (2809 1st Ave. N., 406/248-5231, www.rocketwraps. com, 10 A.M.-6 P.M. Mon.–Fri., 11 A.M.-4 P.M. Sat., $6.50) is an excellent place for a fast and filling meal. The hot and cold wraps and burritos are made from fresh ingredients like roasted chicken, andouille sausage, and albacore tuna. There is an ample selection of salads and kids meals, and diners can wet their whistles with specialty coffees and Italian sodas.

INFORMATION AND SERVICES

The **Visitors Center** is located one floor below the **Billings Chamber of Commerce** (815 S. 27th St., 406/252-4016 or 800/735-2635, www.billingschamber.com, 10 A.M.-4 P.M. Mon.–Sat., 8:30 A.M.-6 P.M. Sun. summer, 8:30 A.M.-5 P.M. Mon.–Fri. winter).

The **main post office** (841 S.26th St., 8 A.M.-5:30 P.M. Mon.–Fri.) is located just behind the Chamber of Commerce. There is also a downtown post office (2602 1st Ave. N., 7 A.M.-5:30 P.M. Mon.–Fri.), and one post office (724 15th St. W.) is open on Saturday (9 A.M.-1 P.M.).

The **Parmly Billings Library** (510 N. Broadway, 406/657-8258, www.billings. lib.mt.us, 10 A.M.-9 P.M. Mon.–Thurs., 10 A.M.-6 P.M. Fri., 10 A.M.-5 P.M. Sat. year-round, also 1–5 P.M. Sun. summer) offers free use of computers with unfiltered Internet access.

You'll find Wi-Fi accessibility at the **Travel Café** (313 N. Broadway, 406/259-0999, 7 A.M.-5 P.M. Mon.–Fri., 9 A.M.-noon Sat.). The first floor is a café, and the second floor is a travel agency. The Starbucks in the Crowne

Plaza Hotel (27 N. 27th St.) also offers wireless Internet.

Two conveniently located coin-op Laundromats are **Speedy Wash** (2505 6th Ave. N., 406/248-4177, 7 A.M.–9:30 P.M. daily) and **The Laundry Room** (3189 King Ave. W., Suite 4, 406/652-2993, 7 A.M.–9 P.M. daily).

For emergency medical assistance, **St. Vincent Healthcare** (1233 N. 30th St., 406/657-7000, www.svh-mt.org) and **Billings Clinic Hospital** (2800 10th Ave. N., 406/238-2500 or 800/332-7156, www.billingsclinic.com) both have 24-hour ER service. For minor medical care, the **Billings Clinic** also has walk-in service at three branch locations: Downtown (8th Ave. N. and N. 28th St., 406/238-2677); West (2675 Central Ave., in Lamplighter Square next to Target, 406/238-2575); and Heights (860 Wicks Lane, across from Wal-Mart, 406/238-2900). All three clinics are open 7 A.M.–7:30 P.M. Monday–Friday, 9 A.M.–5 P.M. Saturday–Sunday.

GETTING THERE

Billings Logan International Airport (BIL) is situated atop the rimrocks off I-90 at the 27th Street exit. Delta, United, Allegiant, Frontier, Horizon, SkyWest, and Great Lakes offer regular flights.

If you arrive early at the airport or have some time to spare before you are picked up, visit the **Peter Yegen Jr. Yellowstone County Museum** (1950 Terminal Circle, 406/256-6811, wwww.pyjrycm.org, 10:30 A.M.–5 P.M. Mon.–Fri., 10:30 A.M.–3 P.M. Sat., free). Once outside the terminal, follow the road around the west parking lot; the museum is on the right before the airport exit. The museum has artifacts and exhibits highlighting the history of the northern plains from early Native American influence through westward expansion and mining up to the 1950s. The museum's deck provides a splendid view of the city below.

The **Greyhound** bus terminal (2502 1st Ave. N., 406/245-5116, www.greyhound.com) and ticket offices are open 24 hours a day year-round.

As the largest city in Montana, I-90 intersects Billings and I-94 begins just outside the town, making it an easy driving destination. It is 142 miles from Bozeman, 81 miles from Big Timber, 60 miles from Red Lodge, and 46 miles from Hardin. In Wyoming, Cody is 106 miles away, and it is 130 miles to Sheridan.

GETTING AROUND

At the Billings airport, **Enterprise, Thrifty, Dollar, Hertz, Alamo,** and **National** have on-site car-rental counters.

There are two taxi services available: **City Cab** (406/252-8700) and **Yellow Cab** (406/245-3033). There is no taxi stand at the airport, so call ahead if you want to be picked up.

MET transit (406/657-8218, www.mettransit.com, 6:45 A.M.–6:30 P.M. Mon.–Fri., 8:10 A.M.–5:45 P.M. Sat., $0.75) offers bus service throughout Billings, and although there are marked bus stops around the city, you can also flag them down at any corner. Booklets with routes and schedules are available at most banks, convenience stores, grocery stores, the library, and government offices.

Crow and Northern Cheyenne Indian Reservations

Southeastern Montana is a ruggedly beautiful part of the state, with vast prairies, dramatic canyons, and stark badlands. The land is dry and brittle in places, but the people here are tenacious, having been ordered to occupy this region in the aftermath of the Fort Laramie Treaty of 1851. The two tribes in this part of the state—the Crow and the Northern Cheyenne—have managed to preserve their cultures and build remarkable, if struggling, communities with little more than steadfast determination. They have done much to showcase people, places, and events that have impacted their own destinies and shaped and defined much of Montana and the West.

CROW RESERVATION

The story of the Crow Reservation is all too familiar and tragic. The 1851 Fort Laramie Treaty recognized almost all of the Yellowstone Valley as Crow territory. Mining claims and a dramatic increase in the number of settlers traveling through the region led to conflict and a second treaty in 1868, which, even though the vast majority of Crows refused to sign it, significantly reduced the size of their territory. The discovery of gold on Crow land shortly after the second treaty led to a third treaty in 1873, which moved the Crow again to a much smaller reservation in central Montana's Judith Basin. Neither the Crow nor the white cattlemen settling in the region were pleased with the arrangement, and after much debate in Washington, D.C., the Crow Reservation was moved farther east and further diminished in size.

Today the Crow Reservation occupies roughly 2.3 million acres of land and is home to some 7,500 Crow Indians, 75 percent of the tribe's enrolled members. The largest settlement by far and the county seat, Hardin (population 3,384, elevation 2,966 feet) is not on the reservation, but the communities on the reservation include Crow Agency, Fort Smith, Garryowen, Lodgegrass, Pryor, and Wyola.

NORTHERN CHEYENNE RESERVATION

Just east of the Crow Reservation is the much smaller Northern Cheyenne Indian Reservation, home to roughly 5,000 people, more than 90 percent of whom are Native American. Of the 9,496 enrolled tribe members, nearly 4,200 live on the 444,000-acre reservation. Lame Deer is the tribal and government agency headquarters; Busby is the other primary settlement on the reservation. Ashland and Birney are just outside the reservation.

The Northern Cheyenne are a division of the great Cheyenne Tribe who once ranged across the Great Plains from South Dakota to Colorado. The first Cheyenne territory dictated by the U.S. government was in the region around what is now Denver. The Cheyenne were repeatedly attacked by the U.S. government and sustained enormous casualties, all while living according to law in the territory the government had put them on. Following the Battle of the Little Bighorn, which the Cheyenne participated in, the Army's attempts to capture the Cheyenne increased in intensity. Several Cheyenne chiefs surrendered, expecting to be returned to Colorado, and were sent to the reservation for the Southern Cheyenne in Oklahoma.

After disease decimated the tribe and starvation threatened the survivors, fewer than 300 Northern Cheyenne slipped out of the reservation with the intent of going back north. Nearly 10,000 soldiers and 3,000 settlers chased the band for six weeks across Kansas and Nebraska. In the fall of 1878, the remaining Northern Cheyenne split into two groups: those who were willing to surrender with Dull Knife and live at Red Cloud Agency, and those under Little Wolf who wanted to continue fleeing. Dull Knife and his people were captured, brutalized, and ordered back to Oklahoma. Dull Knife refused and again made a daring attempt at escape. In the end, only nine of the people with Dull

Knife survived. They were eventually allowed to go to Fort Keogh, near modern day Miles City, Montana, where Little Wolf and his followers had ended up.

After assisting the Army in their pursuit of Chief Joseph and the Nez Perce, the Northern Cheyenne were given a reservation by the U.S. government in 1884. The reservation was established and still exists between Montana's Tongue River and the Crow Reservation. Dull Knife and the survivors and descendants of the 1878 escape from Oklahoma moved to the Northern Cheyenne Reservation. In an atypical move, the government actually expanded the reservation in 1890.

SIGHTS
◖ Little Bighorn Battlefield National Monument
The Little Bighorn Battlefield National Monument (65 miles southeast of Billings, 15 miles southeast of Hardin, 1 mile east of I-90 on U.S. 212, 406/638-2621, www.nps.gov/libi, 8 A.M.–9 P.M. daily June–Aug., call for hours Sept.–May, $10 per vehicle, $5 pedestrians and motorcycles) is a desolate, somber, and terribly meaningful place, commemorating a tragic battle with no true victors, only bloodshed marking the end of an era. The monument memorializes the battlefield made famous by Lieutenant Colonel George Armstrong Custer, more than 200 men from his 7th Cavalry, and the thousands of Native American warriors who fought under Sitting Bull and Crazy Horse for their very way of life against a foreign government that they perceived as dishonest, utterly unreliable, and tyrannical.

In early 1876, thousands of Native Americans from numerous tribes slipped away from their reservations, restless and disgruntled at having been repeatedly lied to and mistreated by the U.S. government. Countless skirmishes throughout the winter and spring reinvigorated the Army's pursuit of the Native Americans, and four centuries of conflict between Native Americans and European Americans came to a head in June 1876 at the battle, when Custer

and his men attacked an enormous force of Cheyenne, Sioux, and Arapaho and were immediately surrounded. Custer's infamous Last Stand actually lasted less than an hour, and every man under his command on that hill was killed.

The Little Bighorn Battlefield Visitor Center and Museum (8 A.M.–6 P.M. daily Apr.–May, 8 A.M.–9 P.M. daily June–Aug., 8 A.M.–6 P.M. daily Sept.–Oct., 8 A.M.–4:30 P.M. daily Nov.–Mar., $10 private vehicle, $5 individuals on foot, bicycle, or motorcycle) is a must for those visiting the site. The compact facility powerfully interprets the events leading up to and following the battle. Exhibited artifacts include weapons, photos of the key players, archeological findings, and, during the off-season, a 17-minute video documentary. Rangers give frequent interpretive lectures, and bus tours of the site are available in summer.

Adjacent to the visitors center is the **Custer National Cemetery** for the military, which resembles Arlington National Cemetery on a much smaller scale. The actual monument on Last Stand Hill is on a paved trail within walking distance of the center, and a 4.5-mile road open to car traffic connects the Custer Battlefield with the Benteen Battlefield.

The granite memorial on **Last Stand Hill** was built in July 1881, and in 1890 marble markers replaced stakes that stood where each soldier had fallen. Starting in 1999, red granite markers were placed to honor the Native Americans who died in the battle, including Cheyenne warriors Lame White Man and Noisy Walking and Lakota warriors Long Road and Dog's Back Bone. For those wanting to do a bit of homework before arriving at the site, the **Friends of the Little Bighorn Battlefield** (www.friendslittlebighorn.com) maintain an excellent website.

A wonderful way to explore the monument, and the starkly beautiful windswept plains that surround it, is by hiring a Native American guide through **Apsalooke Tours** (406/638-7272 or 406/638-3114, www.lbhc.cc.mt.us, standard tours 10 A.M., 11 A.M., noon, 2 P.M.,

PLENTY COUPS, VISIONARY CHIEF OF THE CROW

Born into the Crow Indian tribe in 1848, Chief Plenty Coups had a life that spanned two eras. As a young warrior, he rode across the plains hunting, fighting, and conquering. As a middle-aged leader, he embraced life on the reservation as a farmer, trader, and negotiator. He is considered the last of the great Crow war chiefs and had a tremendous influence on the tribe's relations with white settlers.

Plenty Coups was considered special even as a young child. His grandfather foresaw his role as a chief and named him Alaxchiiaahush, meaning "many accomplishments" or "plenty coups." During his early years he had a vision that seemed not only to foretell the future but also to dictate the path the Crow would have to follow in order to survive.

When he was 11, Plenty Coups went into the mountains on a vision quest. He was gone for three days, and when he returned he shared his dream with the group's elders. He claimed he had seen large herds of buffalo disappearing across the plains and a new strange animal arriving to take their place. He described seeing all the trees in the forest blow over with a great gust of wind until only one remained standing straight and tall. The elders declared that his dream was a vision of the future and that it meant the buffalo would disappear and be replaced by the white men's cattle. They believed the forest represented all the Plains Indian tribes and the white men, like the wind, would tear through their land and way of life. The fallen trees were interpreted as the tribes that resisted and fought the settlers. The sole tree standing represented the Crow; they would survive because they would work with, rather than against, the whites. The Crow used this dream as a guide for the next several years, and when it came time to fight, they joined the side of the whites and fought against other tribes.

Plenty Coups earned several "coups" as a valiant and skilled warrior. He had a reputation for being intelligent and fearless and was believed to have had at least 80 feathers on his coup stick, each representing an act of bravery. In addition, he proved to be an eloquent and moving orator. When the Crows were transferred to their reservation, Plenty Coups advocated that they ought to do their best to adapt to this new way of life. He led by example, cultivating his individual allotment of land, opening a general store, and building a log cabin in which to live. Plenty Coups was also a great promoter of education, reminding his people that "with education you will be the white man's equal; without it you will be the white man's victim." A persuasive advocate for his people, Plenty Coups negotiated a railroad line through the reservation and made several journeys to Washington, D.C., to represent Native American interests. In turn, Washington recognized him as an important American leader. In 1921 he was invited to speak at the dedication of the Tomb of the Unknown Soldier, which was attended by other important international figures.

In 1928, four years before his death, Plenty Coups decided to dedicate a portion of his land as a memorial to the Crow Nation, stating, "It is given as a token of my friendship for all people, both red and white." Today it is a 40-acre state park located on the Crow Reservation called **Chief Plenty Coups State Park** (406/252-1289, 8 A.M.-8 P.M. daily, day use $5 per vehicle nonresidents) and houses a museum of Crow culture, a visitors center, and a gift shop along with Chief Plenty Coups' log cabin home, general store, and grave.

and 3 P.M. daily Memorial Day–Labor Day, $8 adults, $5 seniors, $2 for children 12 and under), organized through the **Little Big Horn College.** The guides can also be hired for group and private tours and as step-on guides; phone for specialized tour options and prices.

Big Horn County Historical Museum and Visitor Center

Located in Hardin, 15 miles north of the Battle of the Little Bighorn National Monument, Big Horn County Museum (3rd St., Hardin, 406/665-1671, www.bighorncountymuseum.

org, 8 A.M.–5 P.M. daily May–Sept., 8 A.M.–8 P.M. daily June–Aug., 8 A.M.–5 P.M. Mon.–Fri. Oct.–Apr., historical buildings closed Oct.–Apr., free except during Little Bighorn Days in June when admission is $3) contains 20 historical buildings outfitted from the periods in which they originated—a 1922 schoolhouse, a 1917 Evangelical church built by German settlers, a 1906 depot, and buildings from a 1911 working farm. The museum offers excellent hands-on educational programs.

Chief Plenty Coups State Park

For his bravery and leadership, Plenty Coups was made chief of the Crow Nation when he was only 28 years old. In 1884, he became one of the first Crow Indians to own and work a farm. Along with his wife, Strikes the Iron, Plenty Coups built a home, worked the land and operated a general store on his 320-acre plot of land, just east of Pryor. Upon his death in 1932, and according to the wishes of the chief and his wife, 195 acres of their land was turned into a public park known as Chief

Plenty Coups State Park (1 mile west of Pryor, off Pryor Road or Pryor Creek Road, 406/252-1289, 8 A.M.–8 P.M. daily, nonresident day use $5 per vehicle). The park is home to a museum of Crow culture, a visitors center, and a gift shop along with Chief Plenty Coups' log cabin home, general store, and grave.

Bighorn Canyon National Recreational Area

Established by Congress in 1966 after the completion of the Yellowtail Dam, the Bighorn Canyon National Recreation Area (north entrance via Hwy. 313, Fort Smith, headquarters 406/666-2414, visitor information 307/548-5406, www.nps.gov/bica, $5, $30 annual pass) includes 71 miles of Bighorn Lake in a spectacular 55-mile canyon. The recreation area itself straddles the Montana-Wyoming border and offers excellent boating, fishing, bird and wildlife watching, swimming, and picnicking. There are 27 miles of hiking on 13 separate trails. Hiking guides and other information are available at the **Yellowtail Dam Visitor**

Chief Plenty Coups State Park in Pryor, Montana

THE PRYOR MOUNTAINS MUSTANGS

One of the most unforgettable things you can do in Montana is to witness the wild mustangs of the Pryor Mountains. The majority of these horses are believed to share the hereditary line of those brought by Spanish explorers to the Americas more than five centuries ago. They share the distinct colors and markings of the Spanish horse, and recent genetic testing has confirmed this lineage. The mustangs are small horses with narrow but deep chests and strong, short backs. They are often distinguished by a solid stripe running down their backs or the unique "zebra" stripes across their legs.

Although initially wary of the animals that the conquistadores rode, Native Americans quickly learned to prize them. Through the years they were traded and often stolen in raids. Horses used by the Indians or white settlers were known to stray if they were not well maintained, and by the mid-1800s enough free stallions and mares had mated that there were more than 2 million wild horses living west of the Mississippi. At the same time, however, homesteaders were staking out their land and settling in the area. The mustangs' land was needed for houses, farms, and cattle grazing. Seen as an impediment to progress, the wild horses quickly began to disappear, hunted for sport with carcasses often left to rot. If captured alive, they were sent to slaughter and used by pet food companies. By the mid-1900s there were just a handful of herds left.

In response to the work of grassroots organizations and public outcry, the U.S. government sanctioned the **Wild Horse Refuge** in 1968. Some 31,000 acres of diverse range were set aside to protect these majestic animals in the Pryor Mountains, on the border of Montana and Wyoming and enclosed by the Big Horn Canyon to the east and Crooked Creek to the west. Three years later the Wild Free Roaming Horse and Burro Act stipulated that these horses were "an integral part of the natural system of the public land" and were to be protected from future harassment.

Today 120-160 mustangs live on this range, which is maintained by the Bureau of Land Management (BLM). The mustangs live in small social units known as harems, which consist of a dominant stallion, a head mare, other mares, and colts. There are currently estimated to be about 30 harems, each producing 20-30 foals each year. In order to balance the well-being of the horses with the well-being of the public land, the BLM has overseen a wild horse adoption program since 1973.

If you drive along Highway 37 north from Wyoming into the Bighorn Recreation Area, you may get lucky and see some mustangs. There are also outfitters willing to take you into the backcountry for a better chance of seeing these wild and beautiful creatures. As is true for the safety and well-being of any wild animal, it is critical that your presence does not impact or change their behavior in any way. The standard distance to keep from mustangs is 100 feet. For more information, you can contact the **Pryor Mountain Wild Mustang Center** (U.S. 14A, Lovell, WY, just east of town, 307/548-9453, www.pryormustangs. org, 9 A.M.-5 P.M. Mon.-Fri.), who can tell you about current sightings and locations, or the BLM's **Billings Field Office** (5001 Southgate Dr., Billings, 406/896-5013, 7:45 A.M.-4:30 P.M. Mon.-Fri.).

Center (off Hwy. 313 near the top of the dam, 406/666-2412 or 406/666-3218, www.nps. gov/bica, 9 A.M.-5 P.M. daily Memorial Day-Labor Day, phone for weekend hours May and Sept., closed Oct.-Apr.). Pontoon boats can be rented from the **Ok-A-Beh Marina** (Hardin, 406/666-2349, 8 A.M.-6:30 P.M. daily Memorial Day-Labor Day, $275 per day). There are numerous free campgrounds within the boundaries of the recreation area, many of which are open all year.

St. Labre Mission and Cheyenne Indian Museum

St. Labre Mission (1000 Tongue River Rd., Ashland, 406/784-4500, www.stlabre.org, tours 8 A.M.–4:30 P.M. daily Memorial Day–Labor Day) began as the St. Labre Indian School in 1884 under the guidance of the Ursuline Sisters. The school and mission were founded before the Northern Cheyenne Indian Reservation was officially set up by the U.S. government. George Yoakum, a former soldier and Roman Catholic from Miles City, requested that Montana Bishop John Brondel go to help the wandering Cheyenne who were congregating in the Tongue River Valley. Brondel purchased the land, and the St. Labre School was founded in March 1884.

The original three-room cabin, of which there is a replica today, served as the church, the school, and the dormitory for both students and nuns. The school has always blended Cheyenne culture with Roman Catholicism; in 1970 the Cheyenne language was added to the elementary curriculum because many of the children had never learned it. The course was so well received that a night course was added for adults. Today the St. Labre Indian School educates nearly 800 Northern Cheyenne and Crow students from kindergarten through high school on three campuses.

A 1971 church on the site was constructed in tipi form, with a cross as the center pole. The Cheyenne Indian Museum on the site offers an opportunity to see various Plains Indian artifacts as well as a short documentary film on the St. Labre School. The museum is open weekdays year-round, 8 A.M.–4:30 P.M., on the Saturdays of Memorial Day and Independence Day weekends, 9 A.M.–3 P.M., and all weekend over Labor Day, 9 A.M.–3 P.M. Admission is free.

ENTERTAINMENT AND EVENTS
(Crow Fair

Crow Fair (406/638-3896, www.crow-fair.com) is an annual powwow held on the Crow Indian Reservation the third week in August to celebrate the past, present, and future of the Crow people. The event is awash in vibrant color, sound, and taste and is certainly one of the best times to visit the reservation; it's called the "tipi capital of the world" for the more than 1,500 tipis that are erected at the site. Crow Fair is a major event not only for Crow Indians but for Native Americans across the U.S., who come to participate in the competitive dancing and drumming and what is considered to be the largest all-Indian rodeo in the United States. There are daily parades, evening grand entries, horse racing of many varieties, and rodeo in addition to nonstop food and music.

The festivities take place mainly at the fairgrounds in Crow Agency, 60 miles southeast of Billings off I-90.

Little Big Horn Days and the Last Stand Reenactment

Little Big Horn Days (Hardin, 406/665-1672 or 406/665-3577, www.custerslaststand.org) entails four days of celebrations—some festive, others sober—commemorating the region's history and, in particular, its proximity to the Battle of the Little Bighorn. The festivities include a quilt show, a book fair, and a historical dance—the 1876 Grand Ball—as well as arts and crafts sales, a symposium, and a parade, all culminating in the dramatic and well-attended Custer's Last Stand Reenactment. It requires more than 200 actors and is performed from the Indian perspective in a script written by historian Joe Medicine Crow. The event takes place on a ranch six miles west of Hardin, not far from the actual battlefield, and tickets ($20 adults, $8 children 6–12, free for children under 6) can be purchased online at www.custerslaststand.org or by calling 888/450-3577.

Powwows on the Northern Cheyenne Indian Reservation

There are two powwows held annually on the Northern Cheyenne Indian Reservation. The largest celebration for the tribe is the **Fourth of July Powwow** (Kenneth Beartusk Memorial Powwow Grounds, 3 miles south of Lame Deer, 406/477-8222, www.cheyennenation.com, camping permitted), which happens over the course of four days around July 4. There are princess contests for princesses from all

CROW FAIR: THE TIPI CAPITAL OF THE WORLD

© DONNIE SEXTON

tipis at Crow Fair near Crow Agency, Montana

Held annually since 1904 in the third week of August, Crow Fair is considered the largest outdoor powwow in the world. The five-day celebration was introduced to the Crow people – their traditional name is Apsáalooke, which means "children of the large-beaked bird" but was misinterpreted to mean "crow" – by S. C. Reynolds, an Indian Affairs agent assigned to the reservation around the turn of the 20th century. His goal was to encourage the nomadic Crow to become more settled and agrarian on the reservation, which was neither their traditional homeland nor particularly well suited for farming. He modeled the concept for the fair after the county fairs that were popular around the country at the time. The tribe's initial reaction was purportedly less than enthusiastic. In an effort to increase their willingness to participate, Reynolds relaxed the strict ban on "Indian doings" for the days of the Crow Fair, giving the Crow their only legal opportunity to dance, sing, and speak in their traditional ways. Recognizing it as an opportunity to openly pass on Crow culture to younger generations, the tribe eagerly accepted the opportunity, and Crow Fair

has been held annually ever since, except during the world wars and the Great Depression. Today, close to 85 percent of the tribe speak Crow as their first language, a much higher percentage than among other Native American groups in the state.

The celebration itself is lively and colorful, with some 12,000 people camping out in more than 1,500 tipis erected on the banks of the Little Bighorn River. Native Americans from various tribes around the country and visitors from around the world come to participate or just witness the competitive dancing and drumming, the all-Indian Championship Rodeo, the pari-mutuel horse racing, and the family reunion-like camaraderie that pervades this time-honored event. The hot, dusty late-summer air is thick with smells – Indian fry bread and Indian tacos – and with the bullhorn whine of the camp-crier and the jingling of the tobacco lids that decorate the elaborate costumes of some of the dancers. Crow Fair is a feast for the senses and a wonderful way to appreciate the traditions and culture of some of the people who were here long before the Europeans.

tribes, open dance and drum competitions, parades, grand entries, and daily gourd dancing. Traditional Native American food is available. Guests are welcome, and photography is allowed.

There is a **second powwow** (at the arbor between St. Labre and Ashland, 0.5 miles off U.S. 212, 406/784-2883, www.cheyennenation.com) every year for four days on Labor Day weekend. Drummers and dancers from tribes across the country participate in the festivities. The flag-raising occurs each morning at 9 A.M., and the dancing concludes each night at midnight. The powwow welcomes visitors and provides an excellent opportunity to learn about and celebrate Northern Cheyenne culture.

FISHING AND OUTDOOR RECREATION

The fishing on the Bighorn River is legendary, and there is no shortage of fly shops and outfitters available to help visitors find big, beautiful trout. The Bighorn is known for trout that are plentiful in both size and number; dry fly fishing is almost always an option, but nymphing and streamer fishing are useful under certain water conditions as well. Although fishing is certainly more popular during the temperate season, the Bighorn is a tail-water fishery—thanks to the Yellowtail Dam—meaning that the river never freezes in winter and stays fishable year-round.

The area's original fly shop and outfitter, **Bighorn Angler** (577 Parksdale Court, Fort Smith, 406/666-2233, www.bighornangler.com) offers complete outfitting service with everything from simple but nice motel rooms ($55–90) to experienced guides, boat rentals, and quality tackle.

In the **Bighorn Canyon National Recreation Area** (north entrance via Hwy. 313, Fort Smith, headquarters 406/666-2414, visitor information 307/548-5406, www.nps.gov/bica, $5, $30 annual pass), fishing can be done from shore or in a boat either in the Bighorn River or on Bighorn Lake—home to brown, rainbow, and lake trout as well as walleye, smallmouth bass,

channel catfish, and even ling and shovel nose sturgeon. There are 27 miles of hiking trails, the majority of which are in the southern portion of the recreation area. A hiking guide is available at the **Yellowtail Dam Visitors Center** (off Hwy. 313 near the top of the dam, 406/666-2412 or 406/666-3218, www.nps.gov/bica, 9 A.M.–5 P.M. daily Memorial Day–Labor Day, phone for weekend hours May and Sept., closed Oct.–Apr.).

On the Northern Cheyenne Indian Reservation, **Cheyenne Trailriders** (past mile marker 28 on U.S. 212, 3 miles east of Busby, 406/592-3520 or 406/740-2779, cheyride@rangeweb.net) affords visitors an opportunity to explore the reservation on horseback. In order to increase awareness and appreciation of Cheyenne history and culture, they offer workshops on history, culture, and ethnobotany. Guides are also happy to teach you about gourd dancing, intertribal hand games, round dancing, and Indian sign language around an evening campfire. There are storytellers and flute players to entertain riders, and wagon trips are available for nonriders.

ACCOMMODATIONS

A safe bet for accommodations in Hardin is the **American Inn** (1324 N. Crawford St., Hardin, 406/665-1870 or 800/582-8094, www.hardinamericaninn.com, from $80), with clean and comfortable guest rooms; the kids will flip for the two-story water slide that dominates the outdoor pool.

A historical and very worthwhile place to stay in Hardin is the **Kendrick House Inn** (206 N. Custer Ave., Hardin, 406/665-3035, from $89), a 1915 Edwardian boardinghouse. There are five guest rooms, and a couple of suites with private baths are available, all meticulously decorated with period furniture.

Just three miles south of Hardin, the Orvis-endorsed **Eagle Nest Lodge** (3100 Eagle Nest Rd., Hardin, 406/665-3711 or 866/258-FISH—866/258-3174, www.eaglenestlodge.com, from $350 d) is a beautiful and traditional log lodge ideally suited for fishing and bird hunting. The lodge has seven well-appointed guest rooms, all with private baths, and the meals—breakfast, field lunch, and dinner—are superb. There are guides on-site, and owners John and Rebecca are exceedingly gracious and always available to point guests in the right direction. Call for information on packages related to fishing, hunting, or cast-and-blast.

CAMPING

Little Bighorn Camp (406/638-2232, $13 tents, $21 full-hookup RV) is immediately adjacent to the Little Bighorn National Monument. In addition to 15 tent sites and 20 RV sites with full hookups, there is a small grocery store, a gas station, a Laundromat, and a small motel.

FOOD

In much of Montana, especially in eastern Montana and on the Indian reservations, dining options are few and far between. Still, there are some good places to be found.

Immediately off the highway near the Little Bighorn Battlefield National Monument is the **Custer Battlefield Trading Post and Café** (406/638-2270, daily in summer 8 A.M.–9 P.M.; daily in winter 9 A.M.–5 P.M., entrées $4–10), a tourist shop and restaurant that obviously appeals to locals. There is quite a selection of Crow Indian handicrafts in the shop, and the restaurant offers Indian tacos, buffalo burgers, and plenty of variations on Montana beef.

The Purple Cow (Hwy. 47, just north of Hardin, 406/655-3601) offers a welcome change from the fast food that dominates cuisine in the area. The shakes and pies are fantastic—as is true across most of eastern Montana—and the family-friendly menu leans toward hefty burgers, sandwiches, and steaks.

Polly's Place in Fort Smith (Fort Smith, 406/666-2255 or 866/658-7688, www.pollysonthebighorn.com, 6:30 A.M.–2 hours after sunset daily Apr.–Sept., phone for off-season

hours, entrées $7–23) is like heaven on earth for anglers, and not because it is the only public restaurant in this tiny fishing town: The chef is creative and offers fresh organic dishes with Southwestern flair. There are always good steaks, pasta, salads, and a nightly special.

INFORMATION AND SERVICES

In some ways, visiting Native American reservations can be a bit like exploring another country. The tribes have worked fiercely to protect their culture and preserve their history. They also live according to their own values rather than any imposed on them. As a result, time can take on a different meaning: Few things happen precisely when it is stated they will. Travelers should adjust accordingly and learn to be more spontaneous. In addition, the technology that many of us reply on is not nearly as critical to some Native Americans; you may not get an answer the first few times you call someone. Persistence pays off, and patience serves travelers well.

The **Crow Tribal Council Headquarters** is a good source of local information (P.O. Box 159, Crow Agency, MT 59022, 406/638-3700, www.crownations.net). The **Tourism Office and Visitors Center** can be reached at 406/638-7272.

The **Northern Cheyenne Tribal Office** can be reached at 406/477-6284. The **Northern Cheyenne Chamber of Commerce** (U.S. 212, Lame Deer, 406/477-8844) is another source of information on the reservation.

GETTING THERE

The Crow Indian Reservation is easily accessed from I-90, which runs the length of the reservation. **The Northern Cheyenne Indian Reservation** is accessed by U.S. 212, which runs east–west, or by Highways 39 or 314, both of which run north–south.

Miles City

Miles City (population 9,000, elevation 2,371 feet) has always been a cowboy town. After the 1876 campaign against the Indians, including the Battle of the Little Bighorn, the 5th Infantry established camp at the confluence of the Tongue and Yellowstone Rivers under the leadership of Col. Nelson A. Miles. In 1881 the arrival of the Northern Pacific Railway assured the longevity of the settlement, and in 1884 the Montana Stockgrowers Association was formed, creating an important and long-lasting link to the cattle market. The brick buildings that line Main Street today are much as they were when this town boomed in the late 1800s and early 1900s.

The biggest event in Miles City and its claim to fame today is the annual Miles City Bucking Horse Sale, which at least doubles the population of the town and reflects its heritage and openness in all its glory. A Montana Mardi Gras with cowboys and chaps, the weekend celebration is probably one of the five best events in the state.

While Miles City has never shed its rough and weathered exterior or its boom-and-bust sensibility, there is something of a subtle renaissance happening. On top of its cowboy culture—stop in any diner before 8 A.M. to see the town's old guard—there is a youthful exuberance to the city that is evident in new cutting-edge art galleries, the vitality of the Range Riders Museum, a plan for greenways throughout the city, and excellent recreation facilities. Indeed, surrounded by badlands and prairie, Miles City unites the best of Montana past and present.

SIGHTS
Range Riders Museum

The fabulous Range Riders Museum (435 L. P. Anderson Rd., 406/232-6146 or 406/232-4483, 8 A.M.–8 P.M. daily Apr. 1–Oct. 31, or

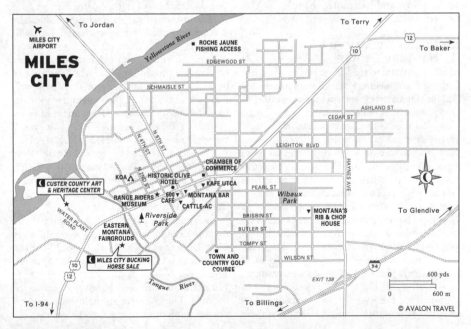

by appointment, $5 adults, $1 students, $0.50 children under 6) is a gem. Plan to spend some time, and don't be bashful about striking up a conversation with caretaker-curator Bob Barthelmess or his wife, Betty Ann, both octogenarians who have been the heart and soul of the Range Riders since 1976.

The museum was founded in 1939 by a group of locals dedicated to preserving their heritage. Today it has 11 buildings and thousands of artifacts that include old saddles and clothing, machinery, dinosaur bones, phenomenal photographs by L. A. Huffman and Christian Barthelmess (Bob's grandfather, an Army photographer born in Germany), and 400 antique firearms in the Bert Clark Gun Collection. Bob commandeered a team of volunteers to build two spectacular dioramas of the 1877 Battle of Lame Deer and Fort Keogh, and an almost life-size replica of Main Street in Miles City circa 1877. **Pioneer Day,** usually held in June, fills the museum with activities, reenactments, food, and entertainment. This museum has been a labor of love for so many, and it captures the spirit of this frontier town.

◖ Custer County Art & Heritage Center

Quite a contrast to the Range Riders Museum but just as compelling is the Custer County Art & Heritage Center (Waterplant Rd., 406/234-0635, www.ccac.milescity.org, 9 A.M.–5 P.M. Tues.–Sun. Feb.–Dec., free). Creatively housed in the concrete basins of the 1910 waterworks that provided the city's drinking water for more than 60 years, the award-winning museum specializes in contemporary Montana artists but has regional and national changing shows. Part museum, part gallery, the center also owns the state's largest public collection of works by photographer L. A. Huffman in addition to photos by Lady Evelyn Cameron, E. S. Curtis, and Christian Barthelmess. Interesting local art, pottery, photos, and books are available in the gift shop. The museum hosts a series of design shows every year or two, focusing on everything from artisanal pieces like handmade

fiddles and furniture to industrial design in iconic cars and motorcycles.

Just outside the center, which is located on the Yellowstone River, is a gorgeous park, the ideal spot for a shaded picnic. Century-old cottonwoods tower over a beautifully manicured lawn with picnic benches and a modest playground. If nothing else, this is a perfect spot to stretch your legs.

ENTERTAINMENT AND EVENTS
◖ Miles City Bucking Horse Sale

Held annually the third full weekend in May, the Bucking Horse Sale (406/234-7700 or 406/853-1700, www.buckinghorsesale.com) is in many ways the granddaddy of all rodeos. Simply stated, it is where the top rodeo contractors come to get their stock, but it has defined Miles City and given it serious swagger since 1914. The image of a headstrong cowboy hitchhiking a lonely highway with nothing in hand but his trusty saddle and the shirt on his back is realized here year after year—they come to ride the best broncs in the business.

In addition to the central bronc sale, the event is rounded out by concerts, bull riding, pari-mutuel horse racing, street dances each night, and a good old-fashioned parade on Saturday morning. The whole affair can be slightly bawdy, and it's true that the town's many bars take out all their furniture to make room for thirsty cowboys. If you arrive Monday morning after the Bucking Horse Sale, you'll see what a hungover town looks like.

The annual **Eastern Montana Fair** (406/234-3848) in late August brings Custer County together with five others for four days of nonstop entertainment, rodeo, concerts, fireworks, exhibits, and a carnival.

In September, as the fields turn golden and there is a crispness to the air, the small **Miles City Bluegrass Festival** (406/234-2480 or 406/853-1678) brings people together. The event is held at the Eastern Montana Fairgrounds and features bands from across the country. The concerts are held indoors, and limited outdoor camping is available.

© DONNIE SEXTON

Miles City Bucking Horse Sale

Shakespeare in the Parks (406/994-3901, www.montana.edu/shakespeare) performs at least one engagement every summer in Miles City at the Pumping Plant Park of the Custer County Art & Heritage Center. And Miles City's own **Barn Players** (406/234-6736) is one of the oldest theater groups in the state, producing a couple of small performances each year.

SHOPPING

Located in an old church listed on the National Register of Historic Places, **Pleasantries** (1720 Main St., 406/234-5644, 10 A.M.–6 P.M. Tues.–Sat.) is a unique little gift shop with great home accessories and everything from purses and jewelry to toiletries. They also carry a few local items, including Montana agate chimes, made of stones from the Yellowstone River.

In business since 1909, **Miles City Saddlery** (808 Main St., 406/232-2512, www.milescitysaddlery.com) is famous for having originated the Coggshall Saddle. The shop is a step back in time with exceptional custom saddles, clothing, boots and belts, hats, tack, and gifts.

FISHING AND OUTDOOR RECREATION

For outdoor recreation, one need not travel too far from town. There are fishing accesses (and in some cases boat launches) on the Yellowstone River at **Roche Jaune** (Truscott St. and N. 6th St.), **Kinsey Bridge** (10 miles east of Miles City, on a gravel road intersecting Valley Dr. E.), and **Pirogue Island State Park** (3 miles northeast of Miles City), where Lewis and Clark camped on their cross-country journey. The 269-acre park is a haven for waterfowl, bald eagles, and white-tailed and mule deer. **Spotted Eagle Recreation Area** (just south of the Eastern Montana Fairgrounds) is a quiet place for walks, picnics, and fishing in the small artificial lake. Disabled-accessible fishing access and picnic benches are being added.

Avid golfers can hit the links in Miles City at the nine-hole **Town & Country Club** (4th St. and Eagle St., 406/234-1500, $15–30), which runs along the Tongue River. There is a driving range and a number of open tournaments during the season.

ACCOMMODATIONS

Although there are a number of larger chain hotels on the way into Miles City (Best Western War Bonnet Inn, EconoLodge, Holiday Inn Express, Motel 6) the **Historic Olive Hotel** (501 Main St., 406/234-2450, $50–75) is a wonderful place to stay. The rooms are hardly fancy or grand, but they are clean and accommodating, and the location is unbeatable. There's also a ghost to be reckoned with—but don't worry, she's friendly.

The Cross M Ranch (406/557-2667 or 877/557-2667, www.crossmranch.com, $1,400 per week includes room, meals, horse, and activities, May 3–Sept. 26) in nearby Cohagen is a working ranch, not a dude ranch, and as such caters more to adult travelers. Guests are expected to participate in the day-to-day operations of running cow-calf pairs on 10,000 acres, which includes checking for strays, doctoring cattle, moving and sorting livestock, checking water, and mending fences. The accommodations are comfortable and traditional in a bunkhouse with four private rooms, and the maximum capacity is eight guests.

CAMPING

There are a few campgrounds in and around Miles City. The **Miles City KOA** (1 Palmer St., 406/232-3991 or 800/562-3909, www.koa. com/where/mt/26114, $18–21 tents, $25–34 RVs, $38–50 cabins) is tucked in the cottonwood trees on the banks of the Tongue River just six blocks from downtown. Free wireless Internet is provided, along with an outdoor swimming pool and bicycle rentals.

FOOD

True to its cow-town status, Miles City is a meat-and-potatoes mecca. The **600 Café** (600 Main St., 406/234-3860, 5 A.M.–2 P.M. daily) is *the* place for breakfast in town. Relatively unchanged since 1946, the café serves hearty breakfasts and lunches, including hand-cut steaks and hamburgers processed on-site daily—no frozen patties here—along with homemade soups, gravy, country sausage, pie, and more. The historic photos on the wall give visitors an excellent introduction to the spirit of Miles City.

The curiously named **Cattle-ac** (420 Pacific, 406/234-6987, entrées from $15) is a favorite steak house–saloon (and casino). The sour cream and chive-spiced fries taste supremely better than they sound.

Although there are a few of these across Montana and Wyoming, **Montana's Rib & Chop House** (3020 Stower St., 406/234-9200, www.ribandchophouse.com, entrées $19) is wildly popular with locals. From pulled pork sandwiches to New York strip and cedar-plank salmon, the Rib & Chop House does simple, hearty Western cuisine very well.

A trip to Miles City would not be complete without a drink at the **Montana Bar** (612 Main St., 406/234-5809). The bar has been serving thirsty patrons since 1902 and has managed to keep its incredible original back bar in beautiful shape all these years. The expansive leather booths, beveled leaded glass, and marble tile floors are all original. The bar stools and the juke box are just about the only additions in the last century. It is a remarkable place to sip a cold drink and reflect on just how much things haven't changed in little pockets like this across the West.

There is free Wi-Fi at **Kafe Utza** (19 S. 9th St., 406/234-9821, 7:30 A.M.–6 P.M. Mon.–Fri., 9 A.M.–2 P.M. Sat.). You can check your email and fill your stomach with mouthwatering freshly baked French pastries; this is Miles City's very own European coffee house.

INFORMATION AND SERVICES

The **Chamber of Commerce** (511 Pleasant St., 406/234-2890, www.mcchamber.com, 9 A.M.–5 P.M. Mon.–Fri.) is a block from Main Street and has maps, brochures for local businesses, restaurant and hotel listings, museum information, and very friendly staff.

The **main post office** is at 106 North 7th Street (8 A.M.–5:30 P.M. Mon.–Fri., 9 A.M.–noon Sat.).

The **Miles City Library** (1 S. 10th St., 406/234-1496, 10 A.M.–6 P.M. Tues.–Fri., 9 A.M.–5 P.M. Sat., www.milescitypubliclibrary.

org) is at Main 10th Streets; computers with Internet access are available.

The **Mudds n' Suds Laundromat** (918 Bridge St., 406/234-9076, open 24-7) also houses an espresso bar (7 A.M.–5 P.M. Mon.–Fri., 7 A.M.– noon Sat.), which allows you to enjoy a hot cappuccino while your clothes rinse and spin.

Holy Rosary Health Care (2600 Wilson St., 406/233-2600, www.holyrosaryhealthcare. org) has a 24-hour emergency room as well as a walk-in clinic (8 A.M.–4:30 P.M. Mon.–Fri.) and urgent care on the weekends (noon–6 P.M. Fri.–Mon.).

GETTING THERE

Two miles northwest of the city, the **Miles City Frank Wiley Field Airport** (MLS, 406/234-1296) is currently only served by Great Lakes Airlines with flights to and from Denver.

I-94 runs through Miles City, making it an easy destination by car. It is 145 miles east of Billings and 78 miles west of Glendive.

The ticket office at the **Trailways** bus depot (in an alley at 515½ Main St., 406/234-3900) is open 9 A.M.–11 P.M. seven days a week. There is daily service to cities in Montana, the Dakotas, and Wyoming.

Miles City to Medicine Lake

The stretch of road from Miles City to Medicine Lake is sparsely populated and subtly beautiful. This is cattle country and the beginning of the badlands. The Yellowstone River cuts through the rugged country as it flows northeast to the North Dakota border. I-94 parallels the river, echoing the Yellowstone's one-time importance as a means of transportation and shipping. This area was once home to the country's last great bison herd, but the slaughter of these animals in the early 1880s nearly wiped out the species, ending a long and important chapter in U.S. history. The hides of the animals were shipped out, first by steamboat and eventually by rail when the Northern Pacific came through in 1881; by 1883 the bison were gone.

Small, colorful towns dot the region and have origins that date back to the Indian Wars and before. **Terry,** named for General Alfred E. Terry, emerged from a dugout that offered food and lodging to soldiers fighting the Sioux. The town later became known for one of its esteemed residents, pioneering photographer Evelyn Cameron, a wealthy Englishwoman who ranched in the area with her husband and captured the often gritty life of local homesteaders. A museum in town honors her art and legacy.

The history of **Glendive** dates back even further. Lewis and Clark camped near the present-day town site in 1806 on their way back from Oregon, and they reportedly shot a huge white grizzly bear four times without killing it. An Irish nobleman hunting bison, bears, and ungulates in the region gave the name Glendive to a small tributary of the Yellowstone River. The town itself sprouted up with the arrival of the Northern Pacific Railway in 1880.

Just this side of the North Dakota border, **Wibaux** is named for French cattle king Pierre Wibaux, who left the family textile empire in Roubaix, France, for the wilds of Montana in 1883. Over time, he amassed a herd of 65,000 cattle. In 1884, with money from his father, Wibaux commissioned the construction of St. Peter's Catholic Church by Norman French immigrants with stunning local fieldstone and lava rock. It is an exquisitely unexpected piece of noble architecture that still stands today.

Farther north, towns such as **Sidney** and **Fairview** survive thanks to a robust sugar beet industry, and across the region, local people's lives are tied to the land through agriculture, ranching, and more recently, energy production.

With intact badlands, grasslands, and wetlands, this part of the state is a birder's paradise. The region is home to a number of national wildlife refuges, wildlife management areas, and tracts of public land, all of which provide marvelous habitat for an enormous number of avian species. Part wetland, part prairie, Medicine Lake National Wildlife Refuge is a spectacular place to see migrating birds at various times of year. Although it is not a common destination, driving through this part of the state is a magnificent way to enjoy the ride on the way from one place to the next.

SIGHTS
Evelyn Cameron Gallery

Located in Terry, adjacent to the **Prairie County Museum** (101 Logan Ave., Terry, 406/635-4040, 9 A.M.–3 P.M. Mon. and Wed.–Fri., 1–4 P.M. Sat.–Sun. Memorial Day–Labor Day), the Evelyn Cameron Gallery (105 Logan Ave., Terry, 406/635-4040, www.evelyncameron.org, same hours as the museum) pays homage to a fascinating woman who captured the spirit of the often hardscrabble life in eastern Montana with captivating photos and meticulous journals. Thousands of Cameron's negatives were discovered in the late 1970s by Time-Life Books editor Donna

Lucey, who published them in her landmark work *Photographing Montana 1894–1928: The Life and Work of Evelyn Cameron*. The gallery is home to many of Cameron's images, both originals and reprints. Her work is a striking testament to the passage of time on the Western frontier, and at the same time a reminder of how much remains the same in eastern Montana.

◖ Makoshika State Park

Montana's largest state park at more than 11,000 acres, Makoshika State Park (1301 Snyder Ave., Glendive, 406/377-MAKO—406/377-6256, www.makoshika.org, 10 A.M.–6 P.M. daily Memorial Day–Labor Day, 9 A.M.–5 P.M. daily Labor Day–Memorial Day, $5 per vehicle, $1 pp, $10 camping, free for Montana residents) is literally at the perimeter of Glendive. The park is an intriguing if not altogether beautiful place, made up of colorful exposed rock layers that look like petrified anthills.

Makoshika (muh-KO-shi-kuh) was created in 1953 and named for the Lakota word that

Makoshika State Park in Glendive, Montana

© DONNIE SEXTON

means "badlands." An impressive **visitors center** gives an excellent overview of the park's geological significance and helps visitors easily navigate the rock layers according to color, distinguishing the Age of Reptiles (dinosaurs!) from the Age of Mammals. Millions of years old, these badlands expose older rock layers than those in North Dakota and have produced some important dinosaur fossils, including a triceratops skull. Hikers have been known to find fossilized shark teeth and alligator teeth, but all rocks and fossils must stay in the park.

The park is well-suited for exploration in a number of different ways. There are four miles of paved roads and 12 miles of unpaved road (which can be impassable at certain times of year). There are three developed trails that offer good hiking opportunities: the **Diane Gabriel Trail,** the **Cap Rock Nature Trail,** and the **Kinney Coulee Hiking Trail.** Trail guide pamphlets and free advice are available at the visitors center. There are also a number of picnic benches, shelters, and an 18-basket **Disc Golf Course.** Although there are pines and junipers throughout the park, there is little shade in this compelling play of light and color, so

bring water and a hat. The park ties the record for hottest place in Montana at 117°F.

Makoshika Dinosaur Museum

For visitors in search of more dinosaur bones and exhibits, Glendive's Makoshika Dinosaur Museum (111 Bell St., 406/377-1637, www.makoshika.com, 10 A.M.–5 P.M. Tues.–Sat. Memorial Day–Labor Day, $5 adults, $3 students and seniors, free for children under 6) is a good bet. In addition to nice displays of fossils, sculptures, casts, and painstaking dioramas, the museum offers daily dinosaur digs geared to aspiring paleontologists age six and up with **Baisch's Dinosaur Digs** (406/635-4133, jsbaisch@wb.midrivers.com, $100 pp, $75 half-day, free for children under 12 with a paying adult). The paleontological day trips take place on a nearby private ranch in view of Makoshika State Park. For visitors who want to take home their own fossil finds, this is really the only legal way to do it.

◖ Medicine Lake National Wildlife Refuge

The Medicine Lake National Wildlife Refuge

THE MONTANA DINOSAUR TRAIL

Before Montana had cowboys, Indians, ranchers, and homesteaders, even before the Missouri and Yellowstone Rivers were formed, this was dinosaur territory. The world's first *Tyrannosaurus rex* was discovered in Montana, as was the world's first baby dinosaur bones. Sites across the state are dedicated to celebrating this unique and rich history, and the Montana Dinosaur Trail, created in 2005, consists of 15 different facilities in 12 communities. The stops along the trail include museums, parks, educational centers, and field stations, all of which are committed to finding and preserving dinosaur specimens. These sites have numerous well-preserved fossils, complete dinosaur skeletons, perfectly honed replicas, and even some active dig sites that are open to the public.

The **Fort Peck Field Station of Paleontology** allows visitors to see how a fossil laboratory works; paleontologists conduct research and prepare molds and casts of fossils. The **Fort Peck Interpretive Center and Museum** boasts the most complete *T. rex* skeleton ever found. You are greeted with a life-size model of the ferocious carnivore when you enter the museum. Glendive is home to the **Makoshika Dinosaur Museum** and **Makoshika State Park,** where at least 10 different dinosaur species have been found; the museum displays an impressive collection of dinosaur fossils from around the world. The furthest eastern stop on the Dinosaur Trail is the **Carter County Museum** in Ekalaka. This is Montana's first county museum and displays complete dinosaur skeletons found in the nearby Hell Creek formation.

is a wetland oasis in a sea of prairie. It is a startlingly beautiful place on a breezy afternoon when the grasses sway in watery waves, or on a stormy night when lightning flashes across the sky, illuminating clouds that are 15 shades of blue and pink, or at any time, really—it is just that beautiful. And like so much of eastern Montana, it is not what you might expect to see in a state known for its mountains.

The Medicine Lake National Wildlife Refuge Complex (406/789-2305, www.fws.gov/medicinelake) comprises two wildlife refuges and a wetland management district. Established in 1935, the area provides a much-used breeding and stopover habitat for an enormous range of migratory birds, including ducks, geese, swans, cranes, white pelicans, and grebes. As such, the refuge is as much an oasis for landlocked ocean lovers and wildlife photographers as it is for migrating birds. The sounds and smells and even some of the sights can immediately conjure feelings of a favorite coastal haunt.

There are plenty of opportunities for birdwatching, and what you see will depend on the time of year you visit. There are roads to cruise along and trails to explore. Hunting and fishing are permitted on the refuge as well; be sure to get up-to-date information about seasons and regulations, licensing, and necessary permits from the **U.S. Fish and Wildlife Service** (223 N. Shore Road, 406/789-2305, www.fws.gov/medicinelake). Camping is not permitted in the refuge, but sites are available in nearby Medicine Lake or Plentywood.

The refuge is located on Highway 16, just south of the tiny town of Medicine Lake, which has very limited accommodations (www.medicinelakemt.com), most of which are modest rentals. The nearest towns with significant hotel and motel accommodations and services—Plentywood and Culbertson—are 20-plus miles away to the north and south, respectively, so be sure to bring what you need for the time you plan to spend exploring the refuge.

RECREATION

Since I-94 parallels the Yellowstone River from Billings to Glendive, you can be sure

there are ample **fishing opportunities** at just about any exit. The Yellowstone is filled with trout and, oddly enough, paddlefish: These prehistoric monstrosities in the sturgeon family can weigh more than 100 pounds and are caught only by snagging and then fighting them, sometimes for hours. The paddlefishing season on the Yellowstone is May 15–June 30. Paddlefish roe is considered a delicacy among caviar connoisseurs but can only be purchased outside Montana.

The Missouri River also flows through the region and offers an abundance of trout, salmon, pike, and the occasional paddlefish.

Despite the abundance of gentle terrain in the region, there are only a few golf courses in the area, most of them nine-holers. The **Cottonwood Country Club** (508 Country Club Dr., Glendive, 406/377-8797, www.cottonwoodcc.com, $19 for 9 holes on weekdays, $23 for 9 holes on weekends, $29 for 18 holes on weekdays, $34 for 18 holes on weekends) in Glendive is a lovely course with long holes, wide fairways, and mature cottonwood trees.

ACCOMMODATIONS AND CAMPING

Wherever you find communities in Montana, most often you'll find at least a couple of roadside motels; options in eastern Montana, however, can be somewhat limited. In Terry, the 1912 **Kempton Hotel** (204 Spring St., Terry, 406/635-5543, $75) has hosted such notable figures as Teddy Roosevelt and Calamity Jane. The hotel is showing its age, and long-range plans are in place to restore it to its original glory.

Glendive is a safe bet for a comfortable, clean room. There are a number of chain motels, but more interesting is the **Charley Montana Bed & Breakfast** (103 N. Douglas St., Glendive, 406/365-3207 or 888/395-3207, www.charley-montana.com, $125–150), a grand old 25-room mansion built in 1907 for stockman Charles Krug, now maintained with period ambience and a casual atmosphere.

In addition to camping at Makoshika State

Park, there are two private campgrounds in Glendive. The AAA-rated **Green Valley Campground** (124 Green Valley Lane, Glendive, 406/377-1944 or 406/377-4156, www.greenvalleycampground.com, $13 tent sites, $15.50 RV sites with electric and water, $16.50 full hook-up) has plenty of greenery and is located near the Yellowstone River. Trout fishing is allowed on the premises without a license, and there are plenty of other activities. There are 60 camp sites as well as hot showers.

FOOD

This is bar-food country and an excellent place for hamburger and chicken-fried steak lovers. Some of the fun is finding the best piece of pie, the juiciest burger, or the strongest coffee. Don't expect gourmet fare, but you can expect big portions and good, simple food.

Pie lovers would do well to stop in Terry at the very red and white **Dizzy Diner** (316 E. Spring St., Terry, 406/635-4666, entrées $5–8), which has a pretty complete menu including wraps, burgers, and pizzas. But the pie's the thing, and the strawberry rhubarb may make you weep. This little joint is clean and very air-conditioned when you want it to be.

For a full menu around the clock, Glendive's historic **Jordan Inn** (222 N. Kendrick Ave., Glendive, 406/377-3333 or 406/377-5555) has two restaurants, including **Café Jordan** which stays open 24 hours and serves breakfast, lunch, and dinner (entrées $4–13) and a coffee shop, at least one of which is open 6 A.M.–9 P.M. Dinner in their **Blue Room** (Tues.–Sat. 5:30–9 P.M., entrées $13–38) is especially good and features steaks, prime rib, and seafood pastas.

INFORMATION AND SERVICES

The Glendive Chamber of Commerce (808 N. Merrill Ave., Glendive, 406/377-5601, www.glendivechamber.com) is an excellent resource for everything from guided excursions to daily fishing reports. One of things that makes this chamber unique is that it offers to clean the paddlefish of any angler willing to donate the fish roe, which the chamber then processes into world-class caviar.

The Glendive Medical Center (406/345-3306 or 800/226-7623) is located at 202 Prospect Drive.

GETTING THERE

Glendive is located off I-94 and at the southernmost point of Highway 16, west of the North Dakota border 35 miles near Beach. Glendive is served by the **Rimrock Stages** (800/255-7655, www.rimrocktrailways.com) bus line.

Fort Peck and the Hi-Line

Located in the extreme northeastern corner of the state, the Fort Peck Indian Reservation and the Hi-Line, a string of towns that are collectively named for their location along the northernmost railroad line in the region, are two interesting and tight-knit places that wear their histories like a badge of honor.

As the state's second-largest, the Fort Peck Indian Reservation encompasses more than 2 million acres of land and is home to some 6,800 Assiniboine and Sioux Indians. The land itself is made up of gently rolling hills and fertile agricultural land. Although the reservation was established in the late 1800s, the government negotiated a treaty with the Indians over the course of nearly 20 years that each Indian on the reservation would be given 320 acres of land, not unlike the Homestead Act. The "surplus lands" were opened up to white settlers, and by the 1920s the Indians retained ownership of about half the original reservation. The integration of white settlers and Native Americans is more pronounced on Fort Peck than any other reservation in the state. The

THE SACRED SUN DANCE

Very little is known about the Native American sun dance, a highly revered and often secretive traditional ceremony performed by various tribes in North America. In Montana, the Arapaho, Sioux, Assiniboine, Crow, and Blackfeet are among the Indian Nations that hold this practice sacred. The sun dance represents a spiritual rebirth and regeneration of the land. Participants acquire spiritual powers, often experiencing visions, and invoke blessings for the whole community. In 1875, Lakota chief Sitting Bull formed an alliance with the Cheyenne during a sun dance in which he had a vision of U.S. soldiers falling from the sky. Many saw his vision as foretelling the defeat of the U.S. Army at the Battle of the Little Bighorn in June 1876.

Although each tribe's sun dance has its own characteristics, there are some common elements. Sun dances involve construction of a lodge, dancing, singing, strict fasting among the dancers and subsequent feasting, the erection of a sacred pole, often body painting, and the sacrificial piercing of the chest or back. The sponsor of the dance, along with other leaders, works for months planning the event and performing certain critical rites beforehand. The sun dances themselves are known to last 3-8 days.

Before the introduction of reservation life, the sun dance ceremony provided an opportunity for the various hunting bands within a tribe to come together. Today, it serves a similar purpose in Native American communities. Often members travel from different regions of the country, and regardless of social status or religious affiliation, it provides an occasion for tribe members to reaffirm their cultural identity. Many would argue that important rituals such as the sun dance contribute to the longevity and preservation of Native American culture.

With the introduction of reservations and the determination of the U.S. government to assimilate Native Americans, many practices, including the sun dance, were banned in 1885. Some tribes did not continue with their rituals and ceremonies, and others did so in secret. When the Commission of Indian Affairs lifted the ban on ceremonies in 1934, certain tribes immediately returned to performing this sacred ceremony in public. The Shoshone in Wyoming had not lost the practice, for example, and they reintroduced it to the Crow. The 50th anniversary performance of the Crow sun dance was held in Pryor, Montana, in 1991. Among the Assiniboine and Sioux, the sun dance is done annually on the Fort Peck Indian Reservation.

---

reservation is the site of the Fort Peck Dam, the largest work-relief project to be undertaken during the Great Depression.

Just north of the reservation, the Hi-Line, which includes such communities as Plentywood and Scobey as well as those along U.S. 2, sprouted up with the arrival of the Great Northern Railway in 1887. The railroad brought the farmers into the region and moved the crops out. U.S. 2 runs parallel to the railroad and is the access point for nearly all the communities of any size in this corner of Montana. During the boom of the 1920s, many of these small towns grew with large numbers of settlers hoping to make a living by farming; Plentywood and Scobey are among the largest. The Great Depression and crop-killing drought of the 1930s nearly decimated the region, and populations began to decline, only to see occasional and short-lived growth spurts starting in World War II and ending with the consolidation of farmland by corporations in the early 1970s. The region today struggles to hold on to its youth—bigger cities and jobs are a siren call—but there is a tenacity among the residents, who have lived through boom-and-bust cycles for generations.

PLENTYWOOD

Like all of the towns dotting the Hi-Line, Plentywood (population 2,061, elevation 2,024 feet) is primarily a farming community, although because of its size and proximity to nothing much larger, it has become something of a trade center and a destination for Canadian bargain-shoppers. Plentywood also attracts a good number of bird hunters every autumn.

The town is proud of some unique chapters in its history—the famous Outlaw Trail ran right through here, bringing with it more than its fair share of unsavory characters; and in the 1920s and 1930s the Communist Party was one of the most active in local politics. An oil boom in the 1970s and 1980s caused a population spike, and for a time, poker chips from the many bars in the area were accepted as legal tender almost anywhere in the county.

Sights

The **Sheridan County Museum** (4642 Hwy. 16 S., 406/765-1733, 10 A.M.–5 P.M. daily Memorial Day–Labor Day) is a small but pleasant county museum, conveniently located adjacent to a 24-hour rest area. The museum houses Montana's largest indoor mural, and nearby a historical monument commemorates Sitting Bull's surrender.

One of only six drive-in movie theaters left in the state, the **Sunset Drive In Theatre** (off Hwy. 16, 1 mile east of Plentywood, 406/765-1233 or 406/765-2078) is open, weather permitting, May 1–Labor Day.

Accommodations

The Sherwood Inn (515 W. 1st Ave., 406/765-2810, www.sherwoodinnplentywood.com, $72–82), complete with a host of Robin Hood–themed businesses (the Robin Hood Lounge, Fryer Tuck's Restaurant, and Maid Marion's Hair Salon) is a rather large hotel with 64 guest rooms and extended-stay apartments across the street. This pet-friendly hotel is a nice place for the night and is ideal for hunters. Wireless Internet is available sporadically, the best reception being in the lounge.

Food

Just about everything in town is within walking distance of the Sherwood Inn, and **Randy's**

Restaurant (323 W. 1st Ave., 406/765-1661, breakfast and lunch $4–9, dinner $8–16) offers three square meals a day. The lemon meringue pie is exceptionally good. **The Blue Moon Supper Club** (4316 Hwy. 16 S., 406/765-2491, 11 A.M.–2 A.M. daily, entrées $7–30) is known for its prime rib and Montana-style fine dining.

SCOBEY

Just down the road from Plentywood is Scobey (population 991, elevation 2,450 feet), an agricultural town with Scandinavian roots, a wealth of wheat farms, and a population of diehard sports fans. The downtown area is compact and cute, with nice places to eat and a very welcoming attitude. There are so many unique features of the town because most of its residents are descendants of those who homesteaded the area around the turn of the 20th century. There are a few legendary feuds, of course, but mostly people get along and are always willing to lend a hand. When Scobey residents get married, for example, invitations are unheard of; rather, the event is published in the weekly paper, and the entire town shows up with hot dishes, salads, and everything else to make a party worth attending. It is as quaint as it is genuine. Scobey is a wonderful example of small-town Montana. The town achieved some minor fame thanks to an award-winning 2008 PBS documentary, *Class C,* that tells the story of vanishing small towns through the lens of five girls' basketball teams.

(Pioneer Town

Just west of town is Scobey's beloved Pioneer Town, an extension of the Daniels County Museum and a significant labor of love. The museum is open daily Memorial Day–Labor Day 12:30–4:30 P.M., and the rest of the year on Tuesdays and Fridays 9 A.M.–3 P.M. or by appointment. Admission during the summer season includes a tour of Pioneer Town and is $7 for adults, $4 for children pre-school to 12 years-old, and free for infants and toddlers. It is a collection of more than 50 buildings from Scobey and the surrounding area that were saved from destruction and, to

© CARTER G. WALKER

Pioneer Town in Scobey, Montana

a lesser extent, the ravages of time. Some 35 of the buildings on-site—including a schoolhouse, a barber shop, two churches, and a saloon—have been restored and furnished with period pieces. Pioneer Town comes alive at the end of June each year with **Pioneer Days,** the town's biggest and arguably best event. The weekend includes the *Dirty Shame Show,* a musical variety show in the vaudeville tradition and still a rite of passage for many of Scobey's young women. There is a parade, plenty of food and celebration, and appropriately dressed pioneer guides will walk you through some of the town buildings.

Accommodations

Just south of town, **The Cattle King Motor Inn** (Hwy. 13 S., 406/487-5332, www.cattleking-inn.com, $75–100) offers clean, comfortable rooms, free Wi-Fi, free continental breakfasts, and free guest laundry. Pets are welcome with a $5 fee. Outside electric outlets are available to plug in your engine block during winter so that the car starts in the morning. No one said the winters were mild this far north.

Food

As you pull into town from the east, you'll encounter **Shu Mei's Chinese** (406/487-5347, call for hours), a wonderful little place for surprisingly authentic Chinese cuisine. Shu Mei herself has been known to select your meal for you; the wise will oblige and will not be sorry. On the other side of town, **Burger Hut** (Hwy. 13 between 1st Ave. and Railroad Ave., 406/487-5030) is a summer-only establishment with classic curb service and a menu that puts full-size restaurants to shame. Don't miss the famous and enormous "Ugly Burgers" or the excellent ice cream. The **Slipper Lounge** (608 Main St., 406/487-9973, Tues.–Thurs. 5–9 P.M., Fri.–Sat. 5–10 P.M., Sun. 5–9 P.M., entrées $7–24) offers sit-down meals (and unfortunately a casino) in the classic supper-club tradition.

WOLF POINT

Nestled on the banks of the Missouri River, Wolf Point (population 2,663, elevation 1,997 feet) has been many things over the course of

Montana history: a fur trading post, a cow town, a refueling stop for wood-burning steamships, an Indian trading post, and, more recently, a community hub for the Fort Peck Indian Reservation and an important storage site for much of the region's grain.

The community is made up of roughly equal numbers of tribe members and nonmembers, just as it was in the early 1900s when the U.S. government opened the reservation to white homesteaders. The Native American population includes primarily Sioux and Assiniboine people.

Events

Among the most celebrated events in Wolf Point is the **Wild Horse Stampede** (Marvin Brookman Stadium, 0.25 miles east of Main St., 406/653-2012, www.wolfpoint.com), Montana's oldest pro rodeo. Held annually the second weekend in July, this event has its origins in Native American celebration and is still an opportunity for participants to show off their equestrian skills. In addition to three nights of spine-tingling rodeo, there are daily parades, a carnival, the famous wild-horse race, and street dances.

The other major event for Wolf Point is the **Wadopana Celebration** (406/650-8724), the oldest traditional powwow in the state, held annually the first weekend in August.

Accommodations

The Homestead Inn (101 U.S. 2 E., 406/653-1300 or 800/231-0986, $60–105) is clean, comfortable, and affordable, and they offer free coffee and doughnuts every morning.

The Meadowlark (872 Nickwall Rd., 406/525-3289, $60–110) is a cozy bed-and-breakfast 16 miles out of town on the Lewis and Clark Trail. There are a couple of very nice suites and an authentic bunkhouse, all set on a farm with splendid views and abundant wildlife. Rates include full breakfast.

Food

Old Town Grill (400 U.S. 2, 406/653-1031, 7 A.M.–8 P.M. Mon.–Sat., 7 A.M.–2 P.M. Sun.,

entrées $6–10) is a clean, well-lighted place with a curious but tasty assortment of Mexican, Asian, and American food.

For more classic Montana fare, try the restaurant at the **Sherman Motor Inn** (200 E. Main St., 800/952-1100, 6 A.M.–10 P.M. daily, breakfast and lunch $6–9, dinner $9–22) or the **Elk's Club Dining Room** (302 Main St., 406/653-1920, 5–9 P.M. Thurs.–Sat., entrées $9–25).

GLASGOW AND FORT PECK

Glasgow (population 2,922, elevation 2,090 feet) is another northeastern Montana town that has seen its share of heart-stopping boom and heartbreaking bust. Founded in the 1800s with the arrival of the Northern Pacific Railway, the town exploded in 1933 with the construction of the Fort Peck Dam, the largest of President Roosevelt's Public Works Administration projects, which employed more than 10,000 workers at any given time. When the dam was complete, the population and the city dwindled until the mid-1960s, when the Glasgow Air Force Base was commissioned. The population doubled, and the city built an entirely new infrastructure to meet the needs of the new residents. The Air Force pulled out suddenly in 1969, and the city was left with the fallout. Today the abandoned and deteriorated base operates as a testing facility for Boeing and is slowly being developed as a retirement community for military personnel.

Both the expansive Fort Peck Lake, with as many miles of shoreline as California has coastline, and the Charles M. Russell National Wildlife Refuge are nearby and offer residents and visitors alike a wealth of outdoor opportunities. And as the largest city in this part of the state, Glasgow has plenty of services for those looking for recreation at Fort Peck Lake.

The town of Fort Peck (population 220, elevation 2,100 feet) was an Indian trading post as late as 1867, and even though the settlement was bypassed by the railroad, it was a hub of activity during construction of the dam. Today the town has a few residents and a significant number of lake visitors.

(Fort Peck Dam

The **Fort Peck Dam Interpretive Center and Museum** (adjacent to the powerhouses on Lower Yellowstone Rd., 406/526-3493, 9 A.M.–5 P.M. daily May 1–Sept. 30, call for hours other seasons, free) is a unique combination of exhibits created in a partnership among Fort Peck Paleontology Inc., the U.S. Fish and Wildlife Service, and the U.S. Army Corps of Engineers. The museum features the state's largest aquariums, with examples of the species native to Fort Peck Lake, a life-size model of the *T. rex* uncovered some 20 miles southeast of Fort Peck, and the construction history of the Fort Peck Dam. The museum offers excellent interpretive programs throughout the summer with weekend nature walks on a nice three-mile paved trail and experiential programs for kids. Visitors can also sign up for tours of the **Fort Peck Power Plants,** next to the interpretive center. There is a great day use area adjacent to the museum, complete with picnic shelters, playground equipment, and horseshoe pits. There is also a Class A campground.

© DONNIE SEXTON

historic Fort Peck Theatre

The **Fort Peck Theatre** (406/526-9943, www.fortpecktheater.org) was built as a temporary movie house in 1934 to entertain the huge number of workers building the dam. Over the years, the structure, designed and built by the Army Corps of Engineers in the style of a Swiss chalet, has become one of Montana's gems. The incredible craftsmanship, right down to the light fixtures, can be appreciated each summer during live theater performances produced by the Fort Peck Fine Arts Council.

Recreation

With 50 different kinds of fish in **Fort Peck Lake Reservoir,** nearly 1,600 miles of shoreline, and more than 1 million acres of public land in the surrounding Charles M. Russell (CMR) National Wildlife Refuge, the area is a nature-lover's paradise. **Hi-Line Charter Fishing** (6820 U.S. 2 E., Havre, 406/262-2195 or 406/390-6892, www.hilinecharterfishing.com) can provide fully equipped boats and guides for fishing expeditions. Marvin and Connie Loomis operate **Trophy's Fishing** (406/557-2787, www.fortpeckfishing.com), providing comfortable lodging on the water in houseboats, great home cooking, and all the equipment and guiding you'll need. Anglers on the reservoir have the chance to catch walleye, sauger, small-mouth bass, northern pike, and even king salmon, among others. To rent a boat, contact the **Fort Peck Marina** (406/526-3442) or the **Rock Creek Marina** (406/485-2560, www.rockcreekmarina.com).

Golfers can hit the links in nearby Glasgow at the fairly level nine-hole **Sunnyside Golf Club** (95 Skylark Rd., 406/228-9519, $15 for 9 holes, $22 for 18 holes).

Accommodations

Right in Fort Peck is the rambling **Fort Peck Hotel** (175 S. Missouri St., Fort Peck, 406/526-3266 or 800/560-4931, Apr.–Dec., $58–112 d), built at the same time and in similar fashion to the Fort Peck Theater. The wooden hotel certainly recalls a time gone by, and though the amenities are simple (double and single beds), they are perfectly suitable and quite charming.

The hotel serves three wonderful meals daily in the quaint dining room.

The **Cottonwood Inn & Suites** (U.S. 2 E., Glasgow, 406/228-8213 or 800/321-8213, www.cottonwoodinn.net, $72–84) in Glasgow is the town's newest and most modern addition. There are 124 guest rooms, an indoor heated pool, free Wi-Fi, a dining room, and an adjacent RV Park.

Food

Foodies are in for a surprising treat in Glasgow: **Durum Restaurant** (309 2nd Ave. S., Glasgow, 406/228-2236, lunch 11 A.M.–2 P.M., dinner 5–9 P.M. Tues.–Sat., lunch $7.50–9.75, dinner $15–35) is an elegant little chef-owned bistro known for its creative fare, handmade pasta, and homemade sauces. Trained at the Colorado Culinary Art Institute, Scott Redstone prepares everything from mouthwatering authentic Italian cuisine to apple-walnut stuffed pork chops with honey balsamic glaze using the freshest and most exceptional local ingredients.

Sam's Supper Club (U.S. 2 E., 406/228-4614, lunch 10:30 A.M.–2:30 P.M., dinner 4 P.M.–2 A.M. daily, entrées $7–23) falls into the category of a classic Montana steak house, and it is a great one: Serving excellent steaks, an array of seafood options, and even some Mexican and vegetarian entrées, the food here is as good as the atmosphere is welcoming.

INFORMATION AND SERVICES

The **Glasgow Area Chamber of Commerce** (23 U.S. 2 E., Glasgow, 406/228-2222, www.glasgowmt.com, 8 A.M.–4 P.M. Mon.–Thurs., 8 A.M.–3 P.M. Fri.) is happy to provide visitors with information for the surrounding area, including Fort Peck.

The **Daniels County Chamber of Commerce** (120 Main St., Scobey, 406/487-2061, www.scobeymt.com, 10 A.M.–2 P.M. Mon.–Fri. May 15–Sept. 15) is located in downtown Scobey.

The **Sheridan County Chamber of Commerce** (108 N. Main St., Plentywood, 406/765-1733, www.sheridancountychamber.org, 9 A.M.–5 P.M. Mon.–Sat.) is in Plentywood. There is also a **Visitors Information Center** rack filled with brochures and pamphlets in the Sherwood Inn Motel (555 W. 1st Ave., Plentywood).

The **Wolf Point Chamber of Commerce and Agriculture** (218 3rd Ave. S., Suite B, Wolf Point, 406/653-2012, www.woldpointchamber.org, 9 A.M.–4 P.M. Mon.–Thurs.) also has information about the Fort Peck Reservation.

The Milk River Valley

The Milk River flows from high in the Montana Rockies, north into Alberta, then east and south, through Havre and across prairie and riparian areas teeming with wildlife, through Fort Belknap, Malta, and Glasgow, eventually joining the Missouri River. The water is indeed milky colored, even late in summer, and it was named by Lewis and Clark, who thought the water looked like "a cup of tea with the admixture of a tablespoonful of milk."

Life along the river seems to follow an equally relaxed pace in nice little towns like Saco, Malta, and Fort Belknap. This is the country of Wallace Stegner, the beloved Western author who spent much of his childhood along Frenchman Creek, a tributary of the Milk River. He didn't always love the austere beauty of the place, but he always appreciated it in his spare, beautiful prose.

This is also prime hunting territory for large game and birds, and there are a number of places to enjoy the water by boat or with a fishing rod. Many people simply come to drink it all in, visiting the scenic wildlife refuges, driving through the open country, stopping in friendly towns along the way, or relaxing at eastern Montana's only hot springs resort.

MALTA

A notable stop on the Montana Dinosaur Trail, Malta (population 1,801, elevation 2,254 feet) is a hub for the myriad ranches in the area and a nice place start day trips into the Bowdoin Wildlife Refuge or to organize an exciting fossil dig.

Just west of town is the site of a great train robbery in 1901 by Kid Curry and his gang of outlaws, many of whom were known to frequent the area. The other most famous residents of Malta were of the scaly variety: a 77-million-year-old mummified *Brachylophosaurus,* a rare and precious find, was unearthed north of town in 2000 and has become something of a local hero, along with Elvis, Roberta, and Peanut, all of whom are on display at the two museums in town.

The **Phillips County Museum** (431 U.S. 2 E., 406/654-1037, www.phillipscounty-museum.org, 10 A.M.–5 P.M. Mon.–Sat., 12:30–5 P.M. Sun., $5 adults, $3 children, free for children under 6, $12 family) is a stop on the Montana Dinosaur Trail and includes exhibits on mining, Native Americans, outlaws, and most notably, dinosaurs. The collection includes Elvis, the aforementioned *Brachylophosaurus,* in addition to a complete *Tyrannosaurus rex* scull and an upright full-size *Albertosaurus,* a relative of the *T. rex* and the primary prey of the *Brachylophosaurus.* A beautifully restored 1903 home, built by New York transplant H. G. Robinson, is adjacent to the museum and available for tours.

Another excellent museum worth visiting and also on the Montana Dinosaur Trail is the **Great Plains Dinosaur Museum and Field Station** (U.S. 2 E., 406/654-5300, www.greatplainsdinosaurs.org, 10 A.M.–5 P.M. Mon.–Sat., $5 adults, $3 children 5–12, free for children under 5), which showcases a selection of dinosaurs that includes duckbills, sauropods, and stegosauruses along with a collection of rare marine fossils found in Montana. The museum also sponsors a number of single-day and multiple-day fossil digs; call for dates and specifics.

The nearby **Bowdoin National Wildlife**

Refuge (194 Bowdoin Auto Tour Rd., 7 miles east of Malta off Old U.S. 2, 406/654-2863, www.bowdoin.fws.gov) was established as a migratory bird refuge in 1936. Both saline and freshwater wetlands offer ideal habitat for the thousands of birds—from waterfowl and shore birds to birds of prey and grassland song birds—that soar along this flyway. A 15-mile self-guided car tour route brings visitors face-to-face with much of the region's wildlife. Fishing and hunting in the refuge is strictly regulated and should be coordinated through the refuge office during business hours.

FORT BELKNAP INDIAN RESERVATION

Set between the Little Rockies and the Milk River, the Fort Belknap Indian Reservation put together the Gros Ventre and Assiniboine tribes in 1888. They had long been enemies and only formed an alliance to fight the nearby Blackfeet. Today the reservation is a peaceful place encompassing vast grasslands and gently rolling hills. There is an 1877 mission in Hays as well as some significant recreation sites and a variety of festive celebrations. The nearby Charles M. Russell (CMR) National Wildlife Refuge is a marvelous place for recreation and to appreciate the wildlife.

CHARLES M. RUSSELL NATIONAL WILDLIFE REFUGE

The CMR National Wildlife Refuge (406/538-8706 or 406/526-3464, www.fws.gov/cmr) was established in 1936, and at 1.1 million acres, it is the second-largest U.S. wildlife refuge outside Alaska. It is home to mountain lions, coyotes, prairie dogs, antelope, and enormous numbers of birds. Twenty-five percent bigger than Rhode Island, there are only two paved roads providing minimal access to the refuge. All other travel is on dirt and gravel roads, on foot, on horseback, or by boat. The region was a frequent hiding place for a number of famous outlaws. The refuge borders the Fort Peck Lake Reservoir and extends more than 100 miles west to U.S. 191.

ENTERTAINMENT AND EVENTS

The **Milk River Indian Days** (406/353-2205, ext. 532, or 406/353-4145) is a traditional powwow with colorfully clad dancers, Native American drummers, and music. The celebration is typically held in late July at the Fort Belknap Powwow Grounds. The **Hays Pow Wow** (406/353-2205, ext. 367) is another excellent celebration of Native American history and culture, staged annually five miles south of Hays in Mission Canyon. The event is free and open to the public.

ACCOMMODATIONS

There are a number of small motels in Malta, the nicest being **The Great Northern Hotel** (2 S. 1st St. E., Malta, 406/654-2100, $67–69). It's not charming in a historic sense, but the rooms are quite comfortable and impeccably clean. There is also a nice steak house and nonsmoking coffee shop on the premises. The pet-friendly **Riverside Motel & RV Park** (8 Central Ave. N., Malta, 406/654-2310 or 800/854-2310, www.riversidemotel-rvpark. com, $49–65) is a good choice for more budget-conscious travelers. The rooms are clean and spacious, and free Wi-Fi is provided.

Just 17 miles east of Malta is eastern Montana's only hot springs resort, **Sleeping Buffalo Hot Springs** (1 mile north of U.S. 2 from the Sleeping Buffalo Rock Monument, 406/527-3370, www.sleepingbuffalo.blogspot.com, $50–100). The resort is centered around two natural pools fed by hot springs, one at 90°F, the other at 106°F. The pools are open year-round, and a handful of modern hotel rooms (with satellite TV and microwaves) are available along with several rustic hotel rooms with different arrangements to accommodate families or larger groups. There is a small café on-site and a pub right next door. The water tends to have some particulate matter and can look a bit red thanks to the iron oxide content, but the minerals are supposedly healing.

CAMPING

In Malta, camping is available at the **Edgewater Inn & RV Park** (47176 U.S. 2, Malta, 406/654-1302 or 800/821-7475). Tent sites (from $12.50) and RV sites ($15.50–36.50) with or without hookups are available.

There are multiple primitive campgrounds in the vicinity of Malta: Fourchette Bay Campground is 60 miles south of Malta, Montana Gulch Campground is 1 mile south of Landusky, and Nelson Reservoir is 17 miles east of Malta. But roads and access can be problematic in wet weather, and most sites advise campers to bring three days' worth of food in case they get stranded.

FOOD

As this is ranch country, diners often have the choice between steaks and burgers, and you can't really go wrong with either. The **Tin Cup Bar and Grill** (1652 U.S. 191 S., Malta, 406/654-5527, 11 A.M.–9 P.M. daily, entrées $7–25) is an elegant full-service restaurant overlooking the Marian Hills Golf Course and the pastoral Milk River Valley. The **Westside Restaurant** (220 U.S. 2 E., Malta, 406/654-1555, 6 A.M.–9 P.M. daily summer, 6 A.M.–8 P.M. daily winter, entrées $7–12) serves award-winning beef but is equally known for its bountiful salad bar. And the **Hitchin Post** (U.S. 2 E., east of Malta, 406/654-1882, 7 A.M.–7 P.M. Mon.–Sat., 8 A.M.–2 P.M. Sun., dinner entrées $8–12) is a favorite for homemade soups, pies, rolls, muffins, and daily lunch specials. Breakfast is served all day.

INFORMATION AND SERVICES

The **Malta Chamber of Commerce** (2 S. 1st St. E., 406/654-1776, www.maltachamber.com) is located in the Great Northern Hotel. The **Tourist Information Center** is open mid-May–mid-September and is located in the Phillips County Museum (431 U.S. 2 E., 406/654-1037, 10 A.M.–5 P.M. Mon.–Sat., 12:30–5 P.M. Sun.).

GREAT FALLS AND THE ROCKY MOUNTAIN FRONT

North Central Montana encompasses much of the geographical diversity that defines the state. There are vast plains along the Hi-Line (a stretch of the state that parallels Montana's northernmost or "highest" railroad line), rolling agricultural fields in Montana's breadbasket (the source of much of the state's wheat crop), and the Rockies practically erupting out of the plains along the Rocky Mountain Front.

Although this stretch of Montana isn't often among the state's primary tourist destinations, there are many reasons why it should be (chief among them that the area is not a tourist destination). The region is rich with natural beauty, culturally significant landmarks, and history. Fort Benton, just east of Great Falls, is considered the birthplace of Montana due to its origins as an important inland port, the westernmost stopping point for steamers loaded with materials and pioneers traveling up the Missouri River. There are two major buffalo jumps (geographical butte-like features that Native Americans used to hunt bison) worth seeing, Egg Mountain with its significant dinosaur discoveries, the vast Bob Marshall Wilderness, the placid Smith River, and outcroppings all along the Missouri River that hold the lore of the fur-trapping era. Great Falls, the largest city in the region, is home to the C. M. Russell Art Museum and some intriguing contemporary art as well as the Lewis and Clark National Historic Trail Interpretive Center. Smaller towns, including Choteau, Lewistown, and White Sulphur Springs, have preserved their culture and history as they have fought to maintain their populations in boom-

© DONNIE SEXTON

HIGHLIGHTS

◖ C. M. Russell Museum: The most beloved and impressive art museum in the state, the C. M. Russell is an extraordinary tribute to the life and work of consummate Western artist Charlie Russell. His contemporaries – including J. H. Sharp and E. I. Couse, among others – are well represented too (page 72).

◖ Lewis and Clark National Historic Trail Interpretive Center: Dedicated to the 8,000-mile journey of Lewis and Clark, this compelling museum enables visitors to learn about the extraordinary challenges faced by the explorers and to appreciate the parallels between what they found and what exists today (page 74).

◖ Fishing on the Missouri River: The river attracts anglers from all over the world, but in this part of the state it winds quietly through rolling plains and craggy canyons as it serves up prolific hatches and thousands of trout per mile (page 78).

◖ The Bob Marshall Wilderness Complex: More than 1 million acres of pristine wilderness straddle the Continental Divide in the isolated Bob Marshall Wilderness Complex, 75 miles west of Great Falls. The topography is dramatic, the wildlife is plentiful, and the opportunities to get lost are endless (page 84).

◖ Fort Benton: Touted locally as the birthplace of Montana, this town was an important early trading post and is recognized today as a National Historic Landmark. A charming hotel, gourmet food, and a riverside setting make Fort Benton an ideal destination (page 85).

◖ Havre Beneath the Streets: Discovered in 1976, practically an entire city exists underneath the streets of downtown Havre. Knowledgeable and passionate guides show you around the 27-bed brothel, saloon, and opium den and the more genteel dentist's office, cigar shop, and bakery (page 88).

◖ Charlie Russell Chew Choo: This three-hour narrated train ride from Lewistown and back takes visitors through some of the most starkly beautiful terrain anywhere. The staged hold-up might be hokey, but the prime rib and splendid scenery are the real deal (page 92).

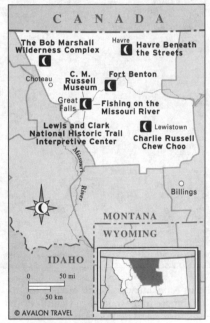

LOOK FOR ◖ TO FIND RECOMMENDED SIGHTS, ACTIVITIES, DINING, AND LODGING.

GREAT FALLS

GREAT FALLS

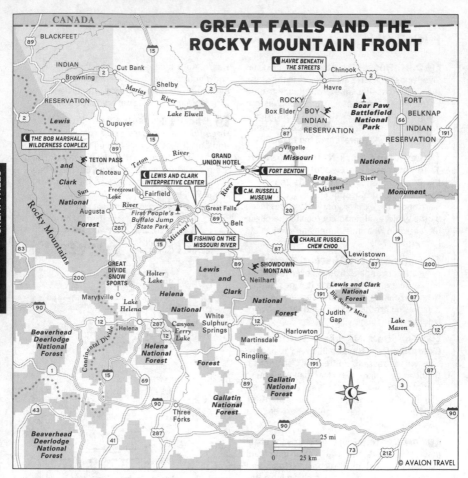

and-bust economies, and each offers a meaningful glimpse into Montana agricultural life past and present. The Rocky Boy's and Fort Belknap reservations offer some wonderful ways to get immersed in Native American culture.

PLANNING YOUR TIME

As with most of Montana, there is as much to do in Great Falls as your time will allow. Visitors should plan at least a day in the city to see some of the excellent museums and nearby natural attractions, including **First People's**

Buffalo Jump State Park. Known for its consistent wind, this city is ideally located on the Missouri River between the Rocky Mountains and Montana's Big Open. Any number of outdoor adventures can be dreamed up and launched from Great Falls.

Other towns in this region, each with its own unique charm, are often best enjoyed en route from one destination to another. One notable exception is Fort Benton, less than an hour's drive from Great Falls. This picturesque hamlet sits in a canyon along the Missouri and is an ideal spot for visitors, with several museums, a quaint downtown, historical sites, and one of the most elegant old hotels in the state. The country opens up significantly east of Great Falls. In places it looks as if the only occupants are cattle and oversize windmills. The **Upper Missouri River Breaks National Monument,** with some of the state's most interesting and isolated terrain, is best explored from the water. Havre is the largest city on the Hi-Line and offers plenty of accommodations and the fascinating **Havre Beneath the Streets Tours.** Farther south, Lewistown is small but colorful, with plenty of good fishing nearby and a couple of good restaurants.

West of Great Falls, the Rocky Mountains soar skyward, with towns such as Choteau and the reservation town of Browning in their shadows. There are dude ranches for those who make this region their primary destination, but at the very least this is a magnificent corner to drive through en route to Glacier National Park or southwest toward Missoula. Dinosaur aficionados will want to allow enough time to visit some of the plentiful paleontological sites, including **Egg Mountain** and **The Old Trail Museum** in Choteau and the **Two Medicine Dinosaur Center** in Bynum.

HISTORY

This vast, largely open stretch of Montana was home to numerous Native American groups, including the Blackfeet, Sioux, Assiniboine, Gros Ventre, and Cree, who took up residence and battled for the land as early as the late 18th century. The Crow, Nez Perce, and Salish were also known to hunt in the region. Louis and Clark famously traveled this area, spending an entire month in 1805 trying to negotiate the myriad cascades around present-day Great Falls.

White settlement was charted by the steamboats that navigated the area along the Missouri all the way to Fort Benton as early as 1859 and the rapid construction of the Great Northern Railway in 1887. Under the direction of James Hill, 643 miles of track were laid in less than eight months by a crew of 9,000 men and 6,600 horses. In an attempt to populate this now reasonably accessible place, in 1908 Hill sent agents and exhibition cars to county fairs across the Midwest and on the East Coast to entice optimistic farmers. Settlers flocked to the region for their 320 acres of "Poor Man's Paradise," a term made famous by Hill's promotional campaign. The campaign—piggybacking on the Homestead Act of 1891, which gave every U.S. citizen the chance to claim 320 acres of unoccupied land—touted that land was abundant and fortunes could be made easily. Generous rainfall prompted enormous harvests of wheat and kept population growth steady until 1917, when a cyclical drought wreaked havoc on the land and broke the spirits of newcomers. Some 80,000 people had moved into the region 1909–1916, and 60,000 of them were gone by 1922. North-central Montana is still subject to harsh weather and the unpredictable boom and bust cycle.

When Meriwether Lewis stood atop the rocks beneath the Great Falls of the Missouri River in June 1805, he pronounced the scene as "the grandest sight I ever beheld," a sentiment shared by Fort Benton businessman Paris Gibson some 75 years later. Gibson, who had made a fortune in Minnesota as a flour and wool merchant before finding success as a merchant in Fort Benton, committed himself to building a city around the site of the falls. In 1883 he did just that, first plotting out the city, then urging his friend James J. Hill to bring his railroad through. Gibson envisioned a "new Minneapolis" on the banks of the Missouri River and worked feverishly to achieve the dream. By 1888, with plentiful industry in town and fertile farmland around it, the city of Great Falls, with Gibson as its mayor, boasted more than 2,000 residents. Two years later the population had doubled. But despite Gibson's best efforts and his intelligent and thoughtful city planning, Great Falls floundered when Hill opted not to bring the railroad to Great Falls. Though it never fulfilled Gibson's ultimate vision, the city did achieve industrial success with power-producing dams, copper smelting, and eventually an Air Force base.

Great Falls

At the edge of the mountains and the plains, Great Falls (population 56,338, elevation 3,674 feet) has more romantic origins than its modern-day grittiness may suggest. A few days ahead of William Clark, Meriwether Lewis stumbled on the region in June 1805, calling the falls themselves "the grandest sight I ever beheld." Seventy-five years later, Fort Benton merchant Paris Gibson sought the same views that had captivated Lewis and later recollected, "I had never seen a spot as attractive as this...I had looked upon this scene for a few moments only when I said to myself, here I would found a city." Just three years later in 1883, the city of Great Falls was named and platted.

With the falls long since dammed to create power—Great Falls is known as the "Electric City" for all its dams and power plants—the city has worked to capitalize on the beauty of the Missouri River with a scenic roadway (River Drive), trails, parks, and picnic areas along the waterway. The Lewis and Clark National Historical Trail Interpretive Center sits atop a bluff and affords visitors an unspoiled view of what the area might have looked like 200 years ago. Another kind of beauty celebrated by this city is art. There are a couple of excellent—and surprising—art museums to visit.

But Great Falls is still a rough-and-tumble Montana town. There is cowboy culture, military culture, and serious wind, all of which give the state's third-largest city a little bit of edge. Its location between the mountains and plains and amid rivers is ideal for lovers of the outdoors, and Great Falls is an excellent launching point for adventures in any direction.

SIGHTS
Great Falls Historic Trolley
If you only have a few hours and want to see as much of the city as possible, the Great Falls Historic Trolley (315 5th St. S., 406/771-1100 or 888/707-1100, www.greatfallshistorictrolley. com, $13–22 adults, $5 children) is a fun way to do so. Carol T. Place, also known as "The Trolley Lady," will keep you entertained as she takes you to the most important natural and human-built places in Great Falls. Don't be surprised if she breaks into song at some point and asks you to join in (this happens more often during the Christmas Luminary Tours in December). They offer a one-hour "city" tour that runs along the Missouri River and into historic downtown, or a two-hour "historic" tour that follows Lewis and Clark's route through the city. During the summer, tours depart from the Visitors Information Center under the huge flag in Overlook Park (15 Overlook Dr.). If you buy your tickets at the center, you get a small discount on the prices.

❰ C. M. Russell Museum
One of the best and most intimate Western art museums in the country, the C. M. Russell Museum (400 13th St. N., 406/727-8787, www.cmrussell.org, 9 A.M.–6 P.M. daily Memorial Day–Labor Day, 10 A.M.–5 P.M. Tues.–Sat. Labor Day–Memorial Day, $9 adults, $7 seniors, $4 students, free for children 5 and under) has amassed the world's largest collection of Charlie Russell art and personal objects, including his illustrated letters. His home and log studio have been meticulously maintained on the museum grounds and are open to visitors. In addition to a significant number of important works by Western masters, the museum takes an interesting approach to art through its permanent bison exhibit. The iconic Western ungulate had significance to Russell himself, and the importance of the animal and its near extinction is traced through more than 1,000 exquisite Native American artifacts. Don't leave Great Falls without spending a few hours at the C. M. Russell.

Paris Gibson Square Museum of Art
Located at the eastern end of downtown Great Falls, the Paris Gibson Square Museum of

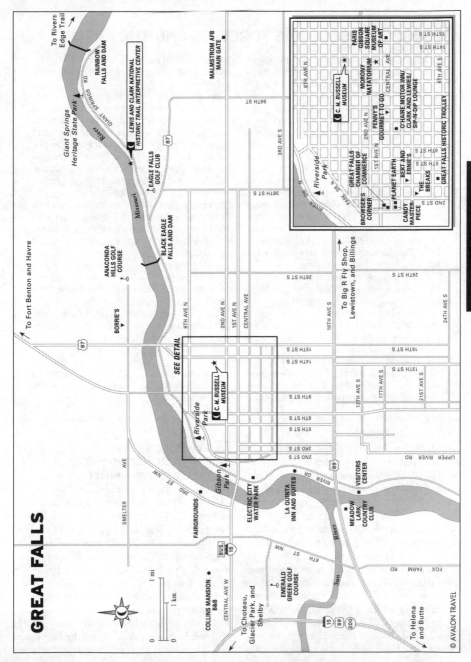

GREAT FALLS

GREAT FALLS

To Rivers Edge Trail

RAINBOW FALLS AND DAM

LEWIS AND CLARK NATIONAL HISTORIC TRAIL INTERPRETIVE CENTER

Giant Springs Heritage State Park

GIANT SPRINGS RD

MALMSTROM AFB MAIN GATE

56TH ST

87

EAGLE FALLS GOLF CLUB

Missouri River

BLACK EAGLE FALLS AND DAM

38TH ST S

3RD AVE S

ANACONDA HILLS GOLF COURSE

To Fort Benton and Havre

87

BORRIE'S

8TH AVE N
2ND AVE N
1ST AVE N
CENTRAL AVE

26TH ST S

To Big R Fly Shop, Lewistown, and Billings

10TH AVE S

24TH AVE S

26TH ST S

SEE DETAIL

C. M. RUSSELL MUSEUM

Riverside Park

15TH ST S
14TH ST S
9TH ST S
6TH ST S
5TH ST S
3RD ST S
2ND ST S

15TH ST S

13TH ST S
17TH AVE S
13TH AVE S
21ST AVE S

UPPER RIVER RD

69

VISITORS CENTER

MEADOW LARK COUNTRY CLUB

Gibson Park

SMELTER AVE
3RD ST NW

FAIRGROUNDS

ELECTRIC CITY WATER PARK

LA QUINTA INN AND SUITES

RIVER DR

Sun River

BUS. 15

1 mi

1 km

COLLINS MANSION B&B

CENTRAL AVE W

To Choteau, Glacier Park, and Shelby

EMERALD GREEN GOLF COURSE

6TH ST NW

FOX FARM RD

15 69 200

To Helena and Butte

0   1 mi
0   1 km

Detail inset

8TH AVE N

C. M. RUSSELL MUSEUM

PARIS GIBSON SQUARE MUSEUM OF ART

15TH ST S
14TH ST S

8TH AVE S

MORONY NATATORIUM

CENTRAL AVE

2ND AVE N

PENNY'S

O'HAIRE MOTOR INN/ CLARK AND LEWIES/ SIP-N-DIP LOUNGE

GOURMET TO GO

1ST AVE N

GREAT FALLS CHAMBER OF COMMERCE

Riverside Park

PARK DR N

PARK DR S

RIVER DR N

1ST AVE S

BROWSER'S CORNER

PLANET EARTH

BERT AND ERNIE'S

CANDY MASTER- PIECE

THE BREAKS

2ND ST S

GREAT FALLS HISTORIC TROLLEY

© AVALON TRAVEL

GREAT FALLS

NANCY RUSSELL: THE FORCE BEHIND THE ARTIST

Charles M. Russell's name is synonymous with great Western art and Montana. He is not only the pride and joy of Great Falls but a hero to the entire state. Although today Charlie Russell's art is heralded around the world, there is little debate that the world may not have known him had it not been for his savvy and determined wife, Nancy.

Born Nancy Bates Cooper in 1878, she was 14 years younger than Charlie and worked as a housemaid for one of his friends when they met. Their pairing seemed an unlikely match, and when news of the engagement spread, it seemed clear that Charlie was marrying beneath himself. What soon became apparent was that not only could Nancy hold her own in any social circle, she would be the single greatest asset to her husband's career.

Nancy Russell had fended for herself from the age of 16, when her mother had died. She was a strong woman capable of achieving whatever she set her mind to; some would argue that's how she nabbed Charlie. In his book *More Rawhide*, Charlie wrote, "It's the women that make the men in this world," and in his case it was true: There is no doubt that he was a talented artist, but his wife's belief in his work and her drive to see him properly recognized is what made him a success. As his

business-minded partner, Nancy ultimately organized the shows that gained him worldwide attention.

Nancy quickly earned the moniker "Nancy the robber" because of the high prices she would ask (and receive) for Charlie's work. Charlie once told a newspaper that the worst fight the couple had ever had was when she had asked for $75 for a painting that he thought would sell for $5. Initially setting up home in the town of Cascade, the couple moved to Great Falls to aid Charlie's burgeoning career. On their arrival, the mayor's wife commissioned a painting, and Nancy asked her husband if she could deliver it. He warned her that the painting was to be sold for $25, and she should not ask for a penny more, or the painting would not sell. Nancy met the mayor's wife, delivered the painting, and with a lump in her throat asked for $35. The mayor's wife replied, "I'll get my checkbook."

Ultimately, it was evident that Charlie was proud of his wife and relieved to have her handle the financial part of his business. In 1919, when asked by a reporter if marriage hinders an artist's expression, Charlie replied, "I still love and long for the Old West, and everything that goes with it. But I would sacrifice it all for Mrs. Russell."

Art (1400 1st Ave. N., 406/727-8255, www.the-square.org, 10 A.M.–5 P.M. Mon. and Wed.–Fri., 10 A.M.–5 P.M. and 7–9 P.M. Tues., noon–5 P.M. Sat. year-round, free) occupies an entire city block. Built in 1896, the impressive structure served the community as Central High School and later as Paris Gibson Junior High until it closed in 1975. Renovated, renamed after the city's founder, and reopened in 1977, this National Historic Landmark houses an impressive collection of contemporary art. In addition to classes, lectures, tours, and performances, the museum has a café, a gift shop, and a branch of the Montana Wilderness Association. Don't miss a stroll through the sculpture garden located on the beautifully landscaped grounds.

◖ Lewis and Clark National Historic Trail Interpretive Center

Beautifully built into a bluff overlooking the Missouri River, the Lewis and Clark National Historic Trail Interpretive Center (4201 Giant Springs Rd., 406/727-8733, www.fs.fed.us/r1/lewisclark/lcic, 9 A.M.–6 P.M. daily Memorial Day–Sept. 30, 9 A.M.–5 P.M. Tues.–Sat., noon–5 P.M. Sun. Oct.–Memorial Day, $8 adults, free for children under 17) provides visitors with a hands-on interpretation of the intrepid explorers' cross-country journey. With a two-story diorama of the monthlong portage at Great Falls, impressive videos by Ken Burns and others, and ranger-led programs, the center does an excellent job of portraying the importance of Native Americans to the journey along with a comprehensive natural history exhibit. The center offers a wealth of worthwhile special events that include concerts, lectures, and reenactments (check the website for upcoming events). There is also a nice outdoor component to the center with a network of self-guided trails, one of which leads you to the nearby Giant Springs Heritage State Park.

Giant Springs Heritage State Park

Among the largest freshwater springs in the world, Giant Springs was discovered by Lewis and Clark in 1805. Every day the spring, now in Giant Springs State Park (4600 Giant Springs Rd., 406/454-5840, www.fwp.mt.gov/parks, 8 A.M.–sunset daily, $5 per vehicle for nonresidents), produces 156 million gallons of water, which stays at a constant 54°F all year, making it an ideal spot for fishing. There is a fish hatchery on-site, a visitors center (8 A.M.–5 P.M. daily), a picnic area, and several trails that wind through the lush area.

First People's Buffalo Jump State Park

Considered to be among the largest buffalo jumps in North America, First People's Buffalo Jump State Park (406/866-2217, www.fwp.mt.gov/parks, 8 A.M.–6 P.M. daily Apr.–Sept., 10 A.M.–4 P.M. Wed.–Sat., noon–4 P.M. Sun. Oct.–Mar., $5 per vehicle for nonresidents) is exceptional in that it offers an extensive on-site education center that houses buffalo culture exhibits, a storytelling circle, a gallery, and an outdoor powwow area. The site itself is impressive, with a mile-long sandstone cliff from which the bison were chased to their deaths, but more than anything, this is the best place in the state to learn about buffalo jumps. Watch your step on or off the trails for both rattlesnakes and prickly pear cacti. An adjacent prairie dog town is home to protected black-tailed prairie dogs and is worth the short detour. The park is located 10 miles south of Great Falls off I-15 at Ulm; follow signs for the state park 3.5 miles northwest on a county road.

ENTERTAINMENT AND EVENTS

The Russell: The Sale to Benefit the C. M. Russell Museum

Held annually at the C. M. Russell Museum over the weekend closest to Charlie Russell's birthday (Mar. 19), The Russell (400 13th St. North, 406/727-8787, www.cmrussell.org) is *the* social event of the year for lovers of Western art. In addition to a number of original Russell works, hundreds of works by Western masters and living greats are available for purchase. Parties, award ceremonies, and a popular Quick Draw round out the weekend events, all of which benefit the museum.

Great Falls Symphony

The Great Falls Symphony (Mansfield Center, 2 Park Dr. S., 406/453-4102, www.gfsymphony.org) is a dynamic organization that has been in existence for more than half a century, offering marvelous year-round entertainment in the form of classical symphonic masterpieces and contemporary compositions, chamber music, a youth orchestra, a symphonic choir, and ballet. For an evening of refined culture in the heart of cowboy country, the symphony is rare treat. All performances are held at the Mansfield Center.

Lewis and Clark Festival

For 20 years, Great Falls has been celebrating the Corps of Discovery's 1806 stay in the city. The Lewis and Clark Festival (4201 Giant Springs Rd., 406/727-8733 or 406/452-5661, www.lewisandclarkia.com) usually takes place each year at the end of June or the beginning of July. For a full weekend, history comes alive in various locations around the city. Highlighting events from Lewis and Clark's experience in Great Falls, the festival is as much about education as it is about fun. There are children's activities such as a discovery camp and storytelling, float trips, tours of Lewis and Clark sites, and presentations by

THE HISTORY OF BUFFALO JUMPS

Used by Native Americans for more than 5,000 years, buffalo jumps are rocky cliff formations that entire herds of bison were driven over, causing mortal injury to the animals and providing the hunters with ample meat, fur, and bones to make into tools. Throughout Montana, the jumps have become significant archeological sites, with discoveries of bones and tools guiding scientists to a better understanding of the various cultures of the people who hunted in this way.

What is surmised about the process is that the hunters would spot herds of bison within a reasonable distance of the jump. Using rock cairns, they would carefully construct an ever-narrowing pathway from the base of the jump, up the gradual slope to the cliff's edge. Several warriors would dress in animal hides and intersperse themselves undetected among the herd. At a specific moment the warriors would throw off their hides and stand up to startle the bison into a stampede, hopefully in the direction of the jump. As the bison headed toward the jump, other hunters would line the way, waving a variety of things to frighten the animals and prevent them from leaving the trail. By the time the animals reached the precipice, they were moving so fast that they were unable to stop at the cliff's edge even when they saw it. Hundreds of bison could go over the jump in one event, providing a substantial harvest for the hunters.

All of the animals were processed on-site, a painstaking process since every piece of the animal was used for meat, clothing, shelter, tools, and even toys. Archeologists have uncovered significant prehistoric camps at the base of many jumps. In some places, bison bones continue to be found more than 15 feet beneath the surface.

Buffalo jumps were used by a great variety of Native American tribes until the 19th century, when the Spanish brought horses to North America and the Indians began hunting on horseback.

© DONNIE SEXTON

First People's Buffalo Jump State Park in Ulm, Montana

Native American groups. Actors help recreate daily life from this period with dramatic readings and plays, and there is a traditional arts and crafts show, concerts, food, and exhibits. One of the culminating activities is the Lewis and Clark Outdoor Gala, which takes place along the banks of the Missouri River and offers a festive dinner, live auction, entertainment, and artists.

Montana State Fair

The Montana State Fair (Montana ExpoPark, 400 3rd St. NW, 406/727-8900, www.montanastatefair.com) takes place in Great Falls around the last week in July. It is one of Montana's largest parties and a true celebration of the state's unique history and culture. It includes a five-day rodeo (the largest in the state), horse racing, carnival rides, and big-name entertainment at the Montana ExpoPark. There are more than 250 vendor booths selling arts, crafts, clothes, music, and plenty of food as well as local, national, and international exhibits.

SHOPPING

Great Falls has a number of unique specialty stores that line either side of Central Avenue downtown. You can start at the beginning of Central Avenue at Park Drive and stroll down the avenue; you are sure to find something that delights you. If you have a sweet tooth, don't miss **Candy Masterpiece** (120 Central Ave., 406/727-5955, 9:30 A.M.–5:30 P.M. Mon.–Fri., 9:30 A.M.–5 P.M. Sat.), truly a treat for your senses. You'll be greeted by friendly staff who are extremely generous with the samples, and you'll find a delicious array of sweets, from childhood favorites straight off the candy rack to mouthwatering handmade chocolates. There are 30 different types of fudge available: Try the Heavenly Goo (chocolate with marshmallow and caramel) or, for the more adventurous, jalapeño fudge.

Next door to the candy store is the fun and funky **Planet Earth** (116 Central Ave., 406/761-7000, 10 A.M.–5:30 P.M. Mon.–Fri., 10 A.M.–5 P.M. Sat.), a shop full of eclectic, unique, and trendy gifts. Browse their

GREAT FALLS

© DONNIE SEXTON

Great Falls Farmers Market vendor

assortment of cards, accessories, and stunning jewelry. They also have a fabulous fragrance bar where you can create your own scent from essential oils and even add it to specific bath or skin-care products.

Just across the street is the aptly named **Browser's Corner** (117 Central Ave., 406/727-5150, 10 A.M.–5:30 P.M. Mon.–Fri., 10 A.M.–5 P.M. Sat.), a delightful antiques store that has a wide variety of merchandise.

During summer, be sure to wander over to **The Great Falls Farmers Market** (Civic Center Park, 2 Park Dr. S., 7:45 A.M.–noon Sat. June–Dec., 4:30–6:30 P.M. Wed. July–Dec.). More than 120 vendors gather to sell their goods, and you'll find the best home-grown fruits and vegetables, delicious jams, tasty baked goods, and handmade gifts and crafts. There are pony rides for the little ones and musicians wandering among the stalls to keep you entertained.

RECREATION
Walking and Biking the River's Edge Trail

The River's Edge Trail is the envy of nearly every town in Montana. With 13 paved miles for wheelchair access as well as single-track, double-track, and graveled paths, the trail winds for 30 miles along both sides of the Missouri River, past such points of interest as Black Eagle Falls, Rainbow Falls, Crooked Falls, and the renowned Great Falls of the Missouri below Ryan Dam. It also provides access to numerous parks, reservoirs, and other attractions, including the Lewis and Clark National Historic Trail Interpretive Center. There are 11 parking areas for easy access, and a trail map can be downloaded at www.thetrail.org.

Swimming

Starting in 2000, the city of Great Falls went to great lengths to renovate all of its municipal pools. The **Electric City Water Park** (100 River Dr. S., 406/771-1265, prearden@ci.great-falls.mt.us, www.greatfallsmt.net, 1–8 P.M. Mon.–Fri., 11 A.M.–6 P.M. Sat.–Sun.

early June–Labor Day, $3–17 depending on age and activities) is a favorite with kids and includes surfing features, giant slides, a lazy river, and a toddler-friendly water-play structure. **Mitchell Pool,** the city's largest, is also within the facility and is open to swimmers of all ages.

When the weather is not conducive to outdoor swimming, **Morony Natatorium** (111 12th St. N., 406/452-3733, www.greatfallsmt.net, call for hours and schedule, $2.50 adults, $1.50 children 4–17, free for children under 4) is a good option for open swimming and classes. The pool is kept at 83–85°F. Life vests are provided free of charge at all municipal pools in Great Falls, but swimmers need to provide their own towels.

Golf

Golfers not afraid of a stiff breeze can find a few places to play in Great Falls. There are two 18-hole public courses: **Eagle Falls Golf Club** (29 River Dr. N., 406/761-1078, $24 all day or 18 holes Mon.–Fri., $27 all day or 18 holes Sat.–Sun.), **Anaconda Hills Golf Course** (E. Smelter Ave., 406/761-8459, $13 for 9 holes or $21 for 18 holes Mon.–Fri., $15 for 9 holes and $24 for 18 holes Sat.–Sun.); **Emerald Green Golf Course** (1100 American Ave., 406/453-4844, $11.50 for 9 holes and $17.50 for 18 holes Mon.–Fri., $7.75 for 9 holes Tues., $12.50 for 9 holes and $18.50 for 18 holes Sat.–Sun.) is semiprivate and open to the public. **Meadow Lark Country Club** (300 Country Club Blvd., 406/454-3553, www.meadowlarkcc.net) is a lovely old private club at the confluence of the Missouri and Sun Rivers that allows reciprocal fees for members of other private clubs.

◖ Fishing

With no shortage of world-class waters in the region, including the Missouri and the Sun Rivers, there are endless opportunities to wet a line in and around Great Falls. The Great Falls Big R, one of the West's best all-around ranch supply stores, selling everything from baby chicks and barbed wire to snakeskin cowboy boots, recently added a fly-fishing shop:

Big R Fly Shop (4400 10th Ave. S., 406/761-7441, www.bigrflyshop.com) is a full-service fly shop staffed by passionate local anglers. Stop in for a few flies and some tips on where to fish locally.

For a guided trip on any number of local waters, try **Fin Fetchers Outfitters** (406/240-3715, www.finfetchers.com, half-day from $375). Owner Brian Neilson was born in Bozeman, raised in Great Falls, and knows as much as you could ever hope to learn about the sport.

Skiing

Although Great Falls is not often considered a prime alpine skiing destination, with the Rocky Mountains in such close proximity, it is no surprise that there are in fact three developed ski areas within a couple of hours' drive. High atop the Continental Divide, **Great Divide Snowsports** (7385 Belmont Dr., Marysville, 95 miles south of Great Falls, 406/449-3746, www.skigd.com, $34 adults, $28 students and senior-, $16 children grades 1–5, free for preschool children, or $8 per hour for anyone) touts itself as "Montana's sunniest ski area" and offers an impressive 140 trails accessed by seven lifts. The hill averages 180 inches of snow annually and offers night skiing and pay-by-the-hour usage. **Showdown Montana** (U.S. 89, south of Neihart, 1 hour southeast of Great Falls, 406/236-5522 or 800/433-0022, www.showdownmontana.com, $35 age 13–69, $25 seniors, $30 students with ID, $20 age 6–12, free age 5 and under) is one of Montana's oldest ski hills, in operation since 1936. In the middle of the not-so-little Little Belts, Showdown sees an average of 245 inches of powder annually. There are four lifts and 34 trails at this family-friendly ski hill, with 40 percent of them geared to intermediates and 30 percent each aimed at beginners and experts. Closest to Great Falls, **Teton Pass Ski Area** (18 miles west of Choteau, 406/466-2209, www.skitetonpass.com, $29 adults, $18 seniors and children, $23 students) is a small ski area—two lifts and 26 trails geared largely to experts—with an enormous amount of snow and some

pretty fierce terrain. The area averages 300 inches of snow annually.

ACCOMMODATIONS

If you are looking for a memorable motel stay in downtown Great Falls, look no further than the 🄲 **O'Haire Motor Inn** (17 17th St. S., 406/454-2141 or 800/332-9819, $70–90), with 72 recently renovated guest rooms, an indoor pool, indoor parking, and free Wi-Fi. Its full-service restaurant, **Clark and Lewies** (6 A.M.–midnight), offers up hearty meals. The biggest draw at the inn is its authentic and unforgettable tiki bar, the Sip-N-Dip Lounge.

The **Collins Mansion B&B** (1003 2nd Ave. NW, 406/452-4444 or 866/939-4262, www.thecollinsmansion.com, $85–125) offers a more tranquil stay in an 1890s Victorian mansion. There are five luxurious guest suites with private baths, cozy sitting areas, and Wi-Fi. The house is filled with detailed woodwork and has two inviting parlors, a generous wraparound porch, and a manicured garden with a gazebo. You can enjoy your gourmet breakfast in the formal dining room or request it served in your room at no extra charge.

Another option just south of downtown is the **La Quinta Inn and Suites** (600 River Dr. S., 406/761-2600 or 800/531-5900, $114–229), one of the city's newest hotels and located on the banks of the Missouri River. Ask for a room with a view of the river. The hotel is styled as a Western lodge, with a fireplace in the lobby, as well as an indoor pool and a fitness center. The guest rooms are large and comfortable with amenities such as high-speed Internet, microwaves, and fridges, and continental breakfast is included.

FOOD

In a historic building downtown, **Bert and Ernie's Tavern and Grill** (300 1st Ave. S., 406/453-0601, www.bertandernies.com, entrées $9–20) is something of a Great Falls institution. The food is simple and hearty with a variety of homemade soups, big salads, sandwiches, and burgers.

Another iconic restaurant in Great Falls is

Borrie's (1800 Smelter Ave., 406/761-0300, entrées $10–60), an old-school supper club with excellent steaks, seafood specials (including the $60 lobster tail), and legendary homemade pasta sauce and ravioli. The atmosphere leaves something to be desired, but this is a classic Montana dining experience with great specials several nights a week.

Newer on the scene and substantially more hip is ⓒ The Breaks (202 2nd Ave. S., 406/453-5980, 11 A.M.–10 P.M. Mon.–Thurs., 11 A.M.–midnight Fri.–Sat., closed Sun., entrées $17–33). An urban eatery in a renovated industrial building, The Breaks offers creative bistro fare, including wood-fired pizzas, along with a wine bar and a nightclub downstairs. There is also a fantastic deck when outside dining is an option.

For a quick, healthy meal to eat in or take out, Penny's Gourmet to Go (815 Central Ave., 406/453-7070, penny@sofast.net, 10 A.M.–4 P.M. Mon.–Fri., $6–10) has a great menu featuring soups, salads, sandwiches, and mouthwatering baked goodies. A fresh fruit and veggie juice bar is a novelty in this part of the state, and Penny's has plenty of offerings for vegetarians.

NIGHTLIFE

An authentic and unforgettable tiki bar, the Sip-N-Dip Lounge (17 17th St. S., 406/454-2141 or 800/332-9819) is located in the O'Haire Motor Inn. You can sip exotic cocktails as you gaze at the glass window into the pool behind the bar; watch exhibitionist guests or, on Friday night, a mermaid and merman perform. Daryl Hannah, the quintessential mermaid, has even taken a dip here. You can catch Piano Pat Spoonheim singing covers of Elvis, Neil Diamond, and other legendary crooners (9:30 P.M.–1:30 A.M. Wed.–Sat.)—she has been a mainstay at the lounge for close to 50 years. Voted the best bar on the planet by *GQ* magazine in 2003 and recognized as one of the world's best bars by *Condé Nast Traveler,* this kitschy, cool watering hole should not be missed.

Another one-in-a-million bar in Great Falls is the **Montana Cowboys Association Museum & Bar** (311 3rd St. NW, 406/761-9299, 11 A.M.–2 A.M. daily, closes earlier when the number of guests drops below 5). Whether this is a bar in a museum or a museum in a bar is open to debate, but either way there is no shortage of cool old stuff to look at while you sip something frosty. An authentic log cabin built in 1941, it boasts two fireplaces and hundreds of artifacts from the Old West, including a sizable gun collection, Charlie Russell's well-worn boots, a rare photo of Jeremiah "Liver-Eating" Johnson, and a handsome collection of saddles. An evening spent bellied up to the bar is bound to be unforgettable.

INFORMATION AND SERVICES

Most services are conveniently located in a walkable downtown area. The **Great Falls Chamber of Commerce** (100 1st Ave. N., 406/761-4434, www.greatfallschamber.org, 8 A.M.–5 P.M. Mon.–Fri.), and the **Visitor's Information Center** (15 Overlook Dr., 406/771-0885, www.visitgreatfalls.net, 10 A.M.–6 P.M. Mon.–Fri., 10 A.M.–4 P.M. Sat.–Sun. summer), under the huge U.S. flag in Overlook Park, both have city brochures, books, made in Montana goods for sale, and friendly, knowledgeable volunteers.

The **Main Post Office** is at 1st Avenue and 2nd Street (215 1st Ave. N., 406/771-2160, 7:30 A.M.–5:30 P.M. Mon.–Fri., 9 A.M.–1 P.M. Sat.).

The **public library** is just two blocks away (301 2nd Ave. N., 406/453-0349, www.greatfallslibrary.org, call for hours) and offers computers and free Wi-Fi for Internet access.

Falls Cleaners & Laundry Center (614 9th St. S., 406/453-9361, open daily) offers same-day laundry service, dry-cleaning service, and coin-op machines to do it yourself.

Benefis Health Systems (1101 26th St. S., 406/455-5000, www.benfis.org) is a first-class hospital with a 24-hour emergency room as well as a walk-in clinic for immediate medical care.

GETTING THERE AND GETTING AROUND

The **Great Falls International Airport** (GTF) lies southwest of the city and is served by Allegiant, Delta, Horizon, and United Express. The airport's on-site rental-car companies are **Alamo/National, Avis, Dollar,** and **Hertz. Budget, Enterprise,** and **Thrifty** also offer car-rental service but are located off-site with shuttles to and from the airport.

Diamond Cab (406/453-3241) serves the Great Falls area and will pick you up from the airport (look for the direct phone in the terminal) or shuttle you around town.

Rimrock Stages/Trailways (station 326 1st Ave. S., 800/255-7655, www.rimrocktrailways. com) offers service to other major towns and cities in Montana.

Great Falls is situated directly off I-15, allowing easy access by car. It is 218 miles from Billings, 186 miles from Bozeman, 155 miles from Butte, and approximately 90 miles from Helena (to the south) or Shelby (to the north).

Rocky Mountain Front

Spanning more than 100 miles from Montana into Canada, the Rocky Mountain Front is the startling merger of prairie and mountain—in places the Rockies literally rise 4,000–5,000 feet. The combination of two ecosystems is fascinating both culturally and in terms of the environmental implications—it is one of the few places in the Lower 48 that grizzly bears still wander onto the plains, much as they did when Lewis and Clark traveled the region. There is a strong cowboy culture in Choteau and a rich Native American culture in Browning. There are agricultural towns with rugged mountain wilderness just a stone's throw away. It is impressive and rare to be able to appreciate natural diversity, undistracted by humankind's homogenous development.

BROWNING

Agency headquarters for the Blackfeet Reservation, home to Montana's largest tribe, Browning (population 1,057, elevation 4,377 feet) has retained much of the culture of the Blackfeet people. The setting is spectacular, at the eastern edge of Glacier National Park, but the town doesn't offer much in the way of striking architecture or high-end hotels. What it does offer, though, is an exceptional opportunity to learn about and experience Blackfeet culture. In addition to the significant Museum of the Plains Indian, there are a number of annual events open to visitors as well as tours given by extremely well-versed local guides. There is even a place where guests can camp in magnificently decorated tipis, feast on gourmet regional cuisine, and enjoy an authentic Blackfeet experience.

Sights

Led by Blackfeet tribe member, historian, and well-known artist Darryl Norman, **Blackfeet Cultural History Tours** (406/338-2787, www. blackfeetculturecamp.com, half-day tours for 1–4 people from $100) offer a remarkable opportunity to explore the reservation and its history. Norman operates as a step-on guide, joining guests in their own vehicles and taking them to various buffalo jumps, tipi rings, and medicine lodges.

Just west of Browning at the junction of U.S. 2 and U.S. 89 is the **Museum of the Plains Indian** (406/338-2230, 9 A.M.–4:45 P.M. daily June–Sept., 10 A.M.–4:30 P.M. daily Oct.–May, $4 adults, $3 seniors over 65, $1 children under 6, free Oct.–May). The museum exhibits the arts and crafts of the northern plains Indians. The permanent collection highlights the diversity of tribal arts and displays artifacts from everyday life, including clothing, weapons, toys, and household implements. There are two galleries dedicated to showcasing contemporary Native American artists. During summer, painted tipis are assembled on the grounds.

Accommodations

Browning itself doesn't offer a lot in the way of accommodations; the best bets are toward Glacier National Park. Just outside town is the interesting **Aspenwood Resort** (U.S. 89, 9.5 miles west of Browning, 406/338-3009, www.aspenwoodresort.com, suites from $95), ideally located close to Glacier National Park between Browning and St. Mary. There are three suites in the rustic lodge in addition to RV sites, a campground, and a restaurant.

The **Lodge Pole Gallery and Tipi Village** (U.S. 89, 2 miles west of Browning, 406/338-2787, www.blackfeetculturecamp.com, tipis $50 pp, plus $15 for each additional person, meals not included) is a rare and special place. Part art gallery, part tipi camp, part gourmet restaurant, the Lodge Pole offers an extraordinarily unique experience and a true taste of Blackfeet culture with traditional meals, Native American art, Spanish mustangs, and various cultural events.

Food

The best local food, including buffalo, deer, and elk, is served in traditional style for guests at the Lodge Pole Gallery and Tipi Village, but there is also a family-owned Mexican restaurant in town: **Tres Hermanas** (108 1st Ave. NW, 406/338-3111, 8 A.M.–6 P.M. daily, entrées $2–9) has been in business for 15 years, which is really saying something in this area.

Information

The **Browning Area Chamber** (124 2nd Ave. NW, 406/338-4015, www.browningchamber.com, 8 A.M.–5 P.M. Mon.–Fri.) is open year-round.

Browning is 123 miles from Great Falls.

CHOTEAU

Established with a post office under the name Old Agency in 1875, Choteau is one of the region's oldest active towns. The name was changed in 1882 to honor Pierre Chouteau, president of the American Fur Company and responsible for bringing the first steamboat up the Missouri River. This ranching town at the edge of the Rockies is a dinosaur-lover's dream, with paleontological museums and sites galore. It also provides unparalleled access to some of the state's most incredible wilderness area. In addition to its obvious attractions, Choteau is simply a charming Montana town—small, friendly, and ideally situated for visitors.

Sights

The remains of the most famous **Egg Mountain** (U.S. 287, between mile posts 57 and 58) inhabitants were discovered by dinosaur guru Jack Horner in September 1983—a discovery that has yielded the largest collection of dinosaur eggs, embryos, and baby skeletons in the western hemisphere. The findings entirely changed our notion of how dinosaurs raised their young. The baby remains were found alongside an enormous number of adult remains, which scientists determined was a monumental herd of *Maiasaura* ("good mother reptile") along with a lesser number of *Troodons* killed in a catastrophic event like a volcanic eruption or a hurricane. Egg Mountain is one of 16 sites in Montana deemed "geological wonders" by a team of historians, geologists, and paleontologists. An interpretive sign on U.S. 287 provides information about the site. There is also a small parking area, and visitors are welcome to wander the site, which is more a hill than a mountain. Naturalist guides occasionally offer narrated tours of the area; for more information contact the Museum of the Rockies (406/994-2251).

Located at the north end of town, the **Old Trail Museum** (823 N. Main St., 406/466-5332, www.theoldtrailmuseum.com, 10 A.M.–4 P.M. daily Memorial Day–Labor Day, $4 adults, $2 children) celebrates both the natural and cultural history of the Rocky Mountain Front. In the Dinosaurs of the Two Medicine paleontology gallery, there are dinosaur bones and fossils aplenty, along with a good *Maiasaura* exhibit. The museum also has a number of other interesting local history exhibits, including Native American artifacts collected by A. B. Guthrie Jr. and details of Choteau's last hanging.

Between Choteau and Fairfield off U.S. 89 is **Freezeout Lake** (406/467-2646, www.fwp. mt.gov, mid-Mar.–autumn), an absolute birder's paradise, and for many Montanans the best place to gauge the imminent arrival of ever-elusive spring. The scenic lake is a staging area for hundreds of thousands of snow geese and thousands of tundra swans on their way north. The snow geese typically arrive at Freezeout in early March. As with most wildlife, dawn and dusk offer the best viewing opportunities. A variety of other birds pass through the area, including raptors and upland game birds in winter, waterfowl in spring and fall, and shorebirds in summer. The interior roads have ample parking and pullouts.

Accommodations

Although this is ranch country with a number of fabulous guest ranches, there are also a couple of quaint motels in Choteau. None are better than the old-school **⟨ Bella Vista Motel** (614 N. Main Ave., 406/466-5711, bellavista@3rivers.net, from $59 d), complete with individual garages beside each unit. All motels should be so smart. Discounted off-season rates start at $59.

The **SK Ranch** (561 31st Rd. NW, Conrad, 406/278-7821 or 406/469-2240, www.realmontanaranchvacations.com) is a 12,000-acre family-run cattle ranch 13 miles north of Choteau. The Skeltons are Montana natives who invite guests to participate in the daily workings of the ranch, although guests are welcome just to tag along for the ride if they are not up to roping and branding. The accommodations—choose a cozy log cabin or a thick-walled tent—are attractive, and Alison Skelton's home-cooked meals are mouthwatering. Horse clinics, excursions to nearby sights, and plenty of opportunities to watch wildlife are offered, and each trip is an authentic experience that can be tailored to individual needs and preferences. Five-day, six-night all-inclusive trips, available June–September, start at $1,250 pp.

Two exceptional guest ranches in the area, both 28 miles west of Choteau, are the **Seven Lazy P Ranch** (2055 Teton Canyon Rd., 406/466-2044, www.sevenlazyp.com, from $1,600 weekly pp d, $1,120 children), located in the heart of Teton Canyon with easy access to the Bob Marshall Wilderness Area, and the **Pine Butte Guest Ranch** (351 S. Fork Rd., 406/466-2158, www.pinebutteguestranch. com, from $1,700 weekly pp, $1,300 children), which is owned by the Nature Conservancy. Both are exceptionally beautiful old dude ranches with specialized amenities that include naturalist hikes and a swimming pool in addition to the classic Western dude experience.

Another favorite family-friendly guest ranch west of Augusta is the **Triple J Wilderness Ranch** (80 Mortimer Rd., 406/562-3653, www. triplejranch.com, $1,900 weekly pp all-inclusive, discounts for children), tucked in the magnificent Sun River Canyon above Gibson Lake. In addition to all-inclusive vacations catering to riders, hikers, and fishers, the Triple J offers fantastic kids' programs and awesome pack trips in the Bob Marshall Wilderness Area.

Food

Choteau has some good options for regional cuisine. The **⟨ Elk Country Grill** (925 Main Ave. N., 406/466-3311, www.elkcountrygrill. com, 11 A.M.–9 P.M. Mon.–Sat., lunch $5–11, dinner $7–26) lives up to its name with wild game selections that include elk medallions. The specialty is steak, but there are plenty of seafood and pasta dishes as well. Treat yourself to one of their Dutch oven concoctions.

The Meeting Grounds (202 N. Main St., 406/466-2667, 6:30 A.M.–2:30 P.M. Mon.–Fri.) is a great little coffee shop and café located in a 1906 bank building, open for breakfast and lunch only.

Information

The **Choteau Chamber of Commerce** (703 Main Ave. N., 406/466-5316 or 800/823-3866, www.choteaumontana.com, 10 A.M.–4 P.M. Mon.–Fri.) has hours that can vary from season to season; call ahead to make sure it is open.

Choteau is 52 miles northwest of Great Falls along U.S. 89.

❰ THE BOB MARSHALL WILDERNESS COMPLEX

With more than 1.5 million acres, the Bob Marshall Wilderness Complex is one of the largest and most remote wilderness areas in the Lower 48. The mountains soar above 9,000 feet, and the Continental Divide splits the region into several headwater drainage areas. Numerous lakes and pristine trout-laden rivers are here along with copious animals, including elk, white-tailed and mule deer, gray wolves, Canadian lynx, bobcats, bighorn sheep, mountain goats, wolverines, and cougars. The area was named for its first and perhaps most vociferous champion, Bob Marshall, a forester, author, explorer, and leader in the protection of wild lands. The area was first set aside in 1940, shortly after Marshall's death, and was designated by the federal government in conjunction with the 1964 Wilderness Act.

What to See

Encompassing three designated roadless wilderness areas, "The Bob," as it is known locally, is a magnificent place to explore. The most famous geological landmark is a dramatic 22-mile-long escarpment known as the **Chinese Wall.** Technically referred to as the Lewis Overthrust, the incredible rock wall—it is 1,000 feet high in places—is the result of a massive geologic upheaval in which the state split from Glacier National Park all the way down to Yellowstone. The Chinese Wall is where the eastern plate slid under the western plate.

Other popular areas for hikers and backpackers include the **South Fork of the Flathead River** valley, where most of the major trails leading in or out of the Bob can be picked up. **Big Salmon Lake** in the South Fork is among the more popular destinations. On the western edge of the wilderness complex, **Holland Lake** in the Swan Valley offers good access for backpackers and outfitters.

The **Sun River Game Preserve,** which lies at the eastern edge of the Bob, is the only portion of the complex where hunting is restricted. The area was established in the late 1920s as a refuge for elk, deer, and grizzlies, among other animals, and remains an important winter range for numerous species.

Access

Though the wilderness complex is roadless by definition, more than 1,000 miles of trails crisscross the region and provide access for private visitors and commercial outfitters. Ten-day trips into the region to take advantage of hunting, fishing, or just unparalleled wild scenery are popular and can be arranged through a number of licensed outfitters. The **Bob Marshall Wilderness Ranch** (Hwy. 83, 21 miles north of Seeley Lake, 406/745-4466 or 406/754-2285, www.wildernessranch.com) offers both a rustic lodge (from $145 pp) bordering the Wilderness area and deluxe guided pack trips into the Bob that cater to hunters, fishers, and nature lovers. The **Seven Lazy P Ranch** (2055 Teton Canyon Rd., Choteau, 406/466-2044, www.sevenlazyp.com) also offers guided trips into the wilderness area. Other outfitters can be found though the **Montana Professional Wilderness Outfitters Association** (www.mtpwoa.com).

Information

Road access to the perimeter of the wilderness complex is on U.S. 2 to the north, U.S. 89 and U.S. 287 to the east, and Highways 200 and 83 to the south and west. The complex is managed by four national forests, including the **Flathead National Forest** (406/758-5200, www.fs.fed.us/r1/flathead/wilderness/Wilderness.htm) in Kalispell, and five ranger districts.

Fort Benton and the Hi-Line

The farther east one travels from Great Falls, the more the landscape opens up. From the edge of the towering Rockies the land is pulled tight into the Upper Missouri River Valley and the rugged breaks that fracture the vast agricultural land and prairie. It is quiet in these parts but stunning, and there is a remarkable quality of light in which the weather can change the landscape in a moment.

Fort Benton, considered the oldest town in Montana, is a picturesque hamlet on the banks of the Missouri. Farther north, on the Milk River, is Havre, a rough-and-tumble railroad town, the largest on the Hi-Line, with a colorful history. Tightly knit communities like Cut Bank, Shelby, and Chinook span the Hi-Line and reflect its boom-and-bust cycle.

◖ FORT BENTON

Established in 1846 as an American Fur Company trading post, Fort Benton (population 1,459, elevation 2,644 feet) became one of the most important trading centers in the Northwest as a critical inland port. Starting in 1860, each year in spring and early summer some 50 steamboats would arrive, loaded with trappers, traders, gold seekers, and mountains of supplies destined for places across the West. When the Great Northern Railway arrived in Helena in 1887, the river traffic to Fort Benton all but dried up. The last steamboat to Fort Benton left in 1922.

The infrastructure created in Fort Benton's heyday—including a glamorous hotel—still lures visitors today. In fact, the entire town is recognized as a National Historic Landmark, and the people of Fort Benton have done much to preserve and promote their storied past. The old steamboat levee, along what was once known as the "bloodiest block in the West," has been transformed into a tranquil walking path. The original fort has been partially rebuilt in the center of town, and there are two wonderful museums and one of the best historic hotels in the state.

Sights

Fort Benton has an inordinate number of museums for its population, all of which are worth seeing. A two-day pass, available for $10 at any of the museums, enable you to visit all three.

Dedicated to the region's 19th century history, the **Museum of the Upper Missouri** (Old Fort Park, 406/622-5316, www.fortbenton.com/museums, 10 A.M.–4 P.M. Mon.–Sat., noon–4 P.M. Sun. late May–late Sept., $5 adults, $1 children) has a number of exhibits that hark back to Fort Benton's glory days as the Northwest's most important inland port. Twice-daily guided tours, leaving promptly at 10:30 A.M. and 1:30 P.M., take visitors on a walk around the fascinating Old Fort.

The **Museum of the Northern Great Plain** (1205 20th St., 406/622-5316, www.fortbenton.com/museums, 10 A.M.–4 P.M. Mon.–Sat., noon–4 P.M.Sun. late May–late Sept., $5 adults, $1 children) pays tribute to the agricultural heritage and homestead era.

The **Upper Missouri River Breaks Interpretive Center** (701 7th St., 406/622-4000 or 877/256-3252, www.mt.blm.gov, 8 A.M.–5 P.M. daily Memorial Day–late Sept., 8 A.M.–5 P.M. Mon.–Fri. late Sept.–Memorial Day, $2) is an impressive new facility celebrating the natural and cultural history of the river and its surrounding environment. A must-see for boaters on the Missouri, the center offers technical information as well as historical and interactive exhibits.

The **Upper Missouri River Breaks National Monument** (406/538-1900 or 877/256-3252, www.mt.blm.gov) comprises 375,000 acres centered on a 149-mile stretch of the Missouri, designated a National Wild and Scenic River. The remoteness of the region adds to its ecological and cultural significance. Boaters have the rare opportunity to travel in an area virtually untouched since Lewis and Clark's era, and the cliffs and sandy beaches have as much appeal today as they did 200 years ago. The water is wide and reasonably flat, so white-

THE LEGEND OF SHEP

A tear-jerking story, Shep has become something of an icon for the town of Fort Benton. Some sort of border collie mix, Shep was born in Montana in the late 1920s. He was a sheepdog and, by all accounts, a very faithful companion. When his sheepherding master fell ill during the Great Depression and had to be taken by buckboard to the hospital in Fort Benton, Shep followed along and waited for days outside the hospital for his owner. A nurse at the hospital, Sister Genevieve, noticed the dog and began to leave scraps of food and drinking water for him. When his master was loaded onto an eastbound train at the Fort Benton depot in a casket, Shep began a nearly six-year vigil, meeting every train, waiting for his master to disembark. Each time a train pulled out of the station, Shep would vanish into the hills, only to return to greet the next arrival.

After several months, Shep stayed closer to the station, carving a little nook for himself under the platform. The son of one of the railroad workers made a point of bringing Shep regular meals, and the depot agent eventually coaxed the wary animal into the station with a warm bed. Another railroad worker recognized Shep as having belonged to a sheepherder whose lifeless body was shipped to his family back East. He explained to Shep's new caretakers that the dog had been waiting at the station since then. Over the span of a few years, the legend of Shep began to grow, along with the number of his admirers.

Shep was written up in newspapers around the world, and the Great Northern Railway had to hire a secretary just to handle the mail – which included everything from money to dog bones – addressed to Shep from people worldwide.

By 1942, Shep was quite old and deaf. Despite his celebrity, he still greeted every train in search of his master. On an icy January morning, Shep wandered out to the tracks and was tragically hit and killed by an inbound train. The whole town mourned his loss, and hundreds came to pay their respects at his funeral. His concrete gravestone still stands sentry high atop a hill next to where the depot once stood.

In 1994, the city fathers presented a beautiful bronze statue of Shep to the people Fort Benton. His sweet story was immortalized in a wonderful children's book, *Shep: Our Most Loyal Dog* by Sneed B. Collard III and Joanna Yardley.

water equipment and expertise is not necessary. However, because of its remoteness, great care should be taken, and careful planning is necessary. Day trips, shuttles, and full-service camping trips can be arranged through a number of outfitters, including **Hole-in-the-Wall Adventures** (Lewistown, 406/538-2418, www.hole-in-the-wall.org), which offers three-day, two-night trips starting at $425 pp, half price for children. **Adventure Bound Canoe & Shuttle Company** (Fort Benton, 406/622-5077 or 877/538-4890, www.adventureboundcanoe. com) offers guided trips and shuttle service as well as canoe, kayak, and camping equipment rentals. Boaters interested in planning their own trips should contact the **Fort Benton River Management Station** (701 7th St., Fort Benton, 877/256-3252, www.blm.gov/mt).

For an altogether different experience, check out the tiny town of **Virgelle,** in the heart of the national monument and accessible by road or river ferry. This former ghost town has been restored without being overly modernized, and accommodations are available. The town and its mercantile store truly offer a step back in time.

Accommodations

If you could only stay in one place in Montana, the **◖ Grand Union Hotel** (1 Grand Union Sq., Fort Benton, 406/622-1882 or 888/838-1882, www.grandunionhotel.com, $120–190) might be it. The hotel was built in 1882 at the height of Fort Benton's steamboat era and a full seven years before Montana became a state. After more than 100 years of operation,

© CARTER G. WALKER

Fort Benton's historic Grand Union Hotel

the hotel closed its doors in the mid-1980s and continued to decay. Montanans Jim and Cheryl Gagnon purchased the once-glorious hotel in 1997 and undertook a massive, award-winning renovation. Today the hotel lives up to its original splendor with gorgeous mahogany woodwork, lofty ceilings, and elegant furnishings throughout. It's interesting to note that the third floor was originally designed for cowboys, workers, and their occasional female companions, and it is accessed by a back staircase rather than the grand central staircase to the second floor, which was occupied by VIPs. The entire hotel is lovely and worth the splurge.

Accommodations in Virgelle, in the heart of the Upper Missouri River Breaks National Monument, are available in rustic but comfy homestead-era cabins or in charming B&B rooms above the **Virgelle Mercantile** (7485 Virgelle Ferry Rd. N., Virgelle, 406/378-3110 or 800/426-2926, www.virgellemontana.com, $115–190 including breakfast).

Food
Located in the Grand Union Hotel, **The Union Grill** (1 Grand Union Sq., Fort Benton,

406/622-1882 or 888/838-1882, www.grandunionhotel.com, 5–9 P.M. daily summers and Wed.–Sun. winters, entrées $19–34) is exquisite and offers some of the most innovative cuisine in this part of the state. In the summer you can sit on the riverside patio and indulge in cocoa-dusted elk loin, grilled buffalo rib eye, or market fresh fish. The menu is ever-changing and incorporates as much fresh local fare as possible. The wine list and the desserts are equally exceptional, and even the bar menu is inspired.

Information
The **Fort Benton Chamber of Commerce** (1421 Front St., 406/622-3864, www.fortbenton.com, 9 A.M.–7 P.M. Mon.–Fri., 10 A.M.–4 P.M. Sat.–Sun. May–Sept.) is part of the Information Center inside the old fire station next to the walking bridge.

Fort Benton is 40 miles east of Great Falls on U.S. 87.

CUT BANK
At the edge of the Blackfeet Reservation between Browning and Shelby, Cut Bank (population 3,105, elevation 3,733 feet) is famous for

being the site of Lewis and Clark's only armed encounter with Native Americans. On July 26, 1806, Meriwether Lewis, joined by George Drouillard, Joseph Fields, and Reuben Fields, met with eight Blackfeet Indians. When Lewis revealed that the U.S. government intended to outfit all of the Plains Indians with hunting rifles, the Blackfeet were angry because they had controlled the firearms trade amongst Native Americans through their relationship with the Hudson's Bay Company. The Blackfeet took off with the men's horses, a fight ensued, and two Blackfeet were killed.

In addition to the town's proximity to the reservation and its cultural influence, there are also five Hutterite colonies in the area that welcome visitors. The **Glacier County Historical Museum** (107 Old Kevin Hwy., 406/873-4904, gcmuseum@sofast.net, 10 A.M.–5 P.M. Tues.–Sat. Memorial Day–Labor Day, by appointment Labor Day–Memorial Day, donation) presents exhibits on Lewis and Clark, homesteading, artist John Clark, and the town's oil boom. On summer weekends, costumed guides reenact homestead life circa 1915.

The **Glacier Gateway Plaza** (1130 E. Main St., 406/873-2566 or 800/851-5541, www.glaciergateway.com, from $69) is the newest and nicest motel in town, with amenities like an indoor pool and high-speed Internet.

SHELBY

The humble story of Shelby's origins involves a discarded boxcar around which a town eventually developed. The town saw enormous growth thanks to the railroad, the Homestead Act, and a 1921 oil discovery. Shelby even hosted the 1923 World Heavyweight Championship fight between Jack Dempsey and Tommy Gibbons. Today, Shelby (population 3,541, elevation 3,086 feet) is a small trade center that attracts plenty of Canadians through the state's busiest port of entry.

The **Marias Museum of History and Art** (206 12th Ave., 406/434-2551, free) is a classic county history museum with dusty but interesting displays of Indian artifacts, dinosaur bones, homestead-era relics, and recreated historic interiors.

The **Shelby Chamber of Commerce** (406/434-7184, www.shelbymtchamber.org, 9 A.M.–noon Mon.–Fri.) and the **Shelby Visitors Information Center** (406/434-9151) are located in the historic Shelby Town Hall (100 Montana Ave.) at the eastern edge of town and can inform you about local events and guided tours. There is free Wi-Fi on the premises.

Shelby is 84 miles north of Great Falls along I-15.

HAVRE

Named for the birthplace of the French homesteaders on whose land the town was sited, Havre (HAV-er, population 9,575, elevation 2,494 feet) is a railroad town anchoring the Hi-Line and with an economy that is increasingly diversifying. As with so many towns along the Hi-Line, the existence of the settlement can unquestionably be attributed to railroad titan James J. Hill, who sent his construction crew to the area in 1887.

The city itself is defined by various natural features: the Bear Paw Mountains to the south, the wide-open plains in every direction, and the Milk River, which borders Havre. With the exception of the Havre Beneath the Streets tour, which is remarkably well done, Havre has not done well in preserving and promoting its historical attractions, many of which, in Havre's defense, were not actually discovered until the 1960s and 1970s. This is an agricultural and college town—Montana State University-Northern—as well as the trade center for many of the smaller towns in the region.

◖ Havre Beneath the Streets

When the city of Havre nearly burned to the ground in 1904, business owners moved underground in an effort to stay afloat while the city was rebuilt. The Havre Beneath the Streets Tours (120 3rd Ave., 406/265-8888, www.havremt.com, 2-hour tours 9:30 A.M.–3:30 P.M. daily late May–mid-Sept., 10 A.M.–4 P.M. Mon.–Sat. mid Sept.–late May, call for specific tour times and reservations, $10 adults, $9 seniors, $7 students) take visitors into this phenomenal maze of turn-of-the-century establishments that include a faithfully recreated saloon, brothel, bakery, sausage factory, and more. The guides are passionate and have juicy stories of Havre's wild days and wilder characters. The underground passages were only discovered in 1976 when the city undertook a street-widening project, but the care with which the businesses have been restored is remarkable, making it one of the best historical tours in the state. Each year in early June, actors in period garb bring the underground city to life with a **Living History Weekend.**

Other Sights and Events

If you don't get your fill of Havre history on the underground tour, visit the **H. Earl Clack Memorial Museum** (Holiday Village Mall, 1753 U.S. 2, 406/265-4000, clackmuseum@co.hill. mt.us, 10 A.M.–5 P.M. Mon.–Sat., noon–5 P.M. Sun. May–mid-Sept., 1–5 P.M. daily mid-Sept.–Apr.), oddly located in a shopping mall, for illustrative dioramas on the development of Havre, an assortment of dinosaur eggs and embryos, and most interestingly, artifacts from the adjacent **Wahkpa Chu'gn Archeological Site** (406/265-6417 or 406/265-7550, www.buffalojump.org, 9 A.M.–2 P.M. daily June 1–Labor Day only, $6 adults, $5 seniors, $3 students, free for children under 6), a 2,000-year-old buffalo jump that was discovered in the early 1960s. Unfortunately the site is located immediately behind the mall behind a chain-link fence that detracts from the perceived significance of the place, but it is one of the best-preserved buffalo jump sites in the state. An hour-long guided tour—the only way visitors are permitted into the site—takes visitors through bison kills areas and campsite deposits, some of which are 20 feet deep.

Winter visitors to Havre, hardy souls indeed, should do whatever they can to ski at **Bear Paw Ski Bowl** (Rocky Boy Reservation, 29 miles south of Havre, 406/625-8404, www. skibearpaw.com, 10:30 A.M.–4 P.M. Sat.–Sun. only Jan.–Mar., $20 adults, $18 students age 9–12, free under age 9 and over age 80). Known as the "Last Best Ski Hill," Bear Paw is

an old-fashioned ski area with two lifts, excellent advanced terrain, and an entirely volunteer staff. There are no rentals available, so be sure to pick them up in Havre at **Master Sports** (301 1st St., 406/265-4712). The hill is open only on weekends, but it's a day of skiing with a side of nostalgia that you will never forget.

The biggest event of the year by far in the Havre area is the **Rocky Boy Pow Wow and Rodeo** in Box Elder, usually held around the first weekend in August. The four-day event includes a rodeo, a dance, and costume and drumming competitions for more than $100,000 in prize money. There are cultural demonstrations, grand entries twice daily, and plenty of food vendors. The venues are decided each year and can be located through the Rocky Boy Agency (406/395-4478 or 800/823-4478, www.rockyboy.org).

Accommodations

Havre has a plentiful assortment of hotels and motels, and surprisingly they are often fully booked with business travelers, so advance reservations are a good idea. On the west end of town, the **AmericInn** (2520 U.S. 2 W., 406/395-5000 or 877/634-3444, www.amercinn.com/hotels/ MT/Havre, $90–160) is the newest and one of the largest, with an indoor pool, oversize rooms, Wi-Fi, and hearty breakfasts.

In the center of downtown, **El Toro** (521 1st St., 800/422-5414, $58–84) is a good bargain in an excellent location. The Spanish architecture is unexpected, but the rooms are basic and nice.

For campers, **Beaver Creek Park** is just 20 miles south of town (17863 Beaver Creek Rd., 406/395-4565 or 406/265-5481, bcpark@ mtintouch.net, permits $7 per night) and has a special site on the north face of the Bear Paw Mountains. At 10,000 acres, it is the largest county park in the United States and offers nature trails, two lakes for fishing, and a private campground.

Food

Murphy's Irish Pub (1465 U.S. 2 NW, 406/265-4700, www.murphysubhavre.com,

11 A.M.–9 P.M. Sun.–Thurs., 11 A.M.–10 P.M. Fri.–Sat., entrées $6–10) has a surprisingly international menu that ranges from the rather Irish fish-and-chips and Gaelic boxty to Asian chicken salad, chicken quesadillas, Philly cheesesteak, and even a Maui Waui burger. The food is good, and the beer and liquor selection is excellent.

Equally inexplicable but just as delicious is **Nalivka's Original Pizza Kitchen** (1032 1st St., 406/265-4050, lunch and dinner Tues.–Sun., large pizza $16–24), owned and operated by a Russian American family since 1957. Nalivka's serves outstanding pizza—the crust is rich and flaky like a quiche—along with sandwiches, soups, and salads. The service is take-out or delivery only.

Riding the Rails Along the Hi-Line

The *Empire Builder* is the most popular Amtrak long-distance train in the United States, traveling between Chicago and either Portland or Seattle. One train passes in each direction daily, and much of the route through Montana, known as the Hi-Line, runs in the north along U.S. 2. The first stop for westbound trains in Montana is Wolf Point, and the last is Whitefish. The route goes over the Continental Divide through Glacier National Park, a portion of the trip that is unforgettable, and trains are supposedly timed so that passengers will be able to enjoy a view of the majestic Rockies regardless of which direction they are traveling. The busiest stops for the train are Whitefish, Shelby, and Havre. If you have plans to travel west and can spare the time, consider taking the train.

Information

One block south of 1st Avenue at the corner of 5th Avenue is the **Havre Area Chamber of Commerce** (139 5th Ave., 406/265-4383, www.havremt.com, 8 A.M.–5 P.M. Mon.–Fri.), which has a good selection of visitor and recreation information.

Getting There

Havre is 114 miles from Great Falls along U.S. 87.

The **Havre City-County Airport** (HVR, 406/265-4671) is located three miles west of the town. Great Lakes Airlines flies to Billings and Denver from Havre.

CHINOOK

With such an auspicious name—*chinook* is a Native American word meaning "warm wind"—it's no wonder that Chinook (population 1,274, elevation 2,428 feet) is a cattle town with more cows than people. Set on the rolling plains alongside the Milk River and just north of the Bear Paw Mountains, Chinook is a lovely and solemn place most closely associated with the heartbreaking battle and subsequent surrender of Chief Joseph.

Bear Paw Battlefield

Fifteen miles south of Chinook and just 40 miles south of the Canadian border on Highway 240 is the haunting Bear Paw Battlefield (sunrise–sunset daily year-round), one of three historic Nez Perce sites in the state and the site of a five-day battle between the U.S. Army and Chief Joseph's band of 700 Nez Perce, who had already traveled 1,300 miles in an effort to escape the Army and were only 40 miles from freedom in Canada. There is a self-guided 1.25-mile trail, and ranger-guided tours can be arranged in summer by contacting the National Park Service (406/357-3130, stephanie_martin@nps.gov, www.nps.gov/nepe).

For a comprehensive introduction to the site, visit Chinook's **Blaine County Museum** (501 Indiana Ave., 406/357-2590, call for hours, free) before you head to the battlefield. The museum offers a gripping multimedia presentation, *40 Miles to Freedom,* as well as maps of the battlefield, and will soon open an extensive series of wildlife exhibits.

Events

Unlike the vast majority of Montana towns, which pack the calendar with events during summer, Chinook offers worthwhile events in the fall and early winter. The **Bear Paw Battle Commemoration** (406/357-3130, www.nps.gov/nepe) commemorates the 1877 battle with

THE BATTLE OF BEAR PAW

Sixteen miles south of Chinook is the historic Bear Paw Battlefield, an area that looks much as it did 130 years ago when the Nez Perce fought the last in a series of battles known as the Nez Perce War of 1877. Originally from the Wallowa Valley in northeastern Oregon, the Nez Perce, under the leadership of Chief Joseph, had refused to relocate to a reservation in Idaho. General Oliver O. Howard planned an attack to force Joseph's band onto the reservation. Before arriving at this site in Montana, the band of 700 Indians, 200 of whom were warriors, undertook a journey that has come to be known as one of the most spectacular military retreats in U.S. history. They spent three months covering more than 1,300 miles, crossed four states, and engaged in numerous skirmishes with the U.S. Army as they fled capture and sought refuge in Canada.

On September 29, 1877, the Nez Perce chose to rest at Snake Creek, just north of the Bear Paw Mountains and 40 miles from the Canadian border. General Howard had pursued them relentlessly, but believing that they had a good lead on his troops, they chose to set up camp. Unbeknownst to the Nez Perce, Colonel Nelson A. Miles and his 7th Cavalry were quickly approaching from the southeast. With the help of Cheyenne and Lakota scouts, they spotted the Nez Perce camp. Although almost 300 troops attacked the Nez Perce, the skilled warriors were able to stand their ground and rapidly fortify the encampment.

The Nez Perce earned great praise not only for their fighting but also for their humane treatment of others. During this battle, as wounded Army soldiers lay on the battlefield, the Nez Perce moved among them looking for ammunition and weapons but did no further harm to the injured men. There is even a legend that an injured soldier kept crying out to his comrades for water. A warrior approached him, removed the soldier's ammunition belt, and left a container of water.

After five days of fighting, Joseph had seen enough. There may have been an opportunity to escape, but he refused to leave the wounded, sick, and elderly behind. On October 5, 1877, Joseph, Howard, and Miles spoke though translators. Joseph made a poignant speech: "From where the sun now stands, I will fight no more forever." Although it was a conditional surrender, and both Miles and Howard assured Joseph that he and his people would be returned to their home in the Northwest, that was not the case: The U.S. government moved the Nez Perce first to a reservation in Kansas and later to Indian Territory in present-day Oklahoma. Not until 1885 were they moved to Washington State, still not their original homeland. Joseph died there in 1904, the cause of death diagnosed by his doctor as "a broken heart."

The Bear Paw Battlefield is one of several sites located within the Nez Perce National Historical Park (406/357-3130, www.nps.gov/nepe, year-round). A ranger is on-site beginning at noon each day late June–September.

GREAT FALLS

a traditional pipe ceremony. It is normally scheduled for the first Saturday in October. Photos and filming of the pipe ceremony are not permitted.

The **Sugar Beet Festival** in early October pays tribute to the region's biggest crop with a Main Street parade, vendors, entertainment, kids' activities, a barbecue, and a street dance. For more information on events and dates, contact the **Chamber of Commerce** (406/357-2394, www.chinookmontana.com).

Worth seeing during summer is the **Blaine**

County Fair & Rodeo (300 Cleveland Rd. W., 406/357-2988 or 406/357-3742), a small-town fair with a great rodeo, a carnival, country music, agricultural exhibits, and even lawn mower races.

Accommodations

The **Bear Paw Motel & RV** (145 Cleveland Rd., 406/357-2221 or 888/357-2224, slharvey@mtintouch.net, $60) has guest rooms with queen or double beds and free Wi-Fi. Pets are allowed for a fee. The nearby **Chinook Motor**

Inn (100 Indiana St., 406/357-2248, www.chinookmotorinn.com, $60–69) is much bigger and slightly more modern, also with Wi-Fi.

Food

Chinook is an excellent place if you have a sweet tooth: **Jean's Old Fashioned Bakery & Sandwich Shop** (315 Indiana St., 406/357-4287, 6:30 A.M.–5:30 P.M. Mon.–Sat., entrées $3–7.50) is a quaint little place with excellent soups and sandwiches as well as a mouthwatering assortment of fresh pastries, including caramel rolls, cream puffs, and pies. The restaurant is something of a shrine to the U.S. Army.

If you don't overload on goodies at Jean's, just a couple of blocks away is **The Creamery** (415 U.S. 2 W., 406/357-4260, noon–10 P.M. daily spring–end of Sept.), a perfect spot for any ice cream concoction imaginable when the weather is warm.

Information

The **Chinook Chamber of Commerce** (info@chinookmontana.com, www.chinookmontana.com) has an informative website. Information is also available at the **Blaine County Museum** (501 Indiana St.) and the **Blaine County Journal** (217 Indiana St.).

Chinook is 135 miles northeast of Great Falls via U.S. 87.

Lewistown and the Central Plains

In many ways, the heartland of Montana doesn't look all that different from the heartland of the United States. Small towns with strong identities and long, hard histories lie amid vast swaths of agricultural land, rolling fields, and—here is where things are different—humble mountains on the horizon. Though Lewistown is charging forward with population growth and the culture that accompanies it, other towns, like Judith Gap, Harlowton, and White Sulphur Springs, have struggled to hold on to their residents, most of whom earn a living on the land. There is great charm in the fact that some places don't change much, and visiting them can be like stepping back in time.

LEWISTOWN

Long the heart of this region both geographically and for trade, Lewistown (population 5,954, elevation 3,950 feet) was built by a diverse group of immigrants, something that is reflected in the town's beautiful architecture. The stonework, using local sandstone, was done largely by Croatians, and the interiors were crafted by Norwegians. The town itself was incorporated in 1899, and the area was settled by landless Métis, gold seekers, farmers, and

ranchers. It is splendidly set amid open fields, rolling prairie, and three mountain ranges. Although there are three ghost towns in the area—access to which is limited because they are almost entirely on private land—Lewistown itself is thriving and has become something of a model for renaissance in Montana. The combination of beautiful scenery, old-fashioned hospitality, good fishing, and great food has served Lewistown well.

Lewistown Art Center

Located across from the historic courthouse, the Lewistown Art Center (810 W. Broadway, 406/535-8278, www.lewistownartcenter.org, 11:30 A.M.–5:30 P.M. Tues.–Sat., free) is the artistic hub of this artsy community. Monthly gallery shows feature primarily Montana artists, and the center is the site of numerous arts-related events throughout the year, including music, theater, and the town's well-loved **Montana Cowboy Poetry & Western Music Rendezvous** (406/535-8278, lac@midrivers.com), held each year in August.

◖ Charlie Russell Chew Choo

One of the best ways to see and appreciate the area is aboard the fabulous and slightly kitschy

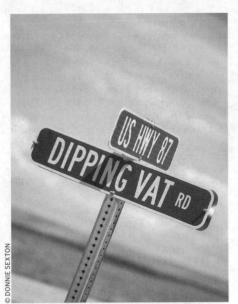

© DONNIE SEXTON

rural road sign west of Lewistown, Montana

Charlie Russell Chew Choo (406/535-5436, www.montanacharlierussellchewchoo.com, Sat. evening late June–Sept., special events in the fall and Dec. holidays, $90 adults, $50 children 12 and under), a three-hour ride that takes visitors on a narrated tour through the mountains and prairies of the region aboard an elegant 1950s passenger train. A full-course dinner featuring prime rib and all the fixings is served. There is also entertainment in the form of musicians, cowboy poets, and the occasional good-natured train robber.

Ghost Towns

There are three primary ghost towns outside Lewistown, all of which were gold-mining towns around the turn of the century. **Maiden** (off U.S. 191, northeast of Lewistown, 406/535-5436) was home to some 6,000 people in 1881 and produced more than $18 million worth of gold in its heyday. By 1896 the population had dwindled to 200, and after a fire destroyed every building in 1905, Maiden was never rebuilt.

The town of **Kendall** (on U.S. 87, north of Lewistown, at the base of the North Moccasin Mountains, 406/535-5436) took off in 1900 with the advent of the Kendall Gold Mining Company. It was among the first mines to use the cyanide process for separating gold. At its height, Kendall had a 23-room hotel complete with hot running water, hot-air heating, and electricity. There was also an opera house, several saloons, two churches, four stagecoach lines, and a number of other businesses. By 1920 the town had died, the mines were closed, and many of the buildings collapsed into the mine shafts.

In 1900, **Gilt Edge** (off U.S. 191, 20 miles northeast of Lewistown, 406/535-5436) was considered to be among the premier towns in the country. Calamity Jane was a frequent visitor, and not unlike Jane herself, who grew quite familiar with the town's jail, Gilt Edge's residents experienced a host of legal problems. The mine manager, Colonel Ammon, was eventually tried and convicted of stealing $25,000 worth of bullion intended as wages for the miners. He ultimately served time in New York's Sing Sing prison for stock swindling.

Before you seek out any of the ghost towns, be sure to call the Lewistown Chamber of Commerce (406/535-5436) for precise directions and information about private lands.

Events

The **Annual Montana State Chokecherry Festival** (Main St., 406/535-5436, www.lewistownchamber.com) is held the first Saturday after Labor Day. Nearly 5,000 people attend the breakfast (pancakes with chokecherry syrup, of course) and other festivities, which include a fun run and walk, chokecherry culinary contests, kids' activities, chokecherry pit-spitting contests, and arts and crafts booths.

The **Central Montana Horse Show, Fair and Rodeo** (1000 Fairgrounds Rd., 406/535-8841 or 800/406-8841, www.centralmontanafair.com) is another great small-town fair with an equestrian bent. In addition, there is musical entertainment, AMX auto racing, and a demolition derby.

Fishing

The land, mountains, and rivers around Lewistown make this area an ideal destination for fishers, hunters, and nature lovers. It's one of the few cities in Montana that offers outstanding fishing within the city limits at **Big Spring Creek,** the area's premier water source, supplying water for the city and a significant trout hatchery. There are also numerous public and privately stocked ponds and springs. For a guided fishing trip, contact David Stuver (406/538-5708, dstuver@midrivers.com, $150–275 for 1 fisher, includes lunch), a longtime teacher and guide with access to some of the region's best private waters; or stop by **Don's Sports and Western Store** (120 2nd Ave. S., 406/538-9408) for some flies and advice.

Accommodations and Camping

For in-town convenience, the **Yogo Inn of Montana** (211 E. Main St., 406/535-8969, www.yogoinn.com, $106–134) has 123 well-appointed guest rooms and suites catering to technologically inclined business travelers. The **Mountain View Motel** (1422 W. Main St., 406/535-3457 or 800/862-5786, $45–75) offers clean, quiet guest rooms in a building that was once a barracks for American and Russian pilots training during World War II.

Food

Lewistown is beginning to establish a reputation for fine dining, and among its newest gems is **The Mint Bar & Grill** (113 4th Ave. S., 406/535-9925, 5–9 P.M. Mon.–Sat., entrées $10–20), housed in a 1940s car dealership. The chefs specialize in savory sauces to accompany succulent steaks, ribs, seafood, and pasta. Like the best Montana restaurants, they use fresh local ingredients and pair hearty meals with an impressive wine list.

Open since 1951, the **Dash Inn** (207 NE Main St., 406/535-3892, 10 A.M.–10 P.M. daily year-round, $4–19) is a classic drive-through-only burger joint with everything you'd expect from a drive-in diner: ice-cream drinks, buckets of crispy chicken, and their famous wagon-wheel sandwich.

Information

The Lewistown Area Chamber of Commerce (406/535-5436, www.lewistownchamber. com, 8 A.M.–5 P.M. Mon.–Fri.) is located in the Central Montana Museum building in Symmes Park, on the east side of town.

Lewistown Municipal Airport (LWT, 190 Terminal Dr., 406/535-3264, www.lwtairport. com) is one mile southwest of Lewistown. It is served by Great Lakes Airlines, which offers flights to and from Denver and Worland, Wyoming. **Budget Rent-a-Car** has an on-site counter, and there is also taxi service available at the airport.

Lewistown is 106 miles southeast of Great Falls on Highway 3 and 125 miles from Billings via U.S. 87.

WHITE SULPHUR SPRINGS

Named for the white deposits found around the hot sulfur springs here, White Sulphur Springs (population 951, elevation 5,043 feet) was a gathering spot for various Native Americans tribes for years before James Brewer stumbled on the area in 1886 and developed the hot springs into a resort. The town boomed, first as the "Saratoga of the West," then with lead and silver mines, and then as a cattle town and commercial region for this vast agricultural area. There is nothing booming about White Sulphur Springs these days, but it does suit its own charm. In the midst of the prairies, it is close to excellent floating on the Smith River and skiing at Showdown Ski Area, and there are wonderful relics from its glory days: A castle sits atop the hill in town, and the hot springs still gurgle with purportedly healing waters.

The Castle

Built in 1892 by merchant Byron Roger Sherman, The Castle is a remarkable Victorian mansion that now houses the **Meagher County Museum** (310 2nd Ave. NE, 406/547-2324, 10 A.M.–6 P.M. daily May 15–Sept. 15). It was constructed with hand-cut granite blocks hauled by oxen from the Castle Mountains, 12 miles away. It is appointed with period furniture and original fixtures—Italian marble sinks as well as crystal and brass light fixtures. Sherman supplied electricity to the entire town, making White Sulphur Springs one of the first towns in the state to have electricity.

Floating and Fishing on the Smith River

One of Montana's most isolated, the Smith River is 59 miles of dramatic canyons, open ranch land, and rugged forest between Camp Baker and Eden Bridge. The high season is when the water is high, typically late spring–early summer. On average, floaters take four days to travel through this spectacular roadless area.

Because of its popularity with Montanans, it is the only river in the state that can be used only with a permit. Permits are issued annually by Montana Fish, Wildlife & Parks (FWP) in a lottery that runs early January–mid-February. For more information, contact the Great Falls FWP office (406/454-5861).

Accommodations

To enjoy White Sulphur Springs in the way the earliest settlers intended, make a point to visit **Spa Hot Springs Hotel** (202 W. Main St., 406/547-3366, www.spahotsprings.com, $59–69). The guest rooms are very basic and clean, but it's the hot springs that make this place special. Outside, the pool is shallow enough in places for toddlers. Inside, the pool is 10°F warmer, and both are drained and cleaned nightly so that no chemicals have to be added to the natural hot water. Nonguests can use the pools for a fee.

For nonswimmers, the nearby **All Seasons Inn & Suites** (U.S. 89 S., at the south end of town, 406/547-8888 or 877/314-0241, www.allseasonsinnandsuites.net, $70–79) is a modern hotel with a hot tub, free Wi-Fi, and continental breakfast. Pets are welcome for a $10 fee.

Food

Dori's Café (112 E. Main St., 406/547-2270, 6 A.M.–1 P.M. Mon.–Fri., 6 A.M.–2 P.M. Sat., 6–11 A.M. Sun., entrées $5–12) is just what

---

FLOATING THE SMITH

In the center of Montana and the middle of nowhere is the Smith River, a blue-ribbon trout stream and one of the most sought-after rivers in the state for float trips. There are no services and no road access along the 59-mile stretch of river between Camp Baker and Eden Bridge. The remoteness of the Smith, coupled with stunning limestone canyons and vast swaths of ranch land, make this river a stunning destination.

Aside from the splendid scenery, the fish add to the river's tremendous appeal. The rainbow and brown trout populations are thriving, as are the native whitefish, which is somewhat unfairly maligned.

Because of the river's popularity, it is closely managed by Montana Fish, Wildlife & Parks (FWP), which oversees a lottery system for the roughly 700 permits released annually. There are 27 boat camps and 52 campsites scattered along the river, which can most often be floated in four days. The season varies dramatically depending on the snowpack, rainfall, and the timing of irrigation use, but mid-April-early July is considered the prime season, and occasionally floaters can hit the Smith as late as September. To apply for a permit, which is due in mid-February, contact the Montana FWP (406/454-5861, www.fwp.mt.gov). Another option for those unlucky in the lottery is to book a Smith River trip with one of a handful of permitted outfitters. **Lewis and Clark Expeditions** (Helena, 406/449-4632, www.lewisandclarkexpeditions.net, 4 day-5 night trips $3,600) offers excellent trips with world-class guides and gourmet grub. In addition to his fantastic commercial trips, owner Mike Geary has teamed with Project Healing Waters to sponsor river fishing trips for disabled veterans.

you'd hope to find in a small middle-of-nowhere Montana town: a friendly place with good hearty food and the ambience of a wildlife museum.

For dinner and a glimpse of the local nightlife, head to the **Stockman's Bar and Steakhouse** (117 Main St., 406/547-9985, 5–10 P.M. daily, entrées $7–25) for a steak or juicy burger.

Information and Services

For information about White Sulphur Springs, contact the **Meagher County Chamber of Commerce** (406/547-2250, www.meagher-chamber.com).

White Sulphur Springs is 75 miles east of Helena and 79 miles north of Bozeman.

GLACIER NATIONAL PARK

Known as the "Crown of the Continent," Glacier National Park is one of the largest intact ecosystems in the Lower 48 and an amalgam of stunning landscapes that, for many visitors, defines the entire state. Think of Montana; picture Glacier.

The beauty of Glacier is rugged, raw, and dynamic. The mountains thrust skyward, and the gravity-defying roads are ribbons that snake toward the summit. The legendary Going-to-the-Sun Road is one of the West's most impressive engineering feats and one of the best scenic drives in the country. There are still 50 glaciers to be found within the park along with countless waterfalls and hundreds of crystalline lakes. In summer the landscape is heavy with huckleberries and dotted with bear grass. While wildlife viewing from the road can be challenging in this mountainous terrain, the animals—grizzly and black bears, mountain goats, bighorn sheep, wolves, and more—are here in abundance. With more than 1,600 square miles of alpine majesty, the scenery, if not the altitude, will leave you breathless.

Glacier National Park is a haven for nature lovers, and there are a number of ways visitors can enjoy the natural beauty—hiking, bicycling, boating, and cross-country skiing, to name a few. There are more than 700 miles of trails throughout the park and a smattering of historic lodges and chalets for cozy accommodations. Yet despite its extensive offerings, Glacier still offers visitors a rare and precious sense of solitude. The crowds are gone as soon as your feet hit the

© DONNIE SEXTON

HIGHLIGHTS

❰❰ Lake McDonald: The largest lake in the park and arguably one of the most beautiful, glacially carved Lake McDonald is easy to access and impossible not to enjoy. Pack a picnic for the rocky beach or cruise the waters on a boat tour (page 104).

❰❰ Going-to-the-Sun Road: Stretching just over 50 miles across the park, this phenomenal feat of engineering gives viewers an extraordinary overview. Shuttles are available and worthwhile for those wanting to view the scenery without driving, and multiple hiking trails start from the road (page 105).

❰❰ Hiking: Glacier National Park was made for hiking. Among the best-loved in the park is the **Highline Trail,** which climbs 200 feet over 7.6 miles to Granite Park Chalet, then drops more than 2,200 feet over the last four miles back to the road. The views are staggering but not for the faint of heart (page 105).

❰❰ Many Glacier: In the shadow of Chief Mountain, Many Glacier is prime hiking, canoeing, and horseback riding country. This stunning area in the northeast section of the park is popular with hikers but is rarely crowded (page 115).

❰❰ Grinnell Glacier: Since scientists anticipate that the glaciers in the park could disappear entirely by 2020, Grinnell Glacier may be a once-in-a-lifetime opportunity. The ranger-led hike is especially worthwhile (page 115).

LOOK FOR ❰❰ TO FIND RECOMMENDED SIGHTS, ACTIVITIES, DINING, AND LODGING.

trail, and there are miles of shoreline where the only other picnickers are four-legged. More than just the Crown of the Continent, Glacier is like no place on earth.

PLANNING YOUR TIME

Depending on the amount of time you have to spend in Montana, Glacier National Park could easily absorb all of it, but often it is a spectacular route to get from one side of the Continental Divide to the other, in which case some sights take priority.

The 50-mile **Going-to-the-Sun Road** is one of the most spectacular drives you will ever take. The breathtaking vistas provide a marvelous sense of the geography, and the park's history comes alive for those who stop to notice the architecture of the road itself. The drive will likely take at least two hours, not accounting for construction, traffic, or weather-related delays, but if time permits even just an extra hour, there are plenty of turnouts and hiking opportunities along the way. **Hidden Lake Overlook** is a wonderful three-mile round-trip hike from the **Visitors Center at Logan Pass** that provides opportunities

SPONTANEOUS GLACIER: HOW TO PLAN A LAST-MINUTE TRIP

Rooms in Glacier's historic lodges and chalets can already be full up to a year ahead, but spontaneous travelers are not necessarily out of luck. Last-minute cancellations and room openings are possible and well worth a couple of phone calls. **Glacier Park Inc.** (406/892-2525, www.glacierparkinc.com) is the park's concessionaire and booking service for the Village Inn Motel, Lake McDonald Lodge, Rising Sun Motor Inn, Swiftcurrent Motor Inn, and the Many Glacier Hotel. Call and ask specifically for cancellations. You may have better luck if you are open to whatever they have to offer, but you just may luck out and get the property you were hoping for. Being flexible with your dates helps.

The **Apgar Village Lodge** (406/888-5484, www.westglacier.com) near Lake McDonald is another possibility. For visitors willing to hike in to their accommodations, **Sperry Chalet** (888/345-2649, www.sperrychalet.com, from $180) and **Granite Park Chalet** (888/345-2649, www.graniteparkchalet.com, from $85 shared) are fantastic options.

For true spontaneity, pitch a tent in one of Glacier's 13 campgrounds, at least some of which are open May-mid-October. With the exception of St. Mary and Fish Creek, all campgrounds are available on a first-come, first-served basis, with nightly fees of $10-23. Apgar is the largest campground, with 192 sites, followed by Fish Creek (180 sites), St. Mary (148 sites), and Many Glacier (110 sites). For advance reservations at Fish Creek or St. Mary, contact the **National Park Reservation System** (877/444-6777, www.recreation.gov).

to view wildlife. Any time in Glacier's backcountry will be time well spent, but visitors should be meticulously prepared for changes in the weather (dress in layers and bring water) and wildlife encounters.

With more than a day, visitors can see some of the park's idyllic corners. **Many Glacier** is a launching spot for day hikes to numerous alpine lakes and glaciers. **Lake McDonald,** the park's largest, is a favorite place to spend the day. The southern section of the park, accessed from U.S. 2, is especially popular in winter with cross-country skiers who make tracks from the **Izaak Walton Inn** in Essex.

Planning is critical in Glacier, as accommodations within and immediately surrounding the park fill up months in advance. The nearly 1,000 campsites throughout the park, on the other hand, are filled primarily on a first-come, first-served basis (with two notable exceptions: Fish Creek and St. Mary). Still, last-minute travelers are not necessarily out of luck. For park brochures, which can be immensely helpful in planning your trip, visit www.nps.gov/glac/planyourvisit/brochures.htm.

HISTORY

Recently discovered evidence indicates that this spectacular area was inhabited as far back as 10,000 years ago, and the Salish, Kootenai, Flathead, and Blackfeet Indians have called Glacier home. The Blackfeet came to the region later than the others, entering the area sometime in the early 1700s and extending their territory through the eastern part of the park and onto the plains. The Blackfeet fought quite a few battles for territory with other Native American tribes, and the French, British, and Spanish fur trappers who journeyed into the region in the 1800s in search of beaver pelts also had to be wary of the Indians. Lewis and Clark's Corps of Discovery came within 50 miles of Glacier as they traveled west.

When the Blackfeet Indian Reservation was created in 1855, it included the eastern part of the park up to the Continental Divide. In 1895 the Blackfeet sold the land to the U.S. government for $1.5 million with the agreement that they would still have unrestricted access for hunting, ceremonies, and other use. Today the Blackfeet Indian Reservation borders the

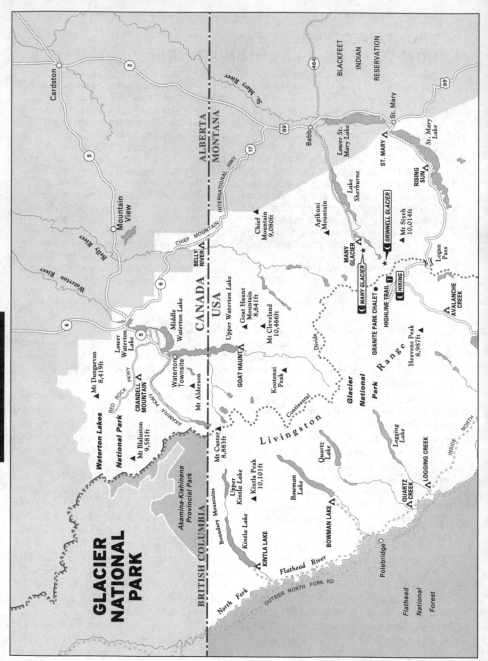

GLACIER NATIONAL PARK

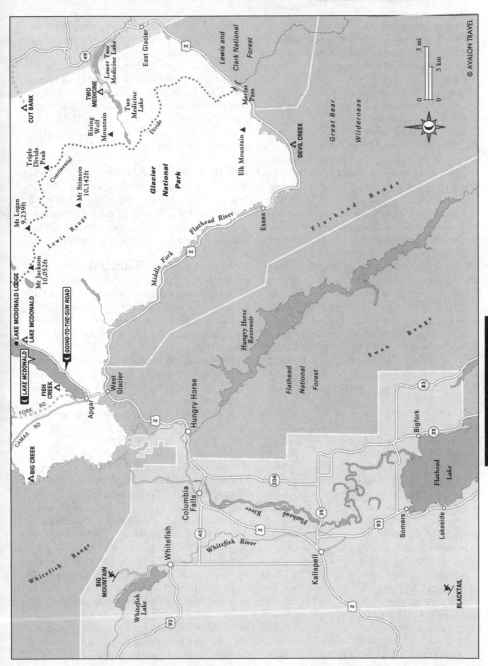

GLACIER NATIONAL PARK

eastern edge of the park, and the Flathead Indian reservation and the Salish and Kootenai reservations lie to the southwest. Buying the land from the Blackfeet opened the area to mining, railroads, and settlers. Mining never proved to be successful in Glacier, although abandoned mine shafts can still be seen scattered through the park.

In 1891 the Great Northern Railway completed its route over Marias Pass in the southern part of the park. The company advertised the area in an effort to attract tourists, and by the turn of the 20th century it had become a tourist destination; visitors arrived by train and ventured into the park on horseback, on foot, or by boat. In 1910 the railroad started building hotels, lodges, and chalets to further entice visitors. There were few roads at the time, and visitors spent days working their way through the mountains, spending nights in different hotels and chalets. As the Great Northern Railway worked to attract visitors, George Bird Grinnell, a journalist who had first come west to cover the plight of the Blackfeet and who also founded the first Audubon Society, worked arduously to see this magnificent area achieve national park status, and in 1910 President Taft made Glacier the nation's 10th national park.

With the railroad, tourist facilities, and national park status, Glacier did attract a fair number of visitors, and soon there was demand for road access into the park. The Going-to-the-Sun Road, a 52-mile highway across the Continental Divide that runs from West Glacier to St. Mary, opened in 1932 after years of treacherous surveying and more than a decade of construction. The road is an impressive engineering feat, now designated a National Historic Landmark, and offers visitors breathtaking (or stomach-churning, depending upon your tolerance of heights) views of the park. With the addition of the road, the number of visitors to the park skyrocketed, and the experience shifted. Now people were able to spend less than a day driving through the park as one of many stops on a cross-country car trip. Fewer in number, rugged adventurers

remained committed to seeing the park—on foot, on horseback, and by boat over the course of several days or weeks.

In 1932, as a gesture of goodwill between the United States and Canada, the park was joined with Canada's Waterton Lakes National Park to become Waterton-Glacier International Peace Park. In 1995 it was designated a UNESCO World Heritage Site, and the park celebrated its centennial with great fanfare in 2010.

FLORA AND FAUNA

With more than 1 million acres, Glacier National Park offers a staggering number of microclimates, including forests, alpine meadows, lakes, rocky peaks, and glacial valleys, that are home to an incredible diversity of plant and animal life.

With two climate zones (Pacific maritime and prairie/arctic), three major watersheds (Pacific, Atlantic, and Arctic), and a range of biomes at various elevations, Glacier is home to a broad selection of plant life. There are 20 different tree species and at least 1,132 species of vascular plants, including 127 nonnative species. There are nearly 900 species of moss and lichen, almost 1,000 species of wildflowers, and more than 100 species of plants that are listed by the state as "sensitive." Amazingly, some of the tiny, seemingly delicate alpine plants that are beaten and battered by the harsh climate year after year can live to be more than 100 years old.

Visitors from the northern part of North America will find familiar flora in Glacier. Divided into four floristic provinces, Glacier's plant species are 49 percent cordilleran (which includes the southern and central Rockies as well as the Cascade Mountains in Washington); 39 percent boreal (which includes much of Canada); 10 percent arctic-alpine; and 1 percent Great Plains. The continent's easternmost hemlock forest thrives in the moist environment around Lake McDonald on the park's west side, offering a stark contrast to the wind-sculpted open forests and grasslands of the east side. There are also significant shifts in plant life from the north to the south as a result of changes in annual precipitation.

Glacier's diversity of habitats is a critical factor in the spectrum of wildlife that calls the park home. From the minute pygmy shrew, which weighs as much as a dime, to indicator species like the grizzly bear, gray wolf, and mountain lion, Glacier is home to 62 species of mammals. Missing are bison and woodland caribou, both of which were grossly overhunted in the region prior to the park's designation in 1910.

Today the park is a safe haven for the Canada lynx and the grizzly bear, both of which are threatened, and the once-endangered gray wolf. There are healthy populations of elk, primarily in the grasslands of the park's eastern side, as well as moose, mountain goats, and

BEAR SAFETY

Glacier has significant concentrations of both grizzly and black bears, both of which can be threatening in any encounter. The keys to safe travel in the backcountry are acting to prevent bear encounters and knowing what to do in the event you do meet a bear. The following are simple guidelines for responsible behavior in bear country:

- **Don't surprise bears.** Make noise, even on well-traveled trails, to allow bears the opportunity to get away from you. Bells can be effective, as can singing, hand-clapping, and loud talking. Never assume that a bear has better senses than you and will see, hear, or smell you coming.

- **Don't approach bears.** Be aware of their feeding opportunities and behavior so that you can avoid potential feeding locations and times of day. Avoid hiking through berry patches, cow parsnip thickets, or fields of glacier lilies. Never approach a carcass, which could be under the surveillance of a bear. Try not to hike before sunrise or at dusk, both active times for bears. Always keep children in close proximity.

- **Minimize the possibility that a bear would be attracted to your belongings or campsite.** Abide by all the park regulations about hanging your food and garbage away from your sleeping area. Don't carry odiferous food, and never bring anything potentially edible, including medicines and toothpaste, into your tent. Take special care with used feminine hygiene products by sealing them in several ziplock bags with baking soda to absorb the odor.

- **Be prepared for an encounter.** Carry pepper spray that is not out of date and know how to use it. Familiarize yourself with the behaviors most likely to ensure your safety in a bear encounter.

If you do surprise a bear, keep your wits about you. While there is no easy and universal answer about how to react – bears are as individual and unpredictable as humans – the following are accepted behaviors outlined on Glacier's website:

- **Talk quietly and calmly.** If you have surprised a bear, don't attempt to threaten it; if possible, try to detour around it.

- **Never run.** Don't turn your back; instead, back away slowly, unless it agitates the bear. Running could trigger its predator instincts.

- **Assume a nonthreatening position.** Turn sideways or bend at the knees to make yourself appear as small as possible.

- **Use peripheral vision.** Bears may perceive direct eye contact as aggressive behavior on your part.

- **Keep your pack on for protection in case of an attack.** If you have bear spray, grab it and be prepared to use it in the event of an attack.

- **Protect yourself if the bear attacks.** Protect your chest and abdomen by falling to the ground on your stomach or assuming the fetal position. Cover the back of your neck with your hands, and most importantly, do not move until the bear has left the scene.

bighorn sheep. Though rarely seen and few in number, wolverines, cougars, and fishers also live here. Glacier's tailed frog is considered the most primitive frog in North America, and the only one that fertilizes the female's eggs internally. It is most closely related to frogs in New Zealand, which has led scientists to believe that its origins date back 250 million years.

The addition of nonnative species and removal of native species can have far-ranging and catastrophic results. The healthy red-backed vole population on the park's west side eats primarily fungus and consequently spread fungal spores as they travel. The rootlets of the spores are almost entirely responsible for the regeneration of conifer trees in the region. Without the voles, there would be no forest. Without the fungus, there would be no voles. The ecosystem is as delicately balanced as it is captivating.

West Glacier Area

A bustling entrance to Glacier, West Glacier (population 426, elevation 3,715 feet) has the feeling of "last chance to get bug spray" and "first non–PB and J in a while." It is clearly not a destination but a portal, and it is a good place to find lodging, dining, and supplies in immediate proximity to the park.

The town itself grew up around the magnificent Belton Chalet, a lodge built by the Great Northern Railway in 1910, the same year Glacier became a national park. The Belton, an arts and crafts gem, was the first permanent lodging on the west side of Glacier, and thanks to a painstaking restoration in 2000 it remains one of the most regal accommodations in the area.

SIGHTS
◖ Lake McDonald
The largest lake in the park at 10 miles long and 472 feet deep, Lake McDonald was gouged out by a glacier that was likely 2,200 feet thick. Surrounded by jagged peaks on three sides, it is bordered by the Lewis Range to the east, which creates a rain block and makes the Lake McDonald Valley one of the mildest and lushest environments in the region. Not unlike the Pacific Northwest, the Lake McDonald Valley boasts dense forests of towering western red cedars and hemlocks.

Although the lake and surrounding forests are exquisitely serene, the area is a hub of activity in the summer months for human visitors and the bear population alike. Modeled after a Swiss chalet, the grand and slightly worse-for-wear **Lake McDonald Lodge** sprawls along the northeast shore and provides relatively expensive lodging with unmatched views. The dining room, lounge, and pizzeria are open to nonguests. Stop in to warm yourself by the massive fireplace, check out the animal mounts that have decorated the place since its 1895 origins, or lounge lakeside on the veranda with a beverage.

There are many great hiking trails around the lake, including those to Fish Lake, Mount Brown Lookout, and the mellow Johns Lake Loop. There are plenty of fish in the lake—17 varieties in all, mainly trout. There are also boat tours departing from the lodge as well as Red Bus Tours and ranger-led activities.

Bowman Lake
Some 32 miles north of the west entrance to Glacier and only 30 miles south of Canada is Bowman Lake, another crystalline alpine gem ringed with mountains and forest. A long bumpy ride is required to get here, and as a result it is never crowded. Also, in the spirit of full disclosure, the density of mosquitoes tends to discourage visitors. But the lake is exceptionally beautiful, and the mosquitoes can be avoided to some extent. Boats are permitted, with restrictions on engines. Kayaks and canoes are a wonderful way to explore this photogenic setting. The lake is filled with fish, primarily kokanee and cutthroat trout, and

the fishing is legendary, particularly in late spring. There are plenty of worthwhile hikes from the area, but be warned that this is the heart of grizzly country, and visitors should come prepared. Camping is available on a first-come, first-served basis at the Bowman Lake Campground (48 sites, late May–mid-Sept., $15).

(Going-to-the-Sun Road

Completed in 1932, the famed Going-to-the-Sun Road is a marvel of modern engineering. Spanning 52 miles from West Glacier to St. Mary, the road snakes up and around magnificent mountains that include its namesake, Going-to-the-Sun Mountain, giving viewers some of the most dramatic vistas in the country. The road, which crosses the Continental Divide, required more than two decades of planning and construction. It climbs more than 3,000 feet with only a single switchback, known as "the loop." Going-to-the-Sun is an architectural accomplishment as well: All of the bridges, retaining walls, and guard rails are built of native materials, so the road itself blends seamlessly into its breathtaking mountain setting.

In addition to being an experience all on its own, Going-to-the-Sun is also the primary access road to the park and the only way to get to some of the park's best-known highlights: the Visitors Center at Logan Pass, the Highline Trail, Lake McDonald, and an array of hiking trails. For visitors who are not keen on driving the road themselves, there are a few excellent options, including free shuttles, vintage tours, and Blackfeet tours, to see the road as a sightseer.

RECREATION
(Hiking

Glacier is a hiker's paradise, and the west side of the park around the Lake McDonald Valley offers a unique opportunity to hike through primeval forests of western red cedars, hemlocks, and other species that thrive in this moist, moderate climate.

Among the most popular and well-traveled trails near Lake McDonald is the **Johns**

© DONNIE SEXTON

Weeping Wall along the Going-to-the-Sun Road

bighorn sheep along the east side of the Going-to-the-Sun Road

© DONNIE SEXTON

Lake Loop, a relatively flat six-mile round-trip through prime moose habitat. It can be found just northeast of Lake McDonald Lodge. Also popular is **Trail of the Cedars,** an easy 0.7-mile loop on a wheelchair-accessible boardwalk through spectacular forest. Leaving from the Avalanche campground, less than five miles east of the Lake McDonald Lodge, the trail crosses an impressive footbridge over Avalanche Gorge. Also leaving from the Avalanche campground, **Avalanche Creek Trail,** four miles round-trip with a 500-foot elevation gain, takes hikers to the picturesque, mountain-ringed Avalanche Lake. Because trailhead parking tends to fill early, the park's free shuttles to both of these trailheads are available from Lake McDonald Lodge or Apgar Village.

A longer and somewhat more strenuous hike is the trail to **Akokala Lake,** climbing roughly 600 feet over 5.8 miles one-way. The trailhead is at the north end of the Bowman Lake Campground (32 bumpy miles north of West Glacier on Bowman Lake Rd.), and the trail runs over moderate terrain, through burned areas, and to the remote Akokala Lake, which is filled with native cutthroat trout. The fishing is great, especially halfway around the west side of the lake, where the water is deep next to the shore. Reuter and Numa Peaks tower over the lake and provide a sublime backdrop. As with many of the trails in Glacier, this one cuts through grizzly country, and hikers should be well prepared.

Leaving from Logan Pass at the summit of the Going-to-the-Sun Road, the high-altitude **Granite Park Trail** is 15.2 miles round-trip, out and back, over moderate terrain with a 500-foot elevation gain. It is well-traveled and breathtakingly scenic. The first three miles of the trail cut into the Garden Wall above the Going-to-the-Sun Road and are not for those with a fear of heights; the ledge can be frightening but provides stunning views. The trail ultimately leads to the Granite Park Chalet but en route passes in the shadow of Haystack Butte, Mount Gould, and Mount Grinnell. Mountain goats and bighorn sheep often share the trail with a good number of hikers. If you're making it a day hike, plan on lunch at the chalet (888/345-2649, www.graniteparkchalet.com) before returning to the trailhead.

Certainly among the best-loved trails in the park, the **Highline Trail** loop, which also departs from Logan Pass, parallels the Garden Wall, climbing 200 feet over 7.6 miles to Granite Park Chalet, then dropping more than 2,200 feet over the last four miles back to the road. The views are staggering, but the precipice is not for the faint of heart.

Boating

Before the Going-to-the-Sun Road was completed, most of Glacier's adventurous visitors saw the park by boat. Today this nostalgic mode of travel offers benefits all its own. Both Lake McDonald and Bowman Lake offer excellent boating and fishing opportunities in the form of kayaking, canoeing, and even semirestricted motorboating. Boat rentals are available at Apgar and Lake McDonald Lodge. For boat tours—think sunset cocktail cruises in a historic wooden boat on Lake McDonald—and rentals, the **Glacier Park Boat Company** (406/257-2426, www.glacierparkboats.com, tours $11.25–22 adults, children half price) is the ultimate resource.

Rafting

Although there is no rafting inside the park, there are a number of white-water outfitting services in West Glacier offering trips on the 87-mile Middle Fork of the Flathead River. The North Fork of the Flathead, which forms the western boundary of the park, can be rafted as well. **Glacier Raft Company** (406/888-5454 or 800/235-6781, www.glacierraftco.com, half-day from $48 adults, $38 children) offers everything from half-day and dinner floats to multiple-day expeditions. The company caters to all floaters, from novices to adrenaline junkies.

Montana Raft Company (406/387-5555 or 800/521-7238, www.glacierguides.com, all-inclusive half-day from $51.36 adults, $41.66 children) is the sister company of Glacier Guides and has some of the most well-rounded and knowledgeable guides in the area. Group

numbers tend to be smaller (9 in a boat as opposed to 14) and the company offers an expansive range of options that include rafting and horseback riding, overnight adventures, family friendly day trips, and more.

Another noteworthy outfitter offering rafting trips in the region is **Wild River Adventures** (406/387-9453 or 800/700-7056, www.riverwild.com, half-day from $48 adults, $38 children).

Bicycling

Biking in Glacier is not for the nonchalant. The climbs are treacherous, the edges precipitous, and the automobile traffic even worse. But the thrill of reaching the summit of the Going-to-the-Sun Road, seeing how far you've come, soaking in the scenery, and whooshing back down again is unrivaled.

Still, as with any activity in Glacier, cyclists should be well aware of the conditions, restrictions, and potential hazards. Common sense prevails: Use helmets and reflectors; wear brightly colored and highly visible clothing; and watch for falling rocks, wildlife, and ice on the road. Bicycles are prohibited 11 A.M.–4 P.M. daily June 15–Labor Day between Apgar Campground and Sprague Creek Campground. From Logan Creek to Logan Pass, eastbound (uphill) bicycle traffic is prohibited 11 A.M.–4 P.M. daily June 15–Labor Day. It takes roughly 45 minutes to ride from Sprague Creek to Logan Creek, and three hours from Logan Creek to the summit of Logan Pass. Bicycles are not for rent in the park. For more information on restrictions and current road closures, check online at www.nps.gov/glac/planyourvisit/bicycling.htm.

Helicopter Tours

If seeing the park from atop Going-to-the-Sun Road is not quite dramatic enough, consider a **Glacier Heli-Tour** (406/387-4141 or 800/879-9310, www.glacierhelitours.net, from $110 adults for groups of 4 or more). The half-hour and hour-long tours cover a terrific amount of ground and can introduce

A MYSTERY IN THE PARK

Although there are a handful of woeful stories about bear attacks, restless ghosts, and freak accidents in Glacier, one of the most chilling is the tale of Joseph and William Whitehead, two brothers from Chicago who vanished without a trace in Glacier's backcountry in 1924.

Joseph Whitehead, 29, was an engineer, and his younger brother, William, 22, was a student at the Massachusetts Institute of Technology. They had come to Glacier as thoughtful adventurers for a well-planned two-week journey. The trip had gone exceedingly well, and in their last letter to the mother, the boys wrote, "Don't worry...we won't go into any danger."

Early in the morning on August 24, 1924, the boys set out from Granite Park Chalet on a reasonably ambitious 22-mile hike to the Lewis Hotel at Lake McDonald. When they failed to return to Chicago on September 1, their mother, Dora, alerted park authorities that her sons were missing. An extensive manhunt followed, with countless park employees and volunteers covering nearly every corner of the park. No trace of them was found.

Dora refused to give up the search; even President Calvin Coolidge got involved, instructing the park service to continue the search with no expense spared. Dora offered a $500 reward, and Louis Hill, son of railroad magnate James Hill, added an additional $1,000 to anyone with information. False leads flooded in, but nothing else.

In late September, nearly a month after the young men had been reported missing, a horse party reported having met the brothers on the afternoon of August 24 hiking along Logan Creek, just 10 miles from their destination and only a few miles from the road to Lake McDonald. As winter set in, the FBI assumed control of the investigation.

The following summer, Dora and her daughter traveled to Glacier to follow the route the young men had taken. They didn't find a single clue, and the following year FBI director J. Edgar Hoover closed the case, which remains unsolved to this day.

There was some initial speculation that the Whiteheads had drowned, but the theory seemed less likely as no bodies were ever found. The prevailing conjecture is that the brothers followed the trail from Logan Creek, where they met the horse party, to the road, northeast of the Lewis Road. It was thought likely that the young men were then abducted in an automobile by unknown assailants for unknown reasons. It is a mystery, and a tragedy, that haunts Glacier to this day.

even Glacier aficionados to unseen corners of this magical place.

Golf

Golfers not afraid of a little distraction in the form of stunning mountain scenery can hit the links at the 18-hole **Glacier View Golf Club** (640 Riverbend Dr., 406/888-5471, www.glacierviewgolf.com, $29 for 18 holes) in West Glacier.

Horseback Riding

Another historic form of transportation in Glacier can be enjoyed even today: Guided horseback rides, from one hour to a full day, are available in good weather late May–late September at the corrals at Apgar and Lake McDonald from **Swan Mountain Outfitters** (877/888-5557, www.swanmountainoutfitters.com, $40–150 plus gratuity).

Cross-Country Skiing

When the white stuff blankets the park, cross-country skiers and snowshoers find themselves in a winter paradise. Many of the hiking trails double as ski and snowshoe trails, but nothing is groomed, so keen and constant orientation is critical. The **Lower McDonald Creek** trailhead is just south of McDonald Creek Bridge, and the trail is 2–3 miles round-trip of gentle, forested terrain that parallels the creek in some spots. Another fairly level but longer option is the **Rocky Point** trail, which is six miles round-trip and rewards skiers with a phenomenal view of Lake McDonald. The trailhead can be found 0.2 miles north of the Fish Creek Campground. Farther north, toward Avalanche Campground, **McDonald Falls** (4 miles round-trip), **Sacred Dancing Cascades** (5.3 miles round-trip), and the **Avalanche Picnic Area** (11.6 miles round-trip) make excellent day trips.

Since many of the roads in the park are unplowed and thus impassable for cars in winter, they can make excellent ski trails. The Going-to-the-Sun Road is one of the best.

Although it's not in the park, one of the region's best-known and beloved areas for cross-country skiing is the **Izaak Walton Inn** (off U.S. 2, Essex, between East Glacier and West Glacier, 406/888-5700, www.izaakwalton-inn.com), which has repeatedly been named one of the best cross-country ski resorts in the Rockies. The resort boasts 20 miles of groomed trails, and its proximity to the park invites backcountry travel. Ski rentals are available, and a night or two at the inn will be something to remember.

ACCOMMODATIONS

There is a good selection of places to stay in the West Glacier area, but once inside the park, or even within view of it, accommodations do not come cheap. If you are on a tight budget, camping is the best option. The hotels listed are only open during the summer season, when Glacier is busiest. However, for avid cross-country skiers who want to take advantage of the park during the winter, the **Izaak Walton Inn** (off U.S. 2, Essex, between East Glacier and West Glacier, 406/888-5700, www.izaakwaltoninn.com, $117–255), a charming old railroad hotel that is on the National Register of Historic Places, is open year-round.

A reasonably priced motel in the area is the **Apgar Village Lodge** (406/888-5484, www.westglacier.com, $85–275), two miles west of Glacier village at the south end of Lake McDonald. There are 28 cabins that sleep up to 10 with Western decor, most with kitchens

with stoves and refrigerators, and each with its own picnic table. Ask for a cabin on McDonald Creek; you can literally fish from your front door. There are also have 20 modestly furnished, clean motel rooms, some overlooking the creek, with either a queen or two twin beds.

West Glacier Motel (200 Going-to-the-Sun Rd., 406/888-5662, www.westglacier.com, $85 s, $150 cabin) is divided between two properties—half the motel units are about one mile from the park entrance in West Glacier, and the cabins and other motel units are on a secluded bluff that overlooks the Flathead River. It's a great value for the price and location.

If you are willing to spend a bit more, there are two historic lodges that are worth a night's stay. **Lake McDonald Lodge** (Going-to-the-Sun Rd., 12 miles from West Glacier, $125–175) was built in 1914 by the furrier John Lewis and adheres to the Swiss-chalet style of architecture. It emanates rustic charm and still has personal touches, such as Lewis's hunting trophies displayed in the lobby. Built before there were roads running through Glacier, visitors arrived at the lodge by boat, and the hotel's original entrance faced the lake. Today most guests arrive by car, and the hotel is conveniently located off the Going-to-the-Sun Road on the shore of Lake McDonald. There are 100 guest rooms in the lodge, a separate motor inn, and cabins. Upon entering the lodge, visitors are immediately struck by its warmth and charm. The large, spacious lobby is surrounded by balconies on three sides. Guests and visitors can enjoy sipping a cocktail on the large veranda, a serene setting that affords a beautiful view of the lake. The guest rooms are rustic yet comfortable, and the location allows easy access to trailheads and boat tours. Fishing lessons and day trips by horseback are available and can be arranged by the hotel.

The most memorable stay in West Glacier is at the family-owned ◖ **Belton Chalet** (12575 U.S. 2 E., 406/888-5000 or 888/235-8665, www.beltonchalet.com, rooms $125–180, cabins $230–325), located at the west entrance to the park. This was the first hotel built by the

BACKCOUNTRY CAMPING

That Glacier National Park is a wild place cannot be understated. Backcountry camping in this spectacularly beautiful and potentially dangerous place requires thoughtful planning and meticulous attention to the rules and regulations. A strong dose of common sense can go a long way. Backcountry campers have to be smart about orientation, wildlife encounters, rapidly changing and adverse weather, and stream and snowfield crossings, all of which can be potentially deadly. Here is a list of simple but critical guidelines and etiquette for backcountry travel.

- **Make a plan and chart your route.** Carefully examine elevation gain and loss. Carrying a heavy pack more than 10 miles in a day with a 2,500-foot elevation change is an extremely ambitious and perhaps overly rigorous endeavor. Topographical maps and hiking guides are available at park visitors centers and ranger stations as well as online through the Glacier National History Association bookstores (www.glacierassociation.org). Make sure you are aware of trail and campsite closures, fire restrictions, weather forecasts, local bear activity, and so on. Glacier offers an excellent online trip planner at www.nps.gov/glac/planyourvisit/backcountry.htm.

- **Secure all your permits.** All backcountry campers must camp in established campsites and must have a backcountry-use permit ($30) for the duration of the trip. Campsites can be reserved in advance when you apply for the permit, or within 24 hours of the trip. Application forms can be downloaded (www.nps.gov/glac/planyourvisit/backcountry.htm) but are accepted starting January 1 by mail or fax (406/888-5819) only, and will be processed randomly after April 15. Applications received after April 15 will be processed in the order they are received. Permits must be picked up at one of five permit issuing stations no sooner than one day before the trip and no later than 4:30 P.M. on the day of departure.

- **Pack intelligently.** All campers should be prepared for a dramatic range of weather conditions by packing appropriate footwear and layered clothing, rain jacket and pants, and footwear for crossing streams. Other items to remember when packing include an appropriate amount of low-odor food, a tent and sleeping bag with pad, a compass and topographical maps, a first aid kit, weatherproof food and garbage bags, 25 feet of rope to hang bags, a water container and purifying system, a camp stove and fuel, an emergency signaling device, and a trowel.

- **Obey all rules and practice the seven principles of Leave No Trace.** Plan ahead and prepare, travel and camp on durable surfaces, leave what you find, properly dispose of waste, minimize campfire impacts, respect wildlife, and be considerate of other visitors. The goal anytime you are in the backcountry is to use your skills and be motivated by an ethic of responsibility for the natural resource, taking care of it conscientiously.

For visitors seeking the backcountry experience without all the preparatory work, guided trips can be arranged through **Glacier Guides** (406/387-5555 or 800/521-7238, www.glacierguides.com).

Great Northern Railway and dates to 1910. It was fully restored in 2000 and is a National Historic Landmark. Guests can experience a piece of history while enjoying the modern amenities. All 25 guest rooms come with a queen bed and are beautifully furnished with antiques. The two cabins on the grounds each have three bedrooms to accommodate up to six people in cozy yet elegant comfort. Although the lodge is closed during the winter season, the cabins are available to rent throughout the year. The hotel does not provide TVs, phones, or air-conditioning as they can detract from the natural setting. There is a spa on-site, a restaurant offering innovative and satisfying meals, and a fully stocked taproom that specializes in Montana brews. You can enjoy a good book in the lobby's reading area, or curl up by the large stone fireplace. The incredibly friendly staff even offer wake-up calls for northern lights and bear sightings.

CAMPING

Glacier has 13 front-country campgrounds with more than 1,000 sites, at least some of which are open May–mid-October. With the exception of St. Mary and Fish Creek, all campgrounds are available on a first-come, first-served basis, with nightly fees ranging $10–23. You'll increase your chances of finding a site by showing up earlier in the day and by scheduling your trip midweek rather than on the weekend. Apgar is the largest campground, with 192 sites, followed by Fish Creek (180 sites), St. Mary (148 sites), and Many Glacier (110 sites). For advanced reservations at Fish Creek or St. Mary, contact the National Park Reservation System (877/444-6777, www.recreation.gov).

FOOD

Even if you are not planning to stay at the Belton Chalet, they offer two distinct and rich dining experiences that are definitely worth a visit in this land of burgers and grilled cheese. **The Belton Grill Dining Room** (12575 U.S. 2 E., 406/888-5000 or 888/235-8665, www.beltonchalet.com, 5–10 P.M. daily summer, 3–8 P.M. Fri.–Sat., 11 A.M.–3 P.M. Sun. winter, dinner $20–35, winter-only Sun. brunch $7–13) provides an intimate and exquisite dining experience in the historic 1910 chalet. The menu changes for summer and winter seasons and offers innovative dishes incorporating the freshest ingredients from local Montana growers and the chalet's own Flathead Lake orchard. For dinner you could sample an elk meatball appetizer, whiskey-and-maple-cured pork chops, or a spicy Thai noodle dish. For equally delicious lighter fare and a more moderately priced experience, you can visit the hotel's **Belton Tap Room** (3–10 P.M. daily summer only, entrées $10–14), where you may choose to accompany a locally brewed Montana beer with Jamaican crab cakes, fried calamari, or a stuffed portobello mushroom.

The **Glacier Highland Restaurant** (U.S. 2, 406/888-5427, www.glacierhighland.com, 7 A.M.–10 P.M. daily late spring–early fall, breakfast $4–9, lunch $6–12, dinner $8–21) is an authentic West Glacier diner experience. Located just before the entrance to the park and across from the Amtrak depot, this is an easy stop if you are craving a five-ounce burger with all the toppings and fresh-cut fries. Hearty homemade soups and a variety of delicious sweet treats, baked each day in their bakery, are also on offer.

GLACIER NATIONAL PARK

East Glacier Area

Located on the Blackfeet Indian Reservation at the southeast corner of the park, East Glacier (population 396, elevation 4,434 feet) has long been a primary entrance into Glacier National Park. Early visitors from the east often arrived by rail at East Glacier and spent the night in the grand Glacier Park Lodge before heading into the wilds of the park.

Today the town of East Glacier bustles year-round and is a hub of activity during the summer months as visitors stream in and out of the park. There are numerous accommodations, including the still-majestic Adirondack-style Glacier Park Lodge, several good restaurants, local outfitters, and a smattering of shops. There is also a tremendous amount of wilderness to be explored both inside the park and in immediate proximity to East Glacier. The stunning Two Medicine Valley is just a few miles away, and there are hiking, skiing, and even snowmobiling trails within steps of the main drag.

SIGHTS
Two Medicine Valley

Geographically, Two Medicine Valley is not at the heart of Glacier, but this remote southeastern corner is staggeringly beautiful and seemingly less known among the masses of summer visitors. The rocky peaks and glacially carved valleys meet in clear alpine lakes, and the area offers plenty of activity for any adventurer. There are boat tours that intersect with hiking trails, numerous waterfalls to ogle, fishing, and a lovely campground.

RECREATION
Hiking

More of a stroll than a hike, the trail to **Running Eagle Falls** is 1,600 feet long, kid-friendly, and wheelchair-accessible. The waterfall is interesting, as it changes from a double fall in spring and early summer to a single one by late summer; it appears to emerge from within the rock wall. The trailhead for this easy but scenic hike is on the park road roughly one mile west of the Two Medicine entrance.

One particularly exquisite, and perhaps nostalgic, way to explore Glacier is by combining a boat ride with a hike. An excellent place to do so is in the Two Medicine Valley. The **Glacier Park Boat Company** (406/257-2426, www.glacierparkboats.com, $11.25 adults, $5.50 children, free for children under 4) offers 45-minute cruises from the Two Medicine Lake boat dock to the far end of the lake, cutting six miles off the hike to **Twin Falls and Upper Two Medicine Lake.** It's backcountry hiking without the blisters. From the upper (unloading) dock, the hike to Twin Falls is just 0.9 miles, and an additional 2.2 miles to the gorgeous upper lake. **No Name Lake,** at the base of the sheer Pumpelly Pillar, is another spectacular hike made easier with a boat shuttle. Instead of five miles one-way, with the boat it is 2.2 miles with an 800-foot elevation gain. For those looking to put more miles on their feet, there are trails on either side of Two Medicine Lake, making a variety of loops possible. Farther north of Two

Medicine, the **Cut Bank Trailhead** offers fantastic hiking with even fewer visitors—perfect for solitude seekers.

Bicycling

There aren't many places in the country where you can hop on a bike, head to the nearest highway, and pedal through spectacular scenery in every direction. Although the inclines can be steep and the declines precipitous around East Glacier, the air is fresh, the traffic relatively limited, and the mountain vistas unrivaled.

For avid cyclists, it's possible to do a 137-mile loop in and around the park: Head southwest from East Glacier on U.S. 2 to West Glacier, then over Going-to-the-Sun Road to St. Mary, then south on U.S. 89 and Highway 49 back to East Glacier. Remember that eastbound Going-to-the-Sun Road is closed to cyclists 11 A.M.–4 P.M. daily June 15–Labor Day, so plan accordingly.

In the vicinity of East Glacier, biking to the Two Medicine Valley, 12 miles northwest of town, is a popular route. Bicycles can be rented in East Glacier from **Scenic View Bicycle Rental** (900 Hwy. 49, 406/226-9238, $3.50 per hour or $15 for 5 hours, helmet included).

Golf

Somewhat surprisingly, there is a unique nine-hole golf course at the Glacier Park Lodge (U.S. 2 and Hwy. 49, 406/226-5642 or 406/892-2525, www.glacierparkinc.com, mid-May–mid-Oct., $18 for 9 holes, $27 for 18 holes). Built in 1927 by Great Northern Railway tycoon James J. Hill, the course is the oldest grass course in Montana. It was designed by a New York architect, but because the course was built within the boundaries of the Blackfeet Indian Reservation, each of the holes is named after a former chief of the Blackfeet Nation. Clubs, carts, and pull carts can be rented from the pro shop.

Horseback Riding

For horseback riding outside the park on the Blackfeet Indian Reservation, **Glacier Gateway**

GLACIER INSTITUTE

Founded in 1983, the Glacier Institute (406/755-1211, www.glacierinstitute.org) is a private nonprofit organization that offers hands-on educational experiences using Glacier National Park and Flathead National Forest as their classrooms. Their mission is to provide "an objective and science-based understanding of the area's ecology and its interaction with people." The Glacier Institute fulfills its mission by providing field-based experiences in and around the park for all ages and levels of fitness.

The Glacier Institute offers 3-5-day youth camps that have a variety of focuses. Whether it is the first overnight camp experience for children away from their parents, an introduction to the basic concepts of ecology, or a focus on art and nature, the institute offers experienced guides and experts to foster each child's learning. They also have a variety of outdoor education courses open to young and old. You can enroll for a full-day or half-day course with expert instructors for a unique learning experience on the owls of the Mission Valley, wilderness first aid, wildflowers along the Rocky Mountain Front, summer mushrooms, and birds of prey, to name just a few of the diverse offerings.

To peruse the institute's extensive and fascinating offerings, visit their website; if you see a course that interests you but is not being offered when you plan to be in Glacier, the Glacier Institute creates custom programs and can plan a half-day to several-day course just for your group based on the courses or expert instructors that you select.

Trailrides (Hwy. 49, across from the Glacier Park Lodge, 406/226-4408, 406/338-5560 off-season, $30–185 pp) offers excellent guided rides through magnificent country. Trips range from one hour to full-day excursions; children must be at least seven. The guides are Native Americans who offer a unique cultural

perspective on places like Looking Glass and Two Medicine River Gorge.

Boating

As on the west side of the park, the **Glacier Park Boat Company** (406/257-2426, www. glacierparkboats.com, tours $11.25–22 adults, children half price) rents kayaks, canoes, and motorboats, and offers guided tours on their fleet of classic wooden launches. There are excellent cruises on Two Medicine Lake at least four times daily mid-June–early September.

ACCOMMODATIONS

There are several small, kitschy motels in East Glacier that are ideal for a night or two before heading into the park, but they are not well-suited for a week's stay. The standout alternative is the stately [(](**Glacier Park Lodge** (U.S. 2 and Hwy. 49, 406/892-2525, www.glacierparkinc.com, late May–late Sept., $129–449), which opened to guests in 1913. An Adirondack-style hotel commissioned by the Great Northern Railway, it was constructed of massive fir and cedar timbers, each weighing at least 15 tons. The local Blackfeet who watched the structure go up called it *omahkoyis*, or "big-tree lodge." The grounds are beautifully manicured—there's even a historic and very playable golf course in addition to a pitch-and-putt. The hotel offers fine and casual dining, a cocktail lounge, a gift shop, an outdoor swimming pool, and a day spa. The rooms are modest but comfortable. Travelers with children will appreciate the family rooms with multiple beds. Although the setting at the edge of East Glacier village is not quite as captivating, the Glacier Park Lodge is certainly in the same class as the Lake McDonald Lodge and even the Old Faithful Lodge in Yellowstone National Park.

Slightly off the main drag is the tidy and comfortable **Mountain Pine Motel** (909 Hwy. 49, 1 mile north of U.S. 2, 406/226-4403, www.mtnpine.com, May–Sept., $67–155), with 25 units and relatively modern amenities.

The **Whistling Swan Motel** (314 U.S. 2, 406/226-9227, www.whistlingswanmotel.com, $58–78) is a long, skinny building that feels a bit like train cars—somewhat appropriate given that the Amtrak station is just across the street. The guest rooms are spotlessly clean and quite comfortable. Hosts Mark and Colleen are exceptionally hospitable and go out of their way to make every guest feel welcome and accommodated. This motel is also within easy walking distance of the local eateries and shops.

If you are willing to hike in to your accommodations, **Sperry Chalet** (888/345-2649, www.sperrychalet.com, from $180) and **Granite Park Chalet** (888/345-2649, www. graniteparkchalet.com, from $85 shared) are fantastic options.

CAMPING

Less than 20 miles from East Glacier are a couple of scenic and quiet campgrounds. **Two Medicine Campground** (early June–mid-Sept., $20), with 99 sites and 13 RV sites, is 13 miles outside town in some of Glacier's most breathtaking wilderness. It is well-developed with potable water and flush toilets, an amphitheater for nightly ranger presentations, and one of the original Great Northern Chalets, which has been converted into a camp store and gift shop. Outside the regular season, primitive camping ($10) is possible late May–early June and late September–late October. Shuttle service, boat tours, and Red Bus Tours are all available from the campground. Sites are available on a first-come, first-served basis, and hiking in the area is as limitless as it is sublime.

Farther north is a smaller (14 sites) and more secluded spot, **Cut Bank Campground** (late May–mid-Sept., $10), accessed five miles down a dirt road from U.S. 89. The site has no water, so campers have to bring their own. Sites are available on a first-come, first-served basis, and day hikes in the area are top-notch.

FOOD

For a town with just 300 year-round residents, East Glacier has a number of good restaurants that cater to Glacier-bound visitors. Often the best way to select a spot to eat is to walk around and see where the wait is shortest. **Serrano's Mexican Restaurant** (29 Dawson Ave., 406/226-9392, www.serranosmexican.com, dinner 5–9 P.M. daily May 1–Memorial Day, 5–10 P.M. Memorial Day–Labor Day, 5–9 P.M. daily Labor Day–first weekend in Oct., entrées $9–18) is charmingly located inside the oldest house in East Glacier. There is nothing old-fashioned, however, about the menu: There are classic and delicious Mexican favorites alongside local offerings that include Indian tacos and huckleberry carrot cake. There is also a selection of American plates, including chicken, steaks, and burgers. The food here is good, and the atmosphere is quite festive.

The **Glacier Village Café** (304-308 U.S. 2 E., 406/226-4464, www.glaciervillagecafe. com, 7 A.M.–9 P.M. daily late May–mid-Sept., breakfast $6–9, lunch $7–11, dinner $11–18) certainly feels like the hub of this community. It's the diner that opens at 6 A.M. and the place that could double as a museum with all its old photos and memorabilia; luckily enough, the food is excellent. From the buffalo sausage for breakfast to the high alpine salad and rainbow trout, the Glacier Village Café uses fresh local ingredients for hearty, healthy, and incredibly inventive dishes. A full coffee bar is also on offer, along with a few wines by the glass or bottle, plenty of Montana microbrews, and a dessert menu that will make you wish you'd hiked longer. This restaurant is both a bargain and a find.

Two Medicine Grill (314 U.S. 2 E., 406/226-9227, www.whistlingswanmotel.com, 6:30 A.M.–9 P.M. daily summer, 6:30 A.M.–8 P.M. daily winter, breakfast $3–5, lunch $3.25–6, dinner $6.75–10.50) is a great spot for budget travelers. The menu has pretty standard fare for the region—bison burgers, chili, chicken fried steak—but the quality is excellent, and the staff is friendly and generous with advice and insights on the area.

St. Mary to Many Glacier

This place feels like it's at the edge of two worlds: mountains to the west, vast plains to the east. St. Mary is a small village nestled between St. Mary Lake and Lower St. Mary Lake that marks another entrance to the park and the start of the Going-to-the-Sun Road. With all the splendor of the jagged peaks and the wide-open vistas created by sparse stands of aspen and sweeping prairie, the recreational opportunities are abundant and the scenery spectacular.

Farther north, Many Glacier is the ideal base camp for avid and active outdoor lovers. There are extensive opportunities for hiking, canoeing, and horseback riding. The popular boat and Red Bus Tours are also accessible from Many Glacier. Grinnell Glacier is a dwindling but still phenomenal work of nature, and daily ranger-led hikes take visitors up to its toe. The Many Glacier Hotel is a historic 1915 Great Northern Railway Swiss Chalet-style lodge that welcomes guests with a rambling veranda and cozy guest rooms.

SIGHTS
St. Mary Lake
One of the most photographed lakes in the park for its absurdly beautiful mountain backdrop, St. Mary Lake is among the best places in Glacier to watch the sunrise. The lake and its many hiking trails are accessible from Going-to-the-Sun Road. The **Sun Point Nature Trail** is 1.4 miles round-trip, and the trailhead is 9.5 miles west of the St. Mary Visitors Center. It is worth the short walk for views of Baring Falls and the lake itself. An even quicker stop is **Sunrift Gorge**, 0.6 miles west of Sun Point, an incredible cascade slicing between two rock walls; it is just 200 feet from the parking area. Baring Falls is another 0.3-mile walk down the trail.

◖ Many Glacier
The Many Glacier region is a palpable reminder of why Glacier has long been known as the Switzerland of America. Marked by grand accommodations and a landscape that was visibly scoured and carved by glaciers, from the U-shaped valleys and milky-blue glacial lakes to the rocky moraines and the last remaining glaciers themselves, this region is among the most dramatic and startlingly beautiful in the park.

This is not a place to be enjoyed from inside a car, although those on a tight schedule would still benefit from making the journey just to walk around the hotel to drink in the stunning surroundings. Many Glacier is best suited for active travelers: The hiking and boating are exceptional, and it is one of the rare places in the Lower 48 where a day hike can lead you to an actual glacier. Come to Many Glacier to see the splendid scenery, but if possible, stay a few days to truly enjoy it.

◖ Grinnell Glacier
Named for conservationist and explorer George Bird Grinnell, Grinnell Glacier lies in the heart of Many Glacier and is a symbol both of the park's wilderness and of the dramatic climatic changes that are occurring. Because the glacier is accessible within a day's hike, its startling shrinkage—from 710 acres in 1850 to 220 acres in 1993—has been captured on film. Still, as long as it exists, this glacier is well worth visiting.

The options for seeing the glacier up close and personal are to hoof it from the Many Glacier Hotel (5.5 miles one-way with a 1,600-foot elevation gain) or to take a boat across Lake Josephine with **Glacier Park Boat Company** (406/257-2426, www.glacierpark-boats.com, $22 adults, $11 children, free for children under age 4) and hike the remainder of the trail from the head of Lake Josephine (3.8 miles one-way with a 1,600-foot elevation gain). There is also an excellent ranger-guided hike to the glacier that makes use of the boat, leaving the Many Glacier dock daily at 8:30 A.M. starting in mid-July (weather and conditions permitting). The 8.5-mile round-trip outing lasts almost nine hours. The trail

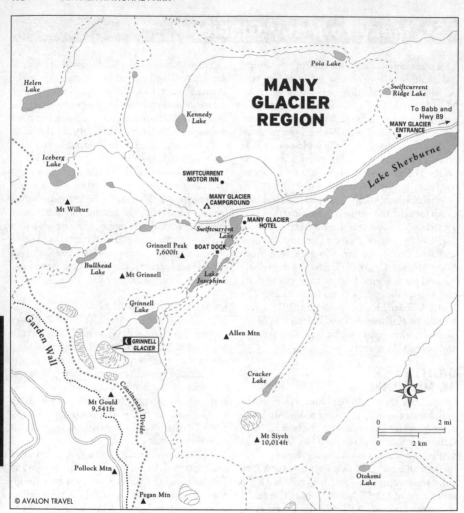

twists and climbs above impossibly blue alpine lakes, and the wildlife is plentiful, but grizzly bears also populate the area. The trail often does not open until late July and is seldom clear of snow until well into August.

Upper Waterton Lake and Goat Haunt

You won't necessarily need your passport to see one of the natural highlights of Canada's Waterton Lakes National Park, although the fjord-like valley is reminiscent of Norway, especially when it is shrouded in fog and mist. Upper Waterton Lake runs north–south, straddling the border. Boats run between the Canadian town of Waterton (headquarters for the park) and **Goat Haunt** at the lake's southern end, accessible only by hiking or by boat.

On the Canadian side, **Crypt Lake Trail** (10.8 miles round-trip) is an ambitious and

© DONNIE SEXTON

Grinnell Lake

spectacular hike that includes a natural tunnel through a rock wall, stomach-dropping heights, waterfalls galore, and a dazzling hidden cirque. There are several hikes, ranging from mellow to death-defying, from the Goat Haunt ranger station, and several ranger-led hikes daily in summer. A few favorites are **Rainbow Falls** (2 miles round-trip, no elevation gain), **Kootenai Lakes** (5 miles round-trip, 200-foot elevation gain), **Lake Janet** (6.6 miles round-trip, 750-foot elevation gain), and **Lake Francis** (12.4 miles round-trip, 1,050-foot elevation gain). For those willing to huff and puff, but only briefly, **Goat Haunt Overlook** (2 miles round-trip, 800-foot elevation gain) offers a phenomenal view of the valley. The isolation and lack of roads tends to keep visitor numbers down around Upper Waterton Lake, but the mosquitoes are abundant; come prepared.

RECREATION
Hiking

One could quite literally spend a lifetime hiking in the St. Mary, Many Glacier, and Upper Waterton Lake region. For a close-up look at a couple of stunning waterfalls in the St. Mary area, head to **St. Mary Falls** trailhead, just west of Sunrift Gorge. The trail is just 0.8 miles one-way, with a 260-foot elevation drop, to St. Mary Falls, and another 0.7 miles one-way, with a 285-foot elevation gain, to the taller **Virginia Falls,** making a relatively easy and lovely three-mile round-trip hike.

For bear-savvy hikers with a penchant for floating ice, **Iceberg Lake** is an extraordinary day hike. The trail, five miles one-way, with a 1,100-foot elevation gain, is well traveled by hikers of the two-legged variety, but it also has one of the densest concentrations of grizzly bears in the park. Bear encounters are not uncommon, and no overnight camping is allowed. The well-marked trailhead is found at the very end of Many Glacier Road, the only road in this section of the park.

The lake itself is a sublime glacial blue with chunks of ice floating in it, often as late as September, but the chunks are bigger and more plentiful in July–August. The elevation is gained slowly, except for a short steep stretch at the beginning, which is enough to turn some hikers around, and passes through meadows bursting with wildflowers. Mountain goats and bighorn sheep are often visible on the last stretch of the hike. Ptarmigan Falls is halfway to the lake—a perfect resting spot. The bridge over Iceberg Creek is erected each summer and taken down each fall to prevent it washing out in spring. Most mornings in July–August, hikers can join a ranger-led hike to the lake, an especially good option for those with more than a healthy fear of bears.

Boating

Boats are permitted on St. Mary Lake, but you'll have to bring your own as there are no rentals on-site. There are 90-minute tours available several times daily through the **Glacier Park Boat Company** (406/257-2426, www.glacierparkboats.com, $22 adults, $11 children, free for children under 4). The tours depart from the Rising Sun Boat Dock, six miles inside the east entrance on Going-

GLACIER NATIONAL PARK

WATERTON LAKES: GLACIER'S CANADIAN SISTER

Just north of Glacier, across the Canadian border in the southwest corner of Alberta, lies Waterton Lakes National Park. Similar in terrain to Glacier, the park is much smaller (about 203 square miles compared to Glacier's 1,600) and houses a small town, Waterton Park, within its borders. Like its neighbor to the south, the stunning landscape of this park was formed by melting alpine glaciers more than 10,000 years ago and later shaped by floods, fires, wind, and its natural wildlife and flora.

Before European settlement, various nomadic groups of indigenous people passed through the area, gathering plants and hunting local wildlife. The most prominent in the area were the Kootenai, who eventually clashed with the Blackfeet that had followed the buffalo into Alberta and taken control of the plains. In 1858 the English explorer Thomas Blakiston was looking for a railroad pass through the Rockies. He encountered some members of the local Kootenai tribe, who directed him to a pass in the south. Traversing this path, he eventually came to an opening that looked on a chain of three lakes. He named the lakes after fellow British explorer and naturalist Charles Waterton, known to be quite eccentric. It became a national park in 1895, and the Great Northern Railway established the Prince of Wales Hotel in 1926, helping put the park on the map for

tourists traveling from Glacier to Banff and Jasper in Alberta.

The star of Waterton's lakes is the **Upper Waterton Lake,** situated on the U.S.-Canada border. It is the deepest lake in the Canadian Rockies and can be explored on a two-hour cruise that leaves from the Waterton marina and dips down into Montana before venturing back. If you have the time, you can disembark from the boat to follow the **Crypt Lake Trail,** considered one of the best hikes in Canada. There are numerous trails around the lake leading past waterfalls, through valleys, and on to spectacular vistas.

Arguably one of the most photographed hotels in the world for its sublime setting, the **Prince of Wales Hotel** (406/892-2525 or 403/859-2231, www.glacierparkinc.com) is a magnificent Swiss chalet-inspired lodge that overlooks the lake and the town below. Although pricey, it is a great place to stay to have the full Waterton experience. If a night's stay is not in your plans, try to stop in for high tea, which is served daily in the hotel lobby.

As you enter the town on Waterton highway, the Visitors Reception Centre (403/859-5133) is on the right. It is open mid-May–mid-October and can provide you with plenty of information on the region. During the off-season, the park's operations building (403/859-2224), located next to the visitors center, provides visitor information and assistance.

to-the-Sun Road, and offer views of various waterfalls, Sexton Glacier, and Wild Goose Island. A 15-minute walk to Baring Falls is also an option on the St. Mary Lake cruise. Twice daily, the cruises can be combined with a guided hike to St. Mary Falls (less than 2 miles roundtrip, 200-foot elevation gain) for a 3.5-hour outing.

In the Many Glacier area, rowboats ($18 per hour), kayaks ($15 per hour), and canoes ($18 per hour) are available to rent at **Swiftcurrent Lake,** adjacent to the Many Glacier Hotel. The **Glacier Park Boat Company** (406/257-

2426, www.glacierparkboats.com, $22 adults, $11 children, free for children under 4) also provides a number of scenic cruises on Swiftcurrent Lake and Lake Josephine. There are up to seven trips daily during summer, and cruises can be combined with guided hikes or used as a shuttle for hiking trips. A highlight for many is seeing the Grinnell Glacier on a cruise across Lake Josephine.

Fishing

While fishing permits or licenses are not necessary in Glacier National Park, it is imperative that anyone fishing abides by the regulations. A brochure can be picked up at any of the visitors centers or downloaded from the National Park Service website (www.nps.gov/planyourvisit/upload/FishingRegs11-12web.pdf).

St. Mary Lake is not especially productive water, but it sure is nice to stand in and soak in the scenery. There are some rainbow trout, brook trout, and whitefish populations in the lake for the patient. In Many Glacier, presumably because of its proximity to the hotel and the road, the trout in **Swiftcurrent Lake** see the most action, but they seem to have wised up. **Lake Josephine** and **Grinnell Lake** have brook trout populations that seem more willing to take the bait or go for flies.

ACCOMMODATIONS

Although there are plenty of options in both St. Mary and Many Glacier for hotels, motels, and cabins, there are not many budget-friendly choices. The prices seem to reflect the scenery, which is spectacular, rather than the amenities, which can be quite modest. **The Red Eagle Motel** (406/732-4453, www.theredeaglemotel.com, May–Oct., rooms and cabins $80–155) is among the more humble. The location is great, the rooms are fine, but this is a place for people who plan to be out and about rather than lounging at the hotel. **The St. Mary Lodge & Resort** (U.S. 89 and Going-to-the-Sun Rd., 406/732-4431 or 888/778-6279, www.stmarylodgeandresort.com, $119–450) is more luxurious—a full resort with all the modern amenities. From tipis to cabins to suites, this resort, which is not operated by Glacier Park Inc., has an array of accommodations to suit nearly every taste.

In Many Glacier, the standout is clearly the **Many Glacier Hotel** (406/892-2525 or 406/732-4411, www.glacierparkinc.com, early June–mid-Sept., $150–289), a historic Swiss chalet–style lodge built in 1915 by the Great Northern Railway. The hotel is located right on the shore of Swiftcurrent Lake, and there is no limit to the natural beauty of the region or the number of ways in which to enjoy it. The guest rooms have not been significantly changed since the hotel's construction, but that only adds to its charm; the prices seem steep, however, for the lack of amenities, but its setting in the Many Glacier Valley is unmatched and memorable. There is nightly entertainment, a wealth of activities that include boat cruises, ranger-led hikes, evening programs, and Red Bus Tours, and horseback riding from the lodge. Note that the hotel is slated for renovations starting in 2011.

Nearby, the **Swiftcurrent Motor Inn** (406/892-2525, www.glacierparkinc.com, mid-June–mid-Sept., $65–137) is decidedly less grandiose and equally less expensive. But this place also has a history; it was established as a tipi camp in 1911 by the Great Northern Railway. There are three main lodgings: motel rooms, duplex-type cottages, and one-bedroom cabins without private baths. It has its own charm as a longtime stopping point for adventurers and road-trippers, and the location cannot be beat. For the price it is an excellent place to stay.

CAMPING

There are two park campgrounds near the village of St. Mary. **St. Mary Campground** ($23) has 148 sites, including 25 sites that can accommodate RVs and truck-trailer combinations up to 35 feet, as well as water and flush toilets. It is the park's largest campground, only 0.5 miles from the St. Mary Visitors Center, and has limited shade but superb views. The regular season is early June–mid-September, but primitive camping ($10) is available early April–early June and mid-September–late November. Winter camping is also possible December 1–March 31. Sites can be reserved for June 1–September 3 online at www.recreation.gov.

The second is **Rising Sun** (early June–mid-Sept., $20), which has 83 sites with 10 sites for RVs, water, flush toilets, and showers. It is halfway along St. Mary Lake in the shadow of Red Eagle Mountain. Some sites are exposed, while others are tucked into the trees. All are available on a first-come, first-served basis.

Not far from the Many Glacier Hotel and the Swiftcurrent Motor Inn, the **Many Glacier Campground** ($20) has 110 sites, including 13 sites for RVs up to 35 feet, as well as water, flush toilets, and showers at the nearby Swiftcurrent Motor Inn. The regular season is late May–mid-September, but primitive camping ($10) is available mid-September–late October, and like most campgrounds in the park, space is available on a first-come, first-served basis. The views are phenomenal, and the access to hiking and boating is amazing. The campground fills up early, so plan accordingly.

FOOD

Without a doubt, the fanciest place to go for a meal in St. Mary is the **Snowgoose Grill** (888/778-6279, www.stmarylodgeandresort. com, 7 A.M.–11 P.M. daily May 25–Sept. 27, breakfast and lunch $9–14, dinner $18–40) in the St. Mary Lodge and Resort. This slightly modern take on the Western steakhouse offers bison steaks, local whitefish, and good salads. They also provide vegetarian options for both lunch and dinner. The adjacent **Curly Bear Café** has more causal fare, including buffalo burgers, wraps, pizza, and chicken dishes. Outside seating is available and highly desirable when the weather cooperates. The nearby **(Park Café** (U.S. 89 and Going-to-the-Sun Rd., 406/732-4482, www.parkcafe.us, 7 A.M.–10 P.M. daily May 25–Sept. 20, breakfast and lunch $5–11.50, dinner $12.25–17) in St. Mary is staffed by people who know and really love Glacier National Park. It is famous for its slogan "Pies for Strength." The pies are indeed mouthwatering and worth every mile on the trail you'll need to work them off. The food is mostly American, and for the most part as healthy as it is inventive and delicious. Up the road in Babb is the **Two Sisters Café** (U.S. 89, 4 miles north of St. Mary, 406/732-5535, www.twosistersofmontana.com, 11 A.M.–10 P.M. daily Memorial Day–Labor Day, lunch $10–14, dinner $15–25), a colorful place that is worth the scenic drive along Lower St. Mary Lake. Although the decor is rather outrageous, the food is sublime—a hiker's dream come true. Try a Red Burger and a slice of home-made huckleberry pie, and if you're in the neighborhood, don't miss the Fourth of July

Crawfish Boil to get a sense of this community along with a full, happy belly.

For those not cooking their own supper over a fire pan in Many Glacier, there are only a few options. The **Ptarmigan Dining Room** (406/892-2525, www.glacierparkinc.com, breakfast 6:30–10 A.M., lunch 11:30 A.M.–2 P.M., dinner 5–9:30 P.M. early June–mid-Sept., breakfast buffet $14, lunch $8–15, dinner entrées $14–27) offers such flavorful entrées as Rocky Mountain trout, buffalo stroganoff, and a wild game sausage sampler. But the fondue is the reason to eat here—try the four-cheese fondue or the Montana-made chocolate fondue. Available on the regular menu, you can also choose to indulge in an après-hike fondue 2–5 P.M. in the **Interlaken Lounge** for $14.95. Each pot comfortably serves two; call for reservations.

In the nearby Swiftcurrent Motor Inn is a casual Italian eatery, **Italian Gardens Ristorante** (406/892-2525, www.glacierparkinc.com, breakfast 6:30–10 A.M., lunch 11:30 A.M.–3 P.M., dinner 5–9:30 P.M. mid-June–mid-Sept., entrées $12–15). It serves standard fare such as pizza, pasta, and chicken, all of which can taste outstanding after a long day on the trail.

INFORMATION AND SERVICES

Entrance to Glacier National Park (406/888-7800, www.nps.gov/glac) costs $25 per vehicle for seven days May–November, $12 for hikers, bikers, and motorcyclists; this is reduced to $10 November–April, when most roads are closed.

If you have questions before arriving in Glacier, be sure to visit the Plan Your Visit section on the National Parks website (www.nps.gov/glac/planyourvisit) or call the Glacier Visitor Information Center (406/888-7800, 24 hours daily summer, 8 A.M.–4:30 P.M. winter).

Visitors Centers and Ranger Stations

At the park entrance, visitors are given a

Vacation Planner, which provides important general information about the park. Once inside the park, visitors centers and ranger stations are the best sources of information. Hours of operation vary, but during the summer the centers and stations are every day.

The **Visitor Information Headquarters Building** (8 A.M.–4:30 P.M. Mon.–Fri. year-round) is located just inside the West Glacier park entrance before the actual entrance station; turn right after passing the "Glacier National Park" sign. They can issue a variety of passes and permits as well as answer most questions.

The park's visitors centers all have knowledgeable staff, guide books and maps, and basic amenities. In West Glacier, visit the **Apgar Visitors Center** in the central part of Apgar Village. It is two doors down from the **Backcountry Permit Office,** which also provides trip planning 8 A.M.–5:30 P.M. daily during summer. The **St. Mary Visitors Center,** located inside the eastern park entrance, is the park's largest and is the only visitors center where you can obtain backcountry permits.

The **Two Medicine Ranger Station** and **Many Glacier Ranger Station,** located close to the campgrounds, provide visitor information and permits.

Glacier Park Inc.

GPI (406/892-2525, www.glacierparkinc.com) is the official concessionaire of the park. You can book accommodations as well as a variety of tours and park transportation online or by phone.

GETTING THERE

The closest airport to Glacier is 30 miles away in Kalispell. The **Glacier Park International Airport** (FCA, www.iflyglacier.com) is served by Delta/SkyWest, Alaska/Horizon, United, and Allegiant. At the airport **Avis, Budget, Hertz,** and **National/Alamo** have car-rentals counters, and **Dollar, Thrifty,** and **Enterprise** have car-rental lots off-site but near the airport. **Flathead-Glacier Transportation Co.**

RANGER PROGRAMS

Some of the best resources on Glacier National Park are the Park Service Rangers – encyclopedias in hiking boots. Their stations are conveniently located at major sites throughout the park, and the rangers host a number of outdoor educational events geared to the whole family. The ranger programs in Glacier begin in late spring and run throughout the summer, with most activities offered at St. Mary, Apgar, Logan Pass, Many Glacier, Goat Haunt, and Two Medicine. Rangers lead several guided hikes each day that allow visitors to learn about the park's geology, history, wildlife, flora, fauna, and more. The St. Mary Visitors Center, Fish Creek Amphitheater, Lake McDonald Hotel, and Many Glacier Hotel host slide lectures as part of the ranger program. There are also full-day hikes, boat tours, and Junior Ranger programs available.

One of the most noteworthy park programs is "Native America Speaks," where members from the Blackfeet, Salish, and Kootenai tribes provide campfire talks about their life, culture, and influence in Glacier. The speakers range from artists and musicians to historians who intersperse their talks with personal stories and Native American legends. These talks are given at the Apgar, Many Glacier, Two Medicine, and Rising Sun campgrounds. During July–August, the St. Mary Visitors Center also hosts weekly Native American dance troupes. For times, locations, and descriptions of the ranger programs offered, pick up the free "Nature with a Naturalist" publication available at any of the park's visitors centers.

For information on ranger stations or programs and to download park brochures, contact **Park Service Headquarters** (406/888-7800, www.nps.gov/glac/planyourvisit/brochures.htm).

GLACIER NATIONAL PARK

(406/892-3390 or 800/829-7039) and **Glacier National Park Shuttle** (406/892-2525, www.glacierparkinc.com) run shuttles from the airport to the park (call for reservations). **Kalispell Taxi** (406/752-4022) is the local taxi service.

Amtrak (800/872-7245, www.amtrak.com) runs the *Empire Builder* from Chicago to Seattle, with daily stops in both directions in East Glacier (summer only), Essex, and West Glacier.

By car, the park is accessible from U.S. 2 and U.S. 89. It is about 150 miles north of Missoula and 150 miles northwest of Great Falls.

GETTING AROUND AND TOURS

Glacier's free shuttle system (406/888-7800, www.nps.gov/glac, 7 A.M.–7 P.M. daily early July–early Sept.) picks up and drops off every 15–30 minutes at 16 different stops, including Apgar Transit Center, Avalanche Creek, Logan Pass, St. Mary Visitors Center, and a number of trailheads.

Scenic interpretive **Red Bus Tours** (406/892-2525, www.glacierparkinc.com, from $45 adults) are another way to see the park. These snazzy vintage buses, known locally as "Jammers," were originally built by the White Motor Company 1936–1939. The vehicles, which have been overhauled for safety purposes, are 25 feet long, seat 17 passengers, and have the added bonus of roll-back canvas tops, ideal for sunny summer days. There are numerous tours available, and informative guides will entertain you with facts and stories about Glacier.

Slightly less flashy but quite comfortable are the air-conditioned and large-windowed coaches of **Sun Tours** (800/786-9220, www.glaciersuntours.com, June 1–Sept. 1, $40–80 adults, $20–25 children). Tours last four, six, or eight hours, and what makes them unique is that they are guided from a Blackfeet perspective. Plants and roots used for Blackfeet medicine are pointed out, for example, as are the natural features that relate to the Blackfeet Nation. The coaches can accommodate 25 passengers and depart daily from East Glacier, Browning, St. Mary, and West Glacier.

Vehicle Restrictions

Vehicles and vehicle combinations longer than 21 feet, including bumpers, and wider than 8 feet, including mirrors, are not permitted on the Going-to-the-Sun Road between Avalanche Campground and the Sun Point Parking Area. Vehicles and vehicle combinations taller than 10 feet may have difficulty navigating the Going-to-the-Sun Road westbound from Logan Pass to the Loop because of rock overhangs. Stock trucks and trailers can access Packers Roost on the west side and Siyeh Bend on the east side.

PETS

Although pets are allowed in drive-in campgrounds, picnic areas, and on roads open to car traffic, they are required to be on a leash no longer than six feet at all times. They are not permitted on any trails within the park, and park officials strongly discourage the presence of pets in Glacier.

MISSOULA AND WESTERN MONTANA

From the towering pines and massive cedar trees to the mountain of huckleberry ice cream clinging to your cone, just about everything is larger than life in western Montana. The craggy Mission Mountains beside Flathead Lake and the Bitterroots, just south of Missoula, are but two of the ranges that make up the spine of the Rockies in this lush, green corner of Montana, the only place in the state that boasts some promising wineries. The area is home to three Native American tribes on one major reservation, an assortment of fascinating wildlife refuges, the National Bison Range, and towns such as Missoula, the ever-growing home of University of Montana, and Whitefish, a skiing and water-sports mecca on the outskirts of Glacier National Park. Western Montana is steeped in Western history, from Lewis and Clark to the Nez Perce Indians and the state's earliest missions, and is home to the state's fastest-growing area, the Bitterroot Valley. Western Montana feels like the Pacific Northwest in some ways—lush greenery, ancient trees, snow-capped peaks, and rather unfortunately, the scars of hyperambitious logging, which often led to catastrophic wildfires that, as recently as 1910, devoured entire cities in a matter of minutes.

As is true of the state in general, western Montana is a slice of paradise for outdoor enthusiasts. From the sublime Flathead Lake in the north with its boating, fishing, and unbeatable swimming and the nearby Jewel Basin, famous for hiking, huckleberries, and grizzly bears, to the Rattlesnake Wilderness and Recreation Area just outside Missoula and the

© DONNIE SEXTON

HIGHLIGHTS

🎠 Carousel for Missoula and Caras Park: Built from the dream of one man and the outpouring of the entire community, this extraordinary hand-built carousel is a reflection of Missoula's spirit and a pretty magical place to spend a beautiful summer day (page 127).

🎠 The St. Ignatius Mission: After more than 120 years, this massive brick Catholic Church set against the backdrop of the Mission Mountains is still enormously impressive, with 58 murals painted by Brother Joseph Carignano, who worked in the kitchen and as a handyman for the mission (page 147).

🎠 Hiking at Jewel Basin: With 27 lakes, 35 miles of trails, and no motorized vehicles or horses permitted, Jewel Basin, high in the Swan Mountains, is a hiker's paradise (page 150).

🎠 Cherry Picking: Planning in advance may be a challenge, but timing your visit to Flathead Lake for the annual cherry harvest promises sweet, juicy memories to savor (page 152).

🎠 Skiing Big Mountain: A phenomenal ski area with a view over Whitefish Lake and perhaps the best après-ski scene in the state, Big Mountain is a highlight of any winter adventure (page 162).

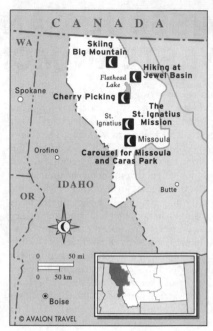

LOOK FOR 🎠 TO FIND RECOMMENDED SIGHTS, ACTIVITIES, DINING, AND LODGING.

HISTORY

Because of harsh winters, unforgiving terrain, and territorial Native Americans, this mountainous and forested land was not as quick to be settled by Europeans as other parts of Montana. The earliest inhabitants of the area were the Salish, Kootenai, and Pend d'Oreille people who fished in the crystal lakes and hunted in the forests and valleys. Fur trappers and traders, attracted by the abundance of beavers in the lakes, entered the area in the

phenomenally rugged Bitterroot Mountains in the south, this corner of the state, some 12,000 square miles of diverse and magnificent habitat, is for many the embodiment of the Wild West and the Montana dream brought to life.

early 1800s. David Thompson, the famous Canadian explorer and fur trapper, set up trading posts in the area 1807–1812, including Saleesh House, the first trading post established west of the Rockies.

The Blackfeet Indians were notoriously in conflict with other tribes in the area. When the Salish traveled through the Missoula valley in search of bison, the Blackfeet would ambush them as they entered the canyon. French trappers who passed through the canyon in the early 1800s encountered the gruesome remains of various massacres and dubbed the area "Hell Gate." Not far from Hellgate Canyon, Lewis and Clark met the Blackfeet, who proved to be of great assistance to the explorers. They introduced them to the main flower of the valley,

WESTERN MONTANA

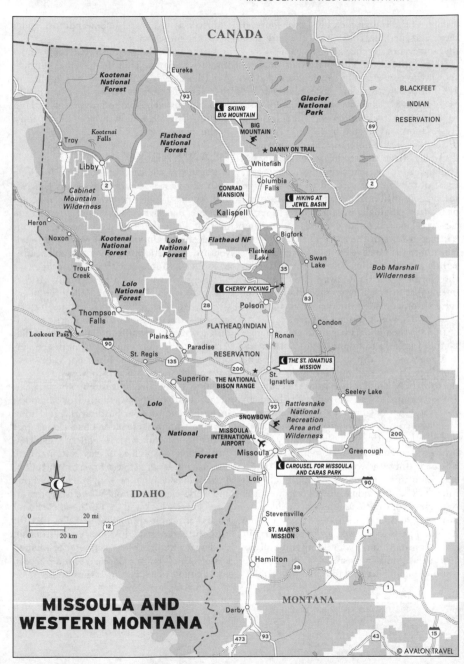

CANADA

Kootenai
National
Forest

Eureka

BLACKFEET

INDIAN

RESERVATION

93

SKIING
BIG MOUNTAIN

Glacier
National
Park

BIG
MOUNTAIN

89

Kootenai
Falls

Troy

Flathead
National
Forest

DANNY ON TRAIL

Whitefish

Libby

2

Columbia
Falls

2

Cabinet
Mountain
Wilderness

CONRAD
MANSION

HIKING AT
JEWEL BASIN

Kalispell

Heron

Noxon

Kootenai
National
Forest

Lolo
National
Forest

Flathead NF

Bigfork

Flathead
Lake

Swan
Lake

Bob Marshall
Wilderness

Trout
Creek

Lolo
National
Forest

35

CHERRY PICKING

83

Thompson
Falls

28

Polson

Condon

Lookout Pass

90

Plains

FLATHEAD INDIAN

Ronan

St. Regis

135

Paradise

RESERVATION

Superior

200

Lolo

THE NATIONAL
BISON RANGE

St.
Ignatius

THE ST. IGNATIUS
MISSION

Seeley Lake

National

93

SNOWBOWL

Rattlesnake
National
Recreation
Area and
Wilderness

MISSOULA
INTERNATIONAL
AIRPORT

200

Forest

Missoula

Greenough

CAROUSEL FOR MISSOULA
AND CARAS PARK

Lolo

90

IDAHO

0   20 mi

0   20 km

12

Stevensville

ST. MARY'S
MISSION

1

Hamilton

38

1

**MISSOULA AND
WESTERN MONTANA**

MONTANA

Darby

473

93

43

15

© AVALON TRAVEL

a staple of the Indian diet, but Lewis found it bitter and inedible, thus giving the bitterroot lily, and eventually the valley, its name.

The Flathead (or Salish) Indians were responsive to conversion by missionaries, and by 1840 St. Mary's Mission was established; the St. Ignatius Mission was moved from Canada to Mission Creek in 1854. The Flathead Reservation was created in 1855 on the condition that the Kootenai, Salish, and Pend d'Oreille share the territory. Although the Indian leaders present begrudgingly agreed, most of the Indians refused to move to the reservation until many years later. Two-thirds of the land originally assigned to the reservation was later taken back to create the many national forests in the area. The Indians did contribute to the development of the area by selling a small portion of reservation land to the Northern Pacific Railway, at the time believing that their willingness to sell would lead the government to expand their reservation territory north, which did not happen.

In 1885 steamboats began to travel across Flathead Lake, and by the 1890s settlements had appeared on the lake's eastern side. The Northern Pacific Railway laid tracks through the town of Missoula at the same time, and by 1891 the railroad had arrived at Flathead. In response, Charles Conrad, a wealthy entrepreneur who stopped his westward travels when he fell in love with the Flathead Valley, established the town of Kalispell, where the main railroad junction would be. The railroad's entry into this region also marked the beginning of its timber industry: Not only were the trees used to lay railroad lines, they could now be transported across the state to the rest of the nation. The wood played an integral part in state's mining industry, building mine shafts and fueling numerous smelters. But like the rest of the state's natural resources, the timber industry would create boom-and-bust cycles up to the present day.

By the 1870s, homesteaders had begun moving into the area. After the Indian Allotment Act (the Dawes Act) of 1887 was applied to the Flathead Reservation in the early 1900s, non-Indians were able to buy parcels of land beginning in 1910, drawing even more people to the region.

PLANNING YOUR TIME

Missoula is a natural stopping point along both east-west I-90 and north-south U.S. 93, and it's easier to get here by air than much of the state, but the city is also a great destination in itself. From boutique shopping and hip eateries near the **University of Montana** to adventurous athletic pursuits in town and nearby, Missoula is Montana with an urban edge.

Using Missoula as a base, many visitors cruise down the **Bitterroot Valley** for an active day-trip with fishing opportunities, historic missions and mansions, and cool little mountain towns like **Hamilton** and **Stevensville.** Another option is to stay at one of the numerous guest ranches in the Bitterroot Valley that have quick and easy access to Missoula.

Almost any part of western Montana can be accessed within a day's drive of Missoula, including the tiny but bustling villages lining the sandy shores of **Flathead Lake**—don't miss charming Bigfork with its galleries, eateries, and theater—as well as Glacier National Park and its gold-letter gateway town of **Whitefish,** a marvelous destination with great restaurants and world-class recreation. Whitefish's proximity to Glacier Park and the **Flathead National Forest** makes it an obvious vacation spot for outdoor enthusiasts. Just south of Whitefish, the larger and slightly less picturesque **Kalispell** has plenty of lodging options, easy air access, and a couple of interesting offbeat museums.

Missoula

Given its location as the hub of five river valleys—Jocko and Big Blackfoot Rivers to the north, the upper and lower Clark Forks, and the Bitterroot—Missoula's longtime status as an important trade center makes perfect sense. About halfway between Yellowstone and Glacier National Parks, Missoula (population 68,202, elevation 3,200 feet) is on the way to just about everywhere in this part of the state and a natural stopping point for visitors to the region.

Originally named Hell Gate by founding fathers C. P. Higgins and Francis Worden, who set up a trading post on the Mullan Road between Fort Benton and Walla Walla, Washington, roughly four miles west of the city's present-day location, Missoula grew quickly when a military post was built in 1870 to protect residents from Indian attacks. When the state legislature agreed to make Missoula the home of the state's university, its status as a city in its own right was secured. The city was built with wood from the forests all around, and logging around Missoula would long define the city with a working-class sensibility and vulnerability to backbreaking and heartbreaking boom-and-bust economic cycles.

The other major defining element of the city—the University of Montana—keeps Missoula young, vibrant, and for this state, liberal. Perhaps because the school is best known for its creative writing, art, drama, and dance programs, Missoula is decidedly arts-oriented. Favorite annual events and organizations include the International Wildlife Film Festival, the International Chorale Festival, and the far-ranging Missoula Children's Theatre.

Not the least of its charms, Missoula is located between the Bitterroot and Flathead Valleys, and there are a host of mesmerizing locales in close proximity. Outdoor enthusiasts have abundant options all around and right in town—hike the M or hang glide off it, kayak the Clark's Fork or bike along its shores. There is world-class fishing on a number of rivers, hot-potting (the art of getting to and swimming in natural hot springs), mountain biking, and no end of places to hike.

SIGHTS
C Carousel for Missoula and Caras Park

Aside from being a beautiful hand-carved carousel, one of the first built in the United States since the Great Depression, what makes the Carousel for Missoula (101 Carousel Dr., 406/549-8382, www.carrousel.com, 11 A.M.–7 P.M. June–Aug., 11 A.M.–5:30 P.M. Sept.–May, $1.50 adults, $0.50 under age 16, $0.50 over age 55, $1 adult and child sharing a seat) so sweet is the way in which it came to be. Local cabinetmaker Chuck Kaparich vowed to the city of Missoula in 1991 that if they would "give it a home and promise no one will ever take it apart," he would build a carousel by hand. As a child, Kaparich had spent summer days in Butte at the Columbia Gardens riding the carousel. For four years, he carved ponies, taught others to carve, and worked to restore and piece together the more than 16,000 pieces of an antique carousel frame he had purchased. The town raised funds and collectively contributed more than 100,000 volunteer hours. In May 1995 the carousel opened with 38 ponies, three replacement ponies, two chariots, 14 gargoyles, and the largest band organ in continuous use in the United States. The jewel-box building opens to the surrounding green of Caras Park in summer and keeps the cold and wind out during the rest of the year. In 2001, a fantastic play area, **Dragon Hollow,** was constructed in just nine days by volunteers.

Missoula Art Museum

With the tagline "Free Expression Free Admission," Missoula Art Museum (MAM, 335 N. Pattee St., 406/728-0447, www.missoulaartmuseum.org, 10 A.M.–5 P.M. Wed.–Fri., 10 A.M.–3 P.M. Sat.–Sun., free) honors the past and celebrates the future. The building

WESTERN MONTANA

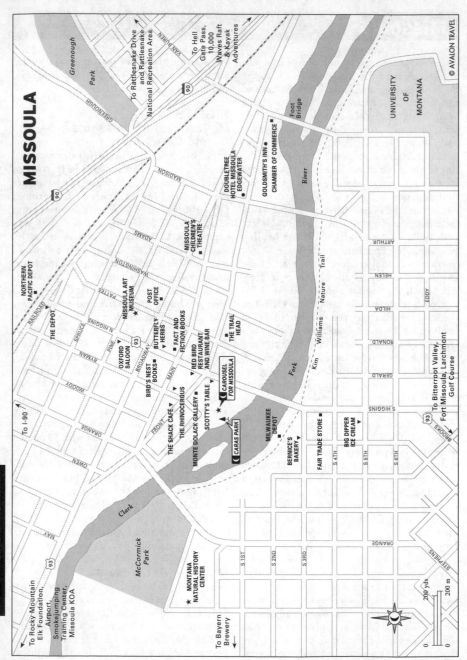

WESTERN MONTANA

MISSOULA

To Rocky Mountain
Elk Foundation,
Airport,
Smokejumping
Training Center,
Missoula KOA

To Bayern Brewery

To I-90

To Hell
Gate Pass,
10,000
Waves Raft
& Kayak
Adventures

To Rattlesnake Drive
and Rattlesnake
National Recreation Area

UNIVERSITY
OF
MONTANA

© AVALON TRAVEL

To Bitterroot Valley,
Fort Missoula, Larchmont
Golf Course

Greenough Park
GREENOUGH
VAN BUREN
MADISON
ADAMS
WASHINGTON
PATTEE
N HIGGINS
RAILROAD
THE DEPOT
SPRUCE
PINE
BROADWAY
RYMAN
WOODY
ORANGE
OWEN
MAY
FRONT
MAIN
Clark
McCormick Park
Fork
Clark Fork
River
Foot Bridge
ARTHUR
HELEN
HILDA
RONALD
GERALD
S HIGGINS
EDDY
S 4TH
S 5TH
S 6TH
S 1ST
S 2ND
S 3RD
ORANGE
STEPHENS
BROOKS

NORTHERN PACIFIC DEPOT ■
MISSOULA ART MUSEUM ★
POST OFFICE ■
MISSOULA CHILDREN'S THEATRE ■
BUTTERFLY HERBS ■
FACT AND FICTION BOOKS ■
OXFORD SALOON ▼
BIRD'S NEST BOOKS ■
RED BIRD RESTAURANT AND WINE BAR ■
THE TRAIL HEAD ■
CAROUSEL FOR MISSOULA 🎠
THE SHACK CAFE ▼
THE RHINOCEROUS ▼
MONTE DOLACK GALLERY ■
SCOTTY'S TABLE ▼
CARAS PARK 🎠
MILWAUKEE DEPOT ■
BERNICE'S BAKERY ■
FAIR TRADE STORE ■
BIG DIPPER ICE CREAM ■
MONTANA NATURAL HISTORY CENTER ★

DOUBLETREE HOTEL MISSOULA
EDGEWATER ●
GOLDSMITH'S INN ●
CHAMBER OF COMMERCE ■

Kim Williams Nature Trail

0   200 yds
0   200 m

itself represents such a marriage, brilliantly combining a 100-year-old Carnegie library with a contemporary glass, steel, and wood addition. The museum has six exhibition spaces that host 20–25 solo exhibitions annually, most of them quite contemporary and provocative. Don't miss the museum's own impressive Contemporary American Indian Art Collection, among the largest of its kind in the country.

Fort Missoula

Originally established to protect settlers against Indian attacks, Fort Missoula (Bldg. 322, Fort Missoula, www.fortmissoulsmuseum. org, 406/728-3476, 10 A.M.–5 P.M. Mon.–Sat., noon–5 P.M. Sun. summer, noon–5 P.M. Tues.–Sun. winter, $3 adults, $1 students, $2 seniors, $10 family, free for children under 6) was never used for its intended purpose. When no attacks occurred, the fort was used to house the African American 25th infantry in 1888 and as an alien detention center for Italian Americans and Japanese Americans during World War II. The museum houses exhibits about the fort's history as well as rotating historical exhibits. The fort grounds are open year-round and admission is free. Although the museum is located in the fort's original buildings, some other historical buildings, including a one-room schoolhouse, an 1860s church, and a homesteader cabin, have been relocated to the grounds.

Montana Natural History Center

The Montana Natural History Center (120 Hickory St., 406/327-0405, www.montananaturalist.org, noon–5 P.M. Tues.–Fri., noon–4 P.M. Sat., $2 adults, $1 children under 12, free for children under 3) is located one block south of McCormick Park. Originally housed on the University of Montana's campus, the center was created by educators who wanted to work with schools and the public to help nurture an understanding and appreciation of nature. They offer workshops, including children's activities, as well as field trips and evening lectures conducted by local scientists

and naturalists. To see what is being offered on specific dates, look under "Community Activities" on the website.

University of Montana

The University of Montana (32 Campus Dr., 406/243-0211, www.umt.edu) was founded in 1895 at the base of Mount Sentinel. To secure Missoula as the site of the state's university, city leaders bribed state legislators with five gallons of whiskey, a case of beer, a case of wine, and 350 cigars. Regardless of its shady beginnings, the university has flourished into a well-respected liberal arts institution with a top-notch football team, a broad interest in the performing arts, a well-known creative writing program, and an ability to produce numerous Fulbright and Rhodes scholars each year.

The university has a fun campus to explore. **University Center,** on the east side of the campus almost directly under the M on the hillside, is the hub of campus life. Wander in to grab a bite at the food court, or peruse the well-stocked bookstore. To find out what lectures, plays, concerts, or other entertainment is happening on campus, visit the website (http://events.umt.edu).

Rocky Mountain Elk Foundation

Strengthening the view that hunters are often the most resolute conservationists, the visitors center of the Rocky Mountain Elk Foundation (5705 Grant St., 800/CALL-ELK—800/225-5355, www.rmef.org, 8 A.M.–5 P.M. Mon.–Fri., 10 A.M.–5 P.M. Sat. Jan.–Apr., 8 A.M.–6 P.M. Mon.–Fri., 9 A.M.–6 P.M. Sat.–Sun. May–Dec., free) has protected and enhanced millions of acres of wildlife habitat across North America since its humble origins in 1984. The center does an impressive job of putting the elk in the context of a wide range of wildlife and emphasizing the importance of habitat conservation. Sure to be a favorite among hunters due to its wealth of trophy mounts, the visitors center is like a natural history museum, and in addition to a pleasant wooded walking trail on the property's 22 acres, there are some great

MISSOULA: MONTANA'S MOST LIBERAL TOWN?

In 1992, when I decided to move to Montana and was vacillating between Missoula and Bozeman, my older brother broke it down according to an age-old and surprisingly right-on generalization when he asked: "Are you more interested in cowboys or hippies?"

Missoula has long been associated with a hippy lifestyle (the herbs store is one of the busiest shops in town), but its origins as a center for labor movements and civil disobedience go back more than a century. In 1909 a pregnant 19-year-old by the name of Elizabeth Gurley Flynn came to Missoula on behalf of the Industrial Workers of the World to organize the region's lumber and migrant farm workers. She and her husband organized heated rallies around town. Eventually city leaders passed a law making public speaking on Missoula streets a crime. Flynn's plan to start a freedom-of-speech battle across the Northwest worked, and before long people willing to be arrested for the cause arrived by the trainload. City jails quickly filled and overflowed, forcing the city to back down and reinstate the right to speak publicly.

Among the Missoula locals who have contributed to its reputation was Jeannette Rankin, in 1916 the first woman to be elected to the U.S.

House of Representatives, two years after Montana granted women the right to vote but four years *before* the 19th Amendment gave women across the country the right to vote. Among the early graduates from the University of Montana in 1902, Rankin was a tried-and-true pacifist, casting one of 50 votes against the resolution to enter World War I in 1917 and the lone vote against entering World War II, a move that sealed her political demise. Rankin famously stated, "You can no more win a war than you can win an earthquake." She was a founding vice president of the American Civil Liberties Union and an outspoken antiwar activist during the Vietnam War era.

The university has also contributed significantly to Missoula's reputation for its liberal leanings. When the school was dedicated in 1895, speaker William Fisk Sanders implored, "Hold not up to these pupils hopes of money or office...their high service is to save the world from shame and thrall." In 1915, the removal of the University of Montana's popular president, Edwin Craighead, triggered the first of many organized protests on campus, including major incidents around freedom of speech, freedom of the press, civil rights, and the Vietnam War.

interactive kid-friendly exhibits and wildlife conservation films.

Smokejumper Visitor Center

Sharing space with the largest active smokejumper base in the country, the Smokejumper Visitor Center (Aerial Fire Depot, 4 miles west of Missoula Airport, 406/329-4934, www.smokejumpers.com, 8:30 A.M.–5 P.M. daily Memorial Day–Labor Day, by appointment the rest of the year, free admission, free tours daily in summer) is a fascinating place for those interested in wildfires and the firefighters who parachute in to battle them. There is a memorial to those killed on duty and a replica of a 1930s fire lookout; visitors on the tour have access to the smoke-jumper loft where

the jumpers work when they are not fighting fires.

ENTERTAINMENT AND EVENTS
Weekly Events in Summer

With an active, outdoorsy, and independent population, Missoula hosts a number of weekly events during summer that encourage everything from outdoor dining to art appreciation. **First Friday Gallery Night** (406/532-3240) is held 5–8 P.M. on the first Friday of every month. Some 15–20 galleries open their doors, often to display new exhibitions, and they provide complimentary hors d'oeuvres and refreshments to art strollers. **Out to Lunch** (406/543-4238, www.missouladowntown.

com, 11 A.M.–2 P.M. Wed. June–Aug.) in Caras Park is a riverside performing arts picnic for the whole city, with talented local musicians and more than 20 food vendors. Also located in Caras Park and run by the Missoula Downtown Association, **Downtown Tonight** (406/543-4238, www.missouladowntown. com, 5:30–8:30 P.M. Thurs. June–Aug.) features live music, food vendors, and a beverage garden.

Known as the Garden City, Missoula boasts three fabulous farmers markets, including the **Clark Fork River Farmers Market** (125 Bank St., 406/396-0593, www.clarkforkrivermarket. com, 8 A.M.–1 P.M. Sat. early May–Oct.), which offers an abundance of local produce, meat, and other products, including hot prepared food. There is live music 11 A.M.–1 P.M., and plenty of parking is available. The **Missoula Farmers Market** (Circle Square, north end of Higgins Ave., 406/777-2636, www.missoulafarmersmarket.com, 8:30 A.M.–noon Sat. May–Oct., 5:30–7 P.M. Tues. July–Aug.) features more than 100 vendors of fresh produce, baked goods, and more. The **Missoula Saturday Market** (E. Pine St. between Higgins Ave. and Pattee St., 406/370-8668, www.missoulasaturdaymarket.org, 8 A.M.–1 P.M. Sat. early May–mid-Oct.) has prepared food and features art and crafts by local artisans.

International Wildlife Film Festival and CINE

For more than three decades, the International Wildlife Film Festival (718 S. Higgins Ave., 406/728-9380, www.wildlifefilms.org, May) has been celebrating conservation and film with an eight-day event based at Missoula's famed Roxy Theatre. The event runs annually in May and features a phenomenal array of wildlife films from around the globe. In October the Montana CINE International Film Festival features films on a broad range of topics relating to the environment and cultures of our planet.

International Choral Festival

Held every three years (the next ones are scheduled for 2012 and 2015), The International Choral Festival (406/721-7985, www.choralfestival.org) is a true Missoula community event. Nonprofit and noncompetitive, it began more than 20 years ago with the goal of promoting cultural awareness and understanding through music. The four-day event takes places at different venues around the city, and the first day usually includes free preview concerts. Hundreds of international and national choral groups apply each year, but only a handful are selected to participate. In 2009 participants came from the Czech Republic, India, Taiwan, and Australia, among others.

Missoula Children's Theatre

Certainly one of the state's most beloved theater companies, the Missoula Children's Theatre (200 N. Adams St., 406/728-1911, www.mctinc.org, Oct.–June) mounts six productions annually of such family favorites as *Hansel and Gretel* and *Snow White and the Seven Dwarfs* with children as cast members. Most significantly, MCT has become known for their performances around the state that include local children. The company arrives in town a week before a performance, casting and rehearsing local children to light up the stage (or the gym, as is often the case in small-town Montana) for an end-of-week performance. At the same time, the company performs pieces that include Broadway musicals and poignant comedies in their home performance space.

SHOPPING
The Fair Trade Store

The Fair Trade Store (519 S. Higgins Ave., 406/543-3955, 10 A.M.–6 P.M. Mon.–Sat.) is operated by the Jeannette Rankin Peace Center and promotes equitable and fair partnerships between producers and distributors of goods. There is a distinctive and colorful selection of merchandise from around the globe, including textiles, pottery, silver, and handmade cards.

Butterfly Herbs

In addition to being Missoula's oldest espresso bar, Butterfly Herbs (232 N. Higgins Ave.,

406/728-8870) is a fun and eclectic gift shop. They sell whole herbs, teas, and spices in bulk as well as soaps, handmade jewelry, candles, and other decorative goods.

The Trail Head

Like the best independent bookstores, The Trail Head (221 E. Front St., 406/543-6966, www.trailheadmontana.net) is a part of the Missoula community and thrives by knowing the area as well as its activities and specific conditions. Trail Head staff participate regularly in volunteer efforts to preserve and enhance recreational opportunities in the region. The store has fantastic gear for nearly every activity in the area, including skiing, boating, camping, and climbing. For more than 35 years, great adventures have started here.

Other Bookstores

In a famously literary town, **Fact and Fiction Books** (220 N. Higgins Ave., 406/721-2881, www.factandfictionbook.com) is a Missoula institution and a good place to learn about local culture and regional authors.

For used, rare, and out-of-print books, **Bird's Nest Books** (219 N. Higgins Ave., 406/721-1125, www.birdsnestbooks.com) is a real find, next door to Fact and Fiction.

Monte Dolack Gallery

One of the most recognizable artists in the region, Monte Dolack shows his work and that of his partner, Mary Beth Percival, at Monte Dolack Gallery (139 W. Front St., 406/549-3248 or 800/825-7613, www.dolack.com, 10 A.M.–5:30 P.M. Mon.–Fri., 11 A.M.–5 P.M. Sat.). The artists travel frequently, which is reflected in their primarily nature-based, often whimsical and witty works, which include tranquil watercolors and vivid posters.

RECREATION
Missoula Osprey Baseball

At Ogren Field in Allegiance Park (700 Cregg Lane), the Missoula Osprey (406/543-3300, www.missoulaosprey.com) take on other Pioneer League teams in some great small-town minor-league baseball. Missoula is known for its softball, so it's no surprise that the community shows up in force to watch their hometown Ospreys, a farm team for the Arizona Diamondbacks.

Trails

Hugely popular with walkers, runners, and bikers, the flat **Clark Fork Riverfront Trail** is 3.8 miles long and provides access to **Caras Park, Bess Reed Park,** and **Kiwanis Park** on the north bank and **McCormick Park, Clark Fork Natural Park, John Toole Park,** the **University of Montana River Bowl,** and **Jacob's Island Park** on the south bank. The trail, graveled in places and paved in others, connects to a number of other intersecting trails and runs on both the north and south sides of the Clark Fork River. It is easily accessible throughout town, but the most abundant parking can be found at Caras Park near the Carousel for Missoula. The trail on the river's south side is about 0.5 miles longer than on the north side but is not paved.

The Clark Fork Riverfront Trail connects to the five-mile **Kim Williams Trail,** a converted railroad bed, near the base of Mount Sentinel (where you can hike the M). The trail is wide and level, and it is open to pedestrians, equestrians, and cyclists. It runs through Hellgate Canyon and connects to the Deer Creek-Pattee Canyon Loop. The trail can easily be accessed from Jacob's Island Park near the Van Buren Pedestrian Bridge.

Hiking the M on Mount Sentinel

For a bird's-eye view of the city, hike up the M Trail on Mount Sentinel. It is a popular trail, so you will likely have others huffing and puffing up the hill in front and behind you. There are 13 switchbacks on the west-facing slope, and the views over Missoula and the Bitterroot Valley at sunset are worth the sweat.

Rattlesnake National Recreation Area and Wilderness

Less than five miles north of town, the 61,000-acre **Rattlesnake National Recreation Area** and **Wilderness** (406/329-3814) is fed by some 50 creeks and has 30 lakes, waterfalls, and many miles of trails. The area is a dream for hikers, runners, mountain bikers, campers, cross-country skiers, and fishers; it is home to deer, elk, coyotes, mountain goats, bighorn sheep, black and grizzly bears, moose, and mountain lions.

To get to the area from Missoula, take the I-90 Van Buren Street exit at the east end of town and travel 4.5 miles north on Rattlesnake Drive.

Skiing

Twenty minutes north of Missoula, **Snowbowl** (1700 Snowbowl Rd., 406/549-9777 or 800/728-2695, www.montanasnowbowl.com, $39 adults, $36 students and seniors, $18 age 6–12, free for children under 6) is a nice little ski hill with an average of 300 inches of snow annually, 2,600 feet of vertical drop, and a run that covers three miles. In summer, the mountain is open Friday–Sunday late June–mid-September for mountain biking, disc golf (folf), and diggler, which is a cross between mountain biking and snowboarding (rentals available).

There is no shortage of cross-country ski trails around Missoula. One unique destination is the **Garnet Resource Area** (406/329-3883 or 406/329-3914, www.garnetghosttown.net), with 50 miles of trails in a ghost town. In summer, hiking and mountain biking are popular. To get to Garnet, follow Highway 200 east of town and turn south at the Garnet Range Road, located between mile markers 22 and 23, about 30 miles east of Missoula. Follow the range road approximately 12 miles to the parking area. The road is closed January 1–April 30, when access is limited to snowshoers, cross-country skiers, and snowmobilers.

There are also more than 150 miles of cross-country ski trails in the **Lolo National Forest** (406/329-3750).

Fishing

While access to the Clark Fork River right in town is easy, the river is still recovering from decades of pollution. Better bets are the Bitterroot River, the Blackfoot River, and Rock Creek. One guiding outfit that does them all is **Five Valleys Fly Fishing Company** (406/544-2135 or 877/783-0218, www.fivevalleysfishing.com). Owner Brandon Henley studied fisheries

HANG GLIDING IN MISSOULA

While it makes some people crazy, for others the combination of wind and mountains in Missoula means only one thing: hang gliding. It's not uncommon to see these colorful oversize-kite contraptions launching off Mount Sentinel and soaring over the city. But what goes up must come down, and when Bill Johnson (widely considered to have been the first hang gliding pilot in the state) landed on top of the university field house, reports of a plane crash swiftly clogged the emergency services switchboard. When the fire department arrived, Johnson had broken down his glider, packed it neatly in a bag, and even asked the firefighters for help getting down. The firefighters were too busy scanning the scene for a crashed plane to realize that they were aiding Johnson in his getaway.

The sport took hold in the state in the 1970s when gear was cheap and mostly homemade. By October 2006 the number of launches off Mount Sentinel gave pause to Missoula's air traffic controllers, who feared a plane-versus-glider crash, and the area was closed to flight for nearly a year. The state's hang glider pilots joined with people in Missoula who appreciated the life and color that the sport brought to town, and in July 2007 Mount Sentinel opened again to hang gliding.

Local pilot Jeff Shapiro from **Five Valley Hang Gliding** (406/531-1955, www.fivevalleyhanggliding.com) keeps the sport alive with his own gravity-defying flights as well as tandem flights ($175) for the curious and lessons packages ($1,000). On a windy day in Missoula, there may not be a more unique way to see the city and the valleys around it.

biology at the university, and it shows. He and his guides fish year-round, have a passion for dry flies, and know the area as well as anyone. Another guide who is also a phenomenal naturalist in addition to being a world-class fishing instructor is Tom Jenni of **Tom Jenni's Reel Montana** (406/539-6610 or 866/885-6065, www.tomjenni.com). Jenni grew up in Missoula and has been fishing its rivers for more than 30 years.

Boating

With five rivers in the vicinity, Missoula is a boater's town. There is even an artificial practice wave right in town for kayakers to play safely in. **10,000 Waves Raft & Kayak Adventures** (8080 W. Riverside Dr., 406/549-6670 or 800/537-8315, www.10000-waves. com) offers everything from scenic rafting to white-water adventures, sit-on-top kayaks, and kayak instruction on numerous sections of the Blackfoot and Clark Fork Rivers. There are also overnight trips and gourmet dinner trips, including full-day trips on the Blackfoot River ($85 adults, $65 children).

Golf

Although there are a couple of nine-hole courses in town, the only 18-hole public course in Missoula is the **Larchmont Golf Course** (3200 Old Fort Rd., 406/721-4416, $28–30 for 18 holes).

Camping

There are only a handful of private campgrounds in Missoula, but the **Lolo National Forest** (406/329-3750) has a wide range of campsites in beautiful settings. Camping is also permitted in certain sections of the **Rattlesnake National Recreation Area and Wilderness** (406/329-3814). For in-town convenience with RV-specific sites, try the **Missoula KOA** (3450 Tina Ave., 800/562-5366, www.missoulakoa.com, year-round, $32–63 RVs, $27–31 tents, $45–52 cabins). The tree-lined property offers 200 RV and tent sites in addition to amenities like a heated pool, two hot tubs, free Wi-Fi, and a café that serves breakfast daily in summer.

ACCOMMODATIONS

As one of Montana's bigger cities, Missoula has plenty of lodging. The old-school independent motels line much of East and West Broadway, while some of the newer chain hotels can be found on Reserve Street.

Twenty minutes north of Missoula is the **Gelandesprung Lodge at Snowbowl** (1700 Snowbowl Rd., 406/549-9777, www.montanas-nowbowl.com, $39 shared bath, $51 private bath, $80 2-room suite), a European-style lodge right on the mountain and open throughout the ski season and on weekends in summer.

For an ultraluxe experience that will thin your wallet considerably, **The Resort at Paws Up** (40060 Paws Up Rd., Greenough, 406/244-5200, luxury tents from $725) in Greenough, about 32 miles east of Missoula, is among the most uniquely glamorous spots in the state. There are luxury homes and luxury tents that are unimaginably elegant, with heated floors, electricity, king-size feather beds, a dining pavilion with a cook, a camping butler, and nightly bonfires with s'mores. This is camping fit for a high-maintenance king. The food is also exquisite, as is the spa, and the activities and adventures are limitless.

In the heart of Missoula on the banks of the Clark Fork River is the pet-friendly **Doubletree Hotel Missoula Edgewater** (100 Madison St., 406/728-3100 or 800/222-TREE—800/222-8733, www.missoulaedgewater.doubletree. com, $159–219), an enormous hotel with all the amenities.

Also on the river is the much smaller **Goldsmith's Inn** (809 E. Front St., 866/666-9945, www.goldsmithsinn.com, $89–129), a charming turn-of-the-century bed-and-breakfast within easy walking distance of the university and downtown.

FOOD

Missoula's dining scene offers more cultural diversity than much of the rest of the state, with plenty of sushi and Thai offerings, but its

WINERIES IN MONTANA

Since 1984, when Tom Campbell Jr. and his father first started experimenting with growing grapes along the shores of Flathead Lake, in prime Montana cherry territory, seven other wineries have sprouted up across the state, primarily in the western region. Though many vintners buy grapes from out of state, there are several growers among them, including a handful that opt for unconventional but delicious base fruits like cherries, huckleberries, chokecherries, apples, pears, currants, and rhubarb.

• **Rock Creek Winery** produces award-winning pinots and syrahs with grapes from Washington and Oregon, and is currently looking for a tasting room in downtown Missoula.

• **Flathead Lake Winery** (Hwy. 486, 8.6 miles north of Columbia Falls, 406/387-WINO – 406/387-9166, www.flatheadlakewinery.com) specializes in small-batch wines made from fruit that was either grown or picked wild in Montana, including huckleberries, cherries, white cherries, chokecherries, and apples. They also produce a pinot noir and a gewürztraminer.

• **Lolo Peak Winery** (2506 Mount Ave., Missoula, 406/549-1111, www.lolopeak.com, 10 A.M.-6 P.M. Mon.-Sat.) also makes wine from Montana fruit, including raspberry wine, plum wine, and spiced apple and honey wine as well as cherry and rhubarb varietals.

• **Mission Mountain Winery** (U.S. 93, Dayton, 406/849-5524, www.missionmountainwinery.com, tastings 10 A.M.-6 P.M. daily May-Oct.) is the state's first bonded winery and produces up to 6,500 cases annually of more than 18 different award-winning varietals. Their vineyards grow the grapes for their highly regarded pinot noir, pinot gris, and small amounts of riesling, chardonnay, and gewürztraminer.

• **Rolling Hills Winery** (U.S. 2, Culbertson, 406/787-5787, 10 A.M.-6 P.M. daily June-Aug., 2-6 P.M. daily Sept.-May), the only winery in the eastern part of the state, is a small family-run business specializing in six varieties of fruit wine, including raspberry and rhubarb grown on the premises as well as chokecherry, honey, plum, and blueberry.

• **Ten Spoon Vineyard and Winery** (4175 Rattlesnake Dr., Missoula, 877/549-8703, www.tenspoonwinery.com, tastings 5-9 P.M. Thurs.-Sat.) is among the fastest growing wineries in the state and has a marvelous origin story. Owner Connie Poten bought some pastureland in the Rattlesnake Valley outside Missoula to protect the rapidly disappearing open space. She met Andy Sponseller on a local preservation campaign, and their shared love of wine led to the backbreaking work that built the vineyard and set the stage for their subsequent success with varietals including sauvignon blanc, petite sirah, and zinfandel.

• **Hidden Legend Winery** (1345 U.S. 93 N., Suite 5, Victor, 406/363-MEAD – 406/363-6323, www.hiddenlegendwinery.com, tours and tastings 11 A.M.-6 P.M. Tues.-Fri., 11 A.M.-8:30 P.M. Sat.), in the Bitterroot Valley, specializes in honey-based mead with Montana twists like chokecherry and elderberry.

• **Trapper Peak Winery** (75 Cattail Lane, Darby, 406/821-1964, www.trapperpeakwinery.com, tours and tastings available by appointment), also in the Bitterroot Valley, produces an affordable selection of cabernet sauvignon, petite sirah, merlot, cabernet franc, and muscat using California grapes.

MONTANA'S LITERARY TREASURE

Few states can boast a nearly 1,200-page, five-pound tome dedicated to the remarkable literature that has come from and defined the state. (The state's "Big Sky" moniker even came courtesy of A. B. Guthrie's classic 1947 novel *The Big Sky*.) Montana's literary anthology, *The Last Best Place*, was published in 1988, and the state's literary status only continues to grow. This may partly be attributed to poet and professor Richard Hugo, who directed the University of Montana's renowned creative writing program from 1964 until his death in 1982. The less prosaic might ascribe the inordinate number of well-known authors and poets to things like the light, space, and quality of life here, or the long cold winters and limited distractions. Among the state's best-known writers are Wallace Stegner, Norman Maclean, Bill Kittredge, James Welch, Tom McGuane, James Crumley, Richard Brautigan, Ivan Doig, Mary Clearman Blew, Richard Ford, David Quammen, and Rick Bass.

Montana's literary heritage is very much alive in Missoula, where one of the area's softball teams goes by the name "The Montana Review of Books," which once had an outfield lineup with 12 published novels among them. The city boasts some fabulous independent bookstores that promote and often host local writers, including **Fact and Fiction** (220 N. Higgins Ave., 406/721-2881). But perhaps the literary spirit is most alive in any number of watering holes, some more savory than others. **Charlie B's** (428 N. Higgins Ave.), a favorite haunt of the late James Crumley, has no sign, tinted windows, and a big wooden door. Crumley was also a regular at **The Depot** (201 W. Railroad Ave.). During his tenure at the University of Montana, Bill Kittredge and plenty of creative writing students frequented **Diamond Jim's Eastgate Casino and Lounge** (900 E. Broadway) just over the Van Buren footbridge from campus. **The Rhino** (158 Ryman St.) was identifiable in Jeff Hull's short stories and his 2005 novel. Probably the best-known among Missoula's thirsty literary geniuses, Dick Hugo often wrote about bars – **The Dixon Bar** (Hwy. 200, Dixon), **Trixi's Antler Saloon** (Hwy. 200, Ovando), and more famously, the **Milltown Union Bar** (11 Main St., Milltown), which is now called Harold's Club and is virtually unrecognizable but for the stuffed mountain goat by the door.

strong suit is still fresh Rocky Mountain cuisine. Among the best is **Red Bird Restaurant and Wine Bar** (111 N. Higgins Ave., Suite 100, 406/549-2906, www.redbirdrestaurant.com, wine bar 5–10:30 P.M. Mon.–Sat., restaurant 5–9:30 P.M. Tues.–Sat., entrées $24–36), an elegant little bistro in a historic hotel building. Everything is fresh, creative, and made on the premises, including steaks, seafood, housemade pasta, and soups.

Serving American bistro fare with a global twist, **Scotty's Table** (131 S. Higgins Ave., 406/549-2790, www.scottystable.net, 11 A.M.–2:30 P.M. and 5 P.M.–close Tues.–Sat., 5 P.M.–close Sun., entrées $8–28) is an upscale dining spot for the whole family. The gourmet kids menu was inspired by the chef's own nine-year-old. Entrées include mouthwatering cioppino and local pork confit, but the appetizers are enchanting—try wild Alaskan salmon cakes, lamb *kofta*, or the charcuterie plate; you might not even make it to the main course.

Far more casual and serving three meals a day in a classic Pontiac-Oldsmobile dealership setting, **The Shack Café** (222 W. Main St., 406/549-9903, www.theshackcafe.com, breakfast and lunch 7 A.M.–3 P.M. Mon.–Fri., 7 A.M.–9 P.M. Sat.–Sun., dinner 5–9 P.M. Thurs.–Sun.) specializes in food that was grown and raised locally. Don't miss the huckleberry pancakes ($9) for breakfast; it may be the best breakfast in town. Lunch includes killer sandwiches ($8–9.25), and dinner entrées ($8.50–16.75) range from sandwiches and salads to steaks and seafood.

For a quick and scrumptious bite with a killer cup of coffee, try **Bernice's Bakery** (190 S. 3rd St. W., 406/728-1358, www.

bernicesbakerymt.com, 6 A.M.–8 P.M. daily, sandwiches $6), a real-butter and from-scratch kind of place featuring high-quality organic ingredients, menus that change daily, and sheer artistry in everything they do. With a strong coffeehouse vibe and a commendable commitment to community, Bernice's also hosts blues concerts the first Thursday of every month.

If you're just starting your Montana adventure, you'll need to get in shape for all of the fabulous ice-cream offerings. A great place to start is **Big Dipper Ice Cream** (631 S. Higgins Ave., 406/543-5722, www.bigdippericecream.com), which has unexpected but out-of-this-world flavors like cardamom, Honey Porter, Irish whiskey, and mango habanero sorbet in addition to the lip-smacking classics. Don't miss daily special flavors like Thai peanut curry (really) and cotton candy. During summer, the walk-up window is open 11 A.M.–11 P.M. daily. Hours vary the rest of the year, so call ahead.

NIGHTLIFE

Home to college students and artists, there is no shortage of watering holes in Missoula, and a brief walk will take you to establishments that are pulsing with activity. Microbrew enthusiasts will enjoy the **Bayern Brewery** (1507 Montana St., 406/721-1482, www.bayernbrewery.com, 10 A.M.–8 P.M. Mon.–Fri., noon–8 P.M. Sat.–Sun.), which always has six of their beers available along with their own coffee blends and a small but delectable sampling of German food. The beer garden is a great place to relax in summer, and brewery tours are available by appointment.

For more of a late-night scene, try tried-and-true favorites like **The Rhinocerous** (158 Ryman St., 406/721-6061), with more than 50 beers on tap; **Feruqi's** (318 N. Higgins Ave., 406/728-8799), an intimate spot known for its martinis and its setting in a historical building; or the **Oxford Saloon** (337 N. Higgins Ave., 406/549-0117, www.the-oxford.com), which no longer serves Brains and Eggs but does offer a pretty tasty Garbage Omelet.

VISITOR INFORMATION

The **Missoula Chamber of Commerce** (825 E. Front St., 406/543-6623, www.missoylachamber.com, 8 A.M.–5 P.M. Mon.–Fri.) and the **Convention and Visitors Bureau** (1121 E. Broadway, Suite 103, 406/532-3250, www.missoulacvb.org) are both great sources of information for visitors.

The **U.S. Forest Service** (200 E. Broadway, 406/329-3511) and the state **Department of Fish, Wildlife and Parks** (3201 Spurgin Rd., 406/542-5500) offices offer good information about hiking, camping and fishing in the national forests.

The **main post office** is at 1100 West Kent Avenue, and the downtown location is at 200 East Broadway. The **Missoula Public Library** (301 E. Main St., 406/721-2665, www.missoulapubliclibrary.org) is open daily; call for hours.

SERVICES

The main hospitals are **St. Patrick's** (500 W. Broadway, 406/542-7271) and **Community Medical Center** (2827 Fort Missoula Rd., 406/728-4100), both of which have 24-hour emergency rooms.

The **Super Wash** laundry (1700 S. 3rd St. W., 406/728-9845) is open daily.

GETTING THERE

Located just four miles northwest of the university, **Missoula International Airport** (MSO, 5225 U.S. 10 W., 406/728-4381, www.flymissoula.com) is served by Alaska/Horizon, Allegiant, Delta, and United. Located on the first floor of the terminal are the **Alamo, Avis, Budget, Enterprise,** and **Hertz** rental-car agencies. **Rent-A-Wreck, Thrifty,** and **Dollar** have shuttles to and from the airport. Most hotels offer free shuttle service to and from the airport; the **Airport Shuttler** (406/543-9416) also provides bus service into town.

The **Greyhound** bus station (110 W. Broadway, 406/549-2339) has several buses in and out of town daily. **Rimrock Stages** (1660 W. Broadway, www.rimrocktrailways.com) also has bus service to major cities within Montana.

I-90 runs directly through Missoula, making it an easy destination by car. Missoula is 115 miles from both Helena and Kalispell, 120 miles from Butte, and about 200 miles from Bozeman.

GETTING AROUND

Alamo (2000 W. Broadway, 406/541-2345), **Thrifty** (3309 W. Broadway, 406/549-2277), **Dollar** (1905 W. Broadway, 406/721-3838) and **Enterprise** (2188 W. Broadway, 406/721-1888) have rental-car offices downtown.

The **Mountain Line** (406/721-3333, www.mountainline.com, Mon.–Sat., $1 adults) is the city bus service. During the summer it offers free shuttles to the farmers market downtown.

For taxi service, call **Yellow Cab** (406/543-6644) or **Green Taxi** (406/728-TAXI—406/728-8294), which only uses hybrid cars.

Hamilton and the Bitterroot Valley

The peaceful and dramatically beautiful valley known as the Bitterroot, named by Meriwether Lewis, has a fascinating history; the region's past has been filled with promise and heartbreak since Lewis and Clark's visit in 1805.

In 1854, John Mullan, who masterminded the Mullan Road overland route to the Pacific, predicted that while much of the region was unpopulated rugged wilderness, the Bitterroot Valley would soon be "one villaged valley, teeming with life, and bustle and business." Nearly 160 years later, his prediction has panned out; the Bitterroot Valley is the fastest growing part of Montana while still remaining a gorgeous swath of green-drenched mountains with sparkling rivers, quaint little towns, and no end of opportunities for outdoor adventures. The drive through towns like Florence, Stevensville, Victor, Corvallis, Hamilton, and Darby is utterly scenic and a splendid way to spend a day or two. The climate is milder than in other parts of the state, sandwiched as it is between the Bitterroot and Sapphire Mountain Ranges. Fishers, cyclists, and hikers will not want to leave, and history buffs and antiques hunters will be content here as well.

LOLO HOT SPRINGS RESORT

Although not among the state's fanciest, the hot springs at Lolo Hot Springs Resort (38500 W. U.S. 12, 800/273-2290, www.lolohotsprings.com, deluxe cabins $85 d, camping cabins $30 d) are among those known to indigenous people long before Lewis and Clark arrived in the region. The area was a natural mineral lick for wildlife and an ancient meeting spot for Native Americans. It was also a well-known rendezvous site for trappers and prospectors. As early as 1888, the springs were advertised in Missoula newspapers for board, room, and bath for $11 per week. Today the resort offers deluxe cabins, camping cabins, tipis, and RV and tent sites. There is also a restaurant on-site.

In summer this is a great camping spot, with immediate access to both the Lolo and Bitterroot National Forests as well as many miles of prime river access. In winter the area is popular for snowmobilers, and snowmobile rentals ($200 full-day, $150 half-day) are available daily on-site. The naturally heated mineral pools (10 A.M.–10 P.M. daily summer, 10 A.M.–8 P.M. daily winter, $7 adults, $5 under age 13) are sublime any time of year. Entrance to the pools is included with cabin rentals.

LEE METCALF NATIONAL WILDLIFE REFUGE

The Lee Metcalf National Wildlife Refuge (4567 Wildfowl Lane, 406/777-5552, www.fws.gov/leemetcalf, year-round) is located about 30 miles south of Missoula on U.S. 93 in Stevensville, along the Bitterroot River. It was established in 1963 by locals in response to the negative effects on wildlife habitat caused by ranches, farms, and the logging industry, and it was named after a local U.S. senator

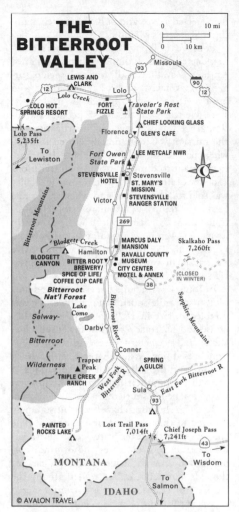

THE
BITTERROOT
VALLEY

the refuge and provides many viewing opportunities from the car.

Traveler's Rest State Park

Located just 0.5 miles west of Lolo on U.S. 12, Traveler's Rest (406/273-4253, www.travelersrest.org, 8 A.M.–8 P.M. daily June–Aug., shorter hours Sept.–May, $5 per vehicle, free with Montana license plates) is a critical stop for any Lewis and Clark buff. The park is a large grassy area with a tree-lined creek that occupies about 50 acres. Historically it was a resting place for Native Americans, who would set up camp here before crossing the Bitterroot Mountains; it is also where Lewis and Clark's Corps of Discovery camped twice. They named the creek nearby "Travellers Rest." In 2002 an archaeological team discovered physical evidence that confirmed the campsite had been used by the Corps of Discovery—it's the only Lewis and Clark campsite with verified physical evidence, which came in the form of high mercury levels. It was determined from the corps's journals that the men were given mercury pills, which caused immediate evacuation of their bowels, to cure any number of ailments. The high mercury content of the soil was limited to a pit that served as the latrine. A kitchen was discovered Army regulation distance away. It was also at this campsite where Lewis and Clark decided to part ways on their return journey east.

STEVENSVILLE

Known primarily for the beautifully preserved mission built by Belgian-born Jesuit priest Pierre-Jean De Smet, Stevensville (population 1,984, elevation 3,370 feet) is surrounded by the Bitterroot and Sapphire Mountains and the **Lee Metcalf National Wildlife Refuge.** It provides superb access to hiking, biking, and fishing for outdoor enthusiasts. The town's history comes to life Fort Owen, the St. Mary's Mission, and the Stevensville Museum.

St. Mary's Mission

As the first permanent settlement in the state, many see St. Mary's Mission (315 Charlos St.,

who was dedicated to the conservation movement. Its main purpose is as a refuge for migratory birds, including ospreys, eagles, and hawks. Larger animals such as white-tailed deer and coyotes can be spotted in the area as well. In the summer, after the nesting season has finished, a two-mile hiking trail that loops through the wildlife viewing area is opened; there are two shorter trails open year-round. Wildfowl Lane, a county road, runs through

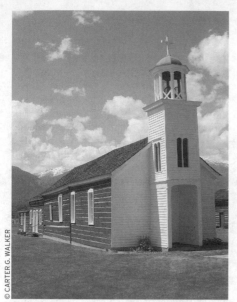
© CARTER G. WALKER

St. Mary's Mission in the Bitteroot Valley

406/777-5734, www.saintmarysmission.org, mid-Apr.–mid-Oct., tours 10 A.M.–4 P.M. Tues.–Sat., gift shop 10 A.M.–5 P.M., grounds free, museum $2, tours $7 adults, $5 students) as the birthplace of modern Montana. Its origin dates to the winter of 1823–1824 when two dozen Iroquois Indians were employed as trappers by the Hudson's Bay Company. Twelve of the Iroquois stayed in the Bitterroot Valley that winter, were adopted by the Salish people, and married Salish women. Having been introduced to Christianity 200 years earlier, the Iroquois shared stories of the men they called "blackrobes," men who could speak to God. The Salish and neighboring Nez Perce were so riveted by the stories that they wanted to bring the blackrobes to their encampments. Four separate missions were dispatched to make contact with the blackrobes in St. Louis; all were futile until 1839, when the Indians met Father Pierre-Jean De Smet. In 1841 De Smet arrived in the Bitterroot Valley with two other priests and three laypeople. When they reached what would become Stevensville, De Smet and his

men erected a cross and built the church, naming it St. Mary's Mission.

Four years later, the mission was commandeered by an Italian Jesuit priest named Anthony Ravalli. Ravalli was a physician, surgeon, pharmacist, architect, and artist who built the first flour mill and saw mill in the state. He respected the Salish people, and although he was also loved by his constituents, the mission was temporarily closed in 1850 when many of the Salish rebelled against practices meant to diminish their own traditions and way of life. During its closure the facility was sold to John Owen, and when the Jesuits could not return, as stipulated in the conditions of the sale, the church was burned; in its place Owen built a trading post known as Fort Owen. Ravalli stayed among the Native Americans in western Montana as their physician and spiritual guide.

In 1866, Ravalli built a new chapel and hospital just a mile south of Fort Owen; it was doubled in size in 1879 to include Ravalli's house and pharmacy, a cabin for Salish chief Victor, and a cemetery where Jesuits and Salish were buried side by side. After Ravalli's death in 1884 and the subsequent forced exodus of the Salish from their homeland, the mission was permanently shuttered.

Today the buildings have been painstakingly restored to their original simple beauty. The chapel's colorful interior reflects the Italian Renaissance and recreates the original colors Ravalli achieved using vermillion clay for the reds, blue from indigo traded among the Native Americans, and yellow from a sacred cave near the Judith River in central Montana. This place has been so lovingly restored that its sacred spirit is palpable; a visit here is time well spent. Mass is said in this historic chapel twice annually, on opening day and the third Sunday in September, in conjunction with the Salish pilgrimage.

Fort Owen State Park

Established in 1850 on the grounds of the original St. Mary's Mission, Fort Owen State Park (0.5 miles east of the intersection of U.S. 93

WESTERN MONTANA

and Hwy. 269, 406/542-5500, free) is a great place for a picnic. The site was a trading post established by Major John Owen, and visitors can wander around the restored rooms of the east barracks, which are appointed with period furnishings. Pets are welcome, and there is a picnic table and a vault toilet. Donations are appreciated.

HAMILTON

The business and trading center of the Bitterroot Valley, Hamilton (population 4,817, elevation 3,572 feet) is a bustling and vibrant little community with a significant historical house, the Marcus Daly Mansion, as well as a museum set in a beautiful old courthouse, an important national research laboratory that arose from government concern over a spotted fever outbreak around the turn of the 20th century, and an abundance of great restaurants and art galleries. If you want to spend more than a day in the area, Hamilton makes an excellent base.

the Marcus Daly Mansion near Hamilton, Montana

Marcus Daly Mansion

Among the original copper kings, Marcus Daly was an Irish immigrant who came to Butte and founded the Anaconda Copper Company, which dominated Montana's economy for more than 50 years. Daly became fabulously wealthy and built a dream life for himself in the Bitterroot Valley, with elaborate horse barns complete with hospitals and Turkish baths for his world-class racehorses, 15,000 acres of farmland that included extensive livestock holdings, and a 24,000-square-foot mansion with more than 25 bedrooms. So many hundreds of people staffed the mansion, the racehorse operation, and the ranching and farming outfits that Daly had to build a town—Hamilton—to accommodate them all.

The home itself was purchased by the Dalys in 1886 and remodeled extensively several times until 1910, when the mansion was transformed into its present Georgian revival style. The mansion (251 Eastside Hwy., Hamilton, 406/363-6004, www.dalymansion.org, tours on the hour 10 A.M.–3 P.M. daily Mother's Day–mid-Oct., holiday tours Nov. 28–Dec. 20, $8 adults, $7 seniors, $5 ages 6–17, free for children under 6) has been impeccably maintained and can be visited only on tours, which include the mansion itself, the laundry house, the greenhouse, the playhouse, the swimming pool, and the tennis courts. Weddings and parties are often held on the magnificently landscaped grounds, known as the **Margaret M. Daly Memorial Arboretum and Botanic Garden.** It is a lovely, quiet place to spend an afternoon imagining the kind of lives that were once lived here.

Ravalli County Museum

The Ravalli Country Museum (205 Bedford St., Hamilton, 406/363-3338, www.brvhsmuseum.org, $3 adults, $6 families, free for children) is housed in the 1900 county courthouse. Operated by the Bitterroot Valley Historical Society, it is dedicated to preserving the cultural heritage of the valley. In addition to their rotating exhibits, the museum's permanent collection focuses on telling the stories of

WESTERN MONTANA

its Native American inhabitants, the Flathead Indians, as well as early white settlers in the area.

DARBY

Once the terminus of the Northern Pacific Railway, Darby is perhaps best known for its place in some of the great logging debates of the 1960s–1980s along with one of the largest pro-logging organized protests in the country in 1988. Referred to as the Great Log Haul, some 300 fully-loaded logging trucks delivered their loads to the Darby Lumber Company on May 13, 1988, to call attention to the plight of the loggers and mill workers who were affected by the big timber companies' flooding of the market, which led to plummeting prices and the subsequent closure of public land to prevent further logging. Much of western Montana and the Bitterroot Valley in particular had relied on logging for nearly a century; layoffs and mill closings had an enormous impact.

ENTERTAINMENT AND EVENTS

There are a number of events throughout the Bitterroot, particularly in summer when the roads can be thick with visitors, including art shows and music festivals; for events listings by community, visit www.visitmt.com.

The **Hamilton Farmers Market** (Bedford St., two blocks south of Main St. between 2nd St. and 3rd St., 406/961-0004, 9 A.M.–12:30 P.M. Sat. early May–early Oct.) offers a bounty of local produce, much of it organic, along with local baked goods, arts and crafts, prepared food, and family entertainment.

The ever-popular **Ravalli County Fair** (406/363-3411) is held in Hamilton over Labor Day weekend.

RECREATION
Fishing

Without a doubt, this valley offers some of the best fishing in the West. The Bitterroot River runs north from Connor, where the East Fork and West Fork (both of which offer great fishable waters) join to form the Bitterroot, up the valley to Missoula, where it flows into the Clark Fork River. In addition to its breathtaking beauty and relatively easy access via close proximity to the road, the Bitterroot River offers diverse waters, with everything from riffles and pools to flats and gravel bars. Rainbow trout are the most plentiful fish, but browns and cutthroats can be found in the upper portion of the river, upstream from Hamilton. The best-known hatch is probably the spring Skwala hatch, which usually starts in March, one of the earliest in the state, and lasts well into April. All fishing during the Skwala hatch is strictly catch-and-release. In late June–early July, after the river has cleared of spring runoff, the big hatches are the Green Drake and Brown Drake hatches, which can last for several weeks. In the fall, September–October, the tiny Trico hatches offers some of the best (and toughest) fishing on the river. In general, the farther you get from Missoula, the fewer the fishers and the better the fishing. Still, there is wonderful wading and floating all along the river.

With so much productive water, it's no surprise that there are plenty of guides in the region. **Western Flies & Guides** (906 S. 1st St., Hamilton, 406/363-9099, www.westernfliesandguides.com, $430 per day for 1–2 anglers) is a good place to start, both for guided fishing and for equipment and flies. Missoula native Tom Jenni of **Tom Jenni's Reel Montana** (406/539-6610 or 866/885-6065, www.tomjenni.com) guides in the area and is an exceptional all-around guide.

Hiking and Biking

With two mountain ranges on either side of the valley, the hiking and biking opportunities in the Bitterroot are endless. The **Stevensville Ranger Station** (88 Main St., Stevensville, 406/777-5461, www.fs.fed.us/r1/bitterroot) and the **Bitterroot National Forest Office** (1801 N. 1st St., Hamilton, 406/363-7100) are great places to get maps and ideas.

It's possible in this valley to hike portions of both the **Lewis and Clark Trail** through the Bitterroot Mountains and the **Nee-Me-**

Poo Trail, the route of the Nez Perce on their fateful 1877 flight from the U.S. Army. The Nee-Me-Poo Trail is at the southern end of the valley near Sula, and the Lewis and Clark Trail is farther north near Lolo Pass.

Among the most popular areas to hike because of its supremely rugged beauty is **Blodgett Canyon,** five miles northwest of Hamilton in the Bitterroot Mountains. The out-and-back hike is spectacular from the get-go with a nice stream and canyon walls. There are several waterfalls along the way, including a beautiful one at 3.6 miles, and the most dedicated can hike a full 12.5 miles to Blodgett Lake, making it a 25-mile trip. The trail is never too steep and there is plenty of wildlife—including moose, deer, and elk—farther into the canyon. To find the trailhead, turn west off U.S. 93 two miles north of Hamilton onto Bowman Road, and follow it for 0.6 miles. Turn left on Richetts Road, follow it for two miles, and then turn west on Forest Road 736 for 2.4 miles to the intersection of Blodgett Canyon Road. Turn right and drive 1.5 miles to the trailhead.

Another wonderful quick hike that offers an excellent overlook of Blodgett Canyon and signs of the great fires of 2000 is the **Blodgett Canyon Overlook.** It is a short three-mile round-trip trail, but it is steep, with 1,100 feet of elevation gain on a switchbacking trail to a heart-stopping overlook. There are benches along the way and an interpretive exhibit on forest-fire ecology. To find the trailhead, follow the directions to the Blodgett Canyon Trailhead above, but at Blodgett Canyon Road, turn left (west) and drive three miles to the trailhead.

The National Forest Service maintains three mountain bike trails in the valley: the 10-mile **Bass Creek Recreation Area Day Use Trail** (Bass Creek Rd., 5 miles northwest of Stevensville); the 17-mile **Hart Bench Mountain Bike Loop** (off Forest Service Rd. 5711) near Darby; and the 19-mile **Railroad Creek Mountain Bike Loop** (Skalkaho-Rye Rd., 16 miles southeast of Hamilton). Road cyclists will be grateful for the paved path between Lolo and Florence that eliminates the need to ride on the highway. Rentals, service, and repairs are available at **Valley Bicycles and Ski** (219 S. 1st St., Hamilton, 406/363-4428). The best resource in town for race-worthy mountain bikes is **Red Barn Bicycles** (399 McCarthy Loop, Hamilton, 406/363-2662, www.redbarnbicycles.com).

Horseback Riding

In addition to numerous guest ranches in the area (listed at www.montanadra.com), guided trail rides are available on an hourly, half-day, and full-day basis from **Wildlife Adventures** (1765 Pleasant View Dr., Victor, 406/642-3262 or 888/642-1010, www.wildlifeadventuresinc.com, $40 one-hour, $85 half-day, $150 full-day), a guest ranch five miles west of Victor that has dozens of horses, including 10 mustangs. Another option in Hamilton is **Lost Horse Creek Lodge** (1000 Lost Horse Rd., Hamilton, 406/363-1460, www.losthorsecreeklodge.com, call for rates), which offers rides along Lost Horse Creek into the 1.6-million-acre Bitterroot National Forest.

Golf

The 18-hole **Hamilton Golf Club** (1004 Golf Course Rd., Hamilton, 406/363-4251, Mar. 1–Oct. 31, $28 for 18 holes, $16 for 9 holes), three miles east of Hamilton, was established in 1924 and is still considered among the best public courses in the Northwest. The mild weather in the valley gives this course more playable days than almost any other in the state. A clubhouse serves three meals daily with incredible mountain views.

Winter Sports

For downhill skiing, head down the valley to **Lost Trail Powder Mountain** (Conner, 406/821-3211, www.losttrail.com, 9:30 A.M.–4 P.M. Thurs.–Sun. Dec.–Apr., extended hours around holidays and in spring, all-day pass $34 adults, $24 ages 6–12, free for children under 6), which sits high atop the Continental Divide and straddles the Idaho-

Montana border. It is a great small-town Montana family-friendly mountain with fantastic terrain and more than 300 inches of snow annually. There are one-ride passes and discounts for afternoon-only and morning-only skiing as well as discounts for seniors and almost-seniors.

Cross-country skiers will be in heaven in the Bitterroot with places like **Chief Joseph Cross Country Ski Trail** (Hwy. 43, 40 miles south of Hamilton, 406/689-3243), which offers 15 miles of groomed trails for every level of ability. Groomed by the Bitterroot Cross Country Ski Club (www.bitterrootxcskiclub.net), the trails and warming hut are open December–mid-April or as the snow permits.

At the end of a long winter's day, why not soak in the warm waters at **Lost Trail Hot Springs** (8321 U.S. 93 S., 406/821-3574, www.losttrailhotsprings.com, $7 adults, $6 seniors, $5 children 2–12, $2 children under 2) in Sula, not far from either ski area. The rustic resort offers a marvelous hot pool in any weather as well as lodging, food, and plenty of history.

ACCOMMODATIONS

The greatest number of hotels can be found in the valley's largest town, Hamilton, but the valley overall offers a handsome range of accommodations, from the ultraluxe adults-only **Triple Creek Ranch** (5551 West Fork Rd., near Darby, 406/821-4600, www.triplecreekranch.com, $650–2,595 d all-inclusive) to the budget-friendly and pet-friendly **City Center Motel & Annex** (415 W. Main St., Hamilton, 406/363-1651, www.remlcsportsmanslodging.com, $48–70), which has standard rooms with microwaves and mini-refrigerators or full kitchenettes.

A historic property that is long on charm is the **Stevensville Hotel** (107 E. 3rd St., Stevensville, 406/777-3087 or 888/816-2875, www.stevensvillehotel.com, $75–135), housed in the 1910 Thornton Hospital building. In bed-and-breakfast tradition, the rooms are individually decorated with period furnishings, and the continental breakfast is delicious. Dogs are welcome in two of the rooms for an additional fee.

For vacation rentals throughout the valley that range from cozy remote cabins to condos and farmhouses, try **Cardinal Properties** (320 S. 2nd St., Hamilton, 406/363-4430, www.cardinalproperties.net).

CAMPING

The camping options in the valley are almost unlimited, with dozens of Forest Service campgrounds in both national forests. A good place to start is on the U.S. Forest Service website for camping in the area, www.fs.fed.us/r1/bitterroot/recreation/campground/campground_listing.shtml.

A pair of really beautiful campgrounds are the **Upper and Lower Lake Como Campgrounds** (County Rd. 82, 4 miles north of Darby, 406/363-7100, early June–early Sept., $8–14), which have 11 tent sites each and well over 100 RV sites between them.

The **Bitterroot Family Campground** (1744 U.S. 93 S., 866/363-2430, www.bitterrootfamilycampground.com, year-round, $12 tents, $24 RVs, $40 cabins) is a pleasant and budget-friendly private campground eight miles south of Hamilton.

FOOD

It is possible to get the impression that Bitterroot Valley residents live on a liquid diet of coffee and beer, as there is plenty of both to be had. But with its comparatively milder climate and abundance of local produce, the valley also boasts some excellent restaurants.

In Hamilton, **Bitter Root Brewery** (101 Marcus St., Hamilton, 406/363-PINT— 406/363-7468, www.bitterrootbrewing.com, 11:30 A.M.–8 P.M. Mon.–Sat., 2–6 P.M. Sun., entrées $7–12.50) offers great local beer, brewed on-site, along with some delicious Mexican-inspired grub and pub food. For eclectic ethnic food, Hamilton's **Spice of Life** (163 S. 2nd St., Hamilton, 406/363-4433, www.thespiceinhamilton.com, lunch 11 A.M.–2 P.M. Mon.–Fri., dinner 5–9 P.M. Tues.–Sun. summer, 5–9 P.M. Wed.–Sun.

winter) has lunch ($6.75–11.50) and dinner ($10–25) and serves a compelling assortment of dishes, as suggested by the giant neon chili pepper outside. Don't miss the daily specials, and both kids and their parents will be happy with the children's menu. For fresh baked goods in Hamilton, you can't go wrong at **Coffee Cup Cafe** (500 S. 1st St., Hamilton, 406/363-3822, 6 A.M.–10 P.M. daily, $4.25–20), which serves breads, cakes, muffins, soups, and more made from scratch daily.

In Florence, **Glen's Café** (157 Long Ave., Florence, 406/273-2534, 9 A.M.–3 P.M. daily year-round), is a wonderful old log cabin that serves up hearty meals, homemade pies, and local art in equally delicious amounts.

For a gourmet splurge, the restaurant at Darby's **Triple Creek Ranch** (5551 West Fork Rd., Darby, 406/821-4231, www. triplecreekranch.com, by reservation only, breakfast $18, lunch $28, dinner $95, includes 4 courses and house wine, fixed-price menu only) is open daily and serves phenomenal contemporary and internationally inspired cuisine with local products and delicacies from around the world.

INFORMATION AND SERVICES

The **Bitterroot Valley Chamber of Commerce** (105 E. Main St., Hamilton, 9 A.M.–5 P.M. Mon.–Fri. year-round, extended hours in summer) is located in Hamilton.

GETTING THERE AND GETTING AROUND

The best way to visit the valley is by car. There are no major bus lines serving the area, and the closest international airport is **Missoula International Airport** (MSO, 5225 U.S. 10 W., 406/728-4381, www.flymissoula.com), which is served by Alaska/Horizon, Allegiant, Delta, and United. **Alamo, Avis, Budget, Enterprise,** and **Hertz** have rental-car offices on the first floor of the terminal.

U.S. 93 runs directly through the valley and can often be congested. To get a beautiful view of the Bitterroot Mountains and a sense of this historic part of Montana, take the scenic Highway 269, which will lead you to Stevensville. From Missoula, Lolo is nine miles, Hamilton is 50 miles, and Darby is 64 miles.

The Flathead and Mission Valleys

Home to the largest freshwater lake in the Western United States, a mountain range that will take your breath away, and the wide open space of the National Bison Range, this part of Montana truly is God's country. Between the wildlife refuges and the 1.3-million-acre Flathead Indian Reservation, the area is of great significance, historically and today. Time spent in these valleys is often quiet and contemplative; there are many opportunities to learn. Flathead Lake has created a culture all its own in towns like Polson and Bigfork. There are endless recreational opportunities as well, including hiking, boating, and soaking in hot springs. On the way to Glacier, these valleys and their small but vibrant communities should not be overlooked.

ST. IGNATIUS

The oldest town on the Flathead Reservation, and among the oldest settlements in the state, St. Ignatius (population 813, elevation 2,939 feet) is the site of the St. Ignatius Mission, built in 1854 by Jesuit priest Adrian Hoecken, who moved from Washington State to be closer to the indigenous people he wanted to reach. The town grew quickly as nearly 1,000 Native Americans moved to be close to the mission, and in 1864 a group of nuns added schools and a hospital to the settlement.

The building considered to be the oldest in the state, built in 1846, is located at Fort Connah, just six miles north of St. Ignatius on U.S. 93. It is all that remains of the last trading post built in the United States by the

WESTERN MONTANA

PRESERVING THE AMERICAN BISON

Before Lewis and Clark set foot in the West, more than 50 million bison roamed the Great Plains and most of North America, from southern Canada into northern Mexico. Early settlers on the plains recorded seeing herds so large that it took a full day for the animals to pass by. Lewis and Clark came across herds that covered entire plains and valleys. By 1900, however, it was believed that less than 100 wild bison existed in the United States.

Indispensable to the Native American way of life, the bison provided Indians with everything they needed — food, clothing, shelter, weapons, and utensils. The eradication of the bison devastated their way of life, making it easier to force them to relocate onto reservations. In addition, the animal's disappearance freed up land for cattle to graze, for railroads to be built, and for pioneers to settle. The 1820-1880 period is known as "the Great Slaughter," when bison were hunted for their meat, hides, or just for sport. Their massive carcasses were often left to rot on the open plains.

At the turn of the 20th century, a few ranchers chose to maintain small private herds of bison. In the 1870s a Pend d'Oreille Indian returning from the plains brought six orphaned bison calves to Michel Pablo and Charles Allard, a pair of ranchers in the Mission Valley of western Montana. By the end of the century these animals had produced the Allard-Pablo herd, one of the largest private herds in the country.

Outraged at the massive slaughter of these majestic animals and convinced of their near extinction, conservationist William T. Hornaday, with the support of fellow conservationist President Theodore Roosevelt, founded the American Bison Society in 1905. Their first priority was to convince Congress to purchase suitable land on which to sustain and preserve bison herds. When the Dawes Act was applied to the Flathead Reservation in 1904, it required that the reservation be divided into individual allotments, one for each family in the tribe. Any remaining land was to be sold to non-Indians six years later. In 1908, before the land was to be made available for sale to the public, the government bought land from the Flathead Nation along with five individual allotments. That same year, the National Bison Range was established, marking the first time a refuge had been created to preserve a single species in Montana.

Once the land was designated, the American Bison Society was responsible for acquiring the bison that would be assigned to the range. They solicited donations through letter-writing campaigns, newspaper ads, and neighborhood women's groups. Many of the donations came from individuals in the amount of $1-5. By year's end, they had raised the equivalent of almost $250,000 in today's dollars. The majority of the first 40 bison to enter the range came from the private herd of Charles Conrad in Kalispell. These bison were direct descendants of the original bison brought to the Mission Valley 20 years earlier. The first bison arrived on the range in 1909, and 11 calves were born by the spring of 1910. Since then, only 12 new bison have been introduced into the herd of the National Bison Range. Between 1910 and 1922, white-tailed and mule deer, antelope, and elk were also donated to the range in small numbers. The last animals to be added to the refuge were mountain goats, donated in 1964. Each new species brought its own needs and challenges, and their adaptation to the range had to be properly overseen by park management. Offspring from animals on the range have been used to replenish herds in other refuges across the nation.

Today there are 350-450 bison on the range with 50-90 bison removed each year. This protects the genetic integrity of the bison and ensures the land can support all of its inhabitants. The bison that are removed are either sold or donated to other refuges or private herds. The range also donates bison to the Flathead tribal government to support bison restoration on Native American land.

Hudson's Bay Company. The post was in operation until 1871.

◖ The St. Ignatius Mission

The beloved redbrick chapel standing today on the St. Ignatius Mission (300 Bear Track Ave., 406/745-2768, 9 A.M.–7 P.M. daily summer, 9 A.M.–5 P.M. daily winter, mass 9:15 A.M. Sun., free, donations accepted) was built in the 1890s, but the mission itself was settled as early as 1854 by Jesuit priest Adrian Hoecken and hundreds of Native Americans who set up camp near him. In 1864, a group of nuns from Montreal, the Sisters of Providence, came to the mission to open a boarding school for girls, a hospital, and eventually, with the help of Ursuline nuns, an orphanage, a kindergarten, and a school for boys. At its peak in the mid-1890s, some 320 children attended school at the mission. Sadly, the schools were burned down by one of the students, and when the federal government ceased federal aid, they were unable to be rebuilt, and shut down altogether.

The handsome brick chapel was completed in 1894 with 58 original murals painted by Joseph Carignano, who worked in the kitchen and as a handyman for the mission. Carignano taught himself to paint and managed to complete the frescoes in only 14 months despite working on them only when he wasn't doing his primary job. The paintings tell the life story of St. Ignatius Loyola and have been well preserved.

In addition to the chapel, there is a small museum and gift shop located in the log house that was the original residence of the Sisters of Providence.

The National Bison Range

Established in 1908, the National Bison Range (58355 Bison Range Rd., 406/644-2211, www.fws.gov/bisonrange/nbr, hours vary by season, year-round, $5 per vehicle May–Oct.) is one of the oldest animal refuges in the country and well worth a visit. Located off Highway 212 in Moiese, the refuge comprises 18,500 acres and is home to around 400 bison, not to mention

white-tailed and mule deer, bighorn sheep, pronghorn antelope, and elk.

There are two driving routes: One is a short five-mile tour that takes about 30 minutes, and the other is a 19-mile loop that climbs about 2,000 feet and takes close to two hours. The longer route, open in summer, is incredibly scenic and definitely worth the time. The roads through the refuge are gravel; no bicycles or motorcycles are permitted on them, but parking is available at the visitors center. Before beginning your tour, be sure to stop in at the visitors center for informative displays, knowledgeable park rangers, and a large relief map of the refuge marked with small lights indicating where bison can likely be seen that day.

RONAN

Named for the first Indian agent, Major Peter Ronan, who wrote the history of the Flathead people and was respected by them, the town of Ronan (population 2,008, elevation 3,047 feet) was once part of the Flathead Reservation before it was opened to sale and settlement in 1910.

Ronan's history is marked by tragedy and travesty. In 1912 a fire erupted in an automobile garage on a particularly windy afternoon. Within hours, the entire town lay in ruins. In June 1929 a robbery at the Ronan State Bank made a group of seven 20-something robbers $3,000 richer. They went on a spree of robberies across the state with police always a few steps behind. Eventually all but the ringleader were caught and either killed during the pursuit or sent to prison. A woman who accompanied them, known dramatically as "the woman in white," was eventually found murdered in a Helena brothel.

Today Ronan is known for its proximity to some of the state's most beautiful wildlife refuges, the Ninepipe National Wildlife Refuge and, farther south, the National Bison Range.

Ninepipe National Wildlife Refuge

Located just north of the Bison Range on land of the Confederated Salish and Kootenai

© DONNIE SEXTON

Mission Mountains near Ninepipe National Wildlife Refuge

Tribe, the Ninepipe National Wildlife Refuge is a waterfowl preserve. Established in 1921, these wetlands are at the base of the Mission Mountains and situated around a large reservoir. The marshlands are difficult to walk through, but good bird-watching is possible from the road that runs along the reservoir. The refuge is situated on a popular migratory path for numerous birds, including mallards, gadwalls, great blue herons, and swans. It has become an important breeding and resting area for the Flathead Valley Canada goose population. The refuge is closed during waterfowl hunting season (fall) and the nesting season (spring).

Ninepipes Museum of Early Montana

The Ninepipes Museum of Early Montana (40962 U.S. 93, 406/644-3455, www.ninepipes.org, $5 adults, $2.50 children) is located halfway between Missoula and Kalispell next to the waterfowl refuge. It documents daily life on the Flathead Reservation over the last 100 years. In addition to Native American life, the history of early trappers, miners, loggers, and ranchers is also on display. There are photos, artworks, costumes, and artifacts from people in these different walks of life. Recently the museum has had trouble obtaining the funding it needs to continue operating; call ahead to make sure it is open.

HOT SPRINGS

At the western edge of the reservation, in the shadow of Baldy Mountain, Hot Springs (population 564, elevation 2,829 feet) is a town whose main attraction is evident from its name. Known as the Little Bitterroot, the region is home to numerous natural hot springs and mud pots that for centuries have been thought to possess healing powers. Native Americans camped in the area to make use of the "big medicine." When the area opened to white settlers in 1910, the springs became increasingly commercial and were advertised around the West. The local newspaper's slogan, printed beneath the masthead, read, "Limp In.... Hop

Out!" The original bathhouse closed in 1985, but if hot mineral water is your thing, there are a number of modern versions worth soaking in.

Wild Horse Hot Springs (175 Camp Aqua Rd., 406/741-3777, 11 A.M.–8 P.M. daily, soaking rooms $5 per hour) offers natural artesian water that can reach 110°F but can be controlled by bathers in individual soaking rooms. Because the rooms are private, skinny-dipping is an option.

The largest and most developed of the local hot springs, **Symes Hot Springs Hotel & Mineral Baths** (209 Wall St., 888/305-3106, www.symeshotsprings.com, 8 A.M.–11 P.M. daily year-round, $7 per day for nonguests, rooms $49–125) was built in 1929 as a grand Mission-style hotel. In addition to the mineral pools outside, spa treatments are offered in private pools. The guest rooms are modest and quaint.

Camas Hot Springs (north end of Spring St. by the abandoned Camas Bathhouse, free) is run by the tribe and offers two outdoor pools and a very laid-back atmosphere. In the distance the original bathhouse has long been shuttered. The water in the pools stays at about 104°F. For information, contact the **Hot Springs Chamber of Commerce** (406/741-2662).

Developed in the 1930s, **Alameda's Hot Springs Retreat** (308 N. Spring St., 406/741-2283, www.alamedashotsprings.com, $50–90) is part motel, part spa with in-room soaking tubs filled with natural hot spring water. The retreat is popular for health-related gatherings and workshops.

POLSON

Polson feels like the kind of town where there is almost always a fair going on or some other reason to celebrate. Historically the economy has been based on lumber, steamboat trade, and ranching. Founded around a trading post at the southern end of Flathead Lake in 1880, the town was named for David Polson, a local rancher who married a Nez Perce woman and who played the fiddle at dances and powwows across the region. White settlement from 1910 greatly increased the size of the town, and when much of the state was losing population during the Great Depression, Polson actually doubled in size with farmers, who came to try their luck with the Flathead Irrigation Project, and people seeking work at the Kerr Dam construction project.

Today Polson (population 5,228, elevation 2,931 feet) is a lakeside town, the heart of Montana's cherry growing district and the busiest town along Flathead Lake. Its proximity to the magnificent lake, the Flathead River, and the Mission Mountains makes Polson a natural playground.

Miracle of America Museum

An eclectic little museum, to say the least, the Miracle of America Museum (36094 Memory Lane, 406/883-6804, www.miracleofamericamuseum.org, 8 A.M.–8 P.M. daily summer, 8 A.M.–5 P.M. Mon.–Sat., 1:30–5 P.M. Sun. winter, $5 adults, $2 children ages 3–12) likes to think of itself as the "Smithsonian of the West." Indeed, the founders were passionate collectors of Western artifacts, and the inspired museum is packed to the rafters with more than 100,000 objects that include moonshine stills, antique motorcycles, entire buildings, and military paraphernalia.

BIGFORK

Arguably the most beautiful of the lakeside hamlets, year-round resort town Bigfork (population 1,650, elevation 2,968 feet) was named for its location along the fork of the Swan River. At the northeast corner of Flathead Lake, Bigfork has unlimited outdoor recreation opportunities, a handsome offering of live theater, art, fine dining, boutique shopping, and elegant accommodations. The feeling here is of an East Coast beach village 50 years ago—small, quaint and lovely.

ENTERTAINMENT AND EVENTS

One of the most important events on the Flathead Reservation is the annual **Fourth of July Powwow** (888/835-8766, www.ckst.org)

WESTERN MONTANA

at **Arlee.** The celebration has played out each year for more than a century with camping, competition dancing, drumming and singing, traditional games, and a host of food and arts and crafts vendors. The **People's Center Annual Powwow** (53253 U.S. 93, Pablo, 406/883-5344 or 800/883-5344, www.peoplescenter.net) is held the third Saturday in August in nearby **Pablo.**

In **Polson,** the **Polson Farmers Market** (3rd Ave. W., 406/883-3595, 9 A.M.–1 P.M. Fri. May–mid-Oct.) features local produce, crafts, jewelry, photography, handmade soaps, and more. The **Mission Mountain PRCA Rodeo** (320 Regatta Rd., Polson, 406/883-1100, www.polsonfairgroundsinc.com) is generally held in late June; the professional rodeo action and small-town fun always ensures a big crowd. The biggest event of the year in Polson is probably the **Polson Main Street Flathead Cherry Festival** (Main St., Polson, 406/883-5800). It has a fair-like environment and celebrates everything cherry, including pie-eating contests, seed-spitting contests, exhibitions, and entertainment throughout the weekend. The event is typically held the third weekend in July, and it is among the best ways to enjoy the phenomenal cherry harvest.

The repertory theater at **Bigfork Summer Playhouse** (526 Electric Ave., Bigfork, 406/837-4886, www.bigforksummerplayhouse.com, performances 8 P.M. Mon.–Sat. plus occasional matinees 2 P.M. Sun., mid-May–Labor Day, $20–26 adults, $15 children) is a standout in the Northwest. For more than 50 years the company has been staging award-winning productions of musical classics like *Fiddler on the Roof, Dirty Rotten Scoundrels,* and *Sugar Babies.* The contemporary theater is quite comfortable and roomy with 400 seats and air-conditioning. Also running all summer in Bigfork is the **Riverbend Concert Series** (Everit Slider Park, downtown Bigfork, 406/837-5888, 6 P.M. Sun. mid-June–mid-Aug., $3), held every Sunday. The bring-your-own-seating concerts range from jazz to big band and light opera. Held annually the first weekend in August, Bigfork's **Festival of the Arts** (406/881-4636, www.

bigforkfestivalofthearts.com) has been attracting visitors and artists alike for more than 30 years with more than 150 booths, food, and entertainment.

RECREATION

The thing about the beauty in this part of the state is that it's all very user-friendly. The mountains can be climbed, the rivers fished, the lake swum. And although public land is harder to find, especially along Flathead Lake, there are still plenty of marvelous places to hike.

Boating

Polson offers rafting opportunities on the warm, clear lower Flathead River. The only outfitter on the river, **Flathead Raft Company** (50362 U.S. 93 N., 406/883-5838 or 800/654-4359, www.flatheadraftco.com, half-day river trips $45 adults, $35 children 8–12), offers great scenic and white-water trips as well as white-water kayak instruction or sea-kayaking trips on Flathead Lake.

There are a couple of outfits that rent boats in Polson, including **Absolute Watersports Rentals** (49708 U.S. 93 N., Polson, 406/883-3900) and the **Flathead Boat Company** (875 Bayview Dr., Polson, 406/883-0999).

In Bigfork, you can rent ski boats, Jet Skis, and pontoon boats from **Bigfork Water Sports** (451 Electric Ave., Polson, docks at 119 Holt Dr., Polson, 406/249-3732, www.bigforkwatersports.com). At **Marina Cay Resort** (180 Vista Lane, Polson, 406/837-5861, www.marinacay.com) you can also rent a variety of watercraft, including fishing charters. For more information on a variety of cruises, sailing tours, charters, and other rentals, contact the **Flathead Lakers** (406/883-1346, www.flatheadlakers.org).

◖ Hiking at Jewel Basin

One of the best and most unique places in the state to hike is the Jewel Basin (Forest Rd. 5392, 10 miles northeast of Bigfork, 406/387-3800, www.fs.fed.us/r1/flathead), a wilderness area with high peaks, lush forests, and plenty of lakes. Camping is permitted, and the trails can

© DONNIE SEXTON

a sailboat on Flathead Lake

be crowded on weekends. Some of the best day hikes include those into **Black Lake** (8 miles round-trip), the **Jewel Lakes** (9 miles round-trip), or the **Twin Lakes** (5 miles round-trip). The best map for the area is published by the **Glacier National History Association** (406/888-5756, www.glacierassociation.org). Note that grizzlies frequent the area, particularly in late summer when the huckleberries are ripe.

Golf

With so many resorts, there are a number of golf courses in the area. The **Polson Bay Golf Club** (111 Bayview Dr., Polson, 406/883-8230, www.polsonbaygolf.com, $30–45 for 18 holes) has two courses with a total of 27 holes. In Bigfork, golfers can hit the links at the renowned 27-hole **Eagle Bend Golf Course** (279 Eagle Bend Dr., Bigfork, 406/837-7310, www.golfmt.com, $32–62 for 18 holes).

SHOPPING

In St. Ignatius, the **Four Winds Indian Trading Post** (U.S. 93, 3 miles north of St. Ignatius,

406/745-4336, 10 A.M.–6 P.M. daily summer, 12–5 P.M. daily winter) is the oldest operating Indian trading post in the state. Opened in 1870, the Fours Winds has long supplied local Native Americans with a variety of wares, including beads, face paint, animal hides, and dance bells. The store is authentic and sells traditional Native American crafts alongside history books and made-in-Montana products. Another wonderful little shop in St. Ignatius is the **Bitterroot Fiber Arts Studio** (55563 Kerns Rd., St. Ignatius, 406/210-5020, www.bitterrootranch.net, by appointment). Proprietor Judy Colvin uses wool from the sheep raised on their ranch to make wonderful felted items that include gorgeous purses, scarves, wraps, and wall hangings. She also teaches workshops and private lessons in felting with wool.

A good place to stop in Polson for some warm Montana bedding is **Three Dog Down** (48841 U.S. 93, 800/364-3696, www.threedogdown.com, 9 A.M.–6 P.M. daily year-round), known in the region for custom-made comforters and

WESTERN MONTANA

pillows. Shopping here is a Montana experience, and bargain hunters should know that singing the *Star Spangled Banner* will earn you a discount.

In Bigfork, art is the thing, so be sure to stop in at a few galleries during your visit. Several artists have their own galleries in town to represent their work exclusively. Other galleries include the avant-garde **Sacred Dancing Gallery** (573 Electric Ave., Bigfork, 406/837-7273, www.sacreddancinggallery.com, 10 A.M.–8 P.M. daily mid-June–Oct., shorter hours May–mid-June), which represents more than 50 renowned contemporary and representational artists including Tom Gilleon, Robert Duerloo, and Karen Bezuidenhout, among others. **The Midnight Sun Gallery** (439 Grand Ave., Suite 332, Bigfork, 406/471-7261, www.midnightsungallery.com, 11 A.M.–5 P.M. Tues.–Sat.) offers original fine art plus jewelry, ceramics, glass, and wood items.

🍒 Cherry Picking

Picking fresh, sweet Flathead cherries, or just eating them, is an idyllic way to spend an afternoon. There are several orchards along the east side of the lake between Polson and Bigfork, so don't be shy about stopping at roadside stands to do a little taste-testing; in this valley, you can't go wrong. The primary harvest is late July–mid-August. Try **Bigfork Orchards** (9392 E. Shore Rd./Hwy. 35, 3 miles south of Bigfork, 406/837-4633) or **Bowman Orchards** (19944 E. Shore Rd./Hwy. 35, 10 miles south of Bigfork, 406/982-3246, www.bowmancherries.com), a family-owned business since 1921 that grows a variety of cherries and sells both the fresh fruit and a number of delicious cherry products.

ACCOMMODATIONS

There are a handful of places to stay in St. Ignatius, including the no-frills **Sunset Motel** (32670 U.S. 93, St. Ignatius, 406/745-3900, www.stignatiussunsetmotel.com, $64–75). The **Bear Spirit Lodge B&B** (38712 St. Mary's Lake Rd., St. Ignatius, 406/745-3089, www.bearspiritlodge.com, rooms $100–115,

Flathead cherries

© DONNIE SEXTON

tipis $75) is a cozy place in a phenomenal setting, and the hosts, Ann and Great Bear, are beyond compare.

There are plenty of choices for lodging in Polson and Bigfork, but a room with a view in these parts can get pretty expensive. Among the best bargains in town is the **Hawthorne House Inn** (304 3rd Ave. E., Polson, 800/290-1345, www.hawthornehouseinn.com, $50–90, plus $5 for full breakfast), a Tudor-style home right in town with views of the Mission Mountains and Flathead Lake. Every nook and cranny is decorated with antiques and family heirlooms, but the four guest rooms are quite comfortable, and the rate for a room with a shared bath ($50) is unmatched in town. The waterfront **Best Western KwaTaqNuk Resort** (49708 U.S. 93 E., Polson, 406/883-3636 or 800/528-1234, www.kwataqnuk.com, $90–160), which is owned and operated by the Flathead Nation, has 112 guest rooms and an extensive menu of activities that include lake cruises, boat rentals, fishing tours, and plenty of gaming at the on-site casino. Pets are permitted for a $25-per-night fee.

Luxuriousness and prices rise as you get closer to Bigfork. Depending on the size of your group, a vacation rental can be the most economical choice. Among several vacation rental companies in town are **Montana's Best Vacation Homes** (7573 Hwy. 35, Bigfork, 888/837-6424, www.montanasbest-vacationhomes.com, from $967 weekly) and **Clearwater Montana Vacations** (459 Electric Ave., Suite J, Bigfork, 866/330-5999, www. clearwatermontanavacations.com, from $349), which offer everything from lakeside studios to cabins in the woods and lakefront lodges.

The **Mountain Lake Lodge** (14735 Sylvan Dr., Bigfork, 406/837-3800 or 877/823-4923, www.mountainlakelodge.com, $125–285) is elegant and cozy with great vistas of the lake and plenty of amenities, including an outdoor infinity pool, a hot tub, a putting green, and a fire pit along with two restaurants on-site. Pets are welcome for $15 per day per pet. Right in town, the **Grand Bigfork Hotel** (425 Grand Ave., Suite 3, Bigfork, 406/837-7377, www.

grandhotelbigfork.com, $69–149, discounts for multiple-night stays) offers nice rooms and easy walking to the lake and the town's shops and restaurants.

CAMPING

If you can get a tent site, camping is one of the best ways to stay as close to Flathead Lake as possible and truly enjoy the region. Among the most popular are **Wayfarers State Park** (Hwy. 35, 0.5 miles south of Bigfork, 406/837-4196, www.fwp.mt.gov/parks, May 1–Sept. 30, $15 tents or RVs), **Finley Point State Park** (Hwy. 35, 11 miles north of Polson, then 4 miles west on County Rd., 406/887-2715, www.fwp.mt.gov/parks, May 1–Sept. 30, $15 tents or RVs), and **Yellow Bay State Park** (Hwy. 35, 15 miles north of Polson at mile marker 17, 406/982-3034, May 1–Sept. 30, $15 tents or RVs).

FOOD

If you cannot survive on cherries alone, there are a number of gourmet restaurants concentrated around Bigfork. Located in the riverside Coyote Riverhouse Inn & Cabins ($125–175), the **Coyote Roadhouse Restaurant** (602 Three Eagle Lane/Hwy. 209, Bigfork, between Bigfork and Ferndale, 406/837-4250 or 406/837-1233, www.coyoteroadhouse. com, seatings 6–9 P.M. Wed.–Sun. mid-June–mid-Sept., dinner $30–60) is a highly acclaimed restaurant with several awards to its credit and a *Mobil Guide* three-star rating. The menu changes nightly and offers a creative and mouthwatering selection of Cajun, Southwestern, Mayan, and Tuscan-inspired specialties. Reservations are required. For breakfast and lunch, the hands-down favorite in the Flathead Valley is the **Echo Lake Café** (1195 Hwy. 83, Bigfork, 406/837-4252 or 406/837-1000, www.echolakecafe.com, 6:30 A.M.–2:30 P.M. daily, entrées $7–10), where everything is homemade and fabulous. Be prepared to wait in line with locals for a table.

In Polson, **Isabel's Fastest Gourmet in the West** (203 U.S. 93, Polson, 406/883-0987,

7 A.M.–3 P.M. daily May–Sept., entrées $3–9) is another wonderful local gem where everything—soups, breads, pastries, and pies—is made from scratch. For a great beer, try **Glacier Brewing Company** (6 10th Ave. E.,

Polson, 406/883-2595, www.glacierbrewing. com, noon–6 P.M. Mon.–Wed., noon–8 P.M. Thurs.–Sat.), a German-style ale house serving their own impressive line of beer, homemade soda, and oddly enough, pizza.

The Seeley-Swan Valley

Much quieter than Flathead, and nestled in between the magnificent Mission and Swan Mountain Ranges, the Swan Valley is a remarkable destination. Visitors feel like they are stepping back in time 50 years or more. There are unlikely to be any towns you've ever heard of in this valley, or chain hotels, fast food restaurants, and interstate highways. Instead, there are pristine lakes and seemingly endless forests, wonderful old lodges, and handsome guest ranches. This is a place to spend lazy lakeside days and cozy fireside evenings, and if lazy isn't your style, there are mountains in every direction for hiking as well as rivers and lakes for boating and fishing. For those who want to venture into the **Bob Marshall Wilderness Area,** this valley is an excellent launching point. If you don't have time to stop and stay awhile, at least plan to drive this route from the Flathead and places north to Missoula, Helena, or Bozeman. In fact, the 91-mile stretch of Highway 83 through the Seeley-Swan Valley is the shortest route between Yellowstone and Glacier. The scenery and solitude make the trip worthwhile.

SEELEY LAKE

Seeley Lake (population 1,577, elevation 4,028 feet) is clearly a recreation town, and the lake itself is among the chain of lakes through which the Clearwater River flows. A resort town in the most classic sense—think rustic lodges and lakeside retreats, cabins dotting the forest—Seeley Lake is popular but relatively uncrowded. There are plenty of fish in the lake, including bass, kokanee salmon, bull trout, perch, and bluegills, in addition to year-round

activities that include boating, hiking, excellent cross-country skiing, and snowmobiling.

Boating

The **Clearwater Canoe Trail** is a 3.5-mile stretch of flat water that takes paddlers down the Clearwater River from north of the town of Seeley Lake into the lake itself. A variety of birds and other wildlife is often seen along the way. A roughly one-mile hiking trail alongside the river leads paddlers back to the trailhead parking lot. Canoes and other sporting equipment, including WaveRunners and ski boats, can be rented from **Seeley Sport Rentals** (3112 Hwy. 83 S., 406/677-3680, www.seeleysportrentals.com, canoe $25 for 4 hours, ski boats $200 for 4 hours).

Hiking and Biking

Among the most popular hiking trails in the region is the **Morrell Lake and Falls,** a five-mile round-trip hike on relatively even terrain to a beautiful mountain lake and a series of towering cascades, the largest of which is 90 feet high. From Seeley Lake, drive north less than 0.5 miles to Morrell Creek Road (also known as Cottonwood Lakes Rd. or Forest Service Rd. 477). Turn right (east), drive 1.1 mile to the junction of West Morrell Road, and turn left. Drive 5.6 miles to another junction, and turn right. Drive 0.7 miles to the trailhead. The trail is well-marked; the trail follows the creek to a pond, Morrell Lake, and then the falls.

Mountain biking is permitted on a variety of Forest Service roads and trails, including a 14-mile round-trip ride at the **Seeley Creek Nordic Ski Trails.** From Highway 83, turn east on Morrell Creek Road (also known as

Cottonwood Lakes Rd. or Forest Service Rd. 477), and drive 1.1 miles to the trailhead on the north side of the road. Bikes can be rented from **Seeley Sport Rentals** (3112 Hwy. 83 S., 406/677-3680, www.seeleysportrentals.com, mountain bikes $10 for 4 hours). For more information on Forest Service trails, contact the **Seeley Lake Ranger District** (3583 Hwy. 83, 406/677-2233, www.fs.fed.us/r1/lolo).

Winter Sports

Seeley Lake is a cross-country skier's paradise. Several of the local resorts, including the Double Arrows Lodge, offer groomed ski trails. The cream of the crop in this region is the **Seeley Creek Nordic Ski Trails.** This trail system has been under development since the 1970s, initially created from old logging camps and logging roads. With 20 miles of groomed classic and skate trails that can be combined to form some impressive routes, the area offers something for every ability level, and an annual 50-kilometer race is held the last Saturday in January. From Highway 83, turn east on Morrell Creek Road (also known as Cottonwood Lakes Rd. or Forest Service Rd. 477), and drive for 1.1 miles to the trailhead on the north side of the road. Nearby are dog-sled and snowmobile trails.

For backcountry skiers who want plenty of adventure with a side of luxury, **Yurtski** (406/721-1779, www.yurtski.com) offers a wide range of services. From their extraordinary guided trips for newer skiers to gourmet catered trips, self-service trips, or just shuttling gear, Carl and his team make use of their awesome backcountry yurts, local knowledge, and mad culinary skills.

Around Seeley Lake are more than 350 miles of snowmobile trails. For information on specific trails and snowmobile-specific maps, contact the **Lolo National Forest** (3583 Hwy. 83, 406/677-2233, www.fs.fed.us/r1/lolo). A variety of snowmobiles and guided tours are available at **Seeley Sport Rentals** (3112 Hwy. 83 S., 406/677-3680, www.seeleysportrentals. com), which has half-day snowmobile rentals from $120, and half-day guides from $100.

CONDON

Just 27 miles up Highway 83 from Seeley Lake is tiny Condon (population 576, elevation 3,220 feet), another gem in the string of lake towns between the Mission and Swan Ranges. Condon is surrounded by the **Mission Mountains Wilderness Area** to the west and the **Bob Marshall Wilderness Area** to the east, making the region a favorite for outdoor recreation. Holland Lake is a gorgeous 400-acre lake with prime opportunities for fishing and boating.

Recreation

The stunning **Holland Lake** is the main attraction in the town and offers plenty of recreational opportunities, including boating, fishing, and swimming. The relatively easy and well-traveled **Holland Falls Trail** leads hikers on a three-mile round-trip hike to a waterfall. From the trailhead on Holland Lake Road just beyond the Holland Lake Campground, the trail skirts the north shore of the lake and climbs roughly 600 feet before reaching the 40-foot falls. There are natural seating areas for picnickers and waterfall gazers. The trail is often used by outfitters packing into Upper Holland Lake and the Bob Marshall Wilderness Area.

SWAN LAKE

An hour's drive north of Seeley Lake and 16 miles south of Bigfork is the quaint little village of Swan Lake (population 1,577, elevation 4,028 feet), on Highway 83 at the southern end of the lake. The area is a natural stopping point for migrating birds, making the Swan River Wildlife Refuge a wonderful place for avid birders. The lake itself offers excellent fishing for northern pike, kokanee salmon, and rainbow trout. There are a few services in town, including lodging and dining options, but most people come to Swan Lake for recreation. There are 50 miles of trails for cross-country skiers and many options for hiking.

Recreation

From Swan Lake, there are numerous lengthy

trails to get hikers and horseback riders into the Bob Marshall Wilderness Area. The **Upper Holland Loop,** from the trailhead at Holland Lake Lodge on the north shore of the lake, is a steep and rugged trail that climbs nearly 4,000 feet over seven miles (13.3 miles round-trip), which can be tackled on a well-planned full-day hike. The trail passes the Sapphire Lakes and Upper Holland Lake before descending again down along Holland Creek. For maps and information, contact the **Swan Lake Ranger District** (200 Ranger Station Rd., off Hwy. 35, Bigfork, 406/837-5081).

The **Swan River National Wildlife Refuge** (Hwy. 83, 1 mile south of Swan Lake, 406/727-7400, www.bisonrange.fws.gov/swan), is just over 1,500 acres of glacially carved grassy floodplain that provides habitat for more than 170 species of birds, including waterfowl, bald eagles, various types of hawks, owls, and songbirds. There are also plenty of other animals—moose, elk, beavers, bobcats, and the occasional grizzly bear—wandering through this quiet and undeveloped place. The refuge is closed for nesting season (Mar. 1–July 15), except for the viewing platforms.

Accommodations

For the most part, the accommodations in the Seeley-Swan Valley are lovely and somewhat rustic. The **Double Arrow Lodge** (301 Lodge Way, 2 miles south of Seeley Lake, 406/677-2777 or 800/468-0777, www.doublearrowlodge.com, cabins range $100–200) is a handsome log lodge with history and character in a ranch-like setting. The accommodations are lovely cabins and lodge rooms, all with private baths. A variety of activities, including fishing, golf, sleigh rides, horseback riding, and winter sports, can be arranged on-site. The **Seeley Lake Motor Lodge** (Hwy. 83, mile marker 14.5, 406/677-2335 or 800/237-9978, www.seeleylakemotorlodge.com, $45–81), on the other hand, is what good roadside motels used to be: comfortable, clean and convenient.

In Swan Lake, there are a handful of lodging options, including the isolated and lovely

Swan Mountain Ranch (26356 Soup Creek Rd., on Hwy. 83 between mile markers 64 and 65, 800/919-4416, www.swanmountainranch.com), which offers both do-it-yourself cabin rentals ($225–275) and bed-and-breakfast packages ($225–233, discounts for multiple rooms). It is a cross-country ski resort in winter, and offers guided hunting trips in fall.

By far the fanciest and most expensive spot in the region is the exclusive **Holland Lake Lodge** (1947 Holland Lake Rd., Condon, 406/754-2282, www.hollandlakelodge.com, cabin $145 pp d, lodge room $125 pp d), where the rates include meals. The activities at this lakefront resort include hiking, canoeing, horseback riding, swimming, fishing float trips, and float plane excursions. The **Laughing Horse Lodge** (71284 Hwy. 83, Swan Lake, 406/886-2080, www.laughinghorselodge.com, May–Dec., $95–125) is a cozy and fun bed-and-breakfast where pets are welcome and the activity menu is unlimited.

Food

For a hearty meal, the **Hungry Bear Steakhouse** (6287 Hwy. 83, between mile markers 38 and 39, Condon, 406/754-2240, 8 A.M.–10 P.M. daily year-round, dinner entrées $13–24) serves steak and seafood with a full-service bar and a kids menu. Breakfast ($4–10) and lunch ($5–10) are served as well. For a real culinary and visual treat, dine lakeside on gourmet fare at **Holland Lake Lodge** (1947 Holland Lake Rd., Condon, 406/754-2282, www.hollandlakelodge.com, breakfast 8:30–9:45 A.M., lunch noon–2 P.M., dinner 5:45–8:45 P.M., call for reservations and to confirm times). The beautiful inn serves breakfast ($4–7), lunch ($5–10), and dinner ($23–30) with entrées like Gruyère egg bake, green chili burger with cheese and lodge salsa, and pecan-crusted pork tenderloin.

In Seeley Lake, the local favorite is the lakefront **Lindey's Prime Steak House** (Hwy. 83, Seeley Lake, 406/677-9229, 5–10 P.M. daily May–Sept., 5–9 P.M. daily Oct.–May, entrées $22–28), where the steaks are of the same caliber as the great view. There is not much on the menu besides steak, but meat lovers will be exceedingly happy with this authentic Montana steak house. Another reliable spot for a meal in Seeley Lake almost any time of day is **The Filling Station Restaurant** (3189 Hwy. 83, 406/677-2080, 11 A.M.–10 P.M. Mon.–Fri., 8 A.M.–10 P.M. Sat.–Sun., entrées $7–17, bar until 2 A.M.), which offers karaoke in the bar on Friday and Saturday nights. The award-winning menu and wine list in the Double Arrow Lodge's **Seasons Restaurant** (301 Lodge Way, 2 miles south of Seeley Lake, 406/677-2777 or 800/468-0777, www.doublearrowlodge.com, entrées $22–29) features fresh, creative cuisine.

Camping

With so much public forest and wilderness in the vicinity, the multitude of camping options in the area attract large numbers of campers on summer weekends. **Placid Lake State Park** (406/542-5500, $12) has 40 sites, flush toilets, and drinking water; it is three miles south of

Seeley Lake on Highway 83, then three miles west on a county road. **Salmon Lake State Park** (Hwy. 83, 5 miles south of Seeley Lake, 406/677-6804, May 1–Nov. 30, $13–15) is another of the better options.

The **Holland Lake Campground** (Holland Lake Rd., 406/837-5081, Memorial Day–Labor Day, $15) has 39 sites, flush toilets, and lake access. The **Swan Lake Campground** (Hwy. 83, Swan Lake, 877/444-6777, www.recreation.gov, $15) is a Forest Service campground 0.5 miles northwest of Swan Lake on Highway 83.

INFORMATION AND SERVICES

The **Seeley Lake Chamber of Commerce** (406/677-2880, www.seeleylakechamber.com) is on Highway 83 at mile marker 12.5, just south of the town. The **Swan Lake Chamber of Commerce** (70942 Hwy. 83, Swan Lake, 406/886-2303) is located in the town.

Kalispell and Whitefish

The northern town of Kalispell (population 21,182, elevation 2,954 feet) exists because of James Hill's Great Northern Railway and survives in spite of it. Freight and mercantile baron Charles Conrad, who made his fortune in Fort Benton and planned to move to Spokane, Washington, before falling in love with the Flathead Valley on his way west, essentially founded the town of Kalispell when he convinced his friend Hill to run the railroad through it in 1891. By 1904, two years after Conrad's death, the Great Northern abandoned its Kalispell route in favor of the more geographically amenable Whitefish line just to the north. The people of Kalispell were furious, but the town's economy survived due to Conrad's National Bank and the booming timber industry that saw 40 sawmills built in Kalispell alone. Today it is still rather industrial compared to Whitefish's resort-like atmosphere—a nuts-and-bolts kind of town that

serves as a natural supply and shopping center and has some wonderful museums, parks, and an ideal location between Flathead Lake and Glacier National Park.

Given a great boost when the train was rerouted from Kalispell in 1904, Whitefish (population 5,844, elevation 3,036 feet) grew up around Big Mountain and the sport of skiing, and today is Montana's largest year-round resort community. The economy bumped along thanks to the train and the timber industry, but when locals started skiing on Big Mountain in the 1930s, an idea was born. At the request of local science teacher Lloyd "Mully" Muldoon, Great Falls skiers George Prentice and Edward Schenck came to town, studied the mountain, and put up $20,000 of their own money to develop the ski area. Whitefish's chamber of commerce raised the rest of the money locally by selling stock. The work was done largely by volunteers in 1947 and 1948. The following year,

WESTERN MONTANA

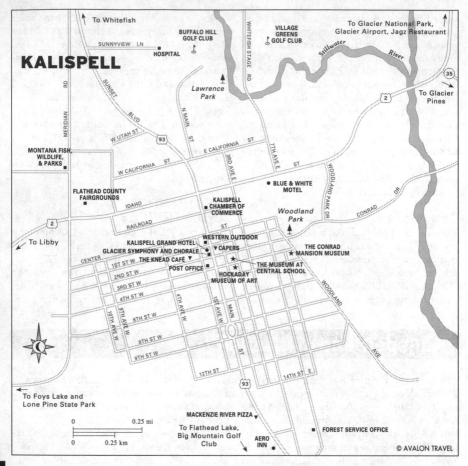

KALISPELL

To Whitefish

BUFFALO HILL
GOLF CLUB

VILLAGE
GREENS
GOLF CLUB

To Glacier National Park,
Glacier Airport, Jagz Restaurant

SUNNYVIEW LN

HOSPITAL

Stillwater River

WHITEFISH STAGE RD

MERIDIAN RD

SUNSET

BLVD

Lawrence
Park

N MAIN ST

W UTAH ST

93

E CALIFORNIA ST

7TH AVE E

To Glacier
Pines

35

2

MONTANA FISH
WILDLIFE,
& PARKS

W CALIFORNIA ST

3RD AVE E

ST

WOODLAND PARK DR

FLATHEAD COUNTY
FAIRGROUNDS

IDAHO

KALISPELL
CHAMBER OF
COMMERCE

BLUE & WHITE
MOTEL

Woodland
Park

CONRAD

DR

2

RAILROAD ST

To Libby

WESTERN OUTDOOR

KALISPELL GRAND HOTEL
GLACIER SYMPHONY AND CHORALE

CAPERS

CENTER

1ST ST W   THE KNEAD CAFÉ

POST OFFICE

THE CONRAD
MANSION MUSEUM

THE MUSEUM AT
CENTRAL SCHOOL

2ND ST W

HOCKADAY
MUSEUM OF ART

WOODLAND

3RD ST W

4TH ST W

4TH AVE W

1ST AVE W

MAIN ST

9TH AVE W

6TH ST W

10TH AVE W

8TH ST W

9TH ST W

12TH ST

93

14TH ST E

AVE

To Foys Lake and
Lone Pine State Park

0   0.25 mi

0   0.25 km

MACKENZIE RIVER PIZZA

To Flathead Lake,
Big Mountain Golf
Club

AERO
INN

FOREST SERVICE OFFICE

© AVALON TRAVEL

Big Mountain hosted the national downhill, slalom, and combined races. Since then, it has gained an excellent reputation, and the town basks in its glory. And although Whitefish is clearly a ski town, it is also an art town, a gateway to Glacier, a summer hot spot, and a great place to find gourmet cuisine.

SIGHTS
The Conrad Mansion Museum

Just a block from Woodland Park sits the palatial historic home of Charles Conrad, the founder of the city of Kalispell. The Conrad

Mansion Museum (330 Woodland Ave., Kalispell, 406/755-2166, www.conradmansion.com, 10 A.M.–5 P.M. Tues.–Sun. May 15–Oct. 15, $8 adults, $7 seniors, $3 children) was completed in 1895 and designed by the renowned Spokane, Washington, architect Kirtland Cutter. The Conrads made sure that the residents of Kalispell felt some connection to the house: On Christmas Day of the year it was finished, the Conrad family invited people from around town who would otherwise have spent the holiday alone to share in their feast. The entire city was invited to a grand New

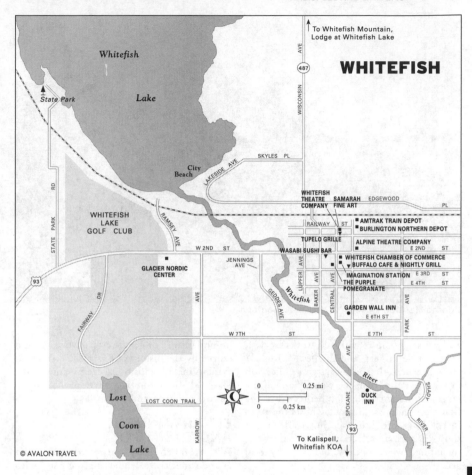

Year's Eve ball a week later. Over the years, Alicia Conrad hosted famous parties, including a Halloween gathering just after a fire had burned through the roof of the mansion. Alicia decorated the hole with Spanish moss, artificial bats, and volcanoes. After her death in 1923, the family continued to occupy the home until the mid-1960s. Conrad himself had only lived in the house for seven years before his death at age 52. In 1974, his youngest daughter donated the residence to the city of Kalispell. The 26-room, nine-bedroom mansion has been beautifully restored and is furnished with the family's original furniture. There is also a large collection of family clothing and three generations of children's toys.

Hockaday Museum of Art

The Hockaday Museum of Art (302 2nd Ave. E., Kalispell, 406/755-5268, www.hockadaymuseum.org, 10 A.M.–5 P.M. Tues.–Sat., $5 adults, $4 seniors, $2 college students, free for children K–12) was originally begun by local artists in the late 1960s, and today it is a well-established public museum known for showcasing some of the region's most important art

© DONNIE SEXTON

Conrad Mansion Museum in Kalispell, Montana

WESTERN MONTANA

and artists. Visitors will find works by T. J. Hileman, John Fery, and Charles M. Russell, among others. It has the largest collection of Glacier Park art in the country and also a large permanent collection dedicated to the Blackfeet Indians. Hockaday hosts the **Arts in the Park** program each July, and the gift shop has a broad selection of original works, including jewelry, pottery, and prints by local artists.

The Museum at Central School

The Central School building was opened in 1894 and for more than 100 years housed different educational institutions. Slated for demolition in the early 1990s, the city of Kalispell instead invested over $2 million renovating the historic building. Since 1999 it has been used by the Northwest Montana Historical Society, which oversees the Museum at Central School (124 2nd Ave. E., Kalispell, 406/756-8381, www.yourmuseum.org, 10 A.M.–5 P.M. Mon.–Fri., $5 adults, $4 seniors, free for children). The museum is dedicated to preserving the

unique history of northwestern Montana and especially the history of Kalispell. Permanent exhibits include a historical examination of the Flathead Valley and the growth of the logging industry in Montana.

ENTERTAINMENT AND EVENTS

With so much to do year-round in this part of the state, the calendar is always full with seasonal events. In northwestern Montana, summertime means farmers markets, and a good one is the **Kalispell Farmers Market** (Center St. and 5th Ave., Kalispell, 406/752-3350, 9 A.M.–12:30 P.M. Sat. mid-Apr.–Oct.). In Whitefish, summer brings two regular farmers markets: the **Farmers Market** (Pin & Cue parking lot, 6570 U.S. 93 S., Whitefish, 406/862-3451, 4–6 P.M. Thurs. early May–mid-Sept.), and the **Downtown Farmers Market** (1 Central Ave., Whitefish, 406/862-2043, www.whitefishfarmersmarket. org, 5–7:30 P.M. Tues. late May–mid-Sept.), both of which offer local produce, local art, handmade crafts, prepared food, and a variety of entertainment.

Another great market, which focuses more on locally made art and crafts, is the **Artists and Craftsmen of the Flathead Summer Outdoor Show** (920 S. Main St., Kalispell, 406/881-4288, www.acfguide.com), held over a weekend in the first part of July. Among the annual festivals celebrating local art, food, and culture are the **Whitefish Arts Festival** (504 Railway St., Whitefish, 406/862-5875, www.whitefishartsfestival.org, usually 4th of July weekend), the **Festival Amadeus** (1 Central Ave., Whitefish, 406/257-3241, www.glaciersymphonychorale.org, late July–early Aug.), and the **Huckleberry Days Art Festival** (1st Central Ave., Whitefish, 406/862-3501, www.whitefishchamber.org, three days in mid-Aug.), which celebrates the juicy purple berry with music, entertainment, an art fair, and lots of family fun.

The annual **Taste of Whitefish** (O'Shaughnessy Center, Central Ave., Whitefish, across from the train station, 406/862-3501, www.whitefishchamber.com, $40 pp) is the region's premier food event, with offerings indoors and outside in early September from more than 20 of the town's best restaurants.

Perhaps the most anticipated event of the year is the **Northwest Montana Fair & Rodeo** (fairgrounds, 265 North Meridian Rd., Kalispell, 406/758-5810, www.nwmtfair.com), usually held in mid-August and kicked off with a parade. The nearly weeklong event includes plenty of local agricultural exhibits, a carnival, three nights of professional rodeo, and a variety of entertainment, all of which attract visitors from across the region. For year-round entertainment, check out the **Glacier Symphony and Chorale** (140 S. Main St., Kalispell, 406/257-3241, www.gscmusic.org), which produces an interesting range of musical events.

In winter, the area celebrates the snow with festivities like the **New Year's Eve Rockin' Rail Jam and Torchlight Parade** (Whitefish Mountain Resort, 406/862-2900, www.skiwhitefish.com) and the **Whitefish Winter Carnival** (www.whitefishwintercarnival.com), a silly and fun event held annually in early February.

Despite its small size, Whitefish has a remarkably savvy theater crowd with offerings from both the **Alpine Theatre Company** (600 2nd St., Whitefish, 406/862-7469, www.alpinetheatreproject.org), a highly respected repertory theater company, and **Whitefish Theatre Company** (1 Central Ave., Whitefish, 406/862-5371, www.whitefishtheatreco.org), which offers eight community plays annually plus concerts, professional dance, and improv performances, workshops, camps, and films.

SHOPPING

Western Outdoor (48 Main St., Kalispell, 406/756-5818 or 800/636-5818, 9 A.M.–6 P.M. Mon.–Sat., 10:30 A.M.–4:30 P.M. Sun. summer, 10 A.M.–6 P.M. Mon.–Sat., 11 A.M.–4 P.M. Sun. the rest of the year) is one of the most popular shopping attractions. This Western goods store boasts more than 3,500 pairs of boots and close to 2,000 hats in every size, shape, and style imaginable. If you've always wanted real cowboy duds, the salespeople here are very attentive and will do their best to make sure you are outfitted properly.

Whitefish is full of small, quaint, and original stores. The **Imagination Station** (221 Central Ave., Whitefish, 406/862-5668, 9:30 A.M.–6 P.M. Mon.–Sat., 11 A.M.–5 P.M. Sun.) began about 15 years ago when the owners realized that they missed the toys of their youth. Their classic toy selection has grown over the years and is a lot of fun for adults and children alike. They also stock their store with the latest wooden toys from Europe, have a good selection of educational toys, and like to keep a lot of puzzles and board games on hand as well.

If you have the time, a stop at **Kettle Care** (6590 Farm to Market Rd., Whitefish, 406/862-9853 or 888/556-2316, www.kettlecare.com, 9 A.M.–5 P.M. Mon.–Sat.) is well worth the visit. This business is committed to producing fine all-natural body-care products while remaining conscious of their carbon footprint. The ingredients come from their certified organic farm and are created, packaged, and labeled for sale on-site. They have a small showroom stocked with products; a trip to this store provides visitors an opportunity to see a successful homegrown green business in action.

The streets of downtown Whitefish are filled with galleries promoting upcoming regional artists. Several galleries line Central Avenue, including **The Purple Pomegranate** (222 Central Ave., Whitefish, 406/862-7227), which showcases a broad selection of art from 150 artists, including jewelry, pottery, musical instruments, toys, and handblown glass. **Samarah Fine Art** (15 Central Ave., Whitefish, 406/862-3339) is a gallery that represents about 30 artists from across the state working in various traditional and contemporary media. Both galleries participate in the popular **Whitefish Gallery Nights** (http://whitefishgallerynights.org), the first Thursday evening of each month May–October. Eighteen galleries are involved, each sponsoring a different artist each night of the event. It's a great way to view art, meet the artists, sample good food, and experience the community.

RECREATION
◖ Skiing Big Mountain
When it comes to skiing in Montana, it doesn't get much better than skiing Big Mountain at the **Whitefish Mountain Resort** (3840 Big Mountain Rd., 406/862-2900 or 800/858-3930, www.skiwhitefish.com, all-day $61 adults, $54 teens, $32 juniors, half-day $54 adults, $47 teens, $25 juniors), which offers 94 trails, 12 lifts, 2,353 feet of vertical drop, and a 3.3-mile run. This is serious skiing and family fun at its best. The mountain stays open year-round for hiking, mountain biking, zipline tours, and an alpine slide, among other activities.

Cross-Country Skiing
For cross-country skiers, fabulous groomed trails can be found locally at the **Glacier** **Nordic Center** (1200 U.S. 93 W., Whitefish, 406/862-9498, www.glaciernordicclub.wordpress.com, $8 ages 13 and up) on the Whitefish Lake Golf Course. There are seven miles of skate and classic trails on gently rolling terrain, and lighted night skiing on two miles of trails until 11 P.M.

Hiking and Biking
In addition to having Glacier National Park as a backyard, both Kalispell and Whitefish have excellent hiking and biking trails. Among the adventures at **Whitefish Mountain Resort** (3840 Big Mountain Rd., Whitefish, 406/862-2900 or 877/754-3474, www.skiwhitefish.com), there are serious mountain biking opportunities for the hard-core and the not-so-hard-core who would prefer to limit their rides to downhill only. For hikers, the **Danny On Trail** winds 3.8 miles from the base of the ski hill to the summit. The gondola is available up ($12) or down (free) the slope, but the forested trail, dotted with wildflower-strewn meadows, is worth the sweat.

Just four miles southwest of Kalispell, **Lone Pine State Park** (300 Lonepine Rd., Kalispell, 406/755-2706, day use $5 nonresidents) has a nature trail, miles of hiking and biking trails with scenic overlooks, and a year-round visitors center with flush toilets and a picnic shelter.

Golf
Both Kalispell and Whitefish are big golfing destinations as soon as the snow melts. There are three public courses in Whitefish, including the North and South Courses at the **Whitefish Lake Golf Club** (1200 U.S. 93 N., Whitefish, 406/862-5960, www.golfwhitefish.com, $40–53 for 18 holes), and five public courses in Kalispell. Among them are **Big Mountain Golf Club** (3230 U.S. 93 N., Kalispell, 800/255-5641, www.bigmountainclub.com, rates vary), the 36-hole **Buffalo Hill Golf Club** (1176 N. Main St., Kalispell, 888/342-6319, www.golf-buffalohill.com, $42–58 for 18 holes), and **Village Greens Golf Club** (500 Palmer Dr., Kalispell, 406/752-4666, www.montanagolf.com, $30–47 for 18 holes).

ACCOMMODATIONS

Kalispell is definitely the best place to find an assortment of more budget-friendly chain hotels and motels, but prices can rise when the town is packed with travelers en route to or from Glacier or Flathead. Next to the airport, the **Aero Inn** (1830 U.S. 93 S., Kalispell, 800/843-6114, www.aeroinn.com, $44–99) has 61 no-frills guest rooms and is reasonably priced. Another good value can be found at the 106-room pet-friendly **Blue & White Motel** (640 East Idaho St., Kalispell, 406/755-4311 or 800/382-3577, www.blu-white.com, $39–90), which, in addition to cool neon signage, has decent rooms, standard amenities, and a 24-hour restaurant next door (making it a favorite with truckers).

For a more historic experience, try the pet-friendly **Kalispell Grand Hotel** (100 Main St., Kalispell, 406/755-8100 or 800/858-7422, www.kalispellgrand.com, $80–150) downtown. It is the last of eight hotels that once lined downtown.

Given its proximity to Big Mountain, Whitefish Lake, and Glacier National Park, it's no surprise that Whitefish has an abundance of accommodations—but true to its resort-town vibe, beds don't come cheap. The grand dame, without a doubt, is the **Whitefish Mountain Resort** (3840 Big Mountain Rd., Whitefish, 406/862-2900 or 877/754-3474, www.ski-whitefish.com, $75–1,500), the resort community around Big Mountain with eight different lodging options, 90 percent of which are condominiums that range from modest guest rooms in the **Hibernation House** to palatial five-bedroom townhouses. Rates are generally higher in winter, and particularly around holidays.

Another sizable full-service resort on the shores of Whitefish Lake and just over a mile from downtown is the **Lodge at Whitefish Lake** (1380 Wisconsin Ave., Whitefish, 406/863-4000 or 877/887-4026, www.lodgeatwhitefishlake.com, low season $109, high season $240). The lodge is pretty spectacular, and the rooms are all luxurious and sparkling new. The immediate lake access is a disincentive to ever leave.

Smaller options for lodging in town include the riverfront 15-room **Duck Inn** (1305 Columbia Ave., Whitefish, 406/862-3825 or 800/344-2377, www.duckinn.com, $144–220) and the charming five-bedroom **Garden Wall Inn** (504 Spokane Ave., Whitefish, 888/530-1700, www.gardenwallinn.com, $155–255).

CAMPING

There are quite a few camping options, both public and private, around Kalispell, but nothing for tent campers in town. Among the largest full-service RV parks and the only one with a heated swimming pool is the shady and private **Glacier Pines** (120 Swan Mountain Dr., Kalispell, 800/533-4029, www.glacierpines.com, $26–31 d), with 80 full-service sites, free Wi-Fi, a playground for small kids, horseshoes, and fire pits. A good primitive option for tent campers is the **Ashley Lake Campgrounds** (N. Shore Rd., off Ashley Lake Rd., 10 miles west of Kalispell, 406/758-5204, www.fs.fed.us/r1/flathead, Memorial Day–Labor Day, no fees for day usage or overnight camping), which offers 11 lakefront sites with no services other than a vault toilet.

By far the most economical accommodations in Whitefish are the campgrounds. There are a number of beautiful National Forest campgrounds as well as two private campgrounds, including the **Whitefish KOA** (5121 U.S. 93 S., Whitefish, 2 miles south of town, 406/862-4242 or 800/562-8734, www.glacierparkkoa.com, $35–43 tents, $45–64 RVs, $68–150 cabins), which has every imaginable amenity. **Tally Lake** (913 Tally Lake Rd., 17 miles west of Whitefish, 406/837-2775, www.recreation.gov, late May–late Sept., $25) is a gorgeous and popular spot with a nice campground. Closer to town, **Whitefish Lake State Park** (0.5 miles west of Whitefish on U.S. 93, then 1 mile north on State Park Rd., 406/862-3991 or 406/752-5501, www.fwp.mt.gov/parks, $15) offers 25 waterfront tent and RV sites that go quickly at this beautiful, convenient spot.

FOOD

In keeping with the number of strip malls in town, Kalispell has quite a few chain restaurants, many of them quite good, like **Mackenzie River Pizza** (2230 U.S. 93 S., Kalispell, 406/756-0060, www.mackenzieriverpizza.com/Kalispell.htm, lunch and dinner daily, entrées $8–16). There are also some fantastic local restaurants that are well worth finding. **The Knead Café** (25 2nd Ave. W., Kalispell, 406/755-7510, www.theknead.com, 8 A.M.–4 P.M. Mon.–Sat., 9 A.M.–3 P.M. Sun.) is a great little Mediterranean-inspired breakfast and lunch joint that rightly calls itself a "spirited fusion of food, art, and music." An excellent choice for a gourmet dinner is the family-friendly **Jagz Restaurant** (3796 Hwy. 2 E., Kalispell, 406/755-5303, www.jagzrestaurant.com, from 4:30 P.M. daily, entrées $7–30), which serves a wide assortment of steaks, seafood, and pasta. More intimate and upscale is **Capers** (121 Main St., Kalispell, 406/755-7687, www.capersmontana.com, from 5 P.M. Tues.–Sat., entrées $15–30), which offers delicious brick-oven pizza plus succulent steaks, fish, and vegetarian dishes.

Whitefish has a surprising number of excellent restaurants. One of the all-around best places to go for a hearty, delicious meal is the budget-friendly ℂ **Buffalo Cafe & Nightly Grill** (514 3rd St., Whitefish, 406/862-BUFF—406/862-2833, www.buffalocafewhitefish.com, breakfast and lunch 7 A.M.–2 P.M. daily, dinner 5–9 P.M. Mon.–Sat., breakfast and lunch $4.50–8.50, dinner $7.50–16). From old-fashioned milk shakes and blueberry granola pancakes to Mexican specialties and baby back ribs, this local favorite has mastered comfort food for more than 30 years.

Although Montana is not known for its sushi, Whitefish residents could not live without **Wasabi Sushi Bar** (419 2nd St. E., Whitefish, 406/863-9283, www.wasabimt.com, from 5 P.M. daily May–Oct., from 5 P.M. Mon.–Sat. Nov.–Apr., rolls $4–15), with classic nigiri and sashimi, a contemporary twist on sushi and tempura, and plenty of grill items that include steak, duck, scallops, and more.

While there are a handful of elegant high-end eateries in town, **Tupelo Grille** (17 Central Ave., Whitefish, 406/862-6136, www.tupelogrille. com, from 5:30 P.M. daily, entrées 18–29) is a unique choice with a wonderfully Southern-inspired menu and an exceptional wine list.

INFORMATION AND SERVICES

The Kalispell Chamber of Commerce (406/758-2800, www.kalispellchamber. com, 8 A.M.–5 P.M. Mon.–Fri.) and **Flathead Convention and Visitor Bureau** (www.fcvb. org, 406/756-9091, 8:30 A.M.–4 P.M. Mon.–Fri.) are located in the historic Great Northern Depot building (15 Depot Park, Kalispell). The **Whitefish Chamber of Commerce** (520 E. 2nd St., Whitefish, 406/862-3501, www.whitefishchamber.org, 9 A.M.–5 P.M. Mon.–Fri.) is open year-round.

The **Flathead National Forest Headquarters** (1935 3rd Ave. E., Kalispell, 406/758-5200, www.fs.fed.us/r1/flathead) has helpful information for campers and hikers.

Kalispell has a **Public Library** (247 1st Ave. E., Kalispell, 406/758-5820, 10 A.M.–8 P.M. Mon.–Thurs., 10 A.M.–5 P.M. Fri., 11 A.M.–5 P.M. Sat.), and the **main post office** (248 1st Ave. W., Kalispell) is at the corner of Third Street.

The **Kalispell Regional Medical Center** (310 Sunnyview Lane, Kalispell, 406/752-5111, www.nwhc.org/krmc) is located just north of downtown.

GETTING THERE

Just 14 miles south of Whitefish, Kalispell is the larger of the two cities and has commercial flights and bus service, while Whitefish has daily train service. Both cities have taxi services.

The **Glacier Park International Airport** (FCA, 4170 U.S. 2 E., Kalispell, www.iflyglacier.com) is served by Delta/SkyWest, Alaska/Horizon, United, and Allegiant. There are on-site car-rental counters for **Avis, Budget, Hertz,** and **National/Alamo; Dollar, Enterprise,** and **Thrifty** are off-site but near the airport.

Both **Greyhound** (1301 S. Main St., Kalispell, 406/755-4011, www.greyhound. com) and **Rimrock Trailways** (406/245-5392 or 800/255-7655, www.rimrocktrailways.com) offer daily bus service in and out of Kalispell. **Amtrak** (500 Depot St., Whitefish, 800/872-7245, www.amtrak.com) runs the *Empire Builder* from from Chicago to Seattle with daily stops in Whitefish in each direction.

Kalispell and Whitefish are easily accessible by car: Kalispell is 115 miles north of Missoula at the junction of U.S. 2 and U.S. 93; Whitefish is just 14 miles farther north on U.S. 93.

GETTING AROUND

Eagle Transit (http://flathead.mt.gov/eagle, 7 A.M.–7 P.M. Mon.–Fri., $1) operates the buses in Kalispell, and there are two companies that provide taxi service; **Jim's Taxi Service** (406/890-8920, www.jimstaxiservice.com, 24-7) covers all of Flathead County from Flathead Lake to Whitefish Mountain, Glacier National Park, and everything in between. **Drive 4 U** (406/730-7879) offers taxi service in both Kalispell and Whitefish.

BUTTE, HELENA, AND SOUTHWEST MONTANA

From the first major discovery of gold along Grasshopper Creek in 1862, southwestern Montana attracted prospectors, miners, and those who would build communities around them. Within a year of that major gold discovery, President Abraham Lincoln signed a bill creating Montana Territory. In many ways, this region gave rise to the state: Two of the state's best-known mining camps, Helena and Butte, prospered and diversified, becoming two of Montana's most interesting and historically significant cities. Others, like Virginia City and Bannack, all but disappeared before rising again as well-maintained tourist attractions. Indeed, history comes to life in southwestern Montana, from the mines in and around Butte to the battlegrounds along the Big Hole River, the ghost towns above

Philipsburg, and the cobblestone streets of Montana's capital city.

But there's much more to this corner of the state than museums and mine shafts. There are vast open spaces, like the glorious Big Hole, dotted with cattle and lined with blue-ribbon trout waters. There are plentiful hot springs, old-school family-oriented ski hills, and some of the region's most scenic drives. And although the region is developing—a hip contemporary art scene in Helena, for example, and a Jack Nicklaus golf course built into the Old Works smelting site in Anaconda—there are stretches that look and feel untouched. The ranchers in the Big Hole Valley still use big wooden beaver-slide contraptions during haying season, and the Beaverhead-Deerlodge National Forest is a vast swath of breathtaking scenery that

© DONNIE SEXTON

HIGHLIGHTS

World Museum of Mining: This museum is packed with artifacts from more than a century of hard-rock mining in the region. Built atop the actual mine yard from the Orphan Girl mine, this museum is the real deal (page 175).

Philipsburg: This fabulous mining town is experiencing a rebirth, with gourmet restaurants and a beautiful hotel; nearby the ghost town of **Granite** has been abandoned to the elements for more than a century. Visited together, they offer two very different studies of Montana history (page 184).

Georgetown Lake: A favorite getaway for Butte residents, this lake's scenery, solitude, and fishing make it a remarkable old-school vacation spot (page 187).

Big Hole National Battlefield: A memorial to the Nez Perce and U.S. Army soldiers who died in battle on August 9-10, 1877, this site is both gorgeous and spectacularly moving. The tipi frames stand where they did the fateful morning of the attack (page 190).

Skiing Maverick Mountain: Clearly a well-kept secret, Maverick is the kind of mountain you might have skied on as a kid – or wish you had. It is tow ropes and Carhartts, the most family-friendly ski atmosphere you can imagine (page 193).

Elkhorn Hot Springs: Set high in the Pioneer Mountains, Elkhorn Hot Springs is a remote, rustic, and wonderfully authentic Montana resort with heavenly outdoor hot springs (page 193).

Fishing: Flowing 155 miles through great little towns like Jackson, Wisdom, and Melrose, the **Big Hole River** is one of the classics in the Montana fishing oeuvre, filled with rainbow, brown, and brook trout as well as rare native grayling (page 193).

Virginia City: A meticulously preserved mining town from the 1860s, Virginia City, along with neighboring **Nevada City,** boasts more than 100 historic buildings, a 1910 steam locomotive, and plenty of locals willing to recreate the rowdy mining era. The vaudeville theater, historic lodging, and good food are icing on the cake (page 196).

Lewis and Clark Caverns: In addition to being the best place by far to get away from the rare blistering Montana heat – think 50°F and damp – the caverns are Montana's first state park and a fine example of limestone caves (page 198).

Last Chance Gulch and Reeder's Alley: One of the few pedestrian malls in Montana, this area is not only the heart of Helena's history but also the center of Helena's modern shopping and culinary scene. Open-air events year-round – like art walks and free concerts – keep the gulch hopping (page 203).

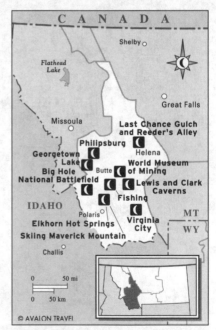

LOOK FOR (TO FIND RECOMMENDED SIGHTS, ACTIVITIES, DINING, AND LODGING.

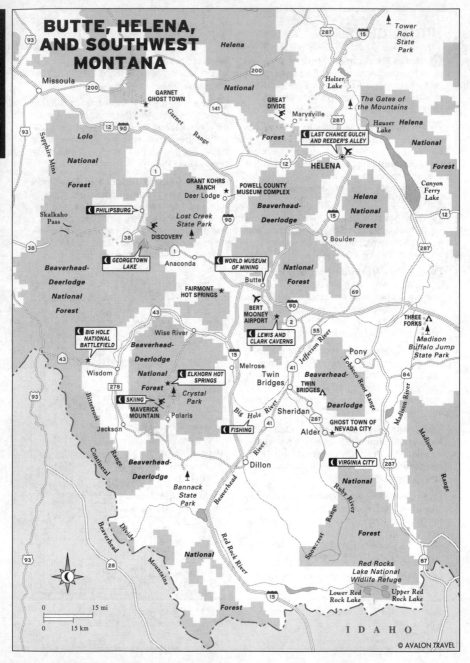

encompasses 3.5 million acres and two pristine wilderness areas. Southwest Montana and its best-known cities offer visitors a unique look into Montana's past and an authentic view of Montana's most appealing present.

PLANNING YOUR TIME

This corner of the state is vast and relatively diverse, both geographically and in terms of its offerings. History buffs will be easily satiated just about anywhere, from the big cities of Helena and Butte to the tiny ghost towns that dot the landscape. And while southwestern Montana could easily absorb a week or more, it can also be appreciated in three days or less for visitors trying to see more of the state.

Butte is a fascinating destination, not so much for its present-day incarnation, which can be fairly described as a bit rowdy and somewhat bleak, but for its older glory: the remarkable architecture that still stands, the underground city that is just coming to light, and the mines that made Butte the "richest hill on earth" and one of the country's largest cities west of the Mississippi for nearly 50 years. Butte is a marvelous place to spend at least a day, and more if you are interested in mining or history.

For good reason, nature lovers and outdoor enthusiasts will be itching to get out of Butte. **The Big Hole,** southwest of the city, is a natural wonderland of wide open spaces, supremely good fishing, a ski hill, an important Native American battle site, and a couple of great hot springs. Indeed, this region could be a vacation on its own, and it requires at least a day to cover the terrain.

Farther west, **Philipsburg,** less than a mile from the ghost town of **Granite** and just 10 miles from **Georgetown Lake** and **Discovery Ski Area,** is an ideal spot to enjoy a sumptuous meal and get a good night's rest, and perhaps even catch a show.

Finally, there are a host of other places in the region that make great add-ons or stand-alone destinations. **Virginia City, Nevada City,** and **Bannack** are meticulously preserved ghost towns. The state's capital, **Helena,** is a

bustling city that has successfully transitioned into modernity while still carefully preserving its past. As is true almost anywhere in Montana, the recreational opportunities just outside the city are plentiful, from the **Gates of the Mountains,** named by Lewis and Clark, to **Holter, Hauser,** and **Canyon Ferry Lakes,** which offer boating, fishing, and only-in-Montana activities like ice sailing during winter.

HISTORY

Although this area's past was dominated by mining, southwestern Montana's history predates the first precious-metal find. The region long had great appeal to both mountaineers and fur trappers. On their epic journey west, this is where Lewis and Clark were given vital assistance by the Native Americans who frequented the region. Just 14 miles north of present day Dillon, Sacagawea recognized Beaverhead Rock as the area where she had been kidnapped as a child. With this information, the men set out to encounter her former people, the Shoshone Indians, who would provide the Corps of Discovery with horses to continue their journey to the Pacific. At the time they traveled this land, Lewis and Clark documented the richness of the wilderness, unaware of the element that would permanently put the region on the map—gold.

The history of Montana's Gold West Country begins in 1862, when gold deposits were discovered in Grasshopper Creek. A year later, the city of Bannack had attracted more than 3,000 residents. Although many initially arrived to try their luck at panning for gold, they stayed to ply their trades—blacksmithing, butchery, or inn keeping—all of which allowed the mining camp to evolve into a small town. A year later, in May 1863, a small group of men set out to explore the area outside Bannack. They struck gold in a stream they named Alder Creek. Alder Gulch quickly had nine mining camps on a 14-mile stretch of the creek. Within a year, Virginia City had been founded and boasted a population of 10,000 (today its population hovers around 130). Alder Gulch would go on to produce almost $120

THE IRISH IN BUTTE

Sometimes referred to as Ireland's fifth province, Butte has long had a significant Irish influence. Of the city's 47,635 residents in 1900, some 12,000 – nearly one-quarter of the population – were Irish. For many years, despite its wildly disparate climate and geography, Butte maintained the largest concentration of Irish immigrants in the United States. Copper king Marcus Daly, himself an immigrant from Ireland, was known to preferentially hire Irish workers in his mines and smelters whenever possible. Other well-known Irish figures in Butte included Cornelius "Con" Kelly, a lawyer who ran both the Anaconda Company and later the Montana Power Company; William McDowell, Montana's lieutenant governor and eventually U.S. ambassador to Ireland; and Jeremiah J. Lynch, a local judge who was an important leader of the Irish community in Butte. At times, being Irish was practically a prerequisite for success. Consider a rug merchant named Mohammed Akara, who in the early 1900s changed his last name to Murphy "for business reasons."

The majority of the Irish in Butte came from western Ireland – Cork, Mayo, and Donegal. Of the 1,700 people who emigrated between 1870 and 1915 from County Cork to the United States, 1,138 landed in Butte. A collection of Irish neighborhoods developed around the mines, Corktown and Dublin Gulch among them. Irish pubs sprung up on just about every corner, many of which still stand today. The Irish Times Pub, a modern-day addition, has booths made out of church pews that originally stood in a Dublin church. A stone at the front door, imported from County Clare, allows patrons to touch Irish rock as they enter. Other bars with Irish influence include Maloney's, the Silver Dollar Saloon, and the M&M Cigar Store.

But Irish culture in Butte extends beyond drinking establishments, thankfully. Each summer the community gathers to celebrate their Irish heritage at the An Rí Rá Montana Irish Festival, an outdoor celebration of Celtic music and dance complete with foot races, concerts, and dance performances. Another Butte program, Project Children, brings Irish children and young adults of different faiths to Butte to work on projects like Habitat for Humanity to show them that religious differences need not prevent cooperation and communication.

Undoubtedly the best-known Irish event in Butte is the annual St. Patrick's Day celebration. Some 30,000 people descend on the city, creating bedlam that some see as a fabulous party. The day kicks off with a parade in uptown Butte led by the Ancient Order of Hibernians. There's a piper luncheon, concerts, and dances, and the city's plentiful bars host massive crowds for green beer and Irish festivities. This Montana version of New Year's Eve in Times Square is more than a little rough-and-tumble: One gets a real sense of what life as a Butte miner must have been like around the turn of the 20th century.

---

million in placer gold ($30 million of which was discovered in the first three years). The mad gold rush was bringing new arrivals to the region daily, and in 1864 Congress created Montana Territory. Although Bannack was its first capital, the legislature quickly moved to Virginia City, where the state opened its first public school in 1866.

Next, another group of men left Virginia City to prospect for gold in uncharted territory. Known as "the four Georgians," they were beaten by their lack of success and planned to return to the South before winter. "OK, boys, just one last chance," one of the miners said as he dipped his pan in the Prickly Pear Creek, and he came up with enough gold to keep them there. The word soon spread, and Last Chance Gulch spawned a small town of saloons, makeshift stores, and boardinghouses.

As was common at the time, these small towns would boom and bust, commerce and government would move from one gold strike to the next, and by 1875 the territory's capital was in Helena, the city that had grown up around Last Chance Gulch. The city of Helena persisted because just as its gold supply dwindled, other valuable materials were discovered, including quartz, silver, and lead. Helena had also established itself as an important center of trade for the region, and when Montana became a state in 1889, Helena had more millionaires per capita than any other city in the country. Although there was a fierce battle with the city of Anaconda, Helena was crowned the new state's capital.

The other city in the region defined by the almost maniacal pursuit of riches is Butte, known for decades as "the richest hill on earth." Originally an assortment of mining camps, with the discovery of silver and copper Butte grew into a bustling city with dozens of mines and 10,000 miles of tunnels beneath its increasingly urban streets. Many big companies moved into town to extract, process, and distribute the metals, making Butte the state's first industrialized city. Urban and fiercely proud, Butte residents were known to describe their city as "Butte, America," rather than "Butte, Montana," to distinguish themselves from the rural sensibilities of the rest of the state. By the late 1800s, Butte was one of the world's largest silver and copper producers and among the most populated cities in the United States. Throughout the boom, a diverse range of immigrants flooded into the area looking for opportunities. Irish, Italian, Eastern European, and Chinese newcomers all contributed to the culture and history of the city.

By the early 1900s, with the introduction of electricity and the demands of World War I, Butte's copper production was in full swing, and big business wanted the largest piece of the pie. In 1899 the Standard Oil Company founded the Amalgamated Copper Mining Company, which would become the Anaconda Mining Company. Clashes between labor and management during the Progressive era set the tone for the labor movement across the country.

When the price of copper sank during the Great Depression, Butte's economy suffered. After a short spike during World War II, the Anaconda Company made the shift to strip-mining in 1955, which involved removing large chunks of earth—and tearing down entire neighborhoods—to open the Berkeley Pit. This hole in the middle of the city grew, swallowing huge amounts of land and scarring every square inch of the city until it was shut down in 1982. The toxic site was declared an environmental hazard, and it is now a Superfund site and a tragic irreparable reminder of the end of the city's mining era.

With the Depression and the plummeting price of metals, most of the mining towns in Montana suffered similar fates, although significantly less dramatically that Butte. While a limited amount of mining is being done today in the region, the state is working to draw visitors interested in the rich history of the area—and, of course, by touting the region's natural splendor. Indeed, there are places in southwestern Montana, including the Big Hole Valley and the Jefferson River Valley, that were unscarred by mining and where time seems to have stood still over the centuries.

SOUTHWEST MONTANA

Butte

I am not afraid to say that I have a tragic (though I won't concede doom just yet) love affair with Butte. The truth is, everyone in Montana is rooting for Butte. Once the cosmopolitan and urban moneymaking center of the state, Butte (population 33,654, elevation 5,700 feet) today is beat-up and a little bleak; "rough around the edges" is putting it mildly. The most far-reaching and present reminder of its former glory, other than the open-pit mining scars that rend the entire valley, leaving nothing untouched, are the car license plates that start with 1, Butte's rank in terms of population when motor vehicles showed up on the scene.

Despite its diminished status, Butte is a remarkable place with the most compelling and diverse history in the state as well as an infrastructure of fabulous old buildings that are just waiting for a renaissance. In fact, Butte is among the largest registered National Historic Landmark Districts in the country, with more than 4,000 historic structures. There is more culture here than just about anywhere in Montana, and there are some marvelous establishments for dining and imbibing—and one hotel in particular that is enjoying a glorious second incarnation.

Unless you are a history fanatic, Butte is not a place you'll want to spend an entire week; to see Montana, you need to get out in the fresh air and enjoy the natural beauty. A weekend in Butte gives visitors to the state an incredible opportunity to learn about Montana's past and see firsthand what happens to a place when all of its natural resources are exploited as quickly as possible. Indeed, there is something of *The Lorax* in Butte, and something of *The Giving Tree*. But no copper king or corporation can rob this place of its fascinating past and modern-day spirit. And no one is willing to rule out a renaissance—least of all the citizens of Butte.

Butte's Berkeley Pit is filled with a rainbow of toxic sludge.

© CARTER G. WALKER

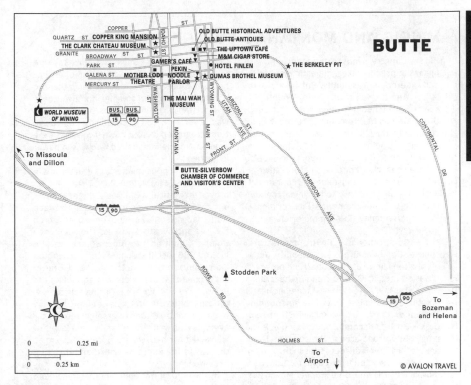

SIGHTS
Old Butte Historical Adventures

If you only have one day to spend in Butte, plan to attend one of the walking tours put on by Old Butte Historical Adventures (117 N. Main St., 406/498-3424, www.buttetours.info, scheduled tours 10 A.M.–5 P.M. Mon., Wed., and Fri.–Sat., 10 A.M.–4 P.M. Tues. and Thurs., 11 A.M.–4 P.M. Sun. May 1–Sept. 3, $10 adults, $8 seniors, $5 children under 12). They offer a variety of 90-minute walking tours of Butte's underground city, complete with a speakeasy, a barbershop, and an old city jail. Other tours stay above ground and visit the gorgeous Finlen Hotel, an old brothel, and Chinatown. What makes these tours so compelling, other than the mind-blowing history, is the passion and knowledge of the guides. Reservations for these tours, which may make you fall in love with Butte, are strongly recommended.

The Berkeley Pit

The transition from underground mining to pit mining in Butte began in 1955. The first open-pit mine dug in pursuit of copper, the Berkeley Pit (east end of Park St., 406/723-3177, www.pitwatch.org, Mar.–Nov., $2 to access the viewing stand) swallowed several of the underground mines along with entire neighborhoods as the Anaconda Company dug deeper and wider for smaller amounts of copper. The ore mined at the Berkeley Pit, for example, was roughly 0.75 percent copper, compared to the original Marcus Daly ore, which was 30 percent copper.

In 1982, because of steadily falling copper prices, the Berkeley Pit was shut down. With it, the pumps from the nearby Kelley Mine, which had kept the pit dry for nearly 30 years, were shut down as well. The mines under the city and the pit itself immediately started to fill

MINING AND MONTANA'S SUPERFUND SITES

Big Sky Country is most often associated with images of pristine lakes, majestic mountains, and wide-open grasslands. But toxic wastelands? And the worst one in the country? It seems far-fetched. However, even this beautiful state has had to come to terms with its complex history. Although Montana's mining industry attracted worldwide recognition and contributed to the state's importance, it also wreaked havoc on Montana's natural environment, scarring the landscape and contaminating both water and soil. Today, in partnership with the U.S. government's Environmental Protection Agency (EPA), a major cleanup is underway.

The Comprehensive Environmental Response, Compensation, and Liability Act is more often known as the Superfund program. It was created in 1980 to clean up hazardous waste sites that posed a threat to public health and the environment. The area surrounding the Upper Clark Fork River, which encompasses Butte, Anaconda, and Missoula, is the largest Superfund area in the country. There are actually four individual sites in the region, all of which resulted from copper production, most of it by the Anaconda Copper Mining Corporation (ACM).

In the late 1800s, Butte's smelters were adjacent to the mines, and the toxic fumes created massive amounts of thick smoke. In mines without smelters, the copper sulfide ore was spread over large piles of logs and ignited. The piles burned for weeks, releasing highly toxic particles and fumes into the air and leaving residue on the ground that would leach into the water table. The mining and smelting in Butte not only contaminated Butte Hill but was carried downstream and downwind as far as Milltown, 120 miles south.

Butte was famously without vegetation – the only green area in town was a small and beloved amusement park named Columbia Gardens that was built by the ACM upwind of the smelters and could thus support green grass – and its citizens were often sick with burning eyes, bloody noses, gagging, and lung disease. The copper baron William Andrews Clark was quoted as saying, "I must say that the ladies are very fond of this smoky city... because there is just enough arsenic there to give them a beautiful complexion." Eventually an antismoke ordinance was passed, but it was never enforced because smelter operators threatened to shut down if the laws were applied. No one questioned who was in power in Butte.

When the copper smelter was erected in Anaconda in 1894 by Marcus Daly, Butte's air improved dramatically. But Deer Lodge ranchers and farmers who lived in the valley between Butte and Missoula suffered devastating crop failures and livestock losses. The Anaconda Company built an enormous smoke stack in 1918 (at 585 feet, it surpasses the Washington Monument) to disperse the smoke, but farmers argued that they were just spreading the poison over a wider area. During this period, the Anaconda smelter was thought to have released up to 36 tons of arsenic into the air every day, as well as alarmingly high levels of lead and other heavy metals. The case went all the way to the Supreme Court, and the company won.

By the 1970s it was apparent that the air and water pollution was still hurting livestock and agricultural soil throughout the Deer Lodge Valley. The reservoir at Milltown, east of Missoula, was so tainted with copper waste that the drinking water was contaminated. Atlantic Richfield Company (ARCO) bought the mines in 1977, inheriting little more than the bill for cleanup, and within a few years had to shut down both the smelter in Anaconda and Butte's Berkeley Pit. The cavernous pit filled with toxic water from the underground mines it was built on. The EPA rated the area the most polluted in the country, worse than Love Canal in New York. Today, visitors to the pit can experience the eerily changing tints of the stagnant pool, which in 1995 claimed the lives of hundreds of snow geese that landed in the water during their migration. The cleanup is well underway but expected to continue for decades, with the final bill running into the hundreds of millions of dollars.

with acidic water. The water depth today surpasses 5,000 feet and continues to climb, with more than 2 million gallons flooding in every day. The water itself is highly toxic and appears various shades of brown, blue, green, and red, depending on the concentration of chemicals and subsequent chemical reactions. In November 1995, a flock of snow geese landed in the Berkeley Pit; fog and snow kept them from flying off, and after several days 342 birds were found dead in the water. Since then, a program has discouraged migrating birds from landing on the pit water.

One curious creature that managed to live in and around the pit for years was a dog known by miners as "The Auditor." He greeted workers daily for 17 years but never came close enough for anyone to touch. He was a white (OK, gray) dog with dreadlocks that dragged on the ground. The miners built him a shanty and left food and water; they pointed to The Auditor as proof that there were indeed things able to withstand the toxicity of the Superfund site. The pit's unofficial mascot died in 2003, but not before the community raised enough money to commission a bronze statue of the mangy mutt. It will eventually be on display at the pit viewing stand.

Our Lady of the Rockies

High atop the crest of the Continental Divide is Our Lady of the Rockies (3100 Harrison Ave., 406/782-1221, www.ourladyoftherockies. net, June–Sept., tours $15 adults, $13 seniors, $11 ages 13–17, $7 ages 5–12, $2 for children under 5), a 90-foot statue of the Virgin Mary meant to watch over this predominantly Catholic town. Between 1979 and 1985, the statue was built and erected entirely by volunteers, many of them miners who had lost their jobs when the Berkeley Pit, Butte's last operating mine, closed down. Bob O'Bill, who worked for the Anaconda Mining Company for years, vowed that if his wife recovered from illness, he would hoist a statue of the Virgin Mary on the East Ridge overlooking the city. When the final piece was set in place by a helicopter, Butte came to a screeching halt to

watch in proud silence. Indeed, the statue is a reflection of this city's indomitable spirit. The roughly 2.5-hour tours leave from the gift shop on Harrison Avenue and include a trip inside the metal sculpture.

◖ World Museum of Mining

Located off West Park Road, across from the Montana Tech campus, is The World Museum of Mining (406/723-7211, www.miningmuseum.org, 9 A.M.–6 P.M. daily Apr.–Labor Day, shorter hours Labor Day–Oct.), which sits on the now defunct Orphan Girl mine yard. It houses numerous large-scale exhibits, and the mine yard is filled with a variety of mining equipment covering a century of use, including smelter cars, ore carts, and trucks. When you purchase your entry ticket to the museum, you may also want to buy a ticket for the **underground mine tours** that take place three times a day. Visitors to the underground mine wear hard hats, cap lamps, and battery belts and descend 65 feet into the mine. The tours are led by former miners who worked in the mine and who tell their personal stories. They also explain how equipment is used and how the ore is mined and removed from the pit. Combined tickets for the museum and the underground are $17 adults, $6 children, discounts for students and seniors, free for children under 5.

A highlight of the museum is its **Hell Roarin' Gulch,** a full-scale, authentic reproduction of an 1890s mining town. There are 50 buildings on the site, 15 of which are original historic buildings that have been relocated to the museum. While on-site, visit a bank, a general store, a school, and even a Chinese herbalist whose shelves are stocked with original herbs and medicines. The buildings have been painstakingly recreated using as many antiques and original materials as possible.

The Copper King Mansion

The Copper King Mansion (219 W. Granite St., 406/782-7580, www.thecopperkingmansion.com, 9 A.M.–4 P.M. daily May–Sept., by appointment Oct.–Apr., adults $7.50, children $3.50) is both a museum and bed-and-breakfast. Guided tours show off this 34-room Victorian home built in 1898 for the infamous King of Copper, William Andrews Clark. Considered one of the wealthiest men in the world in his day, Clark could afford to import all the material for the house's construction as well as the European craftsmen needed to do the work. Each room has a fresco painted on its ceiling by artists personally commissioned by Clark. There is elaborate woodwork throughout the house, including the fireplaces, bookcases, and stairways. Tiffany stained-glass windows and magnificent chandeliers enhance the elegance.

The Clark Chateau Museum

W. A. Clark's son, Charles, also commissioned a house in 1898. The Clark Chateau Museum (321 W. Broadway, 406/491-5636, www.bsbarts.org/chateau, 11 A.M.–5 P.M. Tues.–Sat. summer, by appointment in other seasons, $4 adults, $3 seniors, $2 children) is a replica of a chateau Charles had admired in France. Today the house is a period museum and Butte's community arts center. Up the gorgeous spiral staircase to the second and third floors is the museum's permanent collection, dedicated to showcasing the diverse cultural and ethnic heritage of the city. There are also two galleries with current shows, and the exhibits change every six weeks. Tours are available of the house itself, which is impressive in terms of its architecture, design, and art.

Dumas Brothel Museum

Butte also happens to be home to "America's longest-running house of prostitution." The Dumas Brothel was the center of Butte's red-light district back in its mining heyday. Opened in 1890, it only closed its doors in 1982. The brothel reopened as the Dumas Brothel Museum (45 E. Mercury St., 406/494-6908, www.thedumasbrothel.com), allowing visitors to get a glimpse into the seedier side of the city's history. At its height, the brothel used all 43 rooms and was open 24 hours a day to cater to the miners, who worked around the clock.

There were even underground tunnels that led to other downtown buildings, providing secret entry for some of their more distinguished clientele. Since the building was actually built to serve as a brothel, it has some unique design elements, including windows lining the hallway. The rooms themselves, known as "cribs," are small enough to hold a bed and not much more. The museum had to close its doors for a few years due to a lack of funding. Although it recently reopened, it is best to call before visiting to confirm that it is still operating.

The Mai Wah Museum

The Mai Wah Museum (17 W. Mercury St., 406/723-3231, www.maiwah.org, 11 A.M.–5 P.M. Tues.–Sat. June–Sept.) is dedicated to documenting and preserving Chinese experience in Butte. By 1910, Butte's Chinatown had more than 2,000 Chinese residents, and the 1914 directory listed 62 Chinese businesses that included gambling parlors, noodle shops, herbalists, and grocery stores. The permanent exhibit tells the story of the Chinese immigrants to the city who came in search of lucrative jobs in the mining industry 1860–1940. It houses exhibits containing photos, artifacts, and interpretive materials. The museum is in the Wah Chong Tai and Mai Wah buildings, just off China Alley, the heart of Butte's Chinatown. Originally the buildings were a mercantile store and noodle shop that historically served as meeting places and a major point of social interaction for the Chinese immigrant community.

ENTERTAINMENT AND EVENTS

Chinese New Year

A reflection of Butte's diverse population and cosmopolitan history, each Chinese New Year the community gathers to celebrate with a parade from the courthouse to the Mai Wah Museum. For the year of the dragon, the Mai Wah pulls out its 60-foot paper dragon to dance through the streets of uptown Butte. The event is punctuated by 10,000 fireworks, and in 2009 it was voted among the six most interesting parades in the country by *Reader's Digest*.

St. Patrick's Day

In a town largely composed of Sullivans, Shannons, Harringtons, O'Neills, Sheas, Driscolls, and O'Briens, is it any wonder that the annual St. Patrick's Day celebration is probably the biggest party of the year? Some 30,000 people descend on the city in March to celebrate the strong Irish community with a parade in uptown Butte led by the Ancient Order of Hibernians. There are events all over the city, including a piper luncheon, concerts, dances, and, of course, no shortage of places to fill up on frosty green beer.

An Rí Rá

Held annually the second week of August, An Rí Rá (Park St. between N. Main St. and N. Montana St., www.mtgaelic.org) is the less bawdy cousin to St. Patrick's Day. The event focuses less on drinking (there are no alcohol sponsors and no alcohol sold at the festival itself) and more on Irish culture and traditions, with music and dancing, drama, and historical lectures along with lots of events geared to families with children. The event is sponsored by the Montana Gaelic Cultural Society and includes a one-mile fun run as well as 5K and 10K races. The festival culminates in an Irish mass held outdoors in the Irish language, often to crowds of more than 1,000 people. The Montana Gaelic Cultural Society sponsors education and entertainment opportunities throughout the year as fund-raisers for the festival. Weekend passes for all festival events are $25 in advance or $30 within a month of the event and are available on the website.

Christmas Stroll and Ice Sculpting Festival

Held on successive weekends in December, these two festivals celebrate the past, present, and future of uptown Butte. The Christmas Stroll usually takes place the first Friday evening in December and offers a number of activities for the whole family. It is a community-centered event with food vendors, music, dancing, a parade, a visit from Santa, and a tree-lighting ceremony. Many businesses get involved by offering treats and special events to strollers. There are also plenty of places along the parade route to stop in for a toddy.

Resulting in dozens of marvelous ice sculptures placed around town, the annual Ice Sculpting Contest is another family-oriented event that kicks off with a breakfast with Santa and culminates in the judging of the sculptures. Progress on the carving can be monitored throughout the day as you stroll around uptown Butte.

Information on both events is available from **Mainstreet Uptown Butte** (66 W. Park St., Suite 211, 406/497-6464, www.mainstreetbutte.org).

Mother Lode Theatre

Seeing an event at the Mother Lode Theatre (316 W. Park St., 406/723-3602, http://buttearts.org) is an event in itself. Built entirely with private funds by the Masons in 1923 as the 1,200-seat Temple Theatre, the glorious building was converted into a movie house during the Depression. As the mines were abandoned, so was the theater. In the 1980s, the only other theater in town was condemned and razed. True to form in Butte, people made it a priority to restore the building. The only more pressing project at the time was a complete overhaul of the city's water system. The Butte Center for the Performing Arts formed as a nonprofit organization to raise the funds necessary and oversee the construction work. The Masons donated the building to the city, and $3 million was raised for the overhaul, completed in 1996. A 106-seat children's theater known as The Orphan Girl Theatre (named for a mine in Butte) was added in 1997 thanks to another big donation.

Today, the Mother Lode provides performance space for the Butte Symphony, Montana Repertory Theatre, Missoula Children's Theatre, Western States Opera Company, Montana Chorale, the San Diego

Ballet Company, and numerous other events and organizations.

SHOPPING

Once home to 100,000 people and a number of copper kings, it's no surprise that Butte offers plenty of antiques shopping in the historic uptown. There are seven antiques stores in the area bounded by Main, Montana, Granite, and Galena Streets. **Old Butte Antiques** (123 N. Main St., 406/723-4552, www.oldbutte.com) specializes in small objects ranging from prehistoric fossils to Persian rugs and mining tools.

RECREATION
United States High Altitude Sports Center

A unique facility that has an outdoor speed-skating rink and a training facility for Olympic athletes from all over the world, the United States High Altitude Sports Center (1 Olympic Way, 406/494-7570, free) hosts various competitions and is open to the public.

Stodden Park

During Butte's mining heyday, the only greenery in town could be found at the beloved Columbia Gardens, which sadly burned down. Today there is plenty of green space in town, and Stodden Park (Sampson St. and Utah St., 406/494-3686) tops the list with a swimming pool, tennis courts, and a nine-hole golf course.

Hiking and Bouldering

Hikers and climbers driving into Butte from the east over Homestake Pass might get tingly as they see the hoodoos scattered across the terrain. A wonderful and quite similar place to explore, without the distraction of highway traffic, is the **Humbug Spires** region, 26 miles south of Butte in the Humbug Spires recommended wilderness area. This is primitive Bureau of Land Management land that has granite outcroppings, for which the area is named, in addition to primeval Douglas fir forest and a small stream chock-full of little cutthroat trout. A relatively flat nine-mile round-trip trail can be accessed by taking I-15 exit 99 for Moose Creek, and then heading east on Moose Creek Road for 3.4 miles to the parking lot and trailhead.

ACCOMMODATIONS

Although Butte has quite an assortment of nice chain-type hotels, there are a couple of places that will have significantly more appeal to those caught up in the saga of Butte's past and present. William Andrew Clark's **Copper King Mansion** (219 W. Granite St., 406/782-7580, www.thecopperkingmansion.com, $65–115) is also a bed-and-breakfast. Guests can even sleep in Clark's master bedroom. Because it is a functioning museum, check-in is at 4 P.M. and guests must check out by 9 A.M. to accommodate the tour schedule. Guided tours are free for guests, and a full breakfast is served in the formal dining room.

In the heart of uptown Butte is another fantastic old building striving to achieve its former glory. **Hotel Finlen** (100 E. Broadway, 800/729-5461, www.finlen.com, $56–86) was built in 1924 on the site of the old McDermott Hotel, one of the grandest in the Northwest. Modeled after the Astor Hotel in New York City, the Finlen is a nine-story Second Empire building with a copper-shingled roof. Over the years, Hotel Finlen was visited by Charles Lindberg, Harry Truman, John F. Kennedy, and Richard Nixon.

As is true of all of Butte, Hotel Finlen fell into disrepair and neglect as the mining economy dried up. The Taras family purchased the hotel in 1979 and has worked hard to restore the lobby and mezzanine, both of which are more beautiful than ever. The 30 guest rooms are basic at best, and the 25 guest rooms in the motor inn are dated; still, there is history here, and with some luck, a future.

FOOD

Butte's culinary history is modest but distinctive. The Butte pasty, inspired by the Cornish dish, is a flaky pastry filled with meat and potatoes for the ultimate miner's lunch; when in

Butte, it is the thing to try. The **Gamer's Café** (15 W. Park St., 406/723-5453, 10 A.M.–2 P.M. Mon.–Sat., breakfast and lunch $5–8) is a quaint little spot, founded in 1905, that feels like an old ice-cream parlor. There are no irritating keno machines, despite the name; those are next door in the casino, and the home-cooked food is excellent. Breakfast is served all day, and lunches include homemade soups, burgers, and sandwiches. Still, this is Butte, and you've got to try a pasty: The ones made here are made with New York steak from Montana beef and potatoes grown just down the road in Twin Bridges. Don't miss the apple dumpling for dessert, warm with a scoop of ice cream.

For a rare treat and a step back in time, head to **Matt's Place** (2339 Placer St., 406/782-8049, 11:30 A.M.–6:45 P.M. Tues.–Sat. first Tues. in Mar.–the week before Christmas, burgers and sandwiches $6–9), which reigns as the oldest drive-in in Montana. Open since 1930, Matt's is loaded with antiques—don't miss the old Coke machine—and is famous for their pork chop sandwiches and nut burgers (topped with ground peanuts and mayonnaise), both of which ought to be washed down with one of Matt's world-class milk shakes. Although not exactly healthy, a meal at Matt's is a unique and worthwhile experience.

Another fun and historical establishment is the **Pekin Noodle Parlor** (117 Main St., 406/782-2217, 5–10:30 P.M. Sun.–Mon., 5–11 P.M. Wed.–Thurs., 5 P.M.–midnight Fri.–Sat., entrées $6–12), serving Chinese and American food. The place is casual and utterly authentic.

The locals love **Fred's Mesquite Diner** (205 S. Arizona St., 406/723-4440, 11 A.M.–9 P.M. daily, entrées $7–29), a casual place with ample outdoor seating and the best ribs and kebabs in town.

Long considered the best restaurant in Butte, (**The Uptown Café** (47 E. Broadway, 406/723-4735, www.uptowncafe.com, fixed-menu lunch 11 A.M.–2 P.M. Mon.–Fri., dinner from 5 P.M. Mon.–Sat., from 4 P.M. Sun., lunch $6.50–10.50, dinner $11.50–30) is a gourmet restaurant infused with sophisticated style and plenty of Butte spirit. The creative and mouth-watering dinner menu offers a variety of pasta, beef, poultry, and seafood entrées. If you want to believe the renaissance in Butte is imminent, enjoy a meal at the Uptown Café.

NIGHTLIFE

Like a naughty teenager, Butte's reputation has always preceded it. This is a scrappy town where no one likes to back down. Even the most elegant older women love to tell of carrying pearl-handled revolvers every time they traveled into or through Butte. It's a fighting town, which means that Butte is a drinking town.

There are numerous bars in Butte, many of them good ones, with the best being the **M&M Cigar Store** (9 N. Main St., 406/723-7612, open 24-7), witness to Butte's glory days from a front-row seat. Opened in 1890, the M&M remained unlocked for more than 100 years. There was once a bowling alley in the basement, a dining and drinking room on the first floor, and a gambling lounge upstairs. The cigars were added during Prohibition as a polite show of compliance, but the liquor was never locked up. The M&M fell on hard times over the years and had to close down for a short period, but it reopened in 2005 with a beautiful restoration and the same spirit it has always had. So far, the doors have not been locked again since.

The **Silver Dollar Saloon** (133 S. Main St., 406/782-7367) is another legendary Butte watering hole, established on the border between Chinatown and the red-light district. The adjacent building was both a brothel and a boardinghouse for Chinese laborers. One of the hubs of the St. Patrick's Day festivities, the Silver Dollar is known for its live music offerings.

A more intimate and homey place is **Julian's Bar & Eatery** (113 Hamilton St., 406/782-6500, www.julianspianobar.com), which features piano music nightly. Patrons are always invited to join in, and there are often singalongs. Interestingly, the bar was named for William Julian Dalton (1881–1941), a well-known female impersonator who went by the name Julian Eltinge and is thought to have been the son of a Butte mining engineer.

Jim's Bar (2720 Elm St., 406/782-3431, www.jimsbarbutte.com) is kind of a biker bar, with plenty of fun and rowdy events such as biker rodeos and beach volleyball.

INFORMATION AND SERVICES

The front of the Butte–Silver Bow **Chamber of Commerce and Visitors Information Center** (1000 George St., 406/723-3177 or 800/735-6814, www.buttechamber.org, 8 A.M.–6 P.M. daily summer, 9 A.M.–5 P.M. Mon.–Fri. other seasons) is stocked with brochures, pamphlets, and tour information; in back, you can usually find a helpful chamber employee to answer questions.

The **Butte-Silver Bow Public Library** (226 W. Broadway, 406/723-3361, www.buttepubliclibrary.info, 10 A.M.–5 P.M. Mon. and Fri.–Sat., 10 A.M.–8 P.M. Tues.–Thurs.) is at Broadway and Idaho Street. The **main post office** (Mon.–Sat.) is located at 701 Dewey Boulevard.

The emergency room at **St. James Hospital**

(400 S. Clark St., 406/723-2627) is open 24 hours every day.

For laundry, the **Suds N' Fun Casino & Laundromat** (2721 Harrison Ave., 406/494-7004) is open 24 hours every day.

GETTING THERE

The Bert Mooney Airport (BTM) in Butte is served by Delta carrier SkyWest, with daily direct flights from Salt Lake City, and Horizon, with daily direct flights from Seattle. The car-rental agencies at the airport are **Avis, Budget, Enterprise,** and **Hertz.**

The **Greyhound** (406/723-3287) station is at 1324 Harrison Avenue. Butte is 64 miles south of Helena, 82 miles west of Bozeman, and 120 miles southeast of Missoula.

GETTING AROUND

The Butte-Silver Bow Transit System (406/497-6522, www.co.silverbow.mt.us/transit) offers bus service 6:45 A.M.–6:15 P.M. Monday–Friday, with shorter hours on Saturday. You can pick up a bus schedule at the public library. **Mining City Taxi** (3 S. Main St., 406/723-6511) offers service 24 hours every day.

The Pintler Scenic Route

This stretch of the state is wide open, with sweeping valleys, soaring mountains, and some authentic small communities that were involved in different stages of Montana's boom and bust economy. Philipsburg is by far the most attractive destination—it is quaint rather than past its prime—but Anaconda and Deer Lodge have some fascinating and fun sights to visit, not to mention one of the coolest golf courses in the West.

Set in a grassy valley that was known by Native Americans for its abundance of deer, Deer Lodge was both a mining town and a ranching community during its evolution. It has also long been a county seat, giving Deer Lodge an interesting if somewhat random

collection of specialized museums. There is a museum in the old frontier prison, a museum dedicated to antique cars, one built around a collection of cowboy paraphernalia, and another full of whiskey memorabilia. There is a law-enforcement museum as well as a local history museum.

Philipsburg is itself a study in Montana's boom, bust, and renewal economy. The town was named after mining expert Philip Deidesheimer, who came to the area in the late 1860s to design and run the territory's first smelter, the road to which became the main street of town. In gratitude, the townspeople named their village after Deidesheimer, deciding that Philipsburg was easier than

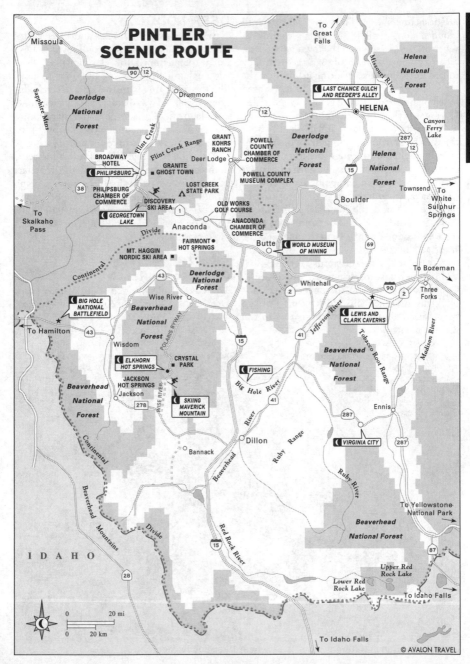

PINTLER SCENIC ROUTE

Missoula

To Great Falls

Helena National Forest

Deerlodge National Forest

Drummond

HELENA

LAST CHANCE GULCH AND REEDER'S ALLEY

Canyon Ferry Lake

Sapphire Mtns

Flint Creek

Flint Creek Range

GRANT KOHRS RANCH

POWELL COUNTY CHAMBER OF COMMERCE

Deerlodge National Forest

Helena National Forest

BROADWAY HOTEL

PHILIPSBURG

GRANITE GHOST TOWN

Deer Lodge

POWELL COUNTY MUSEUM COMPLEX

PHILIPSBURG CHAMBER OF COMMERCE

GEORGETOWN LAKE

DISCOVERY SKI AREA

LOST CREEK STATE PARK

OLD WORKS GOLF COURSE

ANACONDA CHAMBER OF COMMERCE

Boulder

Townsend

To White Sulphur Springs

To Skalkaho Pass

Anaconda

Butte

WORLD MUSEUM OF MINING

Divide

FAIRMONT HOT SPRINGS

MT. HAGGIN NORDIC SKI AREA

Continental

Deerlodge National Forest

Whitehall

To Bozeman

Three Forks

BIG HOLE NATIONAL BATTLEFIELD

Wise River

Beaverhead National Forest

Jefferson River

LEWIS AND CLARK CAVERNS

To Hamilton

Wisdom

POLARIS BYWAY

CRYSTAL PARK

Beaverhead National Forest

Tobacco Root Range

Madison River

ELKHORN HOT SPRINGS

FISHING

Big Hole River

JACKSON HOT SPRINGS

Jackson

Wise River

SKIING MAVERICK MOUNTAIN

River

Ennis

Beaverhead National Forest

Continental

Bannack

Dillon

Ruby Range

VIRGINIA CITY

Divide

Beaverhead Mountains

Beaverhead River

Ruby River

To Yellowstone National Park

IDAHO

Beaverhead National Forest

Red Rock River

Upper Red Rock Lake

Lower Red Rock Lake

To Idaho Falls

0   20 mi

0   20 km

To Idaho Falls

© AVALON TRAVEL

Deidesheimersburg. The town and its mill plodded along until 1881, and a string of silver strikes nearby allowed the town to blossom. The Northern Pacific Railway was eventually routed to Philipsburg, ensuring its place on the map. There were ups and downs, immortalized in a poignant poem by Richard Hugo titled "Degrees of Gray in Philipsburg."

Anaconda took its name and its identity from the Anaconda Mining Company, which established a smelter for the huge amount of copper coming out of the mines in nearby Butte. It was by all accounts a company town, but one that managed to hang on and is working to redefine itself since the company pulled out in 1980. Structures like the **Anaconda City Hall,** the **Deer Lodge County Courthouse,** and the **Washoe Theater** hark back to the town's glory days, when it vied for the status of state capital and narrowly lost to Helena. Its proximity to **Georgetown Lake** and the phenomenal Jack Nicklaus–designed **Old Works Golf Course** keep Anaconda hopping with visitors in the warmer months.

DEER LODGE

Nestled between the Rocky and Deer Lodge Mountain Ranges sits the small town of Deer Lodge (population 3,462, elevation 4,521 feet). Although initially a trading and trapping town like the other towns in the area, Deer Lodge grew when gold was discovered just a few miles outside town. With the gold and quartz mining, businesspeople, among them copper king W. A. Clark, flocked in to set up mills.

Today Deer Lodge is best known for being home to the state penitentiary. But that fact aside, it also proclaims itself the museum capital of Montana, and it does have more museums per capita than any other city in the state. Old West aficionados and collectors will definitely find Deer Lodge worth a stop.

SIGHTS
Grant Kohrs Ranch

The Grant Kohrs Ranch (266 Warren Lane, Deer Lodge, 406/846-2070, www.nps.gov/grko, 9 A.M.–5:30 P.M. daily summer, 9 A.M.–4:30 P.M. daily in other seasons, free) is a

Grant Kohrs Ranch National Historic Site near Deer Lodge, Montana

© DONNIE SEXTON

National Historic Site and a wonderful piece of Montana history. Originally, cattle were grazed in these lush grasslands on the open-range. Canadian Richard Grant and his sons Johnny and James were able to build up their herd trading with pioneers who moved west along the Oregon Trail. They offered travelers a nicely fattened cow for two of their travel-worn brutes.

In 1862 Johnny established a base ranch on the grounds, and as fortune would have it, the area soon flooded with hungry beef-eating gold prospectors. In 1866, Grant sold the ranch to Conrad Kohrs, who went on to become the King of Cattle, making the ranch the head-quarters of a 10-million-acre cattle empire that stretched over three states. Although it was re-duced in size over time, the ranch stayed in the Kohrs family until 1972, when it was bought by the National Park Service to preserve its his-toric significance.

Today it is a 1,600-acre small-scale working cattle ranch with 80 historic buildings, walking trails, guided tours, and ranger-led talks. You can take a tour of the 23-room main house, built in 1862 and later expanded by Kohrs. You have to sign up for the tours at the visitors cen-ter; tour size is limited to 12 people, and they do fill up quickly in the summer months. There are also ranger talks available in summer that cover topics such as the lives of a cowboy on the open range, the importance of the chuck wagon to cowboys on the trail, and the role of the black-smith. Wagon tours ($5 pp, $15 family) are also available Thursday–Monday mid-June–Labor Day. It's a fun way to see a good portion of the park with a ranger as your guide.

Powell County Museum Complex

The real highlight of a trip to Deer Lodge is the **Old Prison Museum** (1106 Main St., Deer Lodge, 406/846-3111, 9 A.M.–6 P.M. daily sum-mer, 10 A.M.–4 P.M. daily Wed.–Sun. in other seasons), which is part of the larger Powell County Museum Complex (www.pcmaf.org, $9 adults, $5 ages 10–15, free for children under 10). Tickets are a two-day pass that grants visitors admission to all the museums.

Deer Lodge was home to the first prison in the Montana territory, built in 1871. The impressive redbrick iron-gated prison you see today was built in the 1890s using inmate labor. Prisoners also made the 1.2 million bricks used to build the cell block and other buildings. Visitors can take self-guided tours through the rows of vacant cell blocks, the maximum-security area, the "galloping gal-lows," and learn about the rules and daily reg-imen for both prisoners and guards. There are a few macabre histories of some of the more interesting characters who occupied these cells. Prisoners who were seen as potential escapees, for example, were forced to wear work shoes with concrete soles, each weighing about 20 pounds, to inhibit their flight. The building it-self is actually impressive and somewhat beau-tiful, resembling a castle with turreted stone towers at each corner. Also housed in this building is the **Montana Law Enforcement Museum,** which pays tribute to officers who have lost their lives in the line of duty.

The **Montana Auto Museum** was recently recognized by *USA Today* as one of the best auto museums in the country. It houses more than 150 cars, many of them beautifully re-stored, hard-to-find vintage models, including a 1911 Ford Model T.

The other museums are open during summer but closed during winter. **Frontier Montana** covers the history of the Old West and dis-plays a vast and impressive gun collection. **Desert John's Saloon Museum** has a large amount of whisky memorabilia and brings the saloons of the Old West to life. **The Powell County Museum** covers local history, which includes mining history, of course; exhibits in-clude antique furniture, historic photos, and a weapons collection from both World Wars. **Yesterday's Playthings** is a toy and doll mu-seum with a fun collection of antique dolls, mohair teddy bears, baby carriages, horse-drawn carriages, and tea sets that date back to the mid-1800s. The newest attraction in the museum complex is **Cottonwood City,** a completely reconstructed historic mining town with a school, a mortuary, and a blacksmith's shop where blacksmithing demonstrations take place daily.

Garnet Ghost Town

About 40 miles outside Deer Lodge, off I-90 at the head of First Chance Creek, you can encounter the tucked-away mining ghost town of Garnet. Named after the semiprecious stone mined in the area, Garnet is an unspoiled, well-restored authentic Montana ghost town. Founded in 1895, there are about 30 buildings on-site along with a visitors center to welcome guests. It is open all year but the road is closed to wheeled vehicles January–April, making it a popular cross-country ski trip. In its heyday, around 1898, the town had a population of 1,000, with a school, hotels, saloons, and even a Chinese laundry. By 1950 the town was virtually abandoned. In the summer, visitors can take guided tours, walk in and out of the buildings, and even rent cabins to stay overnight. If you are interested in ghost sightings, Kelly's Saloon reportedly has spectral sounds of laughter, music, and voices even in the dead of winter.

Accommodations

Most of the accommodations in Deer Lodge fall in the budget-motel category. The most centrally located (across from the Old Prison Museum) is the **Budget Inn** (809 Main St., Deer Lodge, 406/846-2810, www.budget-inndeerlodge.com, $50–75). Formerly the Scharfs Motor Inn, the motel rooms are equipped with microwaves, fridges, and a high-speed Internet connection. The **Western Big Sky Inn** (210 N. Main St., Deer Lodge, 406/846-2590 or 866/244-7590, $55–85) is a slightly nicer motel at the other end of town, better located for a trip out to the Grant Kohrs Ranch.

Food

The **Broken Arrow Steak House** (317 Main St., Deer Lodge, 406/846-3400, $6–28) serves a variety of steak platters for lunch and dinner. **Yak Yaks** (200 Main St., Deer Lodge, 406/846-1750, 7 A.M.–3 P.M. Mon.–Fri.,

8 A.M.–3 P.M. Sat., 9 A.M.–1 P.M. Sun., $4–7) offers fresh deli sandwiches and a plethora of different lattes, Italian sodas, and milk shakes.

Information

A good source of visitor information is the **Powell County Chamber of Commerce** (1109 Main St., Deer Lodge, 406/846-2094, www.powellcountymontana.com, 9 A.M.–6 P.M. daily summer, 10 A.M.–3 P.M. Mon.–Fri. in other seasons). The Old Prison Museum also has a **Visitors Center** (1106 Main St., Deer Lodge, 406/846-3111, 9 A.M.–6 P.M. daily summer, 10 A.M.–4 P.M. daily Wed.–Sun. in other seasons).

◖ PHILIPSBURG

The little town of Philipsburg (population 911, elevation 5,280 feet) is something of a hidden gem. Off the main drag but right on the Pintler Scenic Route, also known as Highway 1, P-burg, as it is known locally, is an 1890s silver-mining town that is ideally located just minutes from recreational hot spots like **Georgetown Lake, Discovery Ski Area,** and the **Old Works Golf Course.** Still, P-burg can stand on its own merits. Surrounded by mountains—the Pintler Range to the south, the Sapphire Mountains to the west, and the Flint Range to the east—Philipsburg is populated by a beautiful collection of brightly painted Victorian brick buildings that have been brought back from the dead—the state's oldest operating school, jail, and theater are all here—by an exceedingly proud and active local population, many of whom are transplants from faraway places. There is a burgeoning culinary scene, a fabulous restored hotel, and many other reasons to come to Philipsburg and stay awhile.

Sights

The **Opera House Theatre** (140 S. Sansome St., 406/859-0013, www.operahousetheatre.com) was built in 1896, complete with a sod basement, elaborate dressing rooms, and indoor plumbing. Countless performers played the stage here for throngs of culture-hungry miners. In 1919 the elegant boxes were removed to make way for sound equipment, and the theater continued to attract a wide range of entertainers. It is still undergoing an extensive restoration that started in the late 1990s. Inside, this is the oldest continually operating theater in the state, with the youngest theater company, **The Opera House Theatre Company,** performing live theater and vaudeville shows to much fanfare every summer. Inside, look for five original backdrops painted by Charlie Russell contemporary Edgar S. Paxson.

Just northeast of town, off Highway 1 near milepost 36, is a marked but rough dirt road that leads four miles up the mountain to **Granite,** once the site of one of the world's richest silver-mining districts. Today it's a fascinating and entirely abandoned ghost town.

Granite's big strike came in 1880. The mine had been open for two years but was due to be closed one night at the end of shift since nothing of substance had been found. As foreman Charles D. McClure prepared to give his workers the bad news, the miners struck silver ore that would produce 1,700 ounces of silver to the ton. Because of a great demand for silver by the U.S. government for coinage, the population of Granite swelled to more than 3,000 almost overnight with miners in pursuit of the $4-per-shift wages. The town grew on the steep mountainside with a two-level main street and many of the buildings built on stilts. Local establishments included the usual abundance of saloons, brothels, and churches, but there was also a sophisticated reading room, a bathhouse, and a toboggan run that zoomed 2,000 vertical feet down the mountain to Philipsburg.

Two mines ran full-bore, making Montana the country's largest silver producer, until 1893, when Congress voted to end silver purchases, leading to a rapid mass exodus from Granite. The barely-staffed mines eventually merged and produced a modest supply of silver for another decade or so until they flooded in 1915. A 1958 fire demolished what was left of the buildings. Today the town is like a graveyard, filled with brick foundations,

rusting equipment, and the faded memories of Montana's biggest silver boom.

By far the most scenic—if somewhat hair-raising—way to get from Philipsburg's Flint Valley to the Bitterroot Valley south of Missoula is by way of **Skalkaho Pass,** a largely graveled 50-mile high-mountain road. Highway 38 heads up through the thickly forested Sapphire Mountains six miles south of P-burg and brings adventurous drivers down three miles south of Hamilton. The road is primitive, not for trailers or the faint of heart (particularly driving east, which puts cars along some pretty precipitous cliffs), seasonal, and well worthwhile.

Skalkaho Pass was long used as a trail by Native Americans traveling between the valleys. A more permanent road was built in 1924 to connect the mining areas around Philipsburg with the agricultural resources in the Bitterroot. There are two campgrounds along the road as well as the spectacular **Skalkaho Falls.** The summit is 7,260 feet, and the region is home to an abundance of wildlife, including moose, elk, deer, black bears, and mountain goats. Though not well traveled due to its altitude and spotty road conditions, the area does offer incredible recreation opportunities, including hiking, mountain biking, cross-country skiing, and snowmobiling on the plentiful trails.

Accommodations

For such a tiny town, P-Burg has no shortage of wonderful and unique accommodations, with nary a chain hotel to be found.

Among several nice bed-and-breakfasts, there are places like **Biker Sanctuary** (208 Kearny Lane, 406/859-1003, www.bikersanctuary.com, $79–109), a mecca for motorcyclists in a beautifully restored church. There are lodge rooms, suites, and private cabins, but it's the camaraderie that keeps people coming back year after year.

New to the area and on the Skalkaho Pass Road is the ultraswanky **Ranch at Rock Creek** (Hwy. 38, 877/786-1545, www.theranchatrockcreek.com, from $825 all-inclusive), which offers an unmatched setting, exquisite

© CARTER G. WALKER

The Broadway Hotel in Philipsburg captures the town's Victorian charm.

service and amenities, and extraordinary accommodations that include riverfront cabins, glamorous walled tents, rooms in a converted hayloft, and a five-bedroom riverfront home. Luxury is infused in every detail.

The frontrunner in town is **The Broadway Hotel** (103 W. Broadway, 406/859-8000, www.broadwaymontana.com, $79.50–140), a cozy hotel with individually themed guest rooms in a beautifully restored 1890 building. There are only nine guest rooms and a couple of cabins, so book early. Guests enjoy amenities that include a continental breakfast, a coffee bar, ample common areas, wireless Internet, and a local library. There are TVs and DVD players in every room.

Food

Visitors to Philipsburg are advised to arrive in town with an empty belly; the town has a couple of great places to eat. The first stop should always be at **The Sweet Palace** (109 E. Broadway, 888/793-3896, www.sweetpalace.com, 10 A.M.–6 P.M. Sun.–Fri. June–Aug.,

10 A.M.–5 P.M. Sun.–Fri. Sept.–May), itself a Victorian confection. The store is all nostalgia and sugar, and it is certainly among the best candy shops in the state.

The **Doe Brothers Restaurant** (120 E. Broadway, 406/859-7677, www.doebrothers. net, 11 A.M.–9 P.M. daily May 1–Dec. 31, entrées $8–13) is a malt shop in its most classic form, housed in a faithfully restored 1887 drugstore. The counter is lined with sweetheart chairs, and the tables come with boards for chess and checkers. The owners, transplants from North Carolina, have lovingly intertwined some of their own family history with that of Philipsburg. The service is beyond compare, and the food is terrific. The homemade bread is dusted with sugar, the ice cream is all Montana-made, and the entrées—ranging from mouthwatering burgers, sandwiches, and Butte-style pasties to crab cakes and specials like teriyaki salmon—are large and savory. Don't miss the onion rings, which are served hanging on little stands, or the beer-battered fried pickles. And whatever you do, don't forgo dessert; it's sublime.

The **Philipsburg Café** (136 W. Broadway, 406/859-7799, www.thephilipsburgcafe.com, breakfast and lunch 8 A.M.–3 P.M. Wed.–Sun., dinner Fri.–Sat.) is truly an unexpected and utterly delightful gem. Breakfast ($4–8) is hearty and classic, and lunch ($5–9) includes a delicious array of burgers, sandwiches, salads, and pasties. But it's the dinners (reservations strongly advised) on weekend nights that blow people's minds. The restaurant itself is unassuming, in a small diner-like setting, but the food is exquisite, and chef Michael Sauer, a Boston transplant who earned both culinary and pastry degrees in Rhode Island, whips up concoctions like pistachio-crusted rack of lamb, seared duck breast with spiced cherries, osso buco, and prime rib. The menus are planned well in advance and posted online (or you can call ahead), but the food is always superb.

Fishing

With all the rivers and lakes in this region, there are plenty of good places to wet a line. You can get geared up in Philipsburg at **Flint Creek Outdoors** (116 W. Broadway, 406/859-9500, www.flintcreekoutdoors.com, 9 A.M.–6 P.M. daily summer, 10 A.M.–5 P.M. Fri.–Sun. in other seasons), a fishing aficionado's version of the Sweet Palace across the street. Then head out to **Rock Creek,** a gorgeous 29-mile stream known for its late May–early June salmonfly hatch, 15 miles west of town.

Information

A good source of information on the local area is the **Philipsburg Chamber of Commerce** (135 S. Sansome St., 406/859-3388, www. philipsburgmt.com).

ANACONDA

The much smaller sibling of Butte, Anaconda (population 8,843, elevation 4,756 feet) boomed with the mines and suffered when the company hurriedly pulled out of the region. The population is still in decline, down more than 6 percent since 2000, but this fierce little town has not given up. They are working to restore some of their most glorious buildings, and they've transformed slag heaps and mining refuse into recreational opportunities like the free **Copper Chute** slide. And the **Old Works Golf Course,** built on the black sand of the slag heap and littered with interesting pieces of equipment, is one of the finest in the state. Anaconda is working to make the most of their location too, just minutes from **Georgetown Lake** and **Discovery Ski Area.** In winter, the scene in the town's central park, **Kennedy Commons**—ice skaters, the community Christmas tree—looks like a tableau in *The Saturday Evening Post.* Not an obvious destination for anything other than golf, Anaconda is a proud and tight-knit community that is not ready to be ruled out.

◖ Georgetown Lake

A vast artificial lake that dates back to the mining era and a longtime respite for residents of Butte, Georgetown Lake is a popular but relatively uncrowded recreation area for boating, fishing, camping, and windsurfing. The elevation here tops 6,000 feet (the local ski area is visible from the lake), so the wind can pick up and the weather can change quickly. In addition to rainbow trout, the lake has a healthy population of kokanee salmon. There are four public boat ramps, a number of campgrounds, and in the winter ice fishing and snowmobiling are among the most popular activities. There are not a huge number of services, but that is part of Georgetown's charm. The lake feels like something out of the 1950s, when people went to their cabins or brought their campers and simply enjoyed the great outdoors.

Boats can be rented, and flies or worms acquired, at the tiny **Moose Marina** (14411 Hwy. 1 W., 406/653-3277, 8 A.M.–8:30 P.M. Mon.–Fri., 7 A.M.–9 P.M. Sat.–Sun. May–Sept.), the only marina on the lake. In addition to docks, a boat launch, and boat rentals that range from canoes to small motorized fishing boats, Moose Marina offers gasoline, fishing licenses, handtied flies, and a small assortment of food and sundries.

Sights

A fantastically pink art deco building, the **Washoe Theatre** (305 Main St., 406/563-6161, movies and frequent live performances daily year-round) was built in 1936 with massive murals as well as silver, copper, and gold leaf to be a movie palace in the truest sense. It is one of the few art deco theaters standing today and was ranked fifth in the nation for its architectural value by the Smithsonian Institution.

The only Jack Nicklaus signature course in the state, the publicly owned **Old Works** (1205 Pizzini Way, 406/563-5989, www.oldworks. org, $29–55 for 18 holes, depending on the season, day, and tee time, carts $15) is a fabulous and challenging course built entirely on a Superfund site. The design makes impressive use of the black slag for all its bunkers along with many relics from the original smelter, including the remains of flues and ovens. The course offers generous fairways and beautifully maintained greens, and the fishable Warm Springs Creek offers water challenges on several holes. If you only play one course in Montana, this is the one.

Skiing and Winter Activities

Just across from Georgetown Lake is **Discovery Ski Area** (180 Discovery Basin Rd., 406/563-2184, www.skidiscovery.com, full-day $35 adults, $18 ages 12 and under), a diverse mountain with varied terrain for all ability levels. There are seven lifts and 67 runs, with a vertical drop of 2,350 feet. This is a very family-friendly ski hill. There is also a terrain park and three miles of groomed cross-country ski trails.

For Nordic skiing enthusiasts, **Mt. Haggin Nordic Ski Area** (Mill Creek Rd./Hwy. 274, 11 miles south of Hwy. 1, 406/498-9615, www.milehighnordic.org, donations appreciated) offers more than 12 miles of groomed trails (six miles for skaters and nine miles for classic skiers) in what used to be a series of logging camps. The trails also provide access to backcountry skiing along the Continental Divide. The trails are maintained by volunteers, usually on Saturday morning, and are not patrolled. There are a number of fantastic loops on varied terrain. This is not an ideal place for new skiers, but hard-core enthusiasts and racers will be delighted. Naturally, the wildlife rich area is ideal for hiking when the snow melts.

Accommodations

Anaconda's glorious hotels are a thing of the past, sadly, and most of the offerings in the area are roadside motels that are decidedly past their prime. A couple of exceptions are the **Celtic House Inn** (23 Main St., 406/560-0338, $48–70), a marvelous brick building that was a bordello at the turn of the 20th century. The hotel has 10 guest rooms, some with kitchenettes; because it is located over the Harp Pub, light sleepers should request one of the quieter guest rooms.

Another historic gem is the **Hickory House Inn** (218 E. Park St., 406/563-5481, www.hickoryhouseinn.com, $80–120), a bed-and-breakfast that has been beautifully maintained.

The house was originally the rectory of St. Paul's Church and offers five individual and lovely guest rooms.

Outside town are some fantastic options for both a rustic cabin getaway and a full-service resort. **Sugar Loaf Lodge and Cabins** (10800 Mill Creek Rd., 11 miles south of Hwy. 1 between Anaconda and Wise River, 406/491-3748, www.sugarloaflodgeandcabins.com, $85–200, 2-night minimum) is a wonderful choice for outdoors people. At the edge of the Pintler Wilderness, the hiking, cross-country skiing, and fishing are literally steps from your front porch, and the camaraderie among fellow adventurers—think nightly bonfires and barbecues—is the real deal.

A much larger and somewhat cushier option is █ **Fairmont Hot Springs** (I-90 exit 211 and follow the signs, 800/332-3272, www.fairmontmontana.com, $134–169, suites $179–405), a sizeable resort built around the hot springs. Guest rooms are nothing fancy, but it's the water that makes this place special. An enormous warm (88–94°F) indoor pool with one end shallow enough for toddlers to walk around is complemented by a smaller indoor hot pool (100–104°F) and two outdoor pools, one warm, one hot. Fairmont's enclosed three-story, 350-foot water slide ($1 per run or $10.50 all-day for adult hotel guests) is a blast, particularly when cold weather causes so much steam that you can't see six inches in front of your face. The pools are open 24 hours daily for hotel guests, for whom entrance is included at no additional charge. Nonguests can swim 8 A.M.–10 P.M. daily ($8.50 adults, $5.25 ages 10 and under, $4.75 ages 65 and older). There are two restaurants and a snack bar in the hotel as well as a small game room. There is also a golf course, a small spa, tennis courts, an outdoor playground, and a small petting zoo. This is a wonderful and easy place for families, even with young children.

At Georgetown Lake, the way to go is vacation rentals, where you can provide your own meals. A couple of websites for perusing vacation rentals in the area are www.georgetownlakevacations.com and www.vbro.com.

Camping

Two miles east of Anaconda is a surprisingly lush and beautiful campground at **Lost Creek State Park** (Galen Rd., 406/542-5500, www. fwp.mt.gov/parks, May–Nov., free), set amid pink and white granite cliffs that soar 1,200 feet above the canyon floor. There is a lovely waterfall, and campers can often spot bighorn sheep and mountain goats on the cliffs. There are 25 sites, vault toilets, fire rings, picnic tables, and drinking water.

There are numerous campgrounds, both public and private, at Georgetown Lake. Among the closest to the lake is **Lodgepole Campground** (Hwy. 1, 406/859-3211, www. fs.usda.gov, small fees determined annually), which has 31 sites, fire pits, picnic tables, and vault toilets. The campground is across the highway from the lake.

Food

Though far from elegant (or even inviting, to be perfectly frank), **Barclay II Supper Club and Lounge** (1300 E. Commercial Ave., 406/563-5541, from 5 P.M. Tues.–Sun. year-round, entrées $13–80) is the most popular fine-dining restaurant in town. In the classic tradition of seven-course meals, what this establishment lacks in ambience it more than makes up for with friendly service and hearty food. Entrées include steak, seafood, chicken, veal, and pasta.

For big burgers, sandwiches, salads, and an extremely family-friendly atmosphere (you can eat in a Volkswagen Bug or on a table made from an engine block), **Classic Café** (627 E. Park Ave., 406/563-5558, www.anaconda-classiccafe.com, 11 A.M.–9 P.M. Tues.–Thurs., 8 A.M.–10 P.M. Fri.–Sat., 8 A.M.–9 P.M. Sun., brunch 9 A.M.–1 P.M. Sun., year-round, lunch and dinner entrées $6–18) is an excellent choice for friendly service and a diverse menu; the food is consistently good.

Information

Visitor information is available from the **Anaconda Chamber of Commerce and Visitors Center** (306 E. Park Dr., 406/563-2400, www.anacondamt.org, 9 A.M.–5 P.M. Mon.–Sat. summer, 9 A.M.–5 P.M. Mon.–Fri. in other seasons). The Visitors Center offers 90-minute antique bus tours of the city (10 A.M. and 2 P.M. daily in summer, $8 adults, $4 children under 6) as well as a 16-minute video of local attractions.

The Big Hole

The Big Hole Valley feels high, wide, and handsome, not unlike Montana's larger breadbasket to the east, but the emphasis here is on high. Most of this massive valley is in fact a relatively high mountain plateau, entirely flat terrain at or above 6,000 feet ringed by mountains that soar more than 10,000 feet into the sky. It's beautiful in the most sweeping sort of way and relatively untouched by the developments of our modern world; technology runs a distant second to tradition.

The valley was explored by Lewis and Clark in the summer of 1806 on their return from the Oregon Coast. They grazed their horses on the 125 different varieties of grass (and some of their animals were stolen while the explorers slept), and they boiled meat in the natural hot springs. While fur trappers and later cattle ranchers did big business here in the summer, no one was eager to weather the harsh winters. The first town in the valley, Wisdom, was settled in 1898. Two local ranchers invented a unique hay stacker, known as the beaver slide, in 1910, and it is still widely used in the valley. It creates large stacks of hay rather than the mechanically bound hay bales we expect to see today.

The Big Hole is a unique corner of the state with virtually all of the attractions Montana is known for: big skies, vast agricultural lands, towering mountains, historically significant sites, world class fishing, and rugged but charming small towns.

◖ BIG HOLE NATIONAL BATTLEFIELD

Among the most moving historical sites in the state, the Big Hole National Battlefield (Hwy. 43, 10 miles west of Wisdom, 406/689-3155, www.nps.gov/biho, sunrise–sunset summer, 10 A.M.–5 P.M. in other seasons, free) is an important stop for visitors interested in the state's Native American history and, more specifically, the flight of the Nez Perce. The site bears the ghosts of the battle on August 9, 1877, between Chief Joseph's band of Nez Perce, often referred to as the nontreaty Nez Perce, who were fleeing the U.S. Army and their own homeland in the Wallowa Valley in Oregon rather than be sent to a reservation, as the U.S. government insisted. Thinking they were safe once they had crossed the border from Idaho into Montana, the Nez Perce set up camp on the picturesque stream to celebrate their freedom and rest after the rugged journey. Thanks to the invention of the telegraph, the Army was able to learn of their movements and catch up to them during the night. The Nez Perce lost an estimated 60–90 people, many of them women and children, in the early morning ambush, and Col. John Gibbon lost 29 of his soldiers. Visitors learn the often tragic details as they amble around the well-preserved battlefield.

DUDE RANCH VACATIONS IN GOLD WEST COUNTRY

Southwest Montana is a natural destination for ranch vacations, with age-old ranching history, wide-open spaces, and spectacular mountain scenery. Indeed, the challenge is choosing among the dozens of wonderful and welcoming ranches in the region. One of the best resources available, aside from a good friend who will steer you to a personal favorite, is the **Montana Dude Rancher's Association** (888/284-4133, www.montanadra.com). In addition to a number of ways to choose a ranch (by location, type of experience, and so on), their website offers some helpful advice in finding the best fit for your family.

- **Location:** Imagine yourself on horseback, and then think about the type of landscape you want to explore. Do you want to lope through open meadows, or wind up mountain trails? Do you want to be out in the middle of sublime nowhere, or would you like to be just a quick ride from town? Determine where you want to be, and then look for ranches in the immediate vicinity.

- **Type of riding:** What is your main objective, and your comfort level, for your time in the saddle? Would you like to be on a working ranch, helping with daily chores like rounding up cattle? Or are you more interested in working on your riding skills in clinics? There

are ranches that can accommodate both. There are also places where you can just ride as the means to take in the incredible scenery. Your choice will come down to working ranches, dude ranches, and ranch resorts.

- **Size and season:** Think about size. Do you want to be among just a handful of guests, or would you like to be among a much larger group of people? And when would you most like to go – summer, spring, or fall?

- **Activities:** Are you exclusively interested in horseback riding, or do you want other options as well – fishing, golf, activities for kids? Sightseeing and day trips away from the ranch?

- **Accommodations:** You'll need to decide whether you want to immerse yourself in ranch life and cowboy style (a working ranch or some dude ranches), whether you just want to casually play cowboy or cowgirl for a week (a dude ranch), or whether you want some serious luxury with a little bit of Western flavor tossed in for good measure (a ranch resort). Accommodations can range from lodge rooms to individual cabins, and amenities vary dramatically, from no cell service or TV to full-on wireless Internet, massages, and luxury accommodations.

All visits should start at the visitors center, where rangers are on hand to answer questions in addition to an excellent video and museum exhibit on the battle, the key players, the events leading up to the Nez Perce War, and the fateful encounter at the Big Hole.

There are several excellent self-guided trails (be sure to buy the printed guide available in the visitors center or at the trailhead; the details it provides are more than worth the $1–2) that lead visitors to various scenes of the battle. On hot summer days or wet spring days when the river bottom is soggy or buggy, one trail leads up into the forest for a firsthand look at location from which the Army mounted its surprise attack. You can still see small mounds, called rifle pits, where the soldiers scratched the earth by hand or with their rifles to protect themselves from the Nez Perce's return fire. The Nez Perce sniper areas are pointed out, as well as the location where the Nez Perce managed to take control of an Army cannon. When the lower trail along the river bottom is dry, visitors can walk among the tipi frames erected where historians have learned the 89 camps stood. Markers indicate where numerous Nez Perce died.

The battlefield is not only a serene and beautiful place today, it is haunting as well. The National Park Service has done an extraordinary job of presenting information about the Nez Perce War and this battle in particular. Because so little has changed in this region—from the actual landscape to the overall view—it is easy to imagine the tragic events that gave this spot its bloody legacy.

MELROSE

Once a mining outpost and then a railroad town, today Melrose (population 336, elevation 5,184 feet) is a fishing town midway between Butte and Dillon. Easy access to both the Wise River and the Big Hole River ensure a steady stream of anglers in this otherwise tiny village.

The Sportsman Hotel (540 N. Main St., 406/835-2141, www.sportsmanmt.com, motel rooms $67 per night or $402 weekly, cabins $100 per night or $600 weekly) offers one-stop shopping: In addition to the motel and cabins, there is an RV park with tent sites ($23 full hook-up, $15 tent sites), plus you can hire a guide and rent a raft on the premises. Hunters are just 10 minutes from the Beaverhead-Deerlodge National Forest. Owners Roxie and Chuck can point you toward some great adventures, including hikes to the otherworldly **Canyon Creek Charcoal Kilns,** a series of beehive-shaped kilns built in the 1870s to produce charcoal for the silver and lead smelters. There are also a few buildings still standing in what was the mining town of **Farlin** on Birch Creek, including some old mining cabins, a school, a butcher shop, and the old smelter.

WISE RIVER

Not even an incorporated town (you won't find it on the Visit Montana website), Wise River is another fishing paradise. The nontown—a collection of modest drinking establishments that are long on character—grew up around the place where the Wise River flows into the Big Hole.

While the area around Wise River offers no end of opportunities for entertainment—fishing, hunting, rockhounding, hiking, snowmobiling—the facilities in Wise River are rather sparse. The notable exception is the **Wise River Club** (65013 Hwy. 43, 406/832-3374, www.wiseriverclub.com, $55 d with shared bath), which is a restaurant, bar, hotel, and unofficial community center all in one. The menu in the restaurant (7 A.M.–8 P.M. Sat.–Thurs., 7 A.M.–9 P.M. Fri. summer, 8 A.M.–8 P.M. Sat.–Thurs., 8 A.M.–9 P.M. Fri. in other seasons) has standard Montana fare, including burgers, steaks, and chicken fried steak; Thursday is pasta night, and Friday is always prime rib night. The bar is open from noon daily. The countless antlers on the ceiling in the club actually came from a single elk that lived across the street for years. People came from miles around to visit the bull, and each year when he shed his antlers, someone would bring them to hang up in the club.

In the nondrinking hours—meaning during

fly-fishing time—the best resource in town is **The Complete Fly Fisher** (66771 Hwy. 43, 866/832-3175), a beautiful facility that caters to discriminating anglers for five-day, six-night all-inclusive guided fishing stays ($4,600). The gourmet meals are exquisite, as are the accommodations. The guides come highly recommended, and everything you could possibly need—from fishing licenses to the latest and greatest fly—is available on-site.

WISDOM

Another great fishing town in a spectacular setting, Wisdom (population 115, elevation 6,050 feet) is the name that Lewis and Clark initially gave to the Big Hole River. The Beaverhead and Ruby Rivers were named Philosophy and Philanthropy. Together the three formed the Jefferson River, and the names were meant to honor the three "cardinal virtues" possessed by President Thomas Jefferson.

In addition to an impressive Western art gallery, Wisdom has more than one place to hang your hat or fill your belly (but no cell phone coverage). The most beloved is probably **Fetty's Bar & Café** (101 Main St., 406/689-3260, 8 A.M.–9 P.M. daily summer, call for variable hours Tues.–Sun. in other seasons, dinner entrées $7–28), which has been serving up "authentic cowboy cuisine since 1932." Never mind that the building dates to 1960; the black-and-white photos tell a treasured history of the area. Fetty's is as famous for its burgers as for its Rocky Mountain oysters (don't ask, just try them). From the kitchen you can hear the muffled sound of the local police scanner, and the snickerdoodles are homemade and always available to go. What could be better than such old-school goodness?

JACKSON

From the cool little town of Jackson (population 134, elevation 6,407 feet), it's 25 miles to Idaho on foot and 45 miles by car. More to the point, though, why leave? There is a great hotel, restaurant, and hot springs complex, not to mention spectacular scenery and terrain worth exploring in every direction along

the Big Hole River near Wisdom, Montana

© DONNIE SEXTON

with fishing access. This is an outdoor lover's paradise at any time of year.

The best place to launch an adventure—or recover from one—is the **〔 Jackson Hot Springs Lodge** (Hwy. 278, 406/834-3151, www.jacksonhotsprings.com, $55 hotel room, $85 cabin with fireplace, $25 RV site with full hookups, and $10 tent site). The rooms are not fancy, by any stretch, but the outdoor pool fed by natural hot springs is divine, and the gigantic Western bar and dance hall are authentic and welcoming. There are often live bands, and the massive Montana-size dance floor invites fancy footwork.

POLARIS

Essentially a ghost town with a surprising number of people (mostly ranchers) still in residence, Polaris (population 239, elevation 6,352 feet) was an important silver-mining center near Grasshopper Creek as early as 1885. The smelter was destroyed in 1922, and by 1955 the only structure left standing was the **Polar Bar,** a small white cabin on the side of the road that served up frosty beers to weary travelers.

Most people coming through Polaris today are headed for skiing at **Maverick Mountain** or soaking at **Elkhorn Hot Springs,** both worthwhile pursuits.

〔 Skiing Maverick Mountain

Maverick Mountain (1600 Maverick Mountain Rd., 406/834-3454, www.skimaverick.com, Thurs.–Sun. and holidays Dec.–late Mar., $30 adults, $20 juniors, $20 adults on nonholiday Thurs.–Fri.) boasts 24 trails, 210 skiable acres, and just over 2,000 feet of vertical drop. There are two lifts, one of which is a rope tow, and a nice breakdown of easier runs (20 percent), more difficult runs (35 percent), the most difficult runs (35 percent), and expert-only runs (10 percent).

An antidote to ski areas like Apsen and Sun Valley, the real charm of Maverick is its total lack of pretense: You're likely to ride a chairlift with a rancher in Carhartt coveralls or a Hutterite girl in a dress and braids. Skiing at Maverick is a little bit like skiing somewhere small but fantastic

in about 1968; it is as family-friendly as a ski hill gets, and the terrain is excellent.

〔 Elkhorn Hot Springs

After a full day of skiing, there is nothing better than to submerge in naturally heated mineral waters, and Elkhorn Hot Springs (Hwy. 284, 13 miles north of Hwy. 278, 800/722-8978, www.elkhornhotsprings.com, $70 rustic cabin, $90 modern cabin, $45 B&B-style room) is just the place to do so. Set in the forest and moderately rustic (the cabins do not have running water, and heat is provided by a fireplace or wood-burning stove), Elkhorn Hot Springs is a playground for outdoor enthusiasts. The two outdoor pools range 102–106°F, and admission is $6 adults, $4 children; admission to the pools, sauna, and bathhouse is included with any lodging package. A restaurant on the premises serves standard Montana fare for three meals daily in summer (breakfast for guests is a complimentary buffet), and lunch and dinner Friday–Sunday in winter.

In addition to all the other amenities at this rustic resort, there is immediate access to more than 200 miles of groomed snowmobile trails and 20 miles of groomed cross-country ski trails.

RECREATION
〔 Fishing

If Butte is a city built on mining, the Big Hole is a region defined by fishing and hunting. For generations, the land and rivers here have provided pristine habitat for an abundance of wildlife and terrific access for anglers and hunters.

The **Big Hole River** is spectacularly beautiful. It is known for early-season salmonfly hatches and then a golden stone hatch in late June–early July. It is also considered the last river where an angler can catch all five species of trout.

There are numerous guides eager to introduce anglers to the trout in the Big Hole River. Among them is Bob Folkedahl of **Big Hole River Guides** (406/782-0567, www.montanatroutflyfishing.com, $425 per day for 2 anglers, $350 for 1 angler).

Hunting

The Big Hole Valley is also an excellent elk-hunting area served by outfitters that include **Beartooth Plateau Outfitters** (800/253-8545, www.beartoothoutfitters.com), who offer a range of pack trips for bow-and-arrow or rifle hunters. Prices for seven-day pack trips start at $3,900.

Rockhounding

There is a reason this part of the state is known locally as Gold West Country. There are a number of places still open to rockhounding. One of the best places to look for gems is at **Crystal Park** (Pioneer Mountains Scenic Byway/Rd. 73, 406/683-3900, Memorial Day–Labor Day, $5 per vehicle day-use), at 7,800 feet elevation high in the Pioneer Mountains, where visitors can dig for quartz crystal and amethyst, among other stones.

Hiking

The Big Hole is surrounded by the **Beaverhead-Deerlodge National Forest** (406/683-3900, www.fs.fed.us/r1/b-d), the state's largest national forest, which encompasses several mountain ranges and innumerable phenomenal hiking trails. Three of the longest running through the region are the **Continental Divide National Scenic Trail,** the **Nez Perce National Historic Trail,** and the **Lewis and Clark National Historic Trail.**

A great day hike near Elkhorn Hot Springs is the trail to beautiful **Sawtooth Lake,** filled with colorful lake trout. It's a four-mile hike to the lake (and four miles back), climbing just over 1,500 vertical feet. The trailhead is off Willman Creek Road (Forest Rd. 7441).

Go east on Willman Creek Road through the Taylor subdivision for 1.8 miles until it forks; keep right for 0.3 miles to the trailhead, where you'll see the parking lot and vault toilet. Be aware that the trail crosses the creek twice, which can be treacherous at high water or anytime the logs are wet.

Camping

There are countless campsites in the vast **Beaverhead-Deerlodge National Forest** (406/683-3900, www.fs.fed.us/r1/b-d). You can choose RV campgrounds, tent sites, or even cabin rentals by location on the website.

The **Boulder Creek Campground** ($8–10 per night in summer, free in winter) near Wise River has 13 sites; another with only five sites but located right on the Big Hole River is the **East Banks Recreation Site** (Hwy. 43, 8 miles west of Wise River, 406/533-7600, no fees for day usage or camping).

INFORMATION AND SERVICES

The website of the **Big Hole Tourism Association** (www.bigholevalley.com) offers information on the towns, businesses, and attractions of the region. Information is also available through the **Beaverhead Chamber of Commerce** (10 W. Reeder St., Dillon, 406/683-5511, www.beaverheadchamber.org).

GETTING THERE

The Big Hole Valley can be accessed most directly from Butte via I-15 to Highway 43 and Highway 278, and from Dillon via I-15 or Highway 278.

Dillon and the Southwest Corner

This part of the state is where mining meets agriculture, and where history and adventure are intertwined. There are wide-open spaces, snowcapped peaks, and limestone caves that snake deep underground. It is an area that will enchant history buffs with preserved mining settlements like Virginia City, Nevada City, and Bannack, and transfix lovers of sports and nature with incredible wildlife habitat, phenomenal fishing in rivers and lakes, and plenty of wild space just to get lost in for a while.

DILLON

The area around Dillon (population 3,595, elevation 5,096 feet) was significant on Lewis and Clark's westward journey. One site earned the name Camp Fortunate when Lewis and Clark met the Shoshone and managed to cache supplies for their return voyage.

After gold strikes in Bannack, Helena, and Butte, the area around what is now Dillon became an important shipping route between the booming mining camps and more developed Utah, often the source of equipment, supplies, and labor. Eventually the railroads came through the region, but not until a deal was struck between Irish rancher Richard Deacon, the railroad owners, and the merchants who made their living following the railroad construction crews. A staunch opponent of the railroad and a shrewd businessman, Deacon raised the price on his land to a whopping $10,500, which the railroad agreed to pay. The town of Dillon, named for Sidney Dillon, president of the Utah and Northern Railway, grew quickly as the construction crews completed the rail line during the winter of 1880–1881. Its longevity was ensured when the county seat was moved to Dillon from nearby Bannack later that year. The town prospered with the construction of a teachers college in 1892, leading some to predict that Dillon would become "the very Athens of the West."

If not quite Athens, today Dillon is a thriving little community and home to the University of Montana Western. The town has preserved its local history—from Native American influences to agriculture and mining—and achieved a reputation as an excellent launching point for outdoor adventures that include hunting, fishing, hiking, biking, and rockhounding. Mostly, though, it is Dillon's proximity to historic mining centers like Bannack, Virginia City, and Nevada City that make it an obvious destination.

BANNACK STATE PARK

Twenty-five miles west of Dillon is Bannack State Park (406/834-3413, www.bannack. org, 8 A.M.–9 P.M. daily May–early Oct., 8 A.M.–5 P.M. daily Oct.–Apr., closed Dec. 24–25, $5 per vehicle nonresidents, $3 pedestrian or bicycle), the original mining settlement of Bannack. First established in 1862 when John White discovered gold on Grasshopper Creek, the town waxed and waned for years until World War II, when all nonessential mining was prohibited. In 1954, much of the area and its 50-plus buildings were donated to the state for preservation.

The town site is well preserved but not restored or commercialized, which makes it an interesting place to visit. Bannack's history is fascinating, and many of its stories come to life in the buildings and grounds in the state park. For example, Henry Plummer, the sheriff of both Bannack and Virginia City, was famously hanged here by a group of vigilantes in 1864. He is reportedly buried at the site. The gallows and cemetery can be visited, and nearly all of the buildings can be entered.

The **visitors center** (10 A.M.–6 P.M. daily summer, 11 A.M.–5 P.M. weekends Labor Day–late Oct.) is open depending on staff availability. There are two campgrounds in Bannack State Park as well, **Vigilante Campground** (406/834-3413) and **Road Agent Campground.** Regular sites are $15 during the regular summer season and $13 October 1–April 30. Restrooms, water, picnic tables, and fire rings are available, and a tipi (mid-May–early Oct., $25) can be reserved at the Vigilante Campground.

RED ROCK LAKES NATIONAL WILDLIFE REFUGE

Known for its alpine and riparian beauty and its phenomenal habitat for birds and other wildlife, including bears, wolves, and moose, the Red Rocks Lake National Wildlife Refuge (27650B S. Valley Rd., Lima, 406/276-3536, 7:30 A.M.–4 P.M. Mon.–Fri. year-round except on federal holidays) is a spectacular area for naturally inspired recreation. Some 232 bird species have been recorded at the refuge, including 53 that are rare or considered accidental. The refuge was founded in 1935 to protect the majestic trumpeter swans, which are still happily in residence. Hunting and fishing are permitted at specific places and seasons within the refuge, but regulations change frequently and can be found through Montana Fish, Wildlife & Parks (406/444-2535 or 406/444-2950 for out-of-state licensing).

© DONNIE SEXTON

Nevada City, Montana

One of the few marshland wilderness areas in the country, the area is in its original natural state. Physical facilities are kept to a minimum, and formal trails are not maintained or designated. This is a place to get away from the crowds and explore at your own pace with minimal impact. To get to the refuge, turn off I-15 at Monida and drive 28 miles east on the gravel and dirt road.

◖ VIRGINIA CITY

Another 57 miles east of Dillon are Virginia City and Nevada City, two thriving ghost towns left over from Montana's glorious gold-mining era. In May 1863, a party of six prospectors left Bannack after a string of bad luck. While they set up camp for the night along Alder creek, the men discovered what would become one of the richest gold deposits in North America. Nine camps grew up along the creek almost overnight, the largest of which would be named Virginia City.

Within a year, the town had upward of 10,000 residents and became the first territorial capital. It was also the site of the state's first newspaper, the first public school, and the first Masonic Lodge. The town's history is intertwined with the Vigilantes of Montana, the group that would hang Sherriff Henry Plummer, among others, in 1864.

By 1875, much of the mining activity in the region had abated, and Virginia City's population had dwindled to less than 800. Over the years, as new technologies developed, including the mining dredges, the area was mined over and over for traces of what might be left. Still, between 1863 and 1889, some $90 million worth of gold had been extracted from the region. Today, that amount of gold would be worth $40 billion.

In 1961, Virginia City was designated a National Historic Landmark and protected as an important historical site. Since then, many of the buildings have been restored to function as shops, restaurants, and a hotel. The display of artifacts in both Virginia and Nevada City constitutes the largest collection of Old West memorabilia outside the Smithsonian. The population of 132 people works hard to recreate the atmosphere of Virginia City at its peak, and throughout the summer there is nightly cabaret entertainment at **Brewery Follies at Gilbert Brewery** and nightly 19th-century melodrama courtesy of the **Virginia City Players at the Opera House.** There are **train rides** on a 1910 locomotive between the cities, and an abundance of living history exhibits scattered around the sites. There are also plenty of services—accommodations and restaurants—for visitors who plan to stay.

Visitor services are available at four staffed areas throughout summer: **Virginia City Depot Visitors Information Center, Virginia City Depot Gift Store, Nevada City Open Air Museum,** and the **Alder Gulch Shortline Railroad.** More information is available from the **Montana Heritage Commission** (406/843-5247, www.virginiacitymt.com). Be aware that while telephone service was introduced to Virginia City as early as 1902, cell service is still not available.

BOULDER HOT SPRINGS AND RADON MINES

In a town that is somewhat jokingly referred to by locals as "Institutionville" for its plethora of, well, institutions (the Montana Developmental Center, Alternative Youth Adventures, and Riverside Corrections, to name a few), Boulder is home to some fascinating therapies indeed.

Indisputably, one of the best is the mineral-rich water at **Boulder Hot Springs** (31 Hot Springs Rd., 406/225-4339, www.boulderhotsprings.com, hours vary daily and seasonally), a historical gem about 30 miles south of Helena off Highway 69. Backing on the Beaverhead-Deerlodge National Forest, the landmark inn was first built as a bathhouse and saloon in 1863 by a prospector who hoped to lure local miners in for a warm bath and a cold drink or two. The Victorian hotel was built in 1881 and enlarged in 1890. In 1910, under the eye of a Butte millionaire and banker, the hotel was renovated and redecorated in Spanish mission style by a snazzy New York firm. The hotel and hot springs attracted presidents and celebrities, among them Teddy Roosevelt. After countless owners and some neglect, including a temporary closure in the late 1980s, the hotel has been renovated (although not to its former glory, it must be noted) and updated, and it provides guests with cozy accommodations, fantastic food, and some of the best soaking waters anywhere.

There are both indoor plunge pools and an outdoor swimming pool, varying in temperature 70-106°F. The indoor pools are separate for men and women and are bathing-suit-optional, giving it almost a European feel. The water is constantly moving, replenishing itself every four hours, so no chemicals are needed. There are also steam rooms available on both the men's and women's sides. Spa services, including massages, are available.

The rooms are simple and "technology-free," and the focus here is truly on healing. Bed-and-breakfast rooms range $99-139 and include a full nutritious breakfast. Guest rooms without breakfast, and often with shared baths, range $65-90 and are more basic than the B&B rooms.

Slightly more controversial than the soothing waters are the **radon mines** in Boulder, which many people believe are the best alternative treatment for relieving chronic pain and diseases that range from gout and lupus to eczema, asthma, arthritis, and even cancer. There are a number of radon mines in town thanks to an abundance of the natural radioactive gas. One of the oldest is the **Free Enterprise Radon Health Mine** (149 Depot Hill Rd., 406/225-3383, hours vary, by appointment, $7 for 1 hour, $225 for 30 hours over 10 days), founded in 1924 as a silver and lead mine. Visitors travel in an Otis elevator 85 feet below the surface to sit or sleep and breathe in the radon. There is even a special area for pets to be treated. Wireless Internet is available even underground, and motel accommodations are available for those undergoing full treatment.

SHERIDAN AND THE RUBY RIVER VALLEY

Nestled between the Ruby and Tobacco Root Mountain Ranges, the Ruby River Valley is lush and fertile, and known for its fishing and bird hunting. Among the small but scenic hamlets in this valley are **Silver Star, Twin Bridges, Sheridan,** and **Alder.** Between Sheridan and Alder is **Robber's Roost,** a notorious hangout for thieving road agents in the gold rush era.

JEFFERSON RIVER VALLEY

The Beaverhead, Big Hole, and Ruby Rivers come together at Twin Bridges to form the Jefferson River, which flows 77 miles through dry, scrubby, and relatively untouched country before flowing into the Missouri alongside the Madison and Gallatin Rivers at Three Forks. Along the way are small, nondescript towns like **Whitehall, Cardwell, LaHood,** and the tiny but charming **Willow Creek.** Much of the valley looks the same as it did when Lewis and Clark made their way through it more than 200 years ago.

◖ Lewis and Clark Caverns

Among the sights Lewis and Clark missed on their travels through the region is the Lewis and Clark Caverns (406/287-3541, www.fwp. mt.gov/parks), a phenomenal limestone cave several hundred yards above the Jefferson River. The caverns are among the largest in the Northwest and were Montana's first state park. Filled with several rooms and lined with stalactites, stalagmites, columns, and helictites, the temperature in these colorful caverns stays at around 50°F year-round, making them the perfect spot to escape the rare blisteringly hot days in southwest Montana.

The caves can only be accessed on a two-hour guided tour (daily May 1–Sept. 30, $10 adults, $5 ages 6–11) that includes a roughly two-mile hike up to and down from the caverns. On hot days, the hike can be grueling, but the cool, dark, moist caverns are the perfect reward. The natural bat nursery inside is daunting to some, but fascinating to others.

A **campground** at the caves has 40 sites

($15), restrooms with showers, a dump station, three cabins, and a tipi for rent. Within the 3,000-acre park there are 10 miles of hiking trails with trailheads at the campground, fishing access, two picnic areas, and a gift shop and restaurant.

ENTERTAINMENT AND EVENTS

Bannack Days

Held annually the third weekend in July, Bannack Days (406/834-3413, $5 per vehicle) is a celebration of the way life was when Bannack was in its prime. The weekend kicks off with a breakfast (7 A.M. Sat.) at **Hotel Meade.** Throughout the day there are a variety of pioneer demonstrations, including quilting, basket making, blacksmithing, and shooting a black-powder rifle. Lots of old-time delicacies—think kettle corn, fry bread, and fresh lemonade—are available, along with live music and an abundance of theatrics.

Annual Labor Day Sale at Patagonia Outlet

More reliable than the first snow, Montanans mark the end of summer with the annual Labor Day weekend sale at the Patagonia Outlet (34 N. Idaho St., Dillon, 406/683-2580, www. patagonia.com, 10 A.M.–6 P.M. Mon.–Sat., 11 A.M.–5 P.M. Sun. year-round). Sales on the already reduced selection of eco-friendly and always cutting-edge outdoor gear jump to 40 percent discounts.

Virginia City Players

For more than six decades, the Illustrious Virginia City Players have been entertaining the crowds at the Opera House (344 E. Wallace St., Virginia City, 406/843-5312 or 800/829-2969, www.virginiacityplayers.com, matinees 2 P.M. Wed. and Sat.–Sun., shows 7 P.M. Tues.–Sat., $18) six nights per week with turn-of-the-20th-century style melodrama and variety acts. They generally offer four shows over the course of the summer season, and also play silent movies on one of only two operating photoplayers in the world. Reservations are strongly encouraged.

Brewery Follies

For more outlandish theater and comedy, the Brewery Follies at the Old H. S. Gilbert Brewery (201 E. Wallace St., Virginia City, 406/843-5218, 406/239-7326 off-season, www.brewery-follies.net, shows 4 and 8 P.M. daily Memorial Day–Labor Day, $18) offers the unique setting of a restored 1864 brewery with bawdy entertainment and excellent microbrews.

FISHING

With so many fantastic rivers in the region, it's no surprise that southwest Montana is known as a fishing paradise. Anglers can choose from the Beaverhead, Big Hole, Jefferson, Ruby, and Red Rock Rivers, all within this corner of the state. The Beaverhead, which is easily accessed from Dillon, is among the state's most productive and prolific tailwaters, with dense bug populations and upward of 4,000 fish per mile. The Jefferson River does not give up its savvy fish easily, but streamer fishing and terrestrial fishing are fantastic. The Ruby River offers great wading and superb caddis and mayfly hatches. It's a serene river that offers small stream-like settings. The Red Rock River flows out from Lillian Lake into the Centennial Valley. Its upper portion, known for cutthroat, rainbows, and grayling, is narrow and ideally suited for wading. There is also great brown and rainbow trout fishing beneath the Lima Reservoir.

With so many fish, there are numerous outfitters in the region eager to get anglers on the water. Among them is Justin Hartman of **Tight Line Adventures** (406/925-1684, www.tightlinemontana.com, half-day for 1 person from $335, full day $435). Another excellent resource is **Frontier Anglers** (680 N. Montana St., Dillon, 800/228-5263, www.frontieranglers.com), a full-service fly shop offering everything from boat and gear rentals to equipment and supplies, guide services, fly-fishing lessons, and even vacation home rentals.

ACCOMMODATIONS

While Dillon is home to what was once a grand railroad hotel, the **Metlen Hotel & Saloon** is much worse for wear: an interesting place to see

and ripe for restoration but not a great place to stay. A better choice is the budget-friendly **Sundowner Motel** (500 N. Montana St., Dillon, 406/683-2375, $48–60), which offers 32 comfortable but basic rooms with continental breakfast and Wi-Fi included. It is the best rate in town.

For a more historic lodging experience, the **Fairweather Inn** (307 W. Wallace St., Virginia City, 406/843-5377 or 800/829-2969, ext. 4, www.aldergulchaccommodations.com, June–mid-Sept., $70–85) is a historic building from 1863 with plenty of charm. There are 14 guest rooms, six of which have en suite baths; the others share facilities. The **Nevada City Hotel & Cabins** (1578 Hwy. 287, Nevada City, 406/843-5377 or 800/829-2969, ext. 4, mid-May–late Sept., $85–100) has a more rustic exterior with slightly more elegant interiors. All of the guest rooms have private baths, and two Victorian suites have their own balconies. The cabins are true sod-roofed pioneer cabins that have been updated with comfortable accommodations and modern amenities. Both hotels offer ideal access to all of the sights in Virginia City and Nevada City plus some local discounts.

A little-known gem for both lodging and dining in the area is ◖ **The Old Hotel** (101 E. 5th Ave., Twin Bridges, 406/684-5959, www.theoldhotel.com, $125 summer, reduced rates winter). This three-story brick building was built in 1879 and restored in 1996. The two suites are supremely comfortable and always filled with fresh flowers. The full breakfast included in the room rate may just be the highlight.

FOOD

Paula and Bill Kinoshita, owners of **The Old Hotel** (101 E. 5th Ave., Twin Bridges, 406/684-5959, www.theoldhotel.com, dinner 5–9 P.M. Tues.–Sat., brunch 8 A.M.–1 P.M. Sat., 9 A.M.–2 P.M. Sun. summer, dinner 5–9 P.M. Thurs.–Sat., brunch 9 A.M.–2 P.M. Sun. winter, dinner entrées $21–29), are phenomenal chefs who have mastered everything from Le Cordon Bleu classics to Pacific Rim flavors and their own brilliant invention, cowboy sushi—a classic nigiri roll filled with thinly sliced vegetables and their own barbecue beef then dipped in tempura batter and fried, served with red chili aioli. The creative menu changes weekly and is always paired with carefully selected wines from around the world. The restaurant's 10 tables serve anglers, ranchers, and range-roving foodies year-round. Because the tiny size and remote location of the Old Hotel is entirely disproportionate to the incredible fusion of flavors, reservations are strongly recommended.

While the cuisine at The Old Hotel is surely the most surprising and remarkable in the region, this is not just steak-and-potatoes country (although the beef in southwestern Montana is notably good). There is fine dining at **Banditos** (300 Wallace St., Virginia City, 406/843-5556 summer, 406/843-5593 off-season, www.banditosmontana.com, 5–10 P.M. Tues.–Sun. mid-May–mid-Sept., entrées $18–26), a fun and upscale Mexican-inspired eatery with entrées like corn husk–wrapped salmon, sweet potato lasagna, and *camarones* chipotle. They frequently have live concerts on Saturday nights featuring everything from jazz to bluegrass to Afrobeat and rock and roll.

In Dillon, a good bet for a relatively quick bite (depending on the crowd of hungry college students) is **Sparky's Garage** (420 E. Poindexter St., Dillon, 406/683-2828, 6:30 A.M.–9 P.M. daily, entrées $7–18), a neat little barbecue joint with tender brisket, mouthwatering pulled pork, and delicious sweet-potato fries.

The 【 **Star Bakery Restaurant** (1576 Hwy. 287, Nevada City, 406/843-5525, 7 A.M.–8 P.M. Mon.–Sat., 7 A.M.–3 P.M. Sun. Memorial Day–Labor Day, breakfast and lunch $6–10, dinner $15–25) has been serving delicious and hearty meals since 1863 when it was a hot spot with miners. Today the clientele is more family-oriented, and the menu has plenty to appeal to everyone, including homemade sandwiches, beer-battered shrimp, and sodas from the early-1900s soda fountain. The emporium offers quick sugary goodies like ice cream, fudge, and penny candy.

In the Ruby River Valley, all roads lead (or ought to lead) to the **Sheridan Bakery & Café** (201 S. Main St., Sheridan, 406/842-5716, 6 A.M.–3 P.M. Mon.–Fri., 6 A.M.–2 P.M. Sun.

year-round, breakfast and lunch $3.50–9), a great little spot for homemade doughnuts and pastries plus excellent sandwiches, homemade soups, and terrific sack lunches for the river.

INFORMATION AND SERVICES

The **Beaverhead Chamber of Commerce** (www.beaverheadchamber.org, 9 A.M.–4 P.M. Mon.–Fri. year-round) is located in the same building as the **Dillon Visitor Information Center** (406/683-6731, 8 A.M.–6 P.M. daily May–Sept.) at 10 West Reeder Street in Dillon.

The **Virginia City Chamber** (406/843-5555 or 800/829-2969, www.virginiacity.com) does not have a physical address but provides information by phone and on their website. The **Montana Heritage Commission** (300 W. Wallace St., Virginia City, 406/843-5247, www.montanaheritagecommission.com, summer) is a good source of information because they manage most of the sights in Virginia City and Nevada City.

For information about the towns in the Ruby River Valley, the **Greater Ruby Valley Chamber of Commerce and Agriculture** (www.rubyvalleychamber.com) makes visitor information available at the public library (206 S. Main St., Twin Bridges) and at the Serendipity Coffeehouse (105 Main St., Sheridan).

GETTING THERE

Dillon is about 65 miles from Butte and 115 miles from Bozeman. Virginia City and Nevada City are both 70 miles from Butte or Bozeman. **The Bert Mooney Airport** (BTM) in Butte is served by Delta/SkyWest and Horizon. The car-rental agencies at the airport are **Avis, Budget, Enterprise,** and **Hertz.** Bozeman's **Gallatin Field Airport** (BZN) is served by Delta/SkyWest, Alaska/Horizon, Frontier, and United Express. Rental-car agencies **Alamo, Budget, Enterprise, Hertz,** and **National** have counters on-site.

Greyhound (800/231-2222, www.greyhound.com) bus service is available to Dillon from various cities in Montana. The station is located at Jim's Smoke Shop (25 E. Helena St., Dillon, 406/683-6703 or 800/454-2487).

Helena

Montana's capital, Helena (population 29,351, elevation 4,090 feet) is an elegant city, the demure little sister to Butte. Founded in 1864 with a gold strike on a site that would become the heart of the city, Helena was initially named Crabtown by the four prospectors who made the discovery. Eventually, as the camp filled with miners, the name was changed to St. Helena after a town in Minnesota. It was a gold-mining town, after all, and the saint was eventually dropped. In 1875, after a bitter battle that pitted copper kings Marcus Daly and William Andrew Clark against each other, Helena was named the capital of Montana Territory, and 13 years later ground was broken on the State Capitol Building.

Helena has done a particularly good job of preserving its history by maintaining architecture. The State Capitol Building, for example, is Greek Renaissance style, and the myriad mansions around town are largely Victorian. With its soaring spires and remarkable stained glass, the St. Helena Cathedral would look at home in Europe. There are also humble miners' cabins and historic businesses lining the streets in Last Chance Gulch. Like Butte, Helena is a fascinating assortment of cultural influences captured over time, and the city has preserved its history beautifully, both on the streets and in its museums.

But Helena is not living in the past. The city is growing rapidly, with a 2000–2008 population increase of nearly 14 percent. And with that growth comes more culture; Helena is becoming recognized as the arts capital of the state, with an edgy, contemporary fine arts scene in addition to extensive performing arts. Located as it is in a wide-open valley surrounded by mountains, lakes, and rivers, Helena also offers endless opportunities to get out of the city and into the wilderness.

© DONNIE SEXTON

Helena, Montana

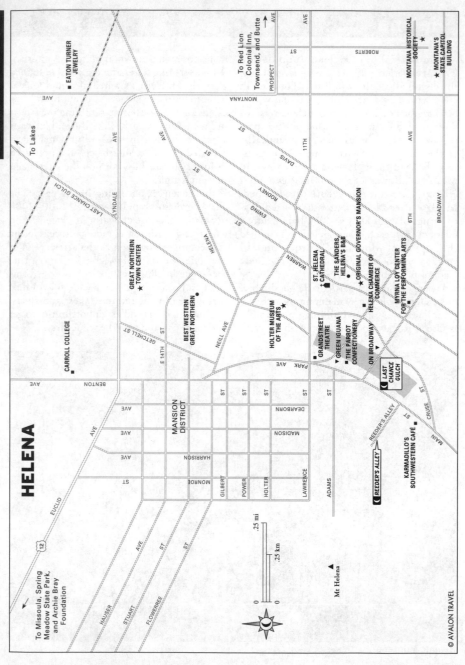

HELENA

To Missoula, Spring
Meadow State Park,
and Archie Bray
Foundation

To Lakes

To Red Lion
Colonial Inn,
Townsend, and Butte

EATON TURNER
JEWELRY

MONTANA HISTORICAL
SOCIETY

MONTANA'S
STATE CAPITOL
BUILDING

CARROLL COLLEGE

GREAT NORTHERN
TOWN CENTER

BEST WESTERN
GREAT NORTHERN

HOLTER MUSEUM
OF THE ARTS

ST. HELENA
CATHEDRAL

THE SANDERS,
HELENA'S B&B

ORIGINAL GOVERNOR'S MANSION

HELENA CHAMBER OF
COMMERCE

MYRNA LOY CENTER
FOR THE PERFORMING ARTS

GRANDSTREET
THEATRE

GREEN IGUANA

THE PARROT
CONFECTIONERY

ON BROADWAY

LAST
CHANCE
GULCH

REEDER'S ALLEY

KARMADILLO'S
SOUTHWESTERN CAFÉ

MANSION
DISTRICT

LAST CHANCE GULCH

Mt Helena

.25 mi

.25 km

© AVALON TRAVEL

SIGHTS

Last Chance Tour Train

One of the best ways to get an overview of the city and some historical perspective is by hopping on one of the Last Chance Tours (tours depart from the Montana Historical Society, E. 6th Ave. and Roberts St., 888/423-1023, www. lctours.com, June 1–Sept. 15, $7.50 adults, $6 ages 4–12, free for children under 4). The wheeled trains and trolley cruise around town with commentary on places like Reeder's Alley, the Old Fire Tower, Last Chance Gulch, and the city's tree-lined Mansion District. Tours depart at 11 A.M., 1 P.M., and 3 P.M. daily in June; there is an additional tour at 5:30 P.M. daily in July–August. Departure times are at 11 A.M. and 3 P.M. September 1–15. Plan to arrive 15 minutes before departure time for any tour.

Montana's State Capitol Building

Visible for miles around with its weathered copper dome, the Montana State Capitol Building (225 N. Roberts St., 406/444-2694, www.montanahistoricalsociety.org) unites Montana's past and present in a very ornate and interesting way. The building itself is something of a Greek Renaissance masterpiece. Started in 1898, the main portion of the building was completed in 1902, and the wings were unveiled 10 years later. The building is filled with dramatic art by some of Montana's most recognizable legends, among them Charles M. Russell and Edgar Paxson.

Self-guided tours are possible 9 A.M.–5 P.M. daily. Guided tours are offered on the hour 9 A.M.–2 P.M. Monday–Saturday and noon–3 P.M. Sunday in summer, and on the hour 9 A.M.–2 P.M. Saturday only in winter. When the legislature is in session, in odd-numbered years, tours are offered 9 A.M.–2 P.M. Monday–Saturday January–April. The Capitol Building is always closed on state holidays and on Sunday when the legislature is in session.

Montana Historical Society

With a phenomenal collection spanning 12,000 years of history, the Montana Historical Society (225 N. Roberts St., 406/444-2964, www. montanahistoricalsociety.org, 8 A.M.–5 P.M. Fri.–Wed. and 8 A.M.–8 P.M. Thurs. summer, 9 A.M.–5 P.M. Mon.–Sat. in other seasons, $5 adults, $1 children, $12 family) is the best historical resource in the state. There is an impressive art gallery, photo archives, a Native American collection, and decorative arts—more than 50,000 artifacts in all. A wonderful long-term exhibit explores what Montana must have been like at the time of Lewis and Clark. There are also several special exhibits and traveling exhibits. The institution was founded in 1865, making it among the oldest of its kind in the western United States.

Original Governor's Mansion

Built in 1888 by a wealthy businessman, this Queen Anne–style mansion was owned by a number of important Helena residents before it was acquired by the State of Montana in 1913 as the Original Governor's Mansion (304 N. Ewing St., 406/444-4789, www.montanahistoricalsociety.org, guided tours hourly noon–4 P.M. Tues.–Sat. summer, noon–4 P.M. Sat. in other seasons, $4 adults, $1 children, combination tickets for museum and tour are $8 adults and $1.50 children). Since 1959, the mansion has been owned, meticulously restored, and maintained by the Montana Historical Society.

◖ Last Chance Gulch and Reeder's Alley

Rarely in the West have important gold or other mineral discovery sites gone on to become the center of big modern cities. Helena is an exception. Four prospectors (known as "the four Georgians") discovered gold in a small tributary of Ten Mile Creek. A mining camp quickly grew up around them, and the discovery site became the camp's main drag. Businesses sprouted up around the creek and never left.

Nearly 150 years after that first discovery, Last Chance Gulch (between W. 6th Ave. and Pioneer Park) is still at the heart of the city. But rather than a dusty collection of saloons and brothels, the area has been transformed into a marvelous three-block pedestrian mall that includes dozens of great eateries, a few museums and galleries, wonderful shopping, and one of the most popular candy shops in the state.

Nearby, Reeder's Alley (between S. Park Ave. and S. Benton Ave., across from Pioneer Park, 406/449-6688, www.reedersalley.com) is a unique little corner of downtown that reflects its more humble origins. The area has remained authentic visually while some of the small miners' shacks, tenements, stables, and other buildings have been transformed into upscale shops and eateries. The buildings have been designated a historic district in the National Register of Historic Places. Both areas are worth spending an afternoon or evening, enjoying a meal and some shopping.

Visual Arts

In a town that is becoming known for its art, the **Holter Museum of the Arts** (12 E. Lawrence St., 406/442-6400, 10 A.M.–5:30 P.M. Tues.–Sat., noon–4 P.M. Sun. year-round, free) is a fascinating place to spend some time. The building was built in 1914 and expanded in 1999 to add 6,000 square feet of art galleries. The museum's contemporary collection includes art in a variety of media that is displayed in over 25 exhibitions annually, creating a unique voice in the Northwestern art scene. The museum makes art education a priority and has managed to keep admission free.

Another cutting-edge artists workshop and gallery is **The Archie Bray Foundation** (2915 Country Club Ave., 406/443-3502, www.archiebray.org, 10 A.M.–5 P.M. Mon.–Fri. Sept.–May, 10 A.M.–5 P.M. Mon.–Fri., 1–5 P.M. Sun. June–Aug.), an international hotbed of ceramic art in what was once a brick factory. Hundreds of well-known artists have come to work and exhibit here.

Marysville

Forty-five minutes northwest of Helena down a long dirt road is the once-booming town of Marysville. The story is familiar: Gold was discovered in the 1880s, and a town grew up around it almost overnight until there were 4,000 souls eking a living out of the earth. Over the course of 20 years, the town exploded with dozens of businesses, including competing newspapers, a dozen saloons, three churches, two doctors, and two hotels. But by century's end, mining had all but ceased and the prosperous town withered quickly as its residents fled elsewhere for opportunities.

Surprisingly, there is a great restaurant to be found amid the slowly decaying ghost town. **Marysville House** (406/443-6677, www.marysvillemontana.com, from 5 P.M. Wed.–Sun. year-round, entrées $15–37) is a rustic but wonderful destination with good food in plentiful quantities. There is quite a selection of seafood and steaks, and they make sure to point out that you won't need a salad with this meal. Dessert is roasted marshmallows over the bonfire out back. You won't find an experience like this anywhere else. The **Marysville Guest House** (406/442-5141, $120) is nearby if you want to spend the night. To reach Marysville, take I-15 north to Highway 279 for 23 miles, and follow the signs for Marysville.

Gates of the Mountains

Just outside Helena is one of the loveliest canyons in Montana. Named Gates of the Mountains by Lewis and Clark in 1805 because of the 1,200-foot limestone cliffs that tower on either side of the Missouri River, it has become a favorite recreation area for Helena residents.

There are many ways to enjoy this scenic area on your own, but for those interested in tours, **Gates of the Mountains Boat Tours** (3131 Gates of the Mountains Rd., 20 miles north of Helena at I-15 exit 209, 406/458-5241, www.gatesofthemountains.com) has 120-minute cruises ($14 adults, $12 seniors, $8 ages 4–12, free for children under 4) from the marina; schedules change daily, so call for details. There is abundant wildlife in the area, including bighorn sheep, mountain goats, and more than 120 bird species. You can bring a picnic lunch and get off the boat, returning later on another one. It is also possible to hike from

YOUNG MEN AND FIRE: THE TRAGEDY AT MANN GULCH

Not far from the Gates of the Mountains is a small but haunting little draw known as Mann Gulch, still reachable only by boat or air. The tragedy at Mann Gulch happened on August 5, 1949, when a small fire grew with blistering hot winds into an inescapable wall of fire.

Fifteen National Forest Service smoke jumpers embarked on a fairly routine call that day. As they departed from their base in Missoula, temperatures in Helena hit 97°F and the winds picked up. The cargo drop did not go as planned – heavy turbulence forced a higher than usual jump, the crew's radio was broken, and much of their equipment was scattered over a wide area – but within about an hour, by 5 P.M., the smoke jumpers gathered their gear, rendezvoused with a local recreation and fire prevention guard who had initially called in the fire, and headed down the slope toward the fire, which was burning up from the river. When their path to the Missouri River was blocked by fire around 5:30 P.M., the crew turned around and headed back uphill. At 5:53 P.M., with the fire rapidly gaining on them, foreman R. Wagner Dodge advised the firefighters to drop their tools in an attempt to speed their flight. The men were literally running up the mountain, a 76 percent grade in places, trying to escape 20-foot flames that were traveling an estimated 280-610 feet per minute. The fire was seconds away when, at 5:55 P.M., Dodge

lit what has come to be known as an escape fire in an open grassy area. Despite his pleas for the men to stay with him in the burned-out area he was creating, the crew continued their mad dash uphill away from the flames. Thirteen of the men were overtaken and burned to death between 5:56 and 5:57 P.M. Dodge survived by laying in his burned-out area, although he was lifted off the ground three separate times by the winds created by the main fire. The only other survivors, Sallee and Rumsey, escaped by taking the shortest and steepest route through a crack in the rimrock to the summit.

The shocking tragedy – the first deaths in the relatively new field of smoke jumping – were not without meaning. Copious research was done at the site to determine more about fire science and, in particular, firefighter safety. The best book on the subject is the posthumously published *Young Men and Fire* (1992) by legendary Montana writer Norman Maclean. Modern safety techniques – including safety zones, individual fire shelters, and survival training – were created in the aftermath of the disaster and are still relied on today. Seventy-three firefighters were trapped while they fought a fire near Salmon, Idaho, in August 1985. Because of the knowledge that came out of the Mann Gulch tragedy, all 73 survived.

here to **Mann Gulch,** where 13 firefighters were killed by a fast-moving wildfire in 1949.

ENTERTAINMENT AND EVENTS

Every Wednesday throughout summer, a different block of Helena comes to life for **Alive at 5** (406/447-1535, www.helenachamber.com), a fun and family-oriented event that combines live music, food, and drink for a fantastic summer evening.

Each summer in late June, the **Mount Helena Music Festival** (406/447-1535, www.

downtownhelena.com, $18 in advance, $20 at the gate) brings a diverse group of musicians to Helena for a celebratory weekend outdoors under the sun and stars.

Once each summer, the Helena Symphony joins Carroll College in presenting **Symphony Under the Stars** (406/442-1860, www.helenasymphony.org) on the hillside at Carroll College.

In late July–early August, Helena puts on the annual **Last Chance Stampede and Fair** (98 W. Custer Ave., 406/457-8516, www.lewisandclarkcountyfairgrounds.com) at the fairgrounds. In addition to big country-music concerts, the fair holds a rodeo, a carnival, food, and a variety of entertainment.

There are two marvelous theaters in town that host both musical and dramatic events. The **Myrna Loy Center for the Performing Arts** (15 N. Ewing St., 406/443-0287, www.myrnaloycenter.com) presents contemporary media and performing arts from its glorious theater in the castle-like old county jail. The **Grandstreet Theatre** (325 N. Park Ave., 406/442-4270, www.grandstreettheatre.com) presents classic plays and musicals in a beautifully restored Unitarian church.

SHOPPING

Eaton Turner Jewelry (1735 N. Montana Ave., 406/442-1940, www.eatonturnerjewelry.com) is the oldest jeweler in the state and has been family owned and operated since 1885. History aside, this is a special store and offers a great selection of jewelry, including local stones like Montana and Yogo sapphires.

A wonderful independent book store, **Montana Book & Toy Co.** (331 N. Last Chance Gulch, 877/844-0577, www.mtbookco.com) offers a diverse collection of books for all readers and children's toys.

For a real taste of Montana, look no farther than [**The Parrot Confectionery** (42 N. Last Chance Gulch, 406/442-1470), an absolute Montana standard when it comes to candy shops and diners. They make 130 different varieties of candy, and their reputation for handdipped chocolates has won them customers worldwide. Try a cherry phosphate from the original soda fountain, and sit up at the bar for a bowl of their secret-recipe chili. A local favorite since 1922, the Parrot should not be missed.

RECREATION
Skiing

Despite the fact that Helena is rather dry compared to many parts of Montana, they do have a pretty impressive ski hill when the weather cooperates. **Great Divide** (7385 Belmont Dr., Marysville, 406/449-3746, www.skigd.com,

$36 adults, $28 students, seniors, and military, cheaper tickets available for less terrain and shorter time) has 140 trails and four terrain parks spread across three peaks and three valleys. There is terrain for everyone from toddlers testing out their ski legs to triple-black-diamond adrenaline junkies. The mountain is 23 miles north of Helena, and in the summer the mountain offers two-hour guided horseback rides (406/439-8742, $49 pp) in beautiful forested and open areas.

Hiking

Considered by many to be the best urban hiking trail in the state, the seven-mile (one-way) trail along the **Mount Helena Ridge** leads gradually up and along the forested ridge overlooking the Helena Valley. It can be accessed five miles south of town from either the Park City trailhead or the Mount Helena trailhead: Drive south of Helena on Park Avenue until you see the sign for Mount Helena City Park. Drive through the Reeders Village subdivision to get to the dirt parking lot. Be sure to arrange a shuttle (or turn around partway) if you don't want to hike the full 14.8 miles round-trip. If you depart from the Mount Helena Park area, there are roughly 20 miles of hiking trails in the 620-acre park. For more information, contact the **Helena Ranger District** (406/449-5490).

Canyon Ferry, Hauser, and Holter Lakes

All three lakes were created by dams on the Missouri River, and all three have become important recreational areas for people from all over southwest Montana.

Located south of Helena off U.S. 287, Canyon Ferry Lake is the largest of the three and the newest, dating to the 1950s. Canyon Ferry covers 25 square miles and offers 80 miles of shoreline along with endless boating and fishing opportunities. The nearby **Canyon Ferry Wildlife Management Area** provides habitat for a diversity of animals that include foxes, moose, ospreys, and geese. There are plentiful camping grounds and services around the lake, but things fill up quickly on hot summer weekends, so be sure to book in advance.

A scenic 3,200-acre reservoir seven miles north of Helena on I-15, then four miles east on Secondary Road 453 and three miles north on the county road, Hauser Lake is home to record-breaking kokanee salmon, rainbow and brown trout, walleye, and perch. Two public campgrounds, **White Sandy Recreation Area** (406/533-7600, $10 per night) and **Black Sandy State Park** (406/495-3260, $20 per night May–Sept., $18 per night Oct.–Apr., $5 day-use for nonresidents) offer terrific access to the reservoir.

The most beautiful of the reservoir lakes is Holter Lake (406/533-7600), within view of the Gates of the Mountains north of Helena. There are three public campgrounds and recreation areas along the shoreline, designated swimming areas, two boat ramps, and plenty of fish waiting to be caught.

ACCOMMODATIONS

While Helena is long on hotels (perhaps for all the legislators who come to govern for four months every other year), most fall into the category of nice upscale chain hotels or nice upscale bed-and-breakfasts. There is no grand dame here waiting to reclaim its former glory.

Still, there are plenty of nice rooms all around town. The **Best Western Great Northern** (835 Great Northern Blvd., 800/829-4947, $129–147) is shiny and new, with decor intended to conjure the Great Northern Railway days. It has all of the amenities you could want in a city hotel, and small pets (under 25 pounds) are welcome for $15 per night per animal for up to two animals. The hotel is ideally located in the relatively new **Great Northern Town Center** and is within walking distance of an eight-plex theater, shopping, a children's museum, and a carousel.

Closer to the highway is the **Red Lion Colonial Hotel** (2301 Colonial Dr., 406/443-2100, www.redlion.com, $140), a large, full-service, very comfortable hotel.

For a more historic option downtown near the state capitol, **The Sanders, Helena's Bed and Breakfast** (328 N. Ewing St., 406/442-3309, www.sandersbb.com, $130) offers seven guest rooms in their beautifully appointed 1875 Queen Anne mansion. Many of the furnishings are original to the home, and the owners are gracious and welcoming.

FOOD

For a quick bite between sights, try the **Green Iguana** (11 W. 6th St., 406/443-7422, 6:30 A.M.–4 P.M. Mon.–Fri., breakfast or lunch $5–11) for healthy smoothies, coffee and tea, and breakfast and lunch items. There is also a full salad bar.

On the top of a hill overlooking Last Chance Gulch and the Helena Valley, **Karmadillo's Southwestern Café** (139 Reeders Alley, 406/442-2595, 11 A.M.–2 P.M. Tues.–Wed., 11 A.M.–8 P.M. Thurs.–Fri., 10 A.M.–8 P.M. Sat.) is a perfect spot to sit outside and enjoy a summer afternoon or evening. The food is sensational, all slow-cooked with the fresh salsas and crèmes prepared fresh daily. Lunch ($5–10) options include nachos, homemade chicken tortilla soup, tacos, enchiladas, and even a savory barbecue-beef sandwich. Dinner ($7.50–12) offers some of the same items as well as tamales, chiles rellenos, and combo plates. As good as their slow-cooked meats are, Karmadillo's also has a number of vegetarian items and a children's menu. Even if the food wasn't so good, you could come just for the incredible view and the spacious outdoor seating.

For fine dining in Helena, **On Broadway** (106 Broadway, 406/443-1929, www.on-broadwayinhelena.com, dinner from 5:30 P.M. Mon.–Sat., bar from 4:30 P.M. Mon.–Sat., entrées $15–37) is the elegant favorite, with mouthwatering pasta dishes, steaks and seafood, and live music on Thursday evenings.

INFORMATION AND SERVICES

A good source of visitor information is the **Helena Chamber of Commerce** (225 Cruse Ave., 406/442-4120 or 800/743-5362, www.helenachamber.com, 8 A.M.–5 P.M. Mon.–Fri.). The **Visitors Information Center** (Memorial

Day–Labor Day) is located in a modular log cabin off U.S. 12 East in the Wal-Mart parking lot.

The **main post office** (406/443-3304, Mon.–Sat.) is at 2300 North Harris Street, and the **Lewis and Clark Library** (406/443-3304, www.lewisandclark.org) is at 120 South Last Chance Gulch.

St. Peter's Hospital (2475 Broadway, 406/442-2480, www.stpetes.org) has a 24-hour emergency room.

The **Clean and Coin Laundromat** (1411 11th Ave., 406/442-9395) is open every day.

GETTING THERE

The **Helena Regional Airport** (HLN, 2850 Skyway Dr.) is just 2.5 miles from the city center and is served by Delta/SkyWest, Alaska/Horizon, United, and Big Sky Airlines. The rental-car agencies available at the airport are **Alamo, Avis, Hertz,** and **National.**

Shuttles to the airport are provided by hotels in town. The courtesy phone to contact them is located in the baggage-claim area. There is also a courtesy phone to call Capitol Taxi (406/449-5525).

Helena is 64 miles north of Butte and 115 miles southeast of Missoula. **Rimrock Trailways** (630 N. Last Chance Gulch, 406/442-5860) runs several bus routes to and from nearby cities, including Bozeman, Billings, and Butte. It connects with Greyhound in Bozeman and Missoula.

GETTING AROUND

In addition to the car-rental agencies at the airport, **Budget** (1930 N. Main St., 406/443-3635) has an office in town.

The Helena Area Transit Service (HATS) operates the **trolley,** which has 10 stops in the downtown area and runs every 30 minutes 11 A.M.–5 P.M. daily, as well as the **Check Point Bus,** with an 18-stop route that runs 7 A.M.–5 P.M., and the **Curb-to-Curb Bus** (pickups are not at fixed stops) that runs every 30 minutes 6:30 A.M.–5:30 P.M.

Capitol Taxi can be contacted at 406/449-5525.

BOZEMAN AND THE GATEWAY TO YELLOWSTONE

Montana's playground and a gateway to the nation's first national park, south-central Montana is bursting with mountains to climb, rivers to fish, and trails to hike. From the Bridgers, Madison, and Gallatin Ranges that ring the Gallatin Valley to the craggy Absarokas of Paradise Valley and the massive Beartooths that bridge Red Lodge and Yellowstone National Park, this region is home to a number of noteworthy mountain towns, including Bozeman, Big Sky, and Red Lodge. Big Timber, Livingston, and Three Forks offer more of a big plains mentality despite their immediate proximity to some very impressive mountains.

The diversity of the region's geography and climate allows for a compelling range of activities. From Bozeman, you can drive 30 miles west and hike the sacred ground at Buffalo Jump State Park; head just 15 miles south from Buffalo Jump and you can fish along the Madison River. Just a few miles north of Bozeman is Bridger Canyon and the legendary Bridger Bowl, where you can ski deep powder on the ridge. Or head 20 miles south of town to find yourself up Hyalite, an impressive recreation area known for its challenging ice climbs. All of these activities are possible in the same month, March; few regions in the state allow you to choose your season as easily as your activities.

While the main draw is the natural splendor and recreational opportunities, as well as the high probability of good weather to enjoy them, there are a multitude of ways to get to know this area: The Sweet Pea Festival of the Arts in Bozeman, the Fourth of July Rodeo

© DONNIE SEXTON

GATEWAY TO YELLOWSTONE

HIGHLIGHTS

◖ Museum of the Rockies: Renowned for its impressive dinosaur collection and its role as the home turf of dinosaur guru Jack Horner, Bozeman's Museum of the Rockies is a gem. Founded with a gift from Dr. Caroline McGill in 1957, the museum is home to 300,000 objects in permanent and traveling displays, a planetarium, and an outdoor living history farm that is open in summer (page 213).

◖ Emerson Center for the Arts and Culture: Just a block and a half off Main Street, The Emerson, as it is more commonly known, is a 1900s school rehabbed as the city's arts hub. Peruse more than 30 studios, a fab restaurant, and any number of special events (page 215).

◖ Madison Buffalo Jump State Park: A hike on this cliff, overlooking the Madison River, is not only a lesson in Native American history but most often an exercise in solitude. Aside from the cacti and rattlesnakes (which can be avoided), this state park sees little traffic and is well worth the visit (page 216).

◖ Floating the Madison River: The section of this blue-ribbon trout stream north of Norris is wide and slow, with plentiful access for floaters. The water is warm for Montana and weaves through some beautiful rolling terrain (page 220).

◖ Chico Hot Springs Resort: A classic Montana joint, Chico has all of the trappings of a resort – hiking, riding, pool, day spa, and sumptuous cuisine – with none of the attitude. You can still get a room here for $49 (page 234).

◖ Beartooth Scenic Highway and Pass: Probably the second-most beautiful highway in Montana (after the Going-to-the-Sun Road), the Beartooth Highway offers a lot more room for spontaneous adventures. Bring your bike, hiking boots, binoculars, even your skis on this summit-topping stunner (page 238).

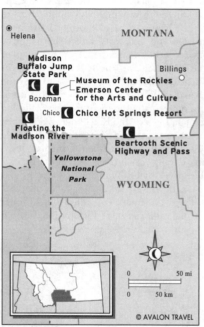

LOOK FOR ◖ TO FIND RECOMMENDED SIGHTS, ACTIVITIES, DINING, AND LODGING.

in Livingston, and the running of the sheep in normally sleepy Reed Point show that south-central Montana is a distinctive blend of the Old West and the new. As the hub of the region, and the home of Montana State University, Bozeman is an increasingly sophisticated mountain town with a welcoming mix of outdoor junkies, old-time cowboys, and blissed-out transplants.

PLANNING YOUR TIME

As is true across Montana and Wyoming in general, this region is vast and can require significant driving to get from one destination to the next. With its fairly central location, ease of air or highway access, and abundance of accommodations, **Bozeman** is a superb launching point for the region. You could easily spend three days here, checking out the arts scene

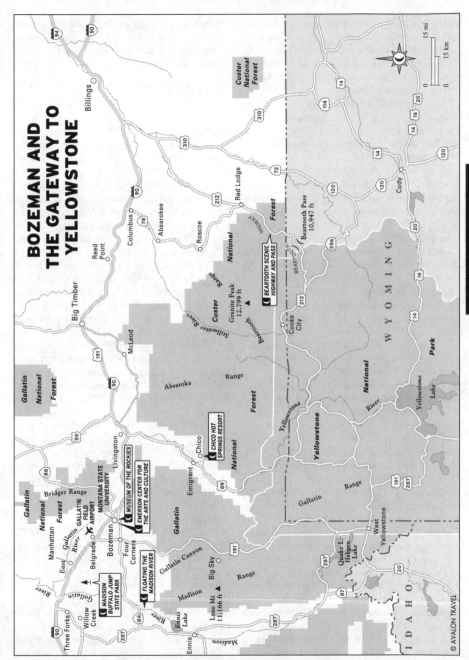

BOZEMAN AND THE GATEWAY TO YELLOWSTONE

Billings

Reed Point

Columbus

Absarokee

Roscoe

Red Lodge

Big Timber

McLeod

Custer National Forest

Custer National Range

Granite Peak 12,799 ft

BEARTOOTH SCENIC HIGHWAY AND PASS

BEARTOOTH SCENIC HIGHWAY

Beartooth Pass 10,947 ft

Cody

WYOMING

Gallatin National Forest

Stillwater River

Beartooth Range

Cooke City

Yellowstone

Yellowstone National Park

Yellowstone River

Yellowstone Lake

Absaroka Range

Gallatin National Forest

CHICO HOT SPRINGS RESORT

Chico

Emigrant

Livingston

MUSEUM OF THE ROCKIES

EMERSON CENTER FOR THE ARTS AND CULTURE

MONTANA STATE UNIVERSITY

GALLATIN FIELD AIRPORT

Bridger Range

Gallatin National Forest

Manhattan

Belgrade

Bozeman

Four Corners

Gallatin River

East Gallatin River

MADISON BUFFALO JUMP STATE PARK

FLOATING THE MADISON RIVER

Gallatin Canyon

Big Sky

Lone Mt 11,166 ft

Gallatin Range

Gallatin

West Yellowstone

Quake L. Hebgen Lake

Three Forks

Willow Creek

Ennis

Madison

Ennis Lake

Madison River

Gallatin River

IDAHO

15 mi

15 km

© AVALON TRAVEL

and nightlife and enjoying the spectacular recreational opportunities in every direction. Nearby **Big Sky** is a popular destination in summer for biking, hiking, and horseback riding as well as for skiing in winter. **Three Forks** and **Manhattan** offer an excellent taste of small-town Montana and are worthwhile stops, especially if you can be there for a favorite local event: the **Three Forks Rodeo,** the **Running of the Horses,** or **Manhattan's Christmas Stroll.**

Just over the pass from Bozeman is **Livingston,** a small but vibrant community with a lot of character (and plenty of characters). You could happily spend a morning or afternoon browsing the shops and galleries downtown, and Livingston has an inordinate number of excellent restaurants to sample. The town explodes with enthusiasm and visitors over the **Fourth of July,** and if you can secure a parking spot for the parade and a ticket to the rodeo, dealing with the crowds (this is Montana, remember) will be well worth the effort.

Aptly named **Paradise Valley** links Livingston with the northernmost entrance to Yellowstone National Park at Gardiner. The mountains are spectacular and beg to be hiked. **Chico Hot Springs** is the place to stay and boasts some of the best dining in the state in addition to a long list of activities.

The plains seem to unfurl themselves, green and then golden, as you drive from Livingston through **Big Timber.** Anyone interested in Norwegian immigrant history in Montana should not miss the **Crazy Mountain Museum,** and a meal at the historic **Grand Hotel** right downtown is a treat. In **Columbus** the sheer bulk of the Beartooths dominate the horizon. There are wonderful side trips en route: a riverside hike in the **West Boulder Valley,** a burger at the **Road Kill Café** in McLeod, and if you time it right (Labor Day Sunday) the **Great Montana Sheep Drive** in Reed Point.

Red Lodge is itself a wonderful destination for skiers, bikers, hikers, and even driving enthusiasts who want to tackle the **Beartooth Highway.** It would be an easy and worthwhile

place to spend a couple of days before heading back to civilization in Billings or Bozeman, or into the wilds of Yellowstone through the northeast entrance at Cooke City.

HISTORY

Called the "Valley of the Flowers" by the Native Americans—including Shoshone, Nez Perce, Blackfeet, Flathead, and Sioux—who lived in, passed through, and traded in the area, the Gallatin Valley around Bozeman was known as a peaceful place; no wars or skirmishes are known to have occurred in the valley. Instead, the region was lush with plentiful rivers and game. White trappers may have entered the valley in the late 18th century, most likely in pursuit of prized beaver pelts. Lewis and Clark camped in the valley in 1805 and 1806.

The discovery of gold at Alder Gulch in 1862 prompted John Bozeman of Georgia to establish the Bozeman Trail, a spur of the Oregon Trail. On July 7, 1864, Daniel E. Rouse and William J. Beall proposed the site for the town that would be named for Bozeman on August 9, 1864. Some of Bozeman's earliest residents include mountain man Jim Bridger, who led the first wagon train through the mountains north of town, now called Bridger Canyon, and cattle baron Nelson Story, who herded his cattle from Texas to Bozeman, mostly at night so that he could avoid Native Americans and the U.S. Army, who did not support the trek.

Founded along the Yellowstone River in 1882 and named for the pioneer director of the Northern Pacific Railway, Johnston Livingston, the city of Livingston grew up around mining, the railroad, and agriculture. Its proximity to Yellowstone National Park, founded in 1872, insured a constant stream of visitors and established Livingston's ongoing reputation as a visitor-friendly town.

In the 18th century, Red Lodge was inhabited by the Crow Indians, who had steadily been moving westward to outrun their Sioux enemies. It is believed the city's name derives from the red clay used to paint the council tipi. Although it was part of the territory assigned to the Crow Nation by the 1851 Fort Laramie Treaty, the U.S. government reneged on its agreement and opened it to settlers and prospectors when coal was discovered in the region. The discovery of this precious resource, attributed to James "Yankee Jim" George, would change the fabric of this town and put it on the map. The town of Red Lodge was officially established in 1884, and by 1887 the Rocky Fork Coal Company opened the area's first mine. By 1889 the Northern Pacific Railway had extended its line to Red Lodge, allowing it to become a major shipping and trade center. During this time a large influx of European immigrants came to work in the mines, and little ethnic neighborhoods sprouted up throughout the town.

In its heyday, Red Lodge was a high-spirited frontier town with miners, ranchers, cowboys, and Indians creating a rather rowdy and at times lawless atmosphere. Both Buffalo Bill Cody and Calamity Jane were known to frequent the town. By the early 20th century, as other mines and sources of energy were being developed, Red Lodge's prominence as a mining town began to fade. When the West Side mine closed during the Great Depression, further economic hardship hit the town. The end of coal mining in the area was marked by the methane explosion in Smith Mine, near Bearcreek, in 1943. This was Montana's worst mining accident, killing 74 miners.

When construction began on the Beartooth Highway in 1931, linking Red Lodge to Yellowstone Park, life came back to the city. The highway was officially opened in 1936 and has insured that the town remains a vibrant destination.

Bozeman and the Gallatin Valley

With Montana State University anchoring it and a geographical setting that has always appealed to outdoor enthusiasts and nature lovers, over the last 20 years Bozeman (population 35,061, elevation 4,810 feet) has grown from a cow town to a town of wine bars and art. The historic downtown is the heart of the community and attracts locals for numerous special events. There are a number of excellent restaurants and bars that appeal to everyone from broke and thirsty students to whisky and wine connoisseurs. A handful of galleries and some very unique shops round out downtown's offerings.

Although the city is growing exponentially and is always on the list of Montana's fastest growing cities, and Gallatin County is among the 100 fastest-growing counties in the United States, the original draw—nature—is still intact. There are two excellent alpine skiing destinations nearby, three blue ribbon trout streams along with numerous smaller streams, and enough hiking and biking trails to satisfy the most hard-core enthusiast. For many, including this writer, Bozeman is the perfect mountain town.

SIGHTS
◖ Museum of the Rockies
Best known for its paleontology exhibit curated by resident dinosaur guru Jack Horner, Museum of the Rockies (600 W. Kagy Blvd., 406/994-2251, www.museumoftherockies.org, 8 A.M.–8 P.M. daily Memorial Day–Labor Day, 9 A.M.–5 P.M. Mon.–Sat., 12:30–5 P.M. Sun. Labor Day–Memorial Day, $10 adults, $9 seniors, $7 MSU students with ID, $7 ages 5–18, free for children under 5) is a fantastic resource for the entire state. The museum tackles 500 million years of history, no small feat, with permanent exhibits that reflect Native American culture, 19th–20th-century regional history, an outdoor living history farm (open only in summer), a planetarium, and, of course, the dinosaurs.

The Siebel Dinosaur Complex includes hundreds of important fossils and an array of impressive life-size reproductions. The traveling

GATEWAY TO YELLOWSTONE

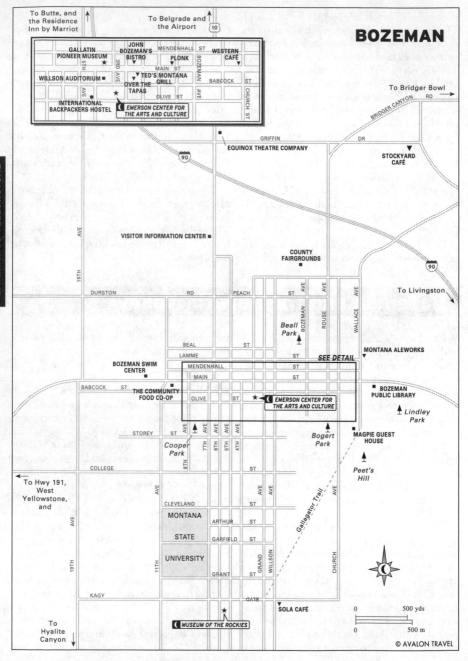

BOZEMAN

To Butte, and the Residence Inn by Marriot

To Belgrade and the Airport

GALLATIN PIONEER MUSEUM

JOHN BOZEMAN'S BISTRO

MENDENHALL ST

WESTERN CAFÉ

PLONK

MAIN ST

WILLSON AUDITORIUM

TED'S MONTANA GRILL

OVER THE TAPAS

BABCOCK ST

OLIVE ST

INTERNATIONAL BACKPACKERS HOSTEL

EMERSON CENTER FOR THE ARTS AND CULTURE

To Bridger Bowl

BRIDGER CANYON

GRIFFIN   DR

EQUINOX THEATRE COMPANY

STOCKYARD CAFÉ

VISITOR INFORMATION CENTER

COUNTY FAIRGROUNDS

To Livingston

DURSTON   RD   PEACH

Beall Park

BEAL   ST

LAMME   ST

SEE DETAIL

MONTANA ALEWORKS

BOZEMAN SWIM CENTER

MENDENHALL   ST

MAIN   ST

BABCOCK   ST

THE COMMUNITY FOOD CO-OP

OLIVE   ST

EMERSON CENTER FOR THE ARTS AND CULTURE

BOZEMAN PUBLIC LIBRARY

Lindley Park

STOREY   ST

Cooper Park

Bogert Park

MAGPIE GUEST HOUSE

COLLEGE

Peet's Hill

To Hwy 191, West Yellowstone, and

CLEVELAND   ST

MONTANA

ARTHUR   ST

STATE

GARFIELD   ST

UNIVERSITY

GRANT

KAGY

To Hyalite Canyon

SOLA CAFÉ

MUSEUM OF THE ROCKIES

Gallagator Trail

0   500 yds

0   500 m

© AVALON TRAVEL

© DONNIE SEXTON

rounding up the horses at a dude ranch not far from Bozeman, Montana

exhibitions vary widely—think tree houses, Egyptian mummies, and Picasso—but typically offer excellent contrast to the permanent exhibits. A children's room upstairs offers limited respite for parents with busy preschoolers, but the museum offers several engaging classes for children as young as infants. Some argue that the admission fees are overpriced, particularly if you come when there is no traveling exhibit, but on a rainy day in Bozeman, the museum can provide hours of compelling exploration.

Downtown Bozeman

Historic downtown Bozeman is interesting architecturally and compelling culturally. It is without a doubt the heart and soul of Bozeman, and more often than not it is the gathering point for the town's most important events. Businesses have faced some stiff competition from big-box stores on the perimeter of town, and there is significant turnover in retail and restaurants, but local residents support downtown in meaningful ways, even starting a

petition campaign to fight to keep staple businesses, like the Owenhouse Ace Hardware, on Main Street. A natural-gas explosion rocked downtown in March 2009, killing one woman and destroying several businesses. Residents showed up in droves to support downtown business owners, workers, and residents alike.

Gallatin Pioneer Museum

Touted as the place "where history and Main Street meet," the Gallatin Pioneer Museum (317 W. Main St., 406/522-8122, www.pioneermuseum.org, 10 A.M.–5 P.M. Mon.–Sat. Memorial Day–Labor Day, 11 A.M.–4 P.M. Tues.–Sat. Labor Day–Memorial Day, $5 adults, free for children under 13, school groups, and researchers) is operated by the Gallatin Historical Society in Bozeman's 1911 county jail building. The museum shared space with the prisoners 1979–1982 before the current jail was completed. The Pioneer Museum boasts a comprehensive permanent collection of items that reflect Bozeman's early history, including an authentic 1870s homesteader's cabin, an agricultural room, substantial historic photographs, and a sheriff's room that houses plenty of artifacts and exhibits related to crime and punishment in the Old West. With no funding from state or local taxes, the museum took a hit with the economic downturn in 2008 and had to raise admission rates. They offer weekly lectures, free with admission, throughout the summer.

◖ Emerson Center for the Arts and Culture

Operated as an elementary school 1918–1991, the Emerson Center for the Arts and Culture (111 S. Grand Ave., 406/587-9797, www.theemerson.org), or The Emerson, as it is more commonly called, is the nucleus of Bozeman's robust arts scene. There are more than 30 studios, galleries, and art-related businesses in the building in addition to Crawford Theater, one of the best in town, and an excellent restaurant, The Emerson Grill. In summer, **Lunch on the Lawn** (11:30 A.M.–1:30 P.M. Wed. July–Aug., free) is a Bozeman tradition with live music, food vendors, and lots of smiling faces.

⟨ Madison Buffalo Jump State Park

Farther afield but well worth the visit is Madison Buffalo Jump State Park (7 miles south of Logan off I-90, 406/994-4042, www.fwp.state.mt.us/parks, sunrise–sunset daily year-round, $5 nonresidents). Used by Native Americans some 2,000 years ago, long before horses were brought to North America, buffalo jumps are a testament to human ingenuity. A covered interpretive display explains the how Native Americans persuaded bison up the hill and off the cliff to their deaths, but the real lesson comes from hiking the mile-long trail (watch for rattlesnakes and cacti, both of which love the sun here) and exploring the site independently. Tipi rings can be identified, as can eagle-catching pits. Splinters of bison bone have been found at the base of the cliff. Aside from the compelling history of the area and the magnificent views from the top, the park's location limits traffic, and you are likely to have the place to yourself.

ENTERTAINMENT AND EVENTS

Held annually the first full weekend in August, **Sweet Pea Festival of the Arts** (406/586-4003, www.sweetpeafestival.org) is Bozeman's answer to Mardi Gras. No one is parading around half-naked—this is Montana, after all—but there is plenty of food (don't miss the tater pigs, a Sweet Pea classic), live music, theater, dance, an arts and crafts fair, both juried and open art shows, and a flower show. The weekend events are held at **Lindley Park** (east end of Main St.). Events leading up to festival include the **Sweet Pea Ball** (Sat. before Sweet Pea weekend), Chalk on the Walk (Tues. before Sweet Pea), **Bite of Bozeman** (Wed. before Sweet Pea), and the Children's Run and Sweet Pea Parade (Sat. morning of Sweet Pea). Packed into three days, the 30-year-old festival is organized by more than 1,500 volunteers and draws more than 16,000 visitors annually. Wristbands

($10 in advance, $15 at the gate) are required for entry to Lindley Park, and one wristband enables you to access all the events in Lindley Park over the course of the weekend.

Although Bozeman residents joke about the "nine months of winter and three months of houseguests," people take summertime recreation very seriously and have created numerous ways to be outside as much as possible. Residents and visitors gather on the lawn at the Emerson Cultural Center for **Lunch on the Lawn** (11:30 A.M.–1:30 P.M. Wed. July–Aug., free), a concert series that attracts 100–200 people and an interesting mix of food vendors. **Music on Main** (6:30–8:30 P.M. Thurs. July–Aug., free) is an opportunity for folks to gather downtown on closed-off streets and enjoy live music, food vendors, and early evening activities for kids. On the second Friday of every month June–September, art lovers gather for the **Downtown Bozeman Art Walk** (406/586-4008, 6–8 P.M.), an opportunity to stroll through the galleries downtown, sipping wine and tasting hors d'oeuvres along the way. Another summer event, **Crazy Days** (downtown, 406/586-4008), is a price-slashing shopping extravaganza that happens each year the third weekend in July.

Other annual events worth checking out are the **Gallatin County Fair** (406/582-3270, fairgrounds@gallatin.mt.gov, $5 adults, free for children under 11), held at the County Fairgrounds (901 N. Black Ave.) the third week in July; October's **MSU Homecoming** and **Downtown Trick or Treat** (both on Main Street); and February's **Wild Winter Fest** (County Fairgrounds, 901 N. Black Ave.). Bozeman's **Christmas Stroll** brings the town out the first Saturday of December to eat, shop, and enjoy the festive season.

Bozeman also boats two **farmers markets.** The original is held in Bogert Park (S. Church Ave., 5–8 P.M. Tues.), and another larger market runs at the Gallatin County Fairgrounds (901 N. Black Ave., 406/582-3270, 9 A.M.–noon Sat.).

As with almost any outdoor activity in Montana, these events are all subject to cooperative weather.

Theater

For a relatively small Rocky Mountain town, Bozeman has a decent number of theater offerings. The best is certainly **Equinox Theatre Company** (2304 N. 7th Ave., 406/587-0737, ext. 06, www.equinoxtheatre.com), which has been around for more than a decade and produces eclectic and original shows, many of which are hilariously funny. The company tours nationally in summer, when there are no performances in Bozeman because people would rather be outside, and offers shows, camps, and classes for kids, teens, and adults. **Broad Comedy** (www.broadcomedy.com), a branch of Equinox that produces irreverent and side-splitting satire by a female cast, has achieved national recognition and plenty of YouTube followers. The **Vigilante Theatre Company** (111 S. Grand Ave., 406/586-3897, www.vigilantetheatrecompany.com) specializes in works by Montana's most gifted playwrights. There are also shows produced by students at **Montana State University** (406/994-3904) and professional theater brought to the Brick Breeden Fieldhouse (1 Bobcat Circle, 406/994-7117) through **Broadway in Bozeman** (406/994-2287, www.brickbreeden.com/broadway).

Music

Bozeman also has an impressive music scene. The **Intermountain Opera** (104 E. Main St., Suite 101, 406/587-2889, www.operabozeman.org) has been producing two professional shows annually since 1978. The shows feature national performers and are staged at the Willson Auditorium (404 W. Main St., 406/522-6042), generally in the spring and fall. The **Bozeman Symphony Orchestra and Symphonic Choir** (1822 W. Lincoln St., Suite 3, 406/585-9774, www.bozemansymphony.org) presents a number of performances each season, starting in September, that range from late Renaissance pieces through the 20th century. They perform annually with the Montana Ballet Company in *The Nutcracker*. **Vootie Productions** (406/586-1922, www.vootie.com) brings outstanding performers to town regularly.

SHOPPING

Like most regional hubs in Montana, Bozeman offers an abundance of shopping opportunities for every taste and budget level. Major stores include Target and Costco on North 19th Avenue as well as Wal-Mart and Murdoch's Ranch & Home Supply on North 7th Avenue. Downtown Bozeman, however, is by far the best place to go for unique items and pure charm.

The Country Bookshelf (28 W. Main St., 406/587-0166, www.countrybookshelf.com) is Bozeman's most beloved bookstore and the state's largest independent bookstore. It is especially geared to local and regional authors, many of whom are willing to show their affection for the place with readings and book signings. On the same block is **Vargo's Jazz City & Books** (6 W. Main St., 406/587-5383), an excellent place to get lost. The shop specializes in slightly more obscure books, CDs, and vinyl, both new and used.

For marvelous gifts and cards, there are three excellent boutiques downtown. **Perspectives** (37 S. Willson Ave. at W. Babcock St., 406/522-7125) offers an adorable selection of baby clothes, shoes, and gifts in addition to distinctive bags, cards, stationery, and jewelry. **Ro Sham Bo** (17 S. Tracy Ave., 406/582-7584, www.roshambomt.com) is an exquisite paper store with works by local and national artisans; there is also an impressive selection of journals, picture frames, baby items, and other gifts. Touted as a shop "for the everyday celebration," **HeyDay** (7 W. Main St., 406/586-5589, www.heydaybozeman.com) specializes in timeless home decor and elegant gifts. From gardening to personal grooming, cooking, and entertaining, this stylish little shop is sure to make you smile.

For the hunter and outdoor enthusiasts, downtown Bozeman offers top-of-the-line shopping. **The Powder Horn** (35 E. Main St., 406/587-7373) has everything from guns and fly-fishing gear to cowboy hats and Saturday-night togs. **Barrel Mountaineering** (240 E. Main St., 406/582-1335, www.barrelmountaineering.com), named in honor of world-class climber and local hero Barry "Barrel" Bishop, is a full-service outdoor store specializing in climbing equipment, backcountry ski gear, functional outdoor apparel, and backpacking supplies. It also has an excellent assortment of climbing books and maps.

Bozeman has a number of notable art galleries. **Thomas Nygard Gallery** (135 E. Main St., 406/586-3636, www.nygardgallery.com) specializes in Western, wildlife, and sports art. Just down the street, **Tierney Fine Art** (127 E. Main St., 406/586-4521, www.tierneyfineart.com) displays an outstanding collection of American, Western, and sports art. **Visions West Gallery** (34 W. Main St., 406/522-9946, www.visionswestgallery.com) is a dynamic space that focuses on contemporary artists in the West.

Bozeman's most significant shopping event is **Crazy Days** (downtown Bozeman, 406/586-4008), a price-slashing extravaganza that happens each year on the third weekend in July. Merchants reduce their inventory prices by up to 75 percent and put much of it out on the street. Early birds are the winners here; it's not uncommon to see several brand-new pairs of last year's skis being carried away by happy new owners.

RECREATION
Pools and Parks
Bozeman is a town of relatively young, active people, a fact that the infrastructure in town reflects. The **Bozeman Swim Center** (1211 W. Main St., 406/582-2910, www.bozeman.net, $4 adults, $3 children and seniors) is a 50-meter Olympic-size pool inside the high school open to the public at designated times daily. The water is kept at a cool 84°F, ideal for lap swimming. **Lone Mountain Gymnastics** (1237 N. Rouse Ave., 406/587-1180) has a smaller and much warmer indoor pool, perfect for little swimmers but not suited for lap swimming; it is open for family swimming ($4 pp, $12 family) on Friday–Saturday. An extensive list of classes is offered at both pools.

During summer, the outdoor pool at **Bogert Park** (303 S. Church Ave., 406/582-0806, $4 adults, $3 children under 14) is packed with families and their children. A couple of waterslides keep the energy (and the crowds) at peak levels. In the park itself, an extensive playground entices children. A band shell is used for Tuesday evening **concerts,** and the pavilion is used as an **ice rink** in winter. Bogert Park is also the venue for the **Farmers Market** (406/539-0216, www.bogertfarmersmarket.com, 5–8 P.M. Tues.), which draws big crowds with food vendors, live music, and family events.

Farther down Church Avenue from Bogert is the **Gallagator Trail,** which follows a former railroad line abandoned in the 1930s. Entirely flat, the gravel trail weaves through some lovely residential and forested areas along Bozeman Creek. Just before the Gallagator is **Peet's Hill,** the city's most popular in-town spot for a hike. A quick cruise up the hill leads you to a network of nice trails, a chance to commune with just about anyone and their dog, and ultimately to **Lindley Park,** an excellent destination year-round. In summer, there is picnicking and the fanfare of the Sweet Pea Festival. During winter, the **Bridger Ski Foundation** (www.bridgerskifoundation.com) grooms miles of trails that bring out racers and novices alike to make tracks around the city's hospital. Two wonderful green areas in the city's historic neighborhoods are **Beall Park** (N. Bozeman Ave. and E. Villard St.), which is popular with kids and has an arts center, a playground, and an ice rink in winter; and **Cooper Park** (S. 8th Ave. and W. Koch St.), a favorite with dogs. The City of Bozeman (www.bozeman.net) has a list of city and county parks online.

Hiking
All across Montana, cities and towns have a tendency to construct an enormous letter on a mountain or hill nearby. Bozeman's B has faded away over time, but the **M** (for Montana State University) is one of the community's favorite, and often most crowded, hiking spots. Accessed from a small parking lot on the west side of Bridger Drive, just past and across the road from the Bozeman Fish Technology

Center, the M is hard to miss and well worth the hike. There is a steep route up (20–30 minutes) or a longer, gentler route (45 minutes–1 hour), making mix-and-match loops a possibility. The diehards can follow the trail 21 miles to the **Fairy Lake Campground** near the end of Bridger Canyon.

Just across Bridger Canyon Drive from the M is the **Bozeman Fish Technology Center** (4050 Bridger Canyon Rd., 406/587-9265, www.fws.gov/bozemanfishtech), one of the community's best-kept secrets. In addition to classes, kid-centered festivals (the Kid Fishing Derby and the Community Watershed Festival), and fantastic architecture, the site offers a great new trail called **Drinking Horse Mountain.** Slightly more shady than the M, and with a summit view that looks north into Bridger Canyon rather than south into the Gallatin Valley, the trail is 1.6 miles to the summit and offers loop options.

South of town is another excellent recreation area, **Hyalite Canyon** (south on S. 19th Ave. to Hyalite Canyon Rd.), one of the most popular in the state. There are excellent opportunities for boating on the reservoir, fishing in Hyalite Creek, and hiking on the various trails, including the stunning **Palisades Falls** trail, which is paved for wheelchair access. Other recreational opportunities include mountain biking, ice climbing, and backcountry skiing in winter.

Skiing

One of only two nonprofit ski areas in Montana, **Bridger Bowl** (15795 Bridger Canyon Rd., 406/587-2111, www.bridgerbowl. com, 9 A.M.–4 P.M. daily during ski season, full-day $45 adults, half-day $37 adults, $37 seniors, $16 ages 6–12, free for children under 6 and seniors over 72) is only 16 miles north of Bozeman and offers 2,000 acres of exceptional terrain and first-class facilities for less than half of what you would pay at Aspen or Vail. Multiple-day tickets and ski school options are available, and there are 71 trails and eight lifts to get you on the mountain, including **Schlasman's,** opened in late 2008, which

summits the ridge, an area long known as an "earn your turns" mecca. The mountain offers diverse terrain but is perhaps slightly more geared toward advanced skiers, with 30 percent of the trails rated "extreme." In the summer, trails are open to hikers and mountain bikers. In early October, usually before the snow flies, the ski hill hosts the **Bridger Raptor Fest** (bridgerraptorfest.org), a series of films, walks, talks, and demonstrations that coincides with the largest golden eagle migration in the United States.

Just north of Bridger Bowl is the **Bohart Ranch Cross Country Ski Center** (16621 Bridger Canyon Rd., 406/586-9070, www.bohartranchxcski.com, $15 adults, $8 ages 7–12, free for children under 7), a wonderful place for novices and racers alike. Bohart boasts 16 miles of impeccably groomed trails suitable for both classic and skate skiers. In summer, Bohart's trails are transformed into excellent hiking, mountain biking, and horseback-riding trails. There is also a championship biathlon course.

In downtown Bozeman, **Lindley Park** (E. Main St. and Buttonwood Ave.) offers extensive groomed cross-country ski trails courtesy of the Bridger Ski Foundation. The best place to park is the northwest parking lot of Bozeman Deaconess Hospital (915 Highland Blvd.). Donation boxes can be found at the entrances to the trail system.

The 18-hole golf course at **Bridger Creek** (2710 McIlhattan Rd., 406/586-9797, www. bridgercreek.com) is also groomed for skiers in the winter. Buttons can be purchased at a variety of locations in town, including **Bangtail Bike & Ski** (137 E. Main St., 406/587-4905, www.bangtailbikes.com), an excellent cycle and Nordic ski shop that also rents cross-country skis.

Fishing

Bozeman is a trout-lover's paradise, with several blue-ribbon streams nearby. The **Gallatin, Jefferson,** and **Madison Rivers** flow through the valley, forming the headwaters of the Missouri River in aptly named Three Forks (31 miles west of Bozeman on

I-90). There is also worthwhile fishing on a private spring creek at the **Milesnick Ranch** in Belgrade. Arrangements and rod fees need to be made through a local outfitter. Al Gadoury of **6X Outfitters** (406/586-3806, www.6xoutfitters.com) is widely considered to be among the region's best, particularly when it comes to spring creeks. As an aside, his shore lunches (think grilled moose burgers) are second to none.

Other local outfitters can offer excellent advice and guide services. **The River's Edge** (2012 N. 7th Ave., 406/586-5373, www.theriversedge.com) is one of Bozeman's oldest and most venerated. **The Bozeman Angler** (23 E. Main St., 406/587-9111, www.bozemanangler.com) offers regular classes and is conveniently located downtown. **Montana Troutfitters** (1716 W. Main St., 406/587-4707, www.troutfitters.com) has been guiding fly-fishing excursions since 1978 and offers excellent online fishing reports. **Yellow Dog Flyfishing Adventures** (406/585-8667 or 888/777-5060, www.yellowdogflyfishing.com) offers first-class trips in the region and mind-blowing fishing adventures around the world.

(Floating the Madison River

In a college town with an active and outdoorsy population, floating the rivers is a popular pastime. The calm and relatively warm **Madison River** is easily the most popular, followed by the slightly more remote **Jefferson River.** For an idyllic half-day float on the Madison, rent an eight-person raft (from $85) or inner tubes (from $9) from **Big Boys Toys All Terrain Rentals** (8254 Huffine Lane, 406/587-4747, www.bigboystoysrentals.com). From Four Corners, drive 30 minutes west on Hwy. 84 (also known as Norris Road) to the Warm Springs access. Float time down to Black's Ford is 2–3.5 hours, depending on the time of year and water flow. If you only have one vehicle, make sure to arrange a shuttle through Big Boys. Try to schedule your float on a weekday, if possible, or early in the morning on the weekend if you don't want to get caught up in the college booze-cruise flotilla.

Golf

There are three private golf courses in and around Bozeman (Valley View Golf Club, Riverside Country Club, and Black Bull Run Golf Club) and two that are open to the public. The 18-hole **Bridger Creek Golf Course** (2710 McIlhattan Rd., 406/586-2333, www.bridgercreek.com, weekdays $19 for 9 holes and $31 for 18 holes, weekends and holidays $21 for 9 holes and $33 for 18 holes) offer 6,511 yards of golf from the longest tees for a par of 71. Special family nights are ideal for little ones just picking up the game, and novice nights provide a nonstressful atmosphere for new players. **Cottonwood Hills Golf Course** (8955 River Rd., 406/587-1118, www.cottonwoodhills.com) offers a nine-hole, 1,181-yard, par-3 course ($14 for 9 holes, $24 for 18 holes) as well as an 18-hole, 6,751-yard course with a par of 70 ($22 for 9 holes, $40 for 18 holes).

Fitness and Yoga

Downtown, **The Club in Bozeman** (448 E. Main St., 406/587-8866) offers guest day passes ($20), which entitle users to all of the facilities and any of the club's impressive list of classes, which include yoga, Pilates, and kickboxing. Longer guest passes are available for this small but very high-end facility. **Be the Change Yoga** (626 E. Cottonwood St., 406/451-3234, www.bethechange-yogastudio.com) is a local favorite with intro classes for only $5 and a $10 drop-in rate. Sweat-inducing Bikram yoga can be found at **Bikram's Yoga College of India/Beyond Boundaries Institute** (705 E. Mendenhall St., 406/522-7008, www.bikramyogabozeman.org). Intro packages are $20 for unlimited classes within 10 days, and drop-ins are welcome for $12. Mats and towels can be rented for $2 each.

ACCOMMODATIONS

At first glance, Bozeman's accommodations seem fairly lacking, at least in terms of charm, for a town with seemingly sophisticated tastes. But for those willing to look, there are some fantastic offerings. The **International Backpackers Hostel** (405 W. Olive St.,

406/586-4659, www.bozemanbackpacker-shostel.com, $20) is open year-round and offers clean shared accommodations in the heart of the downtown residential district.

The east end of Main Street and North 7th Avenue are home to a number of independent motels, some of which have clearly seen better days. **The Rainbow Motel** (510 N. 7th Ave., 406/587-4201, www.rainbowmotelbozeman.com, from $53) offers clean basic rooms.

❰ The Magpie Guest House (323 S. Wallace Ave., 406/585-8223, www.magpiegh.com, $165) offers charming accommodations in an ideal downtown location, sandwiched between the library and Peet's Hill, with all the comforts of home. If you're traveling with friends, the summer rate is $1,155 per week, based on four-person occupancy.

At the 19th Street exit on I-90, visitors will find the extremely comfortable all-suites **Residence Inn by Marriott** (6195 E. Valley Center Rd., 406/522-1535, www.marriott.com, from about $119) with 115 suites. The hotel offers a hot breakfast each morning and social hours Monday–Thursday.

Bozeman Cottage Vacation Rentals (406/580-3223, www.bozemancottage.com) offers a broad array of properties to meet individual preferences for location, price, size, and style—from a lodge near Bridger Bowl to downtown cottages and riverfront cabins. Last-minute bargains can be had for those inclined to wing it.

FOOD

If you have recently traveled through rural Montana, Bozeman seems like a food-lover's mecca. With everything from sushi to tapas, the town affords diners much more than the burgers and steaks for which the state is so well known (although there is an outstanding selection of those as well).

Casual

❰ The Community Food Co-op (908 W. Main St., 406/587-4039, www.bozo.coop, 7 A.M.–9 P.M. Mon.–Sat., 8 A.M.–9 P.M. Sun., deli counter 8 A.M.–8 P.M. daily) is a cornerstone

of the community. Everything the Co-op does—gourmet and often locally produced groceries, mouthwatering prepared foods, and a primo coffee shop, juice bar, and bakery—is done brilliantly. The homemade soups are excellent, as is the salad bar and just about everything in the sprawling deli case. Exotic hot lunches and dinners are often available at prices that cannot be matched elsewhere.

New on the scene and just across the street from the Museum of the Rockies is **Sola Café** (290 W. Kagy Ave., 406/922-SOLA—406/922-7652, www.solacafe.com, 6 A.M.–9 P.M. daily, entrées $6–10), a superb place for fresh, creative cuisine that includes salads, panini, soups, sandwiches, and an assortment of fresh-baked goodies. Sola is also a full-service coffee bar. Online and text ordering along with a drive-through window make gourmet take-home dinners a great option.

Another newcomer worth noting is **Ted's Montana Grill** (105 W. Main St., 406/587-6000, www.tedsmontanagrill.com, Mon.–Thurs. 11 A.M.–10 P.M., Fri.–Sat. 11 A.M.–11 P.M., Sun. 11 A.M.–9 P.M., entrées $12–25) in the historic Baxter hotel. It is the flagship restaurant of local part-time resident and unequivocal philanthropist and land steward Ted Turner. Everything is made from scratch, and each meat cut is available in bison or beef. The apple cobbler dessert is extremely good.

Just up the block is **Over the Tapas** (19 S. Willson Ave., 406/556-8282, www.bozeman-tapas.com, lunch 11 A.M.–2 P.M. Mon.–Sat., dinner 5–10 P.M. Mon.–Sat., tapas 11 A.M.–10 P.M. Mon.–Sat., $3–16), an intimate little bistro serving traditional Spanish-inspired tapas (don't miss the bacon-wrapped dates) and an extensive wine list.

❰ Montana Aleworks (611 E. Main St., 406/587-7700, www.montanaaleworks.com, from 4 P.M. daily, entrées $8.25–36) combines a hip eatery with an extremely popular smoke-free bar and pool lounge. The food is artfully good, with Western staples and an Asian flair. The atmosphere, in a beautifully rehabbed 100-year-old railroad warehouse, is energetic and suitable for everyone from toddlers to grandparents; it can be loud at any time of the week, so a separate dining room is a good option for those with noise issues.

As Bozeman has evolved from its ranching and agricultural heritage, many of the classic diners have been lost to trendier eateries, but two have stood the test of time. The **Western Café** (443 E. Main St., 406/587-0436, 5 A.M.–2 P.M. daily) is an old-timers classic for breakfast and lunch, including their famed chicken-fried steak and cinnamon rolls. Appealing to both cowboys and ski bums is the **Stockyard Café** (1018 E. Griffin Dr., off N. Rouse Ave. as it turns into Bridger Dr., 406/586-9278, 7:30 A.M.–1 P.M. Sat.–Sun. only). The atmosphere is kitschy and intimate—be prepared to help yourself—but anything you order will be sensational; the trick is to find this great old joint.

Fine Dining

John Bozeman's Bistro (125 W. Main St., 406/587-4100, www.johnbozemansbistro.com, lunch 11:30 A.M.–2:30 P.M. Tues.–Sat., dinner 5–9:30 P.M. Tues.–Sat., entrées $8–32) started Bozeman's culinary evolution and continues to set the standard. The menu is diverse, with everything from steak and Alaskan king crab to a Vietnamese *pho* bowl, and features as much local meat and produce as possible through the "Montana Farm to Restaurant Campaign." The bistro occupies a historic 1905 building and went to great lengths to create an elegant and warm ambience.

A few steps off Main Street, tucked into the Emerson Center for the Arts and Culture, the **Emerson Grill** (111 S. Grand Ave., 406/586-5247, entrées $11–29) is a perfect spot for a bite. With walls the color of acorn squash and high-backed wooden booths that recall a 100-year-old schoolhouse, this northern Italian restaurant offers a warm, intimate ambience and excellent, uncomplicated food. The flatbread pizzettes—one of the Grill's signature dishes—are especially good (try the creamed spinach, artichoke, and kalamata olive version), and the extensive boutique-style wine

list boasts descriptions like "Sophia Loren in a glass."

In downtown Bozeman, **Plonk** (29 E. Main St., 406/587-2170, www.plonkwine.com, 11:30 A.M.–2 A.M. daily, entrées $12–30) is an elegant wine bar as known for its tapas and desserts—follow the brie, tomato, and basil panini with the chef's chocolate-board dessert—as for its remarkably global selection of more than 600 wines. The atmosphere is a captivating integration of 100-year-old architecture, contemporary original works of art, minimalist urban design, and an eclectic collection of well-played vinyl records. In the summertime, the crowd spills outside to a handful of sidewalk tables. In a mostly family-friendly town, this is one establishment that does not welcome children or babies.

Nine miles west of Bozeman is the small town of Belgrade, home to one of the best steak houses in the state: The **Mint Bar & Café** (27 E. Main St., Belgrade, 406/388-1100, www.themintmt.com, entrées $17–46) is nearly as famous for its imaginative martinis as for its hand-cut steaks. The fish, complete with dazzling and unexpected sauces, is also noteworthy, and the wine list is extensive.

INFORMATION AND SERVICES

A good place for information, travel services, and maps is **Bozeman's Chamber of Commerce** (2000 Commerce Way, southeast corner of N. 19th St. and Baxter Lane, 406/586-5421 or 800/228-4224, www.bozemanchamber.com, 8 A.M.–5 P.M. Mon.–Fri. year-round). The chamber also runs a log cabin **Visitors Center** (1001 N. 7th Ave., across from K-Mart, 9 A.M.–6 P.M. daily Memorial Day–Labor Day), which offers the same assortment of information, brochures, and maps as at the chamber. Downtown shoppers can find an abundance of information at the **Downtown Bozeman Visitors Center** (224 E. Main St., 406/586-4008).

The main **post office** (2201 Baxter Lane at 19th St., 8:30 A.M.–5 P.M. Mon.–Fri., 9 A.M.–1 P.M. Sat.) offers a 24-hour automated postal service that accepts major credit and debit cards. The old post office still operates downtown at 32 East Babcock Street, one block south of Main Street.

The **Bozeman Public Library** (626 E. Main St., 406/582-2400, www.bozemanlibrary.org, 10 A.M.–8 P.M. Mon.–Thurs., 11 A.M.–5 P.M. Fri.–Sat. June–Aug., 10 A.M.–8 P.M. Mon.–Thurs., 11 A.M.–5 P.M. Fri.–Sat., 1–5 P.M. Sun. Sept.–May) boasts modern and green architectural design with lots of space to work, a nice coffee shop, and an excellent children's section. The library is one of the few places in town that offers **free Internet access.**

Coin-operated washers and dryers can be found at **Duds-n-Suds** (502 S. 23rd Ave., 406/586-3837, 7 A.M.–8 P.M. Mon.–Sat.) and at **The Clothesline** (815 W. Main St., 406/586-3070, 7 A.M.–9 P.M. daily).

Bozeman Deaconess Hospital (915 Highland Blvd., 406/585-5000, www.bozemandeaconess.org) has a 24-hour emergency room. Another option is **Bozeman Urgent Care Center** (1006 W. Main St., Suite E, 406/586-8711, 9 A.M.–8 P.M. Mon.–Fri., 10 A.M.–5 P.M. Sat.–Sun.).

Internet access can be found at the public library, the Community Food Co-op (908 W. Main St., 406/587-4039, www.bozo.coop), and also at a cybercafé, **Homepage** (242 E. Main St., 406/582-9388, www.homepagecaffe.com, 6 A.M.–10 P.M. Mon.–Fri., 7 A.M.–10 P.M. Sat.–Sun.).

GETTING THERE

Bozeman's **Gallatin Field Airport** (BZN) is located eight miles northwest of downtown Bozeman in the nearby town of Belgrade. Delta/SkyWest, Alaska/Horizon, Frontier, and United Express all offer daily nonstop service to and from major U.S. cities, including Salt Lake City, Minneapolis, Seattle, and Denver.

Greyhound travels to almost 40 towns and cities in Montana from the bus depot (1205 E. Main St., 406/587-3110, 10 A.M.–4:30 P.M. and 7:30–8:30 P.M. Mon.–Fri., 2–5 P.M. Sat., 3–4:30 P.M. and 7:30–8:30 P.M. Sun.). In addition, there are several other coach services to choose from:

Northern Transit (406/470-0727), **Powder River Trailways/Coach America** (800/442-3682), **Rimrock Trailways** (800/255-7655), and **Salt Lake Express** (208/356-9796).

Located off I-90, Bozeman is easily accessible by car. It is 142 miles from Billings, 202 miles from Missoula, and 85 miles from Butte. The driving distances are slightly farther from Wyoming: Jackson is 215 miles, Sheridan is 270 miles, and Cody is 214 miles from Bozeman.

Getting Around

From the airport, the Best Western, the Comfort Inn, and the Hampton Inn offer shuttle service. There are also a number of car-rental agencies at the airport; the car-rental center is located next to the baggage claim. **Alamo, Budget, Enterprise, Hertz,** and **National** have on-site counters.

Karst Stage (800/845-2778, www.karststage.com) offers bus and shuttle services. Located next to the National car-rental counter, it provides shuttles to Big Sky ($110), West Yellowstone ($187), and Mammoth Hot Springs ($187) daily during the winter season (during nonwinter months they ask that you make reservations ahead of time).

Greater Valley Taxi (406/587-6303) has a stand outside the baggage claim area. Rides into Bozeman cost $15–35, depending on whether you share the cab with another customer. It is also a good option for getting around town while you are in Bozeman.

VICINITY OF BOZEMAN
Belgrade

Nine miles west of Bozeman on I-90 and often unfairly labeled a bedroom community of Bozeman, Belgrade (population 9,000, elevation 4,454 feet) is a great little Montana town with plenty of character. **Lewis and Clark Park** (Main St.) is the hub of the city and provides a covered picnic area, a wonderful playground, and a wildly popular splash park geared to small children. The **Belgrade Bandits** are the local baseball team, and with Little League and high school offerings, there is always a ball game to watch. Though the Mint Bar & Café (27 E. Main St., 406/388-1100, www.themintmt.com, entrées $17–46) is easily the town's most recommended eatery—diners come from across the state for a martini and a steak—Belgrade is home to a number of good little restaurants.

One standout is Damasco's Pizzeria & Spaghetteria (90 W. Madison Ave., Suite C, 406/388-2724, www.damascos.net, 4:30–9:30 P.M. Fri.–Sat., 4:30–9 P.M. Sun.–Thurs., entrées $9–16). The strip-mall location is nondescript, but owner Tommaso Damasco creates mouthwatering and authentic Italian cuisine. The wood-fired brick oven is a centerpiece and cooks up marvelous pizzas.

The Fall Festival, normally held the third weekend of September, brings out the crowds for a parade, a street dance, and a host of fun family activities. The Festival of Lights, the first Friday of December, is another highlight with a craft show and horse-drawn wagon rides. The Chamber of Commerce (10 E. Main St., 406/388-1616, www.belgradechamber.org) is a good source for local information and a friendly chat.

Manhattan

Twenty minutes west of Bozeman on I-90, Manhattan (population 1,396, elevation 4,200 feet) is a welcoming little (but growing) community surrounded by potato and dairy farms, wheat fields, and mountains. The town was settled by immigrants from the Netherlands but named by New Yorkers who operated the Montana Malting Company. Most folks in the state associate Manhattan with its most famous eatery, Sir Scott's Oasis (204 Main St., 406/284-6929, 11 A.M.–2 A.M. daily, entrées from $18.50), an old-school supper club with relish trays to start and sundaes for dessert. The hearty steak and potatoes you get in between will satiate even the most discerning meat lovers.

During the summer, the Manhattan Farmers Market (406/284-6574, 4:30–7:30 P.M. Wed.) fills the small downtown with local produce, baked goods, arts and crafts, and live entertainment. The third Saturday in August is the annual Potato Festival, which features a pancake breakfast, a parade, a popular annual tent sale from local artisans at Big Sky Carvers, an invitational car show, music throughout the day, and an evening dance. For visitor information, contact the Manhattan Chamber of Commerce (406/284-4162, www.manhattanmontana.com).

Three Forks and Willow Creek

Named for the three rivers that form the headwaters of the Missouri River, Three Forks (population 1,800, elevation 4,130 feet) was put on the map by Lewis and Clark in 1805. The town is rich in fur trapping and trading history and equally distinguished today by a tightly knit community and a mild climate that locals refer to as the "banana belt." The Sacajawea Hotel (5 N. Main St., 406/285-6515, www.sacajaweahotel.com, from $75) is a stately building in the center of town that is a fine place for a drink, a hearty meal, or a comfortable night's rest.

The Three Forks NRA Rodeo is held annually the third weekend in July at the fairgrounds and includes a parade, two nights of rodeo, plenty of food, and entertainment. The Annual Horse Roundup and Drive, held each April, brings the town out with food vendors, entertainment (as if horses galloping down Main Street wasn't enough), and carriage rides through town. The town's Christmas Stroll is what every small town should aspire to: the crowning of a Christmas King and Queen, fireworks, horse-drawn wagon rides, a community cookie exchange, and s'mores around the bonfire.

A couple of great outings just beyond town include Madison Buffalo Jump State Park (off I-90, 7 miles south of Logan, 406/994-4042, www.fwp.state.mt.us/parks, sunrise–sunset daily year-round, $5 nonresidents) and Headwaters State Park (4 miles northeast of Three Forks, Hwy. 205 to Hwy. 286, 406/994-4042), which offers hiking, biking, interpretive trails, camping, and river access for boating and fishing.

Six miles south of Three Forks, the small community of Willow Creek (population 267, elevation 4,153 feet) has plenty of charm. The town's half-dozen artists organize the **Willow Creek Art Walks** the third Friday of each month May–August. A local gallery not to be missed is **Aunt Dofe's Hall of Recent Memory** (102 Main St., 406/285-6996, call for hours), which supports the work of contemporary local artists. Across the street, the **Willow Creek Café and Saloon** (21 Main St., 406/285-3698, 11 A.M.–9 P.M. Tues.–Sat., 8 A.M.–9 P.M. Sun., entrées $6.50–25) draws diners from far and wide for its quaint ambience and savory cuisine, including the valley's best ribs. You can't go wrong with the daily specials—everything is made from scratch. And if you can time your dinner on a night when **Montana Rose** is playing, you're in for a real treat.

Ennis

In the heart of the Madison Valley and in the thick of some of the state's best fly fishing is Ennis (population 1,040, elevation 4,953), 45 miles southwest of Bozeman on U.S. 287. The town hosts a wonderful **Fourth of July Rodeo and Parade** (for reserved-seat tickets, call 406/682-4230 after Memorial Day) each year at the fairgrounds. There is also an excellent weekly **Farm to Fork Farmers Market** (Lone Elk Mall, Main St., www.madisonfarmtofork.com, 9 A.M.–noon Sat. June–Sept.) and the much-touted **Ennis on the Madison Fly Fishing Festival** (406/682-3148, www.

madisonriverfoundation.org) held annually over Labor Day weekend. A benefit for the Madison River Foundation, the three-day event offers plenty of art, food, music, fly-fishing instruction, and camaraderie.

The **fishing** is indeed the thing in these parts, and a number of good outfitters can lead you to gulpers on the Madison River and in Ennis Lake, Hebgen Lake, Quake Lake, Cliff Lake, and Wade Lake. A good place to start is **The Tackle Shop** (127 Main St., 406/682-7729, www.thetackleshop.com).

There is excellent **hiking** in every direction—the Tobacco Roots and Madison Ranges ring the town—and you'll find trail maps and helpful advice west of town at the local **USDA Ranger Station** (5 Forest Service Rd., 406/682-4253).

For dining, Ennis offers a number of good choices, but perhaps none more enticing than the **Continental Divide** (47 Geyser St., 406/682-7600, dinner 5:30–10 P.M. mid-Apr.–Dec.). This sophisticated country bistro is tiny but makes up for its size with exceptionally good food with French flair and a comprehensive wine list. Outdoor seating is available and well worth it.

After filling your belly, the creek-side cabins south of town at **El Western** (4787 U.S. 287, 406/682-4217, www.elwestern.com, $75–155) are an excellent place to hang your hat for the night.

For more information about Ennis, contact the **Ennis Chamber of Commerce** (406/682-4388, www.ennischamber.com).

Big Sky

In the shadow of Lone Peak, tucked in the winding and rugged beauty of Gallatin Canyon, the resort town of Big Sky (population 2,421, elevation 7,218 feet) actually has three resorts: Big Sky, Moonlight Basin, and the entirely private (and dubious, after a 2009 bankruptcy) Yellowstone Club. Although there are not any sights per se, the town and resorts are clearly geographically blessed with mountains for skiing, hiking, climbing, and biking; rivers for fishing and floating; and trails aplenty for horses, hiking, cross-country skiing, and mountain biking. Visitors can take solace in the fact that mountains make up for museums, and the area can be used as a launching point for Yellowstone National Park (51 miles south) or Bozeman (50 miles north).

Although Big Sky has more activities than any visitor could dream of pursuing in a single trip—golf, horseback riding, fishing, skating, skiing, kayaking, wildlife watching—it has a slight identity crisis in that there is no real center of town, which the community is working to remedy. For now, there are enclaves, resorts, and villages dotting the mountainside. The uniting factor in this area is a zeal for outdoor adventuring.

EVENTS AND ENTERTAINMENT

Although it is set up as a winter resort, Big Sky does an excellent job of capitalizing on the relatively short summer with events that draw crowds from near and far. There are few better venues in the state for live music: Concerts are held in a glorious meadow surrounded by rocky peaks at the **Music in the Mountains** series (Meadow Village Concert Stage, 406/995-2742, www.bigskyarts.org, Thurs. evening July–Sept.). Past headliners at the concerts, which are often free, have included Willie Nelson, Bonnie Raitt, and the Doobie Brothers. Other annual musical events sponsored by the Arts Council of Big Sky (406/995-2742, www.bigskyarts.org) include

Strings under the Big Sky (chamber music) and the **Bozeman Symphony Orchestra Pops** concert.

Formerly known as the Big Sky Country Fair, the **Big Sky Arts Festival** (406/995-3000, www.bigskychamber.com, date and venue change each year) is a day-long event that includes a 5K race, a parade, a gathering of local and regional artists and craftspeople, plus kids' activities and plenty of food.

The weekly **Big Sky Farmers Market** (Firepit Park, Big Sky Town Center, 406/570-2417, www.bigskytowncenter.com, 5–7 P.M. Thurs.) features lots of local vendors in addition to prepared food, a great kids area, musical entertainment, and personal enrichment that includes yoga and massage.

For those interested in learning more about the remarkable environment around Big Sky, the **Big Sky Institute** (406/993-9355, www.bsi.montana.edu) is a world-class resource. An interdisciplinary science, education, and outreach institute created by Montana State University in Bozeman, the institute offers regular programs throughout the summer months, including Science and Nature Hikes, Mountains & Minds lectures, Science Family Fridays, and WildWatch Wednesdays geared to children entering 1st–5th grades. There is also a Young Naturalist Camp scheduled annually.

RECREATION
Skiing

One thing that distinguishes Big Sky from other ski destinations in the Rockies is the plentiful elbow room—there are fewer skiers per skiable acre than in most places. **Big Sky Resort** (snow phone 406/995-5900, reservations 800/548-4486, school 406/995-5743, www.bigskyresort.com, $78 adults, $58 students with ID, free for children under 11 with an adult) and **Moonlight Basin** (snow phone 406/993-6666, mountain concierge 866/512-7716, reservations 800/845-4428, www.moonlightbasin.com, $55 adults, $45 students with

ID, free for children under 11) can be combined with the Lone Peak Pass lift ticket ($93 adults) for a total of 5,512 skiable acres and runs up to six miles long with 4,350 feet of vertical drop on 220 named runs. The area averages 400 inches of the fluffy stuff annually, and the ski season generally lasts mid-November–April. With virtually nonexistent lift lines, this is an ideal place for ambitious skiers.

The Lone Peak Tram takes daring skiers 16 feet shy of the mountain's summit, and both resorts offer plenty of terrain for snowboarders with rails and half-pipes. Even with some of the steepest terrain in the country, both Big Sky and Moonlight offer plenty of groomers for beginning and intermediate skiers and snowboarders.

Both resorts have great appeal for families (kids under age 11 ski for free) and have built amenities to keep their guests happy and fully occupied. Big Sky has a **Tubing & Family Fun Zone** (4–8 P.M. Fri.–Sun., $15 adults, $10 children) with a carpet lift as well as a terrain park with boxes, rails, and kickers. Moonlight offers

Family Night with Moonlight (406/995-7716, reservations recommended, $45 includes a family-size pizza and 2 activity bands) 4:30–8 P.M. on certain Fridays that are chosen each year; the event features make-your-own pizza, crafts, games, movies, outdoor sledding, and igloo-building. A traditional bonfire allows for toasty hands and sticky s'mores.

Down the mountain is **Lone Mountain Ranch** (750 Lone Mountain Rd., 800/514-4644, www.lonemountainranch.com, $20 adults, free for kids under 13), a cross-country skier's paradise with 53 miles of beautifully groomed and often forested trails. Snowshoeing is another option, as are guided naturalist tours, lessons and clinics, and telemarking. Skis and snowshoes are available to rent. The trails are sublime, and wildlife viewing can be excellent. For winter solitude and exploration, this is a marvelous place to be.

Fishing and Floating

The Gallatin River runs through the canyon beneath Big Sky and offers up a plethora of

© DONNIE SEXTON

white-water rafting on the Gallatin River near Big Sky, Montana

GATEWAY TO YELLOWSTONE

recreational opportunities. Since U.S. 191 runs parallel to the river for 40 miles, fishing access is easy. The road is not meant for casual driving—no stopping and looking here—but there are several pullouts that can double as parking lots. Float fishing is prohibited, but the wade fishing is enticing, if somewhat tricky given the number of rapids created as the water tumbles down the canyon over beautiful car-size boulders.

Rainbows, browns, and cutthroats can all be found in these chilly waters, and the fish have to be lean and mean to battle the currents. They tend to be slightly less selective than downriver in Bozeman, where the decline slows and the water flattens out. There are caddis hatches practically all summer, and a killer salmonfly hatch in mid-June–early July. Late in the season, whopping terrestrials are the way to go.

Wild Trout Outfitters (U.S. 191, 800/423-4742, www.wildtroutoutftters.com) can offer professionally guided trips. **East Slope Outdoors** (U.S. 191, just south of the Big Sky intersection on the right, 888/359-3974, www.eastslopeoutdoors.com) offers Orvis equipment, rental gear, and guided fly-fishing trips.

If the tranquility of fishing appeals less than the mayhem of white water, rafting on the Gallatin River is a good option. **Montana Whitewater** (U.S. 191, mile marker 64, Gallatin Canyon, 800/799-4465, www.montanawhitewater.com, half-day $51 adults, $41 children under 13, full-day $84 adults, $68 children under 13) offers a range of trips to suit any adrenaline level, including half-day scenic floats, full-day white-water trips, and paddle-and-saddle overnighters. **Geyser Whitewater** (46651 Gallatin Rd., next to Buck's T-4 on U.S. 191, 800/914-9031, www.raftmontana.com, half-day $52 adults, $42 children under 13) is another superb local outfitter that specializes in Gallatin River trips. They also offer kayak trips, horseback riding, and bike rentals.

Hiking and Mountain Biking

In the summer, the mountain at Big Sky unfolds into a network of mountain bike and hiking trails. The **Big Sky Scenic Lift** (406/995-5840, 9:45 A.M.–4 P.M. daily mid-June–Oct., weather permitting, $19 single ride, $30 unlimited full-day, $12 ages 11–17, free for children under 11) gives riders and hikers a lift up (and down, if they choose) and a chance to tackle some thrilling terrain for every skill level. Bikes and helmets are available for rent at **Big Sky Sports** (Mountain Mall, 406/995-5840, www.bigskyresort.com).

The hiking opportunities are endless around Big Sky, with three mountain ranges, the Gallatin National Forest, the Lee Metcalf Wilderness Area, and Yellowstone National Park all nearby. Some local favorites include **Ousel Falls,** an easy up-and-down 1.8-mile stroll to a beautiful waterfall. (Find the parking lot and trailhead on Ousel Falls Road, two miles beyond the intersection of Ousel Falls Road and Spur Road.) Picnic benches along the way make the path a good one for small children. For more ambitious hikers, **Beehive Basin** offers some excellent options. (Find the parking lot and trailhead by following the Beehive Basin turnoff—1.3 miles beyond Big Sky Mountain Village and 30 yards before the entrance gate to Moonlight Basin—for 2.8 miles.) The trail is sky high at 9,200 feet and offers unrivaled 360-degree views. As with all of Montana, the weather can change quickly—snow can fall in July—and hikers need to be fully prepared for whatever Mother Nature sends their way. Farther north in the Gallatin Canyon is **Lava Lake** a somewhat steep hike that leads you to a crystalline icy-cold mountain lake. (From Big Sky, the trailhead is 13.5 miles north on Hwy. 191, just north of the Gallatin River Bridge, but since left turns cannot be made from there, you will need to turn around at the first turn-out and approach the gravel turnoff from the north.) The six-mile there-and-back trail is almost entirely shaded and is an excellent choice on a sweltering day. For guided hikes or backpacking trips, contact **Mountain Ayres Adventures** (406/993-2255, www.mountainayresadventures.com), who will gladly show you the best of the region in style.

For those who choose to hoof it around the links instead of a mountain trail, the 18-hole Arnold Palmer-designed **Big Sky Golf Course** (Meadow Village, 406/995-5780, www.bigskyresort.com, $69 for 18 holes) is open to nonguests and is well worth playing. There is abundant wildlife often sharing the par-72 course. A driving range and full pro shop are available.

ACCOMMODATIONS

Big Sky was built as a resort, and it caters to visitors and vacationers. There is a wide range of accommodations, from ski-in mountainside lodging to rustic roadside motels, inviting guest ranches, luxe resorts, and condo or cabin rentals, that can address your specific needs—staying put or traveling around, skiing or golfing, walking or driving to dinner.

For the best bang for your buck, try the **Corral Motel** (U.S. 191, 5 miles south of Big Sky, 406/995-4249 or 888/995-4249, www.corralbar.com, from $70 s), which also has a terrific restaurant and bar. The guest rooms are basic but clean and comfortable, with honeyed pine paneling that evokes the best of Western hospitality.

Closer to Big Sky is **Buck's T-4 Lodge** (U.S. 191, 1 mile south of Big Sky, 406/995-4111 or 800/822-4484, www.buckst4.com, $99 s or d), a very comfortable hotel with a great bar and one of the best restaurants in the region.

On top of the mountain is the **Summit at Big Sky** (Mountain Village Center, 800/548-4486, www.bigskyresort.com, studio rooms from $192 winter, $252 summer), a deluxe slope-side facility with the convenience of a hotel and the amenities of a condo. It offers both residences and temporary lodging, all in a comfortable and sophisticated atmosphere. There are indoor and outdoor pools, hot tubs, a sauna and fitness facility, and fireplaces in most accommodations.

FOOD

Something about the high mountain air produces serious appetites, and Big Sky has a substantial selection of eateries for every taste.

From the top of the mountain to the bottom, you're never more than a quick jog from your next mouthwatering meal.

The Corral (U.S. 191, 5 miles south of Big Sky, 406/995-4249 or 888/995-4249, www.corralbar.com, summer daily 8 A.M.–10 P.M.; winter Mon.–Thurs. 11 A.M.–9 P.M., Fri.–Sun. 8 A.M.–9 P.M., entrées $16–35) offers up an excellent take on the classic Montana menu. From buffalo T-bones to Delmonico steaks, prime rib, and good ol' hamburgers, the Corral's food is consistently good. There are plenty of chicken, seafood, and pasta options available. You can't go wrong with the smoked trout appetizer.

At the base of the mountain in the Big Horn Center just south of the Big Sky intersection is **(Bugaboo Café** (47995 Gallatin Gateway Rd., Suite 101, 406/995-3350, breakfast 7–10:30 A.M. Tues.–Fri., lunch 11:30 A.M.–2:30 P.M. Tues.–Fri., dinner 5:30–9 P.M. Tues.–Sat., brunch 7 A.M.–2 P.M. Sat.–Sun., entrées $8–32), an unassuming little place featuring comfort food with an inventive twist. The menu changes seasonally to take advantage of local products and includes such favorites as blue crab omelets, chicken pot pie, bacon-wrapped pork tenderloin, and rib eye steak. The Bugaboo is probably the best value in Big Sky.

(Buck's T-4 (U.S. 191, 1 mile south of Big Sky, 406/995-4111 or 800/822-4484, www.buckst4.com, 6–9 P.M. daily summer and winter, call for spring and fall closures, entrées $9–34) is also fairly unassuming but serves up some of the best cuisine in the region. Known statewide and beyond for wild game—think duck, pheasant, bison, and red deer—Buck's menu reflects Montana culinary traditions with more contemporary, lighter fare. The drinks make the most of local harvest; try a huckleberry martini ($7.50).

Located on the mountain in the Moonlight Lodge, **The Timbers Restaurant** (406/995-7777, www.moonlightbasin.com, ski season daily 8 A.M.–midnight; mid-June–late Sept. dinner starting at 5:30 P.M.; closed mid-April–mid-June and late Sept.–Thanksgiving, entrées

$21–37) offers spectacular Western cuisine with a hint of Southern flair. For starters, the pheasant ravioli in saffron pasta and red chili pecan glaze ($13) is an intriguing mix of flavors. The salads are wonderful and fresh, and the entrées are mouthwatering. A few smaller entrées are offered alongside hearty classics like Montana rib eye, Idaho elk chop, and buffalo tenderloin.

INFORMATION AND SERVICES

You can find the **Big Sky Chamber of Commerce** (3091 Pine Dr., 406/995-3000 or 800/943-4111, www.bigskychamber.com, 8:30 A.M.–5 P.M. Mon.–Fri. winter, 8:30 A.M.–5 P.M. Mon.–Fri., 10:30 A.M.–3:30 P.M. Sat.–Sun. summer) in Westfork Meadow.

The **Medical Clinic of Big Sky** has two locations: Meadow Village (11 Lone Peak Tr., 406/993-2797, 10 A.M.–5 P.M. daily), and Mountain Village (100 Beaverhead Tr., 406/995-2797, 10 A.M.–5 P.M. daily). For more serious medical emergencies, **Bozeman Deaconess Hospital** (915 Highland Blvd., 406/585-5000, www.bozemandeaconess.org) has a 24-hour emergency room about an hour's drive from Big Sky.

The **post office** (800/275-8777, 10 A.M.–5 P.M. Mon.–Fri., 10 A.M.–1 P.M. Sat.) is conveniently located at 55 Meadow Center Drive, Suite 2.

The **Wash House Laundromat** is in the Jefferson building in Westfork Meadow.

Your best bet for free **Internet access** is at the **Ophir School library** (45465 Gallatin Rd., 406/995-4281). The library sets aside hours for community use (1–5 P.M. Sun., 10 A.M.–6 P.M. Mon., 4–8 P.M. Tues.–Wed.).

GETTING THERE AND AROUND

Big Sky is 44 miles south of Bozeman off U.S. 191. The closest airport is **Gallatin Field** (BZN) in Belgrade, about 50 miles north.

There are a variety of shuttle services from the airport, including **Karst Stage** (800/845-2778, www.karststage.com), which has a counter next to National Rent-a-Car and provides shuttles ($110) to Big Sky, and **Montana Mountain Express** (888/991-9934), which has fully-equipped luxury vans ($220 per vehicle) that can be chartered for groups of 2–30 people.

Big Sky's only taxi service is **Mountain Taxi** (406/995-4895 or 800/423-4742, www.bigskytaxi.com). It offers transportation to and from Gallatin Field Airport ($140), Big Sky, and West Yellowstone.

Once in Big Sky, take advantage of the new free bus service, **Skyline** (406/995-6287 or 406/539-5858). In addition to covering the Big Sky area, buses also run between Bozeman and Big Sky. Hours vary by season (8 A.M.–10 P.M. daily summer, 6 A.M.–11:30 P.M. daily winter, 10 A.M.–5 P.M. daily spring and fall).

Dollar Rent-a-Car (1 mile from the airport, Belgrade, 877/388-3030) will deliver a vehicle to any Big Sky location.

Livingston and Paradise Valley

Rough and tumble Livingston (population 7,411, elevation 4,501 feet) has always been a crossroads of cultures. A railroad town, it was long the launching point for expeditions—both professional and leisurely—into Yellowstone National Park. Paradise Valley, just south of town, was the stomping ground of the Crow Indians, a prized region for fur trappers, and the end point of the great cattle drive from

Texas. The town was surrounded by mines, which drew a unique crowd, and today it probably has more literary figures and artists per capita than any other community in the state.

At one point in the early 1880s, there were 40 businesses in town, 30 of which were saloons. Such legendary characters as Calamity Jane and Madame Bulldog were residents. Evidence of those wild days is still visible in various establishments,

THE LEGEND OF CRANKY YANKEE JIM

James George, who earned the moniker Yankee Jim as well as a reputation for being more than a little cantankerous, came to Montana Territory as a young prospector in 1863. When gold eluded him, Jim began to hunt professionally, for meat, for the Crow Indian Agency. In 1873, Jim took possession of the road from Bottler's Ranch in Paradise Valley, near present day Emigrant, to Mammoth by squatting in the canyon along the Yellowstone when the road builders stopped construction. Jim set up a toll booth in the narrowest section of the canyon, today called Yankee Jim Canyon, and charged exorbitant fees to all travelers passing through. At the time, it was the only way for travelers to get from Livingston to Gardiner, Montana, and the brand new Yellowstone National Park. By all accounts, Yankee Jim made a lot of money but few friends in those days.

In 1883, the Northern Pacific Railway appropriated his roadbed, much to Yankee Jim's chagrin. He negotiated the construction of another road through the canyon (parts of which are still visible along the west side of Highway 89 south) and used his location above the train tracks reportedly to spit on, curse at, and occasionally fire shots at the passing trains. His tirades were supposedly fueled by copious amounts of whiskey.

By 1893, with his road in disrepair and his penchant for alcohol steadily on the rise, Yankee Jim agreed to surrender his road for a lump sum of $1,000. Local lore inserts Teddy Roosevelt, a frequent visitor to Yellowstone National Park, as the person who convinced Yankee Jim to give up his road and his antics...or else. In 1924, Yankee Jim died penniless in Fresno, California. There are many who believe that his fortune, amassed by all those years of price-gouging in the canyon that bears his name, is buried in the hills between Emigrant and Gardiner.

for example as bullet holes through the ceiling. The town still has a healthy number of bars, but in a nod to foodies, there are now an equal number of excellent restaurants.

Livingston's transformation into a haven for legendary artists, writers, and actors probably started in the 1960s. Iconic film director Sam Peckinpah took up residence in the town's Murray Hotel, and writers Tom McGuane, Doug Peacock, Tim Cahill, and Richard Brautigan all called Livingston home—and some still do. Actors including Peter Fonda, Jeff Bridges, Michael Keaton, and Dennis Quaid have ranches outside town.

Indeed, Livingston has a rich blended culture that is evident in everything from its sophisticated galleries and gourmet restaurants to its bawdy bars, rollicking rodeo, and fly-fishing paradise.

SIGHTS

The town's **Depot Center** (200 W. Park St., 406/222-2300, www.livingstonmuseums.org, 9 A.M.–5 P.M. Mon.–Sat., 1–5 P.M. Sun. late May–mid-Sept., $3 adults, $2 children and seniors) is a

majestic building anchoring the town to its railroad heritage. In addition to being something of a community center where the town gathers for concerts and special events, the depot houses a worthwhile museum featuring history, art, and culture of the region. Electric-train buffs should ask for a tour of the basement, where the region's train fanatics have built a wonderland.

On the other side of the tracks, the **Yellowstone Gateway Museum** (118 W. Chinook St., 406/222-4184, www.livingston-museums.org, 8 A.M.–5 P.M. daily late May–Aug., open year-round by appointment for research, $4 adults, $3.50 seniors, $3 ages 6–12), housed in a historic schoolhouse, holds the county's archives and presents some excellent local exhibits on railroad history, pioneer life, Native American cultures, and military history.

ENTERTAINMENT AND EVENTS

Since 1924, the annual **Livingston Roundup Rodeo** (406/222-3199, www.livingston-chamber.com/rodeo.html) has enticed cowboys from across the country with its fat purse on the Fourth of July holiday. As crowds overtake the town's fairgrounds with rabid rodeo fever, regular events include barrel racing, bareback team roping, tie-down roping, saddle bronc, steer wrestling, and bull riding. The three-day event kicks off with a hometown parade and ends each evening with fireworks. This is without a doubt when Livingston most shines. General-admission and reserved-seating rodeo tickets are available online or by calling, but both sell out well before July.

In a town as food-savvy as Livingston, it's no surprise that there are a handful of great events to sample the local offerings. The wonderful community-centered **Livingston Farmers Market** (at the band shell in Sacajawea Park, River Dr., 406/222-0730, 4:30–7:30 P.M. Wed. early June–late Sept.) offers up the region's fresh local bounty in a friendly and festive environment. Live music is performed until 9 P.M. Sponsored by the Western Sustainability Exchange (www.northrock.org), the event supports a Young Entrepreneur Leadership Program that teaches kids about the intricacies of business and the value of giving back to the community, and a Senior Farmers Market Nutrition Program provides local low-income seniors with $50 vouchers for locally grown veggies, herbs, fruit, and honey at the market.

The **Taste of Livingston** (406/222-8808), held in March as a fund-raiser for local Montessori Island School, began in 2009 and is sure to grow. The elegant event, held in the Depot Center, brings together all of the restaurants in town for a savory evening.

SHOPPING

Downtown Livingston is a wonderful place to shop, with stores all within walking distance of one another offering a convenient escape from the town's ever-present wind along with an eclectic assortment of wares, from art and clothes to books and equipment. Most shops are closed on Sunday.

Sax & Fryer (109 W. Callender St., 406/222-1421) is an anchor for the town and a direct link to the town's origins. Founded in 1883, the year after Livingston was incorporated, and still run by the Fryer family, the store offers a meaty selection of books from regional and local authors as well as magazines, cards, gifts, and office supplies. There is also an excellent section devoted to children's books.

B. Civilized (113 W. Park St., 406/222-5996, www.bcivilized.com) is a hip little boutique that specializes in contemporary art and unique handmade objects. The art blends perfectly with a selection of jewelry and laugh-out-loud T-shirts—perfect for those who don't necessarily want their gifts detailed with rusty nails or old barbed-wire.

The Obsidian Collection (107 S. Main St., 406/222-2022, www.obsidiancollection.com) offers an appealing selection of gifts, children's items, jewelry, and accessories. Customers are loyal, often driving significant distances to see the latest and greatest collections.

ART GALLERIES

Livingston is a railroad town, but to its core it is also an artists' town. There are over a dozen galleries and many more artists, both brilliant amateurs and sophisticated professionals.

The Danforth Gallery (106 N. Main St., 406/222-6510, www.pcfadanforth.org) is the town's oldest gallery and is well respected. The gallery focuses on contemporary art with constantly changing exhibitions, and it even promotes school-age child artists through some inspired installations.

Chatham Fine Art (120 N. Main St., 406/222-1566, www.russellchatham.com) is dedicated to original art by noted local landscape artist and culinary master Russell Chatham.

Local character and talented artist Parks Reece captures the beauty of the region with a delightful and often mischievous sense of humor. The **Parks Reece Gallery** (119 S. Main St., Suite A3, 406/222-5724, www.parksreece.com) should not be missed.

If you want a fantastic overview of the art scene and consequently the entire community, be sure to hit the town **art walks,** held the fourth Friday of every month late

June–September; there is also a single holiday art walk each year in November–December. The town comes out in force to celebrate the arts.

For the most comprehensive listing of arts-related events, check out **Arts Montana** (www.artsmontana.net).

RECREATION
Fishing and Floating

If art defines Livingston, fishing feeds it. The Yellowstone River curves around the town and always makes its presence known. Paradise Valley lives up to its name in countless ways, fishing among them. **Nelson's, Armstrong's,** and **De Puy's Spring Creeks** are just minutes from town and offer some of the best and most consistent fishing in the state. Winter is an especially good time to fish the spring creeks because the springs flow constantly at a consistent temperature, the crowds are gone, and the rod fees go down significantly. Matson Rogers's **Angler's West Flyfishing** (206 Railroad Lane, off U.S. 89 S., Emigrant,

406/333-4401, www.montanaflyfishers.com) is a great resource, with both a fly shop and complete guiding service for the Yellowstone River and waters around the state. In Livingston, **Dan Bailey's Fly Shop** (209 W. Park St., Livingston, 406/222-1673, www.dan-bailey.com, 7 A.M.–7 P.M. Mon.–Sat., 7 A.M.–noon Sun. summer, 8 A.M.–6 P.M. Mon.–Sat. winter) is as venerable a fly shop as ever there was, anywhere. In addition to a living history lesson, the staff at Dan Bailey's can offer superbly qualified advice along with their renowned gear and world-famous flies.

To cover a lot of water in this country, with or without a rod, floating on a raft or drift boat can be a great option. While just about any outfitter can arrange to float and fish, **Flying Pig Rafting Company** (866/807-0744, www.flyingpigrafting.com, half-day trips $39 adults, $29 children under age 13, full-day trips $79 adults, $65 children) and **Montana Whitewater** (406/763-4465 or 800/799-4465, www.montanawhitewater.com, half-day trips $39 adults, $29 children under age 13, full-day

fishing the Yellowstone River between Livingston and Big Timber

© DONNIE SEXTON

GATEWAY TO YELLOWSTONE

trips $75 adults, $55 children) both offer scenic and white-water floats on the Yellowstone River.

Hiking

With mountains towering in every direction—the Absarokas and the Gallatins south of town, the Bridgers to the west, and the Crazies to the northeast—and a stiff wind usually blowing, heading out for a hike is never a bad idea in Livingston. Six miles south of town on the east side of River Road in Paradise Valley, **Pine Creek** is a stunning and popular spot with camping (spots fill up early) and hiking options for every ability level. A nice leisurely amble is the two-mile out-and-back trail to **Pine Creek Falls.** Hard-core hikers could hike the steep but mostly shaded 10 miles to **Pine Creek Lake. Suce Creek, Deep Creek,** and **Mill Creek** all have first-rate trails and stunning scenery, but be aware of bears in the region. For gear or just good ideas, talk to Dale at **Timber Trails** (309 W. Park St., 406/222-9550) on the main thoroughfare into downtown Livingston. His wonderful little gem of a store also rents mountain bikes.

[CHICO HOT SPRINGS RESORT

Built around a natural hot spring that was discovered in the late 1800s, the Chico Hot Springs Resort (off U.S. 89 S., 23 miles south of Livingston, 800/468-9232, www.chicohotsprings.com) has become a Montana icon, as much for its sensational food and raucous saloon as for its heavenly year-round outdoor pools. The resort got its start when Bill and Percie Knowles offered weary miners a clean bed, a hot bath, and fresh strawberries with every meal. The resort has stayed true to its humble origins by offering simple, no-frills guest rooms with shared baths in the main lodge for only $49. Modern accommodations are available in Warren's Wing ($125–179) and in elegant cabins ($209–225). There are also cottages, houses, and chalets ($169–355) to accommodate larger parties.

For travelers in search of more than a memorable meal and a luxurious soak, Chico offers a number of activities, all of which take advantage of its spectacular location just north of Yellowstone National Park in Paradise Valley. From horseback riding and dogsledding to hiking and cross-country skiing, Chico affords every visitor ample opportunity to earn their dinner.

ACCOMMODATIONS

It's true that Livingston has quite a collection of funky roadside motels that have seen better days, but there are some treasures around town and down the valley. Right in town, the **Murray Hotel** (201 W. Park St., Livingston, 406/222-1350, www.murrayhotel.com, from $89) is a Montana standard. It hasn't been glamorously overhauled, but the authenticity works well, and the place is rich with history, including the story of Will Rogers and Walter Hill trying to bring a saddle horse to the third floor in a 1905 hand-cranked elevator. Guest rooms are always clean and well-appointed with elegant details.

Nestled between town and Paradise Valley is the **Blue Winged Olive** (5157 U.S. 89 S., 3 miles south of Livingston, 800/471-1141, www.bluewingedolive.net, June 1–Sept. 30 from $100 s, Mar. 15–June 1 and Oct. 1–Nov. 31 from $90 s, closed Dec. 1–Mar. 14), a cute little B&B geared to anglers. You can hang your waders on your deck to dry while you sip a cocktail and tie tomorrow's flies at one of the fly-tying benches.

FOOD

If the pools are what bring people to [**Chico Hot Springs** (off U.S. 89 S., 23 miles south of Livingston, 800/468-9232, www.chicohotsprings.com, entrées $25–55), the food is what transforms them into regulars. From the first taste of baked Brie en croûte with Montana huckleberry coulis, through the house-smoked rainbow trout and the Gorgonzola filet mignon to the legendary flaming orange, Chico has gone a long way in defining Montana cuisine with fresh local ingredients in simple, hearty, and outstanding dishes.

Closer to town but still set in the grandeur of Paradise Valley, **⟨ The Pine Creek Lodge & Café** (2496 E. River Rd., 10 miles south of Livingston, 406/222-3628, www.pinecreeklodgemontana.com, call for hours and reservations, entrées $9–27) boasts pasta with elk sausage, rainbow trout tacos that you will not soon forget, and a cozy atmosphere that invites community. There is live music and outdoor barbecues on Saturday nights in summer, and local authors read their works on Wednesday nights in winter.

Not gourmet by any stretch of the imagination, **Mark's In & Out Drive-In** (801 W. Park St., Livingston, 406/222-7744) just might be the town favorite. There is no seating at this seasonal walk-up or drive-up joint right out of the 1950s, but the burgers, fries, and shakes are so good that you won't mind.

Located in the venerable Murray Hotel, **2nd Street Bistro** (123 N. 2nd St., 406/222-9463, www.secondstreetbistro.com, dinner from 5 P.M. daily, entrées $10–24) serves simple but inspired cuisine with French flair and Western attitude. The Mediterranean fish stew is a local favorite, as are the upscale pizzas. Sunday night is all-you-can-eat pizza and salad, and a wonderful brunch is served 10 A.M.–2 P.M. Sunday.

Every Western town worth its salt should have a **Stockman** (118 N. Main St., 406/222-8455, lunch Mon.–Sat. 11 A.M.–2 P.M., dinner Mon.–Thurs. 5–9 P.M., Fri.–Sat. 5–10 P.M., entrées $6.50–24.50). It is an old-school bar with the essence of a supper club. The steaks, prime rib, and burgers are second to none; this is the real Montana.

INFORMATION AND SERVICES

Livingston's **Chamber of Commerce** (303 E. Park St., 406/222-0850, www.livingston-chamber.com, 8 A.M.–6 P.M. Mon.–Fri., 9 A.M.–1 P.M. Sat.–Sun. Memorial Day–Labor Day, 8:30 A.M.–5:30 P.M. Mon.–Fri. Labor Day–Memorial Day) is located in the former crew quarters of the Burlington Northern Railroad. They offer a wide assortment of information about summer and winter activities, including a brochure titled "What to Do in Livingston." Stop by to meet the friendly people and pick up information on restaurants, accommodations, fishing, dude ranches, and more. They also have a computer where visitors can check their email or browse the Web.

The **Livingston-Park County public library** (228 W. Callender St., 406/222-0862, www.livingstonpubliclibrary.org, noon–8 P.M. Mon.–Tues., 10 A.M.–8 P.M. Wed.–Thurs., 10 A.M.–6 P.M. Fri., 10 A.M.–5 P.M. Sat.) offers cozy spaces to work or browse through your guide book. They have a terrific collection of fly-fishing material and even offer a genealogy service for visitors in the summer. They also have **free Internet access**; computers are available for up to an hour at a time.

The **main post office** (406/222-0912, 8:30 A.M.–5 P.M. Mon.–Fri., 10:30 A.M.–1:30 P.M. Sat.) is at 105 North 2nd Street.

Livingston Memorial Hospital (504 S. 13th St., 406/222-3541) has a 24-hour emergency room. For nonemergency medical care, visit **Community Health Partners** (126 S. Main St., 406/222-1111, 8 A.M.–5 P.M. Mon., Wed., and Fri., 8 A.M.–8 P.M. Tues. and Thurs.) or **The Park Clinic** (1315 W. Crawford St., 406/222-9970, 8 A.M.–5 P.M. Mon.–Fri.).

Wash clothes at **Off the Cuff** (322 E. Park St., 406/222-7428, 8 A.M.–6 P.M. Mon.–Fri.), which has 12 coin-operated washers and dryers, laundry drop-off service, and dry cleaning. **Scrub Tub at the Livingston Inn** (7:30 A.M.–10 P.M. daily) is at 5 Rogers Lane.

Internet access can be found at the public library, the Chamber of Commerce, and at the Internet café **Chadz** (104 N. Main St., 406/222-2247, 7 A.M.–2:30 P.M. daily).

GETTING THERE AND AROUND

Livingston is 116 miles from the **Billings Logan International Airport** (BIL) and 38 miles from **Bozeman's Gallatin Field Airport** (BZN).

From Bozeman, **Greater Valley Taxi** (406/587-6303) has a stand outside the baggage claim area, and rides to Livingston are around $75. Livingston's lone taxi service, **Amazing Taxi** (406/223-5344), also offers pickup and drop-off service to Bozeman's airport for about $65.

From the Billings Airport, **Phidippides Shuttle Service** (866/527-6789, www.codyshuttle.com) will transport you to Livingston for $165 pp; the cost decreases as the number of people traveling increases.

Both airports have car-rental companies on-site. At Bozeman's airport are **Enterprise, Hertz, Alamo, National,** and **Budget.** At Billing's airport **Enterprise, Thrifty, Dollar, Hertz, Alamo,** and **National** all have a presence.

Livingston to Red Lodge

This stretch of highway is a smooth ribbon between dramatic mountains ranges—the Absarokas, the Crazies, and the behemoth Beartooths. The views stretch for miles in every direction, and although many of the scarce exits off I-90 lead to nothing more than a jumble of ranch buildings, there are some wonderful old towns that appear every now and then. **Big Timber,** still heavily populated by Norwegian immigrants, is a mining town with a railroad history and a grand old hotel. Tiny Reed Point is an agricultural town with big attitude. Columbus and Roscoe, barely dots on the map, offer a well-known watering hole, the **Atlas Bar,** and a great restaurant, the **Grizzly Bar.**

MCLEOD AND THE BOULDER VALLEY

Just east of Livingston is **Swingley Road** (from Livingston, head southeast from E. Park St. before you get to the easternmost entrance to I-90)—as far as this writer is concerned, it is the portal to paradise. The road meanders through age-old farmsteads and stunning ranches, with the Boulder River carving the valley deeper into jagged peaks. The trail at **West Boulder,** which starts from the campground, offers a scenic but moderately easy six-mile round-trip hike through forest and meadow to **Boulder Meadows,** a tranquil spot with the occasional cow that is perfect for wetting a line or setting up camp. You could continue another five miles to the junction of **Falls Creek Trail,** or farther into the **Mill Creek Drainage** of Paradise Valley, but the meadows are a hard place to leave. Right near the trailhead is **West Boulder Cabin** (406/932-5155 for last-minute booking, www.recreation.gov for advance reservations, $35), maintained by the Forest Service. The three-bedroom, no-bath cabin is supremely rustic, complete with mice-eaten mattresses, but there is no better place to wake up if early morning hiking is your thing. Reservations are required and can be made up to six months in advance.

If you can manage to drag yourself out of West Boulder, head northeast on Highway 295 to McLeod and the renowned **Road Kill Café** (Hwy. 298 S., 406/932-6174). The food is fairly decent bar food, but it's the people and the atmosphere (and the name!) that make it worth stopping. From McLeod, Big Timber is only 16 miles north on Highway 298.

BIG TIMBER

Not only is it perfectly situated for a roadway coffee break between Bozeman and Billings, Big Timber (population 1,801, elevation 4,089 feet) is an interesting little town and a worthwhile stop. There are some nice galleries in town, a good shop or two, a great museum, and a beautiful old railroad hotel that anchors the community. An old-school agricultural community with strong mining and railroad ties, it is flat as a pancake but surrounded on either side by dramatic mountains and encircled by the Boulder and Yellowstone Rivers.

Right off the highway is the **Crazy Mountain Museum** (southeast of I-90 exit 367, 406/932-

5126, www.sweetgrasscounty.com/museum, 10 A.M.–4:30 P.M. Mon.–Sat., 1–4 P.M. Sun. Memorial Day–Sept. 30), a thoughtfully laid-out collection that pays tribute to the town's Norwegian heritage. The staff of volunteer docents brings the collection to life with wonderful stories and often personal reflections.

In the heart of town is **The Grand Hotel Bed & Breakfast** (139 McLeod St., 406/932-4459, www.thegrand-hotel.com, from $65 d with shared bath, $90 with private bath), a stately Victorian-style railroad hotel. The guest rooms are traditional and fairly small with period antiques. Downstairs, the restaurant and saloon attract visitors from around the state with butter-knife steaks, elk rellenos, Montana morel chicken breast, and an award-winning wine list. The food is sumptuous, and the atmosphere—with rich, dark mahogany and 1890s furnishings—leaves nothing to be desired.

Just east of Big Timber are two great stops for the littlest travelers. The **Big Timber Waterslide Park** (705 U.S. 10 E., follow signs from I-90, 406/932-6570, www.bigtimberwaterslide.com, 10 A.M.–4:30 P.M. daily, weather permitting, full-day $16 adults, $12 ages 4–12, half-day $13 adults, $10 ages 4–12, credit cards not accepted) has grown significantly over the last 20 years and is a welcome respite on a hot Montana day. There are a number of slides for different ages and adrenaline thresholds, from the Munchkin Slide to Old Faceful, as well as a lazy river, a kiddie pool, and a junior Olympic-size pool; nothing about this place is glitzy.

Greycliff Prairie Dog Town State Park (I-90 exit 377, Greycliff, 406/247-2940, $5 nonresidents) is just what the name suggests—a remarkable metropolis constructed and inhabited by thousands of black-tailed prairie dogs. These furry little creatures are endearing if you watch them interact for even just a few minutes. There is a picnic area, but remember to keep Fido in the car.

REED POINT

Every Labor Day weekend, the population of Reed Point swells from about 100 to more

THE GREAT MONTANA SHEEP DRIVE

It's not exactly Pamplona's Running of the Bulls, but Reed Point's Great Montana Sheep Drive, also known as "Running of the Sheep," is a Montana classic. Though history might suggest this was a reaction to conflict between sheepherders and cattle ranchers, a tongue-in-cheek thumbing of the nose perhaps, the truth is that this event was started in 1980 when the town (population, according to one sign posted in town, "about 100: 99 good folks and one real jerk") gathered to auction off an 89-year-old bachelor in hopes of finding him a companion. The sheep were introduced in 1989, Montana's centennial celebration of statehood during which the relatively nearby town of Roundup was planning a cattle drive. One resident (possibly the jerk?) had the idea of a sheep drive that would actually cross in front of the cattle. The cattle confrontation was quashed, but the idea of the sheep drive took hold and the event has been growing every year since. Roughly 2,000 sheep make their way down Main Street, sandwiched between thousands of spectators and more than 80 food vendors. The annual event also includes a Mutton Cook-Off, a parade, a car show, a street dance, a kids carnival and petting zoo, local crafts sales, and a variety of entertainment. The event is scheduled annually the Sunday of Labor Day. For more information, contact the Waterhole Saloon (406/326-9919).

than 5,000. People come from far and wide to watch a couple of thousand sheep make their way, leaping and running, down Main Street. It's called the **Great Montana Sheep Drive,** and it is an afternoon well spent. The annual event includes a mutton cook-off, a parade and car show, a street dance, a kids carnival and petting zoo, local crafts sales, and a variety of entertainment. For more information, contact the Waterhole Saloon (406/326-9919). Even though it's this one-day event that puts little Reed Point on the map, it is a nice town to explore if you have time.

COLUMBUS, ABSAROKEE, AND ROSCOE

For anglers and adventurers in search of good water, high mountains, and a friendly bar with decent grub, these three hamlets fit the bill brilliantly. With the Stillwater and Yellowstone Rivers nearby, Columbus is a fishing town, and the **New Atlas Bar** (528 E. Pike Ave., Columbus, 406/322-4033) is one of the coolest but least-visited bars in the state. There never seem to be more than a couple of old-timers bellied up to the beautiful old bar, and with more than 60 mounts on the walls and a couple of oddities here and there (a stuffed two-headed calf, for example), this place has the feel of a cool but dingy old museum.

Heading down Highway 78 toward Red Lodge is Absarokee, a quaint little town near the Stillwater River with a handful of B&Bs and a similar number of outfitters. **Absaroka River Adventures** (113 Grove St., Absarokee, 406/328-7440 or 800/334-7238, www.absarokariver.com) offers scenic half-day ($37 adults, $20 children under 13) and full-day floats on the lower Stillwater and on the more dramatic upper section (half-day $45 adults, $25 children), which is only floatable in early summer. **Paintbrush Adventures** (86 N. Stillwater Rd., Absarokee, 406/328-4158, www.paintbrushadvenutures.com) offers guided horseback riding, hiking, and fishing.

The **Grizzly Bar & Restaurant** (1 Main St., Roscoe, 406/328-6789), along the East Rosebud River in Roscoe, offers a perfect setting for a delicious Montana meal. The cuisine is classic—relish trays and steaks large enough to hang off the edges of your plate—and the ambience is idyllic. Diners can enjoy a great meal on the deck overlooking the tumbling river. Ah, summer in Montana—short but so sweet.

INFORMATION AND SERVICES

As you drive west off I-90 exit 367 to Big Timber, you can't miss the Big Timber–Sweet Grass County **Chamber of Commerce** (406/932-5131, www.bigtimber.com, 10 A.M.–6 P.M. daily Memorial Day–Labor Day). In a small log cabin with stunning views of the Crazy Mountains, you will find a well-informed and friendly staff ready to answer any questions you may have about the area. The center also offers a good selection of maps, brochures, and travel magazines.

Red Lodge and the Beartooth Plateau

At the edge of the massive Beartooth Plateau, Red Lodge (population 2,449, elevation 5,553 feet) is a mountain town with the great plains spread out at its feet. There are a couple of great resorts and some world-class skiing just beyond town, but downtown Red Lodge is a worthwhile destination on its own. Cute shops and wonderful restaurants line Broadway, and the spectacle of nature—the rush of Rock Creek and the drama of the Beartooths—is evident from every part of the street. The town's Western hospitality combined with historic zeal for a good time make Red Lodge a wonderful

getaway or a fun launching point to the wildness of the Beartooth Plateau and Yellowstone National Park.

SIGHTS
◖ Beartooth Scenic Highway and Pass

Considered one of the most beautiful roadways in the country, the Beartooth Highway begins in Red Lodge, climbs and twists its way through 60-million-year-old mountains, and ends 65 miles later in **Cooke City** at the **Northeastern Entrance to Yellowstone**

© DONNIE SEXTON

a view of Twin Lakes from the Beartooth Highway

Park. The scenic road has numerous switchbacks and steep grades that, once you're driving on it, clearly demonstrate why it is closed during winter. As you ascend, you come upon magnificent vistas of the Beartooth Plateau, Glacier Lake, and the canyons forged by the Clarks Fork River. After about 30 miles, you reach the mountain summit at 10,947 feet. Here you will encounter the aptly named **Top of the World** rest area, which provides the only services on the route. Keep an eye out for a herd of mountain goats that frequents the area.

If you plan to drive this byway, keep in mind that it is not about getting from A to B but that the drive itself is the destination, and it should be undertaken with plenty of time; it takes about three hours without any stops. You will encounter an array of **wildlife,** including black bears, bighorn sheep, and mountain goats, as well as a broad display of vibrant wildflowers. Take time to pull over and enjoy the vistas, or explore the hiking trails and accessible lakes. With snow falling almost year-round, **skiing** is popular in the area during June–July. Because

of the extreme conditions of the mountains, the highway is only open May–October. It is best to contact the U.S. Forest Service (406/446-2103) or the **Red Lodge Visitors Center** (406/446-1718 or 888/281-0625) to confirm the opening and closing dates.

Beartooth Nature Center

This wildlife refuge is the only one of its kind in Montana. It houses indigenous animals that cannot be released back into the wild due to an injury or unfortunate dependency on humans. The Beartooth Nature Center (Miners Park, 615 2nd St. E., Red Lodge, 406/446-1133, www. beartoothnaturecenter.org, 10 A.M.–5 P.M. daily May–Oct., 10 A.M.–2 P.M. daily Nov.–Apr., $6 adults, $5 seniors, $2.50 ages 5–15) cares for some 75 animals that include black bears, lynx, bald eagles, bison, mountain lions, and many more. The center says in its mission that its "primary focus is to educate the public about the protection and conservation of Montana's wildlife and its habitats" by allowing visitors an up-close and intimate perspective of some of

aerial view at sunrise of the Absaroka-Beartooth Wilderness

© DONNIE SEXTON

Montana's most beautiful species. The center's location also affords some spectacular views of the Beartooth Mountains.

ENTERTAINMENT AND EVENTS

For more than 50 years, **The Festival of Nations** (www.festivlofnations.us) has been a Red Lodge tradition celebrating the wide diversity of ethnic groups that first came to the town during the late-1800s mining boom. The cultural groups honored include both southern and northern Europeans—German, Irish, Finnish, Italian, Norwegian, Scottish, Greek—and a variety of others. The festival takes place in August over two and a half days, with cultural exhibits, dancing, ethnic food, music, children's activities, and a wide assortment of daytime and nighttime entertainment. Contact the **Red Lodge Visitors Center** (406/446-1718 or 888/281-0625) for this year's dates and location.

During the past 20 years, for 10 days in July, Red Lodge has hosted a reenactment of the mountain-man rendezvous that took place in the early 19th century during the fur-trading era. The men in this area made their living hunting, trapping, and fishing. Twice a year they would rendezvous to trade items, swap stories, drink, eat, gamble, and even fight. **Rendezvous at Red Lodge** (U.S. 212, 5.2 miles north of Red Lodge, 406/446-1718, 10 A.M.–7 P.M. daily, $6 adults, $2 children, free for children under 7) is an event the whole family can enjoy, watching dramatic reenactments, browsing authentic trade items from the era, and tasting the selection of food. Participants wear traditional period dress and set up tents where they can barter their goods. There are daily seminars, staged gunfights, period arts and crafts, and much more.

The **Winter Carnival** (305 Ski Run Rd., Red Lodge, 406/446-2610 or 800/444-8977, dates vary each year) takes place at the Red Lodge Mountain Resort and has become a favorite event among locals and visitors alike. Although the carnival selects a different theme each year (a few years ago it was Superheroes), many tried-and-true events make an annual appearance. The Cardboard Classic race tests the skills of its participants as they guide their original crafts—made only from cardboard, duct tape, and glue—in a competitive downhill race. Other popular activities include a scavenger hunt, a snow sculpture contest, a parade of costumes, a jalapeño-eating contest, and a dazzling fireworks show. You may even be crowned King or Queen of Red Lodge Mountain if you can telemark, alpine race, and snowboard yourself to victory.

The Home of Champions Rodeo and Parade (406/446-2422, www.redlodgerodeo. com, July 2–4, $15–30) takes place each year at the fairgrounds west of Red Lodge just off Highway 78, and the parade takes place in downtown Red Lodge. Rodeo competition in the area dates back to the 1890s, when cowboys used to get together on Sunday to ride broncos at the local stockyards. Formed in 1930, the **Red Lodge Rodeo Association** has been hosting this annual celebration ever since. The name, Home of Champions, was coined in 1954 after a local cowboy, Bill Linderman, won his third title as World All Around Champion. There is a different theme selected for the event every year, and a parade takes place at noon each day; participation is open and there are categories for all age groups. The rodeo is part of the Professional Rodeo Cowboys Association circuit, so you will see many of the nation's top champions compete in a number of different events, including bareback, bull riding, calf roping, and barrel racing.

SHOPPING

Shopping in Red Lodge is a leisurely stroll through the historic downtown district. Broadway has still managed to retain the charm and vibrancy of the coal-mining days with a diverse assortment of stores. **Magpie Toymakers** (115 N. Broadway Ave., 406/446-3044, www.magpietoys.com) will delight children and adults alike with a selection ranging from handmade wooden toys and rag dolls to cast iron figurines, along with kites, board games, and books. You won't find a lot of plastic or battery-operated merchandise, but there is plenty to spur the imagination.

Kibler and Kirch (101 N. Broadway Ave., 406/446-2802 or 406/446-2226, www. kiblerandkirch.com) is a home-furnishings store with a nice selection of Western artwork and accessories, including pottery, glassware, and handcrafted leather. Since many of their products are made in Montana, you may find the perfect gift to take home.

Sylvan Peak Enterprises (9 S. Broadway Ave., 406/446-1770, www.sylvanpeak.com) carries a full range of outdoor clothing and gear for getting the most out of the Montana mountains. They carry their own line of clothing as well as more familiar brands such as Marmot, Mountain Hardware, and Osprey. They have an outlet store on their main floor and a Mountain Shoppe downstairs that not only sells equipment but rents cross-country skis, telemark skis, and snowshoes.

Right next door, you'll find the irresistible **Montana Candy Emporium** (7 S. Broadway Ave., 406/446-1119). Their mouthwatering window displays will draw you in to this world of sweets. It is said to be the largest candy store in Montana, which is easy to believe meandering through their selection of more than 800 sugary treats. Located in the former Park Theater, decorated with nostalgic memorabilia, and selling old-fashioned candies, this store will take you back to simpler time.

RECREATION
Skiing

Situated in a glacial valley surrounded by the Beartooth Mountains, Red Lodge offers superb downhill and cross-country skiing. The **Red Lodge Mountain Resort** (305 Ski Run Rd., 406/446-2610 or 800/444-8977, www. redlodgemountain.com) is just six miles from downtown Red Lodge and boasts a mountain free of crowds and with reasonable lift ticket prices ($46 adults, $39 juniors, $16 children, $35 ages 65–69, free for children under 5 and adults over 69) as well as ski runs for beginners to experts. The mountain offers a higher base elevation (7,000 feet) than any other ski hill in the state, a spine-chilling 2,400-foot vertical drop, 70 trails, and five chairlifts to keep you up to your elbows in the white stuff all day. The diverse terrain is groomed regularly and the runs' features are frequently upgraded or even changed. Red Lodge offers a full-service lodge, with ski lessons, ski rentals, child care, a restaurant, two bars, and two cafeterias, all on the hill. The resort also has two cross-country trails that offer about 11 miles of skiing.

Probably the best-known place for cross-country skiing in Red Lodge is the **Red Lodge Nordic Center** (406/446-1771, www.beartoothtrails.org, 8:30 A.M.–4:30 P.M. daily Nov. 30–Mar. 30), located three miles west of downtown off Highway 78 at the base of the Beartooth Mountains. The center is operated by the nonprofit Beartooth Recreational Association; a $5 donation per day is requested. They offer nine miles of groomed trails rated from easy to most difficult. In addition, the center offers equipment rental, lessons, maps, a snack bar, and activities for children.

Hiking and Fishing

There are a number of rivers, creeks, and lakes worth fishing or just ambling along in the vicinity of Red Lodge, and with surroundings as spectacular as these, the catching may not be the point. **Rock Creek** flows through town and is a surprisingly good place to catch rainbows or browns. Public access can be found just north of town. The north-flowing **Stillwater River,** west of town toward Absarokee, is a medium-size tributary of the Yellowstone River with relatively few people fishing it and a healthy number of rainbows and browns.

Wild Bill Lake is stocked regularly and makes a fantastic family outing or introduction to fly fishing. The area is fully accessible for wheelchairs and can be found two miles south of Red Lodge on U.S. 212, then five miles west on Forest Road 2071.

While there are plenty of gnarly trails on the Beartooth Plateau for hard-core hikers, there are plenty just outside town that are a bit more mellow but equally beautiful. The **Nichols Creek Trail** (West Fork Rd. to Forest Rd.

2478), for example, is a four-mile round-trip out-and-back hike that follows Nichols Creek through aspen and pine forests with moderate elevation gain (1,100 feet) and a marvelous view of the West Fork Canyon.

For a professional fishing guide—or just the right gear and good advice—contact **Rocky Fork Outfitters & Guide Service** (108 Obert Rd., Red Lodge, 406/445-2598, www.rockyforkoutfittersguide.com) or **Montana Trout Scout** (213 W. 9th St., Red Lodge, 406/855-3058, www.montanatroutscout.com).

Golf

To hit the links, head to the 18-hole course at **Red Lodge Resort and Golf Club** (Red Lodge Mountain Rd., southwest of Red Lodge, 406/446-3344, www.redlodgemountain.com, Mon.–Thurs. $27, Fri.–Sun. $39). On top of the jaw-dropping scenery around this challenging course, your ball will travel farther because of the altitude.

Recreation on the Beartooth Plateau

High atop these massive mountains is the vast and rugged grandeur of the Beartooth Plateau. It's a nature lover's paradise with spectacular scenery, unrivaled vistas, abundant wildlife, and a tangle of trails and lakes to get out and enjoy. **The Beartooth Highway** makes this remarkable place a Sunday drive destination. But if you have the time, this is a wonderland that begs to be discovered. Take a hike, wet a line—heck, throw on your skis in midsummer; just get out and enjoy this magnificent place.

The truth of the matter is, you're already pretty much on top of the world here, so you don't need to aspire much when planning a hike. The plateau is crisscrossed with trails, and as long as you are amply prepared, you can't choose a bad one. The **Clay Butte Fire Lookout Tower** is only one mile from the highway and can be accessed by a trail that takes hikers up and above 11,000 feet. The views are incredible, and an interpretive display gives great perspective on the 1988 Yellowstone fires and how they impacted the entire region.

Crazy Creek Cascade is another nice short hike, and the Clarks Fork Trailhead, just three miles from Cooke City, offers an abundance of longer trails. Near the summit, an eight-mile loop around Beartooth Lake offers easy terrain and lovely scenery. For trail maps, stop by the U.S. Forest Service Ranger Station (6811 U.S. 212, Red Lodge, 406/446-2103).

Biking the Beartooth is not for the faint of heart. Never mind the insane elevation climbs and descents, the vast grizzly habitat, and the possibility of a blizzard on virtually any day of the year; the real danger is the automobiles, which are plentiful and often wide. You can eliminate that danger by getting off the road and onto a network of trails. A couple of bikes can be rented from the Top of the World Resort (307/587-5368, www.topoftheworldresort.com) or in Cooke City or Red Lodge.

In order to fish any of the sublime mountain lakes on the Beartooth Plateau, many of which have been stocked with trout, you'll need a Wyoming fishing license, which can be purchased at the Top of the World Resort (307/587-5368, www.topoftheworldresort.com) or in Red Lodge or Cooke City.

Thirteen campgrounds along the highway offer 226 sites between Red Lodge and Cooke City. Because of the elevation and volume of snow, many do not open until late June. Beartooth Lake ($15 per night) and Island Lake ($10 per night) campgrounds are two excellent ones very near the summit. Campsites along the Beartooth Highway are managed by the Custer National Forest (406/446-2103, www.fs.fed.us/r1/custer/recreation/campgrounds) and range in price from free to $20 per night, depending on the site.

ACCOMMODATIONS

In historic downtown Red Lodge, **《 The Pollard Hotel** (2 N. Broadway Ave., 406/446-0001 or 800/765-5273, www.thepollard.com, $70–295) should not be overlooked. The hotel was the first brick building constructed in Red Lodge and dates to 1893. It has played host to some of the West's most famous legends, including Calamity Jane, Buffalo Bill Cody, and famed orator William Jennings Bryan. Each of the 38 guest rooms and suites are individually decorated and can come with mountain views, jetted tubs, and balconies. All stays include a full breakfast in the Pollard's excellent dining room.

Rock Creek Resort (6380 U.S. 212 S., 406/446-1111 or 800/667-1119, www.rockcreekresort.com, $125–290) is located about five miles outside Red Lodge in a gorgeous canyon at the base of the Beartooth Mountains. The resort sprawls over a 30-acre site and offers many outdoor activities. The facility has a heated indoor pool, tennis courts, a soccer field, a fully stocked fish pond, and numerous trails for hiking and biking (along with bikes for rent). Most guest rooms have impressive views of the mountains, and the suites come with kitchenettes.

If you want to stay close to downtown Red Lodge without breaking the bank, try **《 The Yodeler Motel** (601 S. Broadway Ave., 406/446-1435 or 866/446-1435, www.yodelermotel.com, $65–129). This Swiss-themed chalet, owned by delightful former guides Mac and Tulsa Dean, is only three blocks from historic downtown; remodeled guest rooms offer nice amenities that include cable TV, free Wi-Fi, jetted tubs, and steam baths.

FOOD

《 Bridge Creek Backcountry Kitchen and Wine Bar (116 S. Broadway Ave., Red Lodge, 406/446-9900, www.eatfooddrinkwine.com, from 10 A.M. daily Memorial Day–Labor Day, from 10 A.M. Tues.–Sat. Labor Day–Memorial Day, entrées $7–33) offers its customers a truly unique dining experience without any pretense. From the layout (the kitchen is open and in the middle of the restaurant) to the menu, it is clear that the restaurant has an innovative approach to food. The focus is on clean flavors, using local ingredients, and producing delicious results (try the bison-stuffed egg rolls). True to their name, they also have an excellent selection of wines. Recommendations are made directly on the menu, pairing each food item with a glass of wine.

GATEWAY TO YELLOWSTONE

For a casual, inexpensive, old-fashioned drive-in—or better yet, walk-up—experience, head to the **Red Box Car** (1300 S. Broadway Ave., Red Lodge, 406/446-2152). Based in an actual 1906 box car from the Rocky Fork Railway, this stand serves some of the best shakes, malts, chili, and burgers you could imagine. Sit outside and enjoy your meal as you take in the views of nearby Rock Creek.

Attached to the Regis Grocery, and known for outstanding breakfasts and organic, whole foods, **Café Regis** (501 S. Word, 406/446-1941, www.caferegis.com, open Tues.–Sun. 6 A.M.–2 P.M., entrées $3–9) is an excellent spot for a hearty, healthy, and very reasonably priced meal. The service is quick and friendly, and every delicious item on the menu—from omelets and breakfast burritos to soup, sandwiches, salads, and mouth-watering daily specials—is available to go. Grab a ready-to-go picnic lunch or find all of the gourmet fixings for whatever adventure you have planned. The Regis Grocery has a huge selection of organic, gluten-free, and other specialty products.

Thirty-five miles northeast of town is the tiny hamlet of Fromberg (drive east of Red Lodge on Hwy. 308 to Belfry, then north on Hwy. 72 past Bridger) and the **(Little Cowboy Bar & Museum** (105 W. River St., Fromberg, 406/668-9502, 8 A.M.–2 A.M. daily), a rare find. Owner, founder, and story-teller extraordinaire Shirley Smith has combined a wonderful collection of rodeo and local memorabilia with a good old-fashioned Montana bar.

INFORMATION AND SERVICES

The **Red Lodge Chamber of Commerce** (601 N. Broadway Ave., 406/446-1718 or 888/281-0625, www.redlodgechamber.org, 9 A.M.–5 P.M. daily June–Sept., 9 A.M.–4 P.M.

Mon., Wed., and Fri. Oct.–May) is located at the intersection of U.S. 212 and Highway 78. They have a 24-hour brochure room that offers a variety of local information. Inside the center you will find knowledgeable staff and plenty of state publications, visitors guides, and maps.

Access the Internet at **Red Lodge Carnegie Library** (3 W. 8th St., 406/446-1905, 10 A.M.–6 P.M. Tues.–Fri., noon–6 P.M. Sat.). They have five Internet-connected computers available to the public. You can also stop by the **Coffee Factory Roasters** (6 S. Broadway Ave., 406/446-3200, 7 A.M.–5 P.M. daily), where you can use the computer for free with the purchase of a drink or snack.

The **Beartooth Hospital and Healthcare Center** (600 W. 21st St., 406/446-2345) offers 24-hour emergency care.

U.S. 212 climbs another 5,000 feet past Red Lodge. If you want to know the road conditions for the Beartooth Highway, you can stop by the chamber of commerce or check with the State of Montana (800/226-7623 or 800/335-7592 TTY, www.mdt.mt.gov/travinfo).

GETTING THERE

The two major airports closest to Red Lodge are **Billings Logan International Airport** (BIL) and Bozeman's **Gallatin Field Airport** (BZN). One of the best options for getting to Red Lodge is by car; both airports have a selection of rental-car companies.

From the Billings Airport, **Phidippides Shuttle Service** (866/527-6789, www.cody-shuttle.com) will transport visitors to Red Lodge for $65.

Driving from Billings, take I-90 west to U.S. 212/U.S. 310 south. Red Lodge is 60 miles from Billings, and the drive time is about an hour. From Bozeman, take I-90 east to Highway 78 south. Bozeman is about 150 miles and 2.5 hours from Red Lodge.

YELLOWSTONE NATIONAL PARK

Yellowstone National Park is at the heart of our country's longstanding relationship with wilderness. The largest intact ecosystem in the Lower 48, meaning that all of the species that have roamed this sweeping mountainous plateau are still (or are once again) in residence, Yellowstone was our nation's first national park, signed into being by President Ulysses S. Grant after a series of important and legendary scouting expeditions through the area. The region's history is lengthy and very much alive, from its prehistoric supervolcanic eruptions, to its occupation by the U.S. Army in the 1880s, to the controversial reintroduction of wolves in the 1990s and the current snowmobile-usage and bison quagmires. And the stories, both far-fetched and true, and characters that have emerged from

the park are as colorful and compelling as the landscape itself.

A vast 2.2 million acres, Yellowstone is indeed a wonderland, filled with steaming geysers and boiling mud pots, packed with diverse and healthy populations of wildlife, and crisscrossed by hundreds of miles of hiking and skiing trails. A stretch of the park called the Lamar Valley is known as the "Little Serengeti of North America," and for good reason: At certain times of the year, in a single day visitors can spot grizzly and black bears, moose, wolves, bison, elk, coyotes, bald eagles, and the occasional bighorn sheep. In fact, the opportunities for viewing wildlife in the park are unparalleled anywhere in the United States, and although Yellowstone may not be as picturesque as Glacier or the Tetons,

© OSAMU HOSHINO/WYOMING TRAVEL & TOURISM

HIGHLIGHTS

◖ Boiling River: In a stretch of the Gardner River between the towns of Gardiner and Mammoth at the park's north entrance, the hot water flows over waterfalls and via springs, mixing with the river water to create a perfect soaking temperature (page 256).

◖ Mammoth and the Mammoth Hot Springs Terraces: The travertine terraces at Mammoth Hot Springs look like an enormous cream-colored confection. Since the springs shift and change daily, a walk around the colorful terraces is never the same experience twice (page 259).

◖ Grand Canyon of the Yellowstone: Since Thomas Moran first painted this breathtaking canyon during the 1872 Hayden Expedition, the Grand Canyon of the Yellowstone has inspired millions of visitors – and quite a few artists – with its sheer cliffs and dramatic coloring. In the summer, visitors get a rare bird's-eye view of several osprey nests. You just have to know where to look (page 261).

◖ Watching the Wolves: Since their return in 1995, the wolves have put on a spectacular show for ardent observers and lucky visitors, with at least one reported sighting daily since 2001. The sagas of the 12 packs and the individuals within the packs are dramatic, heart-wrenching, and utterly captivating. The experts at the Yellowstone Association Institute can often tell you where the wolves are (page 265).

◖ Lamar Valley: Known as the "Little Serengeti of North America," the Lamar Valley is a scenic, glacially carved valley that offers spectacular wildlife-watching opportunities year-round. It is also one of the few areas of the park accessible by vehicle in the winter, and it is prime wolf-watching territory (page 267).

◖ Yellowstone Lake: Touted by early mountain men as perhaps the only place where you could catch a fish and cook it without ever taking it off the line, Yellowstone Lake is a beautiful and has some very interesting things

going on. Too cold for swimming, the lake is open to boating and fishing (page 270).

◖ Old Faithful: If you could see just one thing in Yellowstone, this might be it. The world-famous geyser lives up to its name, with major eruptions every 45–90 minutes. The adjacent Old Faithful Inn is a remarkable example of "parkitecture" and a wonderful place to relax. The geyser basin is fascinating, and the crowds are ever-present (page 273).

◖ Firehole River: The other swimmable thermal feature in Yellowstone, the Firehole River offers a stunning, canyon-like heated swimming area in summer. The twists and turns of the cascading canyon, near Old Faithful, are worth seeing even if you don't get wet (page 274).

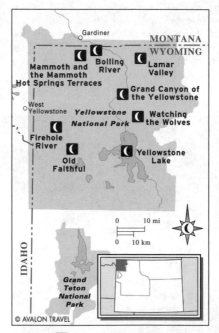

© AVALON TRAVEL

LOOK FOR ◖ TO FIND RECOMMENDED SIGHTS, ACTIVITIES, DINING, AND LODGING.

it is magnificent in its wildness and uniquely American.

Seeing Yellowstone from the back of a cramped station wagon—or these days, a decked-out Winnebago—is almost a rite of passage in this country. What parent doesn't dream of hauling their children out West to see Old Faithful erupt or to catch a glimpse of a grizzly bear? And what kid doesn't want to swim in the Boiling River or lay awake in a sleeping bag, listening to the howl of coyotes? It is not exactly the last frontier that it once was—there are convenience stores, beautiful old hotels, and even places to get a decent latte—but Yellowstone still occupies its own corner of our national imagination, classified somewhere between American wilderness and family vacations; it conjures up foggy but perfect memories.

HISTORY

Evidence from archeological sites, trails, and even oral histories suggests that humans inhabited the region of Yellowstone as far back as 11,000 years ago. And although the land is rich with history, one can argue that not much has changed since the park was created in 1872, the invaluable blessing of having been protected as the nation's first national park. The unique geothermal features, pristine lakes and waterfalls, abundant and varied wildlife, and the different ecosystems have endured through the years.

As with all of the West, Yellowstone was traversed by various Native American groups, including the Crow, Blackfeet, Nez Perce, and Shoshone, whose oral history teaches that they originated in this area. Although these nomads passed through the area, only a branch of the Shoshone, known as the "Sheep Eaters," made Yellowstone their home. The first Europeans to have visited the area were most likely fur traders and trappers who seem to have missed the unusual geothermal activity. Lewis and Clark's expedition bypassed the region completely. On their return voyage in 1806, however, John Colter separated from the group and ventured alone into the region. He is considered the first non–Native American to have seen the wondrous thermal features in the park. When Colter returned home three years later, his stories were considered suspicious. His tales of "bubbling ground," "mountains made of glass" and rivers where you could catch a fish and cook it without ever removing it from the water seemed preposterous to Easterners. Colter's descriptions of fire and brimstone quickly earned the place the nickname of "Colter's Hell." However, as more fur traders moved into the region, the stories of boiling mud, steaming land, and hot pools of water continued. Jim Bridger explored the area in 1856 and is considered by some the "first geographer" of the region. He too shared wild descriptions that were met with similar skepticism.

The first organized expedition into the Yellowstone area was made in 1869 by David E. Folsom, Charles W. Cook, and William Peterson, who witnessed the breathtaking Tower Falls, Mud Volcano, Yellowstone Lake, and the geyser basins of the Firehole River. The Washburn-Langford-Doane expedition followed in 1870. It was the 1871 government-sponsored expedition into the region led by Ferdinand Vandeveer Hayden, however, that produced a detailed account of the area. The Hayden Geological Survey was accompanied by William Henry Jackson photographs and artwork by Henry W. Elliott and Thomas Moran. Photographs and spectacular paintings and drawings were splashed across magazines and newspapers around the East so that people could see the wonders of the region for the first time. It was this report, coupled with the earnest pleas of the men who had seen the area, that prodded Congress to grant the region National Park status in 1872. That year, the park had 300 visitors.

Nathaniel Langford was the park's first superintendent, but without proper funding and staff he had difficulty protecting the land. Poachers and vandals exploited the park's natural resources, creating a state of general lawlessness. By 1886 the U.S. Army had entered the park to help regain control of the region. They built park structures, strengthened and enforced regulations, encouraged visitors, and made sure the land and wildlife were protected. Transportation infrastructure improvements also helped attract more visitors to the park. The Northern Pacific Railway extended to the town of Cinnabar, north of modern-day Gardiner, near the northern entrance of the park, and in 1915 automobiles were allowed into Yellowstone, making it more accessible to the masses. Following World War II, car travel exploded, and more than 1 million visitors came to the park in 1948.

The Army's leadership was not a long-term solution to managing the new national park, and in 1916 the National Park Service was created. (The birthday of the Park Service is still celebrated every year on August 25 with free admission to Yellowstone for the day and a smattering of hilariously decorated Christmas trees around the park.) The rangers took responsibility for management of the park in 1918. Since then, the park's boundaries have been redrawn to encompass 2.2 million acres (roughly equivalent in size to the state of Connecticut) and wildlife management has been continuously refined as new science emerges. One fundamental change came as a result of the 1963 Leopold Report, which suggested that "natural regulation" was superior to the long-held un-natural management in which park managers controlled animal populations and altered the course of naturally occurring events like fire. The Ecological Process Management, as it has come to be called, is still the core philosophy behind park management today.

Yellowstone was named an International Biosphere Reserve in 1976 and a United Nations World Heritage Site in 1978. Both the grizzly bear and the gray wolf (reintroduced to the park in 1995) have seen enormous improvements to their endangered status due to Yellowstone's wildlife policies. In 1988 the park experienced the largest wildfires in its history, affecting more than a third of its land, and once again sparking furious debates about management of public resources and the value of natural ecosystems.

Modern day Yellowstone is every bit as

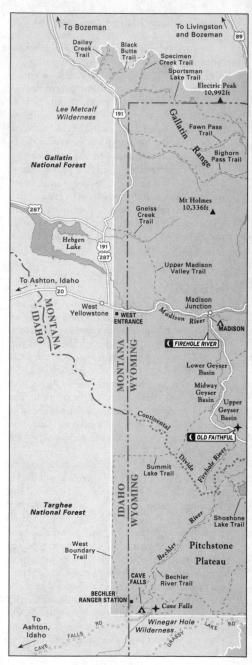

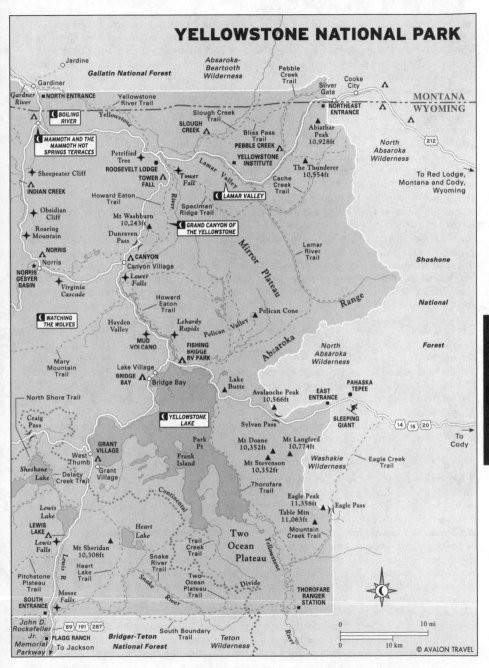

YELLOWSTONE NATIONAL PARK

Jardine

Gallatin National Forest

Gardiner

Gardner River

■ NORTH ENTRANCE

☾ BOILING RIVER

Yellowstone

Yellowstone River Trail

☾ MAMMOTH AND THE MAMMOTH HOT SPRINGS TERRACES

◆ Sheepeater Cliff

Petrified Tree

ROOSEVELT LODGE

TOWER FALL △

Tower Fall

△ INDIAN CREEK

Howard Eaton Trail

◆ Obsidian Cliff

Mt Washburn 10,243ft

Specimen Ridge Trail

◆ Roaring Mountain

Dunraven Pass

△ CANYON

☾ NORRIS

★ Norris

NORRIS GESYER BASIN

◆ Virginia Cascade

Canyon Village

◆ *Lower Falls*

Howard Eaton Trail

☾ WATCHING THE WOLVES

Hayden Valley

Lehardy Rapids

MUD VOLCANO

Mary Mountain Trail

Lake Village

BRIDGE BAY △

Bridge Bay

FISHING BRIDGE RV PARK

Lake Butte

— North Shore Trail

Craig Pass

☾ YELLOWSTONE LAKE

GRANT VILLAGE

West Thumb ○

Grant Village

Shoshone Lake

Delacy Creek Trail

Park Pt

Frank Island

Avalanche Peak 10,566ft

Sylvan Pass

Mt Doane 10,352ft

Mt Langford 10,774ft

EAST ENTRANCE ■

PAHASKA TEPEE

SLEEPING GIANT

14 16 20

To Cody

Mt Stevenson 10,352ft

Washakie Wilderness

Eagle Creek Trail

Thorofare Trail

Lewis Lake

LEWIS LAKE △

Lewis Falls

Mt Sheridan 10,308ft

Heart Lake

Heart Lake Trail

Snake River Trail

Continental

Trail Creek Trail

Two Ocean Plateau

Eagle Peak 11,358ft

Table Mtn 11,063ft

Eagle Pass

Mountain Creek Trail

Pitchstone Plateau Trail

Moose Falls

SOUTH ENTRANCE ■

Lewis R

Two Ocean Plateau Trail

Snake River

Divide

Yellowstone

THOROFARE RANGER STATION

John D. Rockefeller Jr. Memorial Parkway

89 191 287

■ FLAGG RANCH

To Jackson

Bridger-Teton National Forest

South Boundary Trail

Teton Wilderness

River

Absaroka-Beartooth Wilderness

Pebble Creek Trail

Silver Gate

Cooke City

MONTANA
WYOMING

■ NORTHEAST ENTRANCE

212

Slough Creek Trail

SLOUGH CREEK △

Bliss Pass Trail

PEBBLE CREEK △

Abiathar Peak 10,928ft

North Absaroka Wilderness

YELLOWSTONE INSTITUTE

The Thunderer 10,554ft

To Red Lodge, Montana and Cody, Wyoming

Lamar Valley

River

Cache Creek Trail

☾ LAMAR VALLEY

☾ GRAND CANYON OF THE YELLOWSTONE

Lamar River Trail

Mirror Plateau

Shoshone

National

Pelican Cone

Pelican Valley

Range

Absaroka

North Absaroka Wilderness

Forest

0 _____ 10 mi

0 _____ 10 km

© AVALON TRAVEL

spellbinding as it was for John Colter and Jim Bridger and the scores of Native Americans who had traveled through the park long before them. But it is increasingly complex. Issues like bioprospecting, bison management in the face of the disease brucellosis, and the delisting criteria of endangered species loom large. Despite the fact that, thankfully, the physical features of Yellowstone—its mountain-scapes, geothermal features, and wildlife populations—remain largely untouched, an area of this size with more than 3 million visitors annually (more than the populations of Montana and Wyoming combined) cannot be immune to human influence. The challenge as we move forward is to determine a way to let Yellowstone age and evolve in its own way, on its own time, while giving people around the world access to this truly unique and spectacular place. It is we, the visitors, who have an opportunity to be changed forever by time spent in Yellowstone, and not the other way around.

THE LAND

Yellowstone is a living, breathing, evolving ecosystem that is home to a diversity of high alpine, subalpine, and forest plants (1,150 native species of flowering plants, to be exact) and an extraordinary number of animals (including 67 mammal species). It is fascinating to understand how the flora and fauna relate—and react—to one another throughout the park.

Flora

What makes the plant life in Yellowstone so interesting is neither the abundance nor the variety but rather the relationship between the plants and their environment and the way they are determined and shaped by forces of geology, climate, fire, insect infestation, drought, flood, and not least of all, wildlife. In various places throughout the park, for example, visitors will notice small fenced areas where grazing animals like elk, deer, and bison do not have access. The flora is decidedly different when it is protected from herbivores. The massive burns of 1988 have given rise to a plant-lover's paradise where hot pink fireweed

is among the first to recolonize the blackened areas. The geothermal areas have their own rare and unique plant communities. And the reintroduction of the wolves caused the movements of the elk to be more sporadic as they tried to avoid being eaten, which led to an increase in the number of willows and a resulting increase in various animals, including beavers, that thrive on willows. These chains of events linking plants, animals, and the natural forces that control the park are endless and fascinating.

Fauna

For many, the fauna in Yellowstone is the main event. With large mammals such as elk, bison, bighorn sheep, antelope, bears, wolves, and mountain lions, Yellowstone is among the best areas in the country to see wildlife in its natural habitat. For those willing to get up early and be patient enough to wait, sometimes for hours, Yellowstone is like the Discovery Channel brought to life.

There are a few species of reptiles and amphibians known to inhabit the park—10 in all—thanks to Yellowstone's cool, dry climate, and some 318 species of birds have been documented since the park's 1872 founding, ranging from tiny calliope hummingbirds to majestic trumpeter swans.

But it's the big animals that draw more than 3 million people to the park annually. The omnipresent **bison** are the largest animal in the park, with males (bulls) weighing upward of 1,800 pounds and females (cows) averaging about 1,000 pounds. Yellowstone is the only place in the Lower 48 where wild bison have existed since prehistoric times. The herd dropped to near-extinction levels at the turn of the 20th century with only 50 animals within the park boundaries. The importation of 21 bison from private herds and the subsequent 50 years of repopulation efforts led to a marked increase in numbers. By 2006 some 3,500 of these wild, wooly behemoths once again roamed the high prairies of Yellowstone, but significant population fluctuations occur primarily because of fears surrounding the disease brucellosis. In a

PLAYING IT SAFE AND SMART IN THE BACKCOUNTRY

Hiking and camping in the Yellowstone back-country is undoubtedly the best way to understand and appreciate this magnificently wild place. But with this remarkable opportunity comes the very important responsibility to keep yourself safe, protect the animals from human-caused altercations, and preserve this pristine environment.

When hiking, prevent erosion and trail degradation by hiking single file and always staying on the trail. Don't take shortcuts or cut corners on switchbacks. If you do have to leave the trail, disperse your group so that you don't inadvertently trample the vegetation and create a new, unwanted trail.

Chances are good that you will encounter some kind of wildlife in the backcountry, so you need to be prepared to react. Never approach an animal: Remember to always stay at least 25 yards away from all wildlife, and at least 100 yards away from predators, including bears. Make noise as you hike along to give animals the opportunity to depart before an encounter. Do not hike at the edges of day – dawn or dusk – or at night, as these are the most active times for bears and other predators. Always be aware of your surroundings. Look for overturned rocks and logs, dug-out areas, and, of course, carcasses, all of which suggest bear activity.

If you do encounter a bear, know what to do. If there is some distance between you and the bear, give the bear an opportunity to leave, or take the opportunity to redirect your own party. If you run into a bear at close range, be as nonthreatening as possible. Talk calmly and back away. Never turn your back, and never run. Make sure you have your bear spray accessible. If the bear charges, stand your ground. Bears will often bluff charge to determine whether you will run and are thus prey. If the bear does attack, keep your pack on, fall to the ground on your belly, protect your head and neck with your arms, and play dead. When the bear leaves, get up and retreat. In the very uncommon circumstance that a bear provokes an attack or enters a tent, fight the bear with every resource you have.

Go to great lengths to avoid attracting bears by hanging all food, cooking utensils, and scented items (toothpaste, deodorant, and other toiletries) in a bear bag in a tree or atop a bear pole. Designate a separate cooking and eating area away from the sleeping tents. Dispose of your trash and personal waste properly.

You need to plan your trip carefully and secure all permits and backcountry campsites through any one of seven backcountry permit offices: Bechler Ranger Station, Canyon Visitors Center, Grant Village Visitors Center, Bridge Bay Ranger Station, Mammoth Visitors Center, Old Faithful Ranger Station, South Entrance Ranger Station, Tower Ranger Station, and the West Yellowstone Visitor Information Center (307/344-2160, www.nps.gov/yell/planyourvisit/backcountrytripplanner.htm, $20 if reservations are made more than 48 hours ahead). Yellowstone's roughly 300 backcountry campsites can be reserved in advance either in person or through the mail. Backcountry Use Permits are required for all overnight stays and can only be attained in person no more than 48 hours before your trip. A park booklet titled *Beyond Road's End* is available online and will help familiarize you with the backcountry regulations and restrictions.

YELLOWSTONE'S SUPERVOLCANO

It's always interesting to watch visitors' expressions when you tell them that in Yellowstone National Park they are standing atop one of the world's largest active supervolcanos... and that it is overdue for an apocalyptic eruption. While these facts are true, the reality is much less threatening. Indeed there have been three phenomenal eruptions over the course of the last 2 million years, and the patterns do indicate that the volcano is overdue to erupt. But scientists agree that the chances of a massive eruption in the next 1,000 or even 10,000 years are very slight. For the time being, anyway, the supervolcano that gives rise to Yellowstone's extraordinary geothermal features is all bark and no bite – thankfully.

The first supervolcanic eruption 2.1 million years ago was 6,000 times more powerful than the 1980 eruption of Mount St. Helens, spouting rock and ash in every direction from Texas to Canada, Missouri to California. The eruption emptied the magma chamber located just underneath the park and caused a massive sinking of the earth, known as a caldera, within the confines of what is now the park. Small lava flows filled in the perimeter of the Huckleberry Ridge Caldera over the course of hundreds of thousands of years.

The second major, but smaller, eruption occurred 1.3 million years ago and created Henry's Fork Caldera. The most recent massive eruption took place roughly 640,000 years ago and created the Yellowstone Caldera, which is 30 by 45 miles in size. The perimeter of the Yellowstone Caldera is still visible in places throughout the park. Hike up Mount Washburn on Dunraven Pass between Canyon and Tower, look south, and you will see the vast caldera formed by the most recent eruption. The caldera rim is also visible at Gibbon Falls, Lewis Falls, and Lake Butte. As you drive between Mammoth and Gardiner, look at Mount Everts to the east and you will see layers of ash from the various eruptions.

But volcanic activity is not a thing of the past in Yellowstone. The magma, which some scientists think is just five miles beneath the surface of the park in places as opposed to the typical 40, has created two enormous bulges, known as resurgent domes, near Sour Creek and Mallard Lake. The Sour Creek Dome is growing at an impressive rate of 1.5 inches per year, causing Yellowstone Lake to tip southward, leaving docks on the north side completely out of the water and flooding the forested shore of the south side. In addition, there are roughly 2,000 earthquakes every year centered in Yellowstone, most of which cannot be felt. The earthquakes shift geothermal activity in the park and keep the natural plumbing system that feeds the geyser basins flowing. They also suggest volcanic activity. In December 2008 a series of 500 small earthquakes (the largest registered 3.9 on the Richter scale) rocked the park in the course of a single week.

Still, the scientists at the Yellowstone Volcano Observatory have no reason to suspect that an eruption, or even a lava flow, is imminent. For 30 years scientists have been monitoring the region for precursors to volcanic eruptions – earthquake swarms, rapid ground deformation, gas releases, and lava flows – and although there is activity, none of it suggests anything immediately foreboding. Current real-time monitoring data, including earthquake activity and deformation, are available online at http://volcanoes.usgs.gov/yvo/monitoring.html. The bottom line is that the volcano is real and active, but certainly not a threat in the immediate future, and not a reason to stay away from this awe-inspiring place.

given year, the bison population in Yellowstone ranges 2,300–4,500 animals.

There are an estimated 150 grizzly bears living in the park and three to four times as many black bears. Gray wolves were reintroduced to the park (after being entirely killed off in the area) in 1995, and today there are more than 100 wolves in 12 packs. Wolverines and lynx live within the park but are rarely seen. Coyotes are plentiful and often visible from cars. There are fewer than 25 mountain lions. Elk populations soar in the summer months to 10,000–20,000 animals, while moose, hard hit by the fires of 1988, number fewer than 200. There are roughly 250 bighorn sheep in the park and around 200 nonnative mountain goats.

Finding the animals means knowing their habitats, being willing to wait during the edges of daylight, and oftentimes just plain getting lucky. A number of excellent wildlife spotting guides are available through the Yellowstone Association (406/848-2400, www.yellowstoneassociation.org), but the most obvious place to start is by asking any of the rangers at the park's various visitors centers. They can tell you about recent predatory kills, bear and wolf activity, elk and bison migrations, and the most up-to-date sightings of any number of animals.

As is true with nearly every feature of the park, the importance of safety in the face of wildlife cannot be overstated. Be certain to stay at least 25 yards away from bison and elk and at least 100 yards away from bears, wolves, and other predators. If the animals change their behavior because of your presence, if they stop eating to look at you, for example, you are too close and are creating a significant and perhaps even life-threatening hazard for both the animal and yourself. Always remember that you are the visitor here and they are the residents; show proper respect.

Geothermal Features

If the animals are what bring people to Yellowstone, the geothermal features are what transfix them and lure them back year after year. Surprisingly, some 70 percent of adult U.S. citizens are estimated to have witnessed an eruption of Old Faithful.

The world's largest concentration of thermal features—more than 10,000 in all—Yellowstone bursts to life with geysers, hot springs, fumaroles (steam vents), and mud pots. There are six grand geysers, of which **Old Faithful** is the most famous, and more than 300 lesser geysers. Throughout the park, there are a number of basins where visitors can see all four types of thermal features, including **Norris Geyser Basin.**

The thermal features in Yellowstone are an indication of the region's volcanic past, present, and future, and as such they are in constant states of change. Small but daily earthquakes cause shifts in activity and temperature. The travertine **Mammoth Terraces** are literally growing and changing on a daily basis to the point that the boardwalks have had to be altered to protect visitors from different flows of searing hot water.

As miraculous as these water features are to see—with dramatic color displays and water dances that put Las Vegas's Bellagio fountains to shame—and to smell (think hot rotten eggs), what you can't see is perhaps even more compelling: Thermophiles are heat-loving microorganisms that inhabit the geothermal features throughout the park. A source of ongoing scientific study, these thermophiles are modern examples of the earth's first life forms and are responsible for the discovery of DNA fingerprinting.

As spellbinding as they are, particularly in winter when the warm steam beckons, it is critically important to stay on boardwalks in geothermal areas and never touch the water. In addition to being boiling hot, many features are highly acidic or alkaline and could cause extreme chemical burns. The ground around the features is often thin and unstable, occasionally allowing animals to break through and be cooked. Many people have died for failing to use caution when walking near thermal features.

PLANNING YOUR TIME

One could quite literally spend a lifetime in Yellowstone without being able to cover every last corner of this magnificent wilderness, but the reality is that most visitors only have a couple of days, at best, to spend exploring the park. Something like 98 percent of visitors never get more than a mile from the road, but it's easier than you might think—and incredibly worthwhile. Three days in the park is ideal, but if you have less time, there are ways to maximize every minute.

One important consideration in planning your time in Yellowstone is to know the season you'll be traveling. Summer offers magnificent scenery, usually good weather, and the "bear jam," when drivers hit the brakes as soon as someone spots anything resembling a brown furry creature. Summer visitors to Yellowstone need to plan for traffic and often for road construction delays. Fall and spring are fantastic times to see wildlife, but the weather can change in a heartbeat—at Yellowstone's high elevation, blizzards can strike nearly any month of the year. Winter is a magical time in the park, but cars are only permitted on one road in the northeast corner. All other travel is done via snow coach, guided snowmobile tour, or on skis and snowshoes. There is no wrong time to visit the park, but knowing the advantages and disadvantages of the various seasons will help you manage your expectations.

Assuming you'll be in Yellowstone when the roads are open to car traffic, there are five entrances and exits to Yellowstone, making loop trips relatively easy. From Montana, you can enter or exit the park from the northeast at Cooke City, from the north at Gardiner, or from the west at West Yellowstone. From Wyoming, you can enter the park from the east entrance nearest Cody or from the south through Grand Teton National Park. If you're going from one state to the next, there is no more spectacular route than through the heart of Yellowstone.

A cursory glance at a Yellowstone map will reveal the main roads, which form a figure eight in the heart of the park, and the access roads leading to and from the entrances. The majority of the park's big-name highlights— **Old Faithful, West Thumb Geyser Basin,** **Fishing Bridge, The Grand Canyon of the Yellowstone, Norris and Mammoth Geyser Basins**—are accessible from the main loops. Depending on your time and your plan for accommodations, you could easily spend a full day driving each of the two loops. A third day would permit an opportunity for deeper exploration—perhaps a hike—and a leisurely exit from the park.

If time won't permit even one night in the park, it is still well worth driving through, just to get a sense of this magnificent and tremendously diverse place. Consider choosing one feature and pursuing it. To give yourself the best chance of seeing wolves, traveling between the north and northeast entrances is an excellent route during nonsummer months. Geothermal aficionados will have no shortage of choices for seeing the park's impressive features, but to swim in them, try the **Boiling River,** a stretch of the Gardner River near Mammoth, which is swimmable year-round except during spring runoff. The **Firehole River** also offers excellent summer swimming not far from Old Faithful. Landlubbers might prefer a short hike into a less-famous geyser like **Lone Star,** just a few flat miles from Old Faithful.

The best advice is this: Get off the road, get out of your car, be smart, and come prepared to give yourself the opportunity to see and understand what makes Yellowstone America's first wonderland.

Getting There and Around

Yellowstone is about 90 miles from the airports in Bozeman and Billings, 60 miles from the airport in Jackson Hole, and 52 miles from the airport in Cody. The **West Yellowstone Airport** (WYS, 406/646-7631) is served by Delta/Sky West and is only open June–early September. Bus service with **Karst Stage** (800/845-2778) is available from Bozeman to West Yellowstone year-round and to Gardiner during the winter and summer seasons.

Xanterra (307/344-7311, www.yellowstonenationalparklodges.com) offers bus tours of the park during the summer. The Grand Loop Tour departs daily from Gardiner and

Mammoth and covers the entire park in one day. However, your best bet to see the park on your own terms is to go by car. **Budget** (800/426-7669), **Avis** (406/646-7635), and **Big Sky Car Rentals** (800/231-5991) are available in West Yellowstone.

When planning your drive through Yellowstone, it is best to fill up your tank outside the park. Once inside, the gas prices you'll encounter tend to be extremely high, and options are quite limited. Gas stations are located within the park at Canyon, Fishing Bridge, Grant Village, Mammoth, Upper and Lower Old Faithful, and Tower Junction. They are generally open late spring–early fall.

Traffic and Road Construction

One of the things that makes Yellowstone so wild and enchanting is its utter unpredictability—something that relates to wildlife, weather, and unfortunately, road conditions. A 20-year $300-million plan is currently afoot to address the structural deficiencies of Yellowstone's roads. Plan to keep a close watch on road closures and delays that can happen any time of year because of construction, bad weather, or even fire. For a 24-hour road report, check **Road Construction Delays and Closures** (307/344-2117, www.nps.gov/yell/planyourvist/roadclosures.htm). Information on state roads is available from the **Montana Department of Transportation** (800/226-7623, www.mdt.mt.gov/travinfo) and the **Wyoming Department of Transportation** (888/WYO-ROAD—888/996-7623, www.wyoroad.info).

National Weather Service (www.crh.noaa.gov/riw/?n=ynp_gtnp) reports are available for Yellowstone and Grand Teton.

Information and Services

The best resource to familiarize yourself with the park and to help plan your trip is **The National Park Service** (307/344-7381, www.nps.gov/yell). On the website, click on the link titled Plan Your Visit. The site also posts information about the different **Ranger Programs** being offered, including educational lectures and hikes. Admission to the park is $25 per vehicle for seven days, $20 for snowmobiles or motorcycles, and $12 for hikers and bicyclists. The park is open year-round, but during the winter cars can only access the park through the north and northeast entrances.

Xanterra Parks and Resorts (307/344-7901, www.yellowstonenationalparklodges.com) is the official concessionaire of Yellowstone, and all reservations for lodging, dining, and special activities in the park can be made through them.

Emergencies

If you encounter an emergency when traveling through the park, dial 911, but be aware that cell coverage is spotty. Emergency medical services are attended to by rangers. There are three urgent care facilities inside Yellowstone. The clinic at Mammoth (307/344-7965) is open year-round, and the clinics at Lake (307/242-7241) and Old Faithful (307/344-7325) are open seasonally.

Gardiner

Named rather inauspiciously for a cannibalistic mountain man who allegedly got rid of his wives year after year by, ahem, eating them, Gardiner (population 871, elevation 5,314) is actually a cute little town with plenty of places to stay, eat, and stock up, and has ideal proximity to the park. The only year-round entrance to Yellowstone for automobiles, this scrubby little tourist town has a charm and an identity all its own. The Yellowstone River cuts a canyon beside the main drag, which allows for plenty of river-runner hangouts. Few other places in the world have elk congregating in the churchyard or on the front lawns of most of the motels in town. And where else do high school football players have to dodge bison dung as they're running for a touchdown? The town's architecture is a combination of glorious wood and stone "parkitecture" buildings alongside old-school Western style buildings complete with false fronts. The towering Roosevelt Arch, built in 1903 and dedicated by Yellowstone champion Teddy Roosevelt himself, welcomes visitors to the park with its inspiring slogan, "For the Benefit and Enjoyment of the People." Yes, Gardiner is built around its proximity to the park, but the town has maintained its integrity by preserving its history and making the most of its surroundings.

SIGHTS
❰ Boiling River

Halfway between Gardiner and Mammoth Hot Springs, straddling the Montana-Wyoming border and the 45th parallel, the halfway point between the equator and the north pole, is the Boiling River, one of only two swimmable thermal features in Yellowstone. From the clearly marked parking area, visitors amble upstream along a 0.5-mile rocky path running parallel to the Gardner River. Where the trail ends and the steam envelops almost everything, a gushing hot spring called the Boiling River flows into the otherwise icy Gardner River. The hot and cold waters mix to a perfect temperature that can be enjoyed year-round. The area is open during daylight hours only, and all swimmers must wear a bathing suit. The Boiling River is closed each year during spring runoff, when temperature fluctuations and rushing water put swimmers at risk. Alcohol is not permitted.

Kids and adults alike marvel at the floating Day-Glo green algae. The water should not be ingested. Bison and elk frequent the area, and despite the frequent crowds of people (note that 20 people constitute a crowd in this part of the West), this is one of the most unique and unforgettable ways to enjoy a few hours in Yellowstone.

EVENTS

The **Annual NRA Gardiner Rodeo** (406/848-7971, $7 adults, $3 ages 6–12, free for children under 6) is held in mid-June (call for this year's dates) and is one of the town's largest summer attractions. The rodeo is held in the Jim Duffy arena at the northern end of town off U.S. 89 and includes the usual competitions such as bull riding and bareback bronc riding. Women and juniors compete in barrel racing and breakaway roping. The first night of the rodeo is followed by a dance at the Community Center, and the following day the Chamber of Commerce hosts a parade downtown. This is a great small-town rodeo.

RECREATION
Fishing and Boating

The Yellowstone is the longest free-flowing river in the Lower 48, and as such it offers excellent boating and fishing opportunities. With the river plunging through town on its way to Yankee Jim Canyon, Gardiner is home to several outfitters that can whet your appetite for adventure, trout, or both. The **Flying Pig Adventure Company** (511 Scott St., 406/848-

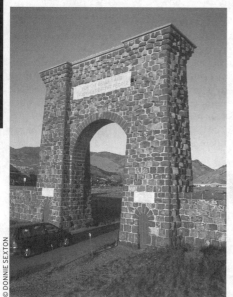

"For the Benefit and Enjoyment of the People" - Roosevelt Arch in Gardiner, Montana

7510 or 866/807-0744, www.flyingpigrafting. com, May–Sept.) is a full-service outfitter offering guided white-water rafting, horseback rides, wildlife safaris, and cowboy cookouts. **Yellowstone Raft Company** (406 Scott St., 406/848-7777 or 800/858-7781, www.yellowstoneraft.com, May–Sept.) was established in 1978 and has an excellent reputation for experienced guides and top-of-the-line equipment. For adrenaline junkies, Yellowstone Raft Company offers sit-on-top kayak instruction and adventures.

For anglers eager to wet a line in or out of the park in search of native cutthroats or brown trout, **Park's Fly Shop** (202 2nd St. S., 406/848-7314, www.parksflyshop.com) is the best place to start. They offer half-day trips for two people starting around $325, and full-day trips for two from around $425. Anglers can pick up their licenses and any supplies in the retail shop, which stays open year-round. And since Park's has been serving the area since 1953, their guides are keenly aware of the spots where the fish greatly outnumber the anglers.

Hiking

Yellowstone is a hiker's paradise, and unless you have a pet that needs to stretch its legs, hiking just outside the park is like spending the day in the Disney World parking lot. Not that there isn't stunning country in every direction, but there is something particularly alluring about hiking within the boundaries of the park.

That said, some 4.7 miles south of the terraces at Mammoth Hot Springs, on the left-hand side after the Golden Gate Bridge, is the **Glen Creek Trailhead** and a small dirt parking lot. There are a range of wonderful hikes that start from this point. Across the street on the west side of the road, a trail leads through **The Hoodoos,** massive travertine boulders that look otherworldly in this setting, and down the mountain 3.8 miles back to Mammoth. If you cannot arrange either a drop-off at the trailhead or a shuttle, the return trip, another 3.8 miles, climbs constantly for nearly 1,000 vertical feet. Another more ambitious hike is the 9.2-mile round-trip to **Osprey Falls.** The

first four miles are easy and flat, following an abandoned road bed popular with mountain bikers. A blink-and-you'll-miss-it spur trail off the south side of the road leads hikers down into Sheepeater Canyon and the remaining 0.6 miles to the mesmerizing 150-foot falls. Relax, have a snack, and save your energy for the 800-vertical-foot climb back up to the road. **Bunsen Peak** offers hikers an interesting walk through an entirely burned forest and all its colorful rebirth, as well as a stunning view from the 8,500-foot summit. The climb is steep: 1,300 vertical feet over 2.1 miles. Try to ignore the hum of the radio tower near the summit, easily accomplished when the summit view fills your senses.

ACCOMMODATIONS

Gardiner is built to accommodate the overflow from the park, but in reality, many of the little motels have more charm and much better value, particularly in nonsummer months, than those inside the park. For the most part, it's hard to go wrong in Gardiner. There are plenty of small cabins and larger vacation rentals in the area. **Above the Rest Lodge** (8 Above the Rest Lane, 406/848-7747 or 800/406-7748, www.abovetherestlodge.com, 2–14-person cabins $125–260) is hardly glamorous, but it is comfortable, and the views over the river and into the park are breathtaking. The folk Victorian **C Gardiner Guest House** (112 Main St. E., 406/848-9414 or 406/848-7314, www.gardinerguesthouse.com, $70–400 depending on the season and number of rooms) welcomes both children and pets and offers three modest but comfortable guest rooms and a cabin. Owners Richard and Nance Parks are longtime residents and an extensive source of information on the area. His fly shop and guiding company, Park's Fly Shop, is one of the oldest businesses in town.

For more standard hotels, there is a good selection ranging from the upscale **Comfort Inn** (107 Hellroaring St., 406/848-7536 or 800/424-6423, www.yellowstonecomfortinn.com, $156–210) to the barebones but clean **Super 8** (702 Scott St. W., 406/848-7401, www.yellowstonesuper8.com, $45–155).

CAMPING IN YELLOWSTONE

As accommodations cannot meet the demand of Yellowstone's 3 million visitors each year, camping is an excellent option, particularly for those spontaneous souls who want to see the park without planning months in advance. There are 12 campgrounds located throughout the park. The five largest – Bridge Bay, Canyon, Fishing Bridge RV, Grant, and Madison – are run by Xanterra. The fees for these campgrounds have additional sales and utility taxes. All inquiries and reservations should be made by calling Xanterra (same-day reservations 307/344-7901, advance reservations 307/344-7311). The other sites are assigned on a first come, first served basis. You should try to arrive early to secure your spot. Sites often fill up by 11 A.M., especially in the busy summer months.

Campground	Number of Sites	Approximate Dates	Fees	RV Sites
Bridge Bay	less than 425	May 28–Sept. 12	$19.50	call for details
Canyon	less than 250	June 4–Sept. 6	$19.50	call for details
Fishing Bridge RV	less than 325	May 14–Sept. 26	$35	call for details
Grant	less than 400	June 21–Sept. 19	$19.50	call for details
Indian Creek	75	June 11–Sept. 13	$12	ten 40-foot, thirty-five 30-foot, pull-through
Lewis Lake	85	June 15–Nov. 16	$12	25-foot
Madison	less than 250	May 7–Oct. 24	$19.50	call for details
Mammoth	85	year-round	$14	all pull-through
Norris	less than 100	May 21–Sept. 27	$14	two 50-foot, five 30-foot
Pebble Creek	less than 30	June 11–Sept. 27	$12	some long pull-throughs
Slough Creek	29	May 28–Oct. 31	$12	fourteen 30-foot (walk through first to check sites after site 16)
Tower Fall	32	May 21–Sept. 27	$12	all 30-foot or less; has a hairpin turn

There are more than 300 backcountry campsites throughout the park. Overnight permits are required for all of the sites. The maximum stay ranges 1–3 nights. Permits are available at all ranger stations and visitors centers, and they are only issued in person up to 48 hours in advance. You may reserve backcountry campsites ahead of time for $20. All requests to reserve sites must be made in person or mailed in. All the pertinent forms and information for backcountry camping in Yellowstone are available online in the NPS Backcountry Trip Planner (www.nps.gov/yell/planyourvisit/backcountrytripplanner.htm).

CAMPING

The difference between camping outside the park and inside Yellowstone is simply that you need to focus on reservations and availability instead of permits and regulations. There are six campgrounds in Gardiner—four National Forest campgrounds and two private ones. The **Yellowstone RV Park & Campground** (121 U.S. 89 S., 406/848-7496, May–Oct.) is ideally situated on the Yellowstone River just 1.3 miles north of the park entrance.

Those in search of a more rustic experience might enjoy the pack-in, pack-out **Bear Creek Campground** (Bear Creek Rd. 493, 10.5 miles northeast of Gardiner, 406/848-7375, 4 sites with no services, mid-June–late Oct. depending on weather, free) or the **Timber Camp Campground** (Bear Creek Rd. 493, 9.5 miles northeast of Gardiner, 406/848-7375, no services, mid-June–late Oct. depending on weather, free), both of which are small, isolated, and pleasantly rustic.

FOOD

◖ **Helen's Corral Drive Inn** (Hwy. 89 S., across from the Super 8 Motel, 406/848-7627, 11 a.m.–11 p.m. daily May–Oct., burgers $6.75–9.25) is the kind of place you might easily drive 100 miles to for the burger, shake, and old-school ambience. Make no mistake—this is a greasy burger joint (albeit with thick, juicy bison burgers) that is not particularly clean, efficient, or healthy in any way. The menu even features "The Hateful Hamburger," a cartoon version of their hamburgers with cigarettes dangling from their mouths. The limited seating is mostly outside. But none of that will matter when you take your first bite of a bison bacon cheeseburger. Helen's is a little slice of hamburger paradise—if you like that sort of thing.

Just over the river toward the park, the **K-Bar Café** (202 Main St., 406/848-9995, lunch 11 a.m.–2 p.m. daily, dinner 5–9 p.m. daily, entrées $8–19) is a classic bar with surprisingly good homemade pizza served for lunch and dinner. They are working on bringing back some Mexican specials a couple of days each week. The **Sawtooth Deli** (220 W. Park St., 406/848-7600, 8 a.m.–9 p.m. Tues.–Sat. May–Oct., breakfast and lunch $4–9, dinner $8–22) serves three meals a day with hearty fresh entrées that include breakfast burritos, brick-oven pizza, hot and cold sandwiches, and homemade soup.

The Northern Loop

With striking panoramas, wonderful thermals, plentiful wildlife, and year-round vehicle access between the north and northeast entrances, this is one of the most underappreciated parts of the park. The accommodations and dining are not as fancy as elsewhere, but the crowds are more manageable, and the experience is just as good. Phenomenal highlights include Mammoth Hot Springs, Tower Falls, Dunraven Pass, the Grand Canyon of the Yellowstone, and Norris Geyser Basin.

SIGHTS
◖ Mammoth and the Mammoth Hot Springs Terraces

Just 5 miles into the park and up the road from Gardiner, Mammoth is the primary northern hub of Yellowstone National Park. It is also an interesting little community in its own right, with a small medical center, the most beautiful post office in the West, a lime-green jail, and a magnificent stone church. The town of Mammoth, once known as Fort Yellowstone, was essentially built by the U.S. Army during their 1886–1918 occupation. Thinking they were on a temporary assignment, the soldiers erected canvas-walled tents and lived in them through five harsh winters. In 1890, Congress set aside $50,000 for the construction of a permanent post, a stately collection of stone colonial revival–style buildings, most of which are still in use today.

YELLOWSTONE NATIONAL PARK

© OSAMU HOSHINO/WYOMING TRAVEL & TOURISM

The terraces at Mammoth Hot Springs are always shifting.

The **Albright Visitors Center** (307/344-2263, 8 A.M.–7 P.M. daily May–early Sept., 8 A.M.–5 P.M. daily Sept., 9 A.M.–5 P.M. daily Oct.–Apr.) is a must-see. There are films, history and wildlife exhibits, and a small but excellent selection of books and videos. While at the center, don't miss seeing some of the artwork produced during the 1871 Hayden Geological Survey of the park. In the Moran Gallery you can see quality reproductions of painter Thomas Moran's famous watercolor sketches, and in the Jackson Gallery, the original photographs by William Henry Jackson. Rangers on staff can usually give you up-to-date animal sightings and activity reports. The flush toilets (the last for a while) are located underneath the building.

The primary ecological attraction in Mammoth (other than the elk often seen lounging around and nibbling on the green grass) can be found on the terraces at **Mammoth Hot Springs.** Since the days of the earliest stagecoach trails into the park, the Mammoth Terraces have been a visual and olfactory marvel for visitors. The Hayden Expedition named

the area White Mountain Hot Spring for the cream-colored, steplike travertine terraces.

Beneath the ground, the Norris-Mammoth fault carries superheated water rich in dissolved calcium and bicarbonate. As the water emerges through cracks in the surface, carbon dioxide is released as a gas and the carbonate combines with calcium to form travertine. The mountain is continuously growing as travertine is deposited and then shifted as the cracks are sealed and the mineral-laden water emerges somewhere else. For frequent visitors to the park, vast changes are noticeable from one visit to the next. In addition to changes in shape and water flow, the colors at Mammoth can vary dramatically from one day to the next. Not only does travertine morph from bright white when it is new to cream and then gray as it is exposed to the elements, the cyanobacteria create fabulous color shifts too—from turquoise to green and yellow to red and brown, depending on water temperatures, available sunlight, and pH levels.

Liberty Cap at the base of the terraces is an excellent example of a dormant spring, where all but the core cone have been eroded away. **Minerva** and **Canary Spring and Terrace** are two other springs worth seeing. Their temperatures average around 160°F, and when they are flowing they often put on marvelous color displays.

Tower Falls

Eighteen scenic miles down the road from Mammoth Hot Springs—past **Undine Falls** and **Blacktail Plateau,** where you can see deer, elk, and bison along with some impressive lookouts—is Tower Junction and the breathtaking Tower Falls. The waterfall itself cascades 132 feet from volcanic basalt. A popular spot with visitors and just steps from the parking lot, this is not the ideal place for solitude, but it is lovely to see.

Dunraven Pass

Between Tower and the dramatic Grand Canyon of the Yellowstone is one of the most nerve-racking and perhaps most beautiful drives in the park. Climbing up the flanks of **Mount**

THE SHEEP EATERS OF YELLOWSTONE

During the early 18th century, the horse was introduced to many of the Native American tribes that frequented the Yellowstone area. With the acquisition of this new, strong, and agile animal, they were able to spread out across the plains, traveling farther and longer to follow the bison. Hunting and warfare became more efficient almost overnight. A small group of Shoshone chose not to use horses or guns, however, and instead remained committed to their traditional mountain living.

The Sheep Eaters, also known as the Tukudika, were forest dwellers considered to be the only Native Americans to have inhabited Yellowstone year-round. They lived in *wikiups* – temporary shelters made of aspen poles, pine bows, and other brush – rather than animal-hide tipis, and they traveled the mountain ridges rather than the river paths as their counterparts on the plains did. Living in small bands of 10-20 people, they relied on their wolf dogs to help them move provisions up and down the mountains. They were named for the animal whose migration they followed: the bighorn sheep. The Sheep Eaters developed highly effective sheep traps, the remains of which can be seen around Dubois, Wyoming, and they utilized the animal for both food and tools. They heated the sheep's horns in the hot springs of Yellowstone to mold them into ex-

quisite strong bows, powerful enough to drive an arrow through a bison. The reputation of these bows spread to other tribes and were highly sought-after. The European outsiders who made their way into the park during the early and mid-1800s described the Sheep Eaters as destitute and forlorn, not owning nor seeming to want the modern trappings of the Plains Indians. Contemporary views suggest that these people revered their environment and ancestors' way of life and were more intent on maintaining their customs than competing and conquering.

Unfortunately, their traditions did not allow the Sheep Eaters to escape the same ultimate fate as other Native Americans. Devastated by smallpox and considered an obstacle to westward expansion, the Sheep Eaters fought the U.S. Army in the last Indian war in the Pacific Northwest. Unfairly accused of murdering five Chinese miners, the last remaining Sheep Eaters, a group of 51 people that included woman and children, were relentlessly pursued in the Idaho wilderness along the Middle Fork of the Salmon River in the fall of 1879. When the Army purportedly captured a woman who had just given birth, the remaining members of the tribe surrendered, exhausted, on October 1, and they were sent to the Wind River Shoshone Reservation in Wyoming and Fort Hall Shoshone Bannock Reservation in Idaho.

YELLOWSTONE NATIONAL PARK

Washburn, Dunraven Pass is the highest road elevation in the park. The spectacular summit tops out at 8,859 feet and offers impressive views of Yellowstone's caldera rim. Eagle eyes can also spot the nearby Grand Canyon of the Yellowstone. Hikers will have no shortage of trailheads to start from. Be aware: The whitebark pines that grow along the road are a critical food source for grizzly bears, so keep your eyes open. Because of its extreme altitude and relative exposure, Dunraven Pass is one of the last roads to open in the spring and one of the first to close when bad weather hits. For current road information, call 307/344-2117.

◖ Grand Canyon of the Yellowstone

Yellowstone's most recent volcanic explosion, some 600,000 years ago, created a massive caldera and subsequent lava flows, one of which was called the Canyon Rhyolite flow, in the area that is now known as the Grand Canyon of the Yellowstone. This particular lava flow was impacted by a thermal basin, which altered the rhyolite and created the beautiful palette of colors in the rock through constant heating and cooling. Over time, lakes, rivers, and glaciers formed in the region, and the relatively soft rhyolite was easily carved away. Roughly

10,000 years ago, the last of the area's glaciers melted, causing a rush of water to carve the canyon into the form it has today. The 20-mile-long canyon is still growing thanks to the forces of erosion, including water, wind, and earthquakes. There are a number of terrific lookouts on both the North and South Rims of the canyon.

Before setting out for the canyon itself, visitors are advised to visit the new **Canyon Visitor Education Center** (307/242-2550), which has an excellent exhibit on Yellowstone's supervolcano, geothermal activity, and other natural history.

On the **North Rim,** don't miss **Inspiration Point,** a natural viewing platform that gives a bird's-eye view both up and down the river. Nathaniel Langford, who would go on to be the park's first superintendent, stood in the same spot with the Washburn Expedition in 1870. He wrote,

Standing there or rather lying there for greater safety, I thought how utterly impossible it would be to describe to another the sensations inspired by such a presence. As I took in the scene, I realized my own littleness, my helplessness, my dread exposure to destruction, my inability to cope with or even comprehend the mighty architecture of nature.

Look down, if you dare, among the nooks and crannies of rock to try to spot nesting ospreys.

Another phenomenal viewing platform can be found at **Lookout Point,** where visitors can gaze from afar at the thundering Lower Falls of the Yellowstone. Visitors who want to get closer to the spray of the falls and don't mind a long hike down, and back up again, can head toward the base of the falls at **Red Rock Point.** It's a 0.5-mile trip one-way that drops more than 500 vertical feet. There is another platform at the top of the 308-foot falls aptly named the **Brink of the Lower Falls.** This lookout also involves a 0.5-mile hike and a 600-foot elevation loss. The **Upper Falls** are

© CARTER G. WALKER

the Grand Canyon of the Yellowstone

just over one-third the size of the lower falls, at 109 feet, but they are worth a gander and can be easily accessed at the **Brink of the Upper Falls.** Mountain man Jim Bridger purportedly regaled friends with tales of the Upper Falls as early as 1846 and urged them to see it for themselves.

From the **South Rim,** visitors can see the Upper Falls from the **Upper Falls Viewpoint.** A trail that dates back to 1898, **Uncle Tom's Trail** still takes hardy hikers to the base of the Lower Falls. The trail down loses 500 vertical feet through a series of 300 stairs and paved inclines, but what goes down must come up again. From **Artist Point,** one of the largest and most inspiring lookouts, visitors get a glorious view of the distant Lower Falls and the river as it snakes down the pinkish canyon. It was long thought that Artist Point was where painter Thomas Moran made sketches for his 7- by 12-foot masterpiece *Grand Canyon of the Yellowstone.* More likely, say historians, he painted from a spot on the North Rim now called **Moran Point.**

Norris Geyser

Both the hottest and the most unpredictable geyser basin in the park, Norris Geyser Basin is a fascinating collection of bubbling and colorful geothermal features. A 2.25-mile web of boardwalks and trails leads visitors through this remarkable basin. From the **Norris Geyser Basin Museum** (307/344-2812), which carefully unravels the geothermal mysteries of the region, there are two loop trails guiding visitors safely through the basin. The 1930s log-and-stone building that houses the museum has been designated a National Historic Landmark. There is also an information desk and a Yellowstone Association bookstore inside the building.

Porcelain Basin is a stark, barren setting with a palette of pink, red, orange, and yellow mineral oxides. Some of the features of note include **Africa Geyser,** which had been a hot spring in the shape of its namesake continent and started erupting in 1971. When it is active, **Whirligig Geyser,** named in 1904 by the Hague Party, erupts in a swirling pattern for a few minutes at irregular periods with a roar and hiss. The hottest steam vent in the hottest geothermal basin in the park is **Black Growler,** which has measured 280°F. The second-largest geyser in Norris, **Ledge Geyser** erupts irregularly to heights up to 125 feet.

In Norris's **Back Basin** you'll find the world's tallest geyser, **Steamboat Geyser,** which can erupt more than 300 feet in the air. The eruptions, which can be separated by days or decades, can last 3–40 minutes. Minor eruptions of 10–40 feet in height are more common. Just down the boardwalk, **Cistern Spring** is linked to Steamboat Geyser and drains in advance of a major eruption. The color is a beautiful blue, enhanced by as much as 0.5 inches of gray sinter deposited annually. By comparison, Old Faithful only deposits 0.5–1 inch of sinter every century. **Echinus Geyser** is the world's largest acid geyser and is almost as acidic as vinegar. Eruptions since 2007 have been rare and unpredictable, typically lasting about four minutes.

HIKING

Yellowstone is indeed a hiker's paradise, with ubiquitous brown signs pointing to trailheads. Look for them anytime your legs need a stretch. In the northern loop, there are some fantastic trails in an otherwise nondescript stretch between Norris and Canyon. Drive east of Norris Junction 3.5 miles (or 8.5 miles west of Canyon Junction) to the **Ice Lake** trailhead on the north side of the road. It is a fairly popular 4.5-mile loop with minimal elevation gain. In fact, the entire trail to Ice Lake is wheelchair accessible and leads to the only wheelchair-accessible backcountry campsite in the park. Avid hikers will want to continue on to **Little Gibbon Falls,** a 25-foot waterfall that is not even on the USGS topographic map. Another way to see this hidden gem is to find the Little Gibbon Falls trailhead 0.4 miles east of the Ice Lake trailhead. There is a small pullout on the south side of the road. The trail starts about 100 feet east of the pullout on the north side of the road. From here, Little Gibbon Falls is a 1.2-mile out-and-back hike.

ACCOMMODATIONS

There are three accommodations in the northern loop. The largest is the **Mammoth Hot Springs Hotel and Cabins** (mid-May–mid-Oct. and mid-Dec.–early Mar., $85–90 with shared bath, $121 mid-range, $427–449 suite, $79–222 cabin), which has 211 Spartan but perfectly decent guest rooms and another 116 cabins, some with hot tubs. Set amid historic Fort Yellowstone, Mammoth provides convenient access to restaurants, gift shops, a gas station, and the visitors center, but visitors may not have the sense that they are out in the wild. Despite human and car traffic in Mammoth, wolves have been known to sneak onto the green watered lawns at night to take down an unsuspecting well-grazed elk. You can imagine the surprise when early risers spotted the carcass on their way to get a breakfast burrito. Both summer and winter packages are available, and outdoor hot tubs can be rented ($15 per hour).

Named for Yellowstone champion Theodore Roosevelt, the **C Roosevelt Lodge Cabins** (mid-June–early Sept.) offer a timeless rustic setting reminiscent of a great old dude ranch in a quiet corner of the park. The Roughrider Cabins (from $68) usually offer double beds and a wood-burning stove. What they lack in amenities they make up for with charming authenticity. Toilets and communal showers are available nearby. The Frontier Cabins (from $113) are slightly larger and include a private bathroom with a shower, toilet, and sink.

Set adjacent to the spectacular Grand Canyon of the Yellowstone, **Canyon Lodge & Cabins** (early June–late Sept.) were built in the 1950s and 1960s, and the two lodges offer more than 80 guest rooms ($173). All guest rooms and cabins have private baths. The most modest Pioneer Cabins ($74) are basic motel-style units, and the slightly larger Frontier Cabins ($101) have been renovated more recently but are simple motel-style units as well. The Western Cabins ($157) are the most spacious.

Reservations for all hotels inside the park should be made through **Xanterra Parks & Resorts** (307/344-7311 or 866/439-7375, yellowstonenationalparklodges.com). Be aware that nature is the draw here: There are no televisions, radios, air-conditioning, or Internet connections.

CAMPING

The only campground in the park's northern loop that can be reserved in advance, operated by Xanterra, the park's concessionaire, is the 250-site **Canyon** (307/344-7901 for same-day reservations, 307/344-7311 for advance reservations, early June–early Sept., $19.50). The other six sites—at Mammoth, Tower Slough Creek, Pebble Creek, Indian Creek, and Norris—are available on a first-come, first-served basis and cost $12–14. These sites fill up quickly; your best bet is to arrive before 11 A.M. Mammoth is the only campground open all year, and all have some RV sites.

In addition to the campgrounds, there are more than 300 backcountry campsites throughout the park. Overnight permits, which are available at all ranger stations and visitors centers, are only issued in person up to 48 hours in advance; they are required for all of the sites. Backcountry campsites can be

reserved by paying a $20 fee. All requests to reserve sites must be made in person or mailed in. Pertinent forms and information for backcountry camping in Yellowstone are available online at the National Park Service Backcountry Trip Planner (www.nps.gov/yell/planyourvisit/backcountrytripplanner.htm).

FOOD

By far the most unique meal available in the park is the [**Old West Dinner Cookout,** which departs daily mid-June–early September from the Roosevelt Lodge and is served in Yellowstone's wilderness. The hearty steak-and-potatoes dinner with all the cowboy trimmings can only be attended on horseback (1-hour rides from $72 ages 12 and over, $61 ages 8–11, 2-hour rides from $87 ages 12 and over, $61 ages 8–11) or via covered wagon (from $60 ages 12 and over, $50 ages 5–11, free for children under 5 if they sit on a lap in the wagon and share a plate with an adult).

Breakfast, lunch, and dinner are served daily throughout the season in the **Roosevelt Lodge Dining Room, Canyon Lodge Dining Room, Cafeteria, and Deli,** and the **Mammoth Hotel Dining Room and Terrace Grill** (866/439-7375, www.yellowstonenationalparklodges.com). Each restaurant has its own flair—Roosevelt Lodge tends to be heartier, with options like barbecue beef, bison chili, and Wyoming cheesesteak, while Mammoth is known for elaborate buffets and inventive small plates like goat cheese sliders, mini-trout tacos, and Thai curry mussels. Canyon offers burgers, sandwiches, and an extensive soup and salad bar. Breakfasts include entrées ranging from pancakes and eggs to biscuits and gravy ($5–9). Lunches range $8–13, and dinners are generally $10–25. The most reasonably priced spot for dinner is the Canyon Lodge Cafeteria, with menu options that include hot dogs, hamburgers, rice bowls, and pasta entrées ($3–10). Generally, breakfast is served 6:30–10 A.M., lunch 11:30 A.M.–2:30 P.M., and dinner 5:30–10 P.M. Hours vary seasonally by restaurant and are subject to change. Call ahead for reservations or to check on hours; menus are available on the website.

The Northeast Corner

With arguably the best wildlife viewing in the park, especially in winter, this region is known as the "Little Serengeti of North America." The wide-open spaces of the Lamar Valley and much of the northeast corner of the park also offer some pretty dramatic mountain vistas. There is excellent fishing and hiking in the region, and just outside the park's northeast entrance is Cooke City, a cool little community with tremendous appeal to backcountry skiers, snowmobilers, and other outdoor enthusiasts.

◖ WATCHING THE WOLVES

When visitors list the animals they most want to see in Yellowstone, wolves rank second, right behind grizzly bears. Since their return to Yellowstone in 1995, wolves have surprised park-goers and wildlife experts alike by being much more visible than anyone anticipated. In fact, in the 15-plus years since their reintroduction, wolves have been spotted in Yellowstone

© DONNIE SEXTON

Canis lupus, gray wolf

by at least one person nearly every day. Much of that is thanks to wolf researchers, including the indefatigable Rick McIntyre, who is out in the field an average of 11 hours per day seven days per week, and the ever-passionate wolf watchers (who tend to follow Rick), armed with massive scopes and camera lenses that look strong enough to spot wildlife on other planets.

The bad news is that there are roughly 100 wolves in 14 packs roaming throughout Yellowstone, an area which is approximately the size of Connecticut. It's always a good idea to bear those figures in mind when you have only a couple of hours and a keen desire to spot one of these majestic canines.

But there's good news too. If seeing the wolves is a high priority for you, here are five ways to improve your odds:

1. **Visit in winter.** Wolves are most active and most visible (nearest to the roads and against a white backdrop) in the winter when they have significant advantages over their prey, including elk and bison. Spring and fall can offer viewing opportunities as well, but summer visitors are at a disadvantage because the wolves are often way up in the high country, far from roads. Whenever you go, don't forget your binoculars or a scope if you have one.

2. **Do your homework or hire a guide.** Stop at the Visitor Center in Mammoth in winter (or any of the visitor centers at other times of year) and inquire about recent activity. Rangers can often tell you where packs have been spotted, if kills have recently occurred and so forth. You could also consider hiring a guide that specializes in wolf watching. **The Wild Side, LLC** (406/223-2152, www.wolftracker.com, $480 per day for up to 6 people) offers 6–8-hour tours led by wildlife biologists. The **Yellowstone Association Institute** (406/848-2400, www.yellowstoneassociation.org) offers a variety of courses that focus on wolves.

YELLOWSTONE NATIONAL PARK

3. **Visit the Lamar Valley.** The only road that is open to car traffic year-round, the stretch of asphalt that winds through the Lamar Valley takes visitors through the heart of some of the park's best winter wolf terrain. There are numerous pull-outs along the road for viewing, but be sure to park safely out of traffic without blocking other visitors.

4. **Be willing to wake up early.** Like most wildlife, wolves are most active at the edges of day. Putting yourself in the heart of the Lamar Valley before sunrise greatly improves your odds of seeing the wolves. The same is true at sunset. In this game, patience pays.

5. **Watch for the wolf watchers.** They often have significant advantages, including radio telemeters which allow them to track collared wolves. These people know so much about the wolves and can often regale you

CINDERELLA: THE REAL-LIFE FAIRY TALE OF WOLF NUMBER 42

In 1926 the last known wolf in Yellowstone was killed, bringing to a conclusion a decades-long campaign to rid the region of the animal that was widely considered a worthless pest. The murderous eviction was a tragic end to a noble creature. It took nearly 70 years for wolves to be seen not only for their intrinsic worth but for their value in making the Yellowstone ecosystem whole again. This was their home, after all, and they had been unnaturally removed. Thirty-one Canadian gray wolves – *Canis lupus* – were reintroduced to the park in 1995-1996 with loud cheers and simultaneous objections.

Among the wolves brought into the park from Canada was a female who would come to be known as wolf number 42. Her sister, wolf 40, was the alpha female of the Druid Peak pack and was known to rule the pack with an iron paw. She was suspected of running off her mother, number 39, and her sister, number 41. Number 42, the pack's beta female, managed to stay in the pack, likely as a result of her unmatched speed and excellent hunting ability, but she could not get into her sister's good graces. The two fought constantly for four years, and despite the fact that both sisters bred with wolf 21, the pack's alpha male, wolf 40 was reported to have killed her sister's first litter of pups in 1999. Wolf watchers nicknamed 42 Cinderella and flocked to the Lamar Valley to watch the drama unfold. Much of Cinderella's life was captured on film by Bob Landis for two National Geographic specials.

In a story that plays out like a fairy tale, wolf 42 got her nieces to den with her in 2000 when she had another litter of pups with 21, and after researchers saw wolf 40 approaching the den just before the pups were weaned, ostensibly to kill this second litter of pups, 42 and her nieces attacked. Wolf 40 was found dying of her wounds, and 42 not only rose to alpha status overnight, paired for life with wolf 21, but she also moved into 40's den and adopted her dead sister's seven pups as her own. That year 42 and 21 raised 20 pups.

Over the course of her life – eight years, which is more than double wolf lifespan averages – she birthed 32 pups and held her alpha-female status over the Druid Pack, which climbed to 37 members in 2000, one of the largest wolf packs ever recorded. She was noted for her faithful and patient parenting, even coaching younger wolves in the middle of an elk hunt. When she was killed by another pack in February 2004, wolf watchers noted wolf 21, her constant companion, atop a ridgeline howling for two days straight. The wolf watchers mourned along with him.

After receiving a mortality signal from 42's radio collar, chief park wolf biologist Doug Smith hiked up the 9,000-foot Specimen Ridge on a blustery winter day. There he found Cinderella dead. She was the last remaining member of the 31 wolves imported from Canada, but her legacy and her story will be forever entwined with the Yellowstone wilderness and the saga of *Canis lupus* finally coming home.

with dramatic sagas of individual animals and entire packs. Don't be shy about pulling over when you see them; they are often willing to let you peer through their scopes. But do be safe and courteous; turn off your engine and remain quiet.

◖ LAMAR VALLEY

One of my favorite corners of the park, the Lamar Valley is stunningly beautiful with wide valleys carved by rivers and glaciers as well as views to the high rugged peaks around Cooke City. Generally uncrowded (save for the ever-growing number of bespectacled wolf watchers), some of the best hiking, fishing, and camping can be had at Slough Creek. And the wolf watching, particularly in the winter, is unrivaled anywhere else in the world. There are also grizzlies, black bears, mountain lions, coyotes, red foxes, elk, bison, bighorn sheep, and pronghorn antelope in the area.

Yellowstone Institute

An arm of the **Yellowstone Association,** the Lamar Buffalo Ranch Field Campus of the Yellowstone Institute (406/848-2400, www.yellowstoneassociation.org/institute) is located away from the large crowds (of two-legged creatures, anyway) in the idyllic Lamar Valley. The institute offers field seminars at this private and unique campus year-round. If you bring your own sleeping bag and pillow, you can stay at the ranch in one of their log cabins ($30). There are propane heaters, a communal bathhouse with individual showers, and a fully equipped kitchen in the common building. It's quite comfortable but not fancy. The best part is waking up each morning in the Lamar Valley, an opportunity very few people have. You can also stay in a nearby campsite or hotel while taking a course at the ranch. Field Seminars also take place at hotels throughout the park. The institute holds rooms in various lodges until 30 days before the course. Call 866/439-7375 for hotel rates and information.

Their courses are broken into summer and winter semesters, and course fees begin around $200 with a $10 tuition discount for YA members. The courses are engaging and are taught by experts in their fields. Using Yellowstone as their classroom, the instructors concentrate on "individual aspects of the ecosystem." During the summer, you can take the "Behind the Scenes of Wolf Management and Ecology" course led by a wolf biologist, or "Mammal Signs: Interpreting Tracks, Scat, and Hair" with an animal tracker. Classes also focus on flora with courses such as "The Art of Wildflower Identification"; other options include "Yellowstone's Geoecosystem" and "Wilderness First Aid." If you take the time to browse through the course catalog, you will likely find something geared to your interests. This is one of the best ways to get an in-depth insider's view of Yellowstone.

COOKE CITY

Named for a miner and populated by hardcore modern-day prospectors in search of snow, **Cooke City** (population 90, elevation 7,600) is a jumble of old buildings and some fairly salty characters, all with true Western flavor. At the end of a one-way road for most of the year (except during the height of summer when the Beartooth Highway leads visitors up and over the towering peaks), Cooke City has a remarkable sense of community, unlimited recreational opportunities, plenty of accommodations, and some excellent places to fill your belly. Nearby **Silver Gate** is equally scenic and even quieter, the Connecticut to Cooke's New York City. Pilot, Index, and Beartooth Peaks are three of the impressive summits that loom over these twin settlements, beckoning adventurers.

Events

Among the biggest events of the year in Cooke City is the annual **Sweet Corn Festival,** a gathering for backcountry skiers and snowboarders usually held in April on the weekend after the nearby ski hills have closed for the season. The weather is often sublime— think blue skies, cold nights, and warm afternoons—and the snow is like, well, sweet corn.

Accommodations are not easy to come by this weekend (even floor space is pretty much spoken for), so plan ahead or bring a tent. There are plenty of snowmobilers on hand to act as taxis, enabling telemark skiers not to have to earn their turns for once. With some of the best backcountry skiing in the West when the conditions are right, this is a welcoming event.

The **Annual Hog Roast** happens in mid-March and attracts a throng of hungry snowmobilers, backcountry skiers, and more recently, a healthy number of cross-country skiers to Cooke City. The event includes an auction, dinner, and live music.

The popular **Firemen's Picnic** is held annually on July 4, just east of town, with fireworks after dark.

For some culture on the periphery of Yellowstone's wilderness, check out **Shakespeare in the Parks** in Silvergate Park in late August. For more information on any of these events, call or visit Donna—who is as knowledgeable as she is friendly—at the brand-new chamber-run **Visitors Center** (406/838-2495, www.cookecitychamber.org, year-round, hours change seasonally) on the west end of town on the north side of the street; the center also has flush toilets.

Recreation

The northeastern corner of the park and the area just outside it is a natural playground for fishing, hiking, cross-country skiing, and snowmobiling.

One short but worthwhile hike can be found 1.8 miles west of the Pebble Creek Campground at **Trout Lake.** The hike itself is short and steep, just 1.2 miles round-trip, and leaves from the Trout Lake trailhead on the north side of the road. Anglers can bring a rod after July 15 when it opens to catch-and-release fishing for native cutthroats. In late spring–early summer, trout can be seen spawning in the inches-deep inlet, a fairly miraculous sight. There is an excellent trail around the 12-acre lake and shallow inlet and a decent chance of spotting playful otters, but hikers should take great care not to disturb the fish, especially during spawning.

Another great place to combine fishing, hiking, and wildlife watching—perhaps the perfect Yellowstone trifecta—is along the trail at **Slough Creek.** East of Tower Junction 5.8 miles (or west of the northeast entrance) is an unpaved road on the north side of the road leading to Slough Creek Campground. The trailhead is 1.5 miles down the road on the right side, just before the campground. The trail itself is a double-rutted wagon trail that leads to Silver Tip Ranch, a legendary private ranch just outside the park. The trail is maintained for 11 miles (one-way) and only gains 400 feet in elevation. All along the trail there is world-class fishing in slow-moving Slough Creek, home to a healthy population of native cutthroat trout. You may meet elk, bison, wolves, and even grizzlies along the trail, so be prepared and be safe.

With an average of 500 inches of snowfall each year, mountainous terrain with elevation that ranges 7,000–10,000 feet, and a nearly interminable winter, Cooke City is a winter mecca with 60 miles of groomed snowmobile trails and endless acres of ungroomed terrain for skiing and snowmobiling. Some favorites trails are **Daisy Pass, Lulu Pass,** and **Round Creek Trail.**

There are a number of places to rent snowmobiles and all the necessary gear. Most important, you'll need to talk with experts about local conditions, trail closures, and avalanche dangers. **Cooke City Motorsports** (203 Eaton St., 406/838-2231, www.cookecitymotorsports.com, snowmobiles from $160 per day) and **Cooke City Exxon** (204 Main St., 406/838-2244, www.cookecityexxon.com, snowmobiles from $165 per day) are obvious choices in town.

The **Silvertip Mountain Center** (115 U.S. 212, Silver Gate, 406/838-2125 or 800/863-0807, www.silvertipmountaincenter.com) has an impressive collection of equipment for purchase and for rent, including skis, snowshoes, ice-climbing and rock-climbing equipment, tents, and more. The staff are local experts in various passions and are a great resource for ideas about any type of adventure you're inclined to plan.

Accommodations

For a town with a population that rarely surpasses 100, Cooke City has an impressive number of places to hang your hat. Lodging runs the gamut from cabins and vacation rentals to roadside motels, chain hotels, and small resorts, although not all of them are open year-round. Most of the photo galleries on the accommodations' websites are images of moose and bears or snowmobiles buried in powder rather than pictures of beds and baths. Clearly, Cooke City has morphed from a mining town into a tourist destination.

Big Moose Lodge (715 U.S. 212, 406/838-2393, www.bigmooseresort.com, $95–110) is three miles east of town and a good place to set up a base camp if you want to explore the region's trails and rivers. Open year-round, the lodge has a small collection of old and new cabins, all of which are quite comfortable and can accommodate up to four people. There are no phones in the cabins (and no cell service in the area), but free Wi-Fi is provided, and you can schedule a Swedish massage on-site.

In the heart of bustling Cooke City is the **Soda Butte Lodge** (210 U.S. 212, 406/838-2253, www.cookecity.com, $88–132), a full-service hotel with 32 guest rooms, a saloon, and a restaurant. The guest rooms are basic, but you didn't come to Cooke City to hang out in your hotel room.

In nearby Silver Gate, **C Silver Gate Lodging** (109 U.S. 212, Silver Gate, 406/838-2371, www.pineedgecabins.com, $79–253) offers 29 great cabins that can accommodate any size group and welcomes pets. The setting is both quiet and communal, with barbecue grills, horseshoe pits, and a playground.

Camping

There are three Forest Service campgrounds in the vicinity of Cooke City. **Soda Butte** (406/848-7375, www.fs.fed.us/ri/gallatin, July 1–Sept. 30 depending on weather, $9 per vehicle) is one mile east of Cooke City on U.S.

212. It has 27 sites, restrooms, and drinking water, and fishing is available nearby. **Colter Campground** (406/848-7375, www.fs.fed. us/ri/gallatin, July 15–Sept. 30 depending on weather, $8 per vehicle) is just two miles east of Cooke City and gives campers access to 23 sites, restrooms, drinking water, and nearby fishing and hiking trails. **Chief Joseph Campground** (406/848-7375, www.fs.fed.us/ri/gallatin, July 15–Sept. 30 depending on weather, $8 per vehicle) is four miles east of town in an open park-like setting. There are six sites, a playground, a fire ring, picnic tables, and a toilet.

Food

There are a million ways to work up an appetite in and around Cooke City. Be assured you won't go hungry (or thirsty, for that matter). **C Beartooth Café** (14 U.S. 212, 406/838-2475, www.beartoothcafe.com, 11 A.M.–9:30 P.M. daily end of May–end of Sept., lunch $5–10, dinner $13–30) offers excellent mountain fare—think steak and trout—with just a hint of Mexican flair. The front-porch outdoor dining is a treat. The **Loving Cup** (Main Street, Cooke City, no phone, 7 A.M.–4 P.M. daily, closing hours may vary, Feb. 1–Oct. 1, entrées $4–10), which used to be the Bike Shack and is still a local hangout, got rid of the bikes to focus more on the coffee and food. They serve breakfast and lunch and offer free Wi-Fi.

The **Prospector Restaurant** (210 U.S. 212, 406/838-2251, www.cookecity.com, 7 A.M.–9 P.M. daily, breakfast $6–10, lunch $7–11, dinner $10–30), inside the Soda Butte Lodge, is open year-round and is particularly known for steak and prime rib—not a stretch in these parts. Finally, for those wanting to pick up some supplies, **C The Cooke City Store** (101 U.S. 212, 406/838-2234, www. cookecitystore.com) is as much a local museum and community center as it is a place to pick up some bread and a bottle of sunscreen. It's a wonderful place and worth a visit; plus the nearest grocery store is 90 minutes away.

Southern Loop

Some of the park's biggest highlights are found in the Southern Loop, along with a significant number of visitors and plentiful wildlife. There are a lot of trees, many of them burned, and not as much dimension to the land as elsewhere, but the southern loop is what many people think of when they think of Yellowstone. From the sweeping Hayden Valley and the otherworldliness of West Thumb Geyser Basin to the sheer size of Yellowstone Lake and the well-deserved hubbub around Old Faithful, this section of the park has an abundance of dynamic features—some world-famous, others hidden gems—for every visitor.

SIGHTS
Hayden Valley
South of Canyon is the expansive and beautiful Hayden Valley, a sweep of grassland carved by massive glaciers, named for the famed leader of the 1871 Hayden Expedition, and occupied by copious amounts of wildlife that includes grizzly bears, wolves, and in summer, thundering herds of bison. The Yellowstone River weaves quietly thorough the valley, and because the soil supports grasses and wildflowers instead of trees, this is one of the most scenic drives in the park, especially during the bison rut and migration in late summer. Besides driving, hiking is an excellent way to explore the valley, either on your own (pay very close attention for signs of bear activity) or with a ranger on weekly guided hikes (4–5 hours, early July–late Aug., free). The hikes are limited to 15 people and reservations must be made in advance at the Canyon Visitor Education Center (307/242-2550) in Canyon Village.

Fishing Bridge
What was once the epicenter of Yellowstone fishing is today a relic of the past and a touchstone for the ongoing struggle between nature and human meddling. Fishing Bridge was built in 1937 and for years was considered the best place to throw a line for native cutthroat trout.

Humans were not the only ones fishing in the area, and human-grizzly encounters led to 16 grizzly bear deaths. To protect the bears and the fish, fishing in the vicinity was banned in 1973. Today, because of the sharp decline of cutthroat as a direct result of the introduction of nonnative lake trout, grizzlies are not seen as often fishing in the river.

There are some services—an RV Park, a gas station, and a general store—and a 1931 log and stone structure that serves as the **Fishing Bridge Visitors Center** (307/242-2450). On the National Register of Historic Places, the visitors center has a collection of stuffed bird specimens worth seeing.

◖ Yellowstone Lake
Covering 136 square miles, Yellowstone Lake is North America's largest freshwater lake above 7,000 feet. In addition to being spectacularly scenic—both when it is placid and when the waves form whitecaps—the lake is a fascinating study in underwater geothermal activity. Beneath the water—or ice, much of the year—the lake bottom is littered with faults, hot springs, craters, and the miraculous life forms that can thrive in such conditions. There is also a rather large bulge, some 2,000 feet long, that rises 100 feet above the rest of the lake bottom. The uplift is related to the ever-present geothermal activity beneath Yellowstone. Whether the bulge is gaseous or potentially volcanic in nature is the subject of ongoing research.

Aside from its geological significance, Yellowstone Lake also offers plenty of recreational opportunities, primarily in the form of boating and fishing. The water is bitter cold, though, typically 40–50°F, and thus not suitable for swimming. Canoes and kayaks can be rented at **Bridge Bay Marina** (307/344-7311 or 866/439-7375) just south of Lake Village or 21 miles north of West Thumb. There is great fishing for native cutthroat trout as well. It's worth mentioning that early visitors to the park loved to tell stories about catching fish

© OSAMU HOSHINO/WYOMING TRAVEL & TOURISM

sunset at Yellowstone Lake

at the edge of the lake and then dipping their catch in the hot springs at West Thumb Geyser Basin to cook them without taking the fish off the line—a practice that would be seriously frowned upon today.

The rambling pale-yellow **Lake Yellowstone Hotel** was built in 1891 and is an elegant reminder of Yellowstone's bygone era. The lobby and deck, which overlook the lake, are worth seeing, even if you are not staying here. Grab an iced tea and soak in the views; this is a stunning spot. If you can, stay for a meal and enjoy the live piano music. The crowds will fade as you gaze on the idyllic scenery, both natural and artificial.

West Thumb

On the western edge of Yellowstone Lake is the stunningly eerie West Thumb Geyser Basin, a collection of hot springs, geysers, mud pots, and fumaroles that dump a collective 3,100 gallons of hot water into the lake daily. An excellent boardwalk system guides visitors through the area, but there have been injury-causing

bison and bear encounters on the boardwalk, so keep your eyes open.

Abyss Pool is a sensational spring, some 53 feet deep, that transforms in color from turquoise to emerald green to brown and back, depending on a variety of factors. Similarly beautiful, **Black Pool** is no longer black because the particular thermophiles that caused the dark coloration were killed in 1991 when the water temperature rose. **Big Cone** and **Fishing Cone,** surrounded by lake water, are the features that led to the stories of fishing and cooking the catch in a single cast. Called "Mud Puffs" by the 1871 Hayden Expedition, **Thumb Paint Pots** are like miniature reddish mud volcanoes (depending on rainfall, after which they can get soupier) and an excellent example of mud pots. **Surging Spring** is fun to watch as the dome of water forms and overflows, unleashing a torrent of water on the lake.

Grant Village

Located on the West Thumb of Yellowstone Lake, Grant Village is a fairly controversial

BISON AND BRUCELLOSIS

Yellowstone is the only place in the continental United States where bison have existed since prehistoric times. Although the bison in the park are free-roaming, many wonder if they are truly wild. Current policy mandates that the animals stay within the park's unfenced boundaries, and how best to do this is a matter of constant debate.

The park's management of the bison has changed throughout the years, just as bison numbers have fluctuated. By the turn of the 20th century, the bison had been so overhunted – or exterminated – that the herd numbers even in Yellowstone were dangerously small. To prevent extinction, park managers agreed to import roughly two dozen privately owned bison, which were bred and ranched like cattle in the Lamar Valley at the aptly named Buffalo Ranch. Once the herd's numbers made a comeback, a decision on how to manage the animals had to be made. Prior to 1967, park authorities would trap and reduce the herd to keep it manageable. After 1967, however, the guiding philosophy changed throughout the park, and the bison were managed by nature alone. By 1996 the number of bison in the park grew to 3,500. The size of the herd, coupled with winters that brought significant snowfall, led many of the bison to migrate out of the park in order to find better grazing and calving grounds. The problem of brucellosis played out on the national stage.

Brucellosis is a bacterial infection present in the bison and elk in the Greater Yellowstone area. The disease can cause spontaneous abortions, infertility, and lowered milk production in the infected animal, but the Yellowstone elk and bison populations seem relatively unscathed by the disease despite the number of animals infected. The same tolerance of the disease is not common among cattle, which is at the crux of the issue. The overwhelming fear is that bison exiting Yellowstone could infect neighboring cattle; this would be gravely detrimental to Montana, Wyoming, and Idaho beef production and the ranchers in those states. Brucellosis cannot be treated in cattle and can be passed on to humans in the form of undulant fever. The government created a fairly simple inoculation program to eradicate the disease in cattle as early as 1934, but brucellosis has never been eliminated from wildlife. Ironically, the common belief is that the Yellowstone bison were initially exposed to the disease when they were fed milk produced by infected cattle during the bison ranching program in Yellowstone sometime prior to 1917.

The park's wildlife management has been challenged to eliminate brucellosis while maintaining a free-roaming herd. Starting in the 1980s, when more than 50 percent of the park's bison tested positive for the disease, the park's approach was to control the borders with hazing to limit the number of bison who left the park. When hazing was unsuccessful, the bison were shot. The winter of 1996–1997 brought record cold and snow, and bison left the park in large numbers to forage for food; 1,079 bison were shot and another 1,300 starved to death inside the park's boundaries. This incident magnified the problem of maintaining a healthy herd while preventing the spread of brucellosis.

The National Park Service, the U.S. Department of Agriculture, and the states of Montana, Wyoming, and Idaho are working together to see how brucellosis can be eliminated and free-roaming bison protected. A vaccination program has been implemented, with a 65 percent success rate, and the use of quarantine has proven fairly successful. Local bison rancher and wildlife advocate Ted Turner has agreed to accept some of the quarantined bison on his property. A small and highly regulated hunting season on bison is carried out each winter just outside the park boundaries. But there are no easy or obvious solutions, just questions: What about elk, which also carry the disease and have been identified as the source of brucellosis outbreaks among horses in Wyoming and cattle in Idaho? No efforts to limit their natural migration in and out of the park have ever been attempted. Why are bull bison – who can carry the disease but cannot spread it through milk or birthing fluids as females do – quarantined and killed? For now, it seems, we watch, wait, and hope for a healthy, wild, and free-roaming bison population.

development dating to the 1970s and built in the heart of excellent grizzly bear habitat and among several cutthroat spawning streams. The architecture is ugly and the location is better suited to wildlife than visitors. In addition to the **Grant Village Visitors Center** (307/242-2650), which houses an exhibit dedicated to fire in the Yellowstone ecosystem, there are accommodations, a campground, and food services.

◖ Old Faithful

Though often crowded, the Old Faithful complex brings together so many of the phenomena—both natural and human-made—that make Yellowstone so special: the landmark geyser and the incredible assortment of geothermal features surrounding it, the wildlife, the grand old park architecture of the Old Faithful Inn, and even the mass of people from around the world who come to witness the famous geyser.

An obvious stop at the Old Faithful complex is the **Old Faithful Visitor Education Center** (307/545-2750, 9 A.M.–5 P.M. daily year-round, extended hours in summer), which showcases Yellowstone's hydrothermal features. The $27 million project hosts 2.6 million visitors annually.

Known as the **Upper Geyser Basin,** the area surrounding Old Faithful is the largest concentration of geysers anywhere in the world. By far the most famous is **Old Faithful** because of its combination of height (although it is not the tallest) and regularity (although it is not the most frequent or most regular). On average, the geyser erupts every 91 minutes for anywhere from 90 seconds to five minutes. It spouts 3,700–8,400 gallons of hot water at heights of 106–184 feet. Signs inside the nearby hotel lobbies and the visitors center keep visitors apprised of the next expected eruptions. Keep in mind that Old Faithful doesn't stop being predictable just because people go to bed or the weather turns cold—some of the most magical eruption viewings can happen without crowds. Choose a full-moon night, any time of year, and be willing to get up in the middle of the

© DONNIE SEXTON

Morning Glory Pool at the Old Faithful complex

night. The vision of Old Faithful erupting in winter with snow and ice, frost and steam in every direction is remarkable.

If you take the time to come to Yellowstone to see Old Faithful, take the time—an hour or more is ideal—to walk through the other marvelous features of the Upper Geyser Basin. **Giantess Geyser** can erupt up to 200 feet high in several bursts. The irregular eruptions happen 2–6 times each year and can occur twice hourly, continuing 4–48 hours. **Doublet Pool,** a colorful hot spring with numerous ledges, is lovely and convoluted. You can actually hear Doublet vibrating and collapsing beneath the surface. Looking something like a fire hose shooting 130–190 feet in the air, **Beehive Geyser** typically erupts twice daily, each eruption lasting 4–5 minutes. **Grand Geyser** is the world's tallest predictable geyser, erupting every 7–15 hours, lasting 9–12 minutes, and reaching heights up to 200 feet. Visible from the road into the Old Faithful complex if you look back over your shoulder, **Castle Geyser** is thought to be the park's oldest. It generally erupts every 10–12 hours, reaches 90 feet in height, and lasts roughly 20 minutes. There is also a 30–40-minute noisy steam phase following the eruptions.

Firehole River

Since swimming in Yellowstone Lake is not an option unless you are a trained member of the polar bear club, a dip in the heated waters of the Firehole River is one of the nicest ways to spend an afternoon. The designated and somewhat popular swimming area is surrounded by high cliffs and some fast-moving rapids both upstream and downstream, so the area is not recommended for new or young swimmers. The water temperature averages 80°F. Parking is accessible from Firehole Canyon Drive, which leaves the main road south of Madison Junction, less than 1,000 feet after crossing the river.

Midway and Lower Geyser Basins

Between Old Faithful and Madison Junction, along the pastoral Firehole River, are the Midway and Lower Geyser Basins, technically

Midway Geyser Basin

THE ECOLOGY OF FIRE

In 1988, wildfires blazed through Yellowstone National Park. To quell the flames, the largest firefighting effort in U.S. history was organized, involving 25,000 people and $120 million, but it was the first snowfall of the season that would eventually reign in the fire. The fires began in July and burned until November. More than 793,000 acres, roughly one-third of the park, were affected, 67 structures were destroyed, and 345 elk and 63 other large mammals died as a direct result of the fire. The entire nation watched in horror as the first national park burned. The park's fire management plan consequently came under intense scrutiny. The question on everyone's lips was, "How could this have happened?"

During the first half of the 20th century, it was widely believed that nothing good came of wildfire. In the 1940s and 1950s, all fires that occurred in the park, whether of natural origin or caused by people, were immediately suppressed. During the 1960s, however, the tide shifted subtly as the ecological benefits of fire were studied. The findings showed that fire was a natural condition that helped maintain balance in the wild. Fires cleaned out understory and residual dead plant matter, creating less competition between tree species for important nutrients and natural elements. It was determined that until recently, wildfires had always been a part of the ecosystem and were in fact necessary to preserve healthy and continuous life cycles of plants and trees. The lodgepole pine, for example, which makes up an enormous percentage of Yellowstone's forests, has two kinds of cones, one of which is called a serotinous cone. The pitch sealing the serotinous cone needs to be heated by fire in order to release the seeds and continue the species. Without fire, the tree would not be able to regenerate as successfully.

By the 1970s, the park decided to allow wildfires caused by lightning to burn under controlled conditions. From the time the park established this natural fire policy until 1988, they had allowed 235 fires to burn; only 10 of those were larger than 100 acres, and in total 33,759 acres had been burned. In June 1988 the park was experiencing a drought, and it turned out to be the driest year in the park's history. Early summer storms produced lightning without rainfall, and 20 fires erupted. Eleven of them self-extinguished, and the rest were monitored; by mid-July only 8,500 acres had burned. Within a week, park managers agreed to extinguish the fires because of the extremely dry conditions. Strong winds made that impossible, however, and within a week 99,000 acres had burned. By September, in order for emergency workers to battle the blaze, the park had to close to visitors for the first time in its history.

When spring came, no one knew what to expect. It was with some trepidation that people went into Yellowstone. Miraculously, the earth was green and vibrant amid the fire-blackened swaths. With the exception of the moose, who lost a significant portion of their forested habitat, the animal populations appeared as if nothing had ever happened. Elk were even reported munching on the burned bark. Yellowstone, it seemed, was different – better and healthier.

As visitors marveled at the park's rebirth, park managers reevaluated their fire management policy and updated it in 1992 with stricter guidelines for managing natural fires. In 2004 they made further additions by defining clear parameters for fires, including size, weather conditions, and the potential for danger. The overriding philosophy today is that naturally occurring fire maintains a balance in the natural ecosystem of Yellowstone and that the land, which has adapted to large wildfires, ultimately reaps its benefits.

YELLOWSTONE NATIONAL PARK

considered part of the same basin. In 1889, Rudyard Kipling dubbed Midway Geyser Basin "hell's half-acre" for its massive hot springs and geysers. Among the most significant features at Midway is **(Grand Prismatic Spring,** a colorful and photogenic spring that was immortalized by painter Thomas Moran on the Hayden Expedition. It releases some 560 gallons of water into the Firehole River every minute. At 250 by 380 feet, Grand Prismatic is the third-largest hot spring in the world and the largest in Yellowstone. Now dormant, **Excelsior Geyser** was once the largest geyser in the world, soaring up to 300 feet high. Major eruptions in the 1880s led to a dormancy that lasted more than a century. In 1985, Excelsior erupted continuously for two days but never topped 80 feet. Today, acting as a spring, it discharges more than 4,000 gallons of heated water every minute.

Compared to the much smaller Midway Geyser Basin, the Lower Geyser Basin is enormous, spanning 12 square miles and including several clusters of thermal features. Among them are the notable **Great Fountain Geyser,** which erupts for up to an hour and sprays an average of 100 feet high; the temperamental **White Dome Geyser;** the almost-constant **Clepsydra;** and the **Pocket Basin Mud Pots,** which are the largest collection of mud pots in the park.

RECREATION
Fishing and Boating
Some 75,000 anglers are lured to Yellowstone each year by the promise of elusive trout, and they are seldom disappointed by the offerings at Yellowstone Lake. In addition to the prized native cutthroat, the lake is home to a population of nonnative lake trout that is sadly devastating the cutthroat. The average lake trout live and spawn in deep waters, feeding on as many as 80–90 cutthroat each year. By comparison, cutthroat trout spawn in the shallow tributaries of the lake, making them an important food source for a variety of creatures that include eagles to bears. Since the lake trout have no enemies in the deep waters of Yellowstone

Lake, they are creating a serious food shortage by devouring the cutthroat. All lake trout caught in Yellowstone Lake must be killed. Be sure to pick up your **fishing permit** at one of the visitors centers along with a copy of the Yellowstone fishing regulations.

There are a number of ways to see Yellowstone Lake by boat. Scenic or fishing boat tours as well as canoe and sea-kayak rentals are available from Bridge Bay Marina, south of Lake Village or 21 miles northeast of West Thumb. Hour-long cruises ($10 adults, $6.50 ages 2–11, free for children under 2) depart regularly from the marina early June–mid-September. Reservations can be made with Xanterra (307/344-7311 or 866/439-7375).

Hiking
The Southern Loop of the park offers plentiful hiking opportunities, most of which can be combined with other interests. There are great trails in the **Hayden Valley** for wildlife lovers, but precautions against bear encounters must be taken. The **Alum Creek Trail,** 4.4 miles south of Canyon at the north end of the Hayden Valley, is a good hike. Wide-open and relatively flat, the trail offers a 10-mile out-and-back trip through prime bison and grizzly habitat. There are also some thermal features along Alum Creek.

Among the geysers in the Upper Geyser Basin is **Lone Star Geyser,** named for its lonely location five miles from Old Faithful. An old once-paved road leads to the geyser and makes a nice level hike or bike trip. The entire out-and-back trip is 4.6 miles. There is parking at the trailhead on the south side of the road, 3.5 miles east of the Old Faithful interchange. Lucky viewers will get to see a 30–50-foot eruption, which happens every 2–3 hours and tends to last 10–15 minutes.

ACCOMMODATIONS
(Lake Yellowstone Hotel and Cabins ($217–227 premium rooms, $151 annex rooms, $135 cabins) is both grand and picturesque, perched on the shores of Yellowstone Lake. Originally built in 1891 and restored in the

1990s to its 1920s elegance, the hotel houses the nicest rooms in the park. As is true everywhere in the park, though, the appeal comes from the location and the views, not the amenities, which are basic. If you are staying in the hotel, be sure to request a room with a view of the lake. There is an annex that offers more modest rooms; individual cabins are located behind the hotel. These duplexes were remodeled in 2004 and are simple and modest.

The **Lake Lodge Cabins** ($157 Western cabin, $70 Frontier cabin) are clean and simple, and some have recently been renovated. Located just off the lake, the cabins are clustered around the main lodge, which is an inviting common area for guests to gather. It has a large porch that beckons guests to take a seat in one of the rocking chairs and soak in the view as well as two fireplaces, a gift shop, and a cozy lounge. The Western cabins are a bit more spacious, with two beds and a shower-tub in each bathroom. The Pioneer cabins are older and more Spartan, with shower-only bathrooms and 1–2 double beds. The setting is tranquil and quiet, and early risers may spot a herd of bison wandering through the property.

The **Old Faithful Inn** ($528 suites, $427 semisuites, $213–240 premium room, $167 high-range room, $160 mid-range room, $125 with shared bath) is the most popular lodging inside the park, and for good reason. The original part of the lodge, know as the Old House, was built in 1904 by acclaimed architect Robert Reamer. Situated close to the Older Faithful geyser, the lodge epitomizes rustic beauty, originality, and strength. It has a large front lobby that houses a massive stone fireplace. The larger rooms are in the wings of the inn, built in the 1920s, while the more modest rooms are in the Old House. The inn has a wide assortment of guest rooms and rates, ranging from two-room suites with sitting rooms and fridges to simple rooms without individual baths. Guest rooms can be booked more than a year in advance, so plan ahead and make reservations.

Located close to the inn is the **Old Faithful Lodge and Cabins** ($113 Frontier cabin, $69

the impressive lobby of the iconic Old Faithful Inn

© XANTERRA PARKS & RESORT

budget cabins) which offers much simpler and rustic lodging. If you are looking for budget-friendly accommodations that put you in the center of the park activity, this is a good option. The cabins are small motel-style units that vary in condition. These are probably very similar to the cabins visitors stayed in during the early part of the 20th century; the walls are thin and amenities sparse. The lower-priced cabins do not come with baths, but there are communal showers nearby. The cabins are scattered around a main log cabin–style lodge. Built in the 1920s, the main lodge has a large cafeteria, a bakery, and a fully stocked gift shop, making it popular with park visitors throughout the day.

The **Old Faithful Snow Lodge and Cabins** ($191 lodge rooms, $140 Western cabins, $94 Frontier cabins) are the newest accommodations in the park. The original lodge was torn down and a new structure was built in 1999. Its architecture is intended to mirror the Old Faithful Inn, and the lodge recently won a Cody Award for Western Design. It offers comfortable, modern rooms decorated with Western flair. They also have a few motel-style cabins, built in 1989. The Western cabins are a good value for the money; they are large rooms with two queen beds and a full bath. This is one of only two lodges (the other is Mammoth Hot Springs Hotel) open during the winter season in Yellowstone.

Grant Village is about 20 miles southeast of Old Faithful on the West Thumb of Yellowstone Lake. Although the accommodations do not have the same rustic feel or character of the other lodges, they do offer a comfortable and modern place to stay away from the crowds. The complex is made up of six small condo-like buildings. Each building has 50 nicely furnished hotel rooms that come with either two double beds or one queen and full baths.

Reservations for all hotels inside the park should be made through **Xanterra Parks and Resorts** (www.xanterra.com, 307/344-7311 or 866/439-7375). Be aware that nature is the draw here: There are no televisions, radios, air-conditioning, or Internet connections.

CAMPING

Five of the 12 campsites in the park are located in this southern region: **Bridge Bay** (between West Thumb and Lake, late May–early Sept., flush toilets, $19.50 per night), **Fishing Bridge RV Park** (at Fishing Bridge north of Lake Village, late May–late Sept., the only campground offering water and sewer, with flush toilets and pay showers, for hard-sided vehicles only, $35 per night), **Grant Village** (at Grant Village south of West Thumb, late June–early Oct., flush toilets, $19.50 per night), **Lewis Lake** (at Lewis Lake south of Grant Village, mid-June–early Nov., vault toilets, $12 per night), and **Madison** (at Madison Junction between the West Entrance and Old Faithful, early May–late Oct., flush toilets, $19.50 per night). Advance reservations (866-GEYSERLAND or 307/344-7311) or same-day reservations (307/344-7901) can be made at Bridge Bay Fishing Bridge RV Park, Grant Village and Madison.

FOOD

As the Southern Loop is generally the most heavily traveled section of the park, there are plenty of dining opportunities. You may want to stop for a quick bite between eruptions at the Old Faithful Lodge cafeteria, pick up a salad or soup to go at the Bear Paw Deli in the Old Faithful Inn, or unwind with a leisurely meal at the upscale restaurant in the Lake Hotel. In the park restaurants, breakfast and lunch are on a first come, first served basis, but reservations are strongly recommended for dinner, particularly if 5 P.M. or 9 P.M. are not your ideal dining hours. In almost all of the venues, you will find some good vegetarian options and many items made with sustainable or organic ingredients; these are identified on each menu. If you are planning a day activity away from the center of things, the restaurants or cafeterias offer box lunches for travelers to take with them. Place your order the night before, and it will be ready in the morning. The General Stores at Grant Village, Lake Village, and Old Faithful also have fast-food service, groceries, and snacks.

The **Grant Village Dining Room** (866/439-7375, breakfast 6:30–10 A.M. daily, lunch 11:30 A.M.–2:30 P.M. daily, dinner 5–10 P.M. daily May 22–Sept. 27, reservations required for dinner, breakfast buffet $11.25 adults, $6 children, entrées $6–9, lunch $7.50–10.25, dinner $16–25) offers a pleasant view of the lake, good service, and a nice variety of American cuisine. Breakfast is buffet or you can opt to order the standard fare à la carte. Lunch and dinner have a lot more originality in the dishes, including a Montana ranch natural burger, bison meatloaf, or grilled vegetable cannelloni. The **Lake House** at Grant Village (breakfast 7–10:30 A.M. daily, dinner 5–9 P.M. daily June 5–Sept. 20, breakfast buffet $11.25 adults, $6 children, dinner entrées $9–17) sits right on the lake and is a low-key casual option. Breakfast is buffet only, and the dinner menu consists mostly of pizza and pasta dishes.

The **◖ Lake Yellowstone Hotel Dining Room** (866/439-7375, breakfast 6:30–10 A.M. daily, lunch 11:30 A.M.–2:30 P.M. daily, dinner 5–10 P.M. daily May 21–Sept. 26, reservations required for dinner, breakfast buffet $13.25 adults, $6 children, entrées $6–11.25, lunch $9–12, dinner $16.75–40) is the most elegant dining room in the park, with a gorgeous view of the lake as you dine on a scrumptious meal. The restaurant is committed to creating dishes with fresh, local, organic, and sustainable ingredients. Lunch is a good way to sample some of the gourmet fare without putting too large a dent in your pocketbook. They have a delicious organic lentil soup, or try the lobster ravioli. Dinner at the hotel is sure to be a memorable experience. One of the most filling dishes on the menu is a surf-and-turf that comes with broiled lobster tail and your choice of Montana beef or farm-raised bison. Directly inside the hotel is the **Lake Hotel Deli** (9:30 A.M.–10 P.M. daily May 21–Sept.), which serves a nice selection of soups, salads, and sandwiches.

The **Old Faithful Inn Dining Room** (866/439-7375, open breakfast 6:30–10 A.M., breakfast buffet 6:30–10:30 A.M. daily, lunch 11:30 A.M.–2:30 P.M. daily, dinner 5–10 P.M.

daily May 8–Oct. 11, reservations required for dinner, breakfast buffet $11.25 adults, $6 children, entrées $5–14, lunch buffet $13.35 adults, $7 children, entrées $7.50–9.25, dinner buffet $29.75 adults, $11 children, entrées $16–29) offers a buffet for each of the main meals daily as well as an à la carte menu. You can dine in the historic inn while enjoying its distinct rustic architecture and Western-style ambience. Lunch is a "Western buffet" with items such as farm-raised pan-fried rocky mountain trout, a chopped barbecue chicken sandwich, and bison chili. If you don't opt for the dinner buffet, featuring the carved roasted steamship round of farm-raised bison, you could try their apple-glazed pork chop, bison and elk Bolognese on rice, and corn cakes with spicy black beans. **The Bear Paw Deli** (10:30 A.M.–7:30 P.M. daily May 8–Aug. 30, 11 A.M.–7 P.M. daily Aug. 31–Oct.10), located in the inn, is perfect for on-the-go meals. They have the standard deli fare of sandwiches and salads but also serve up several flavors of ice cream (until 9 P.M.).

West Yellowstone

West Yellowstone (population 1,511, elevation 6,667 feet) has something of a split personality—hard-core athletes training for the Olympics next to hard-core snowmobilers aiming for high-marking honors; get-too-close tourists alongside bison activists who try to put themselves in the line of fire. The winters are huge, with snow that buries everything but this town's spirit. The region shines with sensational recreation opportunities, from guided snow coach and cross-country skiing excursions to snowmobiling and dogsledding. The winters look interminable with piles of snow still scattered around town well into May and sometimes June, but with so much sun and so much to do, residents never complain about the cold.

The summers tend to be crowded as most people going to Old Faithful come through "West," as the town is known locally. With

crystal-clear alpine lakes and rivers in every direction, there is no shortage of summer recreation—fishing opportunities are phenomenal, and there are plenty of places to cycle. As the hub of the region and the busiest entrance to Yellowstone National Park, there is plenty of good grub and lots of comfortable beds in and around town.

SIGHTS
Grizzly and Wolf Discovery Center
If you have your heart set on seeing a grizzly or a wolf in Yellowstone, here's my advice: Get it out of the way before you even go into the park, like a first kiss on a first date before you even order dinner. The Grizzly and Wolf Discovery Center (201 S. Canyon St., 406/646-7001 or 800/257-2570, www.grizzlydiscoveryctr.org, hours vary, daily year-round, $10.50 age 13 and

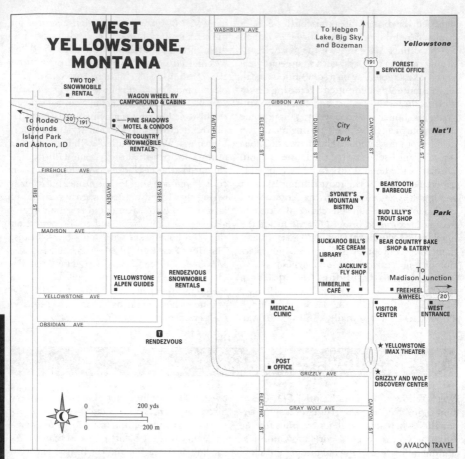

over, $9.75 age 62 and over, $5.50 ages 5–12, free for children under 5, admission valid for 2 consecutive days) is a nonprofit organization that acts something like an orphanage, giving homes to problem or abandoned animals that have nowhere else to go. Although there is something melancholy about watching these incredible beasts confined to any sort of enclosure, particularly on the perimeter of a chunk of wilderness as massive as Yellowstone, there is also something remarkable about seeing them close enough to count their whiskers. The naturalists on staff are excellent at engaging with visitors of all ages and have plenty to teach everyone. The center has gone to great lengths to share the personal story of each animal and why it cannot survive in the wild. They also give the bears all sorts of games and tasks—aiding in the design of bear-proof garbage cans is one example. Ultimately, this is a really nice place to learn a lot about bears and wolves before heading into the park to look for them in the wild.

Yellowstone IMAX Theater

Montana's first IMAX, the Yellowstone IMAX Theater (101 S. Canyon St., 406/646-4100 or 888/854-5862, www.yellowstoneimax.com, $9 adults, $8.50 seniors) boasts a six-story-high screen with stereo surround sound that makes any subject larger than life. Nature-oriented movies rotate in and out, but *Yellowstone* is frequently on the playlist and offers an extraordinary introduction to the park with history, wildlife, geothermal activity, and plain old mountain grandeur that only IMAX can dish out.

EVENTS AND ENTERTAINMENT

There is plenty for visitors to do year-round in West Yellowstone. Before you arrive, you may want to visit the **Chamber of Commerce** events calendar (www.westyellowstonechamber.com/calendar) to scope out the current happenings. The **West Yellowstone Visitors Center** (406/646-7701) also has information on programs like ranger-led educational Yellowstone National Park Afternoon and Evening Programs and Snowshoe Walks through the park in winter, and free Music in the Park evenings and weekly West Yellowstone Rodeo shows in summer.

The **World Snowmobile Expo** (www.snowmobileexpo.com) is the largest snowmobile exposition in the West. All the major manufacturers descend on West Yellowstone in the early spring to unveil their latest and greatest. The show is combined with racing and evening events.

The **Yellowstone Rendezvous Race** (406/599-4465, www.rendezvousskitrails.com or www.rendezvousrace.com), a one-day cross-country ski competition, is the largest event of the year. It usually takes place in early March, and 600–900 skiers come to participate. Six races are held concurrently, based on age and ability, over distances of 2–50 kilometers. The **Youth Ski Festival** is a newer event held right after the Rendezvous Race. To encourage families to stay after the race, there are a series of ski events (including a relay race, an obstacle course, and even musical chairs) for children age 13 and younger. **The Equinox Ski Challenge** is the final ski event each winter, held on one of the last weekends in March.

Skiers can participate as individuals or in relay teams of up to eight people and compete to see how many laps they can complete in the time allotted. There is a 24-minute Kids Race and 3-hour, 6-hour, 12-hour, and 24-hour races for adults. A potluck and bonfire are held on Saturday night to mark the midpoint of the 24-hour race. All proceeds are donated to local charities.

In addition to the **Janet Clarkson Memorial Triathlon** (406/646-9328, www.janetstriathlon.org), the **Annual Mountain Bike Biathlon** (406/599-4464) also takes place in June. There are two divisions, and first-timers are welcome to participate. The Match Class is for participants with experience and their own rifles; the Sport Class is for novices. The race covers 7.5 kilometers with two bouts of shooting. If you'd like to get some practice in before the event, you can sign up for the **Biathlon Shooting Camp** (406/599-4465).

The **Wild West Yellowstone Rodeo** (406/560-6913, www.westyellowstonerodeo.com, $12 adults, $6 children) is another summertime event that runs June–August. Shows begin at 8 P.M. and are held three times each week.

RECREATION
Fishing

The fishing around West tends to be as plentiful as it is phenomenal. In addition to the big-name rivers like the **Madison, Firehole, Yellowstone,** and the nearby **Henry's Fork** across the border in Idaho, there are all sorts of small streams and beautiful lakes of all sizes. **Hebgen Lake** and **Quake Lake** are two favorites for year-round fishing.

You won't have any difficulty finding guides and gear in the town of West Yellowstone. Among the most respected, and certainly the best-known, is **Bud Lilly's Trout Shop** (39 Madison Ave., 406/646-7801, www.budlillys.com), which has been outfitting and guiding anglers for 60 years. Another pretty famous name among anglers is Bob Jacklin of **Jacklin's Fly Shop** (105 Yellowstone Ave., 406/646-7336, www.jacklinsflyshop.com).

SPRING BIKING THROUGH THE PARK

For a few magical weeks between the end of the snowmobile season and the onset of the summer car traffic, Yellowstone's roads are open exclusively to nonmotorized users. This means that bicyclists, walkers, runners, Rollerbladers, and roller skiers can cruise through the park in near silence with eyes focused on bison traffic as opposed to wide Winnebagos. Depending on the seasonal snow, the road between the west entrance and Mammoth Hot Springs typically opens the last Friday in March and stays open to nonmotorized users until the third Thursday in April. Opening can be delayed in heavy snow years due to the need for plowing.

Sometime in May there is normally a brief period of bicycle-only traffic permitted from the east entrance to the east end of Sylvan Pass, and from the south entrance to West Thumb Junction. The roads between Madison Junction and Old Faithful, and Norris Junction to Canyon, remain closed to all traffic during this spring season for human safety and bear management.

There is something truly spellbinding about being on the open road in the park, the wind whistling through your helmet. The relative silence allows some unrivaled wildlife viewing and necessitates great care. As nerve-racking as it can be to be engulfed by a herd of bison while driving in your car, coming across them on your bike is an entirely different scenario. Still, if you are cautious and respectful, being on your bike can allow you to feel somewhat less like an intruder and more like a resident. You can fall into sync with the flow of the rivers, the movement of the breeze, and the calls of the animals. It is truly a remarkable way to experience the park.

With that said: respect, restraint, and absolute caution are of vital importance to your safety and the well-being of the animals. Keep a good distance from all wildlife – 25 yards from ungulates and 100 yards from predators. Remember that bison can run at speeds topping 30 mph, and they can jump a six-foot fence. Harbor no illusions about your immunity from an attack. The fact that you have approached silently allows for more of a startle factor for the animals and increases the likelihood of a conflict. Wear a helmet, and dress in layers: Yellowstone in spring can go from blue skies to blizzard conditions in a staggeringly short period of time. Be prepared for anything, and understand that there are no services in the park at this time. Enjoy this spectacularly unique opportunity to enjoy the park up close. For specific information about road openings, call 307/344-2109.

The roads open in April to bikers only.

Both outfitters are licensed to guide in and out of Yellowstone National Park, and both carry an excellent assortment of top-of-the-line gear. Jacklin's Fly Shop also hosts free fly casting lessons every Sunday evening in summer. Anglers do not need state fishing licenses in Yellowstone, but a Yellowstone fishing permit—available at any of the visitors centers in the park—is required.

Mountain Biking and Cross-Country Skiing

Sandwiched between Yellowstone and the Gallatin National Forest on a high plateau, West Yellowstone offers excellent terrain for mountain biking. Because of its high altitude and location at the top of a reasonably flat plateau, West Yellowstone is also known for its cross-country ski trails. The town's excellent **Rendezvous Ski Trails** (look for the archway at the south end of Geyser St., www.rendezvousskitrails.com) offer roughly 22 miles of gently rolling terrain, groomed for both skate and classic skiers, which easily converts to a single track for mountain bikers when the snow melts. Athletes from around the world have come to train in West thanks in large part to this trail system. And it should be noted that the proximity to Yellowstone opens up a whole new world of opportunity for both mountain bikers and skiers.

The best bike and ski shop in town—which also has surprisingly stylish clothes, great gear, and killer coffee—is the **Freeheel & Wheel** (40 Yellowstone Ave., 406/646-7744, www.freeheelandwheel.com). They rent, sell, and service bikes and skis and can offer any advice you could possibly need on the region's best rides and trails.

Other Winter Recreation

Although snowmobiling inside the park has become something of a hot-button issue, West Yellowstone is still considered the snowmobile capital of the world for its proximity to the 200 miles of groomed trails in the park as well as hundreds of miles of groomed terrain in the national forests surrounding West.

There are numerous places in town to rent a snowmobile, and since the park mandates that all snowmobilers within park boundaries use a guide, several outfits also offer guiding services both in and out of the park. **Two Top Snowmobile Rental** (645 Gibbon Ave., 800/522-7802, www.twotopsnowmobile. com) has rentals for self-guided tours outside the park starting at $119 per day and guided tours into the park from $169. They have licensed guides, Yellowstone-mandated four-stroke engines, and rental equipment. Another full-service rental outfit in West is **Rendezvous Snowmobile Rentals** (415 Yellowstone Ave., 406/646-9564 or 800/426-7669, www.yellowstonevacations.com), renting snowmobiles from $134 per day with a guide fee of $40 per snowmobile. For deep-powder backcountry touring options outside the park, **Hi Country Snowmobile Rentals** (229 Hayden St., 406/646-7541 or 800/624-5291, www.hicountrysnowmobile.com) is an excellent bet, with snowmobile rentals from their entirely new fleet each year starting at $139 per day, guided trail rides from $195 per day for 1–3 people plus the cost of machine rental, and guided backcountry tours from $200 per day.

For those who want to explore the backcountry outside Yellowstone National Park in a slightly quieter way, **dogsledding** might be the perfect choice. **Klondike Dreams** (Yellowstone Rental and Sports, U.S. 20, 8 miles west of West Yellowstone, 406/646-4988, www.klondikedreams.com, $75 over 80 pounds, $50 under 80 pounds) offers two-hour rides and kennel tours featuring their Alaskan huskies with Iditarod bloodlines.

Another amazing way to see the park is on a guided **snow coach tour.** There are numerous providers, but **Yellowstone Alpen Guides** (555 Yellowstone Ave., 800/858-3502, www.yellowstoneguides.com, from $110 adults, $100 seniors, $90 children under 16) offers classic 10-passenger Bombardiers, a fantastic array of tours, and some of the best naturalist guides anywhere. Snow coach tours can be combined with some cross-country skiing in the park.

YELLOWSTONE NATIONAL PARK

ACCOMMODATIONS

In the summer months there are more than 2,000 hotel rooms to be found in West and about 1,300 when the snow covers the ground. There are also guest ranches, bed-and-breakfasts, and cabin rentals to be found. **Yellowstone Tour & Travel** (800/221-1151, www.yellowstonereservation.com) is a full-service travel agency in West Yellowstone that can book everything from accommodations and tours to complete packages.

Just seven blocks from the west entrance to Yellowstone National Park, the pet-friendly **Pine Shadows Motel & Condos** (229 N. Hayden St., 406/646-7541 or 800/624-5291, www.pineshadowsmotel.com) is open year-round and has a selection of motel rooms (from $50) and newly built, spacious condos ($150–230), all of which are clean and comfortable. As is true in much of the town, free Wi-Fi is available. Also open year-round, the **Three Bear Lodge** (217 Yellowstone Ave., 406/646-7353 or 800/646-7353, www.threebearlodge.com, $59–249) offers 70 guest rooms in their pet-friendly motel unit and the lodge, where no two rooms are alike. All guest rooms have a refrigerator, a microwave, and an LCD TV, and all were recently updated with amenities like handmade furniture and new duvets.

CAMPING

With nearly two dozen private and public campgrounds in the vicinity of West, campers have plenty of choice, although most are geared to RV campers. The nearest National Forest Service campground is **Baker's Hole Campground** (U.S. 191, 3 miles northwest of West Yellowstone, 406/823-6961, www.fs.fed.us/ri/gallatin, May 15–Sept. 15 depending on weather, $14 for 1 vehicle, $6 for each additional vehicle, plus $6 for electrical sites), with 73 sites set on a scenic oxbow of the Madison River. Basic services such as water and trash pickup are provided, there is firewood for sale, and the fishing is excellent.

Right in town, just six blocks from the park's west entrance, is **Wagon Wheel RV Campground & Cabins** (408 Gibbon Ave., 406/646-7872, www.wagonwheelrv.com, camping May 15–Sept. 30, cabins May 1–Oct. 30, $33 tents, $45 full-hookup pull-through site, cabins from $114 d), offering an ideal forested and quiet setting that is wonderfully convenient. The nine cabins, reminiscent of the 1930s and 1940s architecture found throughout the park, are especially charming, but they get booked up quickly.

FOOD

For a filling breakfast or lunch, head to the relatively new ❨ **Bear Country Bake Shop & Eatery** (29 N. Canyon St., 406/646-9737, 8 A.M.–2:30 P.M. Mon.–Fri., 9 A.M.–2 P.M. Sat. year-round, extended hours in summer). Their breakfast burritos ($5.25–6.25), lunch sandwiches, wraps, and specials ($4.75–8.25) are delicious, huge, and fresh. Delightful owners Jaime and Danny Hambarian whip up a dizzying array of giant cinnamon rolls, turnovers, and other delectable pastries. Their fisherman's lunch ($11.25) will keep you fueled throughout the day, or you can plunk down with your computer for free Wi-Fi and belly up to the full coffee bar.

For the best soup, salad, and potato bar in town, try the **Timberline Café** (135 Yellowstone Ave., 406/646-9349, 6:30 A.M.–10 P.M. daily mid-May–early Oct., breakfast and lunch $5.25–14, dinner $8.25–31), an old-school establishment that has been feeding Yellowstone visitors and lucky locals during the summer season since the early 1900s. Don't miss the homemade pie.

Another West Yellowstone institution is **Buckaroo Bill's Ice Cream** (24 N. Canyon St., 406/646-7901, 7:30 A.M.–10 P.M. Mon.–Sat. May–Oct., entrées $6.75–26), which has excellent bison burgers in addition to mouth-watering Montana-made ice cream. The joint is popular, though, and it's not always easy to get a seat; the outside patio is a lively place for a meal. **Beartooth Barbeque** (111 N. Canyon St., 406/646-0227, 11 A.M.–10 P.M. daily May–Oct., entrées $9–25) serves excellent slow-cooked meat. For a more gourmet experience, **Sydney's Mountain Bistro** (38 N. Canyon St., 406/646-7660, www.sydneysbistro.com, lunch 11 A.M.–3 P.M., dinner from 5 P.M. daily May–Oct., lunch $8.50–12, dinner $14–38) is undoubtedly the place. They serve exquisite but pricy meals utilizing fresh local ingredients whenever possible. Entrées include the mountain bistro burger ($14.50), Panang chicken ($21), seafood pasta ($23), and porterhouse pork chop ($28). They also offer gourmet salads and sandwiches for lunch ($8.50–13) and boast the most extensive wine list in town.

INFORMATION AND SERVICES

The **West Yellowstone Chamber of Commerce** (406/646-7701), **Montana State Visitors Center**, and **Yellowstone Park Visitors Center** (307/344-2876) are all housed under the same roof at 30 Yellowstone Avenue. You can get all the information you need about the city and the state, and you can even buy your park permits. The visitors center also has a lot of information about the regular and special events held in town.

The **West Yellowstone Public Library** (23 N. Dunraven St., 406/646-9017, from 10 A.M. Tues.–Sat., closing time varies) is located between Yellowstone and Madison Avenues. It offers free Wi-Fi and has three computers with Internet access.

The town's only **post office** (209 Grizzly Ave., 406/646-7704, 8:30 A.M.–5 P.M. Mon.–Fri.) is located at the corner of Electric Street and Grizzly Avenue.

Swan Cleaners (520 Madison Ave., 406/646-7892, 7 A.M.–9 P.M. daily summer, 8 A.M.–9 P.M. daily in other seasons) is located just east of the Running Bear Pancake House. It has coin-operated machines with dry-cleaning and laundry services offered Monday–Friday.

For nonemergency medical care, you can walk into the **West Yellowstone Family Clinic** (236 Yellowstone Ave., 406/646-0200, 8:30 A.M.–noon and 1–4:30 P.M. Mon.–Fri.). There is 24-hour paramedic emergency service available in town.

YELLOWSTONE NATIONAL PARK

GRAND TETON NATIONAL PARK

Just south of Yellowstone in northwestern Wyoming, Grand Teton National Park is even more dazzling than its larger and more prominent neighbor in terms of its mountain splendor. The Tetons soar skyward, three in a sea of 12 peaks topping 12,000 feet. The mountains are young—still growing, in fact—and utterly spectacular, perhaps the most dramatic anywhere in the Lower 48. The park itself contains approximately 310,000 acres (roughly 15 percent the size of Yellowstone), 100 miles of paved road, and much to the delight of hikers, some 200 miles of trails.

Like Yellowstone, Grand Teton is home to healthy populations of wildlife—this is among the best places in the West to see a moose—but the rugged terrain and limited number of roads affords the animals better places to hide. Still, you always need to be aware of and prepared for bear encounters in the park. Beyond the stunning natural and geological history of the region, Grand Teton offers some interesting human-built attractions—including the historic and elegant Jenny Lake Lodge, the Chapel of the Transfiguration, and the Indian Arts Museum—that are well worth seeing. At the end of the day, though, Grand Teton is a place for nature lovers and outdoor enthusiasts. The vistas are unparalleled, as are the natural features and recreational opportunities.

HISTORY

The history of this region dates back 11,000 years, when it was a seasonal hunting ground for such tribes as the Shoshone, Gros Ventre,

HIGHLIGHTS

◖ Colter Bay Indian Arts Museum: Housed unassumingly in the Colter Bay Visitors Center, this museum contains a surprisingly rare collection of American Indian artifacts donated by the Rockefeller family (page 292).

◖ Cruise to Elk Island: As if a sunrise in the Tetons was not reason enough to get up (it is), lure yourself out of bed and into this wonderland with an early morning cruise that features everything from trout to hot cakes for breakfast on Elk Island (page 292).

◖ Oxbow Bend: Home to an impressive number of birds and moose, Oxbow Bend is a hairpin-like curve of slow-moving backwater from the Snake River, perfect for novice boaters, wildlife watchers, and photographers looking to capture the crystalline reflection of Mount Moran (page 295).

◖ Signal Mountain: Grand Teton's answer to Pike's Peak, Signal Mountain offers an exciting five-mile drive, not suitable for RVs and trailers, up for expansive views of the entire valley. Watching a sunset from here is time well spent (page 295).

◖ Jenny Lake: Resting like a mirror at the base of the Tetons, this alpine lake is a gem for hikers, boaters, picnickers, and gawkers alike. It's not a place for those seeking solitude, but its beauty is well worth sharing (page 298).

◖ Hidden Falls and Inspiration Point: There are several ways to get to Hidden Falls and the aptly named Inspiration Point, including a shortcut by boat. The views along the popular and gloriously scenic hike are worth every step (page 299).

◖ Craig Thomas Discovery and Visitor Center: An architectural gem complete with video rivers running beneath your feet and walls of windows that showcase the park's namesake mountains, this visitors center offers a stunning and innovative introduction to the park (page 302).

◖ Laurance S. Rockefeller Preserve: The longtime summer home of the Rockefeller family at the center of Grand Teton National Park, this lovely preserve and its wonderful visitors center personify the family's commitment to stewardship (page 303).

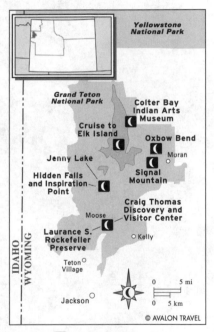

LOOK FOR ◖ TO FIND RECOMMENDED SIGHTS, ACTIVITIES, DINING, AND LODGING.

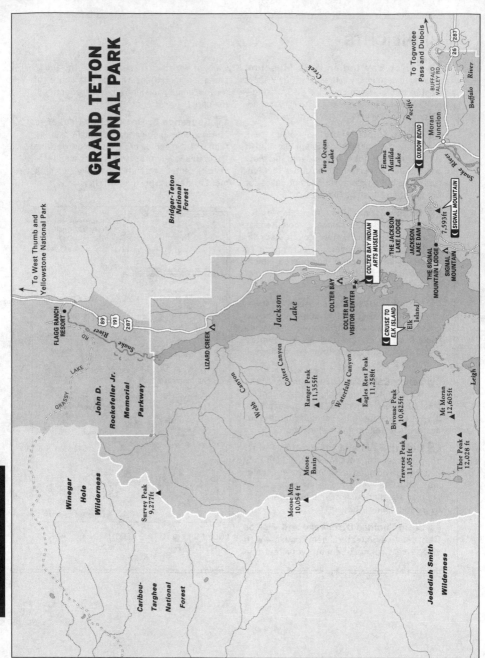

GRAND TETON
NATIONAL PARK

To West Thumb and
Yellowstone National Park

FLAGG RANCH
RESORT

89
191
287

Snake River

GRASSY LAKE RD

John D.
Rockefeller Jr.
Memorial
Parkway

Winegar
Hole
Wilderness

Caribou-
Targhee
National
Forest

Jedediah Smith
Wilderness

Survey Peak
9,277ft ▲

Moose Mtn
10,054 ft ▲

Moose
Basin

Webb Canyon

Cottonwood Canyon

LIZARD CREEK ⋀

Ranger Peak
11,355ft ▲

Colter Canyon

Waterfalls Canyon

Eagles Rest Peak
11,258ft ▲

Traverse Peak
11,051ft ▲

Bivouac Peak
10,825ft ▲

Mt Moran
12,605ft ▲

Thor Peak
12,028 ft ▲

Bridger-Teton
National
Forest

Jackson
Lake

COLTER BAY

COLTER BAY
VISITOR CENTER

COLTER BAY INDIAN
ARTS MUSEUM

CRUISE TO
ELK ISLAND

Elk
Island

Leigh

Two Ocean
Lake

Emma
Matilda
Lake

THE JACKSON
LAKE LODGE

JACKSON
LAKE DAM

THE SIGNAL
MOUNTAIN LODGE

SIGNAL ⋀
MOUNTAIN

SIGNAL MOUNTAIN
7,593ft ▲

OXBOW BEND

Moran
Junction

Pacific Creek

Snake River

BUFFALO
VALLEY RD

Buffalo River

To Togwotee
Pass and Dubois

26
287

To Togwotee
Pass and Dubois

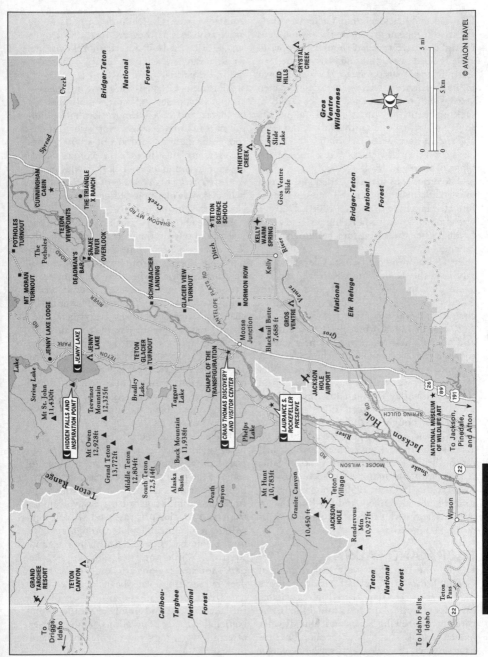

Flathead, and Blackfeet. John Colter was likely the first European to explore the region; he is thought to have traveled though the area in 1808, guided by wildlife and Native American trails. By the 1820s the area was widely known for its abundance of beavers and mountain men arrived with traps in hand. Trapper David E. Jackson spent the winter of 1829 along the shores of Jackson Lake; the valley, the lake, and the nearby town of Jackson bear his name. Many of the park's features were named by the Hayden Survey in 1871.

The region was sparsely settled and farmed due to the climate and the soil, but it was used for cattle ranching in the late 1800s. The area was also well-known among hunters and eventually became the setting for a handful of dude ranches.

In 1897, President Grover Cleveland established the Teton Forest Reserve, and the Teton National Forest was created in 1908. The park itself—96,000 acres in its first incarnation—was set aside by Congress in 1929 and included primarily the mountains and alpine lakes. There were some attempts through the 1930s to add to the park, none of which were successful. John D. Rockefeller Jr., however, was quietly purchasing land in the Teton Valley through his Snake River Land Company. Between 1926 and 1946, Rockefeller bought 35,000 acres adjacent to the park, and in 1949 he deeded all but 2,000 acres to the federal government, which had established the 210,000-acre Jackson Hole National Monument under President Franklin Roosevelt in 1943. In 1950, Congress agreed to merge the monument and the Rockefeller-donated land with the park, bringing it to its current boundaries.

FLORA AND FAUNA

Despite the fact that every square inch of Grand Teton National Park is at or above 6,400 feet in elevation, there is a remarkable diversity of both plant and animal life in the three main growing zones and four distinct habitat regions. Throughout the short but sublime summer, the valleys are awash in colorful wildflowers. And although animals aren't quite as visible as they are in the vast open spaces or burned-out forests of Yellowstone, wildlife watchers will have terrific opportunities in the park.

All three of Grand Teton's growing zones—alpine, subalpine, and valley—fall between 6,400 feet and 13,770 feet in elevation, meaning harsh climates and a short growing season. Still, there are upward of 1,000 species of vascular plants in the park. Porous soil allows for an abundance of colorful wildflowers. And even in the high reaches of the mountains, delicate jewels like alpine forget-me-nots grow close to the ground in mats.

Because of the short growing season, the vast majority of trees in the park are conifers—like Yellowstone, lodgepole pine is the most common tree—but aspens and cottonwoods have chlorophyll in the bark, allowing them to photosynthesize before putting out leaves. As a result, Grand Teton National Park is illuminated in the fall by changing leaves. Sagebrush is everywhere, lending an almost minty smell to the crisp air.

Along with Yellowstone, Grand Teton National Park is a critical part of the more than 11-million-acre Greater Yellowstone ecosystem, considered one of the last nearly intact temperate ecosystems on earth. As such, it provided critical home habitat and migratory routes for a number of species.

The park's four main habitat types are alpine, sagebrush, forest, and aquatic. The alpine habitat, above 10,000 feet, is home to some of the park's hardiest creatures: yellow-bellied marmots, pikas, and bighorn sheep. In the ubiquitous sagebrush areas, with more than 100 species of grass and wildflower, wildlife watchers can look for pronghorn, coyotes, bison, badgers, elk, and Uinta ground squirrels. While not as easy to explore, the park's forested regions are home to elk, mule deer, red squirrels, black bears, and snowshoe hares. And finally, in and around the plentiful lakes, rivers, and ponds of Grand Teton National Park are populations of moose, river otters, beavers, muskrat, coyotes, bison, and mule deer.

© OSAMU HOSHINO/WYOMING TRAVEL & TOURISM

a bull moose in the mist

PLANNING YOUR TIME

Grand Teton National Park is smaller, and in some ways more manageable, than its northerly neighbor. There are only 100 miles of paved road, all of which can be driven easily in less than a day's time. With fewer accommodations than Yellowstone, Grand Teton lends itself to easy day trips from Jackson Hole, but it is a compelling destination on its own. Grand Teton is a paradise for outdoor enthusiasts. Hikers, bikers, boaters, and in winter, cross-country skiers will have no problem coming up with marvelous weeklong itineraries. Still, for those on a time budget, you can get an excellent sampling of the park in two days, but even if you are just driving through, there are a few places that should not be missed.

While summer is by far the busiest time in the park in terms of visitors, spring and fall can be magnificent with wildflowers, golden aspens, and more active wildlife. **Hiking** and **climbing** in the Tetons is best done in summer and early fall, after the winter snow has melted and before it starts flying again. Still, snow squalls and bad weather can surprise hikers any time of year, so be sure to come prepared. Park rangers offer marvelous programs throughout the year that are an excellent way to make the most of the time you have. In the fall, for example, drivers can join ranger-led **wildlife caravans** from the Craig Thomas Discovery and Visitors Center that guide visitors to the best places to see wildlife that day. **Ranger-led hikes and eco-talks** are geared to the seasons and offer visitors a wonderful insiders' look at the park.

The National Park Service offers an excellent trip planning tool online (www.nps.gov/grte/planyourvisit/trip.htm), or you can order a booklet by mail by calling 307/739-3600.

GRAND TETON NATIONAL PARK

Flagg Ranch and Colter Bay

Just south of the Yellowstone border, Flagg Ranch was at one time a U.S. Cavalry outpost. Converted to a guest ranch in 1910, it is ideally situated for visitors looking to explore both Yellowstone and Grand Teton National Parks from one location. In addition to full resort lodging and services, Flagg Ranch offers activities and services—a gas station, a grocery store, a deli and coffee shop—for those just passing through.

One of the busiest spots in the park, with a marina, lodging, a campground, a visitors center, and a museum on the shores of Jackson Lake, Colter Bay is a practical, if not exactly quiescent, place to stay, and it is a worthwhile region to explore.

SIGHTS
(Colter Bay Indian Arts Museum
This unassuming Colter Bay Indian Arts Museum (307/739-3594, 8 A.M.–7 P.M. daily early June–Labor Day, 8 A.M.–5 P.M. daily Labor Day–early Oct., free) is tacked on to the visitors center almost as an afterthought. It is a relatively unknown gem, packed with important Native American artifacts that belonged to tribes across the country. The collection, which includes dolls, shields, pipes, weapons, and photographs, among other objects, was purchased from collector David T. Vernon and ultimately donated by the Rockefeller family with the provision that it be displayed permanently in Grand Teton National Park. It is indeed a remarkable collection that could just as easily be on display at the Smithsonian were it not for the wishes of an extremely generous family. Native American artisans practice their crafts in the museum intermittently through the summer, and there are a number of prominent lecturers and daily educational events scheduled on-site.

RECREATION
Boating and Fishing
On the shores of Jackson Lake, by far the largest body of water in the park, Colter Bay and the **Colter Bay Village Marina** (307/543-2811 or 800/628-9988, www.gtlc.com) are excellent launching points for a variety of boating expeditions. From the marina, you can arrange cruises, canoe or kayak excursions, motorboat rentals, and guided fishing trips.

Guided fly-fishing tours can be arranged through the marina as well. Guided Jackson Lake fishing starts at $80 per hour for 1–2 people with a two-hour minimum and $15 per additional person. Guided fly-fishing trips start at $475 for 1–2 people.

(Cruise to Elk Island
Since nothing builds an appetite like time spent on an alpine lake, there are wonderful breakfast cruises and dinner cruises (800/628-9988, www.gtlc.com) departing from the marina that whisk guests across the lake to Elk Island, in the shadow of Mount Moran. Each cruise takes approximately three hours, and departure times change as daylight hours lengthen and shorten. The breakfast cruise ($36 adults, $22 ages 3–11), offered daily except Friday, serves hearty fare with eggs and trout, pancakes, pastries, fresh fruit, and the all-important cowboy coffee. The dinner cruise ($57 adults, $37 ages 3–11) is offered Monday, Wednesday, and Friday evenings and includes such delectable mountain fare as steak and trout, baked beans, corn on the cob, a salad bar, and mouthwatering fruit cobbler.

Hiking and Biking
There is a lot of marvelous terrain in every corner of the park for hiking and biking, and the northern section near Colter Bay is no exception. The hike to **Hermitage Point** is one of the most significant hikes (and long, at nearly nine miles round-trip). The elevation gain is minimal (980 vertical feet), and the trail, which starts immediately across from the boat launch at the southern end of the parking lot, meanders through forest, meadow, and alongside

FINDING A GUIDE

For nonlocals, setting off into Grand Teton National Park can be slightly intimidating, making guided tours a good option. The park service maintains a list of licensed, permitted, and park-approved guides.

For any type of technical **rock climbing** by nonclimbers, a guide is as necessary as a helmet and rope. **Exum Mountain Guides** (307/733-2297, www.exumguides.com) has been offering instruction and guided mountain climbing since 1931, making it the oldest guide service in North America and certainly one of the most prestigious. Exum offers numerous programs, from easy day climbing for families with kids to guided expeditions up the 13,770-foot Grand Teton. Detailed information, including climbing routes and trail conditions, can be found at www.tetonclimbing.blogspot.com.

For guided **hikes** and **snowshoe or ski tours,** the **Hole Hiking Experience** (307/690-4453 or 866/733-4453, www.holehike.com) offers a range of outings both in and around the park for all interests and ability levels, from sunrise or sunset discovery tours to all-day wildlife watching hikes. Kids will love the family day hikes with fun survival-like activities that include eating "lemon drop" ants and using butterfly nets. Winter cross-country ski and snowshoe tours are guided by naturalists and show off the best winter has to offer.

There are two options for guided **horseback riding** trips in the park. At the north end, closest to Yellowstone, is the **Flagg Ranch Resort** (800/443-2311, www.flaggranch.com), which offers a variety of guided trips in both Yellowstone and Grand Teton National Park. The **Grand Teton Lodge Company** (307/543-2811 or 800/628-9988, www.gtlc.com) can also arrange 1-2-hour horseback tours departing from a number of lodges in the park, including Colter Bay Village and Jackson Lake Lodge.

All riders in the park must be at least eight years old.

With so many varied bodies of water, there are a number of **fishing** outfitters that can guide any type of trip you can dream up. A good place to start is the **Grand Teton Lodge Company** (307/543-2811 or 800/628-9988, www.gtlc.com), which can arrange trips from any of the accommodations inside the park. Fishing trips on Jackson Lake can also be arranged through the lakefront **Signal Mountain Lodge** (307/543-2831, www.signalmtnlodge.com) or **Jack Dennis Fishing Trips** (307/690-0910, www.jackdennisfishingtrips.com).

Rafting is popular in Grand Teton National Park, and there are nine licensed outfitters to guide visitors down the Snake River. As with all activities, **Grand Teton Lodge Company** (307/543-2811 or 800/628-9988, www.gtlc.com) can make arrangements for the park's most popular 10-mile scenic float. Other outfitters include **Barker-Ewing Float Trips** (307/733-1800, www.barkerewing.com), **Solitude Float Trips** (888/704-2800, www.grand-teton-scenic-floats.com), and **OARS** (800/346-6277, www.oars.com).

Throughout the year, Park Service rangers offer excellent **naturalist-guided tours.** From mid-December–March, depending on conditions, daily guided snowshoe hikes depart from the Craig Thomas Discovery and Visitor Center (307/739-3399, reservations required). During the summer months, the range of offerings is vast – from 30-minute map chats and campfire programs to three-hour hikes. For more information on ranger programs, pick up the park newspaper at any of the entrance stations, call 307/739-3300, or check out the visitors centers in Moose, Jenny Lake, Colter Bay, and the Laurance S. Rockefeller Preserve.

ponds and streams. The easy **Lakeshore Trail** is only two miles long round-trip and circumnavigates Colter Bay with stunning views in every direction.

North of Colter Bay, near the Flagg Ranch, is **Grassy Lake Road,** a 52-mile dirt road—great for mountain biking—that follows an ancient Indian thoroughfare all the way to Ashton, Idaho. Along the way are hiking trails, streams, ponds, and splendid scenery.

ACCOMMODATIONS

The **Flagg Ranch Resort** (307/543-2861 or 800/443-2311, www.flaggranch.com, May 18–Sept. 28, $179 d, $189 d with view, children under 17 free with parent, $10 each additional person per night) is touted as the oldest continuously operating resort in upper Jackson Hole. The log cabin rooms are situated in fourplexes and duplexes. If you pay the extra $10, you'll have a beautiful unobstructed view of the valley in a more secluded area of the ranch. All rooms have two queen or one king bed, coffeemakers, private baths, and patios furnished with rocking chairs.

Colter Bay Village (800/628-9988, www.gtlc.com) is located on the northern shore of Jackson Lake and has historic cabins and tent cabins for rent. The original homestead cabins, moved to the area, have been refurbished but still offer a glimpse into the past. Each cabin displays a description of its own history. The private one-room cabins ($109–155) can sleep up to six people, and the two-room cabins ($169–209) up to 10. Prices vary depending on the number of occupants in the room and the arrangement of double, twin, and rollaway beds. If you don't mind sharing a bath in a common hall, the semiprivate cabins ($60) are a good deal, but they cannot accommodate roll-aways or cribs. The **tent cabins** ($50, each additional cot $6) consist of two walls made of logs with the other two walls and roof made of canvas. Each log wall has two pull-down bunks; additional cots can be rented. Each tent has a picnic and grilling area, and showers are located in the launderette with a fee for use.

CAMPING

The **Flagg Ranch campgrounds** (May 22–Sept. 30) are nestled in the woods close to the Snake River. There are 95 pull-through RV sites ($50 for up to 2 adults, each additional adult $5) and 75 tent sites ($25 for up to 2 adults, each additional adult $5). The campgrounds have 24-hour showers and laundry facilities, and each site has a fire pit and picnic table.

The campgrounds at **Colter Bay Village** (800/628-9988, www.gtlc.com, $55 RVs peak season, $42 off-season, $20 tents with vehicle, $8 hikers) are a five-minute walk from the lake. There are 112 RV sites with pull-through access as well as 350 tent sites. Each site accommodates two tents and up to six people; 11 of the sites are specifically reserved for large groups.

Located between Flagg Ranch and Colter Bay Village, the **Lizard Creek Campground** (800/672-6012, early June–late Aug., $18, $5 for hikers or cyclists without vehicles) has 60 individual sites and rarely fills.

FOOD

The main lodge at Flagg Ranch is the center of all activity at the ranch. It has a gas station, a general store, and **The Bear's Den Restaurant** (breakfast 7–10:30 A.M. daily, lunch 11:30 A.M.–2 P.M. daily, dinner 5–9 P.M. daily May 18–Sept. 28, breakfast $4–9, lunch $7–12, dinner $8–24), which serves a solid range of American cuisine in a family-friendly setting.

The **John Colter Café Court** in Colter Bay Village (11 A.M.–10 P.M. daily June–Sept., entrées $2.25–8) offers both Mexican and American food. They have a variety of tacos, burgers, and burritos at reasonable prices, and box lunches are available. Also at Colter Bay is the fairly new **Ranch House Restaurant** (breakfast 6:30–10:30 A.M. daily, lunch 11:30 A.M.–1:30 P.M. daily, dinner 5:30–9 P.M. daily, May 22–Sept. 27, breakfast buffet $12.50 adults, $7.50 children, entrées $5–13, lunch $7.75–14, dinner $16–22). The restaurant offers family-style meals with a Western flavor. The breakfast buffet includes enchiladas and organic oatmeal, or if you want to order à la carte, you can easily fill up on the flatiron steak and eggs. Lunch consists of a good selection of salads, burgers, and sandwiches, while dinner offers hearty steaks, chops, and seafood dishes. They have a "you catch it, we cook it" option

on the dinner menu for $12.25; just make sure you get your trout to the restaurant by 4 P.M., and it will be served to you a few hours later with a side of potatoes and the veggie of the day. The bar is open 11 A.M.–10 P.M. daily and has a small food menu as well.

Jackson Lake Lodge and Signal Mountain

Its stunning setting, coupled with excellent amenities and access to fantastic hiking and sightseeing in the park's northeastern corner, make Jackson Lake Lodge a vacation destination all its own. Though the lodge is not adjacent to Jackson Lake in the way that the Colter Bay Village is, the views over the lake to the Tetons are magnificent. Nearby, the rustic Signal Mountain Lodge is situated immediately on the water, offering unlimited opportunities for enjoying Jackson Lake and its proximity to wonderful hiking and adventuring.

SIGHTS
◖ Oxbow Bend
Just southeast of Jackson Lake Lodge on the main road is Oxbow Bend, a picturesque river area created when the Snake River carved a more southerly route. One of the most photographed areas in the park, the slow-moving water perfectly reflects towering Mount Moran. The serenity of the area attracts an abundance of wildlife, including moose, beavers, and otters along with a vast number of birds. White pelicans can occasionally be spotted passing through, as can sandhill cranes, majestic trumpeter swans, nesting great blue herons, and bald eagles. Avid boaters like to paddle the area in their canoes and kayaks. Don't forget your binoculars and your camera.

◖ Signal Mountain
One mile south of Signal Mountain Lodge is the turnoff to Signal Mountain Road and one of the greatest viewpoints in Grand Teton National Park. The winding five-mile road is completely unsuitable for RVs and trailers.

Along the way, there are ample spots for wildlife viewing—look for moose in the pond on the right as you start up the road, and the pond lilies blooming in June. There are two small parking lots near the summit. The first offers the best view of the Tetons: Sunsets are sensational. From the second, a short walk takes you down to an overlook with a view of Oxbow Bend. Visitors in August might even have a chance to pick some succulent huckleberries as they ripen in the late-summer sun.

The story of Signal Mountain's name is rather a tragic one. Around the turn of the 20th century, a local rancher named Roy Hamilton got lost when he was out hunting. Rescuers agreed to light a fire on the mountain as soon as anyone found Hamilton. After nine days, a fire was lit atop the mountain, signaling the end of rescue efforts. Tragically, Hamilton's body was found in the Snake River, and some speculated his business partner had suggested he cross the river in a particularly dangerous spot.

RECREATION
Fishing
Anglers will be pleased with the varied offerings in this stretch of the park. From the lunkers in Jackson Lake, which can be fished on shore or by boat, to the healthy but discerning trout in the Snake River, guided trips can be arranged through **Grand Teton Lodge Company** (307/543-2811 or 800/628-9988, www.gtlc.com), starting from $80 per hour for 1–2 adults with a two-hour minimum and $15 per additional person; day trips start at $475 per day for 1–2 anglers. From **Signal**

GRAND TETON NATIONAL PARK

Mountain Lodge (307/543-2831, www.signalmountainlodge.com), anglers can go out with experienced guides in pursuit of Jackson Lake's cutthroat, brown, and lake trout for $80 per hour for 1–2 people for a minimum of 2 hours, and $20 per hour per additional person; half-day trips are $280 for 1–2 people and $60 per additional person. Half-day and multiple-day fishing trips on Jackson Lake can also be arranged through **Jack Dennis Fishing Trips** (307/690-0910, www.jackdennisfishingtrips.com). A Wyoming fishing license is required for all fishing in the park and can be purchased at **Snake River Anglers at Dornan's** (307/733-7271, www.snakeriverangle.com), **Signal Mountain Marina** (307/543-2831 or 800/628-9988, www.signalmountainlodge.com), and **Colter Bay Marina** (307/543-3100 or 800/628-9988, www.gtlc.com). Pick up a fishing brochure from any of the visitors centers to learn about all park regulations.

Boating

With so much beautiful water in the park, boating is a fantastic way to explore. Rafting on the Snake River, canoeing or kayaking on any number of lakes, or cruising across Jackson Lake, there are options for adrenaline junkies and die-hard landlubbers alike.

Scenic 10-mile floats down the Snake can be arranged through **Signal Mountain Lodge** (307/543-2831, www.signalmountainlodge.com, $59 adults, $37 ages 6–12), **Grand Teton Lodge Company** (800/628-9988, www.gtlc.com), or **Solitude Float Trips** (888/704-2800, www.grand-teton-scenic-floats.com, $55 adults, $35 ages 6–12, $650 for a private boat for up to 12 guests). Most floats on the Snake River inside the park last about two hours. Both GTLC and Solitude offer a wonderful sunrise float, perfect for spotting wildlife. GTLC also offers four-hour luncheon floats ($65 adults, $45 ages 6–11) and dinner floats ($70 adults, $50 ages 6–11) with fun riverside cookouts.

Human-powered boats like kayaks and canoes are permitted on Emma Matilda Lake and Two Ocean Lake, east of Jackson Lake Lodge.

Jackson Lake is open to motorboats, human-powered boats, sailboats, water-skiing, and windsurfers. Permits are required for motorized boats ($10 for 7 days) and can be purchased at the visitors centers in Moose, Jenny Lake, or Colter Bay. A variety of boats can be rented through **Signal Mountain Lodge** (307/543-2831, www.signalmountainlodge.com), including deck cruisers ($99 per hour, $649 per day for up to 10 people), pontoon boats ($77 per hour, $469 per day for up to 8 people), fishing boats ($36 per hour, $175 per day for up to 5 people), canoes ($17 per hour, $85 per day for up to 3 people) and sea kayaks ($15 per hour, $79 per day single, or $22 per hour, $99 per day for 2 people). The **Grand Teton Lodge Company** (800/628-9988, www.gtlc.com) can also arrange various boat rentals throughout the park.

Hiking and Biking

Sandwiched between Jackson, Emma Matilda, and Two Ocean Lakes, the area around Jackson Lake Lodge offers some wonderful scenic hiking. The **Christian Pond Loop** is a relatively flat and easy 4.3-mile round-trip hike through prime waterfowl habitat. The trailhead is east of the parking lot adjacent to the Jackson Lake Lodge corrals. Nearby, **Two Ocean Lake** offers a moderate 6.4-mile round-trip hike around the lake though forest and meadow. **Emma Matilda Lake** offers an even longer 9.1-mile hike, with fabulous Teton views from the north shore ridge.

A nice area for visitors who travel with their bicycles is in the vicinity of **Two Ocean Road,** southeast of Jackson Lake Lodge and northeast of Signal Mountain Lodge. The road itself is just three miles long, but the scenery is sublime for a short sweet ride. **River Road** is 15 miles of gravel running along the west side of the Snake River between Signal Mountain and Cottonwood Creek.

Horseback Riding

The **Grand Teton Lodge Company** (800/628-9988, www.gtlc.com) can arrange one-hour ($36) or two-hour ($54) horseback tours that depart from Jackson Lake Lodge. All riders must be at least eight years old.

ACCOMMODATIONS

The Jackson Lake Lodge ($224–239, $289–319 with view, $599–775 suites) is one of the largest resorts in the park and commands an unparalleled view of Jackson Lake and the Teton Range from the lobby's panoramic 60-foot-high windows. There are 385 guest rooms in the main lodge and surrounding cottages, and the grounds also house a playground and swimming pool. The cottages are located in clusters and come in a range of styles. The classic cottage guest room has one king bed and sleeps a maximum of three. The cottage guest room with a view of the Tetons can sleep up to five people and has a mini fridge and a patio or balcony. There is also a mountain-view suite that has a spectacular view of Willow Flats, where moose often meander, and the majestic range; it comes with a king bed and a comfortable sitting area. The lodge guest rooms are located on the third floor and also come in three price ranges. Unlike the cottages, these guest rooms do not accommodate roll-aways unless you are staying in the Moran suite, which has two rooms, breathtaking views, a kitchenette, and dining and sitting areas.

The Signal Mountain Lodge (307/543-2831 or 800/672-6012, www.signalmountainlodge. com) is an independently owned resort on the banks of Jackson Lake with a gorgeous view of the Tetons. It has a variety of options for lodging, ranging from rustic log cabins (1-room cabin $132–170, 2-room $185–197, 3-room $300) and decent motel-style rooms ($175–227) to two-room bungalows ($182–266) on the beach. The two-room lakefront retreats ($254–274) are ideal for families; they overlook the lake with fantastic views of the mountains and have kitchenettes. All the rooms in the lodge are carpeted, comfortably furnished, and decorated with a nice homey touch. There is one three-bedroom cabin aptly named Home Away from Home; if you are lucky enough to get it, you'll have a bedroom, dining area, living room with a gas fireplace, kitchen, and

small laundry room all to yourself; the only drawback is that there is no view.

CAMPING

The **Signal Mountain Campground** (800/672-6012, May 7–Oct. 17, $20 with vehicle, $5 hikers) is nestled among spruce and fir trees with views of the mountains, lakes, and hillside. It is also wildly popular and often fills up by 10 A.M. There are 86 smallish sites with no hookups, and RVs up to 30 feet in length are permitted.

FOOD

There are a lot of options for dining at the Jackson Lake Lodge. The **Mural Room** (307/543-2811, breakfast 7–9:30 A.M. daily, lunch 11:30 A.M.–1:30 P.M. daily, dinner 6–10:30 P.M. daily May 18–Oct. 4, dinner reservations recommended, breakfast buffet $14.50 adults, $9 children, entrées $5.50–9, lunch $10–17, dinner $20–28) has terrific ambience with its windowed wall looking out onto the lake, Mount Moran, and the Teton Range along with the colorful murals by famed artist Carl Routers depicting life out West. The food is upscale and innovative—also known as Rocky Mountain cuisine—and when coupled with the view, it makes this one of the most pleasurable dining experiences in the park. Breakfast includes Belgian waffles with huckleberries and a vegetarian eggs Benedict or organic quinoa. Lunch is a mix of gourmet burgers and salads as well as regional cuisine such as peppered buffalo sirloin or vegetarian asparagus and sweet pea Stroganoff. Dinner is a hearty affair with delectable main entrée items including the blue corn and plantain-crusted trout and slow-roasted, grass-fed prime rib, direct from the on-site butcher shop. A delightful end to the meal is the chocolate decadence fudge cake.

Also in the lodge is the **Pioneer Grill** (307/543-2811, 6 A.M.–10:30 P.M. daily May 18–Oct. 4, breakfast $5–8.50, lunch $7–10, dinner $9.50–20), a true-to-style 1950s diner; supposedly it has the largest soda fountain counter still in use. A fun place for a meal, the restaurant is decorated with pioneer artifacts. The Pioneer Grill offers American cuisine with a slight gourmet twist (try the chipotle mashed potatoes) and has a take-out service if you decide you'd rather watch the sunset while munching on your burger. Their famous desserts keep customers returning.

The **Blue Heron Lounge** (307/543-2811, 11 A.M.–midnight daily May 18–Oct. 4, entrées $7–14) is another casual dining experience in Jackson Lake Lodge. They have a bar menu with a good selection of appetizers and creative sandwiches, and they even offer sustainable draft beer from local breweries. Enjoy your meal on the deck while taking in a beautiful view of the mountains.

If you are at the pool or with your kids at the playground, you may want to fill up on the terrific buffet at the outdoor **Pool BBQ** (307/543-3463, May 18–Oct. 4, $24 adults, $12 children 12 and under) which serves up sandwiches and burgers during the day and at night offers authentic barbecue of everything from brisket to chicken, ribs, and bison, all accompanied by live Western music.

There are three options for dining at the Signal Mountain Lodge as well. **The Trapper Grill** (7 A.M.–10 P.M. daily May 7–Oct. 3, breakfast $7–10.25, lunch and dinner $7.50–15) has a large menu for all three meals of the day. They mostly stick to local American fare with some Tex-Mex thrown in. The breakfast menu is vast, with an egg menu, an omelet menu, and griddle options. The lunch and dinner menu is filled with specialty sandwiches, salads, and burgers, but they pride themselves on their homemade desserts. You may want to share an entrée so that you'll have room for the Kentucky bourbon chocolate pecan pie. **The Peaks Restaurant** (dinner 5:30–10 P.M. daily May 7–Oct. 3, entrées $20–35) offers delicious dinners and is committed to offering an environmentally sustainable menu. Dine on their organic vegetable risotto, bison rib eye, or line-caught Alaskan halibut. **Leeks Pizzeria** (lunch and dinner 11 A.M.–10 P.M. daily May 21–Sept. 7, entrées $9.25–16) is located at the marina on Jackson Lake. They serve specialty pizzas and calzones, sandwiches, and salads in a pleasant outdoor setting. For a drink, snack, and a glimpse of television, you may want to stop at **Deadman's Bar,** where they serve the largest plate of fully loaded nachos you have ever seen. They pair perfectly with a blackberry margarita and a Wyoming sunset.

Jenny Lake and Vicinity

Carved some 12,000 years ago by the same glaciers that carved Cascade Canyon, Jenny Lake is perhaps the most picturesque and popular spot in the park. The hiking—to places like Inspiration Point and the even more beautiful Leigh Lake—is sublime, and the water activities—scenic cruising, canoeing, kayaking, swimming, and fishing—are plentiful. The park's fanciest and most expensive lodging and dining can be found at the historic and tony Jenny Lake Lodge.

In much the same way that Old Faithful embodies the Yellowstone experience for many visitors, so too does Jenny Lake conjure up all that is wonderful about Grand Teton. A scenic drive from North Jenny Lake to South Jenny Lake skirts the water and affords breathtaking views of the Grand Teton, Teewinot, and Mount Owen. Those who are more interested in solitude would be well advised to get off the main drag here, away from the crowds and into the wilderness.

SIGHTS
Jenny Lake
In 1872 an English-born mountain man, known widely as "Beaver Dick" Leigh for his enormous front teeth and his penchant for the animal, guided Ferdinand Hayden around the Tetons. Hayden named the lovely alpine lake for Dick's wife, Jenny, a member of the

Shoshone tribe. Tragically, in the fall of 1876, pregnant Jenny took care of an ailing Native American woman, not knowing the woman had smallpox. Jenny and all four of her children became ill. Her baby was born just before Christmas and, along with Jenny and the other four children, died within a week. Beaver Dick buried his family in Jackson Hole.

Despite its tragic namesake, Jenny Lake is indeed one of the most beautiful and beloved spots in the park. From cruising across the lake to hiking along its shores, there are an endless number of ways to enjoy this idyllic spot.

(Hidden Falls and Inspiration Point

One of the area's most popular hikes is to the spectacular Hidden Falls. From Jenny Lake's south shore, the hike follows a moderate 2.5-mile trail to the cascade with 550 feet of elevation gain. Visitors who want to put fewer miles on their feet can take the Jenny Lake Shuttle (307/734-9227, $10 adults round-trip, $7 one-way, $5 ages 2–7 round-trip or one-way, free for children under 2 and seniors over 80) to shorten the hike to one mile with 150 feet of elevation gain. The hike to Inspiration Point, a breathtaking overlook 5.8 miles round-trip with 700 feet of elevation gain from the trailhead, or 2.2 miles round-trip with 420 feet of elevation gain from the boat shuttle, earns its name.

Leigh Lake

Named for mountain man "Beaver Dick" Leigh, Leigh Lake is much quieter and perhaps even more beautiful than the more southerly Jenny Lake. The lake offers unrivaled views of Mount Moran, Mount Woodring, and Rockchuck Peak, and it is dotted with sandy beaches ideal for picnics. The 5.4-mile round-trip (out-and-back) trail is flat and weaves in and out of the forest with a constant water view. The Leigh Lake trailhead is at the northwest corner of the String Lake Picnic Area. The trail can be hiked as early as May–June, depending on snowmelt, and is typically passable well into September. Although popular,

Leigh Lake does not attract the crowds that Jenny Lake does.

RECREATION
Fishing
Fishing is permitted in Jenny, String, Leigh, Bradley, and Taggart Lakes. A Wyoming fishing license is required, and they can be purchased at **Snake River Anglers at Dornan's** (307/733-7271, www.snakeriverangle.com), **Signal Mountain Marina** (307/543-2831 or 800/628-9988, www.signalmountainlodge.com), and **Colter Bay Marina** (307/543-3100 or 800/628-9988, www.gtlc.com). Pick up a fishing brochure from any of the visitors centers to learn about all park regulations.

Boating
Scenic one-hour cruises ($15 adults, $7 children), shuttles to Cascade Canyon hiking trails ($10 adults round-trip, $5 children round-trip, depart every 15 minutes), and canoe or kayak rentals ($15 per hour) can be arranged through **Jenny Lake Boating** (307/734-9227, www.jennylakeboating.com).

Hiking and Biking
Jenny Lake is at the heart of the park's largest concentration of popular hiking trails. In addition to the **Hidden Falls, Inspiration Point,** and **Leigh Lake** trailheads, there are a number of excellent trails in the region. The mostly level **Jenny Lake Loop Trail** circumnavigates the lake with a 6.6-mile round-trip hike. The **Lupine Meadows Trailhead** offers hikers a number of ways to get up into the Teton Range.

The relatively new multiuse pathway from South Jenny Lake to Taggart Lake Trailhead offers bikers (and all nonmotorized travelers) 16 miles round-trip of smooth, level pavement. There are bike racks at Taggart Lake Trailhead and in Moose. Bicycles can be rented from **Dornan's** (in Moose, 307/733-2415, ext. 302, or 307/733-2522, www.dornans.com). In addition to adult mountain bikes ($10 per hour, $22 half-day, $32 for 24 hours or per day, $180 per week), Dornan's rents kids' bikes, Trail-a-Bikes, bike racks, and Burley carriers for toddlers.

ACCOMMODATIONS

A former dude ranch for sophisticated Easterners, **Jenny Lake Lodge** (800/628-9988, www.gtlc.com, May 30–Oct. 11, cabins $599, suites $775–850) is the finest lodging in the park. The cabins have authentic log walls, newly renovated baths, and touches such as handmade bed quilts that add to the rustic elegance of each room. Situated among the three lakes, the lodge is comfortably secluded but offers beautiful vistas in all directions. The rooms are pricey, but guests get a lot for their dime. A gourmet breakfast, five-course dinner, horseback riding, and access to bicycles are all included in the rates. If you are looking for a romantic getaway, consider booking one of the suites, which come with wood-burning stoves.

A much less expensive, and truly rustic, option is the **American Alpine Club Climbers Ranch** (307/733-7271, www.americanalpineclub.org/pt/grandtetonclimbersranch, $10 AAC members, $20 nonmembers), located just three miles south of Jenny Lake. The ranch has small log cabins that serve as dormitories for 4–8 people. Guests must bring their own sleeping bags and pads, towels, cooking equipment, and food. There are cooking and dishwashing facilities, toilets, and showers with hot water available. No tents or camper camping is allowed. There is also a general store on the grounds where you can stock up on groceries as well as hiking and camping supplies.

CAMPING

The **Jenny Lake Campground** (800/628-9988, tent sites mid-May–early Oct., $20 with vehicle, $8 hikers and bicyclists) is the smallest in the park and is available on a first-come, first-served basis only; it is usually full by 8 A.M. It has 49 sites that can each accommodate one vehicle, two tents, and up to six campers. There are 10 additional sites set aside for hikers or bicyclists. There are no large group sites, nor are trailers, campers, or generators are allowed in the area. Because of its size and popularity, the maximum stay is seven days (at the other campgrounds it is 14 days).

FOOD

The **Jenny Lake Lodge Dining Room** (307/733-4647, www.gtlc.com, breakfast 7:30–9 A.M., lunch 12–1:30 P.M., dinner 6–6:45 P.M. and 8–8:45 P.M.) offers a fine dining experience in an original log cabin. Reservations are required for all three meals and should be booked well in advance. Men are required to wear dinner jackets. The food is incredibly creative and incorporates local flavors. Huckleberry pancakes and roasted buffalo hash appear on the breakfast menu ($22), and lunch (entrées $10–13) consists mostly of upscale sandwiches and salads. The main event at the restaurant is the prix fixe five-course dinner ($73 pp not including alcohol or gratuity). There are options for each course that rotate every night. Depending on the day, you may be dining on rosemary gnocchi, Fat Tire–Gruyère soup, coq au vin or seared ahi tuna, shaved muskmelon salad, and grilled elk chop—no matter what's on the menu, it is sure to be a memorable meal.

Moran to Moose

The stretch of road between Moran Junction and the southernmost entrance to the park at Moose is scenic and full of interesting sights, both natural and artificial. From the historic crossing at **Menors Ferry** to the architecturally inspired **Craig Thomas Discovery and Visitor Center** and the wildlife rich **Antelope Flats,** this part of the park is heavily traveled for a good reason: There is so much to see.

SIGHTS
Cunningham Cabin
A relic of hardscrabble ranching days before the turn of the 20th century—and the site of the murder of two alleged horse thieves—Cunningham Cabin is six miles south of Moran Junction. The cabin reflects the common building materials and style of 1890, the year it was built. Known as a "dogtrot," it consists of two small structures connected by a breezeway and topped with a dirt roof.

Pierce Cunningham built a modest home for his family on Flat Creek in the late 1880s or early 1890s. A neighbor introduced Cunningham to two strangers, George Spenser and Mike Burnett, asking if they could buy hay for their horses. Cunningham sold them 15 tons of hay and arranged for them to winter in his cabin near Spread Creek. The rumor among the locals was that the men were in fact horse thieves.

In April 1893, Spenser and Burnett were the target of a posse of vigilantes from Montana. Sixteen men on horseback rode up to the little cabin on Spread Creek under cover of darkness and waited in silence for dawn. Spenser and Burnett's dog barked in the early morning hours, perhaps warning the men of the ambush that awaited them. Spenser dressed, armed himself, and walked out the front door. When the posse called for him to hold his hands up, Spenser fired his revolver in the direction of the speaker

© OSAMU HOSI-INO/WYOMING TRAVEL & TOURISM

Mormon Row

GRAND TETON NATIONAL PARK

and was immediately shot. He propped himself up on one elbow and continued to fire until he collapsed. Burnett came out next, armed with a revolver and a rifle. The men shot at him, but Burnett managed to shoot the hat off one of the posse members and "crease his scalp" with the bullet. Burnett was shot and killed moments later. The two men were buried in unmarked graves a few hundred yards southeast of the cabin on the south side of a draw. Some of their bones were eventually excavated by badgers.

Mormon Row and Antelope Flats

Interesting both for its wildlife and human history, the area around Mormon Row is instantly recognizable from some of the region's most popular postcards, featuring a weathered barn leaning into the stunning mountainous backdrop. Listed on the National Register of Historic Places, Mormon Row is a collection of six fairly dilapidated homesteads that can be explored on a self-guided tour (brochures are available near the pink house). The area was settled around the turn of the 20th century by a handful of Mormon families who built homes, a church, a school, and a swimming hole. The settlement was abandoned and left to the elements when the Rockefellers bought up much of the land and transferred it to the National Park Service. In the 1990s the historical and cultural value of the site was recognized, and steps were taken to preserve the structures.

The Antelope Flats area—excellent for walking or biking on a flat, unpaved road—offers prime habitat for antelope, bison, moose, coyotes, ground squirrels, northern harriers, kestrels, and sage grouse. In the winter, the first mile of Antelope Flats Road is plowed to a small parking area, giving visitors easy snowshoe or cross-country ski access to Moulton Ranch, one of the homesteads on Mormon Row.

【 Craig Thomas Discovery and Visitor Center

Opened in 2007, the Craig Thomas Discovery and Visitor Center (307/739-3399, 8 A.M.–7 P.M. daily June 1–Labor Day, 8 A.M.–5 P.M. daily Labor Day–Oct. 31,

9 A.M.–5 P.M. daily Nov. 1–May 30, reduced hours on Thanksgiving and Christmas Eve, closed Christmas Day), among other things, is an architectural masterpiece, mimicking the nearby natural masterpiece of the Teton Range. The $21.6 million structure has more than 22,000 square feet and is being used as a model for other national parks in that more than half of the funds used to build the center were donated by private individuals. The state-of-the-art facility, including video rivers that flow beneath your feet, places emphasis on the connection between humans and the natural world. Fantastic interpretive displays include a large relief model of the park that uses technology to show glacier movement and animal migration; there is also a photographic tribute to mountaineering in the region.

Menors Ferry Historic District

In 1894, William D. Menor came to Jackson Hole and built a homestead along the Snake River. He built a ferryboat on cables to carry settlers and hopeful miners across the river, which was otherwise impassable during spring runoff. Entire wagon teams crossed on the ferry, paying $0.50 per trip, while a horse and rider paid $0.25. In 1918, Menor sold the ferry operation to Maud Noble, who doubled the fares ($1 for automobiles with local plates, $2 for out-of-staters) in the hope of attracting more tourists to the region. When a bridge was built in 1927, the ferry became obsolete, and in 1929 Noble sold her land to the Snake River Land Company, the same year the park was created. She had already donated a portion of her land for the construction of the Chapel of the Transfiguration.

Today, a replica of the ferryboat and cables has been built on-site, and visitors can meander down the 0.5-mile self-guided **Menor's Ferry Trail** past Menor's cabin, which doubles as a country store (9 A.M.–4:30 P.M. daily late May–early Sept.).

Chapel of the Transfiguration

Built in 1925 to serve the ranchers and dudes in the Teton Valley, the Chapel of the Transfiguration (307/733-2603, services 8 A.M.

In the shadow of the Tetons, services are still held in the Chapel of the Transfiguration.

© WYOMING TRAVEL & TOURISM

and 10 A.M. Sun. late May–early Sept.) is a humble log cabin structure with the most spectacular mountain view framed in the window behind the altar. An Episcopal church, operated by St. John's in Jackson, it was built on land donated by Maud Noble and is a favorite spot for summer weddings.

◖ Laurance S. Rockefeller Preserve

The former JY Ranch and longtime summer home of the Rockefeller family, the Laurance S. Rockefeller Preserve (307/739-3654, trails open year-round, visitors center 8 A.M.–6 P.M. daily late May–Labor Day, 8 A.M.–5 P.M. Labor Day–late Sept.) offers eight miles of trails through forest, wetlands, and meadows on reclaimed property along Phelps Lake and Lake Creek. The preserve is 1,106 acres and was donated to the Park Service in 2007 by the Rockefeller family with the mission of giving people access to the natural world that Laurance Rockefeller found so inspiring and sustaining. Rockefeller himself committed to

returning the old JY to its most natural state by removing more than 30 structures and roads.

The Laurance S. Rockefeller Preserve Center is the first platinum-level LEED-certified building constructed in a national park and was built to give visitors a sensory experience of the natural elements found on the preserve. A poem by nature writer Terry Tempest Williams features prominently, and visitors can learn about the preserve and Rockefeller's beliefs about land stewardship in a comfortable and environmentally sustainable building. Several ranger programs, including sunrise hikes and children's programs, are available from the center daily throughout summer.

Murie Center

The one-time STS Ranch and former residence of wilderness champions Olaus and Mardy Murie, the Murie Center (4 Moose Wilson Rd., 307/739-2246, www.muriecenter.org) is dedicated to connecting people and wilderness. It is where the Wilderness Act was authored in the 1950s and early 1960s. The ranch itself

GRAND TETON NATIONAL PARK

is a National Historic Landmark and the site of ongoing conservation seminars and educational workshops. On-site accommodations are available to participants, and the entire facility can be rented for conservation education programs. There is an excellent library and bookstore on-site, and rangers host naturalist programs throughout the summer.

RECREATION
Hiking and Biking

Like most of Grand Teton National Park, there is an abundance of excellent hiking terrain to be discovered between Moran and Moose, and many easy strolls can combine with historic sites like the Cunningham Cabin, Menor's Ferry, and Mormon Row.

For more substantial hikes, try the **Taggart Lake Trailhead,** three miles northwest of Moose. The trail is 3.2 miles round-trip with 410 feet of elevation gain. If that isn't enough, continue on to Bradley Lake (4 miles round-trip with a 650-foot elevation gain) or Beaver Creek. Three miles south of Moose is the **Death Canyon Trailhead,** not nearly as ominous as the name would imply. The road is not suitable for trailers or RVs and is very rough for vehicles in general. However, the hike to **Phelps Lake** is perfect for families, only 1.8 miles round-trip with 420 feet of elevation gain. Black bears, moose, and marmots frequent the area, so be sure to have your bear spray at the ready.

There are plenty of biking opportunities on the paved and unpaved roads in the region, including **Antelope Flats Road** all the way to Kelly, the **Shadow Mountain Road,** and the **Moose-Wilson Road** linking Moose and the Laurance S. Rockefeller Preserve. The **multiuse pathway** from Moose or the Taggart Lake Trailhead to South Jenny Lake is popular for good reason.

ACCOMMODATIONS

◖ The Triangle X Ranch (307/733-2183, www.trianglex.com, late May–Oct. 31 and Dec. 26–mid-Mar., $1,575–2,225 pp per week summer, $125 pp per night winter) has been in operation for more than 80 years. It is the only authorized guest ranch concessionaire in the entire National Parks System and sits right inside Grand Teton National Park. Not surprisingly, the setting is gorgeous, and you can see the entire mountain range from this secluded getaway.

The lodge, which is the center of activity and meals, is the original main house used by two generations of the Turner family. Their 20 log cabins are also originals that once housed families in different parts of Jackson Hole. The cabins come with 1–3 bedrooms; all have modern amenities and are decorated with cozy Western charm.

The ranch is also the only concession in the park that is open during winter. During the peak season (mid-June–Aug.), the minimum stay is one week (Sun.–Sun.). During the spring and fall seasons, they require a minimum four-night stay but offer reduced rates; and during the winter season visitors can book per night. All meals, served family-style in the main lodge, are included in the price, as are the endless horseback rides, cookouts, square-dancing, and special programs for children. Winter activities include cross-country skiing, snowshoeing, and snowmobiling. Regardless of the season, there are always great opportunities for wildlife viewing.

Dornan's Spur Ranch (307/733-2522, www.dornans.com, year-round) sits idyllically on the Snake River in the middle of a wildflower meadow. There are stunning views in all directions, and the location affords great access to fly-fishing and floating adventures. This is a small, family-owned business that provides quality service with personal touches. There are eight one-bedroom cabins ($175–205 summer, $125–150 in other seasons) and four two-bedroom duplexes ($250 summer, $175 in other seasons) on the premises. The cabins were built in the early 1990s and are bright, airy, and furnished with lodgepole pine furniture. They each have queen beds, kitchens, living-dining areas, and covered porches with a barbecue grill nearby. Also on these 10 acres of property are a grocery and camping store, two restaurants, and an award-winning wine shop. Visitors can rent mountain bikes, canoes, and kayaks during the summer and cross-country

Dornan's has it all, from lodging and food to activities and rentals.

skis and snowshoes in the winter to make the most of the surrounding area.

CAMPING

Gros Ventre (800/628-9988, May 8–Oct. 9, $19) is the largest campground in the park, situated at the southeast end just a few miles from Kelly. The 350 individual sites and five large group sites rarely fill completely. There is a grocery store and service station within two miles of the campground. Each site has a fire pit and picnic table and can accommodate two tents, two vehicles, and up to six people.

FOOD

You'll find most of your food options in this area at Dornan's ranch. **Dornan's Chuck Wagon** (307/733-2415, ext. 203, mid-June–late Sept.) serves up hearty "cowboy cuisine" during the summer. They use beef from their own butcher shop and cook using Dutch ovens heated over wood fires. Breakfast (7–11 A.M. daily, $5–9) offers an amazing order of hot sourdough pancakes (they'll bring you as many as you want), and dinner (5–9 P.M.

Mon.–Thurs., $16–21) is an all-you-can-eat affair. Lunch (noon–3 P.M. daily, $6–12) is served daily as well. The restaurant is used for private events on weekend evenings.

Dornan's Pizza and Pasta Company (307/733-2415, ext. 204, 11:30 A.M.–7 P.M., hours may vary, $4–24) offers a large variety of hot sandwiches, gourmet pizzas, rich pasta dishes, and calzones. If you are looking to pick up something to eat on your hike, stop at **Dornan's Trading Post** (307/733-2415, ext. 201, year-round) for everything from freeze-dried meals and cold drinks to gourmet groceries and any camping equipment you might need. The deli is open May–September and is a good option for a quick meal. If you have the time, don't miss a visit to **Dornan's Wine Shoppe** (307/733-2415, ext. 202, 10 A.M.–6 P.M. daily year-round, longer hours in summer). It is an absolute find for wine connoisseurs and novices alike. They have an award-wining selection of around 1,600 varieties of wines and 150 types of cheese. *Food & Wine* magazine named it one of the 50 most amazing wine experiences in the country.

GRAND TETON NATIONAL PARK

© OSAMU HOSHINO/WYOMING TRAVEL & TOURISM

Information and Services

Be sure to visit the website of the **National Park Service** (www.nps.gov/grte) to help plan your trip to Grand Teton. In the section titled Plan Your Visit, you'll find answers to most of your pressing questions. You can also read the most recent park news releases at www.gtnpnews.blogspot.com. When you enter the park, you will receive a copy of the park newspaper, *Teewinot,* which has a lot of useful information about park facilities, hours of operation, and programs and specific activities offered daily or weekly. If you need additional information before you go, you can call the **visitors information line** (307/739-3300) and **camping information line** (307/739-3603).

Single-entry entrance fees are $25 per vehicle, $12 pp for hikers or bicyclists, and $20 per motorcycle for seven days in both Grand Teton National Park and Yellowstone National Park.

The main concessionaire in the park is the **Grand Teton Lodging Company** (800/628-9988, www.gtlc.com), which operates lodging, restaurants, tours, and activities. Their website can also be a great aid in planning your visit. The Grand Teton Lodge Company's mission is to preserve, protect, and inspire, and to do so in part by following sustainable business practices. They are responsible for the lodging, restaurants, tours, and activities at Jackson Lake Lodge, Jenny Lake Lodge, Colter Bay Village, and the Jenny Lake and Gros Ventre campgrounds. In their restaurants they use free-range, naturally raised meat and dairy, organic coffee, and produce, and they support sustainable farming practices.

A great educational opportunity is provided by the **Teton Science Schools** (307/733-1313, www.tetonscience.org), based in Jackson. They are committed to creating a deeper appreciation and understanding of the wilderness and natural ecosystems found in the Greater Yellowstone area. Their experts provide classes and programs to engage every type of learner from small children to adults. The courses focus on everything from ecology and geology

to unique plant and animal life. Even if you only plan to be in the park for a day or two, visit their website to see what is being offered. Regular programs can include hikes, campfires, canoe tours, and wildlife viewing. The school also offers renowned **wildlife expeditions** (307/733-2623, www.wildlifeexpeditions.org). These can be half-day, full-day, or multiple-day guided tours with professional wildlife biologists, who provide you with an up-close and unique opportunity to experience the natural wonders of the park.

There are three main visitors centers in the park. The impressive **Craig Thomas Discovery and Visitor Center** (307/739-3399, 8 A.M.–7 P.M. daily June 1–Labor Day, 8 A.M.–5 P.M. daily Labor Day–Oct. 31, 9 A.M.–5 P.M. daily Nov. 1–May 30, reduced hours on Thanksgiving and Christmas Eve, closed Christmas Day) is located 0.5 miles west of Moose Junction and serves as the park's headquarters. The **Jenny Lake Visitors Center** (307/739-3392, 8 A.M.–7 P.M. daily June 1–early Sept., 8 A.M.–5 P.M. last three weeks of Sept.), is eight miles north of Moose Junction on Teton Park Road. West of Colter Bay Junction 0.5 miles is the **Colter Bay Visitors Center and Indian Arts Museum** (307/739-3594, 8 A.M.–7 P.M. daily early June–Labor Day, 8 A.M.–5 P.M. daily Labor Day–early Oct.). Close to the northern entrance of the park, there is an **information station** at Flagg Ranch (307/543-2372, 8 A.M.–3 P.M. daily early June–early Sept.).

With more than 230 miles of maintained trails in the park, backpacking and backcountry camping provide a unique way to explore the area. Permits are required and can be obtained for free at the Craig Thomas Visitor Center, the Colter Bay Visitors Center, or the Jenny Lake Ranger Station. Roughly one-third of backcountry campsites in heavily used areas can be reserved in advance January 1–May 15. Reservations cost $25. All campers are required to use bear-proof canisters below 10,000 feet and at sites without bear boxes. Free canisters are provided when registering for a permit.

For medical emergencies within the park dial 911. **St. John's Medical Center** (625 E. Broadway, Jackson, 307/733-3636) is open year-round, and the **Grand Teton Medical Clinic** (307/543-2514, May–Oct.) is located in the Jackson Lake Lodge.

Getting There and Around

Grand Teton National Park is immediately south of Yellowstone and 175 miles southwest of Cody. If you are driving from Yellowstone, take U.S. 89 south, which will lead you directly into the park. If you are coming from Idaho Falls, from I-15 take U.S. 26 east to Idaho Highway 31 east, continuing to Highway 33 east. This will take you through the scenic Teton Pass, where it becomes Wyoming Highway 22. Continue until you reach U.S. 89, taking it north into the park. An alternate route, flatter but slightly longer, is to take U.S. 26 until it hits U.S. 89 and head north.

If you are driving through the park, don't forget to keep an eye on your fuel gauge. The only gas station open year-round is at **Dornan's** (gas pumps available 24 hours if paying with a credit card) in Moose. Other gas stations are open May–October and are at Signal Mountain, Jackson Lodge, and Colter Bay.

Jackson Hole Airport (1250 E. Airport Rd., Jackson, 307/733-7682, www.jacksonholeairport.com) is only nine miles from the south entrance to the park and is served by American, Delta, SkyWest, United, and United Express. There are daily flights from Salt Lake City and Denver.

The airport has on-site car rentals from **National, Avis, Alamo,** and **Hertz. Dollar** and **Thrifty** are available off-site.

Alltrans/Gray Line Buses (307/733-3135 or 800/443-6133, jacksonholealltrans.com) offer shuttles to and tours of Grand Teton National Park from Jackson. The **Grand Teton Lodging Company** (800/628-9988, www.gtlc.com) also offer four-hour tours of the park departing from Jackson Lake Lodge during summer.

JACKSON HOLE, CODY, AND THE WIND RIVERS

Northwest Wyoming swings dramatically from stunning vistas and a sublime outdoor culture to the arts scene and high style of Jackson and Cody. Some of the state's most exquisite lodgings and legendary ranches can be found in this breathtakingly beautiful corner of Wyoming. The area is jam-packed with obvious destinations such as world-class museums—Cody's Buffalo Bill Historical Center and Jackson's National Wildlife Art Museum are among the best—as well as landmarks like Sinks Canyon near Lander, Hot Springs State Park near Thermopolis, the Wind River Range, and a string of scenic drives. The region provides a marvelous launching point into both Grand Teton and Yellowstone National Parks. Naturally, opportunities to explore the great outdoors here are abundant and include rafting, fishing, skiing, and hiking.

While bigger towns like Jackson and Cody are natural attractions in themselves, other towns in the region, such as Pinedale, Thermopolis, and tiny Ten Sleep, offer an authentic Wyoming experience with great museums, hot springs, historical monuments, and hole-in-the-wall cafés. Though towns like Lander and Powell lack the glitz and pomp of Jackson and Cody, they possess so much of what defines the state—rugged beauty, open space, rich history, and unrivaled wilderness access. In Wyoming, the journey from one town to the next is often the destination itself, and is by far the best way to appreciate this sparsely populated state.

© WYOMING TRAVEL & TOURISM

HIGHLIGHTS

◖ Jackson Hole Town Square: Surrounded by impossibly cool archways constructed entirely out of found elk antlers, this is the heart of the community and the best place for shoppers, art lovers, and diners to gather (page 312).

◖ National Museum of Wildlife Art: An architectural wonder that seems to grow out of the hillside, this museum's real genius is their collection, dedicated to all things wild, that spans from George Catlin's bison to Picasso's sketches to incredible works by Georgia O'Keeffe, Charlie Russell, and some marvelous contemporary artists (page 314).

◖ National Elk Refuge: Most magical in winter under a blanket of snow, the National Elk Refuge is home to more than 5,000 of these nobly beautiful creatures, and visitors can tour the area by horse-drawn sleigh (page 314).

◖ Rafting on the Snake River: With both white-water and more scenic options, the Snake winds through the valley, giving floaters unparalleled access to the area's most stunning views (page 319).

◖ Sinks Canyon State Park: This natural wonder occurs where the middle fork of the Popo Agie River "sinks" into a cave and then emerges again half a mile away in a great spring. Bighorn sheep and other wildlife here make for splendid scenery (page 331).

◖ Hot Springs State Park: Like a mini Mammoth Hot Springs, this park has fabulous limestone terraces as well as public baths in the therapeutic waters (page 337).

◖ Buffalo Bill Historical Center: Arguably the best in the West, the center is home to five remarkable museums that cap-

ture the art, natural history, Native American cultures, firearms, and the legends of the Old West. If you can visit only one museum in the West, this should be it (page 342).

◖ Chief Joseph Scenic Highway: This is the Wyoming you've dreamed about: high mountain plateaus speckled with wildflowers, cascading rivers and narrow canyons, all of it teeming with far more four-legged creatures than two. This really is what you call a scenic drive (page 346).

LOOK FOR ◖ TO FIND RECOMMENDED SIGHTS, ACTIVITIES, DINING, AND LODGING.

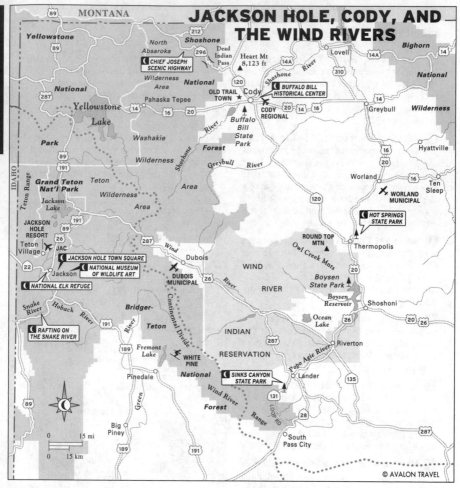

PLANNING YOUR TIME

Jackson Hole and Cody are obvious destinations, with easy air access; each could easily occupy visitors for 2–3 full days, and both are excellent launching pads for day trips into Yellowstone and Grand Teton National Parks. Both have their own distinctive cultures that include art and entertainment, the great outdoors, and elegant accommodations and eateries. The dude ranches outside both Jackson and Cody offer tremendous opportunities to experience the state's vast open spaces in close proximity to the hustle and bustle of town. For many people, this is the ideal way to spend a week enjoying the best of Wyoming's offerings.

The charm of Jackson is that it is pretty much anything you want it to be. Boutique shopping? Check. Gallery strolls? Check. Kitschy bars with saddle-topped stools? Check. Gourmet dining? Hard-core outdoor pursuits? Quiet afternoons in the museum? Check. Jackson is a great destination because it is geared to visitors who want to be entertained, pampered, challenged, and wined and dined. A few hours in the **National Museum of Wildlife Art** is time well spent. And you will want to allow an afternoon to stroll around town, browsing the shops and galleries—but don't let Jackson's shopping sirens lure you away from the majestic wilderness in every direction. In winter, try skiing at **Snow King**, right in town, or **Jackson Hole Mountain Resort** in nearby Teton Village. In summer there are trails to hike and dirt roads to bike, and two of the world's most incredible national parks are just up the road. Make sure to book a raft trip on the Snake River, and consider a wagon or sleigh ride on the sprawling **National Elk Refuge.**

Decidedly less glitzy than Jackson and more for the working cowboy than the urban variety (except during Rendezvous Royale), Cody is a rugged Western town with a rich history and just enough refinement to appeal to sophisticated travelers. The **Buffalo Bill Historical Center** is far and away the heart of Cody and should not be missed. A quick tour at a breakneck pace could probably be accomplished in two hours, but history buffs and Western art lovers could spend several days in the museum and not see the same exhibit twice. Cody's **nightly rodeos** in summer are a treat for the entire family, and a trip to Buffalo Bill's town would not be complete without a visit to the beautiful old hotel he built and named for his daughter, **The Irma Hotel.** The restaurant and saloon are open to nonguests, and if you go in the evening, be sure to see the old **Cody gunslingers** hash it out right outside the hotel nightly at 6 P.M.

While disparate in philosophy, perhaps, the energy boomtown of Pinedale and the outdoor mecca of Lander both offer excellent access to the spectacular Wind River Mountains. The region is absolutely worth exploring as a destination for outdoor and nature lovers, and as a beautiful setting for travelers en route from one place to the next.

HISTORY

While Wyoming had long been home to such Native American groups as the Sioux, Crow, Cheyenne, Arapaho, Shoshone, Gros Ventre,

Bannock, and Ute, a party of Frenchmen, traveling and trapping in the northwestern corner of the state as early as 1743, are thought to be the first Europeans in the area. The oldest dated carving in the state is on a rock outside Pinedale and bears the initials M. A. and the year 1791. Perhaps the most influential visitor in encouraging other trappers and mountain men to visit the region was John Colter, a member of the Lewis and Clark Expedition who plied his skills as a trapper in the vicinity of what is now Jackson Hole in 1807–1808. His exploits and subsequent stories opened the area to an influx of mountain men, trappers, and traders, and by 1825 men like Jedediah Smith, David Jackson, and Bill Sublette had made names for themselves as fearless explorers and shrewd at business.

By 1840, the demand for beaver pelts had bottomed out, leaving little incentive for mountain men in the region. The population somewhat temporary swelled with pioneers headed west on the Oregon Trail, including the Applegate Wagon Train, the largest ever assembled, which brought more than 875 people and 5,000 animals through the state in 1843. Conflicts with Native Americans were inevitable as white settlers encroached on traditional hunting grounds and, more importantly, nearly wiped out the bison altogether. There were great battles that always ended tragically, most often for the Native Americans, and a series of unfair treaties that reduced the size of their lands until there was virtually none left. Today Wyoming is home to two recognized tribes—the Shoshone and Arapaho—that share the Wind River Reservation.

By the 1880s, cattle ranching had taken hold across much of the state, and sheep ranchers moved in just over a decade later. Both Jackson and Cody were settled much later, closer to the turn of the 20th century, because of the harsh snowy winters in Jackson and the desertlike conditions around Cody. What irrigation did for Cody in terms of increasing the population, the creation of Grand Teton National Park did for Jackson in 1929 by attracting tourists and jumpstarting dude ranching in the area.

Wyoming's biggest boom, however, came in

the form of energy—oil, gas, and coal, the production of which dominates the state's economy. Oil was discovered outside Cody in 1904. The largest coal deposits in the country are being mined in the Powder River Basin, and much of the western portion of the state produces natural gas. After energy, the state's second-largest source of income is tourism, and among Jackson, Cody, and the national parks, the northwestern corner of the state attracts visitors in great numbers.

Wyoming has a couple of surprising historical events as well. The state's motto—Equal Rights—attests to the fact that Wyoming was the first territory to grant voting rights to women, in 1869, more than 20 years before its statehood was established. It was also the first state to elect a woman as governor, Nellie Tayloe Ross, who served 1923–1925.

A darker time in Wyoming's history includes the creation of the Heart Mountain Relocation Camp, located between Powell and Cody, where more than 10,000 Japanese Americans were held during World War II. Amid tremendous fear and racism across the country, politicians opposed the camp but citizens welcomed it, seeing it as a relief to 15 years of economic recession. With 2,000 laborers needed to build the camp and then 10,000 inmates who could work in the area, the Cody and Powell economies rebounded virtually overnight. Detainees arrived in August 1942, and the last ones left when the camp closed in November 1945. White homesteaders and farmers moved into the area immediately, taking advantage of the impressive irrigation system the inmates had built.

Jackson Hole

Visitors love Jackson (population 8,647, elevation 5,672 feet) because it encompasses the best of the West in a charming town with a spectacular setting. Western indeed, Jackson boasts a classic boardwalk around town, saloons with swinging doors and saddles for bar stools, and architecture built on elk antlers. At the same time, Jackson is clearly mountain chic, with a number of high-end boutiques and art galleries, gourmet dining, and ritzy accommodations.

The valley itself, known as Jackson Hole because it is entirely surrounded by mountains, is 48 miles long and 6–8 miles wide. With the Tetons as the most significant landmark, Jackson Hole gives rise to the headwaters of the Snake River, fed abundantly by numerous mountain streams. Because of its remarkable setting, Jackson Hole is a natural playground with offerings for just about anyone. In winter, outdoor enthusiasts can ski downhill at two well-known ski areas, Snow King and Jackson Hole Mountain Resort, or go the cross-country route just about anywhere, including nearby Grand Teton National Park. For those less interested in working up a sweat, a sleigh ride in

the National Elk Refuge is a memorable experience. When the snow melts, there is no end to the amount of adventurous options this valley offers, with fly fishing and wildlife watching among the less exhausting. From hiking and mountain biking to rafting and rock climbing, Jacksonians do it all.

SIGHTS
◖ Town Square
Almost European in its layout with a central square, Jackson's Town Square is uniquely distinguished by four dramatic archways constructed in 1932 entirely from naturally shed and sun-bleached elk antlers. It is the focal point of town and a good meeting spot, with shady trees and the occasional musician. In the summer, late May–early September, Town Square is the site of the free **Jackson Hole Shootout,** a spirited reenactment of frontier justice, that plays for crowds nightly at 6 P.M. In winter, the arches are illuminated by strings of lights, creating a magical setting.

Within easy walking distance of the square are more than 70 eateries—from

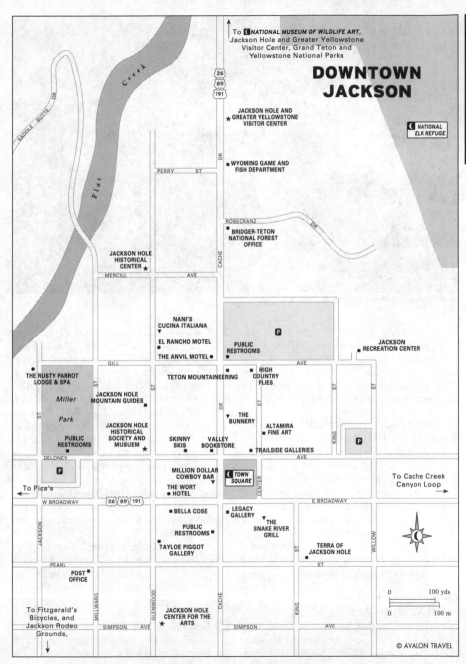

To **(** *NATIONAL MUSEUM OF WILDLIFE ART*,
Jackson Hole and Greater Yellowstone
Visitor Center, Grand Teton and
Yellowstone National Parks

DOWNTOWN
JACKSON

26
89
191

JACKSON HOLE AND
★ GREATER YELLOWSTONE
VISITOR CENTER

(*NATIONAL
ELK REFUGE*

PERRY   ST

DR

■ WYOMING GAME AND
FISH DEPARTMENT

ROSECRANZ

DR

CACHE

■ BRIDGER-TETON
NATIONAL FOREST
OFFICE

JACKSON HOLE
HISTORICAL
CENTER ★

MERCILL   AVE

NANI'S
CUCINA ITALIANA
▼
● EL RANCHO MOTEL

● THE ANVIL MOTEL ●

P

PUBLIC
RESTROOMS

JACKSON
■ RECREATION CENTER

● THE RUSTY PARROT
LODGE & SPA

GILL

AVE

TETON MOUNTAINEERING

■
■ HIGH
COUNTRY
FLIES

ST

ST

ST

Miller

JACKSON HOLE
MOUNTAIN GUIDES ■

Park

PUBLIC
RESTROOMS

JACKSON HOLE
HISTORICAL
SOCIETY AND
MUSUEM ★

SKINNY
SKIS ■

VALLEY
BOOKSTORE ■

DR

▼ THE
BUNNERY

ALTAMIRA
■ FINE ART

■ TRAILSIDE GALLERIES

KING

P

DELONEY   AVE

P

To Pica's

MILLION DOLLAR
COWBOY BAR
▼
THE WORT
● HOTEL

(TOWN
SQUARE

CENTER

To Cache Creek
Canyon Loop

W BROADWAY   26 89 191

E BROADWAY

JACKSON

■ BELLA COSE

PUBLIC
RESTROOMS ■

■
TAYLOE PIGGOT
GALLERY

■ LEGACY
GALLERY
▼ THE
SNAKE RIVER
GRILL

ST

TERRA OF
JACKSON HOLE

WILLOW

PEARL

ST

POST ■
OFFICE

MILLWARD

GLENWOOD

CACHE

KING

0   100 yds

0   100 m

To Fitzgerald's
Bicycles, and
Jackson Rodeo
Grounds,

JACKSON HOLE
CENTER FOR THE
★ ARTS

SIMPSON   AVE

SIMPSON   AVE

© AVALON TRAVEL

Traditional transportation is available in the Town Square.

mouthwatering pizza joints with ski-bum prices to the very tony—and a number of fine art galleries and shops that sell everything from high-end furs to T-shirts and knickknacks. There are also plentiful espresso and ice cream shops for those in need of instant energy.

Jackson Hole Historical Society and Museum

Just off Town Square, the Jackson Hole Historical Society and Museum (105 N. Glenwood St., 307/733-9605, www.jackson-holehistory.org, 10 A.M.–6 P.M. Mon.–Sat., noon–5 P.M. Sun. Memorial Day–mid-Sept., $3 adults, $6 families, $1 students, $2 seniors) is full of interesting historical photos of the region, Indian artifacts, fur trade–era tools, and firearms. The historical society offers free walking tours of Jackson in summer.

(National Museum of Wildlife Art

Just three miles north of Town Square overlooking the National Elk Refuge, the National Museum of Wildlife Art (2820 Rungius Rd., 800/313-

9553, www.wildlifeart.org, 9 A.M.–5 P.M. daily summer, 9 A.M.–5 P.M. Mon.–Sat., 11 A.M.–5 P.M. Sun. winter, $12 adults, $10 over age 60, $6 ages 5–18) is an absolute find. In existence in various forms since 1984, the museum's 14 galleries represent the lifetime study and collection of wildlife art by Bill and Joffa Kerr. There are more than 5,000 objects in the permanent collection, primarily paintings and sculpture by artists that range from early Native American artists to masters both past and present, including Pablo Picasso, Carl Rungius, John James Audubon, Robert Bateman, and Kent Ullberg. Audio guides are included with paid admission, and coupons for discounts on admission are offered on the museum's website.

The museum itself is a work of art: Inspired by the ruins of a Scottish castle, the red Arizona sandstone building emerges from the hillside like a natural outcropping of rock and often reminds visitors of Anasazi ruins.

(National Elk Refuge

During the winter months, more than 7,000 elk descend from their mountain habitat to the

THE ELK CONUNDRUM

Established in 1912, the National Elk Refuge was the first Wyoming state-run feeding ground for elk. In the 1930s and 1940s, more feeding grounds were created to help the animals survive the harsh winters and in part to keep them from entering areas reserved for cattle grazing. The thriving herd in Jackson ultimately was used to replenish other herds of elk and aid the reintroduction of elk throughout the country. However, as a result of the large number of elk concentrated in these feeding grounds, the animals are much more susceptible to contagious diseases – the biggest threat being brucellosis. Wyoming lost its federal brucellosis-free status in 2004 when cattle acquired the disease after coming into contact with elk from the refuge.

In 2005 the U.S. Department of Agriculture's Animal Plant Health Inspection Service reported that there was a 50-80 percent rate of infection among elk on feed lots, and though that number has dropped to 28-50 percent in more recent reports, it is still substantially higher than the 1-3 percent infec-

tion rate in wild free-ranging elk. Before the Elk Refuge was created, the elk from southern Yellowstone would migrate and spread past the area of the refuge into southwestern Wyoming. As the winter came to a close, they moved back to their summer habitat. Today it's believed that the elk that migrate to and from the refuge are carrying and spreading the brucellosis virus.

The question now is, what can be done? The argument has been made that the elk should return to their historic migration routes and original winter ranges rather than being concentrated in the feed lots. Today, however, many of those routes and ranges have been developed for housing, ranches, or other businesses. Furthermore, the idea of elk and cattle competing for food on the open range is worrisome to many Wyoming ranchers. So, although the scientific consensus is that it would be best for the elk to return to their natural migration patterns, the challenge is finding places in the wild that can sustain them throughout the year.

National Elk Refuge (307/733-9212, www. fws.gov/nationalelkrefuge) located in Jackson Hole. The large number of elk make the refuge a popular wintertime attraction (in the summer, birds and other wildlife populate the range). Horse-drawn sleigh rides through the refuge are offered mid-December–March. The elk are accustomed to the vehicles, allowing visitors to travel easily through the herds. Tickets can be purchased at the **Jackson Hole and Greater Yellowstone Visitor Center** (532 N. Cache Dr., $18 adults, $14 ages 5–12, free for children under 5), and a free shuttle will take visitors three miles north of Jackson to the departure point. Tours run 10 A.M.–4 P.M. daily and last about an hour. Be sure to dress warmly as the wind can be quite biting during the tour.

Jackson Hole and Greater Yellowstone Visitors Center

A terrific place to start any type of exploration of

the area, the Jackson Hole and Greater Yellowstone Visitors Center (532 N. Cache St., 307/733-9212, 8 A.M.–7 P.M. daily Memorial Day–Sept. 30, 9 A.M.–5 P.M. daily Oct. 1–Memorial Day) is a phenomenal resource with seven agencies represented, including the local Chamber of Commerce, the National Park Service, and the Bridger-Teton National Forest. Visitors can obtain annual park passes, hunting and fishing licenses as well as get trip planning assistance, directions, and maps aplenty. Talk about convenient one-stop shopping. The wildlife exhibits inside are matched by sweeping wildlife observation decks outside that overlook the National Elk Refuge. The real treasure here, though, is the staff, all of whom are friendly, knowledgeable, and more than willing to roll up their sleeves for whatever help you need. Short interpretive talks are offered throughout the season, and naturalists are often on-hand at the upper viewing deck with spotting scopes, binoculars, and field guides.

Teton Village

Twelve miles northwest of Jackson is Teton Village, an Alps-like enclave nestled around the state's largest and most popular ski hill. The area pulses with energy and activity as soon as the snow flies, and although it quiets down in the shoulder seasons, it is an enormously popular destination in summer as well. In addition to the abundant lodging, shopping, and dining options, the area is a hub for outdoor activities such as hot air ballooning, paragliding, horseback riding, and, of course, a myriad of mountain-oriented sports. There are also plenty of concerts and special events held year-round.

National Bighorn Sheep Interpretive Center

Set in Dubois, 85 miles east of Jackson on Highway 287/26, the National Bighorn Sheep Interpretive Center (907 W. Ramshorn. Dubois, 888/209-2795 or 307/455-3429, www. bighorn.org, summer Mon.–Sat. 9 A.M.–7 P.M., Sun. 9 A.M.–5 P.M.; winter Mon.–Sat. 9 A.M.–5 P.M., $2.50 adults, $0.75 children, $6 families) is dedicated to educating the public about these remarkable, majestic creatures and their habitats. Visitors are welcomed by a stunning bronze of a ram, and led inside to several hands-on exhibits, 16 mounts of wild sheep from around the world, and a great little gift shop with everything from T-shirts to children's toys and wares by local artists. From November–March, the center offers tours to the winter range of the Whiskey Mountain herd, providing an excellent opportunity to see the bighorn sheep in their natural, windswept habitat. Reservations for the 3–5-hour tours should be made at least 24 hours in advance by calling the center. The cost is $25 per person.

ENTERTAINMENT AND EVENTS

Among the most impressive facilities in the state is the relatively new **Jackson Hole Center for the Arts** (240 S. Glenwood St., 307/413-0458, www.jhcenterforthearts.org), a truly inspired art campus in the heart of downtown that offers educational programs and facilities along with professional theater, dance, and music as well as a remarkable space for major community events. Check out the schedule online—there is always something happening. Of particular note at the Center for the Arts is the **Off Square Theatre Company** (307/733-4900, www.offsquare.org), which produces excellent and wildly diverse shows ranging from classic American musicals (*Man of La Mancha*) and dramatic masterpieces (*Uncle Vanya*) to side-splitting comedies (*The Second City*) and even childhood favorites (*Peter Pan*). Regardless of the offerings, a night at the theater in Jackson is a night well spent.

Weekly events in Jackson during the summer season (Labor Day–Memorial Day) include the **Jackson Rodeo** (447 Snow King Ave., 307/733-7927, www.thejacksonholerodeo.com, 8 P.M. Wed. and Sat., $19 reserved seating, $14 general seating, discounts for families and kids, free for children under 5), a fun family event with bull riding, team roping, barrel racing, bareback broncs, and plenty of other action. Food and refreshments are sold at the chuckwagon.

For one of Jackson's favorite regular events, check out the **Town Square Shootout** (6 P.M. Mon.–Sat.) on the Town Square. It's free and a lot of fun for visitors.

An annual event built around the well-known Boy Scout Elk Antler Auction, where the boys sell the shed antlers they collect from the National Elk Refuge, **Elk Fest** (307/733-3316, www.elkfest.org) takes place the weekend before Memorial Day and includes plenty of food, community concerts, children's activities, and many opportunities to learn about elk.

Happening each year over Memorial Day weekend all around town is Jackson's long-running **Old West Days** (307/733-3316, www.jacksonholechamber.com), which features a horse-drawn parade, old-town entertainment, a rodeo, a mountain man rendezvous, and a host of other events that celebrate Jackson's rough-and-tumble origins.

Happening in late July–early August, the nearly weeklong **Teton County Fair** (Teton County Fairgrounds, 307/733-5289, www.

tetoncountyfair.com) includes family-friendly events like pig wrestling, a rodeo, a demolition derby, concerts, a carnival, and plenty of agricultural and animal exhibits.

The equivalent of Cody's Rendezvous Royale, Jackson's **Fall Arts Festival** (307/733-3316, www.jacksonholechamber.com) is a 10-day event in mid-September that unites the community and attracts a crowd of art lovers with a phenomenal range of art-related events, including the prestigious **Jackson Hole Art Auction** (www.jacksonholeartauction.com) and **Western Design Conference** (www.westerndesignconference.com), gallery walks, open-air art fairs, historic ranch tours, and culinary coups.

The **Grand Teton Music Festival** (McCollister Dr., Teton Village, 307/733-1128, www.gtmf.org, $20–50) takes place annually during July–August. It is held in the all-wooden Walk Festival Hall, which recently underwent a $4.85 million renovation to improve the intimate setting and provide top-notch acoustics. Known as one of the top music festivals in the country, it showcases an impressive list of musicians and singers. Past performers have included Sarah Chang, Itzhak Perlman, the New York Philharmonic, and the Mormon Tabernacle Choir. In addition to the summer festival, the organization hosts concerts during the winter. The festival celebrates its 50th anniversary in 2011.

One of the most renowned bluegrass festivals in the country takes place on the western slopes of the Grand Tetons in Targhee during mid-August. The **Grand Targhee Bluegrass Festival** (www.grandtarghee.com/summer/music-festivals/bluegrass-fest.php, day pass $59–69, all weekend pass $139, camping $30 pp) draws a large number of the best bluegrass musicians in the country, including Brother Mule, Danny Barnes, and Sarah Jarosz, along with a large number of fans. Held at the Grand Targhee Resort (800/827-4433), tent and RV camping is allowed in the national forest during the festival weekend. In addition to performances all day long, there is also plenty of food, arts, and crafts available.

Also taking place at the Targhee Resort, in mid-July the newer **Targhee Fest** (day pass $59–69, all weekend pass $139, camping $30 pp) is a lively three-day music festival with an eclectic mix of artists such as Shawn Colvin and David Lindley. Camping is also allowed in the national forest during this event.

The Jackson Hole Film Festival (www.jacksonholefilmfestival.org) is a biennial event dedicated to nature conservation held annually in late September–early October. The six-day festival attracts leaders in science, conservation, and media as numerous films are screened and related social events and activities are organized throughout the week. The festival is held at the Jackson Lake Lodge, except for the final event, which screens selected finalists at the Center for the Arts in downtown Jackson.

Winter Carnival (307/413-3662, www.jacksonholewintercarnival.com) gives residents and visitors alike one more reason to celebrate the snow. Happening over four days in late January, the carnival includes events like a Quick Draw, film screenings, a sled-dog race, a torchlight parade, and fireworks.

Another winter event everyone looks forward to is **The International Pedigree Stage Stop Dog Race** (307/734-1163, www.wyomingstagestop.org). It takes place from the last weekend in January through the first week of February. Begun in 1996, it is the largest U.S. dog-sled race outside Alaska. The race begins in Jackson and runs 500 miles to Park City, Utah. It is unusual in that the participants stop for the night in 10 different towns along the way, including Lander, Pinedale-Cora, Big Piney–Marbleton, Alpine, Kemmerer, Evanston, and Mountain View–Lyman. Each town along the route celebrates with different festivities as they greet and cheer on the racers.

SHOPPING

For those with time and money, shopping can practically be an athletic pursuit in Jackson, particularly in the streets and alleyways around **Town Square**. In the early 1990s, Jackson was populated with a number of outlet stores, but today most of those have been pushed out by more sophisticated boutiques. There are so many fascinating little shops to pop into, from gorgeous high-end art galleries to the few remaining tacky but fun T-Shirt and tchotchke shops.

For an independent bookstore, **Valley Bookstore** (125 N. Cache Dr., 307/733-4533, www.valleybookstore.com) is pretty great and has been providing local readers with fabulous books and stellar recommendations for nearly 50 years. The owners grew up in Jackson and have a superb local and regional section.

For top-of-the-line women's and children's clothes in a spacious, almost Zen-like setting, visit **Terra of Jackson Hole** (105 E. Broadway, 307/734-0067) which would not be out of place in Manhattan or San Francisco. Another glorious place filled with beautiful things is **Bella Cose** (48 E. Broadway, 888/733-3338, www. bellacose.com), which offers elegant home decor as well as kitchen and dining items; it clearly caters to the second-home crowd.

The art scene in Jackson is both rarefied and approachable, and it is an increasingly important part of both the community and the local economy. There are more than 30 galleries in town. Among the favorites are **Trailside Galleries** (105 Center St., 307/733-3186, www.trailsidegalleries.com) and **Legacy Gallery** (75 N. Cache St., 307/733-2353, www.legacygallery.com), both with classic examples of Western art in its traditional and contemporary forms. **Altamira Fine Art** (172 Center St., 307/739-4700, www.altamiraart. com) has a more loftlike urban feel and represents groundbreaking contemporary artists, including Rocky Hawkins, Duke Beardsley, John Felsing, Amy Ringholz, and John Nieto. The **Tayloe Piggot Gallery** (62 S. Glenwood St., 307/733-0555, www.jhmusegallery.com) is cutting-edge cool with both emerging and mid-career artists in a variety of media.

RECREATION
Fishing

Surrounded by abundant rivers and streams, including the Snake River and its myriad mountain tributaries, plus Grand Teton and Yellowstone parks, Jackson has become something of a fly-fishing mecca.

The best-known trout stream in the region is the Snake River, which winds more than 60 miles on lazy flats and then blasts through the Snake River Canyon, which offers more white-knuckle rafting than graceful casting. The Upper Snake, much of which is in Grand Teton National Park, is characterized by braided channels with cut banks and log jams, and the water holds native cutthroats. Drift boating is popular as a way to maximize the water covered (and scenery enjoyed), but there are ample opportunities to get out and wade-fish. The section of the river that goes through the canyon is almost exclusively fished by boat (self-bailers come in handy in the Class II and Class III rapids), and despite the action of the waves, the fish are more plentiful in the canyon, though not always easy to catch.

Jackson has no shortage of fly-fishing guides or fly shops. Among the best is a small outfit, **Teton Fly Fishing** (307/413-1215, www. tetonflyfishing.com) run by Nate Bennett, who loves teaching his clients about the art of fishing as much as he loves hooking a fish. He books only one trip daily so that the pace can be less breakneck and far more enjoyable. Bennett gets his clients on a variety of types of water and, like a good fish whisperer, somehow gets the fish to bite. An artist by training, Bennett ties all his own flies and loves to share. His full day trips ($450–500) on the Snake, Salt, and Green Rivers include all equipment, flies, transportation, streamside lunch, and full access to his unlimited knowledge and expertise.

A great resource for fishing are the friendly folks at **High Country Flies** (185 N. Center St., 307/733-7210 or 866/733-7210, www. highcountryflies.com, 8 A.M.–8 P.M. daily summer, 9 A.M.–6 P.M. Mon.–Sat., 10 A.M.–5 P.M. Sun. winter), which has been in business for nearly 40 years. The staff are experts on waters all over the region, and in addition to guiding services, the shop has a great selection of flies, equipment, and clothing.

◖ Rafting on the Snake River

One of the greatest attractions for summertime visitors to Jackson is rafting the Snake River. There are close to two dozen rafting companies to choose from in the area, and most are open mid-May–September. Below are a few options for those who are interested in experiencing the river, whether it be a tranquil day float through Grand Teton National Park or a white-water adventure a little farther south in the canyon. Most adult fares average $65 for an eight-mile trip. A popular option, available with all three companies listed below, is a trip that combines a float trip and white-water trip in the same day. These tend to be about $90 pp (less for children). If booking a combination trip, be sure to confirm whether there is a bus ride between the two trips or if it is continuous.

Barker-Ewing (800/448-4202, www.barker-ewing.com) is a family-operated business that has been running small trips for close to 50 years.

Dave Hansen Whitewater (800/458-7328, www.davehansenwhitewater.com) has been in the business since the late 1960s. Dave actually named two of the largest waves on the river, the Lunch Box and the Big Kahuana.

Another option with a variety of trips down the Snake River is **Mad River Boat Trips** (800/458-7328, www.mad-river.com).

For experienced floaters who want to tackle the Snake unguided, **Rent-a-Raft** (U.S. 89, Hoback Junction, 13 miles south of Jackson, 307/733-2728, www.rentaraft.net) offers 11-foot and 16-foot rafts, sit-on-top kayaks, and shuttle service from their headquarters.

Hiking and Mountain Biking

Although plenty of hikers choose to hit the phenomenal trails in Grand Teton and Yellowstone National Parks, with so many mountains in every direction around Jackson there is no shortage of amazing hikes outside the parks. Many of the trails outside the parks are open to mountain bikers as well.

One trail with immediate proximity to town that skirts the Gros Ventre Wilderness Area is the **Cache Creek Canyon Loop,** which is part of the Greater Snow King Trail Network. It is a popular trail for hikers, mountain bikers, and in winter, cross-country skiers. To get to the trailhead, drive east on Broadway to Redmond Street, across from the hospital; turn right and go 0.4 miles to Cache Creek Road. Turn left and continue just over one mile to the parking lot at road's end. Hikers can amble along both sides of the creek on this four-mile loop, gaining only 350 vertical feet. Connecting trails lead to Game Creek and Granite Falls, or back to Snow King in Jackson.

Ten miles west of town near Teton Pass is **Phillips Pass,** an incredible and somewhat strenuous day hike at the edge of the Tetons and the Jedediah Smith Wilderness Area. The trail is open to hikers and mountain bikers. To get to the trailhead, head west to Teton Pass on Highway 22. Two miles east of the summit is Phillips Canyon Road (Forest Rd. 30972). There is no parking at the trailhead, which is 0.5 miles down this road, so park safely across the highway in a small pullout or on Phillips Canyon Road close to the highway. The eight-mile out-and-back trail is spectacularly beautiful, particularly in late summer, and winds through flower-drenched meadows and forest to the alpine country above the tree line. As always in this part of the country, be prepared for significant weather changes and encounters with wild animals.

For excellent guided hiking in the Tetons and around the valley, contact **The Hole Hiking Experience** (307/690-4453 or 866/733-4453, www.holehike.com), which offers a wide variety of trips from half-day naturalist-guided trips geared to families to strenuous all-day hikes and even yoga-hiking combinations. For guided mountain bike trips for the whole family (including kids on Trail-a-Bikes and in trailers) or more extreme riders, contact **Teton Mountain Bike Tours** (800/733-0788, www.tetonmtbike.com) for their half-day, full-day, multiple-day, and specialty trip offerings.

For the best mountain-bike map of the region, highlighting more than two dozen rides in the area, look for *Adventure Cycling's Mountain Biking in the Jackson Hole Area,* available at local sporting goods stores. **Fitzgerald's Bicycles**

(245 W. Hansen St., 307/734-6886, www. fitzgeraldsbicycles.com, 10 A.M.–6 P.M. Mon.– Fri., 10 A.M.–5 P.M. Sat., 10 A.M.–3 P.M. Sun.) has all kinds of rental bikes and can point bikers in the direction of any kind of ride they seek.

Horseback Riding

Another popular way to experience the great outdoors in Jackson is on horseback. There are several options, including hourly rentals, half-day trail rides, or overnight pack trips, available from the many local outfitters in and around town. For half-day trail rides, expect to pay around $90 pp.

Located 35 miles south of Jackson, **Jackson Hole Outfitters** (307/654-7008, www.jacksonholeytrailrides.com) start their trail rides in the secluded Greys River camp and follow trails through the Bridger-Teton National Forest.

Spring Creek Ranch (307/733-8833 or 800/443-6139, www.springcreekranch.com) offers 1–4-hour rides along the East Gros Ventre Butte.

Mill Iron Ranch is located 10 miles south of Jackson and offers two-hour, four-hour, or full-day trips that can be combined with breakfast, lunch, or a steak dinner for an additional charge.

Golf

Golf is becoming increasingly popular in Jackson Hole, and there are a couple of world-class public courses. The **Jackson Hole Golf & Tennis Club** (5000 Spring Gulch Rd., 307/733-3111, www.jhgtc.com, $65–190) offers an award-winning 18-hole course designed by Robert Trent Jones II that recently underwent a $15 million renovation. The 18-hole course at **Teton Pines Country Club** (3450 N. Clubhouse Dr., 307/733-1005 or 800/238-2223, www.tetonpines.com, $57–90 depending on the season, higher rates for nonguests) in Teton Village was designed by Arnold Palmer and has been highly ranked by *Condé Nast Traveler,* among others.

Skiing

Jackson's reputation among the West's premier ski towns is not hard to explain. There are three developed downhill ski resorts, the closet one to town being right in town.

Snow King Resort (400 E. Snow King Ave., 800/522-KING—800/522-5464, www. snowking.com, all-day $42 adults, $32 juniors and seniors, $5 for children under 6, discounts for lodging guests) soars skyward just six blocks from Town Square, making Jackson a ski town in the most literal sense. The mountain was developed for skiing in 1939, making it the first in the Jackson area and one of the first in the country. The area boasts 1,571 feet of vertical drop over 400 acres with two double chairlifts, one triple lift, a surface tow, and the ever-popular **Snow Tubing Park.** The area is open for day and night skiing and offers an innovative two-hour lift ticket that can be used anytime during the day. Nonskiers can pay to ride the lift just to enjoy the breathtaking views of town and the valley from the summit. In the summer, the trails and lifts are open for hiking and mountain biking.

In nearby Teton Village, the ski area at **Jackson Hole Mountain Resort** (307/733-2292, www.jacksonhole.com, $55–91 adults, $40–60 seniors, $32–54 age 14 and under, prices rise as the season progresses) is in fact two mountains, Apres Vous and Rendezvous, which together offer skiers 2,500 skiable acres, a vertical drop of more than 4,000 feet, and open access to another 3,000-plus acres of backcountry terrain. There are 116 named trails on the map, of which a whopping 50 percent are geared to experts, 40 percent for intermediate skiers, and 10 percent for beginners. The ski hill averages 459 inches of snow annually. In Jackson, this is the mountain to ski and be seen.

The **aerial tram** (307/733-2292, single ride $20–25 adults, depending on the season, $16–20 age 65 and older, $15–19 ages 13–17, $10–12 ages 6–12, free for children under 6) known as Big Red takes hikers, bikers, paragliders, backcountry skiers, and lookie-loos up to the summit of Rendezvous Peak (4,139 feet in 9 minutes). The tram is generally open 9 A.M.–6 P.M. mid-June–early September, and

9 A.M.–5 P.M. daily late May–late September. At the top, a fabulous little waffle hut, **Corbet's Cabin,** makes you wish you had hiked the whole way.

Although you need to go to Idaho to get there, **Grand Targhee Resort** (300 E. Ski Hill Rd., 800/TARGHEE—800/827-4433, www.grandtarghee.com, prices vary each year) in Alta, Wyoming, is a destination in itself. The skiing in winter is out of this world, with huge dumps of powder and expansive terrain. The resort also offers Nordic skiing, tubing, guided snowcat tours, sleigh-ride dinners, snowmobile tours, and ice climbing. In summer, the mountain stays awake for hiking, mountain biking, horseback riding, and a couple of renowned musical events, including **Targhee Fest** and the **Grand Targhee Bluegrass Festival.**

For avid Nordic skiers, the blanket of snow transforms many favorite local hiking trails into first-rate ski trails. From hitting the groomers at local golf courses, including **Teton Pines** (3450 N. Clubhouse Dr., 307/733-1005 or 800/238-2223, www.tetonpines.com) to hoofing into the backcountry in Grand Teton National Park, there is terrain for everyone. The **Jackson Hole Nordic Center** (3395 Village Dr., 307/739-2629, www.jacksonhole.com) at Teton Village offers 11 miles of groomed trails for classic and skate skiers. Rentals are available on-site. In town, gear can be purchased or rented from **Skinny Skis** (65 W. Deloney Ave., 307/733-6094 or 888/733-7205, www.skinnyskis.com) or Teton Mountaineering (170 N. Cache Dr., 800/850-3595, www.tetonmtn.com).

ACCOMMODATIONS AND GUEST RANCHES

While there are plenty of places to hang your hat in Jackson, during the prime seasons those places will not come cheap. The best deal in town is **The Anvil Motel** (215 N. Cache Dr., 800/234-4507, www.anvilmotel.com, $55–128 d), just a block off Town Square. The rooms are cute and comfortable with microwaves, mini refrigerators, and air-conditioning. Tucked right behind the Anvil is the even more

bargain-friendly **El Rancho Motel** ($45–104 s, $60–137 d), which is slightly more Spartan and does not have air-conditioning. Check-in for both properties is at the Anvil's office, and both offer Wi-Fi.

Almost as close to Town Square but quite a bit higher on the luxury scale is **The Wort Hotel** (50 N. Glenwood St., 800/322-2727, www.worthotel.com, $179–329), built in 1941 and a landmark in town, complete with the legendary Silver Dollar Bar & Grill, which has more than 2,000 inlaid silver dollars as time capsule–type decorations. The rooms are plush, and the location is great. Just down the street, **The Rusty Parrot Lodge & Spa** (175 N. Jackson St., 307/733-2000 or 888/739-1749, www.rustyparrot.com, $185–725) is like a little oasis at the edge of town. From the on-site spa to the world-class dining at Wild Sage Restaurant, every little detail is well-considered. The 31 rooms and suites are luxurious; some even have fireplaces and jetted tubs.

Away from the hustle and bustle of town, perched on a ridge overlooking the entire valley is the **Spring Creek Ranch** (1800 Spirit Dance Rd., 307/733-8833 or 800/443-6139, www.springcreekranch.com, $170–340), which boasts a variety of accommodations, including hotel rooms, cabins, condos, and exclusive mountain villas. The property is entirely self-contained with two restaurants on-site, a spa, and a slew of activities. The views from here trump just about everything else in the region, and the quiet gives Spring Creek Ranch tremendous appeal.

At Teton Village, **Hotel Terra** (3335 West Village Dr., 307/739-4000 or 800/631-6281, www.hotelterrajacksonhole.com) is a hip choice, at once luxurious and sustainable. The ecofriendly rooms have clean lines, retrofunky appointments, and lots of gadgets for techies, including iPod docking stations, flatscreen high-definition TVs, and Bose surround sound. The 132 guest rooms and suites range in size and style from urban studios ($119–349) and Terra guest rooms ($119–349) to 1–3-bedroom suites ($320–1,400). There are two restaurants on-site, a lively bar, a rooftop swimming pool and hot tub, a day spa, and a new fitness center.

For many visitors, the best way to enjoy Jackson Hole is to while away the days at a scenery-soaked dude ranch somewhere in the valley. After all, it was the dude ranches that jump-started Jackson's economy in the 1920s and 1930s. There are a multitude of wonderful choices that range from the historic and rustic, like the **Flat Creek Ranch** (15 bumpy miles from Jackson in isolated splendor, 307/733-0603 or 866/522-3344, www.flatcreekranch.com, $525–625 for 2 people, all-inclusive), and the extravagant, like **Lost Creek Ranch & Spa** (U.S. 89, Moose, 30 minutes north of Jackson, 307/733-3435, www.lostcreek.com, $6,015–14,120 per week), to the family-oriented, like the **Heart Six Guest Ranch** (Moran, 35 miles north of Jackson, 307/543-2477, www.heart-six.com, $1,995 pp per week, all-inclusive, reduced rates for children). There are options for every preference: proximity to town, emphasis on riding, this century or last, weekend or weeklong stays, and more. For a comprehensive listing of the dude ranches in the vicinity of Jackson Hole, contact the **Dude Ranchers' Association** (866/399-2339, www.duderanch.org).

CAMPING

Camping is by far the most economical way to stay in and around Jackson, and there are 14 campgrounds within a 15-mile radius of downtown. Among the closest to town is the **Curtis Canyon Campground** (Flat Creek Rd., 7 miles northeast of Jackson, 307/739-5400, www.fs.fed.us/r4/btnf, late May–late Sept., $12), which offers phenomenal views of the Tetons, immediate access to the National Elk Refuge, and terrific mountain hiking trails.

For more information on specific public campgrounds, contact the **Bridger-Teton National Forest** (340 N. Cache Dr., Jackson, 307/739-5500, www.fs.fed.us/r4/btnf).

For RV parks in Jackson, try the large and conveniently located **Virginian Lodge** (750 W. Broadway, 307/733-2792 or 800/262-4999, May 1–Oct. 15, www.virginianlodge.com, full

hookups $57–69), which has both motel rooms and 104 RV sites in addition to all the amenities you could want, including laundry, a pool, a hot tub, a salon, a restaurant, and a saloon.

FOOD

For every opportunity this region provides to exert energy by skiing, hiking, biking, or other pursuits, Jackson offers many more ways to replenish your supply. The number of outstanding restaurants in this town puts just about every other town in Wyoming—and many Western states—to shame.

As a rule, every day in Jackson should start with a trip to **The Bunnery** (130 N. Cache Dr., 307/734-0075, www.bunnery.com, 7 A.M.–9 P.M. daily, entrées $6.50–9), open for three meals daily (if you consider a coffee break at 6 P.M. a meal). The food is entirely made from scratch and utterly scrumptious. The baked goods—including their trademark OSM (oats, sunflower, millet) bread and homemade granola—are beyond compare, and the enormous and diverse menu offers plenty of healthy options as well as a few decadent ones. The "Get Your Buns in Here" bumper stickers are also good for a laugh. Be prepared to wait, however; the Bunnery is well loved by visitors and locals alike.

A relatively new, hip, and delicious arrival on Jackson's culinary scene is **Pica's** (1160 Alpine Lane, 307/734-4457, www.picastaqueria.com, 11 A.M.–10 P.M. daily summer, 11 A.M.–10 P.M. Mon.–Sat. winter, entrées $7–15), which offers the freshest take on tacos, burritos, great salads, and authentic Mexican dishes. There is another Pica's in Wilson (5755 W. Hwy. 22, Wilson, 307/734-7422, 11 A.M.–10 P.M. daily summer, 11 A.M.–10 P.M. Tues.–Sun. winter).

For carb loaders, the best spot in town is undoubtedly **Nani's Cucina Italiana** (242 N. Glenwood St., 307/733-3888, www.nanis.com, lunch Mon.–Fri. 11:30 A.M.–2 P.M., entrées $7–9; open nightly for dinner 5 P.M., closing hours vary, entrées $13–33), a gem of a place run by a woman and her daughter, who grew up in this kitchen and is now the head chef. The menu changes monthly—each one features a different region of Italy—and they serve up authentic dishes with farmers market–fresh ingredients. Everything is made from scratch, and the flavors cannot be overpraised. The ambience is quiet and comfortable, and the outside decks are a treat in good weather.

Although it is every inch a Four Seasons, this is still Wyoming, and there is casualness that puts visitors at ease here. The hotel has some exquisite restaurants, Westbank Grill and The Peak among them, but a great little spot is the **Lobby Lounge** (7680 Granite Loop Rd., Teton Village, 307/732-5000, www.fourseason.com/jacksonhole, 3–11 P.M. daily, $10–39), which feels like an oversize light living room and serves casual but still elegant light fare that ranges from sushi to burgers. It's smaller than the resort's other restaurants, with seating for 38. As it's quite popular with the locals, the overflow spills out onto the gorgeous heated mountainside patio.

Right on the Town Square is one of Jackson's most celebrated eating establishments, **The Snake River Grill** (84 E. Broadway, 307/733-0557, www.snakerivergrill.com, from 5:30 P.M. daily summer, from 6 P.M. daily winter, entrées $21–42). A visual feast in addition to being a gastronomical delight, the Snake River Grill has largely defined Jackson Hole cuisine with offerings like buffalo hanger steak, sautéed morel mushrooms with sherry and cream, and roasted bone marrow with rye crisps and sea salt. The menu is diverse, constantly changing, and completely mouthwatering.

INFORMATION AND SERVICES
Visitor Information
The most comprehensive spot to get information on the area is the **Jackson Hole and Greater Yellowstone Visitor Center** (532 N. Cache St., 307/733-9212, 8 A.M.–7 P.M. daily Memorial Day–Sept. 30, 9 A.M.–5 P.M. daily Oct. 1–Memorial Day), which has representatives from the Chamber of Commerce, the National Park Service, the Bridger-Teton National Forest, and four other agencies all under the same sod roof.

Post Office
Not wanting to forgo the unofficial community center that is the post office in small Western towns, Jackson residents balked years ago when the postal service tried to implement home delivery service. There are two main post offices in Jackson: the old one (220 W. Pearl St., 307/739-1740) and the new one (1070 Maple Way, 307/733-3650).

Public Library
The impressive **Teton County Library** (307/733-2164, www.tclib.org, 10 A.M.–8 P.M. Mon.–Thurs., 10 A.M.–5:30 P.M. Fri., 1–5 P.M. Sat.–Sun.) is located at 125 Virginian Lane.

Laundry
At **Soap Opera Laundromat** (850 W. Broadway, 307/734-7627) there are both do-it-yourself and drop-off options.

Internet
Many of the lodges and resorts around Jackson provide Wi-Fi to their guests, and Internet service is also available in town at a variety of places, including **The Hard Drive Café** (1110 Maple Way, 307/733-5282, www.harddrivecafe.biz, 5:45 A.M.–3 P.M. daily), which offers free high-speed connections for customers as well as time-based paid computer use, and the **Teton County Library** (125 Virginian Lane, 307/733-2164, www.tclib.org, 10 A.M.–8 P.M. Mon.–Thurs., 10 A.M.–5:30 P.M. Fri., 1–5 P.M. Sat.–Sun.).

Medical
St. John's Medical Center (625 E. Broadway, 307/733-3636, www.tetonhospital.org) has a 24-hour emergency room and specialized orthopedists who regularly deal with skiing injuries. There are also two walk-in clinics: **Emerg-A-Care** (982 W. Broadway, 307/733-8002) and **St. John's Urgent Care** (1415 S. U.S. 89, 307/739-8999).

GETTING THERE
By Air
Nine miles north of town off U.S. 89, entirely within the borders of Grand Teton National

Park, is the **Jackson Hole Airport** (1250 E. Airport Rd., 307/733-7682), which offers daily flights on **American** (800/433-7300, www.aa.com), **Delta/SkyWest** (307/732-0364 or 800/221-1212, www.delta.com), and **United/United Express** (307/732-0364 or 800/241-6522, www.united.com).

By Bus
The only buses that serve Jackson Hole are with **Alltrans** (307/733-3135, www.jacksonholealltrans.com), which offers service to and from Salt Lake City, Idaho Falls (Idaho), and Pocatello (Idaho).

By Car
The major routes into Jackson Hole—including U.S. 89/191/287 from Yellowstone and Grand Teton National Parks, U.S. 26/287 from the east, Highway 22 from the west over Teton Pass, and U.S. 189/191/89 from the south—can all experience weather closures in the winter, particularly over Teton Pass. There is no car traffic in the southern portion of Yellowstone during the winter. For Wyoming road reports, call 800/WYO-ROAD—800/996-7623.

Jackson is roughly 240 miles from Bozeman, 177 miles from Cody through Yellowstone National Park, and 275 miles from Salt Lake City. Keep in mind that while distances through the national parks may be shorter in terms of distance, the time is often extended by lower speed limits, traffic congestion, and animal jams. In addition, most of the park roads are closed in winter, and car travel is not possible between Bozeman and Jackson or between Cody and Jackson. Driving distances around the parks increase significantly.

GETTING AROUND
Car Rentals
Rental agencies operating at the Jackson Hole Airport include **National** (307/733-0671 or 800/227-7368, www.nationalcar.com), **Alamo** (307/733-0671 or 800/327-9633, www.alamo.com), **Avis** (307/733-3422 or 800/831-2847, www.avis.com), and **Hertz** (307/733-2272 or 800/654-3131, www.hertz.com). Off-airport rental agencies include **Dollar** (307/733-9224, www.jacksonholedollar.com) and **Thrifty** (307/734-8312 or 800/367-2277, www.thifty.com).

Taxis and Shuttles
In town, **Alltrans** (307/733-3135, www.jacksonholealltrans.com) provides airport shuttles and a variety of tours. **Buckboard Transportation** (307/733-1112 or 877/791-0211, www.buckboardtrans.com) and **Taxi Tim Cab Service** (307/734-5744) both offer regular taxi service around the valley.

Pinedale

Like so many small communities that dot the West, Pinedale (population 1,658, elevation 7,201 feet) started as a ranch that doubled as a post office. Organized in 1904 and incorporated in 1912, the small community has an interesting mix of people and, thanks to the state's energy boom and extraction of natural gas nearby, some unavoidable growing pains.

Nestled between the western flank of the staggeringly beautiful Wind River Mountains and the 11-mile-long Fremont Lake, Pinedale is a natural playground for hiking, climbing, sailing, and fishing. The other great pastime in these parts is history, and the town has done an excellent job of preserving it with the **Museum of the Mountain Man** and annual events like the **Green River Rendezvous** in July. Not necessarily a well-known destination, Pinedale, which is the county seat for Sublette County, is a natural stopping point between Jackson (78 miles north) and Rock Springs (100 miles south), with great access to some of Wyoming's most extraordinary mountains and lakes.

SIGHTS
Museum of the Mountain Man

The Museum of the Mountain Man (700 E. Hennick St., 307/367-4101 or 877/686-6266, www.museumofthemountainman.com, 9 A.M.–5 P.M. daily May–Sept., 10 A.M.–noon and 1–3 P.M. Mon.–Fri. Oct., by appointment only in winter, $5 adults, $4 seniors, $3 ages 6–12) is dedicated to preserving the history of the fur trapping and trading era. Its exhibits are full of interesting artifacts and interpretive materials related to the Western fur trade and the life of Native Americans in the region during this period. Visitors can view Jim Bridger's rifle, learn about beaver trapping and the processing of fur, and see a full-size buffalo hide tipi (there are not many of these remaining in the U.S.) that has been extensively and authentically furnished. The museum also houses exhibits related to local history, including the settling of Sublette County and the development of Pinedale over the last 100 years.

Granite Hot Springs

En route from Jackson to Pinedale, some 12 miles south of Hoback Junction on U.S. 189/191, is the turnoff for Granite Hot Springs (10 A.M.–8 P.M. daily June–Oct., 11 A.M.–5 P.M. daily mid-Dec.–Mar., $6 adults, $4 children). The 10-mile-long scenic drive is on a gravel road that ends at the parking lot for the hot springs. Camping is allowed along the road but not within the last 1.5 miles before the springs. In the winter the road is groomed to allow access on skis, snowshoes, snowmobiles, or dog sleds. The pool is situated below the Gros Ventre mountain range and was built by the Civilian Conservation Corps in 1933. The water is usually about 93°F in the summer and 110°F in winter. There is a nice deck for lounging, and changing rooms are available. There is also a nearby campground (June–Sept., $15), run by the same people who manage the hot springs.

If you are visiting during the winter, a popular way to access the hot springs is by dog sled. **Jackson Hole Iditarod Sled Dog Tours** (307/733-7388 or 800/554-7388, www.jhsleddogs.com) offer full-day trips to the hot springs and include a hearty lunch and a steak or trout dinner (prepared on-site while you are enjoying a dip in the springs).

the Museum of the Mountain Man in Pinedale, Wyoming

JACKSON HOLE

ENTERTAINMENT AND EVENTS

The Green River Rendezvous (307/367-4101 or 877/686-6266, www.meetmeonthegreen. com) is a huge community event that takes place the second weekend of July. The city prides itself on the fact that six of the 15 Rocky Mountain Rendezvous were held here in the Green River Valley at Horse Creek. The first rendezvous was held in 1825 and continued each summer until 1840. For about three weeks trappers, traders, and Native Americans would come together to trade and resupply their outfits, exchange stories, catch up with old friends, get incredibly drunk, and participate in all sorts of boisterous behavior.

Today the Green River Rendezvous is more family-friendly while still bringing the era of the mountain man to life. There are plenty of games, crafts, living history demonstrations, guest speakers, a mountain man encampment, programs for children, and a rodeo. The pageant, which is usually held on Sunday, should not be missed. It is an entertaining reenactment of an 1830s rendezvous. The participants, in original costumes, are lively characters who barter, trade, and duel.

The Green River Winter Festival originated in 2002 with one purpose in mind: "to fend off the winter blahs." This is a fun-filled five-day event catering to the whole family. There are winter Olympic events for kids, an arm-wrestling tournament, a wood chopping and stacking race, and a variety of other contests. It begins with a large bonfire, and there is a lot of food, music, and entertainment throughout the week, including the must-see drag queen beauty pageant.

RECREATION
Fremont Lake

The second-largest natural lake in the state, Fremont Lake (4 miles north of Pinedale, 307/367-4326, www.pinedale.com/destinations/fremontlake.htm) was formed glacially and is more than 600 feet deep in places. The lake was named for John C. Fremont, who mapped the area in 1842 in advance of the

Oregon Trail. The lake is a natural recreation site with opportunities for boating, sailing, water-skiing, fishing, and camping. Though there are no designated hiking trails around the lake, most of the shoreline is undeveloped and can be walked on. The RV and tent campsites at **Fremont Lake Campground** ($12), operated by the Forest Service at the lower end of the lake, are generally open mid-June–early September and can be reserved through www.reserveUSA.com. Also at the lower end of the lake, the **Sandy Beach** picnic area is for day use only.

For an incredibly scenic drive or bike ride, **Skyline Drive** is a 16-mile paved road along the lake's eastern shore that leads to a campground and hiking trails at the edge of Bridger Wilderness.

The only commercial facility at Fremont Lake is the idyllic **Lakeside Lodge Resort & Marina** (877/755-5253, www.lakesidelodge. com, year-round), which offers 12 beautiful deluxe cabins ($75–169), six rustic cabins (call for rates), a full-service restaurant (307/367-3555, lunch and dinner daily summer, dinner Wed.–Sun. winter), and rental of fishing boats, pontoon boats, and ski boats ($15–60 per hour).

Fishing and Boating

There are literally hundreds of lakes in the vicinity of Pinedale that contain several species of trout and a few Montana grayling as well as an assortment of freestone waterways that include the world-class Green, Hoback, and New Fork Rivers. Wild trout abound in smaller streams too, including Faler Creek, Fish Creek, and North Cottonwood Creek in the Wyoming Range, some of which are private-lease streams.

The best place to start any fishing expedition is at **Two Rivers Emporium** (211 W. Pine St., 307/367-4131 or 800/329-4353, www.2rivers. net), which can outfit you from rod to leader to fly and offers a range of guided trips (from $425 per day for 1–2 people), including on private waters, and can include lodging and gourmet meals.

With so many lakes in the region, canoe-ing is a wonderful and quiet way to navigate the myriad waterways. Lake-use canoe rentals ($35 for a full day) are available in town from the **Great Outdoor Shop** (2332 W. Pine St., 307/367-2440, www.greatoutdoorshop.com, 7 A.M.–9 P.M. daily summer, 8 A.M.–8 P.M. daily winter). They also offer an amazing range of services, including guided fishing trips and gear rental, shuttles to the best trailheads and the airport in Jackson, backpacking, and gear rentals for rock or ice climbing.

Motorized and nonmotorized boats are available for rent on both Fremont and Half Moon Lakes at **Lakeside Lodge Resort & Marina** (877/755-5253, www.lakesidelodge.com, $15–60 per hour) and **Half Moon Lake Resort** (307/367-6373).

Hiking and Rock Climbing

The Wind River and Wyoming Ranges, which include the Jim Bridger and Gros Ventre wilderness areas, offer some of the best hiking and climbing in the state. Hundreds of miles of trails crisscross the area and give hikers and backpackers access to hundreds of thousands of acres of gorgeous alpine and subalpine terrain. Many of the trailheads are at 9,000 feet and higher, so be prepared for significant and immediate changes in the weather. Prime hiking season this high is short—mid-July–mid-September—and it can snow any day of the year. Average daytime summer temperatures peak in the 70s and 80s, with nighttime lows dropping into the 30s. Afternoons often bring rainstorms with lightning, so be prepared to get lower in a hurry. Also, always be aware that this is black bear and grizzly bear country, so plan ahead to bring pepper spray.

Among the favorites in the area is the easily accessible **Elkhart Park** trail, the only one accessed by a paved road, just 15 miles northeast of Pinedale. The heavily hiked trail departs from the **Trails End Campground** at 9,100 feet in elevation. Great day hikes will lead you into the Wind River Mountains and places like **Photographer's Point** and **Miller Lake.** A staffed Forest Service visitors center at the Elkhart Park trailhead can provide information about trails and trail conditions.

Another excellent series of trails is in the **Green River Lakes,** 52 miles north of Pinedale (31 paved miles and 21 miles of good gravel). The **Hiline Trail,** among others, starts at a 39-site campground at 8,000 feet in elevation and runs almost the length of the Winds, 80 miles south over jaw-droppingly beautiful terrain. There are several fishable lakes in the area and an abundance of ways to enjoy a day hike.

For more information on specific trails, conditions, and maps, contact the **Bridger-Teton National Forest Office** (29 E. Fremont Lake Rd., Pinedale, 307/367-4326, www.fs.fed.us/r4/btnf/offices/pinedale-trail.shtml).

Mountain Biking

The 2,700-mile **Great Divide Mountain Bike Route** from Banff, Alberta, to the U.S.-Mexican border, along the spine of the Rockies, passes directly through Pinedale. There is plenty of good rugged terrain to be explored by mountain bike. Due to the weather, however, most trails are only good for biking 3–5 months of the year. **Sweeny Creek** and **Grouse Mountain Trails** have some good short rides, or for the more adventurous (and fit), try the ride up **Half Mountain**; from the top you can bike almost the entire length of the ridge and take in some spectacular views.

During the summer, **White Pine Ski Resort** (Skyline Dr., 10 miles northeast of Pinedale, 307/367-6606, www.whitepineski.com) is open to mountain bikers. The chairs on the ski lift can accommodate riders and their bikes; bikes are available for rent at the resort as well. Special biking trails for all levels of experience have been groomed for the ride downhill. For a more tranquil and scenic ride, opt for one of the leveler cross-country trails.

Skiing

The state's oldest ski area, **White Pine Ski Area and Resort** (Skyline Dr., 10 miles northeast of Pinedale, 307/367-6606, www.whitepineski.com, all-day $40 adults) is tucked in the Bridger-Teton National Forest above

Fremont Lake. Though relatively small when compared to others in the Jackson area, the resort is a wonderful family-oriented ski hill with lodging, two restaurants, rentals, and free cross-country skiing in winter.

In summer, the mountain is open for mountain biking, scenic chairlift rides, hiking, horseback riding, and because of its proximity to the lake, fishing.

Horseback Riding

The Bridger-Teton National Forest is a wonderful experience on horseback. The **White Pine Ski Resort** (Skyline Dr., 10 miles northeast of Pinedale, 307/367-6606, www.whitepineski.com) offer trail rides; horses are available for hourly rentals or half-day and full-day trips. Overnight pack trips, which last 1–4 nights, can be arranged. **Half Moon Lake Resort** (10 miles northeast of Pinedale, 307/367-6373) also offers trail rides and pack trips with horses suited for all levels of experience.

Golf

At the west end of town, **Rendezvous Meadows Golf Course** (Club House Rd., 307/367-4252, $19 for 9 holes, $25 for 18 holes) is a nice nine-hole public course.

ACCOMMODATIONS

Because of a population boom driven by the energy industry, there are quite a few accommodations in and around Pinedale, particularly given the size of the town. **The Log Cabin Motel** (49 E. Magnolia St., 307/367-4579, www.thlogcabinmotel.com, $49–169) is as charming as it is conveniently located. Built in 1929, the motel lives up to its name by remaining true to Pinedale's architectural style. The cabins vary in size, but most are quite spacious with partial or full kitchens, covered porches, satellite TV, and Wi-Fi.

The **Half Moon Lake Resort** (10 miles northeast of Pinedale, 307/367-6373) was between owners at press time, but another great lakeside resort is the **Lakeside Lodge Resort and Marina** (3.5 miles northeast of Pinedale, 877/755-5253, www.lakesidelodge.com, year-

round), with 12 beautiful deluxe cabins ($75–169) and six rustic cabins (call for rates), all with immediate waterfront access and splendid views.

CAMPING

Sublette County is 80 percent public land, making camping in the region a viable option. Among the closest (and happily, the most scenic) RV and tent campsites can be found at **Fremont Lake Campground** (5 miles northeast of Pinedale, www.reserveUSA.com, mid-June–early Sept., $12) and the **Half Moon Lake and Boat Ramp** (10 miles northeast of Pinedale, $10). There is no potable water at Half Moon Lake, and none of its 19 spots can be reserved.

For more information on Forest Service campgrounds and backcountry camping, contact the **Bridger-Teton National Forest Office** (29 E. Fremont Lake Rd., Pinedale, 307/367-4326, www.fs.fed.us/r4/btnf/offices/pinedale-trail.shtml).

FOOD

Among Pinedale's oldest and most favorite restaurants is the **Patio Grill and Dining Room** (35 W. Pine St., 307/367-4611, 7 A.M.–2 P.M. Sun.–Mon., 6 A.M.–8 P.M. Tues.–Thurs., 6 A.M.–4 A.M. Fri.–Sat., entrées $9–22), known for home-cooked food, great gravies, pies, Greek breakfasts, and staying open until four in the morning on the weekend.

For a fun evening with excellent beer, try the **Wind River Brewing Company** (402 W. Pine St., 307/367-BEER—307/367-2337, www.windriverbrewingco.com, 11 A.M.–11 P.M. Sun.–Thurs., 11 A.M.–midnight Fri.–Sat., entrées $8–26) with great salads, appetizers, sandwiches, burgers, and steaks. Their award-winning hand-crafted ales are the icing on the cake.

A unique dinner option that reflects the people and culture of Pinedale is the family-run **Pitchfork Fondue** (9888 U.S. 191, 307/367-3607, www.pitchforkfondue.com, 5:30–8:30 P.M. Thurs.–Sun.), an ingenious Western outdoor cookout at the fairgrounds south of town. Tender steaks are seared in large cast iron cauldrons of oil (yes, on pitchforks) and served with fondue sauces, hot homemade potato chips, fruit salad, green salad, beverages, and homemade brownies. The picnic tables can accommodate 240 people, but call ahead for reservations and current pricing.

INFORMATION AND SERVICES
Visitors Center
The relatively new and sizeable **Sublette County Visitors Center** (19 E. Pine St., 307/367-2242 or 888/285-7282, www.sublettechamber.com, 9 A.M.–6 P.M. daily summer, 9 A.M.–5 P.M. Mon.–Fri. winter) can provide information about the local area and the region for everything from hiking trails to fishing guides and up-to-date event calendars.

A comprehensive website for activities and businesses in the area is www.pinedaleonline.com.

Library
The **Sublette County Library** (155 S. Tyler Ave., 307/367-4114, www.sublettecountylibrary.org, 10 A.M.–5:30 P.M. and 7–9 P.M.

Mon.–Fri., 10 A.M.–5 P.M. Sat.) offers plenty of interesting events in addition to its sizeable collection. Free Wi-Fi is provided, and public computers with free Internet access are available for 30 minutes at a time.

Medical
Though the nearest hospital is 78 miles north in Jackson, Pinedale is served by the **Pinedale Medical Clinic** (619 E. Hennick St., 307/367-4133, 24 hours daily).

GETTING THERE AND AROUND
The nearest commercial airports are in Jackson (78 miles), Rock Springs (100 miles), Idaho Falls, Idaho (190 miles), and Salt Lake City (250 miles). Private jets can be accommodated at **Pinedale Wenz Field** (307/367-2290).

Rental-cars are available in Jackson and Rock Springs. The closest Greyhound bus service is also in Rock Springs.

For shuttle service in Pinedale, **The Great Outdoor Transportation Company** (307/367-6440) offers taxi service, gear drops, and fishing shuttles.

Lander

Tucked in the foothills of the Wind River Mountains on the banks of the Popo Agie (po-PO-shuh) River and adjacent to the Wind River Indian Reservation, Lander (population 7,181, elevation 5,357 feet) is an outdoor lover's town and a vibrant, growing community. The area was first visited by white fur trappers as early as 1811, and oil was discovered in 1824 but not developed until the mid-1880s. The area was the home ground of Chief Washakie and his Shoshone people. In 1869 a small military post was established here to protect the Shoshone from enemies that included the Sioux and Arapaho. The valley, once known by Native Americans as Pushroot for its fertile soil, was farmed early on to great success thanks to the soil, relatively mild winters, and little wind.

Not a large town by any stretch, Lander is a welcoming place with friendly people, a decidedly outdoors-oriented culture, and immediate access to some of the most stunningly rugged wilderness in the country.

SIGHTS
The Wind River Reservation
The Wind River Reservation (307/455-2466, www.wind-river.org) sits on 2.2 million acres and is home to both the Northern Arapaho and Eastern Shoshone tribes. It surrounds the city of Riverton, with the towns of Lander, Shoshoni, and Thermopolis close to its borders. There is not a lot of intermingling between the native and nonnative communities, or between the Arapaho and Shoshone themselves, for that

CHIEF WASHAKIE AND THE SHOSHONE

The Shoshone Indians have inhabited the United States for thousands of years. Their language is one of the Uto-Aztecan languages spoken by indigenous people throughout the Western United States, extending through Mexico and into South America. Also known as the Snake Indians by early European traders and explorers, they were one of the first tribes to acquire horses from the Spanish. On horseback they spread out to cover much of Wyoming, Utah, Montana, and Colorado. The tribe that occupied most of western Wyoming was known as the Eastern Shoshone, and their most famous leader was Chief Washakie.

Born around the turn of the 19th century to a Flathead (Salish) father and a Shoshone (Lemhi) mother, Washakie would live through the most tumultuous century for Native Americans. At an early age his father was killed during a Blackfeet raid, and he and his mother returned to live with the Lemhi people in Idaho. During his adolescence, Washakie joined a nomadic band of Bannocks, since they shared similar languages, and eventually settled with the Shoshone who called the Green River Basin in southwest Wyoming

their home. During the early 1820s Washakie met and befriended a young Jim Bridger, who would later become a celebrated explorer and mountain man. Together they hunted, trapped, and traded. Their friendship was so great that one of Washakie's daughters became Bridger's third wife. Although trading and trapping ingratiated him with the white settlers and explorers, Washakie was also earning the respect of his fellow Indians as a skilled warrior by participating in numerous raids.

By the mid-1800s, before Washakie became a chief, it was clear he was an influential leader; he had been recognized by the U.S. government, who engaged him in various discussions. Unlike other Native American groups, the Shoshone didn't enter into any formal treaties with the government to protect settlers crossing Native American lands, although the Shoshone did not attack travelers. Under Washakie, who had learned the benefits of befriending and trading with the newcomers, there was a much-needed alliance. During the 1840s, the Shoshone actively traded with travelers and settlers. There are even stories of the Eastern Shoshone helping pioneers

matter; the arrangement to leave both tribes on the same reservation was decided by the U.S. government without their consent. The western part of the reservation, including the towns of Fort Washakie, Burris, and Crowheart, is occupied by the Shoshone, and the eastern part, including the towns of Ethete and Arapaho, are occupied by the Arapaho. Although the reservation struggles with problems of poverty and unemployment, it is also home to an incredibly rich history, important traditions, and pristine wilderness.

A drive through the reservation affords visitors magnificent views of Wyoming's undeveloped natural beauty and the majestic Wind River Mountains. The reservation is easily accessible by car, and its roads are open to visitors. If you'd like to hike, fish, camp, or boat, however, access is restricted to certain parts of

the reservation, and a recreation fee or fishing permit is required. Hunting by nonnatives is not allowed. The **Tribal Fish and Game Office** (307/332-7207), located in Fort Washakie, can provide more information about fees and permits, as can the Chambers of Commerce in Lander, Riverton, and Dubois. Fort Washakie is also the location of the **Shoshone Tribal Cultural Center** (307/332-9106) and the gravesites of the two most prominent Shoshone Indians, Chief Washakie (it was his hometown) and Lewis and Clark's fearless guide, Sacagawea.

The biggest draw to the reservation are the powwows held throughout the summer season. These large cultural celebrations usually take place over a three-day weekend and include dancing, singing, parades, and traditional games. Competitors come from across traverse difficult streams and round up stray cattle as they crossed through Wyoming. The skills Washakie acquired through his friendship with Bridger and other traders and trappers served him well as an Indian leader. He was able to negotiate ardently for the best interests of his people, getting them much needed supplies, tools, and food. At some point, perhaps seeing their chief's gestures as an indication of weakness, younger warriors questioned his leadership. In response, Washakie left camp and headed east, only to return a week later with seven Sioux scalps, challenging anyone who questioned him to match the feat.

Washakie was also considered to be forward-thinking. When it became clear in the early 1850s that their land was being threatened by the constant flow of migrants and settlers, he suggested to leaders, including Brigham Young, that land be set aside for the Shoshone Indians. By the end of the decade, he was again negotiating directly with the government to acquire this land. It was not until 1863 that the Treaty of Fort Bridger designated land for the tribe. Chief Washakie enthusiastically signed the document. In 1883, U.S. President Chester Arthur paid a visit to Washakie's tipi to meet the famed Indian leader in person.

On the reservation, Washakie continued to lead his people. He maintained a fine balance between the new reservation life and their traditions. Living in a log cabin rather than tipi, Washakie sent his children to the agency schools and even farmed a small piece of land. But he also made sure his children joined him on the important buffalo hunts. He defended Native American practices and led his fellow Shoshone warriors in the U.S. Army battles against the Sioux and Cheyenne. Washakie never stopped advocating for the needs of his people.

Toward the end of his life, Washakie was baptized twice, first as a Mormon in 1880 and later as an Episcopalian in 1899, a few months before his death in 1900. Chief Washakie was buried with full military honors, and his funeral procession stretched for miles. A warrior and peacemaker, a diplomat and an advocate for change, Chief Washakie is considered the last of the great Shoshone leaders. Wyoming has paid tribute to the influential man by naming various public places in his honor.

the country, and both tribes host their own powwows. The largest Shoshone powwow is the **Eastern Shoshone Indian Days Powwow and Rodeo,** an all-Indian rodeo usually held the fourth weekend in June. The largest Arapaho powwow is the **Ethete Powwow** in late July. For additional information about the powwows, contact the **Wind River Heritage Center** (307/856-0706).

(Sinks Canyon State Park

A place that is as beautiful as it is fascinating, Sinks Canyon State Park (3079 Sinks Canyon Rd., 6 miles south of Lander, 307/332-6333 or 307/332-3077, www.wyopark.state.wy.us, visitors center open daily Memorial Day–Labor Day, day-use $6 pp) is filled with recreational opportunities and one of the state's geological wonders. Here in the canyon is where the Middle Fork of the Popo Agie River plunges into a cave, only to emerge 0.5 miles away in an area known as the Rise. What makes it so interesting is that geologists have determined that it takes more than two hours for the water to make the journey. In addition, there is plenty of water emerging at the Rise that did not enter at the Sinks. Adding yet another layer of mystery is that the water is a couple of degrees warmer when it emerges than when it disappeared.

Aside from its geological and scenic attributes, Sinks Canyon is a fantastic place for hiking, rock climbing, fishing (but not in the trout laden waters at the Rise, where vending machines dole out food for these lunkers), and wildlife watching. Keep your eyes peeled for transplanted bighorn sheep, moose, and any number of bird species.

SINKS CANYON AND SOUTH PASS AREA

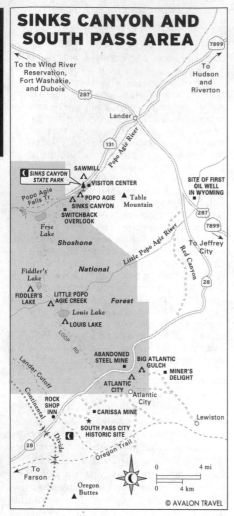

Loop Road

Among the most scenic drives in the region, and perhaps the state, is a roughly 75-mile round-trip seasonal route known locally as the **Loop Road.** From Lander, follow the signs to Sinks Canyon State Park via Highway 131. Just beyond Bruce's Camp parking area, the 32-mile Loop Road climbs past Frye Lake, Fiddler's Lake, and Louis Lake to a junction

that leads south to South Pass City Historic Site or north to Atlantic City and Highway 28, which brings travelers 35 miles back to Lander. Along the way, the Wind River Range unfolds in all its majesty, and hikers will have no shortage of trailheads to amble down. Because of its extreme altitude, the road is often not open until July due to snow, and it closes as early as September again because of snow.

South Pass City Historic Site

One of the region's few gold mines, South Pass City Historic Site (35 miles south of Lander, 2 miles off Hwy. 28, 307/332-3684, www. southpasscity.com, May 15–Sept. 30, $4 per person out-of-state, $2 per person residents) is a beautifully restored site with 20 original log, frame, and stone structures, including the jail, a livery, a stable, a school, saloons, and homes. The city was founded in 1867 and, in addition to its mining legacy, is well remembered for its pivotal role in women's suffrage. A territorial representative from South Pass City, William Bright, introduced the bill that made Wyoming the first territory to grant women the right to vote in 1869; South Pass City's justice of the peace, Esther Hobart Morris, was the first woman to hold political office in the United States.

The South Pass Hotel has been refurbished to give visitors a sense of 1880s Wyoming. The Smith-Sherlock General Store is open for shopping, and the Miner's Exchange Saloon offers visitors a chance to shoot pool on an 1840s billiards table.

Every year in mid-July **Gold Rush Days** celebrates the town's heritage with a vintage baseball tournament, food, entertainment, and interpretive programs. The town's **Carissa Mine** was purchased by the state, overhauled significantly for safety, and can now be toured.

ENTERTAINMENT AND EVENTS

The most popular event in Lander is their **Pioneer Days** festival. It takes place around the Fourth of July and includes a parade,

PEACEFUL CO-EXISTENCE: THE SHOSHONE AND THE ARAPAHO

The Treaty of Fort Bridger, signed in 1863, designated 44 million acres as "Shoshone Country." This large parcel of land not only included territory in Wyoming but crossed into Colorado, Utah, and Idaho. However, there was no formal demarcation and settlers and migrants continued to settle the land in the south, up into the Green River Valley, forcing the Shoshone into enemy territory in order to hunt. Furthermore, gold was discovered near South Pass, coal near Rock Springs, and both mining towns and farms were popping up along the Wind River drainage.

In 1868, another treaty was signed, establishing the much smaller 2.2-million-acre Wind River Reservation. For a variety of reasons, however, land continued to be ceded to the government, including the Popo Agie Valley and the present-day towns of Shoshoni and Thermopolis. Chief Washakie knew much of the fertile valley was in demand and that if it was not surrendered, it would be taken by force. He chose instead to barter determinedly to improve life on the reservation for his people. He asked for specific physical improvements, goods, and protection from their Indian enemies. Fort Brown, renamed Fort Washakie in 1878, resulted from this bargaining. Today the reservation stretches 70 miles west to east and 55 miles north to south and is home to about 2,500 Eastern Shoshone and 5,000 Northern Arapaho Indians.

Understanding why two tribes, historically great enemies, would share the same reservation requires a history lesson and some imagination. By 1877, most Native Americans had been relocated to reservations, yet the Northern Arapaho remained landless. With winter rapidly approaching, the U.S. Government turned to the Shoshone leader, Chief Washakie, requesting that the Shoshone share their reservation with the Arapaho just for the winter. Washakie conceded, but made it clear that by spring the visitors must be relocated. Spring came and went with Washakie repeatedly demanding that the Arapaho be removed from the reservation. His pleas fell on deaf ears, and the former archenemies were forced to make the best of an already challenging situation.

They each established their own governments and mostly occupied separate parts of the reservation. The Arapaho settled the eastern part of the land, with the towns of Ethete and Arapaho as their hubs; the Shoshone developed the west portion, which includes the towns of Fort Washakie, Burris, and Crowheart. Although there have been few major conflicts, the two cultures tend to keep to their own with little interest in intermixing.

Today the reservation has some incredibly beautiful vistas of the Wind River Valley and its craggy mountains. Standing in the middle of its pristine wilderness, it's not evident that oil and gas fields are the primary source of revenue for the reservation. Although plagued by unemployment and poverty, there is also a great sense of cultural pride. This is explicitly expressed each May–September through a series of powwows and other cultural celebrations.

For more information on the Wind River Reservation, or to plan a visit, contact the **Wind River Heritage Center** (307/856-0706, www.wind-river.org).

Indian dancing, a buffalo barbecue, fireworks, and a nightly rodeo. The celebration is more than 115 years old, making it the oldest paid rodeo in the world.

A much younger but also entertaining event is the **Lander Brew Fest,** which takes place in mid-June. More than 15 breweries from the Rocky Mountain region participate, allowing visitors to sample more than 50 different types of beer while enjoying great music.

The **International Climber's Festival** (307/349-1561, www.climbersfestival.org) is held each July and attracts outdoor enthusiasts from around the country. There are lectures, activities, social events, and a trade show. Visit the website to check which events require tickets.

Lander is also a stop on the **International Pedigree Stage Stop Dog Race** (307/734-1163, www.wyomingstagestop.org) that takes place in late January–early February.

Stop by the **Lander Area Chamber of Commerce** (160 N. 1st St., 307/332-3892 or 800/433-0662, www.landerchamber.org) to get more information or to buy tickets for any of the events in town.

RECREATION
Hiking and Rock Climbing

Known as the roof of Wyoming and the spine of the Rockies, the Wind River Range offers phenomenal hiking and climbing from Lander. Among the trails accessible from the Loop Road between Sinks Canyon State Park and South Pass City are the easy seven-mile **Christina Lake Tail,** the easy-to-moderate 6.5-mile **Louis Lake Trail,** and the difficult 17-mile multiuse **Shoshone Lake Trail.**

For hiking that is somewhat closer to Lander, with scenery no less dramatic, Sinks Canyon State Park offers six miles of easy to moderate trails in a figure-eight layout.

For expert guidance and equipment related to rock climbing, the best resource in town is

© WYOMING TRAVEL & TOURISM

Welcome to Lander.

Wild Iris Mountain Sports (307/332-4541 or 888/824-5968, www.wildirisclimbing.com), named for one of the region's best-known climbing areas. Another renowned spot for climbers is Sinks Canyon State Park.

For more information on trails and conditions, contact the Shoshone National Forest's **Washakie Ranger Office** (333 E. Main St., 307/332-5460, www.fs.fed.us/r2/shoshone, 8 A.M.–4:30 P.M. Mon.–Fri.).

Fishing

With the Wind River Range as an impressive backdrop to Lander, the fishing in this part of the state varies from crystalline alpine lakes to small but productive rivers, including the Wind River, Bull Lake Creek, the Sweetwater River, and various forks of the Popo Agie River. Unlike most of the state, the fishing around Lander is exclusively wade fishing.

Daily guided fishing trips can be arranged through **Sweetwater Fishing Expeditions** (307/332-3986, www.sweetwaterfishing.com), who offer a variety of adventures that include day trips ($375–430), 5–10-day expeditions ($1,550–2,200 pp), and horseback and llama pack trips.

Golf

The **Lander Golf Club** (1 Golf Course Dr., 307/332-4653, $30 for 18 holes) is an 18-hole, par-71 course.

ACCOMMODATIONS

The most charming place in town is the **Blue Spruce Inn** (677 S. 3rd St., 307/332-8253 or 888/503-3311, www.bnblist.com/wy/bluespruce, brown@bluespruceinn.com, $70 s, $95 d), a 1920 arts and crafts home built by a local sheep rancher. There are only four spacious guest rooms, each with a private bath, so make reservations well in advance. The house has beautiful grounds and is within walking distance of downtown, shopping, and restaurants.

Also close to downtown shopping and restaurants is the **Best Western Inn at Lander** (260 Grand View Dr., 307/332-2847, www.

bestwesternwyoming.com, $80–131), which has 100 guest rooms offering amenities that include free Wi-Fi, free cook-to-order breakfasts, a restaurant, an outdoor pool, and a year-round hot tub.

CAMPING

As evidence of the community's commitment to the outdoor experience, free overnight camping is permitted in Lander's **City Park**

(405 Fremont St.). RVs are invited to park in the parking lot.

The best public camping is found in **Sinks Canyon State Park** (3079 Sinks Canyon Rd., 6 miles south of Lander, 307/332-6333 or 307/332-3077, www.wyopark.state.wy.us, $17 nonresidents, includes day-use) which has three campgrounds, all with restrooms and drinking water. Advance reservations are not accepted.

Sleeping Bear RV Park and Campground

NOLS AND THE WIND RIVER RANGE

In 1965, one year after the Wilderness Act had passed, an Outward Bound instructor named Paul Petzoldt founded the National Outdoor Leadership School (NOLS) in Sinks Canyon near Lander, Wyoming. Having spent much of his youth in the nearby Tetons, where he climbed The Grand in cowboy boots at the age of 16, and the Wind River Range, much of which was not even mapped, Petzoldt wanted to create a school specifically to train outdoor leaders, educators, and conservationists. A small group of all-male students departed in June of that year to spend a full month in the Wind River Range. For the most part, their gear consisted of Army surplus from the Korean War.

Within a year, female students were admitted to NOLS for the 30-day outdoor leadership training in the Winds, and by 1970, more than 750 students enrolled in summer courses. Having taken all of their students into the Winds since 1965, NOLS started branching out in the 1970s with programs and eventually bases in Alaska, East Africa, Mexico, Idaho, and Washington's Northern Cascades. Still, the school never lost touch with Wyoming and the Winds, and in 2002 an impressive world headquarters (284 Lincoln St., Lander, 307/332-5300 or 800/710-NOLS – 800/710-6657, www.nols.edu) was completed in Lander.

So what are these mountains that gave rise to the one of the world's most esteemed wilderness education programs and the largest backcountry permit holder in the United States?

The Wind River Range cuts through Wyoming with 100 miles of jagged peaks, crystalline lakes, boulder-strewn meadows, two national forests, and three pristine wilderness areas. The range has 48 summits topping 12,000 feet, eight above 13,500 feet, and seven of the largest glaciers in the Lower 48. At 13,804 feet, Gannett Peak is the crown of this magnificent range and the highest peak in the state. The Cirque of the Towers, 10 miles into the Bridger Wilderness at the southern end of the range, offers some of the most dramatically scenic hiking in the Lower 48, and plenty of technical rock-climbing. The Winds are bisected by the Continental Divide to form three major drainages for the Columbia River, the Colorado River, and the Missouri River.

The area has long been a favorite backpacking destination for the adventurous, beyond just NOLS students, and access is possible from both the east and west sides. In addition to the Continental Divide Trail, which traverses the range from South Pass to Union Pass on its way between Canada and Mexico, there are hundreds of miles of hiking trails crisscrossing the Winds. Among the more popular trailheads are Big Sandy, Boulder Creek, Elkhart Park, and Green River Lakes. For more solitude, try some of the low-use trailheads like Burnt Lake, Half Moon Lake, and Meadow Lake. For information on trails and backcountry regulations, contact the **Bridger-Teton National Forest Office** (29 East Fremont Lake Rd., Pinedale, 307/367-4326, www.fs.fed.us/r4/btnf/offices/pinedale-trail.shtml).

(715 E. Main St., 307/332-5159 or 888/757-2327, www.sleepingbearrvpark.com) offers 10 tent sites ($20), 22 full RV hookup sites ($32–35), 23 water and electric hookup sites ($22.50–28.50), cabins with shared bath ($46), and cabins with private baths ($56). Amenities include Wi-Fi, picnic tables, and fire rings, plus access to clean bathrooms with showers.

FOOD

With so many ways to burn energy, it's not surprising that there are a number of great places to refuel. For healthy breakfast and lunch options, try **Wildflour Bagels & Breads** (545 Main St., 307/332-9728) or **The Magpie** (159 N. 2nd St., 307/332-5565), a de facto coffee shop and Internet café.

The **Gannett Grill/Lander Bar** (126 Main St., 307/332-8228, www.landerbar.com, lunch and dinner 11 A.M.–9 P.M. daily, entrées $7–25) is a local favorite offering hand-tossed pizzas, juicy burgers made from local beef, gorgeous salads from the on-site organic garden, and locally brewed beer. The outdoor dining option is insanely popular when the weather is good. Right next door and under the same ownership, **Cowfish** (128 Main St., 307/332-8227, www.landerbar.com, dinner 5–9 P.M. daily, entrées $13–29) offers an assortment of fresh seafood, salads, steaks, pasta, and homemade desserts that is impressive enough to make you forget you are in Wyoming; it's impossible to leave hungry.

INFORMATION AND SERVICES

The **Lander Area Chamber of Commerce** (160 N. 1st St., 307/332-3892 or 800/433-0662, www.landerchamber.org, 8 A.M.–5 P.M. Mon.–Fri., 9 A.M.–2 P.M. Sat. summer, 8 A.M.–5 P.M. Mon.–Fri. in other seasons) acts as a visitors center.

For information and maps related to backcountry hiking and camping, contact the Shoshone National Forest's **Washakie Ranger Office** (333 E. Main St., 307/332-5460, www.fs.fed.us/r2/shoshone, 8 A.M.–4:30 P.M. Mon.–Fri.).

Library

The **Fremont County Library** (307/332-5194) is located at 451 North 2nd Street.

Medical

The largest medical facility in the area is the **Lander Regional Hospital** (1320 Bishop Randall Dr., 307/332-4420, www.landerhospital.org), which has a 24-hour emergency department.

GETTING THERE AND AROUND

The closest commercial airport to Lander is 26 miles away, the **Riverton Regional Airport** (RIW, 4690 Airport Rd, Riverton). **Great Lakes** (800/554-5111, www.flygreatlakes.com) operates daily flights and offers code shares with United and Frontier. Private air travel is available at **Hunt Field Airport-Lander** (307/332-3119).

The **Wind River Transportation Authority** (800/439-7118, www.wrtabuslines.com) offers fixed route bus service around town plus transportation to and from airports in Riverton ($25 pp one-way), Jackson ($100 pp one-way) and Casper ($100 pp one-way).

By road, Lander is 163 miles from Cody, 160 miles from Jackson, 157 miles from Yellowstone National Park, 136 miles from Pinedale, and 79 miles from Thermopolis.

Thermopolis

At the south end of the Big Horn Basin, **Thermopolis** (population 3,172, elevation 4,504 feet) is a notably sunny town with 321 sunny days on average each year; it also has natural hot water forming the world's largest mineral hot spring.

The town was originally called Old Town Thermopolis, one of two Wyoming settlements built around mineral hot springs; the other is Saratoga. Around the turn of the 20th century, when an analysis of the water suggested potential health benefits, the town's name was shortened to Thermopolis in a calculated marketing move. Local mineral deposits—including coal, copper, and oil—plus the arrival of the railroad bolstered the Thermopolis economy, but for the most part tourism was and continues to be the major economic force. Teddy Roosevelt and Butch Cassidy and his gang are among the most famous frequent visitors to Thermopolis.

There are a surprising number of fantastic attractions in this small, friendly town surrounded by the Owl Creek Mountains. At **Hot Springs State Park,** mineral terraces create a stunning background for herds of grazing bison. The **Wyoming Dinosaur Center** is among the best paleontology sites in the state. And the **Legend Rock Petroglyphs** (which can only be opened with a key from the Chamber of Commerce!) is one of the most compelling examples of prehistoric rock art in the state. From fishing and rafting on the Big Horn to horseback riding in the Owl Creek Mountains, there are a variety of ways to enjoy the natural beauty surrounding town.

SIGHTS
◖ Hot Springs State Park
Hot Springs State Park (307/864-2176, www.wyoparks.state.wy.us) is a natural phenomenon featuring terrain with brilliant hues, unique rock formations, and, of course, hot springs. The mineral deposits and various life forms paint the park different shades of red, orange, green, brown,

and yellow. In summer the park explodes with vibrant flower gardens. Because the two national parks in the state's northwest corner draw the large crowds, if you make it to this park, you're guaranteed a more leisurely, chaos-free visit.

Originally part of the Wind River Reservation, the hot springs were believed by the Shoshone to be a gift from the Great Spirit. The U.S. government bought Big Springs and the surrounding territory from the Arapaho and Shoshone in 1896. Chief Washakie, who signed the agreement, had one stipulation: The waters should be freely available to all so that anyone could receive the great health and healing benefits. As a result, Wyoming's first state park was created along with the State Bath House, which is free and open to the public to this day.

Big Springs, considered the largest hot spring in the world, is the main attraction in the park. The water's temperature is 135°F, and more than 8,000 gallons per day trickle and

Hot Springs State Park in Thermopolis, Wyoming

gush freely over large mineral-painted terraces into the Bighorn River. Boardwalks allow visitors to walk along the terraces, springs, and cooling pools; they lead to a long suspension bridge that crosses the Bighorn and provides great views of this remarkable area.

The **State Bath House** (307/864-3765, 8 A.M.–5:30 P.M. Mon.–Sat., noon–5:30 P.M. Sun.) has the only free thermal pools in the park. There is an indoor and outdoor soaking pool, although the outdoor pool is closed in the winter, along with smaller private tubs in the locker rooms. The water from the hot springs is piped to these mineral pools and is kept at 104°F. Open year-round, the pools are small but clean and well maintained. Lockers, towels, and even swimsuits are available for a nominal charge. If you are looking for more elaborate swimming facilities (including slides, steam rooms, and hot tubs), there are several commercial facilities inside the park, including **Hellie's Teepee Spa** (307/864-9250) and **Star Plunge** (307/864-3771).

Hot Springs County Museum and Cultural Center

This small town has done an impressive job of collecting and displaying artifacts from its lively past. Hot Springs County Museum and Cultural Center (700 Broadway, 307/864-5183, www.hschistory.org, 9 A.M.–5 P.M. Mon.–Sat. Memorial Day–Labor Day, 9 A.M.–4 P.M. Tues.–Sat. Labor Day–Memorial Day, $4 adults, $2 seniors and children) consists of the two-story main museum building and five additional structures in the vicinity. The museum building was, in various incarnations, a Ford garage, a Coke bottling plant, and a technical college before opening as the county museum in 1980.

One of the museum's more interesting exhibits is dedicated to the outlaws of Wyoming. Thermopolis was frequented by outlaws such as Butch Cassidy and the Sundance Kid. The museum has the cherrywood bar from the Hole in the Wall Saloon and the stained glass windows from Hack Hollywood's Saloon, two of their favorite watering holes in town. There are also exhibits highlighting the town's varied sources

of revenue, including coal mining, oil drilling, and petroleum extraction. The first floor of the main museum recreates businesses from an early 1900s Main Street, including a dentist's office, a post office, a general store, and a jail. They have been designed mostly using artifacts from the time period and even from the original stores. The Cultural Center has rotating exhibits by local artists.

The Wyoming Dinosaur Center and Dig Sites

Located at the Warm Springs Ranch, where dinosaur fossils from the Jurassic period have been unearthed, the Wyoming Dinosaur Center (110 Carter Ranch Rd., 307/864-2997 or 800/455-3466, www.wyodino.org, 8 A.M.–6 P.M. daily May–Sept., 10 A.M.–5 P.M. daily Oct.–Apr.) is a 12,000-square-foot complex that houses more than 200 displays. In addition to 20-some full-size dinosaur skeletons and casts from the local site and from around the world, there is also a preparation lab on-site. Visitors can watch technicians cleaning recently discovered fossils. One of the special features of the museum is its proximity to the **Warm Springs Dig Site.** Excavations still take place here each summer.

During the summer, visitors can take a tour of the site, or participate in the **Dig for a Day program** ($150 adults, $80 children with a paying adult), which allows you to work at the actual dig site, learning about the process and the science involved. There are also specific days throughout the summer set aside for the **Kids' Dig Program,** which caters to budding archeologists.

Admission to the museum is $10 adults and $5.50 children and seniors. The dig site tour is $12 adults and $8.75 children and seniors. The best option is to purchase the combination package, which includes entrance to the museum and the tour, for $18.50 adults and $11.75 children and seniors. Families of four can pay a flat rate of $50, which includes both the museum and the tour.

Legend Rock Petroglyph Site

Although it may seem like a small adventure just to find these prehistoric drawings 21 miles outside Thermopolis, the sheer number and variety make it a worthwhile visit. The easiest way to visit the petroglyphs is first to stop at the Hot Springs State Park office (located at the corner of Park St. and Hwy. 789, 307/864-2176) where you can pick up a gate key and a map to the site (the unmarked route is otherwise difficult to locate). Once at the parking lot for Legend Rock, you can choose to hike 0.5 miles to the petroglyphs or use the key to the gate and drive down the hill. Etched along the sandstone cliffs are numerous animal and human figures that have been linked to different time periods throughout history, some dating back 2,000 years. Unfortunately, not all visitors to the site have treated the paintings respectfully, and it's important not to touch or try to remove the petroglyphs.

ENTERTAINMENT AND EVENTS

The **Gift of the Waters Pageant** is held during the first weekend in August and recreates the selling of the hot springs by the Shoshone and Arapaho Indians to the U.S. government, based on a play written in 1925. The pageant suggests it was a fair transaction between equal partners, which wasn't exactly the case. However, Native Americans from the Wind River Reservation do participate in the event, which is followed by a powwow. Contact the Thermopolis Chamber of Commerce (307/864-3192) for more information.

RECREATION
Hiking

Although there is no national forest in immediate proximity to Thermopolis, the locals like to hike around their landmark **Round Top Mountain.** In Hot Springs State Park, there are 6.2 miles of accessible walking and hiking trails, the most popular being **Spirit Trail,** which meanders through the park.

Boating and Fishing

Both white-water and scenic river trips are offered on the Wind and Big Horn Rivers and can be arranged exclusively through the Indian-owned **Wind River Canyon Whitewater and**

Fly Fishing (307/864-9343 or 888/246-9343, www.windrivercanyonraft.com). Roughly two-hour white-water trips on the dramatic upper or lower canyon sections start at $45 pp, and all-day trips covering the whole canyon are $90 pp. Scenic two-hour trips are $30 pp. They also offer a variety of guided fishing trips as the only outfitters on the Wind River.

Golf

There is a nine-hole public course at **Legion Town and Country Club** (141 Airport Rd., 307/864-5294, $16–18).

ACCOMMODATIONS

With its history of attracting visitors to its medicinal waters, Thermopolis has quite a large, if not necessarily diverse, number of accommodations.

The snazziest hotel by far is the **(Best Western Plaza Hotel** (116 E. Park St., 307/864-2939, www.bestwesternwyoming.com, $91–121), a historic hotel in Hot Springs State Park.

Some of the more budget-friendly options in town include the 12-room **El Rancho Motel** (924 Shoshoni St., 307/864-2341, $50 d), with air-conditioning, Wi-Fi, refrigerators, and microwaves; and the recently remodeled **Paintbrush Inn** (605 S. 6th St., 307/864-3155, www.paintbrushinn.com, $39–59), which features basic air-conditioned rooms with Wi-Fi and kitchenettes. Both motels accept dogs upon approval and for a fee.

CAMPING

While there is no camping permitted in the most desirable of spots—Hot Springs State Park—there are a few RV parks in Thermopolis that allow tent camping as well. The **Fountain of Youth RV Park** (250 U.S. 20 N., 307/864-3265, www.fountainofyouthrvpark.com) is open year-round and offers RV sites ($33–35 d), tent sites ($30 d), a cabin and a guest house ($125 for up to 6 people), and a bunkhouse ($45 d). There is also a large hot springs pool on-site, laundry facilities, and free Wi-Fi.

The **Eagle RV Park** (204 U.S. 20 S., 307/864-5262 or 888/865-5707, www.eaglervpark.com)

features a shady campground with RV sites ($31.25 d), tent sites ($20 d), and camping cabins ($40–69 d). Amenities include free Wi-Fi, a game room and playground, and laundry facilities.

The nearest public campgrounds to Thermopolis are 17 miles south of town in **Boysen State Park** (307/876-2796, www.wyoparks.state.wy.us, $17 for nonresidents) in the Wind River Canyon.

FOOD

Serving breakfast, lunch, and dinner, **Pumpernicks Family Restaurant** (512 Broadway St., 307/864-5151, www.pumpernicksfamilyrestaurant.com, 7 A.M.–8 P.M. Mon.–Fri., 7 A.M.–9 P.M. Sat., entrées $7–21.50) is known for homemade breads, savory crepes, and a vast selection of pies. The food is fresh and hearty. Special kids and seniors menus will delight the whole family.

Newer on the scene and open daily in summer for lunch and dinner, **Stones Throw Restaurant** (143 Airport Rd., 307/864-9494, www.stonesthrowwyoming.com, entrées from $7) offers everything from homemade soups and salads to burgers, steaks, and seafood. Their specialty dish is Jäger-schnitzel.

INFORMATION AND SERVICES

The **Chamber of Commerce** (220 Park St., 877/864-3192, www.thermopolis.com) is open 8 A.M.–5 P.M. Monday–Friday in summer and 9 A.M.–5 P.M. Monday–Friday in winter.

Library

The **Hot Springs County Library** (344 Arapahoe St., 307/864-3104, http://www-wsl.state.wy.us/hotsprings) is open 9 A.M.–6 P.M. Monday–Friday year-round, closed on holidays.

Medical

There is a 24-hour emergency room at **Hot Springs County Memorial Hospital** (150 E. Arapahoe St., 307/864-3121, www.hscmh.org).

GETTING THERE AND AROUND

The closest commercial airports to Thermopolis are in Worland (30 miles) and Riverton (65 miles). **Great Lakes** (800/554-5111, www.flygreatlakes.com) operates flights out of both airports, and in Riverton offers code shares with United and Frontier.

Daily **bus service** is available to and from points north (Billings) and south (Denver) at **Shell Southside Travel Center** (167 S. U.S. 20, 307/864-3108).

By road, Thermopolis is 82 miles from Cody, 150 miles from the east entrance to Yellowstone National Park, and 190 miles from Billings.

Cody

It seems somehow fitting that this Western town was the brainchild of one of the West's most colorful and dynamic showmen. Indeed, Cody (population 9,309, elevation 5,088 feet), named for Buffalo Bill Cody, is a small town that packs a lot of punch. Set as it is in the arid Big Horn Basin, you might expect Cody to be all dust and tumbleweeds. But that couldn't be farther from reality, although there are plenty of both when the Wyoming wind kicks up. Cody is high style with shiny boots and fringe on almost everything. Cody is Molesworth furniture, a little gaudy sometimes but an absolute classic. Cody is a nightly rodeo and old-time gunslingers. In many ways, Cody is the old West, the *real* West, that visitors want to see and experience.

An obvious destination in and of itself, Cody is home to what is arguably the best Western art and history museum in the world. The Buffalo Bill Historical Center is beyond compare. Visitors could spend a week in the

THE LEGEND OF BUFFALO BILL

When it comes to Buffalo Bill Cody, born William F. Cody, it can be difficult to discern fact from fiction. The man was legendary in every sense of the word, and for the most part he earned the reputation that still follows his name. Born in Iowa in 1846, Cody made his way out west in 1857 with his father. Cody's father died en route, leaving the boy to fend for himself, finding work as a cowboy and Pony Express rider. He became an Army scout at the end of the Civil War and even earned the Congressional Medal of Honor in 1872 for valor in action during the Indian Wars. He reportedly earned his nickname after the Civil War when he shot 4,280 bison in the span of 18 months on behalf of the Kansas Pacific Railroad.

Cody was a natural hunter and was frequently asked by the Army to guide visiting dignitaries. The hunts were greatly publicized, and an eager public greedily consumed tales of Cody's adventuresome pursuits. In 1873, with a string of dime-store novels glorifying him, Cody agreed to perform a melodramatic stage show highlighting his exploits alongside other legendary figures Wild Bill Hickok and Texas Jack Omohundro. In July 1876, just weeks after Custer's defeat at the Little Bighorn, Cody and the Fifth Regiment for whom he was scouting at the time met a band of Cheyenne warriors. Cody killed and scalped a warrior named Yellow Hair, avenging Custer's death and securing his place among the country's military heroes of the day.

In 1883, Cody produced his well-known Wild West Show, which would travel the world for more than three decades, earning him both fame and fortune. Cody became a shrewd businessman, investing in an Arizona mine, hotels in Sheridan and his namesake Cody, ranching, coal and oil development, film-making, publishing, and tourism. He used his wealth and reputation to espouse such causes as women's suffrage, and eventually, the just treatment of Native Americans.

As a symbol of the burgeoning West, Cody's expertise was relied on by every U.S. president from Ulysses S. Grant to Woodrow Wilson. He mingled with world-famous artists and dined with kings. Indeed, Buffalo Bill lived a life quite worthy of the legends that continue to define the man.

© WYOMING TRAVEL & TOURISM

Buffalo Bill Historical Center in Cody, Wyoming

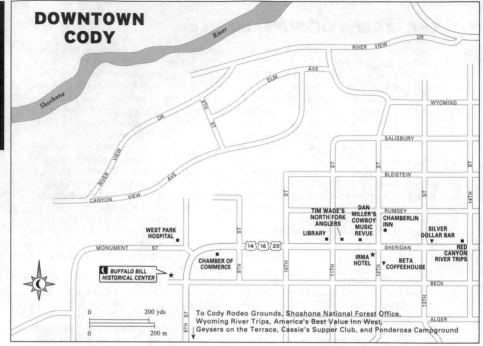

complex's five separate museums and never see the same exhibit twice. The compact downtown is scenic and historic, with world-class art galleries, fun tourist shops, and great eateries. There are plenty of Western entertainment options as well across the valley.

Just outside town, the landscape shifts into the lush South Fork and into the high country the closer one gets to Yellowstone National Park. There are a hundred reasons to go to Cody, including its proximity to Yellowstone.

SIGHTS
◖ Buffalo Bill Historical Center

The West's version of the Smithsonian, the Buffalo Bill Historical Center (720 Sheridan Ave., 307/587-4771, www.bbhc. org, 10 A.M.–5 P.M. Thurs.–Sun. Dec.–Feb., 10 A.M.–5 P.M. daily Mar.–Apr., 8 A.M.–6 P.M. daily May–Sept. 15, 8 A.M.–5 P.M. daily Sept.16–Oct., 10 A.M.–5 P.M. daily Nov., $15 adults, $13 seniors and students, $10 ages 6–17, $45 families, free for children under 6) is a collection of five extraordinary museums plus a research library. The **Buffalo Bill Museum** celebrates the private and public life of town father W. F. "Buffalo Bill" Cody. The **Whitney Gallery of Western Art** reflects the diverse history of art of the American West from the early 19th century to today with original paintings, sculpture, and prints by some of the best-known deceased masters and contemporary geniuses. The **Plains Indian Museum** examines the culture and history of the Arapaho, Crow, Cheyenne, Blackfeet, Sioux, Shoshone, and others through an impressive collection of Native American art and artifacts. The **Cody Firearms Museum** is home to the world's largest assemblage of American arms along with some European arms dating back to the 1500s. The **Draper Museum of Natural History** offers exhibits that interpret the Greater Yellowstone ecosystem from human and natural science

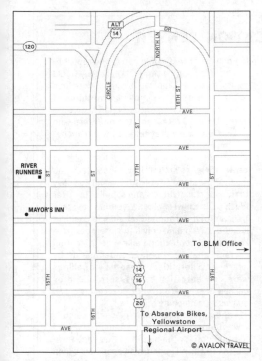

© AVALON TRAVEL

perspectives. Finally, the **Harold McCracken Research Library** is an extraordinary resource for studies of the American West.

This complex is indeed the grand dame of Western history and art. In addition to their own unrivaled permanent collections, the museums feature a constantly shifting assortment of compelling traveling exhibits and special events. Be sure to check the website for events before you arrive. If you only see one museum on your journey out West, this one is it.

The BBHC also has two restaurants, the Mustang Grill and the Pony Express, for quick bites.

Cody Trolley Tours

From early June through late September, one of the best ways to get an overview of Cody, its founding father, and the natural environment that rolls out in every direction is the Cody Trolley Tours (307/527-7043, www.codytrolleytours.com, $34 adults, $20 ages 6–17, free

for children under 6, call for tour schedules), which offer hour-long narrated tours and covers 100 years of history in 22 miles. Highlights include stories about Buffalo Bill, Annie Oakley, the Crow Indians, and a 1904 bank robbery in Cody by the Hole-in-the-Wall gang. The tour includes a "Best of Cody" souvenir guide and admission to the Buffalo Bill Historical Center. Reservations can be made and tickets can be purchased on the front porch of the Irma Hotel (1192 Sheridan Ave.), which is also where the tours depart. As an added service, free transportation can be provided to and from your hotel. Call to make reservations.

Old Trail Town and the Museum of the West

Located on the site of the original Cody City (about two miles west of Cody), Trail Town (307/587-5302, www.museumoftheoldwest.org, 8 A.M.–8 P.M. daily mid-May–Sept., $7 adults, $6 seniors, $3 children) is a fascinating collection of historic buildings from the Wyoming frontier. The recreated town is the result of local historian and archaeologist Bob Edgar's hard work and dedication. In total, there are 26 buildings dating to 1879–1901 and at least 100 wagons, maintained in nearly original condition, helping create an authentic feel of the bygone pioneer era. Among the highlights is the old Rivers Saloon, its walls still marked by bullet holes; it was a favorite meeting place of Butch Cassidy and the Sundance Kid. There is also a cabin from Hole-in-the-Wall country.

Housed in its own larger building on-site, the Museum of the West displays artifacts from frontier life, including guns, carriages, clothing, and an excavated canoe that might have been used by Lewis and Clark on their journey west. There is also a graveyard in the Old Trail Town complex that has the reinterred bodies of many infamous characters of the Old West, including that of John "Liver Eating" Johnston (frequently spelled Johnson). The reburial of his body in Old Trail Town was attended by more than 2,000 people including the actor Robert Redford, who played

HEART MOUNTAIN RELOCATION CENTER

Situated between the towns of Cody and Powell, in the midst of some overgrown barley fields, stand a few dilapidated buildings, including one with a tall brick chimney. Utterly abandoned and somewhat inexplicable at first sight, they strike an odd picture in this high desert. These shells are remnants of a dark period in U.S. history.

With the bombing of Pearl Harbor in December 1941, war hysteria and anti-Japanese fervor reached new heights in the United States. There had been anti-Asian sentiment along the West Coast for decades, primarily directed at hard-working Chinese laborers who would work anywhere doing anything for nearly nothing. When the government virtually stopped all Chinese immigration, Japanese immigrants quickly took their places as the targets of racism. For many Americans, the attack on Pearl Harbor somehow justified the racial prejudice. President Roosevelt signed Executive Order 9066 in February 1942, creating a War Relocation Authority and authorizing the roundup and removal of all people of Japanese ancestry, regardless of their U.S. citizenship status.

By the early spring, Japanese aliens and Japanese Americans were given 10 days to wrap up their livelihoods and families, packing only what they could carry, and report to makeshift assembly centers where they would be assigned and deported to camps. More than 120,000 people were moved. Two-thirds of those with Japanese ancestry had been born in the United States, and the one-third who were aliens were prevented by law from becoming citizens.

Wyoming was home to one of 10 relocation centers. Heart Mountain was isolated, had means for a steady water supply, and was easy to transport individuals and supplies to. After much political wrangling, Wyoming governor Nels Smith determined that a camp could be located in Wyoming only if the internees were kept in "concentration camps, not reception centers" and were "worked under guard." By nearly any definition, these new dwellings were concentration camps, surrounded by barbed wire, guard towers, searchlights, and guards with machine guns.

Although the decision to place the camp in Wyoming was not initially popular, it proved to be a boon for the people of Cody and Powell. The towns had been in an economic slump for 15 years, but with the camp construction project, thousands of jobs were created literally overnight. The camp covered more than 4,600 acres and housed 468 barracks. These

---

the famous mountain man in the 1972 movie *Jeremiah Johnson*.

Irma Hotel

Naming it after his beloved youngest daughter and calling it "just the sweetest hotel that ever was," Buffalo Bill built the stately Irma Hotel (1192 Sheridan Ave., 800/745-IRMA—800/745-4762, $100–132, suites $150–172) in 1902 with the idea that tourists from around the world could stay here en route to Yellowstone National Park. The hotel was designed by a well-known church architect from Nebraska, and some exterior walls are made of local river rock. The cherrywood bar, one of the most photographed features in town, was

built in 1902 as well. Additions were added in 1929 and 1976–1977.

Still the heart of downtown, the Irma is starting to show her age. The rooms are basic and a little creaky, but it's fun to stay in Buffalo Bill's original suite or imagine the royalty that stayed in many of the other rooms. You don't need to spend a night, though, to get a real sense of the history. Visitors can enjoy a drink at the bar or a full meal at **The Irma**, serving breakfast ($4–14), lunch ($5–17), and dinner ($8–32), which is known for prime rib and delicious steaks. The atmosphere alone is worth the price of the meal.

Heart Mountain

Heart Mountain lies halfway between Cody

poorly assembled, tar-papered buildings were divided into sections. The average room was 20 by 20 feet and was shared by one family, equipped only with cots, one unadorned hanging light, and a potbellied stove, which didn't always work due to fuel shortages. The shelters provided little relief from Wyoming's searing summers and frigid winters. Also constructed on the site were mess halls, communal bathrooms and showers, laundry rooms, a hospital, a sewage plant, two places of worship, and even a high school. The camp at Heart Mountain became Wyoming's third-largest city.

Construction began in June 1942, and by August 11, 1942, the first trainload of internees arrived. More than 14,000 internees entered the camp during 1942–1945. Its largest population at any given time was nearly 11,000. Despite the dire circumstances and violation of their rights, life at Heart Mountain proved to be a testament to the human spirit. The internees demonstrated a deep resilience and determination to create and maintain a community within its ragged confines. There were general stores, two movie theaters, barbershops, high school athletic teams, a weekly newspaper, and a democratically elected camp government. They also made the most of their barren surroundings, extending the irrigation system, planting 27 different types of fruits and vegetables, and raising profitable hog and poultry farms. The cities of Powell and Cody, although never entirely welcoming to these outsiders, benefited economically from the camp and its internees by purchasing inexpensive but necessary goods, like meat and produce, and by hiring the internees as cheap labor to pick their crops. During the three years the camp was open, 552 births and 185 deaths were registered.

The West Coast exclusion order was revoked in December 1944, and internees were allowed to leave beginning the following January. Each internee was granted $25 and a bus ticket to his or her destination. The problem for many was that they no longer had a place to call home. The last internees left the camp on November 10, 1945. After the camp closed, homesteaders quickly moved into the territory, taking advantage of the cleared land and irrigation systems already in place. The only signs that remain of the Heart Mountain Relocation Center are three decrepit buildings leaning into the Wyoming wind.

In 1990, all survivors of Heart Mountain were issued a check for $20,000 and a signed apology from President George H. W. Bush.

and Powell and takes it name from the twin summits atop the mountain range that slightly resemble a heart. Driving east on U.S. 14A, the mountains become clearly visible, and the feature is easily identified on the maps created by Lewis and Clark. The range is a puzzle for many geologists and has inspired heated debate. It seems to be part of rock formations found in Yellowstone National Park, 60 miles away, but how they ended up in their present location is unclear. Furthermore, it is an "upside down" mountain, with strata of limestone appearing at the top with younger strata below.

Heart Mountain was the site of a Japanese-American internment camp during World War II. Between 1942 and 1945 more than 10,000 people of Japanese descent (at least two-thirds of whom were American citizens) were relocated to this isolated terrain. Confined by barbed-wire fences and armed prison guards, they did their best to create a sense of community and normalcy under difficult living conditions. Of the 120,000 people detained in the 10 internment camps across the country, not one was ever found guilty of espionage or conspiring with the enemy. The camps were a result of heightened wartime hysteria, the fear-mongering of politicians, and acute racism. **Heart Mountain, Wyoming Foundation** (307/754-2689, www.heartmountain.net) is dedicated to preserving the memory of this dark period in American history and telling

Old Trail Town near Cody, Wyoming

the stories of those it affected. They are still in the money-raising phase with the goal of building an interpretive center.

Today all that remains at the site of the camp are three buildings in various stages of decay and different plaques noting the location of the site and the memories of the victims, including one honoring the more than 600 internees who left the camp to fight in the U.S. Army during the war.

Also in this region is the **Heart Mountain Ranch** (307/754-8446, www.nature.org/wyoming), a 15,000-acre plot of land managed by the Nature Conservancy. It has a large number of rare plants, numerous species of birds, and large mammals such as elk and mule deer. There is a seven-mile easy-to-moderate hiking trail that takes hikers to the mountain's summit.

◖ Chief Joseph Scenic Highway

Linking Cody with the northeast entrance to Yellowstone National Park is the seasonally-open 47-mile Chief Joseph Scenic Highway. It

is a winding and at times hair-raising drive that cuts through mountainous country, providing views of spectacular waterfalls and mountain vistas of the Absarokas, Cathedral Cliffs, and the mouth of Sunlight Basin, and occasionally a glimpse of wildlife. Interpretive signs along the way tell the story of the Nez Perce's 1877 flight from the U.S. Army under the leadership of Chief Joseph, for whom the highway is named. For adventurers, the highway gives unparalleled access to some incredible hiking trails.

From Cody, drive north 17 miles on Highway 120, turning left (west) Highway 296, known as the Chief Joseph Scenic Highway. The road climbs over Dead Indian Summit, above 8,000 feet, and then drops into the magnificent Clark's Fork Valley. The road ends at Crandall, Wyoming, the only place on the highway to buy provisions or find lodging. Ten miles west of Crandall on the Beartooth All American Road (known locally as the Beartooth Highway) is Cooke City and the northeast entrance to Yellowstone National Park. Plan on spending at least two hours to drive the full 74 miles or so from Cody to Cooke City.

Buffalo Bill Scenic Byway

The shorter of two routes to Yellowstone, this one to the east entrance, the 52-mile Buffalo Bill Scenic Byway winds through the rugged North Fork Canyon along the Shoshone River. President Theodore Roosevelt was among its admirers, calling the road the most beautiful 50 miles in the United States.

From Cody, head west on U.S. 20/14/16. The road ends at the east entrance to Yellowstone.

ENTERTAINMENT AND EVENTS

Making this Western town one of the best places in the state to see rodeo, the **Cody Nite Rodeo** (519 Yellowstone Ave., 307/587-5155, www.codystampederodeo.com, June 1–30 and July 6–Aug. 31, $18 adults, $8 ages 7–12, free for children under 7) is held nightly in summer at the rodeo grounds except July 1–5 during the Cody Stampede. Running every summer since 1939, the rodeo is two hours filled with daring cowboys and cowgirls looking to make a name for themselves on the circuit. Gates open at 7 p.m., and the action begins at 8 p.m.

The town's rodeo fever hits its high over the Fourth of July during the annual **Buffalo Bill Cody Stampede Rodeo** (519 Yellowstone Ave., 307/587-5155, www.codystampederodeo.com, grandstand seats $16–24). The stampede has been running for nearly 100 years and was inspired by Buffalo Bill's own Wild West Show. This is one of the biggies for pro rodeo cowboys and cowgirls, with the bull-ride purse alone bringing the winner $50,000. For world-class rodeo action, it's hard to beat.

One of the few towns to stage nightly gunfights in summer (Jackson is another), Cody enchants visitors with Old West characters that stage a hilarious, silly, and at times gripping street performance and gunfight known as the **Cody Gunfighters** (307/202-1113, www.cody-gunfighters.com, 6 p.m. Mon.–Sat.). The shows are free and are performed at adjacent to the Irma Hotel (1191 Sheridan Ave.).

Produced annually in mid-July, the **Yellowstone Jazz Festival** (www.yellow-stonejazz.com) brings some of the biggest names in jazz and big band to Cody.

By far the biggest arts-related event of the year in Cody is the **Rendezvous Royale** (888/598-8119, www.rendezvousroyale.com), which happens in mid-September and ushers in the last hurrah of Cody's almost manic summer season. The week is packed with events that include **Cody High Style,** which celebrates Western design in its myriad forms, and the **Buffalo Bill Art Show and Sale,** which boasts it own impressive line of events. The town is full of style icons, design gurus, and blissed-out art collectors, and the energy pulses nearly around the clock. Several galleries and shops host concurrent events. Some of the best shows by contemporary Western masters open at **Simpson Gallagher Gallery** (1161 Sheridan Ave., 307/587-4022).

RECREATION
Hiking

Even though Cody itself is in something of a desertlike bowl, there is abundant hiking in the beautiful forests and mountains to the north, south, and west of town. There are several districts of the Shoshone National Forests within relatively close proximity to town. Trails worth pursuing include the **Bald Ridge Trail** (County Rd. 7RP, off Hwy. 120, 18 miles north of Cody). The five-mile trail climbs nearly 4,000 vertical feet through Bureau of Land Management land to the summit of Bald Ridge. The views, naturally, are breathtaking. The area is closed December–April to protect critical winter habitat for elk and mule deer. And remember, this is grizzly bear territory, so you should take all necessary precautions.

For more information on trails and conditions, contact the **Shoshone National Forest** (808 Meadowlane Ave., 307/527-6241, www.fs.fed.us/r2/shoshone) or the **Bureau of Land Management** (1002 Blackburn Ave., 307/578-5900, www.blm.gov/wy).

For less vigorous hiking, visit the **Chamber of Commerce** (836 Sheridan Ave., 307/587-2777 or 800/393-2639, www.codychamber.org)

and pick up the "Cody Pathways" brochure and map of nonmotorized trails in the region.

Fishing and Rafting

The Shoshone River runs right through the heart of Cody, offering both white-water rafting opportunities and plenty of excellent fishing. Among the rafting companies in town that offer everything from two-hour whitewater floats to half-day scenic tours and weeklong trips are **River Runners** (1491 Sheridan Ave., 800/535-RAFT—800/535-7238, www.riverrunnersofwyoming.com), **Wyoming River Trips** (233 Yellowstone Ave., 307/587-6661, www.wyomingrivertrips.com), and **Red Canyon River Trips** (1374 Sheridan Ave., 307/587-6988 or 800/293-0148).

There is an abundance of prime fishing waters within an easy drive from Cody, including the Shoshone River, the Clarks Fork of the Yellowstone River, and hundreds of lakes. For fishing gear or advice on local hatches and water conditions, head to **Tim Wade's North Fork Anglers** (1107 Sheridan Ave., 307/527-7274, www.northforkanglers.com). In addition to all of the gear, they offer guided wading trips ($350 per day) or float trips ($400 per day).

Mountain Biking

If you are looking to do some exploring on bikes, **Absaroka Bikes** (2201 17th St., 307/527-5566) offers bike rentals, guided bike tours, and maps of bike trails around the area.

Horseback Riding

Head out 1.5 miles past the rodeo grounds to **Cedar Mountain Trail Rides** (12 Spirit Mountain Rd., 307/527-4966, $35 for 1 hour, $45 for 2 hours), where you will be attended by knowledgeable and friendly guides who are especially good with beginners. The trails wind up Cedar Mountain and provide great views of the town below. If you are interested in a full-day ride, they take the horses and riders by trailer 35 minutes north to Elk's Fork; lunch is provided.

Golf

Golfers can hit the links at the 18-hole semiprivate **Olive Glenn Golf & Country Club** (802 Meadow Lane, 307/587-5551, www.oliveglenngolf.com, $70 for 18 holes) or at the **Powell Golf Club** (600 U.S. 114, 7 miles east of Powell, 307/754-7259, www.powellgolfclub.com, $49–59 for 18 holes).

There is also a great miniature course for the whole family at **Cody Miniature Golf** (Cody's City Park, 307/527-7511, $4 pp).

ACCOMMODATIONS

Geared as it is toward the flocks of visitors headed to Yellowstone, Cody has an abundance of accommodations, many of them new. Among the best deals in town is the basic but appealing **America's Best Value Inn West** (720 Yellowstone Ave., 307/587-4208, www.americasbestvalueinn.com, May–Oct., $45–134). For significantly more charm and a bit more money, the **C Chamberlin Inn** (1032 12th St., 307/587-0202 or 888/587-0202, www.chamberlininn.com, $115–165) is a stately complex built in 1904 and beautifully restored in 2007. There are 21 individual rooms, including several suites, all of which are unique. Ernest Hemingway spent the night in one of them in 1932—his signature is still in the guest register.

Another unique option is the **Mayor's Inn** (1413 Rumsey Ave., 888/217-3001, www.mayorsinn.com, $85–215), a bed-and-breakfast in a turn-of-the-20th-century home known as Cody's first mansion. Inquire about their scrumptious set-menu dinners.

Just outside Yellowstone's east entrance, **Pahaska Tepee Resort** (183 Yellowstone Hwy., 307/527-7701 or 800/628-7791, www.pahaska.com, $70–180) is another of Buffalo Bill's historic lodges. The complex is vast, with the old 1904 lodge, newer housekeeping cabins, and deluxe modern condos, but so are the recreational opportunities. From horseback riding to cross-country skiing, Pahaska Tepee is like a giant playground with immediate proximity to Yellowstone.

Guest Ranches

Since Cody is cowboy country, after all, it's

fitting that there are a number of guest ranches in the area. Most are geared heavily toward horseback riding and provide lodging in individual and often charmingly rustic cabins. Other activities such as fishing and hiking are regularly available. Things like cell phone coverage, satellite TV, and Wi-Fi are simply not on the menu. These ranches provide true opportunities to get away from life as you know it in some of the most spectacular country on the planet.

Forty miles west of Cody, the **Absaroka Mountain Lodge** (1231 Yellowstone Hwy., 307/587-3963, www.absarokamtlodge.com, $100–160 cabins) is one of the largest and best-known. Unlike most guest ranches in the area, the Absaroka Mountain Lodge is not all-inclusive; guests select and pay for activities, including fishing and horseback riding, and eat meals in a restaurant.

Founded by the grandson of Buffalo Bill, the **Bill Cody Ranch Resort** (2604 North Fork Hwy., 26 miles west of Cody, 307/587-2097 or 800/615-2934, www.billcodyranch.com) is exactly halfway between Cody and Yellowstone in the magnificent North Fork Valley. Cabins rent for $100–175, and meals and activities are paid separately. Packages are also available.

Closer to Yellowstone, the **Crossed Sabres Ranch** (829 North Fork Hwy., 307/587-3750 or 888/587-3750, www.crossedsabresranch.com, 6-day trip $1,500 adults, 3-day trip $750 adults, all-inclusive) was established in 1898 as the first dude ranch in Wyoming. Strongly geared to families with good rates for children and plenty of activities, Crossed Sabres is in a remarkable setting at the edge of Yellowstone National Park.

The **7D Ranch** (774 Sunlight Rd., 307/587-9885, www.7dranch.com, $1,610–1,820 pp per week) is a small, remote ranch in the Sunlight Basin, 50 miles northwest of Cody, offering cozy, rustic accommodations, horseback riding and fishing, pack trips, and hunting trips.

Camping

Buffalo Bill State Park (47 Lakeside Rd., 307/587-9227, May–Sept., $17 for nonresidents), 11 miles west of Cody, offers the closest public campgrounds. Situated below the Absaroka Mountains, the park has two campsites: The North Shore Bay campground has 37 sites, and the North Fork campground has 62 sites. A small number of sites in each campground can be reserved (877/996-7275, www.wyo-park.com) ahead of time.

A good, fully equipped private facility in town is the **Ponderosa Campground** (1815 8th St., 307/587-9203, www.codyponderosa.com, $22 tents, $31–36 RVs, $25 tipis, $42 cabins for 4 people). There is a cowboy cappuccino bar, a convenience store, a playground, clean restrooms and showers, and many other amenities in this large complex.

FOOD

Although much of the state can be classified as meat and potatoes only, Cody leans toward slightly more variety. For a great cup of coffee and a light breakfast of homemade pastries and bagels (admittedly the homemade cinnamon rolls may not count as light), stop into the **Beta Coffeehouse** (1132 12th St., 307/587-7707, 7 A.M.–6 P.M. Mon.–Fri., 7 A.M.–4 P.M. Sat.–Sun.). A favorite community gathering spot, the Beta often hosts live music and open-mike nights. In the winter, their homemade soups are beyond compare.

Cody's best-kept culinary secret is likely **Geysers on the Terrace** (525 W. Yellowstone Ave., 307/587-5868, dinner from 5 P.M. Mon.–Sat., entrées $9–26.50), an American bistro with inventive creations like Reuben egg rolls, Irish pizza with fennel cream sauce, hazelnut shrimp, and of course plenty of savory Wyoming steaks. There is a great children's menu too.

It doesn't get more local or more traditional than **Cassie's Supper Club** (214 Yellowstone Ave., 307/527-5500, www.cassies.com, 11 A.M.–10 P.M. daily, lunch $8–13, dinner $12–36), named for its original proprietor, Cody's most beloved madam. When the city asked her to close her brothel in the early 1930s, Cassie complied, sort of: She opened her supper club at the west end of town, where it stands today. The atmosphere is dark, the mood light, the food hearty, and the history rich. It is Cody's hot spot for two-stepping and has three bars to help lubricate the dancers. It should be stated that Cassie's brothel business died with her in 1952.

NIGHTLIFE

Although drinking while driving was only outlawed in Wyoming in 2002, believe it or not, drive-through liquor stores are still a surprise to many visitors. People often take their parties to go. For traditionalists who like to have a drink in a more stationary location, Cody offers plenty of great bars. Among them are the historic **Irma** (1192 Sheridan Ave., 800/745-IRMA—800/745-4762) and the **Silver Dollar Bar** (1313 Sheridan Ave., 307/527-7666), which often has live country music and serves food.

For family-oriented nightlife, try **Dan Miller's Cowboy Music Revue** (1171 Sheridan Ave., 307/272-7855, www.cowboymusicreview.com, 8 P.M. Mon.–Sat. May–Sept., $14 pp), which features a night of music, comedy, and poetry.

INFORMATION AND SERVICES

The **Cody Country Chamber of Commerce** (836 Sheridan Ave., 307/587-2777 or 800/393-2639, www.codychamber.org, 8 A.M.–5 P.M. Mon.–Fri. Oct. 1–Memorial Day, 8 A.M.–6 P.M. Mon.–Fri., 9 A.M.–5 P.M. Sat., 10 A.M.–3 P.M. Sun. Memorial Day–Sept. 30) acts as a visitors center and a ticket outlet for events around town. Excellent planning tools are also available online at www.yellowstonecountry.org.

For information on recreational trails and public camping in the region, contact the **Shoshone National Forest** (808 Meadowlane Ave., 307/527-6241, www.fs.fed.us/r2/shoshone) or the **Bureau of Land Management** (1002 Blackburn Ave., 307/578-5900, www.blm.gov/wy).

The main **post office** (307/527-7161) is located at 1301 Stampede Avenue.

The airy and bright **Cody Library** (307/527-1880, www.parkcountylibrary.org, 9 A.M.–8 P.M. Mon.–Thurs., 9 A.M.–5:30 P.M.

Fri., 9 A.M.–5 P.M. Sat., 1–4 P.M. Sun.) is located at 1500 Heart Mountain Street.

Visitors can do laundry at **Cody's Laundromat** (1728 Beck Ave., 307/587-8500) or **Eastgate Laundry** (1813 17th St., 307/587-5355).

Cody's **West Park Hospital** (707 Sheridan Ave., 307/527-7501 or 800/654-9447, www.westparkhospital.org) has a 24-hour emergency room. The hospital's **Urgent Care Clinic** (702 Yellowstone Ave., 307/587-7207) is open daily and evenings for walk-in patients.

GETTING THERE

The Cody area is served commercially by **The Yellowstone Regional Airport** (COD, 3001 Duggleby Dr., 307/587-5096, www.flyyra.com), just two minutes' drive from downtown, which has daily flights by **Delta/SkyWest** (307/587-9740 or 800/221-2121, www.delta.com, www.skywest.com), **United** (800/UNITED-1—800/864-8331, www.united.com), and **United Express/Mesa** (307/587-9740 or 800/864-8331, www.mesa-air.com, www.ual.com). The airport is 52 miles from the east entrance to Yellowstone National Park. Air and shuttle services are also available from Billings (107 miles).

By road, Cody is 177 miles from Jackson, 163 miles from Lander, 84 miles from Thermopolis, and 52 miles from Yellowstone National Park.

GETTING AROUND

Rental-car companies operating at the Yellowstone Regional Airport include **Avis** (307/587-4082 or 800/331-1212, www.avis.com), **Budget** (307/587-6066 or 800/527-0700, www.budget.com), and **Hertz** (307/587-2914 or 800/654-3131, www.hertz.com).

For service between Cody and Billings, local taxi service in town, and tours to Yellowstone, contact **Phidippides Shuttle Service** (307/527-6789 or 866/527-6789, www.codyshuttle.com).

For regular taxi service, contact **Cody Cab** (307/272-8364, www.codycab.llc@gmail.com). Tours of Yellowstone and Grand Teton National Parks can also be arranged.

SHERIDAN, DEVILS TOWER, AND NORTHEAST WYOMING

Northeast Wyoming is a vast swath of diverse terrain, from rocky peaks and meadows blanketed by wildflowers to river-carved canyons and wide-open spaces; from Sheridan, a classic Western town timeless in its appeal, to the Powder River Basin, which includes the working-class towns Gillette and Buffalo. Long a prime buffalo hunting territory for Native Americans, the area has seen great conflict between Indians and encroaching settlers. Today that relationship is dynamic and evident throughout much of the region, even at Devils Tower, where climbers are making strides toward working in cooperation with the Native Americans who consider the feature sacred.

The economy here is based almost entirely on natural resources: coal and coal-bed methane, livestock production, and tourism in these vast and beautiful places. There are tiny museums in towns like Sheridan and Big Horn, among many others, that celebrate a way of life that seems in no danger of disappearing, with the relative vastness and remote feel of the region. Although towns like Gillette are multiplying as quickly as trains can haul coal, there are plenty of places where time stands still in northeast Wyoming. From horseback riding and fishing to hiking and rock climbing, the region has no shortage of recreational opportunities.

PLANNING YOUR TIME

Travelers heading east or west on I-90 will have easy access to much of the region. **Sheridan** is a wonderful town to visit and a terrific hub for many of Wyoming's **dude ranches.** Although

© WYOMING TRAVEL & TOURISM

HIGHLIGHTS

◖ King's Saddlery: Part museum, part Western tack store, King's Saddlery in downtown Sheridan is the hub of this cowboy town (page 358).

◖ Medicine Wheel National Historic Landmark: High in the Big Horns on a narrow ridge overlooking two cirques is the mysterious, almost Stonehenge-esque feature known as Medicine Wheel. Thought to be 500-800 years old, this sacred spot swirls with theories (page 359).

◖ Eatons Ranch: The oldest dude ranch in the world, and certainly one of the most traditional, Eatons Ranch in tiny Wolf, Wyoming, is tried and true (page 363).

◖ Big Horn: This tiny little town nine miles south of Sheridan and set on Little Goose

Creek in the Big Horn Mountains is full of character, with a gem of an art museum, plenty of polo, and wonderful Western celebrations (page 365).

◖ Cloud Peak Scenic Byway: From Buffalo to Ten Sleep, this stunning road climbs over and cuts through the Big Horn Mountains, passing by beautiful spots like Tensleep Canyon and the Tensleep Preserve, and providing access to historic sites including Fort McKinney and Medicine Lodge State Archeological Site (page 368).

◖ Hiking and Climbing at Devils Tower: Rising more than 1,200 feet above the Belle Fourche River, the nation's first national monument is a magnet for hikers and climbers (page 379).

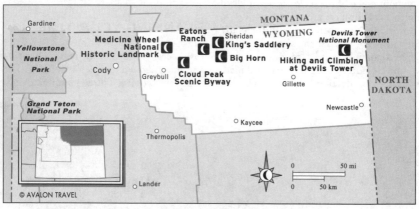

LOOK FOR ◖ TO FIND RECOMMENDED SIGHTS, ACTIVITIES, DINING, AND LODGING.

most ranches are busiest in summer, a few open in May, and some stay open into fall for hunters. Just down the road from Sheridan, the tiny town of Big Horn is home to the cool **Bradford Brinton Memorial and Museum,** on a gentleman's ranch where you could easily while away an afternoon. Nearby Buffalo, the starting point for the 64-mile **Cloud Peak Scenic Skyway,** has a historic downtown with a great

little museum and easy access to a number of sites that feature prominently in Wyoming history, including **Fort Phil Kearney** and the infamous **Hole in the Wall** region where Butch Cassidy and the Sundance Kid were known to hide out. Though not exactly a touristy destination, Gillette offers nice parks, a terrific public pool and waterslide, and one of the region's best culinary experiences, **The Chophouse**

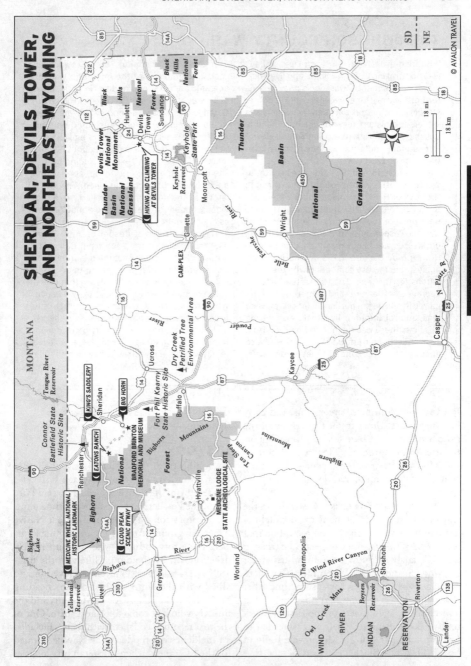

SHERIDAN, DEVILS TOWER, AND NORTHEAST WYOMING

NORTHEAST WYOMING

© AVALON TRAVEL

THE JOHNSON COUNTY WAR

With lush grasslands and rich river valleys ideal for grazing by both wildlife and livestock, Powder River country was long a popular area for both Native Americans and early homesteaders. The battles between the Indians and settlers for this territory are well documented. But the confrontations among white settlers were equally contentious, none more so than the Johnson County War.

Between 1875 and 1884, hundreds of thousands of cattle were brought to or through the Powder River Basin. Ranchers were quick to realize that the rich, wide-open grasslands were perfect to sustain their herds. Many of the men responsible for these large ranching businesses were known as the cattle barons. However, by the late 1870s and early 1880s, homesteaders were competing with the cattle barons for the land. The Homestead Act encouraged settlement, and numerous settlers moved in and began putting up fences, plowing land, and raising their livestock. Also during this time, there was further competition from smaller cattlemen known as rustlers who also appropriated land, and at times stray cattle, for their herds.

In 1892, The Wyoming Stock Growers Association, made up of the influential and important ranchers, planned to rid themselves of this ever-increasing problem in Johnson County. The plan was simple: hire men who would terminate anyone infringing on their territory – meaning the settlers and the rustlers. They gathered a group of about 50 gunmen, half hired from Texas, including former sheriffs, lured by the offer of $5 per day and a $50 bonus for each man killed. The Regulators, as the gunmen were called, were provided a "dead list" that named about 70 men as their targets.

The men arrived at Casper on April 5 and planned to sweep the area from Casper to Buffalo. On arrival they cut the telegraph lines so news of what they were about to do would not reach other towns. They heard that over a dozen men on their list were at the KC Ranch. When they arrived, there were in fact only four men, two of whom were not on the list and were left unharmed. The two other men, Nate Champion and Nick Ray, were believed to have stolen a few stray calves during their time as rustlers. The Regulators set upon the

---

Restaurant. Summer, late spring, and early fall are the best times to hit this corner of the state because of the blue skies and easy opportunities to be outdoors. They're still here in the winter, of course, but one gets the feeling that everyone is hunkered down, waiting for spring.

Though **Devils Tower** is not exactly on the way to anywhere, it is for many the highlight of a trip to Wyoming as an obvious recreation spot for climbers, hikers, and campers. The trip can be made fairly easily in a day from just about anywhere in northeast Wyoming. It's wise to plan your visit to Devils Tower sometime other than June, when the voluntary ban on hiking and climbing is in place, or the first and second weeks in August, when bikers headed to or from the huge Sturgis Motorcycle Rally in South Dakota's Black Hills can descend on

the tower in crowds of hundreds and even thousands.

HISTORY

Stretching from the eastern flank of the Big Horn Mountains east to the Black Hills and bordered on the south by the North Platte River, the Powder River Basin was prime hunting territory for a number of different Native American groups. Among the early inhabitants were the Crow Indians, who were ultimately driven north by the Sioux, likely in the mid-1800s. Arapaho and Cheyenne moved in and allied with the Sioux against miners heading hurriedly to the gold fields in Montana and the military who had come to protect them. One of the first recorded conflicts with whites included an incident near modern-day Kaycee (named for the KC ranch) when Lutheran missionaries house with their guns, killing Ray but unable to hit Champion, who remained holed up in the house. He wrote poignant notes about the attack, predicting he would never make it out alive. By early evening the gunmen had set fire to the house and fired on Champion, killing him as he ran from the flames. Two fellow rustlers had passed the house during the shootout and word soon spread of the imminent onslaught.

The Regulators saw these initial kills as a success and set their sights on Buffalo. They pulled into the T-A Ranch, just 14 miles outside town, to rest briefly. Unbeknownst to them, however, their journey had ended.

The people of Buffalo and settlers outside town had heard about the shoot-out at the KC Ranch and made a call to arms. The townsmen were committed to defending themselves and exacting revenge. The 200 "Home Defenders" rode out of town and surrounded the Regulators at the T-A Ranch. The Regulators believed their death was imminent. However, one man escaped and word reached the Wyoming governor, Amos W. Barber, who supported the cattle barons in their miscalculated efforts

to rid the state of rustlers. In turn, Barber contacted two state senators, who were also supporters of the Wyoming Stock Growers Association, the bastion of the cattle barons, and they called on the president for help. President Harrison ordered the troops from Fort McKinney to calm the riot and arrest the invaders being held inside.

Ultimately justice was never served to the Wyoming Stock Growers Association for their harebrained plan, nor to those who attempted to carry it out. The troops who arrested the Regulators did not turn them over to Johnson County, fearing retaliation by the townspeople. Instead they took them to Cheyenne to await trial. The prisoners were held in Cheyenne at the expense of Johnson County, and when Johnson County could no longer manage the expense of keeping them locked up, they were released on their own recognizance. The Texas gunmen fled home, and those from Wyoming quickly slipped under the radar. Due to the difficulty and expense involved, the court eventually threw the case out. The tensions between the ranchers and the rustlers would not dissipate for years.

set up a mission to convert Crows. When the missionaries arrived and set up camp in 1860, the Crow were no longer in the area, and the Sioux and Cheyenne did not want the missionaries around. One of the missionaries quickly deserted the mission; another was killed by the Indians, and the others fled for their lives. The Indians felt justified running the missionaries off and burning the mission because the Treaty of 1851, signed at Fort Laramie, had declared everything east of the Big Horns to the Black Hills and north of the North Platte River to be Indian territory.

In order to bypass inevitable conflict, most miners traveling through the region to Montana's gold fields traveled south of the Powder River Basin on the Oregon Trail. In 1864, however, as mining towns were booming overnight in Montana, John Jacobs and John

Bozeman built the first trail through the area, saving prospectors weeks of travel time. The Bozeman Trail became known as "The Bloody Bozeman" for numerous mortal conflicts. Jacobs and Bozeman dealt with their fair share of Indian encounters during the completion of the trail, including one in which Jacob's daughter, herself half-Indian, was beaten for traveling with white men.

The area was essentially a war zone 1865–1868, during the first of three Sioux wars. Only after the 1874–1876 second Sioux War, which included Crazy Horse's surrender and the Battle of Wounded Knee in 1890, did the Sioux commit to living on the reservation. During those 25 years numerous battles flared between significant leaders on both sides, including Sioux Chief Red Cloud, Dull Knife, and Col. H. B. Carrington. The 1876 Dull

Knife Battle robbed the Cheyenne of all their winter supplies, including lodge poles, canvases, and clothes, and even their winter food storage. Part military tactic, part revenge for the recent death of Custer and his men at the Battle of the Little Bighorn in June of that year, the Army destroyed everything the Cheyenne had gathered for winter, and the surviving Indians, women and children included, fled on foot in temperatures that dipped below -30°F. The Cheyenne surrendered a few weeks later. The reservation spread into the Black Hills, much of which was thought to be gold-rich, and was purchased by the government from the Sioux in 1876. Although the Indian Peace Commission had originally offered $6 million, and the Sioux, understanding the value the white men saw in the soil, had asked for $70 million, a final sale price of $4.5 million eliminated Indian ownership of the land.

With the Indian Wars essentially over, a new type of conflict arose between the moneyed cattlemen and the hardscrabble homesteaders across the Powder River Basin. Texas cattle had come into the region between 1875 and 1884. They were grazed on the open range until homesteaders started fencing off pastureland and watering holes. The cattle herds continued to increase while the open rangeland decreased. With drought followed by freezing temperatures, cattle numbers sustained cataclysmic losses over the winter of 1886–1887, later referred to as the "Great Die-up." Cattlemen became even more resolved to make their outfits profitable.

While the cattlemen were trying to rid themselves of pesky rustlers and homesteaders, a hired group called the Regulators pursued a "Dead List" of ambitious and outspoken homesteaders and people believed to be rustlers. Known as the Johnson County Wars, there were major conflicts between cattlemen and townspeople who supported the outspoken homesteaders.

The last Indian battle in Wyoming took place on October 30, 1903, southwest of Newcastle, when Sioux returning to their reservation from Montana ran into lawmen from Newcastle. At stake was the issue of whether or not the Indians were violating game laws by hunting off the reservation. Three lawmen were killed, and the Indians eventually surrendered, were put on trial, and were ultimately acquitted.

Throughout the 20th century, the story of this corner—and certainly the economy—of the Wyoming centered around cattle and sheep production, and more recently and far more lucratively, coal and coal-bed methane production. With wide-open ranch country and Devils Tower as the country's first national monument, it's not a stretch to see why tourism too continues to play an important role in the region.

Sheridan and Vicinity

Although Sheridan (population 17,197, elevation 3,745 feet) continuously touts itself as the midpoint between Yellowstone National Park and the Black Hills, they are selling themselves short. It's true that it is conveniently located, but this authentic Western town has much more to offer.

Rich with history, Sheridan is the town where Martha Jane Canary transformed herself into Calamity Jane. In an 1872 battle, she heroically rescued Captain Egan, who dubbed her "Calamity Jane, the heroine of the plains." The town's first building was erected in 1878 by trapper Jim Mason. In 1881 the tiny cabin was converted into a post office and store named Mandel. The town was eventually platted by J. D. Loucks, who named it for his Civil War commander, General Philip H. Sheridan, and with the coming of the railroad in 1892, Sheridan quickly became a cattle town. The iconic Sheridan Inn was opened in 1893 and was the town's unofficial center with Buffalo

claims to be the lowest town in Wyoming at 3,745 feet.

SIGHTS

Trail End State Historic Site

The Trail End State Historic Site (400 Clarendon Ave., Sheridan, 307/674-4589, www.trailend.org, daily Mar. 1–Dec. 14, hours vary seasonally, $2 nonresidents, $1 residents) is situated high on a bluff overlooking town. The four-acre grounds are impeccably manicured and have retained much of their original landscaping, designed nearly a century ago. The museum is the former home of John B. Kendrick, one of Wyoming's most famous sons. Kendrick was orphaned early in life and got his start at age 15 as a ranch hand. Originally from Texas, he followed cattle into Wyoming and, taken with its beauty, decided to stay. He went on to become a successful rancher and businessman, accumulating more than 200,000 acres of land. Kendrick would become Wyoming's first governor and later a U.S. Senator. Kendrick referred to the house, begun in 1908 and completed in 1913, as the "end-of-the-trail mansion," and it's where he would spend the last 20 years of his life when he wasn't in Washington, D.C.

The house is built in the Flemish Revival style, with rich mahogany walls, exposed-beam ceilings, and 18 beautifully decorated rooms. What is unique to this historic house is that almost everything on display (furniture, rugs, magazines, books, and photographs) is the original property of the Kendrick family. Self-guided tours are available; for groups larger than eight, reservations for guided tours can be made two weeks in advance.

Sheridan Inn

When the Sheridan Inn (856 N. Broadway, Sheridan, 307/674-5440, www.sheridaninn.com) opened in 1893, it was considered the finest hotel between Chicago and San Francisco. Designed after a Scottish inn and with a bar imported from England, the inn was the only hotel in Sheridan to have electric lights (200 of them, to be exact). The porch runs the full

Bill as its operator for two years. Sheridan has weathered cattle, coal, and tourist economies; today there is an interesting mix of all three with a couple of coal mines in nearby Decker, Montana, serving as important employers.

One of the most charming towns in the state, with an extensive historic downtown, Sheridan has the feel of the old West, although that is slowly beginning to change as traditional Main Street businesses are gradually being replaced by high-end art galleries and gourmet eateries. Still, Wyoming's best-known saddlery is here and in no danger of leaving, as are some classic watering holes like the Mint Bar, along with numerous historic sites. Surrounded by dusty but beautiful countryside and the pastoral and magnificent Big Horn Mountains, Sheridan

130-foot length of the hotel, and there are 62 dormer windows.

Buffalo Bill Cody helped inaugurate the hotel—chilled champagne was served—and went on to become a co-owner. He would hold auditions for his Wild West Show on the hotel's veranda, and the Sheridan Inn quickly became the social center for Sheridan's affluent residents.

The hotel has hosted famous guests, including presidents Theodore Roosevelt, Howard Taft, and Herbert Hoover. Its longest resident, however, is said to still reside in the hotel: Catherine B. Arnold worked and lived at the Inn for 64 years, from her arrival in 1901 until she left, only when the hotel closed, in 1965. She had worked as a desk clerk, seamstress, housekeeper, and hostess, and her dying request was to be buried in the hotel. When she died three years later, her ashes were placed in the wall of the third floor room she often occupied. Today, the staff say the presence of "Miss Kate" is still felt. From the sound of footsteps and lights turning on and off to doors being opened and shut, the rumor is that she still likes to manage the inn.

The hotel reopened in 1967 and continued to operate for another 20 years before closing its doors again. In 1991 a restaurant opened in the inn, but it no longer functioned as a hotel. A new restaurant, **1893 Grille and Spirits** (307/673-2777, open for lunch and dinner), recently replaced the older one; the hotel is under renovation and will eventually reopen as a 22-room boutique hotel. Visitors can buy a $2 brochure for a self-guided tour of the first floor. To see other floors, you must take the guided tour ($5 adults, $2 seniors, free for children).

◖ King's Saddlery

In a town full of Western stores, King's Saddlery (184 N. Main St., Sheridan, 307/672-2702 or 800/443-8919, www.kingropes.com, 8 A.M.–5 P.M. Mon.–Sat.) is indeed aptly named. A legendary tack store founded by the King Family in the late 1940s, founder Don King is a local hero and was a renowned saddle maker. Many of his saddles are on display in the store's **Don King Museum** (8 A.M.–5 P.M. Mon.–Sat., donation requested) as well as at the National Cowboy Hall of Fame and the PRCA Rodeo Hall of Fame. For six years, Don handcrafted the PRCA World Championship saddles.

In addition to the store's dizzying selection of rope, hats, and Western tack, the museum houses hundreds of saddles, wagons, coaches, Indian artifacts, cowboy memorabilia from around the world, and original art. Don't leave without a King Ropes baseball cap, which promotes the saddlery's most famous product; it will connect you with other cowboy aficionados the world over.

Sheridan Trolley

The Sheridan Trolley (307/751-3472, Memorial Day–Labor Day, charter rides year-round, $1), is a good way to see the historic highlights in town. The two trolleys are replicas of the original electric trolleys that ran 1911–1926. The trolleys depart from and return to the Visitors Information Center (E. 5th St., Sheridan, 307/672-2485 or 800/453-3650), where you can also pick up a map of the trolley route and schedule. The loop stops at many of the city's main attractions, and riders can disembark and climb aboard the trolley as many times as they'd like (just ask the driver for a transfer token). There is also a night route that runs 5–8 P.M. and stops at many of the hotels and bars downtown.

Ucross Foundation

Twenty-seven miles east of Sheridan, nestled in the midst of a 20,000-acre working cattle ranch (half of the land is protected by the Nature Conservancy), is the artists haven known as Ucross (30 Big Red Lane, 307/737-2291, www.ucrossfoundation.org). About 80 artists from around the globe are invited to take up residence at the foundation each year for a few weeks at a time. The foundation's mission is simply to provide a workplace where writers, composers, painters, or other artists can live and work uninterrupted for an extended period of time. There are usually eight or nine residents on the grounds at the same time. Respected local author Annie Proulx has been a significant supporter of Ucross, and Elizabeth Gilbert wrote part of her novel *Eat, Pray, Love* while in residence.

Big Red was the main house of the original ranch and now serves as the artists' residence. It is decorated with antique furniture and houses a gallery where there are four exhibitions annually. Visitors and townspeople alike descend on the campus each Fourth of July for the spectacular fireworks show. The on-site art gallery (8:30 A.M.–4 P.M. daily year-round) is open to the public.

Big Horn Scenic Byway

One stretch of stunning road between Yellowstone to the west and Mount Rushmore and the Black Hills to the east is the Big Horn Scenic Byway, a 57-mile stretch of road that starts at Shell, Wyoming, in the dramatic Shell Canyon. Winding up through the Bighorn National Forest past the stunning Shell Falls, the byway slips through narrow canyons past red chimney rocks and towering cliffs. The highest point on the drive is Granite Pass, just above the Antelope Butte Ski Area. North of the pass, the byway intersects with U.S. 14A, known as the Medicine Wheel Passage for its access to Medicine Wheel National Historic Landmark. In addition to a diversity of landscapes—rangeland, forest, subalpine, and alpine—there is an abundance of wildlife in the region; travelers can watch for elk, moose, and deer. The access to public campgrounds and hiking trails is better on this byway than just about anywhere in the Bighorn National Forest. The byway starts or ends (although U.S. 14 continues on) just west of Ranchester, where the Connor Battlefield State Historic Site is located.

🄲 Medicine Wheel National Historic Landmark

High atop a bluff in the Big Horn Mountains, some 70 miles (about a 90-minute drive) west of Sheridan on U.S. 14A, Medicine Wheel National Historic Landmark is a 74-foot-wide stone circle with 28 interior spokes connecting the exterior with an interior circular mound. Made of limestone slabs and boulders, the Medicine Wheel is a mysterious landmark that has spiritual but unexplained significance to many Native American groups. First seen by white explorers in the late 1800s, thoughts on its origins are vast and varied: Some link it back to the worship of the Aztecs; others attribute it to early French or Russian explorers. The most common viewpoint, however, is that is was built by one of the tribes in the region: Crow, Arapaho, Shoshone, Sheepeater, or Cheyenne. The star alignments suggest the medicine wheel could have been constructed as early as the 13th century, and the solstice alignments are accurate even today. The only carbon dating from the site, done on a piece of wood, suggests a minimum age of 1760. There are tipi rings around the site and worn travois trails to the site, suggesting heavy usage. Stone markers in the shape of arrows point to a number of nearby medicine wheels, including those in Meeteetse and Steamboat Mountain in southwest Wyoming near Rock Springs.

Although the site was designated a National Historic Landmark in 1970, little was done to protect the artifacts from the elements, livestock, and, rather unfortunately, disrespectful visitors. Today the U.S. Forest Service (2013 Eastside 2nd St., Sheridan, 307/674-2600, www.fs.fed.us/r2/bighorn) is responsible for protecting and preserving the area, and Native American guides have been hired to interpret the site for visitors. Driving to the site itself is restricted, so plan to park at the ranger station and walk about 1.5 miles on a gravel road.

ENTERTAINMENT AND EVENTS

Sheridan is a strong community of locals and regular yearly visitors that supports a multitude of weekly events, including the Thursday **Sheridan Farmers Market** at the Whitney Commons and Tuesday evening **Concerts in the Park** at Kendrick Park. Sheridan is also home to two theaters, **The Carriage House Theater** (419 Delphi Ave., 307/672-9886) and the **WYO Theater** (42 N. Main St., 307/672-9084), the oldest vaudeville theater in the state.

Each year in mid-June the **Bozeman Trail Days** (307/684-7629, www.bozemantrail.org) commemorates the historic trail and the conflicts surrounding it with educational symposiums, living history demonstrations, and tours of the Fort Phil Kearny State Historic Site and various battlefields.

For more than 80 years, the **Sheridan WYO Rodeo** (www.sheridanwyorodeo.com) has been one of the most celebrated events in the state, and its renowned posters hang as graphic art all across the West. The mid-July event entails four nights of PRCA rodeo, multiple concerts, the Chris LeDoux Spurs and Spikes Memorial Golf Tournament, a traditional Indian Relay with a $25,000 payout, a parade, and a foot race.

Held annually the last week of July, the **Sheridan County Fair** (1650 W. 5th St., Sheridan, 307/672-2079, free) offers games, contests, and events scheduled to entertain the whole family, including a pancake breakfast, horse and livestock shows, community exhibits, inflatable games and slides, and the usual 4-H and FFA events.

Later in the summer, typically in mid-August, the **Sheridan County Rodeo** (www.sherfair.com) is held at the local fairgrounds. Less flashy than the Sheridan WYO Rodeo, this old-school small-town rodeo showcases the abundant local talent the region is known for. Events are open to adults and kids in more than two dozen events, including roping, racing, pole bending, goat tying, and steer wrestling.

The Big West Arts Festival (307/674-6446, www.bigwestartsfestival.com) is a relatively new but rapidly growing event; started in 2004, it ranks as one of the top 50 art festivals in the country. It takes place the second weekend of August on the Sheridan College campus and attracts traditional, contemporary, and even postmodern art. One of the festival's stated purposes is not only to showcase Western art and artists but to bring the rest of the country's art to the West. Admission to the event is free and includes live musical performances each day.

SHOPPING

After a requisite stop at **King's Saddlery,** shoppers can stroll up and down historic Main Street with its abundance of art galleries, boutiques, and classic Western stores.

A fun shop worth visiting is the **Crazy Woman Trading Company** (120 N. Main St., Sheridan, 307/672-3939, www.crazywoman-trading.com) which sells clothing, gift items, home decor, and more.

For appropriate cowboy and cowgirl duds, stop into the authentic **Dan's Western Wear** (226 N. Main St., Sheridan, 800/817-3267, www.danswesternwear.com) or the **Custom Cowboy Shop** (1286 Sheridan Ave., Sheridan, 800/487-2692, www.customcowboyshop.com), which was started more than 30 years ago as a way to make ends meet by cattle rancher and saddle maker Don Butler. Today these stores carry everything from saddles and tack to hats, buckles, scarves, clothing, and jewelry.

RECREATION
Hiking

With the Big Horn Mountains looming so close to town, there is plenty of country to get lost in within an easy drive from Sheridan. To plan a good hike or backpacking trip, visit the **U.S. Forest Service** (2013 Eastside 2nd St., Sheridan, 307/674-2600, www.fs.fed.us/r2/bighorn) for maps and advice. Right downtown, **Big Horn Mountain Sports** (176 N. Main St., Sheridan, 307/672-6866, www.bighornmountainsports.com) can outfit hikers and backpackers or just offer friendly advice.

For adventurous types keen to head out, there are hundreds of trails in the Big Horn National Forest, many of which can be accessed from the Big Horn Scenic Byway on U.S. 14. One such trail is the **Tongue River,** an 18.2-mile out-and-back hike that leaves from a trailhead roughly nine miles west of Ranchester on County Road 92 in the Tongue River Canyon. Though the trail climbs more than 3,000 vertical feet over 9 miles, hikers looking for a shorter route will be delighted with the two-mile round-trip hike along the gushing river and up a set of switchbacks to a rather large limestone cave that can be explored if you have the right equipment (headlamps are essential). Be on the lookout, however, for livestock, poison ivy, and rattlesnakes; even with them, this is a beautiful spot.

A map of the paved and unpaved trails that cover much of the town of Sheridan is available online at www.city-sheridan-wy.com/info/pathways.php.

Fishing

There is no shortage of fantastic fishing spots around Sheridan. Anglers have long flocked to the region to wet a line on the **Tongue River, Little Goose Creek,** and **Big Goose Creek** as well as any of the dozens of pristine alpine lakes in the region, including **Sibley Lake** and **Lake DeSmet.**

For up-to-date information and all the gear you could possibly need, stop into **Fly Shop of the Big Horns** (227 N. Main St., Sheridan, 307/672-5866 or 800/253-5866, www.troutangler.com). They offer guided trips to blue-ribbon trout waters on both public and private lands. All-day trips for two people start at $445, all-inclusive.

Horseback Riding

While Sheridan is surrounded by some of the best guest ranches in the country that focus on riding, there is an option for visitors to town who are looking for a riding opportunity without the full-on ranch experience. **Canyon Ranch** (59 Canyon Ranch Road, Big Horn, 307/674-6239, www.canyonranchbighorn.com) is located 15 miles south of Sheridan (take Hwy. 335 to County Road 77 to Canyon Ranch Road) and has been run by the Wallop family for more than a century. In addition to offering a guest ranch experience, they are among the only ranches to offer trail rides by the hour. Riders can choose from trails at Canyon Ranch or the nearby Rafter Y Ranch, both of which offer incredible views of the Big Horn Mountains. They have horses that are

well-suited for all levels of riding ability. Rides are $50 pp per hour, and there is a half-day option that runs about four hours and includes lunch for $150 pp.

Golf

There are three golf courses in the vicinity of Sheridan. **The Powder Horn Golf Community** (161 Hwy. 335, 307/672-5323 or 800/329-0598, www.thepowderhorn.com, $64–84 for 18 holes, rates vary seasonally, discounts for Sheridan County residents) offers a nationally recognized and semiprivate 27-hole course with three distinct nines, one of which is modeled after St. Andrews in Scotland. The nine-hole course at the **Sheridan Country Club** (1992 W. 5th St., 307/674-8135, www.sheridancountryclub.com, $30 for 18 holes) is open to the public during the week only, but not on holidays. Work is underway on another nine holes to make this an 18-hole course. The municipal **Kendrick Golf Course** (65 Golf Course Rd., 307/674-8148, www.city-sheridan-wy.com, $28 for 18 holes) offers 18 holes with discounts for families and twilight play.

ACCOMMODATIONS

Sheridan has a broad assortment of roadside hotels and motels. The most unique is probably the **Mill Inn** (2161 Coffeen Ave., 307/672-6401 or 888/FLR-MILL—888/357-6455, www.sheridanmillinn.com, $60–89 s), cleverly built in an 1890s flour mill and listed on the National Register of Historic Places. The modern rooms are standard and comfortable.

Among the most budget-friendly options in town is the **Super Saver Inn** (1789 N. Main St., 307/672-0471, eshelby@q.com, $44 s, $55 d) near the VA Medical Center; it is clean and very basic, offering microwaves, coffeemakers, refrigerators, free Wi-Fi, and a Laundromat onsite. The 37 guest rooms are pet-friendly, and their rates are the lowest in town.

At the other end of the spectrum, the new **Wingate by Wyndham** (1950 E. 5th St., 307/675-1101, www.wingateinnsheridan.com, $85–140 d) is geared to business travelers (although kids will love the Nintendo and video

THE NATION'S FIRST DUDE RANCH

In 1868, a trio of brothers left Pittsburgh in pursuit of more adventure than their father's dry good store promised. Howard Eaton settled in the Badlands of North Dakota; his brothers Alden and Willis joined him a few years later, and together the three established a small ranch by invoking squatter's rights near what would become the town of Medora, North Dakota. On the Custer Trail Ranch, the brothers made their living by supplying wild game to railroad workers and hay to the nearby Army fort, all while establishing their own herds of horses and cattle.

Stories of their adventures trickled back East, and before long the much-loved brothers hosted an endless string of friends. In 1882, realizing the financial strain he and others were placing on the hospitable Eatons, Bert Rumsey of Buffalo, New York, insisted on paying for the privilege of staying on the ranch. In so doing, Rumsey became the world's first "dude," a term coined by the eldest Eaton brother, Howard. Modest as it was – guests slept several to a bed or on the floor, paying $25 per month for the right to do chores – the dude ranching industry was born.

The brutal winter of 1886-1887 changed dude ranching from a practicality to a necessity: The Eatons lost all but 150 of their 1,500 cattle to the cold and snow. The paying guests kept the Eatons afloat.

In 1904, the Eaton brothers bought 7,000 acres of land on the northeastern slope of the Big Horn Mountains. They announced to their friends that they'd be taking a year off to build structures on the ranch: cabins, barns, and a dining hall. Some 70 dudes showed up anyway and for about $100 apiece built many of the cabins that stand today. Although Howard and Willis remained lifelong bachelors, Alden married and set into motion the family that would run the ranch for more than a century. His great-great-grandson, Jeff Way, is the ranch general manager today, and like his family before him, he welcomes guests every summer as part of the extended Eatons family.

The beauty of Eatons is in its simplicity. Not much has changed since 1903. Days start early with the thunder of horses being brought down from night pasture. The clanging of an old locomotive wheel signals the start of hearty meals served family style in the old dining hall. There are still Saturday-night cookouts and Western dances, picnics, softball games pitting the dudes against the wranglers, rodeos, and more riding than the horsiest Easterner could ever dream of.

The dude season at Eatons runs late May-September, and the ranch can accommodate 125 guests in 51 cabins. Depending on the dates and cabin selected, adult nightly rates for a six-night stay range $210-235, children under 18 are $180 per night, and children under 6 are $145 night. Rates include transportation to and from Sheridan, accommodations, all meals, and riding.

© CARTER G. WALKER

Dudes at Eatons, even little ones, always wear a smile.

games) and has spacious oversize rooms with exceptionally nice amenities, including a complimentary deluxe continental breakfast buffet, a fitness room, free Wi-Fi, a pool, and a self-service business center. Every room offers either a view of the Big Horn Mountains or the prairie. Located on a hilltop east of I-90, the Wingate is quiet with easy access to town.

GUEST RANCHES

One beloved dude ranch in the area is the **Spear O Wigwam** (888/818-3833, www.spear-o-wigwam.com, $1,500 per week or $225 per day adults double occupancy, all-inclusive) northeast of Sheridan. The cabins are at once rustic and comfortable, and activities include horseback riding, fishing, hiking, and pack trips, among others. The ranch was founded by Wyoming senator Willis Spear in 1923, and Ernest Hemingway was a frequent visitor.

For a comprehensive list of dude ranches across the region, contact the **Dude Ranchers' Association** (307/587-2339, www.duderanch.org) which represents more than 100 of the West's most respected ranches. Another excellent resource for finding the ideal dude ranch vacation is **Gene Kilgore's Ranchweb** (www.ranchweb.com).

(Eatons Ranch

A half-hour's drive from Sheridan nestled along Wolf Creek in the Big Horn Mountains is Eatons Ranch (270 Eaton Ranch Rd., 307/655-9552, www.eatonsranch.com, $185–235 pp all-inclusive), the oldest dude ranch in the world and, frankly, the cream of the crop. The cabins are old and charming, and the wonder of Eatons is that it rarely changes through the decades. The founding family is still running the ranch, which can accommodate up to 125 guests, and many of the dudes' families have been coming for generations as well. The riding is excellent, and Eatons is among the only ranches where riders can take to the mountains or prairies without a wrangler (although one is always available). The setting is magnificent and diverse—with mountains,

canyons and prairies to ride—and the traditions here are time-tested.

CAMPING

There are numerous public campgrounds in the Bighorn National Forest, many of which are easily accessed from the Big Horn Scenic Byway. For information about specific sites and, in some cases, to make reservations, contact the **U.S. Forest Service** (2013 Eastside 2nd St., Sheridan, 307/674-2600, www.fs.fed.us/r2/bighorn). Reservations can be booked at some sites through www.recreation.gov.

There are also a handful of RV parks scattered around town. The **Sheridan KOA** (63 Decker Rd., 307/674-8766, www.koa.com, $24–68) offers tent and RV sites, 1–2-room cabins, bike rentals, fishing, miniature golf, a swimming pool, and free Wi-Fi.

FOOD

Unlike much of rural Wyoming, Sheridan is quite cosmopolitan when it comes to dining options. There is plenty of variety—think Chinese, Korean, and Mexican—plus some very sophisticated gourmet eateries. Even so, it's never hard to find a juicy burger or steak in this cattle country.

A classic local favorite for breakfast, lunch, or dinner, the **Sheridan Palace** (138 N. Main St., 307/672-2391, 6 A.M.–9 P.M. Mon.–Sat., entrées $4.50–21) is the quintessential Main Street café that doubles as an unofficial community hub. The food is almost entirely homemade and includes Friday and Saturday night prime rib, plus made-from-scratch barbecue, sandwiches, excellent meat-filled omelets, and daily specials. The can't-miss-it yellow-and-red building has been home to the restaurant for nearly 100 years, and from time to time a ghost affectionately known as Tex is heard ambling about with his spurs jingling. This is such a comfortable place that regulars feel free to come in and out the back door. Longtime owners Jane and Steve give back to the community with their free Thanksgiving dinner each year.

Equally a part of the Sheridan community

is the knock-your-socks-off gourmet cuisine at **Oliver's Bar & Grill** (55 N. Main St., 307/672-2838, oliversbarngrill@qwest.net, lunch 11 A.M.–2 P.M. Tues.–Fri., dinner 5–10 P.M. Mon.–Sat., lunch $7–15, dinner $9–35). Opened in 2002 by local son and genius chef Matt Wallop, Oliver's offers American bistro cuisine with Asian and Mediterranean influences. From the bar burgers, pizzas, and pastas to juicy steaks, the menu here is creative, fresh, and utilizes local ingredients when possible. Long known as *the* fine dining establishment in town, Oliver's shook things up a bit in 2010 with a remodel and a new emphasis on more casual but still fabulous meals, including lunches.

NIGHTLIFE

Whether you are cruising in a beat-up pickup truck or on foot, you don't have to leave Main Street for a taste of Sheridan's nightlife. The most famous of all the watering holes, and for good reason, is the **Mint Bar** (151 N. Main St., 307/674-9696), which boasts hundreds of artifacts and mounts, furniture made in the tradition of Thomas Molesworth, hundreds of local

The Mint Bar in Sheridan is a timeless spot.

© WYOMING TRAVEL & TOURISM

cattle brands on the wall, and ambience that cannot be beat. Don't leave without a pair of satin underpants that touts the Mint as a place "where good friends meet."

INFORMATION AND SERVICES

The office of **Sheridan Travel and Tourism** (307/673-7120, www.sheridanwyoming.org, 8 A.M.–5 P.M. daily summer, 8 A.M.–5 P.M. Mon.–Fri. in other seasons) is conveniently located at the State of Wyoming Information Center, just east of I-90 at exit 23.

For information on hiking, camping, and other recreation in the Bighorn National Forest, contact the **U.S. Forest Service** (2013 Eastside 2nd St., Sheridan, 307/674-2600, www.fs.fed.us/r2/bighorn). Information on fishing and hunting is available through the **Wyoming Game and Fish Department** (307/672-7418, www.gf.state.wy.us).

The main **post office** (307/672-0714) in Sheridan is located at 101 East Loucks Street.

The **Sheridan County Fulmer Public Library** (335 W. Alger St., 307/674-8585, www.sheridanwyolibrary.org, 9 A.M.–9 P.M. Mon.–Thurs., 9 A.M.–5 P.M. Fri.–Sat. June–Aug., 9 A.M.–9 P.M. Mon.–Thurs., 9 A.M.–5 P.M. Fri.–Sat., 1–5 P.M. Sun. Sept.–May) has both Internet-connected computers and free Wi-Fi available.

Sheridan Memorial Hospital (1401 W. 5th St., 307/672-1000, www.sheridanhospital.org) has a 24-hour emergency room. There are also two urgent care facilities in town: **Big Horn Urgent Care** (813 Highland Ave., 307/673-5501, www.bighornurgentcare.com) and **Urgent Care Clinic of Sheridan** (1842 Sugarland Dr., Suite 103, 307/673-5586).

Do laundry at **Sheridan Econ-O-Wash** (19 E. 5th St., 307/672-7899).

GETTING THERE

The tiny **Sheridan County Airport** (SHR, 908 W. Brundage Lane, 307/674-4222) offers daily flights to and from Denver on **United** (800/UNITED-1—800/864-8331, www.united.com), **Frontier** (800/432-1359, www.frontierairlines.com), and **Great Lakes**

(800/554-5111, www.flygreatlakes.com). The nearest larger airport is about 135 miles away (2 hours by car) in Billings.

Bus service in the region is provided by **Jefferson Bus Line** (307/674-6188 or 800/767-5333) and **Arrow/Blackhills Stage Line** (307/674-6188), which offers service to and from Billings, Denver, and the Colorado communities of Greeley, Fort Collins, and Longmont as well as the Wyoming communities of Buffalo, Casper, Douglas, Wheatland, and Cheyenne.

By car, Sheridan is 103 miles from Gillette, 147 miles from Cody, 199 miles from Yellowstone National Park, and 324 miles from Jackson.

GETTING AROUND

Rental cars are available from **Avis** (307/672-2226 or 800/831-2847, www.avis.com), **Budget** (307/673-1240 or 800/527-7000, www.budget.com), or **Enterprise** (307/672-6910 or 800/736-8222, www.enterprise.com).

In addition to the **Sheridan Trolley** (307/751-3472), which runs limited hours during summer, local taxi service is available by calling **Sheridan Taxi** (307/674-6814).

◰ BIG HORN

Located on the eastern flank of the Big Horns, the tiny town of Big Horn (population 208, elevation 4,081 feet) packs a lot of punch. The town was initially settled by upper-class ranchers and European aristocrats; among them was the Moncreiffe family, who raised prize sheep in the region. Although the town never officially incorporated, at one time the population purportedly passed 1,000 but rapidly dwindled in 1893 when the railroad came to Sheridan, nine miles northeast. Still, with its heritage of gentleman ranchers, Big Horn has an assortment of fascinating sites and a unique culture that makes a stop in town worthwhile.

Sights

For starters, the **Bradford Brinton Memorial and Museum** (239 Brinton Rd., 307/672-3173, www.bradfordbrintonmemorial.com, 10 A.M.–4 P.M. Mon.–Sat. Memorial Day–Labor Day, $4 adults, $3 seniors and students, free for children under 13) is an exquisite little museum housed in a genteel 1920s and 1930s working ranch. Bradford Brinton was a wealthy businessman from Chicago when he bought the ranch in 1923. He built it into an elaborate estate to showcase his ever-growing collection of art and then left it to his sister when he died. She meticulously maintained it and left it to the Northern Trust Company of Chicago, which administers it today. Tours through the 20-room Brinton home are given, and this magnificent gem has a surprising number of works by Charlie Russell, Frederic Remington, and numerous other legendary Western artists.

Another surprising museum in this tiny little town is the **Bozeman Trail Museum** (335 Johnson St., 307/674-6363 or 307/674-8050, jslack@wyoming.com, 11 A.M.–4 P.M. Sat.–Sun. Memorial Day–Labor Day). Built in what was a log blacksmith shop to serve travelers along the trail, the museum includes Indian artifacts, photos, pioneer clothing, book, tools, and other artifacts.

Polo

Big Horn is also the polo hotbed of Wyoming. There are practice games on Wednesday and Friday, and tournament games on Sunday June–August at the noteworthy **Big Horn Equestrian Center** (932 Bird Farm Rd., www.thebhec.org). Admission to the announced matches (twice on Sun. July–Aug.) is free, and concessions are available. Every year on Labor Day Sunday–Monday, the center closes out the season with **Don King Days**, a classic Western celebration with polo, championship steer roping, bronc riding, and wild-cow milking. The center is also one a local favorite places to spend the Fourth of July, with a phenomenal fireworks display.

Buffalo and Vicinity

A neat little Western town with a lot of history and a surprising Basque influence, Buffalo (population 3,900, elevation 4,645 feet) was settled in 1879. Historically it is among Wyoming's biggest sheep towns, which was true as recently as the 1980s, until a late-spring storm after shearing in 1984 caused major losses and reminded locals of the Great Die-up of 1886–1887. Political and environmental conditions never allowed ranchers to recover. Instead, Buffalo makes the most of its beautiful location in the foothills of the Big Horn Mountains, its easy access to scenic drives and outdoor adventures, and its historic buildings and museums.

SIGHTS
Jim Gatchell Memorial Museum
The origins of the Jim Gatchell Memorial Museum (100 Fort St., 307/684-9331, www. jimgatchell.com, May–Oct., days and hours vary) can be traced back to the opening of the Buffalo Pharmacy in 1900, the first of its kind in town. People from all walks of life—cattle barons, outlaws, and homesteaders—frequented Jim Gatchell's drugstore, and many would give him small mementos that he kept. Over time, they began entrusting him with pieces of Johnson County history. He also befriended the local Indians, and they too would bestow on him different cultural and personal artifacts.

After Gatchell passed away in 1954, his family donated his collection to Johnson County with the condition it would be shared with the public. The museum was established three years later. Its focus is on Johnson County's frontier era history, and more than 15,000 pieces are on display. There is a large array of Native American artifacts and many pieces that can be traced back to the U.S. Cavalry. There are a variety of wagons, historic photos, a model of Fort Phil Kearny, artifacts from the fateful Fetterman Fight, and many interpretative materials related to the Bozeman Trail. The museum is being remodeled in stages, and after the renovation is complete in 2011, it will be open year-round.

Occidental Hotel
Entering the Occidental Hotel (10 N. Main St., 307/684-0451, www.occidentalwyoming. com), many visitors feel as if they've stepped back in time. The hotel has been painstakingly restored to its original 1880s splendor, which includes many of its original furnishings such as light fixtures, the back bar, tin ceilings, a piano, and stained glass. Even the bullet holes throughout the bar are mementos of rowdier days. The place is said to be part museum, part hotel, part bar and restaurant. Visitors can follow a brochure for a self-guided tour or take a free 15-minute guided tour. Hotel guests have a variety of individual suites to choose from, each uniquely decorated with different antiques and features to match the original era. On Thursday nights, the saloon hosts a jam session featuring high-caliber bluegrass, Western, and folk musicians.

Dry Creek Petrified Tree Environmental Area
To find the unusual Dry Creek Petrified Forest, drive east from Buffalo on I-90, take the Red Hills Road exit (exit 65), and follow the road for seven miles. In the midst of this sagebrush country, you can follow a 0.8-mile loop that winds through the remnants of petrified trees. They date back 60 million years to when the area was swampland covered by metasequoia trees. Some of the stumps are larger than four feet in diameter, and the numerous rings can be identified. The loop that takes visitors through the area is also an eight-station ecological trail with information about the process of petrifaction and the unique history of the land.

Fort Phil Kearny State Historic Site
Located between Sheridan and Buffalo off I-90, the Fort Phil Kearny State Historic Site

THE BOZEMAN TRAIL

Although the Bozeman Trail was not given a name until John Jacobs and John Bozeman plowed through the region to give optimistic miners and settlers access to the quickest route through the Powder River Basin, in fact the trail is an ancient migratory route long used by animals and Paleo-Indians. Today this modern transportation corridor is rich with evidence from the past: pictographs, petroglyphs, and ledger art. There are oral histories of trappers and traders in the area that date back to the mid-1700s; written records from Lewis and Clark, who zigzagged across the trail; and evidence that mountain men, missionaries, and the U.S. military all used the trail that, until the first gold rush in southwest Montana in 1862, probably resembled a well-used age-old game trail.

Enter Jacobs and Bozeman in 1863. Leading a wagon train toward the gold fields in Montana, the men were just 140 miles beyond Deer Creek when they met a large party of Northern Cheyenne and Sioux warriors. Although the bulk of the wagon train turned back toward the Oregon Trail crossing southern and central Wyoming, Bozeman and a few of the men continued on horseback through the region. The following year, Bozeman again led a wagon train through the region, this time with help from Allen Hurlbut and mountain man Jim Bridger. Although nonnative traffic through the area was illegal under the Fort Laramie Treaty of 1851, and indeed there were conflicts, military support for the Bozeman Trail was evident in various campaigns throughout the region. The treaties signed at Fort Sully in 1865 gave the military unchecked authority to build roads and forts along the Bozeman Trail, and in 1866 alone, more than 2,000 people traveled on it to Montana, with Fort Reno and Fort Phil Kearny established to protect civilians. On December 21, with tensions high between Native Americans and the military, an entire command of 81 men under Captain William J. Fetterman was demolished by Sioux warriors.

In 1868, after several more battles, the Bozeman Trail and the forts along it were abandoned as indefensible by the U.S. Army. Still, the trail saw traffic from expeditions sent to scout the Yellowstone area and the Black Hills. When the Cheyenne were ultimately defeated by General Crook in November 1876 and forced to live on a reservation, the Bozeman Trail once again opened the region to significant settler traffic. Gradually, it became the preferred route for telegraph lines, stagecoaches, and eventually, an interstate highway.

(528 Wagon Box Rd., 307/684-7629, www. philkearny.vcn.com, grounds dawn–dusk daily, museum and visitors center 8 A.M.–6 P.M. daily May 15–Sept. 30, noon–4 P.M. daily Oct. 1–May 14, or by appointment, $4 per person out-of-state, $2 per person residents, children under 18 free) commemorates the fort that stood on the site 1866–1868.

The fort was commissioned at the height of the Indian Wars when the Sioux stood by their vow to fight for their traditional hunting grounds against anyone who dared cross into the Powder River Basin. Although Col. H. B. Harrington attempted to get permission for the fort's construction from Sioux chief Red Cloud, it was never given, and the Cheyenne warned that the Sioux would indeed go to battle with anyone who crossed the North Platte River. Still, Carrington moved forward and built the fort on a plateau between Big and Little Piney Creeks in an effort to protect travelers on the Bozeman Trail. Because the soldiers had to go into the nearby Big Horn Mountains to get wood to build the log and adobe fort, and had less than adequate supplies and ammunition, they lived with nearly constant attacks by the Sioux. In the first six months, some 154 people were killed by Indians and 700 head of horses, mules, and cattle were stolen.

At 17 acres, the fort was a complete settlement, with a stockade, a variety of living quarters, a social club, a guard house, a hospital,

THE FETTERMAN FIGHT OF 1866

During the 1860s onslaught of eager gold seekers looking for a quick route to riches in Montana, John Bozeman led many travelers along the trail that would eventually bear his name, taking them from southeast Wyoming across the Powder River Basin into Montana. The Sioux who inhabited the region had fought and removed the Crows and were determined to prevent white settlers from moving in as well. Travelers were warned not to venture past the Northern Platte River, and the military felt in order to protect the Bozeman Trail, new forts would need to be established.

In June 1866 the military met with the Sioux chief Red Cloud, hoping to attain permission to build forts in the area. Though he refused, and despite a warning by the Sioux, the commander of the area, Colonel H. B. Carrington, gave orders to build a fort at the fork of Big Piney and Little Piney creeks. The fort was named after Civil War general Phil Kearny. Both the Cheyenne and Jim Bridger had warned Carrington that it was a death wish to build the fort in the middle of the Sioux's hunting ground. But the warnings went unheeded.

True to their word, the Sioux made numerous attacks on the fort. Within the first five months, there were numerous civilian and military losses as well as the theft of horses,

A memorial marks the site of the Fetterman Fight.

mules, and cattle. The Sioux were savvy warriors and were skilled at luring soldiers away

and even a laundress row. But the structures alone were little help in keeping the soldiers safe. The battles that took place in close proximity to the fort include the Fetterman Fight and the Wagon Box Fight. By 1868 the railroad had made the Bozeman Trail obsolete, and the military abandoned the fort as indefensible. It was burned to the ground, likely by the Cheyenne, in 1868.

At the site of the fort today are a visitors center and museum that provide information for self-guided tours of the grounds and outlying sites. A cabin built by the Civilian Conservation Corps was crafted to resemble officers' quarters. Several of the battlefields are accessible within five miles of the fort.

◖ Cloud Peak Scenic Byway

Traveling from Buffalo on U.S. 16 over the southern portion of the Big Horn Mountains toward Ten Sleep and Worland, the 64-mile paved Cloud Peak Scenic Byway offers breathtaking scenery of the Cloud Peak Wilderness and the only view of Cloud Peak itself, the highest mountain in the Big Horns. The summit is at 9,666 feet, and the road also winds through the spectacular Tensleep Canyon. There are multiple turnouts for travelers to stretch their legs and enjoy the view; the road also passes Fort McKinney and runs just 20 miles south of Medicine Lodge State Archeological Site, known for its ancient petroglyphs, pictographs, and idyllic campgrounds.

from the fort. The soldiers would often run to defend workers or deliveries under attack only to realize it was a trap. The fort's construction required plentiful timber and logs to be shipped in from the nearby Big Horn Mountains, and the trains were an easy target for the Sioux.

In mid-December 1866, Captain William J. Fetterman and his 18th cavalry were stationed at the fort. Fetterman did not think highly of the Sioux's fighting skills and was convinced that if given the opportunity, his 80 men "could ride through the whole Sioux nation." In response, Jim Bridger reminded Fetterman and his men that although they had fought in the South during the Civil War, "they don't know anything about fighting Indians."

On December 21, 1866, the Sioux attacked a lumber train heading toward the fort. Fetterman and his men responded to the cries for help intending to ward off the attackers. Colonel Carrington gave them specific orders not to pursue the attackers past Lodge Trail Ridge, but there had been dissention in the ranks, and some troops, including Fetterman's, felt Carrington's cautiousness was unwarranted. The 18th cavalry pursued the attackers across the ridge, chasing the Indians who dared to taunt them, and rode right into a well-designed ambush about five miles from the fort. The 81 men were dead within 30 minutes. Troops back at the fort heard the gunfire and ran to their colleagues' defense only to encounter their brutally destroyed bodies halfway down the ridge. No one would see such an obliteration of U.S. troops until General Custer's last stand at the Battle of the Little Bighorn 10 years later.

When General Sherman heard about the loss of U.S. troops, he demanded retribution, saying, "It's not necessary to find the very men who committed the acts but destroy all of the same breed." However, for this brief period, the Sioux had successfully defended their territory. The Bozeman Trail was no longer used, and by 1868 Fort Kearny was abandoned.

Today the site of the fight, which lies between I-90 and I-87, is marked by a stone monument, and the site of Fort Phil Kearny has been designated a national historic landmark. Although the original fort was burned to the ground, most likely by Indians, it was partially reconstructed in 2000. There is also a small museum (528 Wagon Box Rd., Big Horn, 307/684-7629, www.philkearny. vcn.com, grounds dawn-dusk daily, museum and visitors center 8 A.M.-6 P.M. daily May 15-Sept. 30, noon-4 P.M. daily Oct. 1-May 14, or by appointment).

There is also ample access to hiking trails in the Bighorn National Forest.

ENTERTAINMENT AND EVENTS

The biggest event in Buffalo is the weeklong annual **Johnson County Fair and Rodeo** (307/684-7357, www.bighornmountains. com/jcf&r.htm), held at the Johnson County Fairgrounds during the first week of August; it culminates with a three-day rodeo. There are also two rodeos weekly June–August at the fairgrounds: The **Cowgirl Rodeo,** with only women contestants, is held each Tuesday night, and the **Lion's Club Rodeo** is held every Wednesday night. Call the **Buffalo Chamber of Commerce** (307/684-5544) for more information.

The **Big Horn Mountain Music Festival** (www.bighornmountainfestival.com) is also held at the fairgrounds around the second weekend in July. The three-day event showcases bluegrass, country, folk, and old-time music. In addition to the concerts, performers also conduct workshops throughout the day for musicians and nonperformers alike. Mandolin, banjo, guitar, and fiddle contests are held during the weekend. Camping is available at the grounds. Ticket prices range $25–45, or $85 for all three days. You can save $5–10 by purchasing tickets in advance on the website.

RECREATION
Hiking

In addition to the wealth of trails in the nearby **Bighorn National Forest** (www.fs.fed.us/r2/bighorn), Buffalo has an excellent 13-mile trail system in town. Known as the **Clear Creek Trail System,** the well-marked trails can be accessed around town at various spots, including the historic shopping district on Main Street, the motel circle near the intersection of I-25 and U.S. 16, the city park, and the Mosier Gulch picnic area. Maps are available through the Chamber of Commerce (www.buffalowyo.com).

Swimming

Buffalo has a wonderful free public swimming pool that attracts locals and visitors alike on warm summer days. The enormous pool at **Washington Memorial Park** (S. Burritt Ave. and W. Angus St.) is surrounded by trees, walking trails, and prime picnic spots. There is also a water park for kids and a snack shack. The pool is open mid-morning–sunset June–August.

Fishing

For fishing gear and current conditions on such varied water as **Clear Creek, Rock Creek,** the **Powder River,** and a variety of mountain and prairie lakes, stop in to **The Sports Lure** (66 S. Main St., 800/684-7682, www.sportslure.com).

For guided trips to any of 200 mountain lakes and streams in the Big Horns, contact **South Fork Mountain Lodge and Outfitters** (U.S. 16, 16 miles west of Buffalo, www.southfork-lodge.com, 307/267-2609, $55 for 2 hours, $90 for 4 hours, $150 full-day). Their guides know how to find the rainbows, brookies, native cutthroats, browns, and golden trout.

Horseback Riding

For trail rides that will take you into the Big Horn Mountains, contact **South Fork Mountain Lodge and Outfitters** (U.S. 16, 16 miles west of Buffalo, www.southfork-lodge.com, 307/267-2609). They have rides by the hour or pack trips and drop camps that take you into the Cloud Peak Wilderness Area in

the Bighorn National Forest. The half-day and full-day rides include lunch.

Another option is the **Little Piney Ranch** (430 Wagon Box Rd., Banner, 307/683-2667, www.littlepineyranch.com) located close to Fort Phil Kearny in Banner. They offer guided trail rides into the mountains ($50 for 2 hours, $80 half-day); experienced riders are allowed to take their horse and explore the ranch's hundreds of acres on their own.

Golf

Golfers can hit the links at the 18-hole municipal **Buffalo Golf Course** (550 W. Hart St., 307/684-5266, www.buffalowygolf.com, $28 for 18 holes).

ACCOMMODATIONS AND GUEST RANCHES

For such a small town, Buffalo has a surprising number of chain hotels and motels, which indicates its popularity with travelers. A great mom-and-pop option with the best rates in town is the **Arrowhead Motel** (749 Fort St., Buffalo, 307/684-9453, www.arrowheadmotel.com, $45–65). Rooms are clean and comfortable and come with a refrigerator and microwave; kitchenettes are available.

At the other end of the spectrum, the **❮ Occidental Hotel** (10 N. Main St., Buffalo, 307/684-0451, www.occidentalwyoming.com, $80–165) is an upscale historical gem that is worth every penny. From its historical ties to such figures as Owen Wister and Teddy Roosevelt, among others, to its fantastic restaurant, this is a uniquely Wyoming getaway.

For an authentic cowboy and cowgirl experience at a working ranch, try the **T-A Guest Ranch** (307/684-5833, www.taranch.com), south of Buffalo off I-25 on Crazy Woman Creek. Established in 1883, this 8,000-acre working cattle ranch offers beautifully restored Victorian accommodations, gourmet meals, riding twice daily, fly fishing, and a variety of other dude-ranch activities. The ranch focuses on local history and takes guests to tipi rings and Bozeman trail sites on the property as well as important battlefields nearby. Since guests

© WYOMING TRAVEL & TOURISM

the historic Occidental Hotel in Buffalo, Wyoming

get to work, ride, and even share meals with the ranch crew, there is a real sense of camaraderie. The T-A Ranch is one of the few in the area that does not require a weeklong stay, so visitors can enjoy the ranch's activities and amenities for as little as one night. All-inclusive rates start at $252 per day for adults; bed-and-breakfast rates that do not include riding or meals start at $125 per night based on double occupancy.

Another wonderful family-oriented ranch in the area is the H F Bar Ranch (1301 Rock Creek Rd., Saddlestring, 307/684-2487, www. hfbar.com, from $260 per day age 5 and up, all-inclusive), which offers wonderful riding and an assortment of fun activities for kids. The H F Bar is the second-oldest dude ranch in the country after Eatons Ranch in Wolf.

Camping

Inexpensive public campgrounds ($9–12) may be found nearby in the **Bighorn National Forest** (www.stateparks.com/bighorn.html), about 15 miles west of Buffalo on U.S. 16. Closer to town is the **Big Horn Mountains Campground** (www.buffalaocamping.com,

$20 tents, $26 RVs), owned and run by Paul and Bev Chaffee. Tent sites are available with or without electricity, the restrooms are always clean, there is a 24-hour laundry room, and discounted weekly rates are available.

FOOD

Known for their hearty breakfasts, great steaks, and burgers, **Tom's Main Street Diner** (41 N. Main St., Buffalo, 307/684-5627, Tues.–Fri. 7 A.M.–2 P.M., Sat. 7 A.M.–12 P.M., Sun. 8 A.M.– 12 P.M., $4–10) has a full menu and a great small-town feel.

In what used to be the old drug store and soda fountain, the **Udder House** (38 S. Main St., Buffalo, 307/621-7002, www.udderhouse.net, Mon.–Fri. 9 A.M.–8 P.M., Sun. 11 A.M.–4 P.M., entrées $7–10, pizzas up to $18) is a fun spot offering New York–style pizza whole or by the slice, homemade soup, pasta, and fantastic ice cream concoctions that include soda fountain drinks, malts, and floats.

Only open on Friday–Saturday evenings (4 P.M.–midnight), **Up in Smoke** (94 S. Main St., Buffalo, 307/217-2290, $8–19) offers a unique approach to barbecue. They use organic produce, dairy, and chicken whenever possible; all of their dishes are made from scratch; and their take-out containers, made from cornstarch, are biodegradable. In other words, if there is such a thing as healthy and green barbecue, this is it. Sit outside on warm summer evenings and savor the delicious food with a cold beer. Be aware that they accept cash and local checks only, no credit cards.

By far the most upscale dining experience in town is **The Virginian** (10 N. Main St., Buffalo, 307/684-5976, www.occidentalwyoming.com, open daily), named for Owen Wister's iconic novel and located in the historic Occidental Hotel. The ambience is 1890s chic, and the food is globally gourmet with offerings that include bison rib eye ($32), Caribbean duck breast ($20), Powder River prime rib ($22–30), and surf-and-turf. The beer and wine list is impressive too. For an unforgettable meal in a one-of-a-kind setting, this is a marvelous place for dinner.

NORTHEAST WYOMING

INFORMATION AND SERVICES

The **Buffalo Chamber of Commerce** (307/684-5544 or 800/227-5122, www.buffalowyo.com) is located at 55 North Main Street.

For information on hiking, camping, and other recreation in the Bighorn National Forest, contact the **U.S. Forest Service** (2013 Eastside 2nd St., Sheridan, 307/674-2600, www.fs.fed.us/r2/bighorn).

The **Johnson County Library** (307/684-5546, www.jclwyo.org) is located at 171 North Adams Avenue.

The **Johnson County Healthcare Center** (497 W. Lott St., Buffalo, 307/684-5521, www.buffalohealthcare.vcn.com) has a 24-hour emergency room.

GETTING THERE

Although Buffalo does have a small airport, the nearest commercial air service is available in Sheridan (33 miles) and Gillette (72 miles).

Bus service throughout the region is provided by **Powder River Transportation** (307/682-1888).

By car, Buffalo is 123 miles from Thermopolis, 182 miles from Cody, 234 miles from Yellowstone National Park, and 341 miles from Jackson.

Gillette

Founded as a livestock center and transformed into a minerals hub with one of the largest and most easily accessible coal seams in the world, Gillette (population 23,405, elevation 4,550 feet) was organized in 1869 and named for a railroad engineer, Edward Gillette. After a significant oil boom in the late 1960s, coal extraction in the area was boosted by the 1970 Clean Air Act, which mandated cleaner-burning low-sulfur coal, most of which is produced in the West. The Thunder Basin mine opened in 1978, producing 6 million tons of coal that year, and by 1993 was producing upward of 34 million tons annually, the largest amount from any mine in the world at that time. Because the seams are closer to the surface, mines in the Powder River Basin quickly outproduced mines in the southern part of the state. Currently, the city is in the throes of a coalbed methane boom, which is again increasing the population with modern-day prospectors working as miners and drillers.

This is a working and rapidly growing town with all sorts of growing pains related to coal, oil, and gas extraction. While it certainly has the infrastructure for people traveling through, Gillette is not typically on the top of the vacation radar. Still, it does make an excellent launching point to some of northeast Wyoming's wide-open spaces, and with its enormous tax base, it has managed to develop some phenomenal recreational facilities, many of which are free. The rapidly spreading Avenue of Arts on 4J Road, for example, is a walking path lined with ever-changing sculptures. Visitors will learn quickly that community means everything here—and Gillette residents are quick to point out that people come for the job, stay for the money, then never leave because of the community.

SIGHTS
Campbell County Rockpile Museum

The exhibits at the Rockpile Museum (900 W. 2nd St., 307/682-5725, www.rockpilemuseum.com, 9 A.M.–5 P.M. Mon.–Sat., free) are focused on the local history of Campbell County. The museum has accrued a wide array of artifacts and displays them creatively. Visitors can see the inside of a general store, the tools and trade of an early medical clinic, and a large rifle collection. An actual homestead cabin and tiny one-room schoolhouse have been moved to the grounds, and there is an impressive collection of wagons, carriages, and even an old horse-drawn hearse. There are hands-on activities for children, including a fun dress-up area with old-time garb. Since this is the heart of coal country, watch the short film about coal excavation and distribution; the large-scale explosions are sure to catch any viewers' attention.

CCSD Science Center

The Campbell County School District's Science Center (525 W. Lakeway Rd., 307/686-3821, www.ccsd.k12wy.us/adventuarium) is free and open to the public. Located in the Lakeway Learning Center, the science center occupies almost 10,000 square feet and offers young visitors numerous opportunities to discover, inquire, experiment, and learn. There are live animal displays (children can visit with an African pygmy hedgehog, an African bullfrog, ferrets, exotic birds, and even a python) and more than 60 interactive exhibits. During the school year, hours are 9 A.M.–noon and 1–3 P.M. Monday–Thursday, 9 A.M.–1 P.M. Friday; because it caters mostly to schools, during the summer it is only open Tuesday–Thursday.

Wright Museum

Located 35 miles south of Gillette in the small town of Wright, the Wright Museum (104 Ranch Court, Wright, 307/464-1222, www. wywrightmuseum.org, 10 A.M.–5 P.M. Mon.–Fri., 10 A.M.–2 P.M. Sat. May–Sept.) houses a small collection of artifacts from the surrounding area. The museum's collection has been largely amassed from the donations of residents. On display are vintage clothes, kitchen and bathroom furnishings from old homesteads, tools, saddles, and even a prostitute's "dresser box" with her personal items (including a gun). The town was established by the Atlantic Richfield mining company, and so there are many exhibits and interpretive materials dedicated to the mining industry. During the summer, visitors to the museum can sign up for tours of a local coal mine to witness the process firsthand.

ENTERTAINMENT AND EVENTS

Most of Gillette's large-scale events take place in the massive facility known as **Cam-**

Plex (1635 Reata Dr., 307/682-0552, www. cam-plex.com), which hosts concerts, conventions, expos, sporting events, public ice skating, and good ol' Wyoming rodeos. Visit the website to see what events are scheduled when you're in town.

Rodeos are held almost every weekend during the summer at Cam-Plex. The **PRCA Rodeo,** which takes place in late July or early August, is quite popular, and the **National High School Rodeo Finals** in July are also a huge draw. Almost 6,000 people descend on Gillette for this annual weekend event.

Also during the summer, there are the silly yet entertaining **melodramas** at Cam-Plex each Saturday night, and free **Concerts in the Park** each Thursday night at Cam-Plex. If you head out to the **Gillette Thunder Speedway** (Hwy. 51, 307/689-1287, www.gillettespeedway.com), there are stock-car races almost every Saturday night during the summer; check the website for the current schedule.

In the winter, **The Powder River Symphony**

Downtown Gillette gets gussied up for the Fourth of July.

NORTHEAST WYOMING

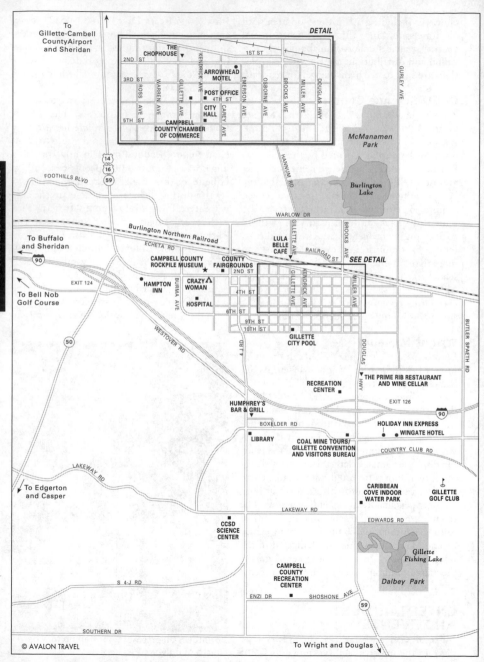

DETAIL

To Gillette-Cambell County Airport and Sheridan

2ND ST
THE CHOPHOUSE
1ST ST
3RD ST
ARROWHEAD MOTEL
POST OFFICE
4TH ST
CITY HALL
5TH ST
CAMPBELL COUNTY CHAMBER OF COMMERCE

ROSS AVE
WARREN AVE
GILLETTE AVE
KENDRICK AVE
EMERSON AVE
CAREY AVE
OSBORNE AVE
BROOKS AVE
MILLER AVE
DOUGLAS HWY

GURLEY AVE

FOOTHILLS BLVD

14
16
59

McManamen Park

Burlington Lake

WARLOW DR

Burlington Northern Railroad

ECHETA RD

To Buffalo and Sheridan
90

LULA BELLE CAFÉ

GILLETTE AVE
RAILROAD ST
BROOKS AVE

SEE DETAIL

EXIT 124

CAMPBELL COUNTY ROCKPILE MUSEUM
COUNTY FAIRGROUNDS
2ND ST
4TH ST
6TH ST
9TH ST
10TH ST

HAMPTON INN

BURMA AVE

CRAZY WOMAN
HOSPITAL

CITY

GILLETTE AVE
KENDRICK AVE
MILLER AVE

GILLETTE CITY POOL

To Bell Nob Golf Course

50

WESTOVER RD

DOUGLAS HWY

BUTLER SPAETH RD

RECREATION CENTER

THE PRIME RIB RESTAURANT AND WINE CELLAR

EXIT 126

90

HUMPHREY'S BAR & GRILL

BOXELDER RD

LIBRARY

COAL MINE TOURS/ GILLETTE CONVENTION AND VISITORS BUREAU

HOLIDAY INN EXPRESS
WINGATE HOTEL

COUNTRY CLUB RD

To Edgerton and Casper

LAKEWAY RD

CARIBBEAN COVE INDOOR WATER PARK

GILLETTE GOLF CLUB

LAKEWAY RD

EDWARDS RD

CCSD SCIENCE CENTER

Gillette Fishing Lake

CAMPBELL COUNTY RECREATION CENTER

Dalbey Park

S 4-J RD

ENZI DR
SHOSHONE AVE

59

SOUTHERN DR

To Wright and Douglas

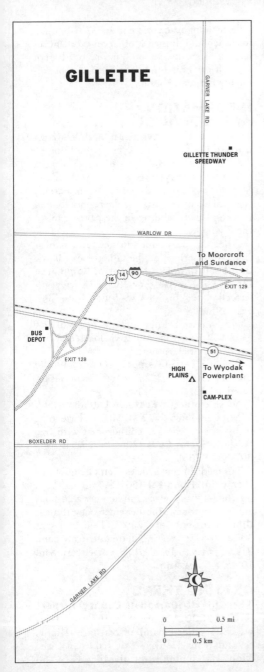

GILLETTE

GARNER LAKE RD

GILLETTE THUNDER
SPEEDWAY

WARLOW DR

To Moorcroft
and Sundance

16 14 90

EXIT 129

BUS
DEPOT

EXIT 128

51

HIGH
PLAINS

To Wyodak
Powerplant

CAM-PLEX

BOXELDER RD

GARNER LAKE RD

0   0.5 mi

0   0.5 km

Orchestra (307/686-5767, www.prs.vcn.com) performs concerts at Cam-Plex, and there are a host of holiday craft fairs as well.

RECREATION
Swimming
With a soaring tax base, it's no surprise that Gillette has a wealth of terrific public facilities, including the outdoor **Gillette City Pool** (909 Gillette Ave., 307/682-1962, Mon.–Sat. early June–early Sept., call for swim session hours, including open swim and lap swim, free). Admission is free to the massive outdoor pool and all of its facilities, which include a deep-diving well, zero-depth entry for toddlers, water slides, a bathhouse, a concession area, a sand playground, climbing structures, and a sunbathing area. The **Campbell County Recreation Center** (250 W. Shoshone Ave., 307/682-8527, www.ccprd.com, call for hours, activities, and admission) is a phenomenal facility that has a climbing wall, a kids' zone, an aerobics room, a gymnasium, a lap pool, a leisure pool, and a sports complex.

Kids will be deliriously happy at the **Caribbean Cove Indoor Water Park** (2577 S. Douglas Hwy., 307/682-1717, noon–10 P.M. Mon.–Fri., 8 A.M.–10 P.M. Sat.–Sun. summer, call for winter hours, $6 pp Mon.–Fri., $8 pp Sat.–Sun.), an 11,000-square-foot indoor water park with a lazy river, waterslides galore, a kiddie pool, and an activity pool. The water park is located inside the Fairfield Inn and Suites.

Golf
Golfers do not lack options in Gillette. The nine-hole **Gillette Golf Club** (1800 Country Club Rd., 307/682-4774, $20–25 for 9 holes) and the 18-hole **Bell Nob Golf Club** (4600 Overdale Dr., 307/686-7069, $35 for 18 holes) are both open to the public; there are additional courses in nearby Wright.

ACCOMMODATIONS
Because of the influx of workers in the mining industry, Gillette has an abundance of accommodations, most of which are chain hotels. One notable exception is the friendly **Arrowhead**

Motel (202 S. Emerson Ave., 307/686-0909, $45–80), which offers clean, basic rooms with microwaves, refrigerators, and a daily continental breakfast.

Among the most popular upscale chain hotels, appealing to business travelers and families alike, are the **Holiday Inn Express** (1908 Cliff Davis Dr., 307/686-9576, www.holidayinnexpress.com, $129–199), **Hampton Inn** (211 Decker Court, 307/686-2000, www.hamptoninn.com, $129–199), and the **Wingate Hotel** (1801 Cliff Davis Dr., 307/685-2700, www.wingatehotels.com, $99–269), all of which offer a multitude of plush amenities for road-weary travelers.

CAMPING

If you are attending an event at Cam-Plex, they have campgrounds available on-site. Otherwise, the two other campgrounds in town are the **High Plains Campground** (1600 Garner Lake Rd., 307/687-7339, year-round), with 65 RV sites, tent sites, a laundry, showers, and grills, and the interestingly named **Green Tree Crazy Woman Campground** (1001 W. 2nd St., 307/682-3665, year-round), with 85 RV sites, tent sites, a pool, clean restrooms, and especially important in the summer, shaded sites.

FOOD

A great but tiny spot for breakfast, lunch, and sensational homemade pies, among other specialties, is **Lula Belle Café** (101 N. Gillette Ave., 307/682-9798, $4–10). Another popular spot for lunch and dinner is **Humphrey's Bar & Grill** (408 W. Juniper Lane, 307/682-0100, www.humphard.net, entrées $8–23), which has an enormous menu and more than 50 beers on tap. After a fairly recent and significant expansion, **The Prime Rib Restaurant and Wine Cellar** (1205 S. Douglas Hwy., 307/682-2944, www.primeribgillette.com) is a nice place for lunch ($8–20) or dinner ($8–20), and a perfect choice for wine lovers.

The best and by far the best-known restaurant in Gillette is **The Chophouse** (113 S. Gillette Ave., 307/682-6805, www.

gillettechophouse.com, entrées $7–30); open for lunch and dinner, it offers an excellent selection of steaks, seafood, pasta, and Italian specialties. This restaurant has a serious following for good reason.

INFORMATION AND SERVICES

The **Gillette Convention and Visitors Bureau** (1810 S. Douglas Hwy., Building A, 307/686-0040 or 800/544-6136, www.visit-gillette-wrightwyo.org, 8 A.M.–8 P.M. daily May 1–Sept. 30, hours vary in other seasons) is an excellent resource for the region, located in a log-sided building in the parking lot of the Flying J.

Another source for business and relocation information for the Gillette area is the **Campbell County Chamber of Commerce** (314 S. Gillette Ave., 307/682-3673, www.gillettechamber.com, 8 A.M.–5 P.M. Mon.–Fri. year-round).

The main branch of the **post office** (307/682-3727) in Gillette is located at 311 South Kendrick Avenue.

The wonderful **Campbell County Public Library** (307/682-3223, www.ccpls.org) is located at 2101 South 4J Road.

Wash clothes at **Eastside Laundry** (1500 U.S. 14, 307/685-2722). Last loads have to be in by 9 P.M. Another Laundromat with free Wi-Fi is **Surf'n Suds** (203 S. Richards Ave., 307/686-9266).

For medical emergencies, **Campbell County Memorial Hospital** (501 S. Burma Ave., 307/688-1000, www.ccmh.net) has a 24-hour emergency room. Another emergency clinic is **Gillette Urgent Care** (2007 S. Douglas Hwy., 307/686-5750, www.gilletteurgentcare.com, 8 A.M.–8 P.M. Mon.–Fri., 8 A.M.–6 P.M. Sat., 10 A.M.–6 P.M. Sun.).

GETTING THERE

The **Gillette-Campbell County Airport** (GCC, 2000 Airport Rd., 307/686-1042, www.iflygillette.com) offers daily flights to and from Denver, Salt Lake City, the Montana communities of Miles City and

Lewistown, and the Wyoming community of Rock Springs. Carriers include **United** (800/UNITED-1—800/864-8331, www.united.com), **Delta** (800/221-1212, www.delta.com), and **Great Lakes** (800/554-5111, www.flygreatlakes.com).

Bus service in the region is provided by **Jefferson Bus Line** (307/674-6188 or 800/767-5333) and **Powder River Transportation** (307/682-0960).

By car, Gillette is 70 miles from Buffalo, 136 miles from Casper, 250 miles from Cody, 301 miles from Yellowstone National Park, and 411 miles from Jackson.

GETTING AROUND

Car rentals are available in town from **Enterprise** (603 E. 2nd St., 307/686-5655, www.enterprise.com) and **Avis** (2000 Airport Rd., 307/682-8588, www.avis.com).

Taxis are available through **City Cab** (307/685-1000).

Devils Tower National Monument

Rising 1,267 feet above the Belle Fourche River, Devils Tower is an iconic rocky sentinel that was formed some 50–60 million years ago and has fascinated people for generations. The tower was instantly recognizable in the 1977 film *Close Encounters of the Third Kind,* where it bridged human and alien life forms. Comprised of phonolite porphyry, which is a volcanic rock created by magma and similar to granite without the quartz, the massive columnar feature looks likes an otherworldly cat scratching post. Scientists refer to it as an igneous intrusion, meaning that magma welled up into a pocket of sedimentary rock, where it cooled and hardened. Over millions of years, the sedimentary rock was eroded away by natural forces, leaving the phenomenal tower.

The country's first national monument, Devils Tower is both a sacred site to many Native Americans and a climbing mecca for rock hounds from around the globe. The two groups have managed a hard-won, if somewhat delicate, respect for each other through a voluntary climbing closure in June every year, the month traditionally known for the greatest number of Native American ceremonies. Climbers are strongly encouraged to refrain from climbing or hiking around the tower during the closure.

Still, Devils Tower is a recreational hot spot with several climbing routes for beginners and experts alike, plus some eight miles of hiking trails that circle the tower and wind through the nearby forests and meadows. Although it's not exactly conveniently located, 33 miles north of I-90, Devils Tower is the type of destination—like Mount Rushmore—that visitors are happy to go out of their way to see. Especially for those with an interest in hiking or climbing, it's easy to make a day of Devils Tower.

Devils Tower rises from the rolling hills like an otherworldly spire.

© WYOMING TRAVEL & TOURISM

HISTORY

According to the National Park Service, more than 20 Native American tribes have historically attached cultural and spiritual significance to Devils Tower. Many of the tribes have sacred stories related to the tower, which often determined their name for the feature. The Arapaho, for example, called the tower "Bear's Tipi." Similarly, the Cheyenne referred to it as "Bear's Lodge," "Bear's House," and "Bear Peak." The Crow are known to refer to it as "Bear's Lair," and the Lakota, who often had winter camps at the tower, called it a variety of names that include "Bear Lodge," "Grizzly Bear's Lodge," "Ghost Mountain," and funnily enough, "Penis Mountain." The Kiowa called the feature "Tree Rock" or "Aloft on a Rock," and their origin story for the rock is among the best known. The story goes that the tribe was camped along the river, and seven sisters and their brother were playing when the brother turned into a bear, forcing the sisters to flee in search of safety. They climbed onto a rock and prayed for divine intervention. The rock began to grow skyward as the bear clawed at it to get to the sisters. Eventually, the girls were so high that they became the stars in the Big Dipper, and the tower still bears the scars of the bear's ferocious claws.

Many tribes conducted their most sacred events—including sun dances, sweat lodges, vision quests, and funerals—in the shadow of the tower, and they still do.

First studied in 1875 by scientists H. Newton and Walter P. Jenney, who were commissioned to complete a geological survey of the area, the land surrounding the tower was wisely pulled from homestead acreage in 1892, and the government created Devils Tower Reserve the following year. President Theodore Roosevelt dedicated Devils Tower as the country's first national monument in 1906.

Although it is constantly overrun by people, the area around and on top of the tower is ecologically significant. A colony of threatened black-tailed prairie dogs, who today occupy only 2 percent of their former habitat, make their home in the soft soils around the tower. Prairie falcons are known to nest in the cracks of the tower, requiring temporary closures to protect their young. Even on the grassy top of the tower, which is about the size of a football field, many wildlife species have been recorded, including chipmunks, mice, pack rats, and snakes.

Playing into the "because it's there" mentality, adventurers have long looked at ways to climb the soaring monolith. The first recorded ascent involved an oak peg ladder on July 4, 1893, by local ranchers Bill Rogers and W. A. Ripley, much to the delight of local revelers. Rogers's wife, Linnie, was the first woman to climb it (using the ladder) two years later on July 4, 1895. Both spectacles included crazy patriotic costumes, some 2,000 spectators, and live music. Although the ladder was no longer used after 1927, portions of it are still visible on the southwest side of the tower.

Technical rock climbers made the first ascent in 1937 in just four hours and 46 minutes, opening the tower to scores of climbers and dozens of firsts. Since then, numerous routes have been established up the rock, and the fastest free climb of Devils Tower was in the 1980s by Todd Skinner, who made the climb without ropes or protection in an astonishing 18 minutes. Today's average climb for two people requires 4–6 hours up and two hours for the rappel down.

EVENTS

A tradition since the early 1880s, when settlers would descend on the area for a few days at a time to camp, picnic, and enjoy one another's company, the **Old Settler's Picnic** was formalized as an annual event in the 1930s on Father's Day weekend. The tradition continues today, after a 40-year lapse starting in the 1960s, with a large gathering of locals and visitors who come to enjoy food, Western music, cowboy poetry, kids' activities, and nondenominational church.

The annual **Cultural Program Series** changes from year to year but consistently offers fascinating lectures, entertainment, and living history displays over the course of the summer season (May 31–Aug. 31). For information on current happenings, contact the visitors center at the base of the tower (307/467-5283) or look online at the Park News newsletter (www.nps.gov/deto/parknews).

The National Park Service hosts a fantastic spectrum of ranger-guided programs throughout the summer season. Offerings include a 1.3-mile guided **Tower Walk,** a variety of 20-minute **ranger talks,** hour-long **Evening Programs,** and fantastic 90-minute **Full Moon Walks.** For information on any of the regularly scheduled events, contact the visitors center at the base of the tower (307/467-5283, www.nps.gov/deto/planyourvisit/rangerledactivities.htm).

◖ HIKING AND CLIMBING

Nonclimbers interested in hiking will delight in the 1.3-mile trail around the base of the tower, plus the additional seven miles of trails that meander through the nearby forest and meadows. Trail maps are available at the visitors center. The three-mile **Red Beds** trail winds through meadows and ponderosa pines to the Joyner Ridge.

Each year the tower is climbed by 4,000–5,000 people who come to slip their fingers and toes into the hundreds of parallel cracks that divide the hexagonal columns of Devils Tower. Although the entire tower offers more than 200 routes with technical difficulties ranging 5.7–5.13, the **Durrance Route,** first pioneered in 1938, is the most common. A few bolted face climbs were established in the 1980s and 1990s, but new bolts and fixed pitons are prohibited. Only a handful of fatalities have occurred over the years, most of which happened on the descent.

All climbers must register at the **climber registration office** next to the visitors center; registration is free.

Be aware that climbing is strongly discouraged during the **June voluntary climbing closure,** advocated by the National Park Service out of respect for many Native American cultures that recognize the tower as a sacred place.

Climbing Guides

For inexperienced climbers, hiring a licensed guide is the best way to approach the monolith. There are about 10 companies licensed to guide climbers on Devils Tower. Among them is Frank Sanders and his **Devils Tower Climbing School** (307/467-5267 or 888/314-5267, www.devilstowerclimbing.com, guided one-on-one climbs $350 per day). Frank has

© WYOMING TRAVEL & TOURISM

Climbers share a ledge on Devils Tower.

been guiding climbers up the tower for nearly 40 years. His school offers excellent instruction and guiding through play days, instruction days, and summit days. Combination specials are available. Other guiding companies licensed to work in the monument include **Above Ouray Ice and Tower Rock Climbing Guides** (888/345-9061, www.towerguides.com, group summit climbs from $209 pp) and **Sylvan Rocks Climbing School and Guide Service** (605/484-7585, www.sylvanrocks.com), which requires two-day courses ($600 pp, $440 pp for 3 people) to climb to the summit.

ACCOMMODATIONS

Other than the Belle Fourche Campground, there are no accommodations inside the monument. The **Devils Tower Lodge Bed & Breakfast** (just north of the monument, 307/467-5267 or 888/314-5267, www.devilstowerlodge.com, $175–225, discounts for multiple nights) is owned by climbing guide Frank Sanders and offers comfortable rooms with unparalleled access to the tower.

CAMPING

The only campground in the monument proper is the **Belle Fourche Campground** (307/467-5283, $12), open in the summer season for tent campers and RVs on a first-come, first-served basis. Running water is available, but there are no RV hookups.

Just outside the monument, the **Devils Tower KOA** (307/467-5395 or 800/562-5785, www.devilstowerkoa.com) has RV hookups ($45), cabins ($70–111), and tent sites($29), plus an on-site swimming pool, snack bar, and free Wi-Fi.

FOOD

Be aware that no food is sold inside the monument, so you will have to bring your own supplies or eat before you arrive at Devils Tower. There are restaurants and grocery-convenience stores in Moorcroft (33 miles), Sundance (28 miles), and Hulett (8 miles).

INFORMATION AND SERVICES

Vehicular **entrance fees** for seven days are $10. Pedestrians, bicyclists, and motorcyclists can enter for seven days for $5.

The National Park Service operates a great **visitors center** (307/467-5283, www.nps.gov/deto, hours vary, daily May 1–Nov. 1, Wed.–Sun. Nov. and Apr., closed Dec. 1–mid-Apr.) in the parking lot beneath the tower. Housed in a classic 1938 Park Service log cabin constructed by the Civilian Conservation Corps, the visitors center is staffed and has a number of interesting geological, natural, and cultural history exhibits.

The nearest health care facilities are the **Hulett Medical Clinic** (122 Main St., Hulett, 307/467-5281) seven miles from Devils Tower, and the **Moorcroft Clinic** (101 W. Crook St., Moorcroft, 307/756-3414), 33 miles south of Devils Tower.

Be aware that the speed limit in the monument is 25 mph. Each year, dozens of wild animals are hit and killed by cars, and reduced speed can positively impact the number of fatalities.

Also, do not feed the wildlife. This point cannot be overstated. Prairie dogs are especially sensitive and can die from eating any human food.

GETTING THERE

The nearest commercial airports are located in Gillette (61 miles southwest) and Rapid City, South Dakota (120 miles east).

By car, Devils Tower is 33 miles northeast of the I-90 exit at Moorcroft. The monument is 61 miles from Gillette, 131 miles from Buffalo, 309 miles from Cody, and 363 miles from Yellowstone National Park.

While the number of visitors to the monument continues to grow (it grew more than 16 percent in 2009 alone), it is generally not overcrowded. That changes in August, and be prepared to wait in long entrance lines in the weeks surrounding the Sturgis Motorcycle Rally in nearby Sturgis, South Dakota, each summer. If you don't like crowds, this is not the time to go to Devils Tower. To check on this year's dates for the rally, visit www.sturgismotorcyclerally.com.

SOUTHERN WYOMING

An enormous expanse of diverse terrain that includes everything from vast prairie and rugged mountain peaks to red desert and wind-blown dunes, southern Wyoming in many ways defines the state, with celebrated events, important intellectual culture, and a wealth of historical sites. This region is at the heart and soul of Wyoming's agricultural tradition, both past and present. But interestingly, the lower half of the state is less traveled *to* and more often traveled *through*.

With I-80 in the far south and a series of smaller roads bisecting the landscape east–west and north–south, it seems this section of Wyoming is thick with travelers on their way someplace else, which has been true for more than a century. Most of the West's great travel routes—the Oregon Trail, the Overland Trail, the Bozeman Trail, and eventually the Northern Pacific Railway—cut through this dramatically shifting landscape, exposing travelers, if only briefly, to the diversity of terrain.

In the southeast corner around Cheyenne—the state's capital, known for its festive, even rowdy, rodeo, called Frontier Days—the landscape shifts, greens, and begins to look more like Colorado. Just north and west of Cheyenne, Laramie presents an interesting blend of university counterculture and age-old Western tradition in a literary-meets-cowboy dance. Beyond town, three impressive mountain ranges offer prime climbing opportunities, then give way to the plains and prairies where sheep and cattle rather than trees dot the horizon. Farther north on I-25, the frontier town of

HIGHLIGHTS

❨ Flaming Gorge National Recreation Area: Fed by the Green River, this 207,363-acre natural playground comprised of cliffs and Technicolor desert rock formations surrounds a 91-mile-long reservoir, which is popular for fishing and boating (page 389).

❨ Nicolaysen Art Museum and Discovery Center: With an impressive collection of more than 6,000 works by contemporary artists in the Rocky Mountains, the Nic is an important part of Casper's community and a phenomenal tribute to the current art scene in the West (page 394).

❨ National Historic Trails Interpretive Center: Among the best museums in the state, this place gives visitors a real sense of pioneer life on many of the historic trails that crisscross the state, including the Oregon Trail, Mormon Trail, Bozeman Trail, and Pony Express Trail (page 396).

❨ Casper Mountain: The mountain makes getting out of town as easy as it is delightful.

The skiing, hiking, camping, and fascinating local folklore give this area its own magical identity (page 397).

❨ Laramie Plains Museum at the Historic Ivinson Mansion: A terrific museum in a beautifully restored setting, this museum is a labor of love for the people who continue to operate it and a gift to visitors who can enjoy it (page 405).

❨ Fort Laramie National Historic Site: Dating back to 1834, this post was a fur trading fort, a military outpost, and an important witness to the dramatic conflicts and sweeping change of the 19th century in the American West (page 415).

❨ Frontier Days: The big daddy of Wyoming rodeos draws thousands of eager spectators to its big-name country music concerts, carnival, parades, and world-class professional rodeo action. This is the week Cheyenne shines brightest (page 416).

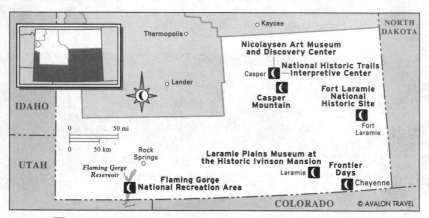

LOOK FOR ❨ TO FIND RECOMMENDED SIGHTS, ACTIVITIES, DINING, AND LODGING.

SOUTHERN WYOMING

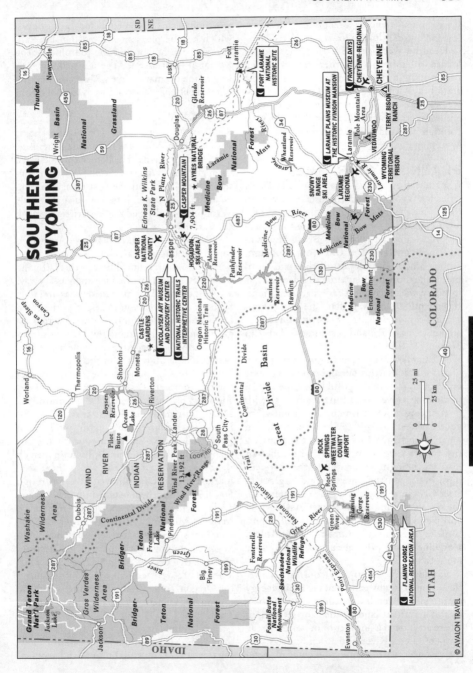

SOUTHERN WYOMING

© AVALON TRAVEL

Casper is experiencing a renaissance as a fishing and outdoor-loving town.

Heading west on I-80, the landscape is loaded with minerals, and the entire area is rich with mining history, dinosaur fossils, and the stark beauty of the Flaming Gorge National Recreation Area. There are wildlife refuges, endless spots to wet a line, and little ranching communities and outposts that give southern Wyoming its flavor.

PLANNING YOUR TIME

Cheyenne, Casper, and Laramie are all sizeable cities for Wyoming and could occupy visitors for at least a full day each. In Cheyenne, there are a number of museums that are worth seeing, including the **Wyoming State Museum** and the **Frontier Days Old West Museum,** among others. In this part of the state, summer is the most popular time to travel thanks to sunny, warm days and easy road conditions. Bear in mind, however, that Cheyenne's population explodes during **Frontier Days,** the second half of July, and accommodations can be tough to find.

In Laramie, there are more museums, plenty of opportunities to get out and experience some of Wyoming's most beautiful landscapes, and a fascinating university culture that brings with it abundant entertainment and some darn good eateries. Laramie can be a bit windy and bleak, even frigid, in winter, but the university culture keeps things lively with concerts, lectures, sporting events, and other happenings. In Casper, the state's second-largest city after Cheyenne, there is a growing interest in the region's fishing on the **North Platte River** and plenty of year-round recreational opportunities in the nearby **Laramie Mountains, Medicine Bow National Forest,** and **Casper Mountain.**

Southwest Wyoming, by contrast, is a series of small towns experiencing a big energy extraction–driven boom and a vast swath of starkly beautiful land primed for recreation. There are indeed a number of museums in the areas of Green River and Rock Springs, but the vast majority of people who come to spend any time in this region come for the outdoors, which can be pleasant mid-spring–late fall. Summer can be hot, but the **Flaming Gorge National Recreation Area** is a striking gateway to the dramatic Green River country and offers plenty of places and ways to cool down.

HISTORY

Southern Wyoming is a land of corridors, home to the Oregon, Mormon, California, Cherokee, and Overland Trails. The Pony Express crossed through here, as did the nation's first transcontinental railroad and the first transcontinental automobile route. It makes sense that early Wyoming was defined not by settlers so much as by travelers.

What initially attracted Native Americans to this region also attracted traders, trappers, and immigrants. The North Platte and Sweetwater Rivers created natural passageways across the land. They provided water and food for both men and livestock and kept the grasslands well irrigated. Buffalo grazed across the grassy plains with Indians always in close pursuit. The Shoshone, Arapaho, Cheyenne, and Sioux Indians all hunted in the region.

Fur trappers, known as the Astorians, were the first nonnatives to see South Pass. They stumbled on this crossing of the Continental Divide during their return trip east to St. Louis. It was later found again by Thomas Fitzpatrick in 1824 and subsequently used by many trappers, traders, and mountain men on their journeys west. By the 1840s there were marked trails that followed rivers through South Pass. But the movement into Wyoming really picked up after 1843, when a large wagon train left Missouri and arrived in Washington six months later. Hundreds of thousands of immigrants, following their "manifest destiny" and in search of gold, religious freedom, or just a better life—passed through Wyoming over the Oregon Trail. Today Wyoming is home to the longest unchanged portion of the Oregon Trail.

Fort Laramie in the east and Fort Bridger in the west became important way stations, allowing travelers to stock up on food and supplies, repair wagons, trade goods, and even swap their tired livestock for fresh animals. Troops were stationed in the forts to provide protection from Native Americans.

Initially, the Indians did little to prevent the travelers from crossing the land they used. Realizing that the wagons were just moving through with no intention of staying, the migrants were not viewed as a threat. But it soon became evident that the migration was taking a toll on the land as well as their way of life. The grass that sustained the buffalo was being destroyed by wagons and consumed by livestock. The buffalo themselves were being killed to make way for cattle grazing land and railroad tracks. The Indians were not ready to give up their traditional way of life; confrontations ensued, and by the 1860s military stations were established along the trail. By the time the transcontinental railroad entered Wyoming, it was evident that the land no longer belonged to the Indians.

In the early 1860s, stagecoaches, freight, and mail wagons ran along the Overland Trail, which loosely followed the Cherokee Trail of 1848. When the railroad arrived in Wyoming in 1867, it also followed this route. The railroad changed Americans' perception of Wyoming— rather than a passageway, it had become a destination. It no longer took months, only days to arrive in Wyoming. It was easier to export goods from the territory and target destinations that were farther away. With its prime grazing land and natural resources, Wyoming began to attract settlers.

Beginning in 1867, tent cities sprung up overnight wherever railroad crews laid tracks. These small "hell on wheels" towns consisted of ramshackle houses, brothels, saloons, and gambling tents. Cheyenne, Laramie, Carbon, and Rock Springs were all initially settled in this manner. As the tracks moved west, the makeshift towns would often close up and follow suit. However, the more innovative found other ways to remain relevant or remain linked to the railroad business, and they prospered. The southern part of the state housed the first five original counties of the Wyoming territory,

which extended all the way from Colorado to Montana.

The first makeshift railroad town to be settled was Cheyenne in July 1867. Initially a boisterous, mayhem-filled tent city, it soon began to blossom. By November it had 4,000 residents and was dubbed the "magic city" for its large population boom. Fort D. A. Russell was established nearby, and the military presence helped to settle things down. Cheyenne became an important shipping center, exporting cattle and supplies to the East and importing the latest fashions and desirables. By the 1880s, Cheyenne was considered one of the wealthiest cities per capita in the world.

Laramie became a permanent town when the Union Pacific Railroad decided to locate its division headquarters there. Like Cheyenne, it had wild and rowdy days, but by 1887 Wyoming University was established, opening its enrollment to both women and men. Laramie went on to hold the distinct honor of having the first women voters in the country. Like most of these towns in southern Wyoming, Laramie's future was intrinsically tied to the railroad, and when Union Pacific established a rolling mill in town, it immediately brought with it new improvements.

Union Pacific was awarded mineral rights to tracts of land along the railroad, and this also shaped the character of southern Wyoming. When coal was discovered at Carbon, miners from England and Finland came to work the mines, as well as those in Rock Springs and Evanston. Since Union Pacific coal sold at cheaper prices (and the company could ship it at almost no cost), it eventually monopolized the industry, and Rock Springs became the biggest coal producer in the West.

A mixture of railroad and natural resources also led to the establishment of Casper. Originally it was set up as station for the Fremont, Elkhorn and Missouri Valley Railroad, with its first residents creating a town site in 1888. After a relatively common and lawless beginning, Casper prospered with the discovery of oil. When the first oil well was drilled in 1887, an onslaught of land speculators and other investors arrived, looking get rich. When the Salt Creek Oil Field was established 40 miles north of Casper, the town responded by building a refinery and went on to become a booming town. Casper's wealth peaked in the 1920s and crashed heavily with the rest of the country in 1929. Like cities all across the West, Casper seemed destined to repeat this boom and bust cycle through the rest of the 20th century.

Coal, oil, and natural gas are still important sources of income for Wyoming. But Casper, like many of Wyoming's towns, has realized the need to diversify in order to protect its economy. The tourism industry has grown in this part of the state, and if you can take the time to veer off I-80, which runs parallel to the Union Pacific transcontinental route, you will find yourself crossing century-old trails, exploring abandoned trading posts, and experiencing traditions that bring southern Wyoming's unique history to life.

Sweetwater County

Sweetwater County in the southwest corner of Wyoming is a fascinating mix of the desert Southwest—think kaleidoscopic rock formations, mesas, and canyons—and the rugged Western appeal of Wyoming with rodeo, wild mustangs, and vast open spaces. Though not a tourist destination in the way that northwest Wyoming is, this region of the state is growing rapidly with the explosive growth of the energy sector and abundant recreational opportunities, which add up to an appealing lifestyle. This is not so much cowboy country as it is mining country, mountain biking country, and river rafting country.

A high alpine desert, **Rock Springs** (population 27,000, elevation 6,271 feet) parallels Gillette in some ways—it is in the thick of an energy boom and the subsequent rapid growth—but it is located next to some pretty phenomenal country, including the unrivaled and scenic **Flaming Gorge Recreation Area.** The city itself has a few good museums and an interesting international flavor that dates back to coal mining and railroad development around the turn of the 20th century.

Green River (population 12,149, elevation 6,109 feet) is an old railroad town that got its start as a station along the Overland and Pony Express routes. It has a rather industrial history spanning the railroads and mines in the region, but it is best-known for its namesake river, which courses speedily through town.

The Green River forms the headwaters of the Colorado River basin and was for years a prime shipping route for timber. Major John Wesley Powell launched two of his biggest expeditions from here, including his first into the unexplored Grand Canyon in 1869. Surrounded by magnificent multicolored buttes and outcroppings, the town is still very much centered around the river and is a popular launching spot for raft and kayak expeditions.

Economically speaking, Sweetwater County owes its growth to the world's largest known deposit of trona ore (a type of soda ash used in chemicals, laundry detergent, kitty litter, and glass), the production of which employs more than 2,000 people at five local mines. Coal mining continues, and large reserves of oil and natural gas in the area are relatively untapped but being eyed by Halliburton and Exxon.

SIGHTS
Museums
There are a number of museums in this region worth a visit. **The Sweetwater County Historical Museum** (3 E. Flaming Gorge Way, Green River, 307/872-6435, www.sweetwatermuseum.org, 10 A.M.–6 P.M. Mon.–Sat., free) will surprise visitors with its vast and thorough displays. The museum has done a good job of documenting the history of the region and exhibits many artifacts from the daily life of ranchers, miners, and the numerous

THE CHINESE MASSACRE

Mining was essential to the ultimate success of the Union Pacific Railroad: Closed mines threatened coal supplies, which would be disastrous because trains required a steady supply of fuel to meet their schedules. In 1875 when miners in Rock Springs and Carbon organized to demand better wages, their strike shut down Union Pacific's two largest mines. It was no surprise that the railroad looked for a quick yet cheap solution. Until this point, all the miners in Rock Springs had been white, but two weeks after the strike started, Union Pacific brought in 150 Chinese men to work the mines. By month's end, some 50 white miners had returned to work, strike organizers had been fired, and the two races were expected to work side by side. Although there was underlying resentment – Chinese miners worked for less and were therefore more employable – and racism – this was the era when the Chinese Exclusion Act of 1882 was passed – tensions did not come to a head until a decade later.

By 1885 the number of Chinese miners at Rock Springs had increased to 331, nearly double the number of white miners. Since the miners were paid by the ton, mine assignments were important. On September 2, some white miners were upset that Chinese miners had been assigned to prime areas. They met the Chinese men outside the mine and prevented them from entering. The altercation quickly turned violent, with one Chinese miner dying from his injuries.

The mob mentality quickly picked up momentum, and soon many more white miners were vengefully hunting down Chinese miners. Many victims were scalped, mutilated, dismembered, and even burned alive. In an effort to escape the violent persecution, many Chinese miners ran into the surrounding desert.

The white miners entered Chinatown, attacking its occupants and setting fire to the buildings. The entire neighborhood burned to the ground: 79 homes were destroyed, 28-51 Chinese were dead, and 15 were injured. The violence shocked the nation, but it also ignited anti-Chinese violence in other small towns in the West. Reaction in Wyoming was mixed. The local newspaper supported the attacks; other papers criticized the massacre while empathizing with the plight of the white miners. The territorial governor, Francis E. Warren, requested federal help to restore peace.

Federal troops entered Rock Springs on September 5. Troops were also deployed to Evanston, where many of the Chinese had fled. Emergency troops were pulled out of the area one month later; the temporary post at Camp Pilot Butte remained occupied until 1899, however.

When the mines eventually did reopen, 45 men were fired by Union Pacific for their role in the violence. Sixteen men were arrested in conjunction with the riot and held in Green River. Although a grand jury was called in Green River, no indictments were handed out, and the men were released a month later to a heroes' welcome.

The only form of justice came as a response by the U.S. government to appease the Chinese government. With much finagling, President Grover Cleveland persuaded Congress to issue financial compensation to China for $149,000. During the 1920s and 1930s, the Union Pacific Coal Company paid retirement packages and purchased tickets for retired miners to return to China. Only one of the miners chose to live his final days in Rock Springs.

SOUTHERN WYOMING

immigrants who came to the region. Visitors can see everything from a dinosaur's fossilized footprint to a rifle from Butch Cassidy's gang, to a RCA Victor Victrola phonograph, and a wedding dress from 1903. There is also an engaging video and display about the Chinese massacre in Rock Springs.

In Rock Springs, the **Rock Springs Historical Museum** (201 B St., Rock Springs, 307/362-3138, 10 A.M.–5 P.M. Mon.–Sat., free) is situated in the old city hall. It documents the city's diverse immigrant population, its coal-mining history, and the illegal activity and outlaws it also attracted. The **Wyoming Community College Natural History Museum** (2500 College Dr., Rock Springs, 307/382-1600, 10 A.M.–10 P.M. daily, free) houses a small collection of fossils, minerals, and Native American artifacts from the area. There is also a large number of big-game heads from around the world on display. The **Community Fine Arts Center** (300 C St., Rock Springs, 307/362-6212, 10 A.M.–6 P.M. Mon.–Thurs., noon–5 P.M. Fri.–Sat., free) has works by Norman Rockwell, Conrad Schwiering, and Grandma Moses, among other prominent American artists.

Pilot Butte Wild Horse Scenic Tour

There are 1,100–1,600 wild horses roaming the stark landscape around Rock Springs and Green River. Although they can often be spotted from I-80, there is a scenic road that affords better opportunities for wild horse sightings. County Road 4-53 can be accessed either from Rock Springs or Green River; it is a 24-mile gravel road that takes about 90 minutes to drive as it winds across the White Mountains with spectacular vistas. The most likely view of the horses comes at the top of the mountains, and early morning or late afternoon are the best times to view wildlife. The road is only open May–October. For more information about the scenic drive, contact the Bureau of Land Management's Rock Springs Field Office (307/352-0256).

Rich Nobles of **Green River Wild Horse Tour & Eco Safari** (307/875-2923 or 307/875-

5711, www.greenriverwildhorsetours.com) guarantees his customers views of the mustangs. For $65 he takes passengers off the normal route in his imported all-terrain vehicle to view the wildlife up close. The trip usually covers about 70 miles and lasts up to six hours.

Seedskadee National Wildlife Refuge

The Seedskadee National Wildlife Refuge (www.fws.gov/seedskadee) sits along 36 miles of the Green River and encompasses over 26,000 acres of the land. It consists of marshes, wetlands, and uplands, and more than 200 different bird species have been sighted in the area. The riparian areas have become an important nesting ground for a variety of migratory birds, including Canada geese, great blue herons, and swans. The refuge is a popular spot for fishing, wildlife viewing, and short float trips. It is 37 miles north of Green River on Highway 372. The refuge headquarters is just two miles north of the junction of Highways 372 and 28.

Killpecker Sand Dunes

Thirty-seven miles from Rock Springs is one of Wyoming's most unique natural wonders. The Killpecker Sand Dunes are the largest active dunes in the United States. The massive hills of white sand stretch more than 55 miles and offer a fun playground for hikers to explore. However, be sure to go prepared with water, food, a compass, and a map—people can easily get disoriented in the desert setting. If approaching the dunes from Rock Springs, you will pass the area office of the **Bureau of Land Management** (280 U.S. 191 N., Rock Springs, 307/352-0256); it's worth stopping in to get more information and a map of the area.

Also at the dunes, rock climbing enthusiasts will enjoy a visit to the volcanic plug known as **Boar's Tusk.** This towering rock formation measures 400 feet in height; Devils Tower is the only other geological feature like this is the state. Another trek in the area can take you to the **White Mountain Petroglyphs,** where hundreds of drawings depicting animals and hunters are etched to into the sandstone cliff.

Fossil Butte National Monument

Fossil Butte National Monument (U.S. 30, 80 miles west of Green River, www.nps.gov/fobu) sits in the middle of what was once a subtropical habitat. During the Eocene Epoch, 50 million years ago, this was a large lake area home to alligators, turtles, fish, and even palm trees. Over the eons, animal and plant remains sank to the bottom of the lake bed, where they were covered with sediment and fossilized. When the lake dried up and the bed was eventually pushed to the surface, some of the best-preserved fossils in the world were revealed.

The visitors center (9 A.M.–5:30 P.M. daily May–Sept., 8 A.M.–4:30 P.M. daily Oct.–Apr., closed holidays in winter) displays more than 80 fossils, including two types of bats, numerous species of fish, and even a 13-foot crocodile. There is also an area where visitors can handle the fossils and make rubbings of them. During summer, experts conduct fossil preparation demonstrations and take questions from the public. There are two short trails that take visitors through the unique history of the park and allow for some wildlife viewing. During summer, plan to visit 11 A.M.–4 P.M. Friday–Saturday to assist paleontologists as they collect fossils at the research quarry.

◖ Flaming Gorge National Recreation Area

The Flaming Gorge National Recreation Area is full of beautiful rock formations, spectacular land, and rich natural colors. The area was aptly named by a group led by Major John Wesley Powell who started their famous journey down the Green River from where the town of Green River now stands. The explorers floated through the rocky canyons and were stunned by the striking red hues, primarily in Utah.

The area consists of more than 200,000 acres and crosses southwestern Wyoming into northeastern Utah. The landscape in Wyoming is primarily high desert, and the more impressive and dramatic sights are found over the border in Utah. There are three roads—Highway 530, U.S. 191, and Utah Highway 44—that connect to form a loop around the National

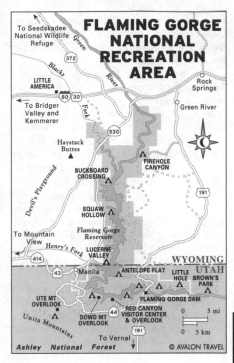

Recreation Area. The visitors center is on the Utah side at Red Canyon.

Activity in Wyoming is largely based around the 91-mile-long **Flaming Gorge Reservoir,** constructed in 1964 and a popular destination for water-skiing, fishing, camping, and boating. Its trout-filled waters make it an attractive year-round fishing spot; licenses may be bought in Wyoming or Utah. There are also campgrounds nearby, and many boat launches around the reservoir.

If approaching the reservoir from Highway 530 south of Green River, the road follows the west side of the lake just a few miles from the shore. There are various dirt-road turnoffs that lead to the water. Many end at isolated beaches where you can camp for free. There are also commercial services, Lucerne Marina and Buckboard Crossing Marina, that take visitors to the recreation area's campsites and docks. If you continue south, heading to Utah, the road passes **Haystack Buttes,** rocky mound-like formations that resemble haystacks, and **Devil's Playground,** a barren badlands of rough terrain.

The loop can also be started at U.S. 191, heading south from Rock Springs. This approach is more mountainous and therefore more scenic, but it is also farther from the reservoir. Early on, a paved road turnoff will take you to **Firehole Canyon.** Here you can see the rocky spires known as **North and South Chimney Rocks** and other interesting geological features. U.S. 191 continues south, climbing 8,000 vertical feet, and has good views of the rolling hills and valleys to the east and west. From here the reservoir is about 15 miles from the road. However, when crossing Spring Creek, the water becomes visible, and there is a turnoff leading four miles to the shore.

Both routes cross the Wyoming-Utah border and lead to Utah Highway 44, which takes visitors through the dramatic canyons. One other approach to the loop is from Highway 414, heading southeast from the town of Mountain View. This road traverses badlands, fields filled with sage and juniper, and large open pastures and leads to Henry's Fork, the site of the first mountain man rendezvous in the country.

ENTERTAINMENT AND EVENTS

Known as **Wyoming's Big Show,** the Sweetwater County Fair, held annually at the Sweetwater Events Center (3320 Yellowstone Rd., Rock Springs, 307/352-6789, www.sweetwaterevents.com, $8 adults, free for children under 6), is a 10-day event that includes rodeo action, 4-H livestock competitions, entertainment, and a carnival. Comparable in size to the Wyoming State Fair, the event attracts some 80,000 attendees annually. The Sweetwater Events Center is also home to a variety of rodeo, stock-car, motocross, and BMX racing.

Rock Springs has a healthy representation of the performing arts, including the **Sweetwater County Concert Association** (307/352-3468), which produces four musical performances annually as well as fund-raisers that pair music with

festive dining. The **Actors' Mission** (307/382-0019) produces five plays each season in addition to some dinner theater offerings at the Elks Lodge (307 C St.). The city also hosts regular **Rock Springs Concerts in the Park** (307/352-1423) throughout the summer as well as **Movies in the Park** (Bunning Park, Evans St. between Elk St. and Noble Dr.). Also in Bunning Park in mid-August is the **Annual Sweetwater Blues 'n Brews Festival** (307/352-1434, www.sweetwaterbluesnbrews.com, $4 pp, free for children under 14), which pairs a daylong lineup of blues music with local hoppy libations.

As a nod to the town's 56 different ethnicities, the Rock Springs Chamber hosts a free **International Day** (307/382-2538, www.rockspringswyoming.net) in Bunning Park in early–mid-July. The daylong family-oriented event includes international food and beer plus entertainment and activities.

In Green River, the biggest event of the year is **Flaming Gorge Days** (800/FL-GORGE—800/354-6743, www.flaminggorgedays.com), held annually the last weekend of June. The event includes a country concert and a rock concert along with basketball and volleyball tournaments, a parade, a festival in the park, and children's entertainment. Concert tickets are available in advance at discounted rates from the chambers of commerce in Rock Springs (1897 Dewar Dr., Rock Springs, 307/362-3771, www.rockspringschamber.com) and Green River (1155 Flaming Gorge Way, Green River, 307/875-5711, www.grchamber.com), or at full price at the gate.

Another big event in Green River is the **Annual River Festival** (800/FL-GORGE—800/354-6743, www.grchamber.com) held at the end of August. This three-day event includes an art show and auction, a Cajun shrimp boil, kids' games, concerts, nightly fireworks, a number of races that include the Run with the Horses Marathon, a poker run, and plenty of food.

SHOPPING

Rock Springs has an excellent assortment of art galleries and gift shops for shoppers. **Local**

Color Gallery & Gifts (513 Bridger Ave., Rock Springs, 307/382-0990) is the largest artist-owned gallery in the state and has an impressive collection of pottery, paintings, jewelry, photography, and handmade crafts. The gallery is housed in the historic Slovenski Dom, which was a social meeting spot for Slovenians in the early 1900s when Rock Springs was indeed a melting pot. **West of Center Studio & Gifts** (204 Center St., Rock Springs, 866/654-2523, www.westofcenter.com) is owned by painter R. C. Jones and represents more than 35 artists and artisans.

RECREATION

Thanks to the local economy, recreational opportunities in Rock Springs are plentiful. The **Rock Springs Family Recreation Center** (3900 Sweetwater Dr., Rock Springs, 307/352-1440, www.rswy.net, 5 A.M.–7 P.M. Mon.–Fri., 9 A.M.–5 P.M. Sat., closed Sun.) offers an indoor swimming pool, a full-size ice arena, a full gym with basketball, volleyball, racquetball, and handball courts, an indoor putting course, and various classes and fitness programs. Admission for nonresidents is $6 adults, $3.75 youth, and free for children.

Golfers can tee off at the 27-hole championship **White Mountain Golf Course** (1501 Clubhouse Dr., Rock Springs, 307/352-1415, www.rswy.net, sunrise–sunset daily late Mar.–early Nov.), considered among the best public golf courses in the state. Nonresidents pay $32 for 18 holes. There is also a nine-hole course in Green River, the **Rolling Green Country Club** (Country Club Rd., Green River, 307/875-6200, $12 for 9 holes).

Hiking and Mountain Biking

Although this is wide-open desert, there are some interesting places to hit the trail. For starters, the **Green Belt** and **Scotts Bottom Nature Area,** running through Green River, offer lovely trails to stretch your legs and enjoy the views. The trails are easily accessed from **Expedition Island,** the launching point for Powell's famous river trips through the Grand Canyon.

For more of an adventure, Sweetwater County has more still-visible pioneer trails running through it that anywhere else in the country, and hikers and mountain bikers can follow the double ruts at a variety of points in the big open countryside. Trails in the region include the Oregon and California Trails, the Mormon Trail, and the Pony Express Trail. A fantastic free

GREAT DIVIDE MOUNTAIN BIKE ROUTE

The Great Divide Mountain Bike Route is the longest off-pavement bicycle route in the world, running 2,745 miles from Banff, Canada, down to Antelope, New Mexico. Developed by the Adventure Cycling Association, the trail is roughly 90 percent unpaved and crosses the Continental Divide as many as 30 times. The elevation gains and losses are equivalent to 200,000 vertical feet, which compares to riding up Mount Everest nearly seven times.

One stretch of the trail in southern Wyoming from South Pass City near Lander to Rawlins cuts through an area known as the Great Basin, since the water in this area does not drain into the Atlantic or Pacific but rather stays in the playa lakes here or evaporates in the heat. In fact, the Continental Divide splits and is on both sides of the Great Basin. It's the only portion of the route where the terrain is consistently level. But that doesn't make it easy. Riders will need to carry plenty of water on the 131-mile stretch and will likely have to deal with significant wind. Temperatures in this high desert can plummet quickly, and rainstorms can make the double track nearly impassable. Possible wildlife encounters in this stretch of the trail can include prairie dogs, antelope, coyotes, and even wild horses.

The Great Basin is a starkly picturesque place that will appeal to those who love wide, open spaces.

SOUTHERN WYOMING

interpretive booklet on the historic trails across Wyoming is available online from the National Park Service at www.tourwyoming.com/pdf/ NationalHistoricTrailsAcrossWY.PDF. All adventurers need to be well-prepared for the vast undeveloped stretches of land and should bring maps, adequate clothing, and plenty of water.

The mountain biking in the area is sublime, with hundreds of miles of trails from the scenic to the gnarly. Green River is known for some of its hairier trails, including the extremely technical **Lunatic Fringe** and the slightly less insane **Macbones Trail**, both of which can be scouted on www.singletracks.com.

Among the most popular trails is the 20-mile **Cherokee Trail/Currant Creek Ranch Loop**, which starts and ends at the Currant Creek Ranch off County Road 33. It is part of a wider 250-mile network of trails on Little Mountain, south of Rock Springs.

For excellent advice or service, visit **The Bike and Trike** (612 Broadway, Rock Springs, 307/382-9677, www.bikeandtrike.com, 7 A.M.–6 P.M. Mon.–Fri., 8 A.M.–3 P.M. Sat.).

Without a doubt, the **Flaming Gorge Recreation Area** offers the densest concentration of recreational opportunities, including miles upon miles of trails for hikers and mountain bikers. The scenic five-mile **Canyon Rim Trail** is accessible from the Red Canyon Visitors Center and is open to both hikers and mountain bikers. The **Dowd Mountain-Hideout Canyon Trail** is significantly steeper and is also open to both hikers and mountain bikers. A trail map for these and other trails in the gorge is available for free at the Forest Service offices in Green River (1450 Uinta Drive, 307/875-1646) and Manila, Utah (intersection of Hwys. 43 and 44, 435/784-3445). For **mountain bike rentals** in the Flaming Gorge, visit the **Red Canyon Lodge** (2450 W. Red Canyon Lodge, Dutch John, Utah, 435/889-3759, www.redcanyonlodge.com, $10 per hour, $20 half-day, $35 full-day), four miles west of the junction of Highways 44 and 191.

Fishing

There are a couple of ways to fish this part of the state, but for anglers looking to hook the big one—a really big one—**Flaming Gorge Reservoir** is the place to go. The lake trout in the reservoir can grow to weigh more than 50 pounds, and 20-pounders are common. Lake trout generally like deeper waters and are more easily fished from boats. The rainbows in the reservoir, on the other hand, can be fished from shore. Other fish in the reservoir include smallmouth bass, kokanee, and burbot. Be aware that the reservoir drops into Utah, and fishing licenses are required in both Wyoming and Utah; special-use stamps are available for fishing in both states.

The fishing on the **Green River** around its namesake town produces cutthroat, lake trout, and the occasional whitefish. For current conditions, information, and licenses, visit the Wyoming Game and Fish Department (351 Astle Ave., Green River, 307/875-3223).

For equipment and guided fishing trips on the Green River, contact **Trout Creek Flies** (U.S. 191 and Little Hole Rd., Dutch John, Utah, 435/885-3355 or 435/885-3338, www.fishgreenriver.com). In addition to a full-service fly shop, Trout Creek Flies offers half-day ($325) and full-day ($425) float trips.

Rafting and Boating

For a high desert, Sweetwater County has an awful lot of ways to enjoy the water. Kayakers get their thrills at the **white-water park** near Expedition Island in Green River.

Most of the boating action in the area, however, happens at Flaming Gorge, and boats can be rented at three locations: **Buckboard Marina** (Hwy. 530, 25 miles south of Green River, 307/875-6927, www.buckboardmarina.com), **Cedar Springs Marina** (U.S. 191, 2 miles from the dam, 435/889-3795, www.cedarspringsmarina.com), and **Lucerne Valley Marina** (5570 E. Lucerne Valley Rd., off Hwy. 530, 435/784-3483, www.flaminggorge.com).

ACCOMMODATIONS

Rock Springs has a number of chain hotels, but among the best is the pet-friendly **Best Western Outlaw Inn** (1630 Elk St., Rock

Springs, 307/362-6623, www.bestwestern.com, $84–104), which has a variety of room configurations, standard amenities, a pool, an on-site restaurant, and complimentary breakfast.

The **Western Inn** (890 W. Flaming Gorge Way, Green River, 307/875-2840, $55–70) offers clean, basic accommodations with friendly staff, Wi-Fi, refrigerators, microwaves, and a nice continental breakfast included that seems like a bonus at this price.

The most appealing place to stay in the region is actually over the border near Dutch John, Utah. The ◖ **Red Canyon Lodge** (2450 W. Red Canyon Lodge, Dutch John, Utah, 435/889-3759, www.redcanyonlodge.com, $110–140 cabins, discounts in winter) offers attractive and cozy cabins with front porches perfect for enjoying the tranquil scenery. The resort offers excellent dining with stunning views and daily wild-game specials, plus a host of activities that range from horseback riding and mountain biking to boat trips and fishing tours.

CAMPING

The **Rock Springs/Green River KOA** (86 Foothill Blvd., Rock Springs, 307/362-3063, www.koa.com) is open year-round and offers tent sites ($31), RV sites ($34–42), and cabins ($60). The campground also has Wi-Fi, a swimming pool, a playground, and a variety of games. Pets are permitted.

There is phenomenal public camping in the Flaming Gorge Recreation Area. Among the favorites is the ◖ **Red Canyon Campground,** which offers front-row seats for the area's spellbinding sunsets. To reserve one of the more than 600 campsites throughout Flaming Gorge, visit www.recreation.gov or call 877/444-6777.

FOOD

For a relatively remote Wyoming town, Rock Springs has an impressive number of international eateries, the origins of which date back to the town's population diversity. **Siam King Thai and Japanese Cuisine** (1679 Sunset Dr.,

307/382-7288, 11 a.m.–9:30 p.m. Mon.–Thurs., 11 a.m.–10 p.m. Fri.–Sat., 11 a.m.–9:30 p.m. Sun., entrées $8–16) feeds the community's appetite for Asian cuisine. In addition to Chinese and Thai specialties, the restaurant serves decent sushi.

For southwest Wyoming's favorite hamburgers, fries, and shakes, hit **Grub's Drive In** (415 Paulson St., Rock Springs, 307/362-6634, Mon.–Fri. 6 a.m.–8 p.m., entrées $5–12). It's not healthy, and you may have to wait in a good-size line, but the shamrock burgers are juicy, the fries come with a side of brown gravy, and the milk shakes are something to write home about.

Among the hippest dining options in town is ◖ **Bitter Creek Brewing** (604 Broadway, Rock Springs, 307/362-4782, www.bittercreekbrewing.com, 11 a.m.–10 p.m. Mon.–Sat., 5–9 p.m. Sun., entrées $8–28), which offers a large and varied menu—think chicken wings, Thai nachos, pizza, and mouthwatering baby back ribs—in a casual, fun, and family-friendly environment.

Hungry diners head to **Peggy's Diner** (1170 W. Flaming Gorge Way, Green River, 307/875-3500), a classic '50s-style diner open 24 hours a day that serves up everything from omelets and sandwiches to burgers and salads.

INFORMATION AND SERVICES

The **Rock Springs Chamber of Commerce** (1897 Dewar Dr., Rock Springs, 307/362-3771, www.rockspringschamber.com) doubles as a visitors center. The **Green River Chamber of Commerce** (1155 Flaming Gorge Way, Green River, 307/875-5711, www.grchamber.com) also operates as a visitors center.

There are **post offices** in Rock Springs (422 S. Main St., Rock Springs, 307/382-4391) and in Green River (350 Uinta Dr., Green River, 307/875-4920).

Wash clothes at the **Sweetwater Laundry** (2528 Foothill Blvd., Rock Springs, 307/382-6290) or the **9th Street Laundromat** (1215 9th St., Rock Springs, 307/382-6092). Machines or drop-off service are available at

Sunshine Laundry (1315 Bridger Dr., Green River, 307/875-8134).

Medical care is available 24-7 at **Memorial Hospital of Sweetwater County** (1200 College Dr., Rock Springs, 307/362-3711, www.sweetwatermedicalcenter.com).

GETTING THERE AND GETTING AROUND

The **Rock Springs-Sweetwater County Airport** (RKS, Hwy. 370, 307/352-6880, www.rockspringsairport.com) has daily nonstop flights to Denver and Salt Lake City on **United** (800/241-6522, www.united.com), **Delta** (800/221-1212, www.delta.com), **Frontier** (800/432-1359, www.frontierairlines.com), and **Great Lakes** (800/554-5111, www.greatlakesav.com).

Daily bus service is provided by **Greyhound** (1695 Sunset Dr., Suite 118, Rock Springs, 307/362-2931 or 800/231-2222, www.greyhound.com).

Public transportation across Sweetwater County is available through **STAR Transit** (307/382-7827, www.ridestartransit.com).

Rental cars are available at the Rock Springs–Sweetwater County Airport from **Avis** (307/362-5599, www.avis.com), **Enterprise** (307/362-0416, www.enterprise.com), and **Hertz** (307/362-3262, www.hertz.com).

For public transportation in and around Sweetwater County, including sightseeing trips around the Flaming Gorge Dam and the Wild Horse Loop, contact **City Cab Wyoming** (307/382-1100, www.citycabwyoming.com).

Green River is 14 miles from Rock Springs, 113 miles from Pinedale, 209 miles from Thermopolis, 240 miles from Casper, and 247 miles from Yellowstone National Park.

Casper

A sprawling town near the center of the state, in many ways Casper (population 51,240, elevation 5,123 feet) has long been a hub for people traveling the region, first the Native Americans and later the settlers making use of the multiple pioneer trails in the region. Casper's booms and busts came with the trails, the railroad, and eventually oil and gas exploration. Its reputation as a rough-and-tumble town is well-earned, and one can't help but chuckle to think of Butte, Montana's minor league baseball team, the Copper Kings, ditching one of the roughest towns in the West to become the Casper Ghosts.

Although Casper is indeed industrial, rather large, and perhaps overly spread across the landscape, the town is experiencing something of a renaissance. There is a world-class contemporary art museum and a couple of professional sports teams. The beautiful North Platte River, once hopelessly polluted, has been cleaned up and is earning a reputation as one of the best fisheries in the West. There are wonderful museums and a wealth of incredible outdoor opportunities just outside town at the city's unofficial year-round playground, Casper Mountain. Casper is indeed worth a visit; you may well be surprised by all that is here.

SIGHTS
◖ Nicolaysen Art Museum and Discovery Center

The museum around which Casper revolves is the impressive Nicolaysen Art Museum and Discovery Center (400 E. Collins Dr., 307/235-5247, www.thenic.org, 10 A.M.–5 P.M. Tues.–Sat., noon–4 P.M. Sun., $5 adults, $3 ages 5–17). Focusing solely on work by contemporary artists in the Rocky Mountains, The Nic, as it is known locally, has a permanent collection of more than 6,000 works that include paintings, sculpture, textiles, drawings, photos, and prints; it features the region's most important traveling exhibitions related to their mission. The Discovery Center offers hands-on art activities for visitors of all ages along with a lineup of classes and special programs. The museum is very invested in the Casper

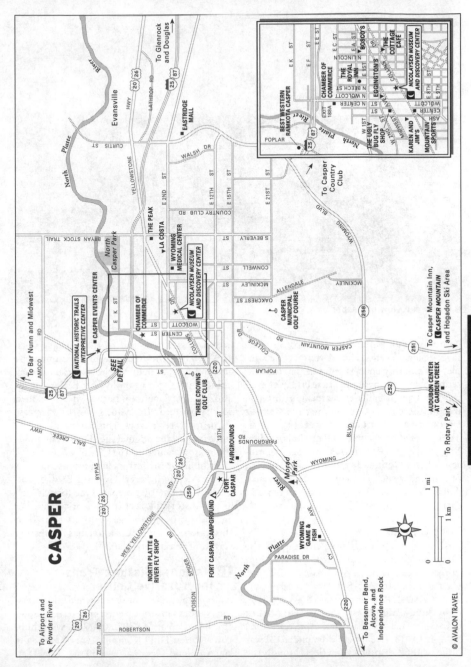

CASPER

SOUTHERN WYOMING

© AVALON TRAVEL

© WYOMING TRAVEL & TOURISM

a bird's-eye view of Casper

SOUTHERN WYOMING

community and often serves as host to some favorite local events. **Nic at Noon,** for example, is a monthly concert series held in the museum lobby at noon on the first Friday of each month. The art galleries charge no admission during the concert. In summer the **Casper Downtown Farmers Market** (5–8 P.M. Tues.) is held on the museum grounds, and on Wednesday evening during summer the museum hosts **Wednesday Night Live,** a series of musical, visual, and edible outdoor events. There's also a wonderful art show and sale in early November.

Fort Caspar

Positioned at a critical river crossing for the Oregon, Mormon, Pioneer, California and Pony Express trails, Fort Caspar (4001 Ft. Caspar Rd., 307/235-8462, www.casperwy. gov, 8 A.M.–5 P.M. daily May, 8 A.M.–6 P.M. daily June–Aug., 8 A.M.–5 P.M. daily Sept., 8 A.M.–5 P.M. Tues.–Sat. Oct.–Apr., $3 adults, $2 ages 13–18, free for children under 13) was built in 1862 to protect travelers through the

area and was occupied by the military until 1867. When the Army decommissioned the site and took as many of the materials as they could with them to build Fort Fetterman in 1867, Native Americans burned what remained to the ground. In 1936, a Works Progress Administration crew rebuilt several of the buildings on the original site. The fort and museum are operated by the City of Casper.

Exhibits at the fort include reconstructions of the Mormon Ferry, Guinard Bridge, and Richard Bridge that predated the fort, as well as fort history, pioneer trail history, and other agricultural, oil, and gas exhibits related to the region. The museum also hosts interesting traveling exhibitions.

◖ National Historic Trails Interpretive Center

Among the state's most renowned museums, the National Historic Trails Interpretive Center (1501 N. Poplar St., 307/261-7700, www.blm. gov/wy/st/en/NHTIC.html, 8 A.M.–5 P.M. daily late Apr.–mid-Oct., 9 A.M.–4:30 P.M. Tues.–Sat.

THE WYOMING JACKALOPE

As much a design staple as statewide lore, the famed jackalope is to Wyoming what Big Foot is to the Pacific Northwest. Does it exist? Could it possibly? Stop into nearly any roadside tavern and you are bound to see a mount of the creature. Ask around and the locals will gladly play along.

Popularized by Douglas Herrick in 1939, the jackalope is supposed to be an extinct antlered rabbit species, a cross between a pygmy deer and some sort of killer rabbit. Among the beliefs surrounding these legendary creatures are that jackalopes can travel at speeds of 90 mph and can mimic human sounds when chased.

Sighted in Colorado, New Mexico, and Nebraska in addition to Wyoming, jackalopes have cousins in Germany (called the *wolperdinger*) and in Sweden (the *skvader*). Drawings of antlered rabbit-like creatures date back to the 16th century in scholarly European works, so it is not just the stuff of goofy Wyoming calendars.

Those who sit on the fence between believing and not believing cite a disease called papillomatosis, which indeed causes parasite-caused growths on the top of a rabbit's head to harden, perhaps resembling antlers.

For those who prefer lore to science, the story of Douglas Herrick, a taxidermist from Douglas, seems a believable origin. Herrick and his brother Ralph returned from a hunt one day and slid their catch onto the floor. A hare landed next to a set of antelope antlers, and a pop-culture idea was born. The brothers mounted the antlered bunny, and the rest is history.

Jackalopes became so popular in the 1940s that Douglas was known far and wide as the "Jackalope Capital of the World." The city has stayed true to the legend with public art and signage all over town, as well as an annual Jackalope Day in June. Each year the local chamber issues thousands of jackalope hunting licenses, which specify that hunters cannot have an IQ higher than 72 and can only hunt between midnight and 2 A.M. on June 31. In the works now? A giant 80-foot fiberglass jackalope sculpture to tower over I-25. This is a story so entwined with Wyoming culture that it will never fade away.

mid-Oct–late Apr., $4–6, free for children under 16) tells the gritty story of Manifest Destiny and westward expansion on the historic pioneer trails through interactive exhibits and multimedia presentations. The museum's exhibits are both indoors and outside, and they succeed in giving visitors a real sense of what day-to-day life was like for the early pioneers. The museum's seven distinct galleries are dedicated to four of the trails that cut through the region, as well as Native Americans, mountain men, explorers, and the trails today. There's even a virtual river crossing experience.

Ayres Natural Bridge

Some 50 miles southeast of Casper and 10 miles west of Douglas is one of Wyoming's earliest tourist attractions, Ayres Natural Bridge (208 Natural Bridge Rd., 307/358-3532, 8 A.M.–8 P.M. daily Apr.–Oct., free), a natural arch where the LaPrele Creek worked its way through a 100-foot-long, 50-foot-high solid rock wall over the centuries. It is set in a lovely 22-acre park. The Native Americans of the region thought of the natural bridge as a sinister place because of a tale about a young brave being struck by lightning in the canyon. The legend developed until it was widely believed among the Indians that an evil spirit lived beneath the bridge. Travelers on the Mormon Trail, which crossed the creek two miles north of the site, discovered the bridge and the legend, and often visited the area to escape the Native Americans.

There are 12 beautiful campsites within the park boundaries; pets are not allowed in the park.

◖ Casper Mountain

When Casper residents are eager to flee the

city, particularly in the heat of summer, they head to Casper Mountain, an alpine oasis just minutes from town. In addition to a popular downhill ski area, several campgrounds and parks, and miles of beautiful hiking and biking trails, Casper Mountain is also rich with history and culture.

An early settler from Missouri, Elizabeth "Neal" Forsling, fled a horrible marriage with her two young daughters to homestead on the top of Casper Mountain in the 1920s. An artist and writer, Forsling was strong, independent, and loved the mountain with all of her being. She fell in love with and married a local rancher, Jim, who joined her in her happy life on the mountaintop, but when he froze to death at just age 38 while skiing home from town with supplies, Neal dedicated herself even more to the land on which she lived. She painted and wrote stories about the spirits, trolls, fairies, and other beings that lived on Casper Mountain. She hosted a summer solstice party in 1930 that would become the Mid-Summer's Eve Celebration that continues today. Singlehandedly, Neal Forsling created a mythical culture on the mountain that persists today.

Forsling donated her land and cabin to Natrona County in 1973. She died a few years later, and the county turned her home into a wonderful museum named for the book of stories she created about the mountain: The **Crimson Dawn Museum** (1620 Crimson Dawn Rd., 307/235-9311, call for open days and hours) is at the center of the Mid-Summer's Eve Celebration.

Somewhat surprisingly, there is also a great little restaurant atop the mountain. The **◖ Casper Mountain Inn** (8455 Casper Mountain Rd., 307/473-8707, 11 A.M.–8 P.M. Fri., 8 A.M.–8 P.M. Sat., 8 A.M.–6 P.M. Sun., entrées $7–25) serves killer breakfasts, hearty lunches, and delicious dinners in a charmingly rustic setting.

ENTERTAINMENT AND EVENTS
Rodeo
Rodeo is serious business in this part of the state—or anywhere in Wyoming, for that matter. One of the biggest is the **College National Finals Rodeo** (307/577-3030 or 800/442-2256, www.cnfr.com), held annually at the Casper Events Center in mid-June. More than 400 cowboys and cowgirls from 100 universities and colleges compete for champion status in saddle bronc riding, bareback riding, bull riding, tie-down roping, steer wrestling, team roping, barrel racing, breakaway roping, and goat tying.

Another big rodeo in Casper is the **PRCA Rodeo** held annually in conjunction with the **Central Wyoming Fair** (1700 Fairgrounds Rd., 307/235-5775 or 888/225-2600, www.centralwyomingfair.com) in mid-July. The fair has been in operation since 1904 and comes with all the hoopla and community spirit you'd expect.

Stage III Community Theatre
Performing in an intimate, theater-in-the-round, Casper's Stage III Community Theatre (900 N. Center St., 307/234-0946, www.stageiiitheatre.org) is an entirely volunteer organization that produces six productions annually between September and June. The company has been entertaining Casper for more than 30 years, with offerings ranging from classic dramas to mysteries and comedies.

Midsummer's Eve Celebration
Held each year on June 21, the summer solstice, **Mid-Summer's Eve Celebration** (Crimson Dawn Park, 1620 Crimson Dawn Rd., 307/235-9311) is a unique event that showcases the history and spirit of Casper. Marked by a bonfire that everyone is invited to throw red dirt into, in hopes of seeing their fondest wish granted, the event dates back to 1930 and celebrates the witches, spirits, and trolls said to inhabit the mountain.

Undoubtedly one of the best outdoor music festivals in the region, the **Beartrap Summer Festival** (307/266-5252, www.beartrapsummerfestival.com) brings Casper Mountain to life with bluegrass music the first weekend in August. The event hosts big-name bands and musicians for two days from mid-morning until dusk. Rounding out the festival are musical workshops, an arts and crafts marketplace, an open-air food court, and supervised children's activities. Pets are welcome on a leash. Discounted tickets can be purchased in advance by phone.

SHOPPING

A central shopping locale for much of the region, Casper has every sort of shopping imaginable, from big malls and shopping centers to box stores and downtown boutiques. The largest facility in the region by far is the **Eastridge Mall** (601 SE Wyoming Blvd., 307/265-9392, www.shopeastridge.com), anchored by Target, Best Buy, Macy's, Bed Bath and Beyond, Sears, and J. C. Penney.

There are some smaller stores too that should not be missed. **Blackberry Mountain Gift Shop** (251 S. Center St., 307/234-6605, www.bbmgs.com, 10 A.M.–5 P.M. Tues.–Fri., 10 A.M.–2 P.M. Sat.) is a quirky little place with everything from home decor and seasonal decorations to candles, jewelry, and incredible china. A terrific place to find work by local artists is the **Casper Artists Guild/West Wind Art Gallery** (1040 W. 15th St., 307/265-2655, www.casper-business.com/ArtistsGuild, noon–4 P.M. Tues.– Sat.), which hosts regular shows in a variety of media and has a gift shop.

For a sweet tooth, the best spot in Casper is **Donnells Candies** (201 E. 2nd St., 307/234-6283 or 877/461-2009), which has been churning out delectable handmade chocolates, savory nuts, and all flavors of popcorn since 1956. The store is still owned and operated by the founding family, and with brisk Internet sales it has found admirers the world over.

RECREATION

Casper is one of the few cities in Wyoming where spectator sports include more than just rodeo. The **Casper Ghosts** (Mike Lansing Field, Poplar St., off I-25, 307/232-1111, www.ghostsbaseball.com, $6.50–9) are a minor league affiliate of the Colorado Rockies that play more than 70 games per season to enthusiastic and family-friendly crowds.

Football fans can check out the **Wyoming Cavalry** (307/232-8170, www.wyomingcavalry.com), members of the National Indoor Football League.

Hiking and Biking

In addition to the abundance of hiking and biking trails just outside the city in places like Casper Mountain, there are a number of green trails within city limits. The **Platte River Parkway** winds nearly 10 miles along the river's edge and can be accessed in a number of parks, including Morad Park and Casper Whitewater Park, as well as at the Holiday Inn on the River. **Rotary Park** just south of town at the base of Casper Mountain is home to the beloved Garden Creek Falls and the 4.5-mile **Bridle Trail.**

Just six miles east of town on Highway 252, **Edness K. Wilkins State Park** (S. Poplar St., 307/577-5150, www.wyoparks.state.wy.us/EWslide.htm, day-use $6 nonresidents) is a serene spot with giant cottonwoods, river access, ideal picnic spots, fishing, boat access, and a playground. There are also 2.8 miles of paved trails for walkers, and birders will delight in the more than 40 species that can be counted in a single day in the park. Another tranquil spot for walks and birding is the **Audubon Center at Garden Creek** (101 Garden Creek Rd., 307/473-1987, www.audubonwyoming.org, 8 A.M.–5 P.M. Mon.–Fri.). There is a nice visitors center open year-round and a variety of nature programs open to the public.

Casper Mountain is the best place for serious hiking and biking. Among the many popular trails in the area is the unique **Lee McCune Braille Trail** for both sighted and visually impaired hikers.

Avid bikers without wheels can rent great mountain bikes from **Mountain Sports** (543 S. Center St., 307/266-1136, www.wyomap.com/mtnsports.html, $25 per day, $5 per additional day).

Skiing

Casper's easy access to the mountains makes this town an ideal winter getaway. Just 15 minutes from town is **Hogadon Ski Area** (Casper Mountain, 307/235-8499, www.hogadon.net, Wed.–Sun., full-day $40 adults, $35 youth, $25 children), a small, family-friendly mountain that offers 20 percent beginner terrain and 40 percent each intermediate and advanced. There are 15 major trails and three lifts, and a snowboard terrain park for adventurous riders. Group and private lessons are available.

For Nordic skiers, the **Casper Nordic Center** (Casper Mountain, 307/235-4772, www.caspernordic.com, Wed.–Sun.) offers 26 miles of groomed trails plus a lighted loop for night skiing. There are an additional 30 miles of backcountry and snowshoe trails in the area as well.

For equipment rentals for just about any sport in any season, head to **Mountain Sports** (543 S. Center St., 307/266-1136, www.wyomap.com/mtnsports.html).

Rock Climbing

As Casper's status among outdoor junkies continues to climb, rock climbing is another of the region's well-known offerings. **Fremont Canyon** has world-class granite climbing for people of all ability levels, ranging 40–400-plus feet. To get to the canyon, which overlooks Alcova Reservoir, head south from Casper on Highway 220 to the town of Alcova; the canyon is 10 miles farther south, accessed by the Fremont Canyon Bridge.

To practice or get information on other area climbs, visit Casper's in-town climbing gym, **The Peak** (408 N. Beverly St., 307/472-4084).

Fishing

Fishing in the North Platte River is something of a comeback story. Around the turn of the 20th century, the North Platte was known as one of the great trout fisheries of the West; as an example, a celebration in Saratoga in 1907, known as the Railroad Days Celebration and Fish Fry, required more than 3,000 fish to be caught in two days to feed visitors. The river was thick with trout, and anglers flocked to

the area to catch them. As industrialization spread across the country, feedlots and oil refineries increasingly dotted the landscape and polluted the North Platte until it was nearly uninhabitable. Only in the last 15–20 years have sweeping measures been taken to restore the river, an effort that has, by all accounts, been enormously successful. In fact, *American Angler* magazine voted the Grey Reef section of the North Platte River the number one big fishery in the world.

Today, in part because of its shallow depth and slow current, the river can be fished for hundreds of miles, and anglers can expect to see the noses of rainbows, browns, Snake River cutthroats, walleye, and the occasional cutbow, a rainbow-cutthroat hybrid.

Casper offers an abundance of fly shops and guides. A good place to start for a license and regulations is **Wyoming Game and Fish** (3030 Energy Lane, Suite 100, 307/473-3400, www.gf.state.wy.us). For gear or guided trips, contact **The Ugly Bug Fly Shop** (240 S. Center St., 307/234-6905, www.crazyrainbow.net), which has full-day ($380 per boat) and half-day ($280 per boat) guided fly-fishing trips. The **North Platte River Fly Shop** (7400 Hwy. 220, 307/237-5997 or 866/548-FISH—866/548-3474, www.wyomingflyfishing.com) offers all-day guided trips ($350–390 for 2 anglers).

Golf

Casper has 90 holes for avid golfers to play, including a world-class course designed by Robert Trent Jones Jr. built on an old remediated oil refinery: The **Three Crowns Golf Club** (1601 King Blvd., 307/472-7696, www.threecrownsgolfclub.com, $65 for 18 holes Sat.–Sun., $60 for 18 holes Mon.–Fri., includes golf cart) is a par-72 course that opened in 2005 and has a resort-like feel.

Another course worth playing is the **Casper Municipal Golf Course** (2120 Allendale Blvd., 307/237-9470, www.casperwy.gov, $25 for 18 holes, $16 for 9 holes), which has 27 holes on three distinct nines. Opened in 1929, the course is consistently ranked among the best municipal courses in the state.

For some of the most unique golfing in the state, try the **Salt Creek Country Club & Golf Course** (Hwy. 387, Midwest, 307/437-6207, www.pasturegolf.com, $2 for 9 holes), which offers nine holes of mowed prairie grass fairways and sand greens at only $2 per round. Golfers share the course with antelope, deer, and prairie dogs.

ACCOMMODATIONS

Casper has no shortage of places to stay, and many chain hotel options are available. The **Best Western Ramkota Casper** (800 N. Poplar St., 307/266-6000 or 800/528-1234, www.casper.ramkota.com, $110) is a large facility that caters both to business travelers (in-room desks, free Wi-Fi, and a business center) and to families with the astaway Bay Indoor Water Playground, geared to young children.

A more budget-friendly option downtown is **The Royal Inn** (440 E. A St., 307/234-3501, www.caspermotel.com, $40–54), which offers clean, basic rooms with microwaves and refrigerators, free Wi-Fi, and on-site laundry machines. They also provide gas barbecue grills and a briquette for guests who want to cook out.

For an unforgettable wilderness B&B experience just out of town, **(Sunburst Lodge** (2700 Micro Rd., 307/235-9086, www.sunburst-lodge.com, $135–165) is located on Casper Mountain next to Hogadon Ski Area and just 20 minutes from town. There is much exploring to be done year-round just outside the lodge along with cozy accommodations and sumptuous meals inside. You can also sleep in a wonderful yurt ($150).

CAMPING

The closest public camping in the vicinity of Casper is 10 miles south of town on **Casper Mountain,** a breezy, forested all-season playground for locals. There are four campgrounds on the mountain; **Beartrap Meadow** (Casper Mountain Rd., 307/235-9311, $7) is the only one with water and is also the nicest of the four. Various campsites maintained by the Bureau of Land Management (307/261-7600, www.wy.blm.gov, $5) include the **Rim** and

Lodgepole Campgrounds, which can be accessed from gravel roads off Casper Mountain Road.

For a scenic lakeside campground 28 miles west of Casper on County Road 407, off Highway 220, **Alcova Lake Campground** (307/235-9311, www.natronacounty-wy.gov, $15 full hookup, $7 unserviced) is a beautiful spot; unserviced sites are first-come, first-served, and sites with hookups are by reservation only.

There are also a few private campgrounds and RV parks right in town. Set along a beautiful bend in the North Platte River, the **Fort Caspar Campground** (4205 Fort Caspar Rd., 307/234-3260 or 888/243-7709, www.ftcasparcamp.org, $21–40) offers tent and RV sites, a lodge, ponds, and several walking trails; they also provide free Wi-Fi.

FOOD

Casper is a breakfast lover's town: There are a number of great places to start the day right. **Eggington's** (229 E. 2nd St., 307/265-8700, until 2 P.M. daily, entrées $3–13) serves breakfast and lunch to a bustling crowd. They offer everything from omelets and pastries to burgers and salads. A somewhat hidden but marvelous spot is **(The Cottage Café** (116 S. Lincoln St., 307/234-1157, lunch Tues.–Sat., entrées $9) which is tucked into a residential neighborhood and serves delicious homemade soups, paninis, pastas, and more.

For good Mexican food, which southern Wyoming seems to have no shortage of, try **La Costa** (1600 E. 2nd St., 307/235-6599, Sun.–Thurs. 11 A.M.–9 P.M., Fri.–Sat. 11 A.M.–10 P.M., entrées $6–14). **Bosco's** (847 E. A St., 307/265-9658, lunch 11 A.M.–1:30 P.M. Tues.–Fri., dinner from 5 P.M. Tues.–Sat., entrées $6–20) serves wonderful Italian meals in an intimate setting. Another favorite in town is **Karen and Jim's Restaurant** (520 S. Ash St., 307/266-4976, Tues.–Sat. 10:30 A.M.–8:30 P.M., bar open later, entrées $7–20), which specializes in Greek fare, including gyros, but offers plenty of American entrées such as burgers, steaks, and pasta.

About five miles southwest of town en route to the Mormon Trail, the **Goose Egg Inn** (10580 Goose Egg Rd., 307/473-8838, dinner 5:30–9:30 P.M. Wed.–Sat., $9–32) is a family-friendly treat with plenty of juicy Wyoming beef on the menu as well as specialties like fried chicken and catfish.

A word of caution: Don't come to Casper on a Monday with an empty belly. For whatever reason, most restaurants stay closed on Monday. Many of the town's menus can be seen online at www.caspermenus.com.

INFORMATION AND SERVICES

The **Natrona County Travel and Tourism Council** (992 N. Poplar St., 307/234-5362 or 800/852-1889, www.casperwyoming.info) has a wealth of information for visitors. The **Casper Area Chamber of Commerce** (500 N. Center St., 307/234-5311 or 866/234-5311, www.casperwyoming.org) is an excellent resource for local businesses and relocation information.

Post offices are located at 411 North Forest Drive (307/237-8556) and at 150 East B Street.

The **Natrona County Public Library** (307/237-4935, www.natronacountylibrary.org) is located at 307 East 2nd Street.

Laundry facilities are available at **Hilltop Laundromat** (2513 E. 3rd St., 307/234-7331) or **Lux Laundry** (1333 S. Conwell St., 307/237-5491).

Wyoming Medical Center (1233 E. 2nd St., 307/577-7201 or 800/822-7201, www.wmcnet.org) is the largest health care facility in the state and offers everything from 24-hour emergency medicine to highly specialized care.

GETTING THERE AND AROUND

The **Casper/Natrona County International Airport** (CPR, 8500 Airport Pkwy., 307/472-6688, www.iflycasper.com) is located on U.S. 20/26 approximately nine miles west of downtown. Two carriers, **United** (800/864-8331, www.united.com) and **Delta** (800/221-1212, www.delta.com), provide daily flights to and from Denver, Salt Lake City, and Minneapolis–St. Paul.

Regular bus service to and from Casper is available on **Greyhound** (601 N. Center St., 307/266-1904, www.greyhound.com) and **Black Hills Stage Lines** (601 N. Center St., 877/779-2999, www.blackhillsstagelines.com).

By car, Casper is 145 miles from Lander, 148 miles from Laramie, 178 miles from Cheyenne, 240 miles from Green River, 242 miles from Gillette, 284 miles from Jackson, and 267 miles from Yellowstone National Park.

Rental-car agencies at the airport include **Avis** (307/237-2634 or 800/831-2847, www.avis.com), **Budget** (307/266-1122, www.budget.com), and **Hertz** (307/265-1355, www.hertz.com). **Enterprise** (120 S. Forest Dr., 307/234-8122 or 800/261-7331, www.enterprise.com) has an office in town.

The easiest public transportation in Casper is **The Bus** (307/265-1313, www.casperareatransportation.com, 6:30 A.M.–6:30 P.M. Mon.–Fri., $1 adults, $0.50 seniors, free for children under 5), a fixed-route transit system. The Casper Area Transportation Coalition also offers **Dial-a-Ride,** which must be reserved before 3 P.M. at least one day in advance; it's better to reserve two days early. The cost is $5, or $2 for seniors and people with special needs. Local taxi service is provided by **Casper Cab** (307/234-8294) and **RC Cab** (307/235-5203).

Laramie

Nestled in a high basin between the Laramie and Medicine Bow Mountains, Laramie (population 27,523, elevation 7,173 feet) is a charming combination of Old West frontier town and sophisticated university town, all with immediate proximity to a phenomenal natural playground that envelops the city.

Like so many cities in the region, Laramie can trace its roots back to a fort, Fort John Buford, built in 1866 to protect travelers on the pioneer trails, most notably the Overland Trail. In 1867, railroad workers plotting the course through the Laramie Valley rumbled into town, bringing with them numerous businesses to support their way of life. When the first passengers disembarked from the Union Pacific train in Laramie City in 1868, there were 23 saloons ready for them to wet their whistles.

Fort Buford, by then known as Fort Sanders, was abandoned in 1882, but other significant structures had been built in Laramie. The Wyoming Territorial Prison was first built in 1872 as a response to the lawlessness of the area. And in 1887, Wyoming University, now known as the University of Wyoming, opened its doors to both men and women. Incidentally, women in Laramie were the first in the United States to sit on a jury and to vote, both in 1870.

Today, Laramie continues to be among the most progressive cities in the state, although it hasn't lost any of its cowboy swagger. The nearly 150-year-old downtown buildings are beautiful and authentic examples of the finest frontier architecture. The town is full of important historic sites and an arresting spectrum of museums. The university gives Laramie just enough academic culture to keep the town young and vibrant with concerts, lectures, sports, and coffeehouses, and the surrounding wilderness is well used without becoming overcrowded.

the red brick buildings of downtown Laramie

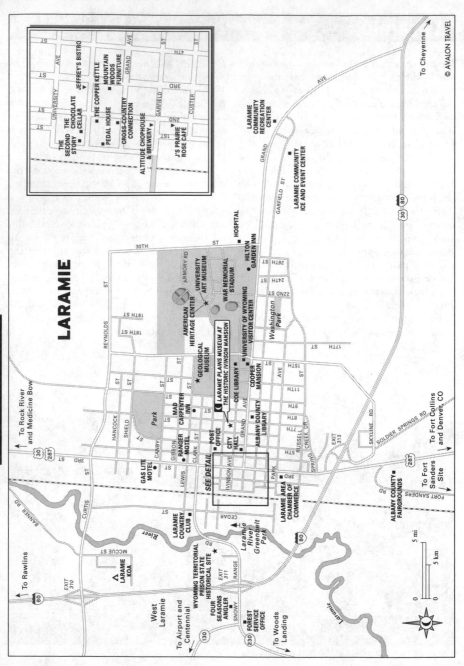

SOUTHERN WYOMING

LARAMIE

© AVALON TRAVEL

SIGHTS
American Heritage Center
Established in 1945, the American Heritage Center (2111 Willett Dr., 307/766-4114, www. ahc.uwyo.edu, Mon.–Fri., hours vary, free) houses one of the most extensive nongovernmental historical collections in the country. In addition to the manuscripts collections, a rare book center has more than 55,000 items that date back to medieval times. Topics range from the American West, an obvious and natural specialty, to British and American literature, natural history, conservation, women authors, and book arts, among countless others. The center is open to the public and is utilized constantly by scholars from all over the world. The center also hosts an array of fascinating events from lectures and symposia to rare and important exhibits. The website offers viewers a meaningful look into the digital collection, audio-visual collection, and virtual exhibits.

University of Wyoming Art Museum
Located in the same architecturally stunning complex as the American Heritage Center, the University of Wyoming Art Museum (2111 Willett Dr., 307/766-6622, www. uwyo.edu/artmuseum, 10 A.M.–9 P.M. Mon., 10 A.M.–5 P.M. Tues.–Sat., free) brings art from around the world to Wyoming. Their permanent collection houses more than 7,000 objects, including European and American paintings, prints, and drawings; 19th-century Japanese prints; 18th–19th-century Persian and Indian miniature paintings; 20th-century photography; and African and Native American artifacts. They also host important exhibitions focused on everything from regional art to international museum collections.

University of Wyoming Geological Museum
In a university with several compelling museums covering everything from anthropology to insects, another great one is the Geological Museum (West Campus, near N. 9th St. and E. Lewis St., 307/766-3386, www.

uwyo.edu/geomuseum, 1–4 P.M. Tues.–Fri., 10 A.M.–2 P.M. Sat., noon–4 P.M. Sun., free). The museum houses some of the best fossils in the country and dedicates plenty of space to Wyoming's earliest inhabitants: the dinosaurs. In addition to the usual suspects—from *Allosaurus* to *T. rex*—the museum lays claim to one of only six *Apatosaurus* skeletons on display worldwide. This one is 145–160 million years old and was discovered in Albany County in 1901. There are also skeletons of *Diatryma gigantea,* a prehistoric carnivorous flying dinosaur more than seven feet tall, found in 1876. Dozens of displays tell the stories of the more than 50 species of dinosaur whose remains have been found in Wyoming soil.

❰ Laramie Plains Museum at the Historic Ivinson Mansion
Entrepreneur and banker Edward Ivinson was a local hero in Laramie, not only for his ethical business practices and his community-minded role in the construction of the prison and the university, but also for the home that he built in 1892, the same year he lost the Wyoming gubernatorial race. Indeed, the Ivinson Mansion (603 E. Ivinson Ave., 307/742-4448, www.laramiemuseum.org, 1-hour tours 9 A.M.–5 P.M. Tues.–Sat., 1–4 P.M. Sun. summer, 1–4 P.M. Tues.–Sat. in other seasons, hours can change for private events, $10 adults, $7 seniors, $5 students, free for children under 6, discounts for families, AAA, and military) is among Laramie's most impressive buildings. The house was designed by architect W. E. Ware and built for $40,000 with then-unheard-of amenities that included central heating, electricity, and running water. Jane Ivinson, Edward's wife, decorated the home with elegant appointments from around the world. After his beloved wife died, Ivinson donated their regal residence to the Episcopal Missionary District of Wyoming with the understanding that it be used as a school-home for teenage ranch girls who otherwise might not be educated. The school operated until 1958, at which point the house sat vacant at the mercy of vandals for more than a decade.

In 1972 the Episcopal Church sold the mansion to the Laramie Plains Museum Association. Under the museum's care, the home has been beautifully restored and is open to the public as the Laramie Plains Museum. The home is filled with artifacts from all over the state, including the largest collection of Wyoming Territorial Prison furnishings, gorgeous wood pieces made by Swedish prisoner Jan Hjorth, a regional gun collection spanning more than a century, period furnishings, and more. Seeing the artifacts in such a stunning home setting makes this museum absolutely worth seeing.

Wyoming Territorial Prison State Historical Site

Built in 1872 to deal with the ruffians in lawless Laramie, the Wyoming Territorial Prison (975 Snowy Range Rd., 307/745-6161, www.wyoparks.state.wy.us, 9 A.M.–6 P.M. daily May–Oct., call for winter hours, $5 adults, $2.50 ages 12–17, free for children under 12) was restored in 1989 and made into a 190-acre state historic site. The prison was in use 1872–1903, during which time more than 1,000 men and 12 women were imprisoned there. Among the most famous residents was Butch Cassidy. When Wyoming achieved statehood in 1890, work was already underway on a new state prison in Rawlins. When the Wyoming Frontier Prison opened in 1901, the transition began, and prisoners in the Territorial Prison were slowly replaced by animals from the University of Wyoming's experimental stock farm, which were housed in the prison for more than 70 years.

Rounding out the historic site are an entirely recreated frontier town; a number of buildings in various stages of restoration, including the broom factory where many of the prisoners worked on a variety of different jobs; authentic pioneer cabins; a schoolhouse; and agricultural buildings.

Still, the prison is the main attraction, and visitors should plan to spend at least an hour touring the facility. A brochure in the gift shop provides a self-guided tour through furnished cells, the prisoner dining room, guards' quarters, women's quarters, the warden's office, and

© WYOMING TRAVEL & TOURISM

the Wyoming Territorial Prison in Laramie

a number of other rooms and exhibit galleries. The warden's house on the grounds can also be toured.

ENTERTAINMENT AND EVENTS

With such a young, vibrant population, Laramie has loads of events going on year-round. From scholarly lectures on campus to concerts and meditation gatherings, the offerings are plentiful and diverse.

On Wednesday nights throughout summer, the **Laramie Municipal Band,** made up primarily of students and teachers from the university, puts on free concerts in Washington Park (Sheridan St. between S. 18th St. and S. 21st St.) starting at 7:30 P.M. On Friday afternoon and evening July–September, the town comes downtown for the weekly and festive **Farmers Market** (307/742-2212, www.laramiemainstreet.org, 3–7 P.M.). For cultural events held throughout the year at the university, including the **University of Wyoming Symphony Orchestra,** theater and dance

WIND POWER: WYOMING'S NEXT BOOM?

Having prospered from the boom and then endured the bust of energy production cycles countless times over the last century or more, Wyoming is at the forefront of a new boom, this one based on what has for eons been at the center of the state's frequently harsh climate: wind. Wind power technology as we now know it started in the early 1980s. As the eighth windiest state, Wyoming ranks 12th in terms of wind power installations, and their numbers are growing steadily – in 2009 the energy produced by wind was double the 2008 figures. The benefits of wind power to Wyoming include jobs and electricity produced without greenhouse gases.

Spend a few days in Wyoming, particularly in the southern half of the state, and it will come as no surprise that Wyoming has some of the most consistent wind in the country. As much as 90 percent of energy produced will be exported at a cost of $107 per megawatt hour to states like California, for example, which is committed to getting one-third of its power from renewable sources by 2020. Montana produces the cheapest wind, at $77 per megawatt hour, and Wyoming is second at $82 per megawatt hour. New Mexico, by comparison, is among the more costly producers, at $89 per megawatt hour. In May of 2010, there were 777 wind towers in Wyoming, according to the American Wind Energy Association, and another 207 more were under construction. Estimates put the eventual tally as high as 10,000 towers across the state, which will clearly change the landscape of Wyoming.

Somewhat controversially, Wyoming is the first state to put a tax on wind energy production. Proposed by Governor Dave Freudenthal, the $1 per megawatt hour tax is due to go into effect in 2012, and a sales tax exemption for renewable energy projects expires in 2011. The tax is expected to generate roughly $4 million annually for the state, for starters, 60 percent of which will go to the county where the electricity is generated and the other 40 percent to the state's general fund. The crux of the controversy is that some feel this makes Wyoming unfriendly to wind power producers, but the governor and his supporters argue that the producers are going to make a lot of money but that Wyomingites will bear the environmental – primarily visual – and socio-economic burden. They point to the benefits gained statewide by tax revenues from oil, gas, coal, and coal-bed methane.

As the wind power boom takes off, something of a land rush in southeastern Wyoming, where the greatest number of wind farms exist, is transforming the local agricultural and ranching culture. In an effort to prevent bad deals with a strength-in-numbers approach, ranchers and farmers have joined together to form associations to bargain collectively. One of a dozen or so such cooperatives, the Bordeaux Wind Energy Association asserts that everyone is going to be impacted, whether the turbines are on their property or not, so everyone should benefit. Just as the massive wind turbines are undoubtedly shifting the landscape of Wyoming, so too are the proactive ranchers and farmers working together to transform the business of agriculture. Indeed, income from wind farms can often be the deciding factor in whether a family can hold on to their ranch or not. As a result, some argue that wind farms are in fact strengthening Wyoming's agricultural tradition by keeping farmers and ranchers on their land.

performances, and major concerts, contact the **Fine Arts Box Office** (307/766-6666, www. uwyo.edu/finearts).

For more than 70 years, **Laramie Jubilee Days** (www.laramiejubileedays.com) has been Laramie's annual hometown celebration that draws revelers from across the region. Scheduled around the anniversary of Wyoming's statehood on July 10, the event frequently spans more than a week and includes Fourth of July events, including the biggest fireworks display in the state. Other Jubilee Days events include street dances, a classic parade, bull riding, and three nights of professional rodeo.

The **Albany County Fair** is held annually in late July–early August at the fairgrounds (3520 U.S. 287) and includes all the family-friendly fun visitors expect from a Western fair, including a carnival, entertainment, and 4-H activities.

SHOPPING

While the shopping options are quite varied around town, from marvelous bookstores to hippie outposts and classic Western saddleries, the experience of shopping in Laramie's historic and charming downtown cannot be beat. **The Second Story** (105 Ivinson Ave., 307/745-4423, www.personallyrecommendedbooks.com), for example, is a gem of an independent bookstore housed in a public hall built in 1889. Since then, it has been a hotel, a bordello, a saloon, a seniors center, and now a bookstore. Their children's book selection is particularly good. As a bonus, with every book purchase comes a free espresso drink, made to order.

For a delectable treat, stop by **The Chocolate Cellar** (113 Ivinson Ave., 307/742-9278, www.christieschocolatecellar.com), which has been creating handcrafted goodies for more than 30 years. **Mountain Woods Furniture** (206 S. 3rd St., 307/745-3515, www.mtswoodsfurniture.com) sells rustic wood furniture handcrafted by local artisans. **The Copper Kettle** (209 2nd St., 307/742-1800, www.mycopperkettle.com) is a glorious kitchen shop in a wonderful environment.

RECREATION
Rock Climbing

A mecca for rock climbers and nature lovers alike, **Vedauwoo** (off I-80 exit 329, 17 miles east of Laramie, 307/745-2300, www.vedauwoo.org) is an otherworldly jumble of enormous boulders that offer some of the best wide-crack climbing in the West. More than 500 sport climbs were documented in the first guidebook for the area, written in 1994 and no longer available. Today there are more than 900 climbs, many of which are detailed on the Vedauwoo website, and the number continues

to grow. For nonclimbers, the area is ideal for hiking, trail running, and even wildlife viewing. Among the animals sighted here are antelope, deer, moose, and even black bears and cougars. A Forest Service campground is available at the site.

Hiking and Biking

In addition to meandering hikes in town along the Laramie River Greenbelt and at nearby Vedauwoo, the **Pole Mountain Area** (Forest Rd. 705, off I-80 exit 323, 13 miles east of Laramie) in the Sherman Mountains offers terrific trails for hiking and biking. The **Headquarters National Recreation Trail Loop** can be a four-mile or eight-mile round-trip loop, depending on your time and energy level. The trail winds through a number of environments, from sage and grassy meadows to pine forests, and there is plenty of opportunity for bouldering among the pink granite rocks that are reminiscent of Vedauwoo. A "Pole Mountain Summer-use Trails" brochure is available at the Laramie Ranger District (2468 W. Jackson St., 307/745-2300).

You'll have to bring your own bike to Laramie, unless you are a student or faculty member of University of Wyoming, in which case you can rent from the ingenious Bike Library through the Outdoor Program (307/766-2402), but if you need service, repairs, or just some good advice, head into the **Pedal House** (207 S. 1st St., 307/742-5533, www.pedalhouse.com).

Fishing

While Laramie isn't quite the hotbed of fishing that can be found in other parts of the state, its location makes access to varied waters relatively easy. For lake fishing, options include **Laramie Plains Lakes** (15 miles west of town off Hwy. 230) and **Lake Hattie** (20 miles southwest of Laramie off Hwy. 230). Nearby rivers filled with trout include the **Big Laramie River** and the **Upper North Platte River.** For fishing gear or guided trips, contact **Four Seasons Angler** (334 S. Fillmore St., 307/721-4047, www.fourseasonsanglers.com). Half-day trips for two anglers start at $350; full-day trips for two start at $400.

Golf

Golfers can hit the links in Laramie at the nine-hole **Laramie Country Club** (489 Hwy. 230, 307/745-8490, www.thelaramiecountryclub.com, $20 for 9 holes) or the **Jacoby Park Golf Course** (3501 Willett Dr., 307/745-3111, www.jacobygc.com, $22 for 9 holes, $28 for 18 holes).

Skiing

Thirty-two miles west of town in the Medicine Bow National Forest, **Snowy Range Ski Area** (3254 Hwy. 130, Centennial, 307/745-5750, www.snowyrangeski.com, full-day $39 adults, $24 children under 13) has five ski lifts covering 27 trails on 250 acres.

A terrific store for all kinds of gear and first-rate advice for Nordic skiers is the **Cross-Country Connection** (222 S. 2nd St., 307/721-2851, www.crosscountryconnection.com).

Spectator Sports

When it comes to recreation, one cannot forget that Laramie is a college town and somewhat fanatical about its football. Attending a **Wyoming Cowboys** game at War Memorial Stadium (E. Grand Ave and N. 22nd St.) is a true Wyoming experience. It's likely the only place in Wyoming you'll ever feel crowded. For schedule and tickets, contact the Athletic Ticket Office (307/742-2427 or 800/922-9461, www.wyomingathletics.com).

Perhaps small beans compared to the Cowboys, the **Laramie Colts** (www.laramiecolts.com, $5 adults, $3 children under 12) play collegiate baseball to family-friendly crowds, at Cowboy Field (2623 Willet Drive, just east of War Memorial Stadium).

Recreation Centers

When the wind blows in Laramie, as it will, the **Laramie Community Recreation Center** (920 Boulder Dr., 307/721-5269, www.ci.laramie.wy.us) offers an indoor leisure pool, an eight-lane lap pool, an outdoor pool with

water slides and a lazy river, a full-court gymnasium, weights, an indoor playground, and an abundance of classes and activities. Daily fees for nonresidents are $8 adults, $6.50 ages 13–18, $4.50 ages 3–12.

Accessed from a trailhead at West Garfield Street and South Spruce Street, the **Laramie River Greenbelt Park** offers 5.75 miles of paved walking, running, biking, and Rollerblading paths.

When winter comes to town, the **Laramie Community Ice and Event Center** (3510 Garfield St., 307/721-2161, www.ci.laramie.wy.us) offers ice skating and skate rentals.

ACCOMMODATIONS

Laramie has nearly 2,000 guest rooms in town, of which 500 are just a few years old. Accommodation options include hotels, motels, bed-and-breakfasts, and guest ranches.

For the best value in town with a convenient downtown location, the **Ranger Motel** (453 N. 3rd St., 307/742-6677, rangermotel@wyo2u.com, $50 d) offers clean no-frills guest rooms with air-conditioning, microwaves, and mini refrigerators.

At the other end of the spectrum, the new **Hilton Garden Inn** (2229 Grand Ave., 307/745-5500, www.uwconferencecenter.com, $129–189) offers all the frills you are going to find in Laramie. From Egyptian cotton sheets and ergonomic chairs to flat-screen TVs and cushy bathrobes, this hotel sets the standard for luxury.

Two unique lodging options are the pet-friendly and roadside **Gas Lite Motel** (960 N. 3rd St., 307/742-6616, $40–66), filled to the brim with Western knickknacks; and the fabulously quirky **Mad Carpenter Inn** (353 N. 8th St., 307/742-0870, www.madcarpenter.home.bresnan.net, $85–115, includes gourmet continental breakfast), a B&B near the university where the creative and delightful innkeepers have a passion for carpentry, cooking, and poetry.

CAMPING

There are plenty of fantastic opportunities for camping or renting a cabin in the **Medicine**

Bow-Routt National Forest, which surrounds Laramie to the east (Pole Mountain) and west (Snowy Range). The closest public campgrounds to town are the nicely forested **Yellows Pine Campground** (Forest Rd. 719, 13.2 miles west of Laramie, $10) and the otherworldly **Vedauwoo Campground** (Vedauwoo Rd., 17.3 miles east of Laramie, $10). Both campgrounds have potable water. For information on sites in the Laramie Ranger District or other nearby areas, contact the U.S. Forest Service (2468 W. Jackson St., 307/745-2300, 8 A.M.–5 P.M. Mon.–Fri.).

Just north of I-80, the **Laramie KOA** (1271 W. Baker St., 307/742-6553, www.koa.com/where/wy/50110) has tent sites ($20), RV sites ($34), and cabins ($42–52) in addition to free Wi-Fi, various organized activities, and a playground.

FOOD

Like all college towns worth their salt, Laramie has an abundance of good, relatively cheap places to enjoy a meal. For breakfast or lunch, a local favorite is **J's Prairie Rose Café** (410 S. 2nd St., 307/745-8140, 7 A.M.–3 P.M. Mon.–Thurs. and Sat., 7 A.M.–8 P.M. Fri., breakfast only 7 A.M.–noon Sun., entrées $6–10). The Prairie Rose, as it is known, has the best green chili in town, plus phenomenal breakfast burritos. Their off-menu specials include everything from Italian dishes to eggs Benedict, and their Friday night dinners are most often delicious twists on juicy Wyoming steak.

For a smattering of reasonably priced global cuisine, try **Jeffrey's Bistro** (123 E. Ivinson Ave., 307/742-7046, www.jeffreysbistro.com, lunch and dinner 11 A.M.–9 P.M. Mon.–Sat., lunch about $10, dinner about $15), which offers hearty salads, creative daily specials like ancho-cherry barbecue chicken or hot-and-spicy Thai shrimp, and delicious entrées such as pot pie, enchiladas, Thai burritos, and Indian *dopiaza,* many of which can be made vegetarian.

Serving upscale brewpub cuisine that ranges from the traditional (hickory burgers, seafood pasta, bacon-wrapped tenderloin, and cedar-plank salmon) to the unusual (Vietnamese barbecue, orange-braised pork loin, and Thai salmon burgers), 🍺 **Altitude Chophouse & Brewery** (320 S. 2nd St., 307/721-4031, www.altitudechophouse.com, 11 A.M.–10 P.M. Mon.–Sat., entrées $8–20) perfectly pairs sensational beer with delicious and creative cuisine; don't miss the desserts.

INFORMATION AND SERVICES

The **Albany County Tourism Board** (210 E. Custer St., 800/445-5303, www.visitlaramie.org) operates a convention and visitors bureau and is happy to send a visitors guide in advance of your trip. The **Laramie Area Chamber of Commerce** (800 S. 3rd St., 866/876-1012, www.laramie.org) can provide useful information on local businesses and relocation.

For information on recreation in the nearby **Medicine Bow-Routt National Forest** and the **Thunder Basin National Grassland,** both of which are managed by the U.S. Forest Service, visit the headquarters (2468 W. Jackson St., 307/745-2300, 8 A.M.–5 P.M. Mon.–Fri.).

The **Albany County Public Library** (310 S. 8th St., 307/721-2580, www.acpl.lib.wy.us, 10 A.M.–8 P.M. Tues.–Thurs., 1–5 P.M. Fri.–Sun.) has nine Internet terminals available for free.

The **post offices** are located at 152 North 5th Street (307/721-8837) and 1409 South 3rd Street.

This is a college town, with no shortage of Laundromats, including **Laundry Land** (864 N. 4th St., 307/742-0192).

Ivinson Memorial Hospital (255 N. 30th St., 307/742-2141, www.ivinsonhospital.org) offers 24-hour emergency care plus specialized medicine.

GETTING THERE AND AROUND

The **Laramie Regional Airport** (LAR, 555 General Brees Rd., 307/742-4164, www.laramieairport.com) offers daily service to and from Denver and Worland, Wyoming, on **Great Lakes** (307/742-5296 or 800/554-5111, www.flygreatlakes.com), which also has code share agreements with **Frontier** (800/432-1359, www.frontierairlines.com) and **United** (800/864-8331, www.united.com).

Greyhound (1300 S. 3rd St., 307/742-5188, www.greyhound.com) serves Laramie with daily buses to Denver and the Wyoming communities of Cheyenne and Rawlins.

Car-rental agencies with locations at the airport include **Hertz** (307/745-0500, www.hertz.com) and **Avis** (307/745-8395, www.avis.com). **Enterprise** (517 S. 3rd St., 307/721-9876, www.enterprise.com) has a location in town.

Laramie's only **taxi service** can be reached at 307/761-8294.

By car, Laramie is 49 miles from Cheyenne, 130 miles from Denver, 148 miles from Casper, 207 miles from Rock Springs, 380 miles from Yellowstone National Park, and 383 miles from Jackson.

Cheyenne

Just a few miles from the Colorado border is Cheyenne (population 56,915, elevation 6,062 feet), the state capital and an important historical and modern crossroads. The town was named by the Sioux, who used the word to define another tribe, which we know as the Cheyenne, that they considered alien. A settlement sprung up on July 4, 1867, in advance of the Union Pacific Railroad; the town's population thrived and culture flourished. Influential people and performers traveling across the West by train often stopped in Cheyenne, making it a rather progressive town. Today I-80 and I-25 cross in Cheyenne, bringing visitors from every direction into its historic folds.

The city's defining event, Frontier Days, was founded in 1897 and today brings nearly

© WYOMING TRAVEL & TOURISM

Wyoming State Capitol building

SOUTHERN WYOMING

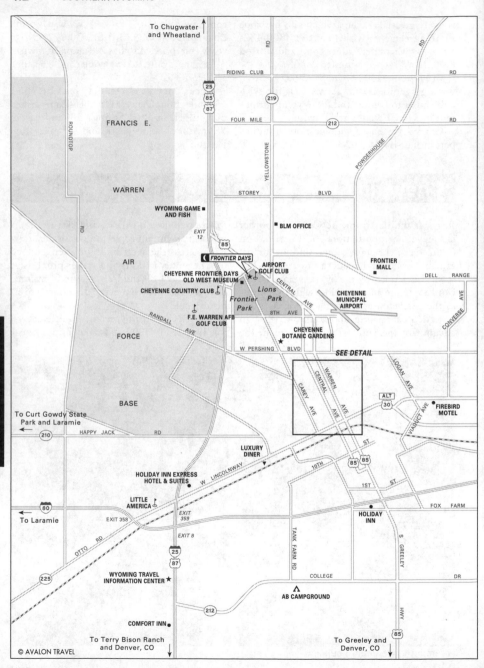

To Chugwater
and Wheatland

RIDING CLUB

FRANCIS E.

ROUNDTOP

WARREN

FOUR MILE

YELLOWSTONE

STOREY   BLVD

WYOMING GAME ■
AND FISH

■ BLM OFFICE

AIR

EXIT
12

85

FRONTIER DAYS

AIRPORT
GOLF CLUB

FRONTIER
MALL

CHEYENNE FRONTIER DAYS
OLD WEST MUSEUM ■

CHEYENNE COUNTRY CLUB

Lions
Park

Frontier
Park

CENTRAL   AVE

DELL   RANGE

CHEYENNE
MUNICIPAL
AIRPORT

CONVERSE   AVE

RANDALL

AVE

F.E. WARREN AFB
GOLF CLUB

8TH   AVE

FORCE

CHEYENNE
BOTANIC GARDENS

W PERSHING   BLVD

SEE DETAIL

POWDERHOUSE

LOGAN   AVE

BASE

WARREN   AVE

CENTRAL   AVE

CAREY   AVE

ALT
30

VIADUCT AVE

● FIREBIRD
MOTEL

To Curt Gowdy State
Park and Laramie

210

HAPPY JACK   RD

LUXURY
DINER

ST

80

To Laramie

HOLIDAY INN EXPRESS
HOTEL & SUITES

W LINCOLNWAY

10TH

85 85

LITTLE
AMERICA

EXIT 358

EXIT
359

EXIT 8

1ST   ST

FOX   FARM

HOLIDAY
INN

S. GREELEY

225

25
87

WYOMING TRAVEL
INFORMATION CENTER ★

OTTO   RD

TANK FARM RD

COLLEGE

DR

212

Λ
AB CAMPGROUND

HWY

85

COMFORT INN ●

To Terry Bison Ranch
and Denver, CO

To Greeley and
Denver, CO

© AVALON TRAVEL

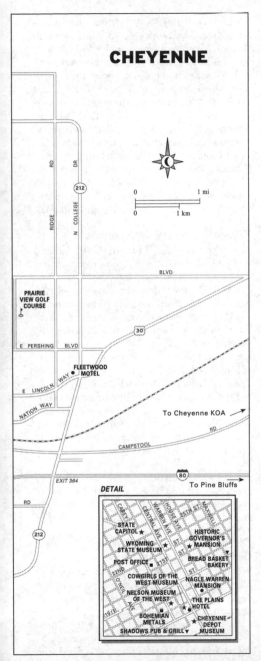

200,000 people to town for 10 days in late July. Cheyenne is still a rodeo town, with one of the only visitors bureaus that lists horse-boarding stables along with hotels and motels. After all, if you're coming to Cheyenne, why not bring your horse?

High and windswept, Cheyenne is not a classic Wyoming beauty in the same way as Jackson Hole or Sheridan, but it is a compelling setting with more urban culture than in most of the state, some wonderful museums, and a smattering of ways to enjoy the great outdoors.

SIGHTS

As a wonderful prelude to this historic city, jump on the **Cheyenne Street Railway Trolley** (121 W. 15th St., 307/778-3133 or 800/426-5009, www.cheyenne.org, departs 10 A.M., 11:30 A.M., 1 P.M., 2:30 P.M., and 4 P.M. Mon.–Fri., 10 A.M. and 1:30 P.M. Sat., 1:30 P.M. Sun. early May–Sept., $10 adults, $5 ages 2–12) departing from the beautiful old rail depot. The ride gives visitors a 90-minute narrated overview of the city, stopping by many of the best sights. Visitors are welcome to hop off and hop on the next trolley, 90 minutes later.

State Capitol

The cornerstone of the State Capitol (W. 24th St. and Capitol Ave., 307/777-7220, http://ai.state.wy.us/capitoltour, 8 A.M.–5 P.M. Mon.–Fri.) was laid on May 18, 1887, when Wyoming was still a territory. Modeled after the Capitol in Washington D.C., this National Historic Landmark went through various phases of construction, the last being the addition of the senate and house chambers, completed in 1917. The building measures 300 feet in length, and its gold dome is 146 feet high. The capitol underwent a $7.6 million renovation during the 1970s, and the dome has been gilded six times, most recently in 1988. When celebrating its centennial in 1987, the original cornerstone was removed, and the documents that had been buried inside—a map and a list of territorial officers, among others—were removed and entrusted to the state archives.

From the first floor, visitors can enter the

rotunda and gaze up three stories to the dome, created from stained glass imported from England. The governor's office is off the rotunda on the first floor. The second floor houses the legislative chambers, decorated by four large Western murals with ceilings of Tiffany stained glass inlaid with the state seal. The balconies on the third floor are always open, and visitors can view the senate and house chambers while they are in session. From the third floor it is also easy to appreciate the Renaissance revival architecture of the entire building. Don't miss the 1,000-pound Tiffany chandelier in the conference room, and look at the ornate hinges on the large cherrywood doors. Guided tours can be arranged by calling ahead for an appointment, but if time permits, walk-in requests may be accommodated.

Union Pacific Railroad Depot

At the southern end of Capitol Avenue sits the historic Union Pacific Railroad Depot (121 W. 15th St., 9 A.M.–7 P.M. Mon.–Fri.). Built in 1886, this was once considered the finest train depot between Omaha and Sacramento. The building occupies an entire city block and was reopened in 2004 after undergoing a major renovation. It has been restored to its original beauty, and the sandstone structure is worth a visit just to appreciate the architecture and design. During the summer there are free evening concerts and other events in the depot plaza.

In addition to housing the Cheyenne Visitors Center and a fun restaurant, the structure is also home to the **Cheyenne Depot Museum** (121 W. 15th St., 307/632-3905, www.cheyennedepotmuseum.org, 9 A.M.–7 P.M. Mon.–Fri., 9 A.M.–6 P.M. Sat., 10 A.M.–5 P.M. Sun., $5 adults, free for children under 12). The museum focuses on the important role the railroad played in the city's development and to the West as a whole. There are fantastic old photographs, exhibits with models, and artifacts from the station's busiest railroad days.

Historic Governors' Mansion

The Historic Governors' Mansion (300 E. 21st St., 307/777-7878, 9 A.M.–5 P.M. Wed.–Sat.

Sept.–May, 9 A.M.–5 P.M. Mon.–Sat. June–Aug., free, donations welcome) was home to each of Wyoming's governors 1905–1976. It is a state historic site and recently underwent a $1 million renovation project. Today visitors will see original decor from 1905, 1937, 1955, and the 1960s. The home was the height of modernity when it was constructed in 1905, with indoor plumbing, hot water, central heating, and electrical and gas fixtures. The most interesting tidbit about this Georgian style building is that it housed the country's first woman governor, Nellie Tayloe Ross, 1925–1927. Visitors can view a short video about the house and its residents before beginning their self-guided tour.

Wyoming State Museum

The Wyoming State Museum (2301 Central Ave., 307/777-7022, www.wyomuseum.state. wy.us, 9 A.M.–4:30 P.M. Mon.–Sat. May–Oct., 9 A.M.–4:30 P.M. Mon.–Fri., 10 A.M.–2 P.M. Sat. Nov.–Apr., free) is dedicated to documenting the state's history from its earliest inhabitants to the present day. In addition to the permanent collection, 3–4 traveling exhibits are showcased at a time. Always on display are exhibits dedicated to prehistoric Wyoming and its dinosaurs, the wildlife of Wyoming, the state's mining history (including an explanation of how coal is created in nature), and a social history of the state. Other exhibits include beautiful Native American beadwork and pottery, a vast firearms collection, and a copy of the act granting women the right to vote in the Wyoming Territory. A hands-on history room for children is well-equipped with vintage clothing, a child-size tipi, a chuck wagon, and dinosaur and other interactive displays.

Cheyenne Frontier Days Old West Museum

Frontier Days is such an important part of Cheyenne's local history that a museum was created to tell the story of this Western celebration. The Old West Museum (4610 Carey Ave., 307/778-7290, 9 A.M.–5 P.M. Mon.–Fri., 10 A.M.–5 P.M. Sat.–Sun. year-round, $7 adults, free for children under 12) is filled with memorabilia from the rodeo and focuses on frontier life in Wyoming. It has more than 150 horse-drawn carriages and wagons dating back over a century along with large Western art exhibits. There is also a fun children's history room with clever interactive displays. The museum has extended hours during the Frontier Days festival and is conveniently located in Frontier Park adjacent to the rodeo.

Nelson Museum of the West

If you are interested in viewing more cowboy and Native American memorabilia, head over to the Nelson Museum of the West (1714 Carey Ave., 307/635-7670, www.nelsonmuseum.com, 9 A.M.–4:30 P.M. Mon.–Fri. May–Oct., 9 A.M.–4:30 P.M. Mon.–Sat. June–Aug., $3 adults, $2 seniors, free for children under 13). There are more than 20 exhibits created from the eclectic personal collection of Robert C. Nelson, including the art of the Plains Indians, firearms of the West, and furnishings from the homes of cattle barons. There are also a number of stuffed big-game animals scattered throughout the three floors.

Cheyenne Botanic Gardens

Should the days get hot and dusty in Cheyenne, find a stunning oasis at the Cheyenne Botanic Gardens (710 S. Lions Park Dr., 307/637-6458, www.botanic.org, call for days and hours, free). The plant diversity is stunning, and there is a unique children's village with drop-in activities, a pond and labyrinth, a solar conservatory, community gardens, and more.

◖ Fort Laramie National Historic Site

An indelible part of Wyoming's history, Fort Laramie (307/837-2221, www.nps.gov/fola, 8 A.M.–7 P.M. daily Memorial Day–Labor Day, 8 A.M.–4:30 P.M. daily Labor Day–Memorial Day, adults $3, seniors and children under 16 free) sits at the confluence of the Laramie and North Platte Rivers. It was a major trading center, a military garrison, and the site where the infamous Treaty of 1868 between the U.S. government and the Plains Indians was signed. People from all walks of life, including Indians,

Fort Laramie National Historic Site

trappers, missionaries, and homesteaders, passed through the fort during its almost 50 years of existence.

Today there are 22 original structures on the 830 acres of this National Historic Site. The first stop at the fort should be the **visitors center,** located in the old commissary building. There is an 18-minute video that describes the fort's rich history along with exhibits with artifacts from frontier times, including weapons, uniforms, and historical photos. A free brochure is available to help visitors with a self-guided tour, or experience the audio tour ($3), which includes voices and sounds from the past.

While at the fort, be sure to visit the **cavalry barracks,** which clearly gives a sense of the cramped living quarters of the soldiers, and **Old Bedlam,** initially the fort headquarters and later used as officers quarters. The officers were known to host wild parties in the building, hence its name. Also on the grounds is an old stone **guardhouse** where prisoners were kept, a model of the original **Fort John** building erected in 1841, and the old fort **bakery.**

SOUTHERN WYOMING

THE GRAND OLD POST

Originally built as a fur trading post in 1834, Fort Laramie was established as a military fort in 1849 when the U.S. Government purchased the old Fort John. As was true of most of the forts across the region, its mission was to ensure the safety of pioneers traveling west on the established trails, the closest of which was the Oregon Trail. The second military fort constructed for this purpose, Fort Laramie was unique in that it was always an open fort, meaning there was no wall or fence enclosing the structures.

In 1854, three years after the Treaty of 1851, which was meant to bring peace between the Native Americans and the United States, 29 soldiers from Fort Laramie, an officer, and an interpreter were killed in the Grattan Fight. The event fueled a new ferocity in the war that raged throughout the 1860s and 1870s between Native Americans and the U.S. military. As the battles grew larger, Fort Laramie was often a staging ground and a command post.

By the late 1880s, when the Indian Wars were mostly a thing of the past, Fort Laramie became more of a village than a fort. Trees were planted on the otherwise barren landscape. Boardwalks were built in front of the officers quarters. In March 1890, when the Union Pacific Railroad was routed south of the fort, with no enemy to fight and no trails to protect, the military decommissioned the fort and sold many of its buildings at auction.

For decades, Fort Laramie existed as a small village, attracting a few curious history buffs, but not much else. Three homesteaders secured and used some of the existing buildings for businesses or agricultural purposes, preventing them from the fate of many of the buildings, which were to be stripped and sold for valuable lumber and other materials. By the numbers, nine original buildings survived by being useful while more than 50 were demolished, moved, or stripped for lumber. In 1938, after much wrangling among federal and state officials and private landowners, including a battle over turning the fort into a golf resort, the 214 acres that had once been Fort Laramie were made a national monument. In 1960, the monument was increased to 571 acres and named a national historic site by Congress. A great deal of restoration took place at the fort 1950-1970.

Today, visitors can amble around the grounds and peek into several of the restored buildings. A very worthwhile audio tour ($3), including readings from journals of people who lived at the fort, is available at the Visitors Center (8 A.M.-7 P.M. daily Memorial Day-Labor Day, 8 A.M.-4:30 P.M. daily Labor Day-Memorial Day). The fort offers a Living History Military Weekend (check the website for dates and details), which brings the fort to life with reenactments and various educational events. The weekend is also the time for the annual Moonlight Tour. Other events throughout the year include Haunted Prison Tours in October and Horse Barn Dinner Theater evenings in summer.

To get to the fort from Cheyenne, head north on I-80 for 80 miles to exit 92 for Guernsey and Torrington. Drive east for 27.9 miles, turn right on Hwy. 160, and follow the signs. The drive is just over 113 miles and should take about an hour and 45 minutes.

ENTERTAINMENT AND EVENTS

◖ Frontier Days

The biggest event in Cheyenne—the biggest in Wyoming—is Frontier Days, an affair that has been defining Wyoming's capital city since 1897. The largest outdoor rodeo in the country today, the celebration's origins are rather humble. Union Pacific passenger agent F. W. Angier and the editor of the local Cheyenne newspaper claimed to have dreamed up the idea based on Greeley, Colorado's "Potato Day."

The first Frontier Days was held on September 23, 1897, and drew a substantial crowd for events that ranged from a bucking horse contest to a mock stagecoach robbery and mock hanging. The troops from Fort Russell lit cannons, and the crowd quickly followed suit by firing their own guns, sending horses and other livestock into a panic. No one was killed, and the event only reinforced Wyoming's reputation for rowdiness.

By far the most popular event at early Frontier Days was the bucking bronc contest, which allowed ranchers to pit their cowboys against each other to determine who had the best ones. Although riders could use a saddle, they had to wait until the horse came to a complete standstill before finishing their ride. They weren't allowed to hold on to any part of the saddle, but they could fan the horse with their hats, whip it, or use their spurs.

More than 100 years later, Frontier Days carries on with much the same spirit. It is now a 10-day event spanning two weekends. In recent years nearly 200,000 people have shown up to attend events that include parades, major rock and country music concerts, free pancake breakfasts, tours of an Indian village, a Western art show, a carnival, dances, and nine days of PRCA rodeo. This event has clearly earned its nickname, "the daddy of 'em all."

The event is held annually the last two weekends in July at the rodeo grounds (4610 Carey Ave.) and around town. For more information, contact the Frontier Days Office (307/778-7222 or 800/227-6336, www.frontierdays.com).

Other Events

Happening over a weekend each year in mid-June, Cheyenne gathers on the beautiful Depot Plaza to celebrate beer at the **Wyoming Brewer's Festival** (307/432-5395, www.wyomingbrewersfestival.com). The event includes a delicious Taster's Party, which pairs beer with food from Cheyenne's varied culinary scene. There is also live music both nights and plenty of festivities.

For eight days in early August, the **Laramie County Fair** (3967 Field Station Rd., 307/637-4534, www.laramiecountyfair.com) offers up family entertainment with everything from a demolition derby and dock diving for dogs to horse events and 4-H. After all the flash and

sparkle of Frontier Days, the Laramie County Fair is bunny shows over bronc riding, a refreshingly traditional small-town event.

For regularly scheduled events such as Tuesday-night **Movies in the Park** or **Symphony Orchestra concerts** in the amphitheater at Lions Park, check out the City of Cheyenne website (www.cheyennecity.org).

SHOPPING

Because of its size, Cheyenne has plenty of the major superstores, but there are also some smaller and wonderful boutiques to check out. **Bohemian Metals** (314 W. 17th St., 307/778-8782, www.bohemianmetals.com) specializes in handmade jewelry, including vintage Native American pieces, gemstones and minerals, and fossils.

A wonderful place for browsing and shopping is the **Cowgirls of the West Museum & Gift Shop** (205 W. 17th St., 307/638-4994), a nonprofit museum dedicated to informing visitors about the contribution that women made to the settlement of the Old West and the contributions being made by women today. The gift shop and museum (11 A.M.–4 P.M. Mon.–Sat., free) features Wyoming-made collectibles, jewelry, Western art, antiques, and wonderful kids' items.

The largest shopping mall in the region is **Frontier Mall** (1400 Dell Range Blvd., 307/638-2290, www.frontiermall.com, 10 A.M.–9 P.M. Mon.–Sat., 11 A.M.–6 P.M. Sun.), which has more than 80 stores.

RECREATION

For a city known for its rodeo, Cheyenne has a surprising number of sports teams to support, and a vast array of recreational opportunities beyond the chutes.

The **Cheyenne Grizzlies** (www.cheyennegrizzlies.com) are the local affiliate of the Mountain Collegiate Baseball League and play some 24 home games each season. The **Cheyenne Wranglers** play semipro football at Miller Field June–August as part of the Colorado Football Conference and the American Football Association.

Hiking and Biking

For being in the middle of a high desert, Cheyenne has a remarkable number of green parks to explore and enjoy on two feet or two wheels. The **Greater Cheyenne Greenway** links several of the parks with 10 miles of paved trails open to hikers and bikers. Sections of trail wind through Crow Creek, Dry Creek, Sun Valley, Lions Park, and Allison Draw, among other parts of town. The trails also serve as a wildlife corridor, so keep your eyes peeled.

Located halfway between Cheyenne and Laramie on the Happy Jack Road, **Curt Gowdy State Park** (1319 Hyndes Lodge Rd., 307/632-7946, www.wyoparks.state.wy.us) contains more than 35 miles of trails connecting three reservoirs as well as four open free-ride areas. The trails were given an Epic designation by the International Mountain Biking Association, and all are open to both hikers and bikers. Among the longer trails are **Canyon's Trail** (5.43 miles), **Stone Temple Circuit** (3.75 miles), **Lariat** (2.92 miles), and **Shoreline** (2.63 miles). The area is also open to horses. A map is available online or at the park.

Golf

Cheyenne has a number of golf courses, including the 18 hole **Airport Golf Club** (4801 Central Ave., 307/638-3700, $22 for 18 holes), the **Cheyenne Country Club** (800 Stinner Rd., 307/637-2200, www.cheyennecountryclub.com, $60 for 18 holes as an unaccompanied guest), the 18-hole **F. E. Warren AFB Golf Club** (6110 Golf Course Dr., 307/773-3556) at the Air Force base, the nine-hole municipal **Prairie View Golf Course** (3601 Windmill Rd., 307/637-6420) and the nine-hole **Little America Golf Course** (2800 W. Lincolnway, 307/775-8500).

ACCOMMODATIONS

Built in 1888 when Cheyenne was among the richest cities of its size in the world, the **Nagle Warren Mansion** (222 E. 17th St., 800/811.2610, www.naglewarrenmansion.com, $98–155) is an exquisite bed-and-breakfast boasting 12 rooms in the mansion and the adjacent carriage house. While the ambience and furnishings are a wonderful reflection of the elegant Victorian era in which the mansion was built, the amenities—including central air conditioning, private baths, telephone, TV, and wireless Internet in each room—are decidedly 21st century. Each room is uniquely appointed and named for an important figure in the mansion's fascinating history. A sumptuous breakfast is served each morning; lunches and dinners can be arranged as well. The mansion's Murder Mystery Dinners are great fun and wildly popular, as are a variety of getaway weekends and special events.

Undoubtedly one of the coolest signs at any motel just about anywhere is the one at the **Firebird Motel** (1905 E. Lincolnway, 307/632-5505, $40–50). The rooms are as basic as can be, and the motel has been hit hard by the economic downturn, but the sign is worth seeing. A good and perhaps more reliable budget-friendly choice in town is the **Fleetwood Motel** (3800 E. Lincolnway, 307/638-8908, $55–95).

An important part of the Cheyenne community since 1911, **The Plains Hotel** (1600 Central Ave., 307/638-3311 or 866/2-PLAINS—866/275-2467, www.theplainshotel.com, $69–114) is a handsome establishment with 130 lovely rooms and suites. The hotel is decorated with art by Wyoming artists and offers a full restaurant, bar, coffee shop, and an on-site fitness center and spa. A multi-million-dollar renovation in 2003 restored the hotel to its glory, and The Plains is by far the best value for your money in Cheyenne.

Cheyenne also offers a number of chain hotels that are comfortable and convenient. Both the **Holiday Inn** (204 W. Fox Rd., 307/638-4466, www.holidayinn.com, $119–157) and the **Holiday Inn Express Hotel & Suites** (1741 Fleischli Pkwy., 307/433-0751, www.holidayinn.com, $108–142) are excellent choices.

The website for the **Cheyenne Convention and Visitors Bureau** (www.cheyenne.org) has a handy tool where travelers can input their travel dates to see all available accommodations in the city. The tool is particularly useful the closer one gets to Frontier Days, as accommodations fill up entirely.

CAMPING

Thanks to the massive numbers of people that roll into town for Frontier Days, Cheyenne has abundant RV and tent campgrounds, not all of which are necessarily great. Among those that are really special is (**Curt Gowdy State Park** (1319 Hyndes Lodge Rd., 307/632-7946, www.wyoparks.state.wy.us, day use permits required, $4 residents, $6 non-residents, camping permits include day use, $10 residents, $17 non-residents), 24 miles west of Cheyenne, half-way to Laramie at the edge of the Laramie Mountains. The area was prime hunting and camping ground for numerous Native Americans tribes. There are 24 RV sites that can be reserved, 15 with water hookups, none with electricity. The remaining sites are first-come, first-served. Located on three lovely reservoirs, this park offers trout and kokanee salmon fishing as well as hiking and biking trails in addition to camping and prime picnicking spots.

Another worthwhile camping spot, particularly for families with children, is the **Terry Bison Ranch Campground** (51 I-25 Service Rd. E., 307/634-4171, www.terrybisonranch.com), just seven miles south of Cheyenne. There is an abundance of activities available, including horseback riding, fishing, train tours to see the ranch's population of bison, ostriches, and even camels, and even bison hunts in winter. With a restaurant on-site, the place is fully self-contained. Accommodations options include cabins ($90), bunk rooms ($60), RV sites ($20–35), and tent sites ($20). Rates go up significantly during Frontier Days.

Other options right in Cheyenne are the nicely shaded **AB Campground** (1503 W. College Dr., 307/634-7035, www.campcheyenne.com, tent and RV sites $25–45 per night), which offers nightly barbecues, and **Cheyenne KOA** (8800 Archer Frontage Rd., 307/638-8840, www.koakampgrounds.com, tent and RV sites $33–49 per night, cabins $60 per night), which has an outdoor swimming pool in summer.

FOOD

As Wyoming's largest city by far, Cheyenne has quite a few restaurants and no shortage of chain establishments to choose from, and there are some wonderful gems worth seeking out.

One of the best local spots for breakfast or lunch is **Luxury Diner** (1401 W. Lincolnway, 307/638-8971, 6 A.M.–4 P.M., entrées $5–10), a tiny railroad-themed place announced by a "Wyoming Motel" sign that is almost larger than the restaurant. The ambience is crowded but completely delightful, and the food explains the crowds; try the corned beef hash and eggs or the Santa Fe breakfast burrito. The **Bread Basket Bakery** (1819 Maxwell Ave., 307/432-2525, www.breadbasketbakery.com, 6 A.M.–6 P.M. Mon.–Fri., 6 A.M.–4 P.M. Sat., lunch $3–6) offers wonderfully fresh pastries, breads, cakes, and other goodies along with a selection of sandwiches and soups.

Located in the east wing of the historic Depot, **Shadows Pub & Grill** (115 W. 15th St., 307/634-7625, www.shadowspub.com, 11 A.M.–11 P.M. Mon.–Thurs., 11 A.M.–2 A.M. Fri.–Sat., 11 A.M.–8 P.M. Sun., entrées $8–20) is a popular and noisy spot with a huge menu and great food, including salads, sandwiches, pizza, burgers, fish, and steaks.

INFORMATION AND SERVICES

Cheyenne's well-organized Convention and Visitors Bureau has a downtown **Visitors Center** (121 W. 15th St., Suite 202, 307/778-3133 or 800/426-5009, www.cheyenne.org, 8 A.M.–7 P.M. Mon.–Fri., 9 A.M.–5 P.M. Sat., 1–3 P.M. Sun. summer, 8 A.M.–5 P.M. Mon.–Fri., 9 A.M.–5 P.M. Sat., 1–3 P.M. Sun. in other seasons).

The **Wyoming Travel Information Center** (1520 Etchepare Circle, 7 A.M.–7 P.M. daily May 15–Oct. 15, 8 A.M.–5 P.M. daily Oct. 16–May 14), the state's tourism department, is headquartered in Cheyenne and is a phenomenal resource.

SOUTHERN WYOMING

The main downtown **post office** (307/772-7080) is located at 2120 Capitol Avenue. The **Laramie County Library** (307/634-3561, www.lclsonline.org, 10 A.M.–9 P.M. Mon.–Thurs., 10 A.M.–6 P.M. Fri.–Sat., 1–5 P.M. Sun.) is at 2200 Pioneer Avenue. Wash clothes at **Easy Way Laundry** (900 W. Lincolnway, 307/638-2177, 7 A.M.–10 P.M. daily).

The **Cheyenne Regional Medical Center** (214 E. 23rd St., 307/634-2273, www.crmcwy.org) is a major medical facility with 24-hour emergency care. Another option is **College Drive Urgent Care** (4136B Laramie St., 307/637-2800, www.collegedriveurgentcare.com, 9 A.M.–6 P.M. Mon.–Fri.).

GETTING THERE AND AROUND

Cheyenne Regional Airport (CYS, 300 E. 8th Ave., 307/634-7071, www.cheyenneairport.com) offers daily nonstop service to Denver and Dallas–Fort Worth on **Great Lakes** (307/742-5296 or 800/554-5111, www.flygreatlakes.com) and **American Eagle** (800/433-7300, www.aa.com). Denver International Airport (DEN) is just 90 miles by car from Cheyenne. For shuttle service between Denver and Cheyenne airports, contact **Super Shuttle** (307/638-3940 or 866/482-0505, www.rideshamrock.com).

Daily bus service in and out of Cheyenne is provided from the Rodeway Inn by **Greyhound** (5401 Walker Rd., 307/635-1327, www.greyhound.com) and **Black Hills Stage Lines** (5401 Walker Rd., 307/635-1327, www.blackhillsstagelines.com).

Local transportation is available in Cheyenne from **Cheyenne Transit** (307/637-6253, www.cheyennecity.org) and six taxi companies, including **BC Cab** (307/632-4444) and **Capitol City Cab** (307/632-8294 or 877/632-8294).

Car rentals are available from **Avis** (307/632-9371, www.avis.com), **Enterprise** (307/632-1907, www.enterprise.com), and **Hertz** (307/634-2131, www.hertz.com).

By car, Cheyenne is 49 miles from Laramie, 100 miles from Denver, 256 miles from Rock Springs, 291 miles from Rapid City, 393 miles from Cody, 429 miles from Yellowstone National Park, and 456 miles from Billings.

BACKGROUND

The Land

Not only do Montana and Wyoming share borders, they share many of the same characteristics when it comes to the geographic and cultural lay of the land. While both are well known for their spectacular mountains, rivers, and valleys, the eastern part of both states is remote, rural, and based on agriculture. Both states have Native American reservations and the stories that go with them—many of the West's greatest battles took place here—and they share many of the same industries: agriculture, mining, oil and gas, tourism, and forestry. Although Montana and Wyoming have many similarities, it's their subtle differences that make them stand out on their own.

GEOGRAPHY

Montana is the fourth-largest state in area, with just over 147,000 square miles of land, but ranks near the bottom in population—44th, to be exact, with an estimated 975,000 people as of 2009. To the north is Canada, with Montana sharing borders with Saskatchewan, Alberta, and British Columbia, while Wyoming is to the south. The western and southwestern part of the state is bordered by Idaho, and North and South Dakota flank its eastern edge. Montana is bisected by the Continental Divide, which runs diagonally from the northwest to the south-central part of the state. The big peaks and expansive

© DONNIE SEXTON

valleys dominating the landscape of western Montana, from Yellowstone to Glacier National Park, inspired the state's name, which comes from the Spanish word for mountains. Central Montana acts as a transition to the flatter part of the state, with the Yellowstone and Missouri Rivers flowing out of the mountains and into the wide-open spaces that make up remote eastern Montana and the northern plains. Eye-catching badlands, buttes, terraces, and old grain silos dominate the horizon here, a stark contrast to the coniferous forests found farther west. Granite Peak in the Beartooth Mountains is the highest point in the state at 12,799 feet.

Wyoming is the least populous state in the union with only 544,000 people, but is 10th in terms of land area—just over 97,000 square miles. One of only three states (Colorado and Utah are the others) that have borders along straight latitudinal and longitudinal lines, Wyoming is bordered on the north by Montana and on the south by Utah and Colorado. Nebraska and South Dakota border Wyoming on the east, while Idaho makes up most of the western border with a little slice of Utah. Like Montana, the western part of Wyoming is made up of mountainous terrain covered by coniferous forests, and similarly the Continental Divide continues its diagonal run through the state. Eastern Wyoming consists of the High Plains, an expanse of high-elevation prairie home to large cattle ranches and oil and gas wells. Wyoming is the third highest-state in the nation (behind Alaska and Colorado), with a range of 3,125–13,804 feet. Gannet Peak in the Wind River Range is the highest point in the state.

CLIMATE

Montana and Wyoming have similar weather patterns, influenced predominantly by each state's diverse topography. Generally, summers are hot and dry, often punctuated by brief but intense thunderstorms. Winters are cold and see a healthy amount of snow, particularly in the western portions of the state. Daytime highs in a Montana and Wyoming summer are in the 80s and 90s, with triple digits occasionally setting in. During the winter, it can get downright cold in either state—the coldest recorded temperature in the Lower 48 states was -70°F at Rogers Pass in Montana on January 20, 1954. For both states, July–August are the warmest months, while January–February are the coldest. Snow can fall at any time of the year, but most occurs November–March. May–June are often the rainiest months of the year. Humidity is generally on the low side, making the hot summer days a little more bearable. It's important to realize that when engaging in outdoor activities during the summer, always plan for bad weather—it can happen almost instantly at any time in Montana or Wyoming, even during the hottest part of the summer.

Temperatures decrease with higher altitude, so it's not uncommon in the mountains for the weather to be drastically different from lower elevations. Storms can move in on a moment's notice and can often be fierce—driving hail in the summer and blizzard conditions in the winter. Rain in the valleys can often mean snow in the mountains, especially in the spring when a storm can dump several feet of heavy snow in a relatively short amount of time.

Chinook winds can blow in both states. These unusually warm, dry winter winds blow down the east slopes of the Rockies and across the plains. They occur when moist Pacific air rises over the mountains, loses its moisture in the form of precipitation, and then warms rapidly on the leeward side. Chinooks can quickly melt snow and raise the temperature, as evidenced in January 1972, when the temperature in Loma, Montana, went from -56°F to 49°F in 24 hours.

In general, both states are known for being on the windy side. Great Falls, Montana, and Casper and Cheyenne, Wyoming, all rank among the top 10 windiest cities, and by some accounts Cheyenne is number 1 and Great Falls number 2. Winter winds can turn an average cold day into a bone-chilling one, while summer gusts often keep outdoor event planners working overtime.

Flora and Fauna

Montana and Wyoming (as well as parts of Idaho) converge around the Greater Yellowstone ecosystem, widely regarded as the largest biologically intact temperate ecosystem in North America. Centered around Yellowstone National Park, this 20-million-acre area consists of a diverse landscape with geothermal activity and native wildlife; it is considered by scientists as a natural laboratory for landscape ecology, geology, and wildlife preservation.

Visiting the Greater Yellowstone area provides the opportunity to see a natural environment much like it was hundreds and even thousands of years ago. Yellowstone National Park itself is on a high plateau, the remnants of a volcano that last exploded more than 640,000 years go, leaving a giant caldera. Yellowstone is the most geothermic place on earth, containing a majority of the world's types of geothermal features, including geysers, hot springs, mud pots, and fumaroles.

If you are worried that Yellowstone could explode, you're not alone. Scientists are constantly measuring the amount of pressure in the magma chamber, which actually raises the floor of the caldera plateau—nearly three inches from 2004 to 2008, or about the pace at which our fingernails grow. Theoretically, the volcano could burst again, but most scientists seem to think there is little evidence that a cataclysmic explosion will occur anytime soon. Due to its volcanic nature, the Yellowstone area experiences upward of 2,000 measurable earthquakes each year, but you are unlikely to feel one.

Outside Yellowstone Park, the rest of the ecosystem is mountainous and filled with large tracts of roadless land, jagged peaks, broad valleys, and flowing rivers—exactly why many people live here and even more choose to visit. Wildlife abounds, offering a rare glimpse into the lives of everything from the pine marten to the grizzly bear. Of course, people live here too, and the interaction between humans and nature is important not only historically but in contemporary matters as well.

In addition to mountains, both states have large tracts of prairies that contain mostly dry grasses and shrubs. The iconic sagebrush plant can be found at nearly every elevation—more sage grows in Wyoming than anywhere else—and many land areas seem almost desertlike, right down to the tumbleweeds that roll along in the breeze. Wyoming actually includes two areas that are classified as desert: the Red Desert near Rock Springs, and a large part of the Bighorn Basin.

HERBIVORES

Both Montana and Wyoming are known for their abundant wildlife, and it's only fitting that residents and visitors want to see them in their natural habitat. Both herbivores and predators roam the land, and with the right information a savvy traveler can seek out views of these animals. Keep in mind that it is not acceptable to approach wildlife for any reason—keep a safe distance away and never feed any animal.

A herd of nearly 4,000 **bison** roams within the borders of Yellowstone National Park, a far cry from the millions that once lived throughout central North America from Canada to Mexico. These massive creatures graze on grasses and can weigh more than 2,000 pounds. Bison can commonly be seen almost any time of the year in Yellowstone, often causing traffic jams as they stand on the road. The National Bison Range Wildlife Refuge in Moiese, Montana, also supports a herd of 500 animals and has a visitors center and interpretive displays.

Elk are found throughout the mountainous region, and more than 30,000 roam free in Yellowstone National Park. These regal creatures are fairly common and can be found at higher elevations in the summer and lower elevations in the winter. The Northern Yellowstone elk herd numbered about 6,000

CARTER G. WALKER

This mountain goat begs the question, "Who is watching whom?"

animals during the winter of 2009–2010, where the herd spends its winter just north of the park. The National Elk Refuge in Jackson, Wyoming, is home to more than 5,000 wintering elk, as well as an educational visitors center and winter sleigh rides that travel among the herd.

White-tailed deer and the large-eared **mule deer,** as well as the **pronghorn antelope,** can be found throughout the region and are as often seen on the sides of highways as they are in the wild. **Bighorn sheep** are impressive, stocky animals. The rams (males) are known for their massive curled horns and give the rugged creatures their distinctive look. Large herds of bighorn sheep can be found in and around Yellowstone—near the north entrance of the park and around Big Sky, in particular—and Wyoming's Whiskey Basin Habitat Area near Dubois.

Mountain goats inhabit many of the high peaks of Montana and Wyoming and can often be seen clinging to impossibly steep sides of rocky cliffs. The high country is also home

to the smallish **pika** and the larger, fuzzier **yellow-bellied marmot.** Both can be spotted running along rocky outcrops and scree fields at higher elevations.

Some of the largest animals you'll encounter are **moose,** which typically inhabit river bottoms, wetlands, and willowed areas and graze on grasses, brush, and leaves. Moose can surprise you on the trail, as they are typically quiet and private creatures. Their docile nature can quickly turn deadly if they charge; give them plenty of room, especially if you encounter a female moose with its young.

Both states have numerous species of birds, including raptors. Attentive visitors can expect to see bald and golden **eagles, ospreys, hawks, falcons, owls, woodpeckers, grouse, herons, pelicans,** and more. Smaller species include **jays, mountain bluebirds, warblers, western tanagers,** and **magpies.** The Red Rock Lakes National Wildlife Refuge in southwestern Montana is home to the one of the largest habitats of the majestic **trumpeter swan.** For information on the excellent birding opportunities, visit www.audobonwyoming. org or www.mtaudobon.org.

The region is also home to a large herd of **wild horses,** located in the Pryor Mountains south of Billings along the Montana-Wyoming border. One of just 10 herds left in the country, many of the Pryor Mountain horses have primitive striping on their backs, withers, and legs; they are thought to be descendants of colonial Spanish horses. In 1968, interested individuals and groups convinced the government to set aside 31,000 acres in the Pryor Mountains as a public range for the wild horses, who had been living there for more than a century. The Pryor Mountain Wild Mustang Center in Lovell, Wyoming, houses a museum where visitors can learn about the history, behavior, and life of the animals. The center can also direct visitors on where and how to catch a glimpse of these beautiful creatures running free in the wild.

PREDATORS

Montana and Wyoming are perhaps best known for the predators that most visitors try to catch a glimpse of. **Black bears** can be found in forested areas and often see much more human interaction than their larger counterpart, the **grizzly bear.** Grizzlies once roamed the entire northern hemisphere, and when the first settlers arrived there were more than 50,000 in the Lower 48 alone. Although there are still healthy populations in western Canada and Alaska, grizzly numbers in the rest of the U.S. declined to less than 1,000 by 1975. Since the U.S. Fish and Wildlife Service listed them as a threatened species, the population has recovered to include an estimated 600 bears in the Greater Yellowstone ecosystem—most of them in Wyoming and the rest in southwest Montana around the park. The Northern Continental Divide ecosystem in

western and northwestern Montana is believed to be home to the largest number of grizzlies— more than 750 when the last population study was completed in 2004. One fascinating thing to be aware of is that the grizzlies along the Rocky Mountain Front have, in the last several years, started coming out of their alpine habitat to regain their status as residents of the plains, something not seen since Lewis and Clark traveled the region at the turn of the 19th century. Indeed, grizzlies today have been reported east of Great Falls, more than 100 miles from the nearest mountain range.

The reintroduction of the **gray wolf** is one of the greatest—and most controversial—wildlife success stories of the 20th century. Numbers went from zero—gray wolves were last seen in Montana and Wyoming in the 1930s—to more than 1,700 now living throughout Montana, Wyoming, and Idaho. Yellowstone National Park is the best place to catch a glimpse of the elusive wolf. The Lamar and Hayden Valleys are especially good places to view one of the 100-plus wolves that roam through Yellowstone in 14 different packs.

You'll often see **coyotes** walking along the roadsides in Yellowstone or strolling in an open meadow stalking its prey. These dog-like predators have a longer and more pointed nose than wolves, a much fluffier tail, and are noticeably smaller and more delicate in appearance. **Mountain lions** also are present in the region. These elusive cats are becoming slightly more common, and human confrontations have risen over the years. If you see one in the wild, chances are it will be crossing the road on a late-night hunting excursion. The **prairie rattlesnake** is found in the eastern part of the region, typically in open arid country. They often den on south-facing slopes with rock outcrops and consume rodents as their main meal.

Environmental Issues

As in many Western states, the environment is a controversial topic in Montana and Wyoming. While both states are on the conservative side politically, many of the people who have moved here in the past two decades have a decidedly more liberal political view, particularly when it comes to land, air, and water issues.

The effects of irresponsible hard-rock mining operations can be found throughout Montana, marked by a scarred landscape and contaminated water. The mile-wide Berkley Pit, a former open-pit copper mine in Butte, is one of the country's largest Superfund sites. Since it closed in 1982, contaminated water has been filling the pit, which could eventually contaminate the entire Clark Fork River basin. In 1998, voters in Montana approved a law that phased out the process of cyanide leaching in open-pit mines, although mining companies are trying to get the decision reversed. Twelve of the 17 Superfund sites in Montana are related to mining operations.

One of the most tragic reminders of the mining industry's legacy is the situation of the northwest Montana town of Libby, where a former vermiculite mine was found to have poisoned the town's residents with a rare form of asbestos that was present in the mining dust. Many miners and townspeople have died from asbestos-related cancers, and nearly 20 percent of those residents tested for asbestos were found to have abnormal lung function. There was local and national outrage when the news was made public in 2000 that the W. R. Grace Company, which owned the mine. The company has since filed for bankruptcy, blaming the large number of personal-injury lawsuits, and an emergency cleanup of the town is being managed by the Environmental Protection Agency. Two documentary films have been made, and several books have been written about the case and the tragic events surrounding the town.

Air quality in Montana is another concern, in particular emissions from proposed coal-fired power plants and tire burning at a cement plant near Three Forks. Proponents of banning snowmobiles in Yellowstone National Park have succeeded in lowering the number of machines allowed to enter, as well as requiring all snowmobiles to be the cleaner four-stroke variety. This has divided towns where the winter economy has traditionally relied on the snowmobile tourism industry. Global warming has also affected Glacier National Park, as the number of glaciers larger than 25 acres has decreased from 150 to 25 in the past 100 years—and some models predict that some of the largest of the park's glaciers could disappear altogether by 2030.

Perhaps nothing divides Westerners more than how to use and manage the forests. Whether it is the creatures that live in them, logging operations, forest fires, recreation, or potential wilderness, residents are passionate about their beliefs. Both sides of any issue typically have ardent followers, making legislation a painstaking process. Whether it's wolf reintroduction or motorized-vehicle access, they can be touchy subjects at the lunch counter. Check any newspaper in the state and you're bound to see articles and letters to the editor about these topics.

Another contentious issue in both states is the government-sponsored reintroduction of the wolf, which started in 1995 when 66 Canadian wolves were transplanted to Yellowstone National Park and central Idaho. The population has rebounded, and in some people's minds, become a threat to humans and livestock. At last count, there were close to 1,700 wolves in the three-state region and about 125 in Yellowstone Park alone. Area ranchers say wolves decimate livestock and elk herds; environmentalists say the animals have a right to thrive on land that was once theirs. Wolves were relieved of their endangered-species status in Montana and Idaho, but Wyoming could not agree

LEAVE NO TRACE IN THE BACKCOUNTRY

Leave No Trace is an educational program that teaches outdoor enthusiasts how to protect the places they love from human-caused recreational impact. However, the Leave No Trace ethic extends far beyond backcountry and wilderness areas. As more and more people are recreating in "front country" settings, knowledge of how to apply Leave No Trace becomes increasingly important.

Planning ahead is the easiest way to protect outdoor places and to enjoy a safe visit. Use a map, bring a small first aid kit, remember to bring additional clothing to keep you warm and dry, and wear suitable shoes or boots on the trails. When hiking, stay on designated trails, especially if they pass through private property. Shortcutting around corners causes erosion and damages trailside plants, especially if it's wet or muddy. Dispose of trash and biodegradable materials, such as orange peels, apple cores, and food scraps, in a bear-proof trash container. Remember, animals that become dependent on human food often have to be relocated or destroyed. Two easy slogans to remember are "Pack it in, pack it out," and

"Leave it as you find it." By leaving the natural world as you found it, you will be protecting the habitat of plants and animals as well as the outdoor experience of millions of visitors.

In the backcountry, you must carry all trash out with you, and use a biodegradable soap when washing dishes. Avoid using soap within 200 feet of a stream or spring. Allow others a sense of discovery by leaving rocks, plants, archaeological artifacts, and other objects of interest as you find them. Minimize campfire impacts by instead using portable camp stoves or fire pans. Use designated fire grates if available, and always make sure the fire is completely out before you leave camp. If you make a fire ring with rocks, disperse the rocks before you leave camp, and try hard to "leave no trace" of your being there.

Finally, always respect wildlife and be considerate of other visitors to help protect the quality of their experience. The last thing you want to do is ruin somebody else's trip of a lifetime. Keep noise to a minimum and let nature's sounds prevail; everyone will be happier for it.

---

to a management plan that was acceptable to the government. Residents of that state wanted to be able to shoot wolves on sight. A hunting season was enacted in Montana and Idaho in 2009, only to be rescinded in 2010. Changing legislation about the wolves is ongoing, and it could be some time before policies are clearly resolved.

Major environmental issues in Wyoming also include water quality, especially associated with coal-bed methane, a form of natural gas. Wyoming is the country's third-largest coal-bed methane producer, much of it coming from the Power River Basin in the northeast part of the state. Wyoming is also the seventh-largest oil-producing state, with five large refineries and the fourth-largest volume of oil reserves. And like Montana, Wyoming faces issues with hard-rock mining and coal-fired power plants.

History

MONTANA

When examining the history of Montana, it's important to note the role geology played in creating the mountains, rivers, lakes, and valleys that are so treasured by residents and visitors alike. The Rocky Mountains were created about 100 million years ago, when giant masses of molten rock deep inside the earth began to push to the surface. The ensuing tectonic pressure stretched the land in every direction, allowing large blocks of rock to thrust upward and create the massive jumble of mountains we see today.

These new mountains were eventually buried under ice and water during several ice ages—the last one starting roughly 20,000 years ago—that carved out many of the details of today's landscape. The remnants of these glaciers can still be seen throughout the high country of Montana and Wyoming, particularly in Glacier National Park, Grand Teton National Park, and the Wind River Mountains.

Prehistoric Residents

Dinosaurs played an important role in the region's early history. Some of the most recent and important fossil discoveries have been made here, including the largest known skull of a *Tyrannosaurus rex*. Well-known paleontologist Jack Horner—consultant on the popular *Jurassic Park* movies—resides at Bozeman's Museum of the Rockies, where an excellent exhibit highlights Montana's prominent role in dinosaur discovery.

Because of the region's geologic history, it has made a perfect laboratory for finding fossils from the Cretaceous and Jurassic periods. As the dinosaurs were dying off, the formation of the mountains caused sediment to slough off the rising peaks to form a layer over their remains. Receding glaciers then scoured the land and removed many of the layers, leaving behind fossils that can be found at or near the surface. And since much of the region remains undeveloped, most fossils have been undisturbed by humans.

The first humans most likely appeared 10,000–30,000 years ago, when Asiatic people came to North America across the Bering Strait land bridge. These people traveled south from Alaska to the Great North Trail, which ran along the eastern slopes of the Rockies. Some wandered all the way to South America. Those who stayed in the north hunted big game, including the extinct mammoth, and used tools made of chipped stone. They lived on the plains and foothills until a climatic change around 5000 B.C. turned the plains into a desert, and the people and animals all but disappeared.

As the climate slowly became more moderate, people returned from the south and northwest, bringing with them new techniques and cultural ideals. Buffalo roamed the land, providing a much-needed food source. These last prehistoric migrants are thought to be the direct ancestors of today's Native Americans. Evidence of their culture can be found in the tipi rings, pictographs (rock paintings), and petroglyphs (rock carvings) that still adorn the landscape. Buffalo jumps (also called *pishkuns*) were used during this period; entire herds were stampeded off rocky cliffs and then slaughtered for their meat and hides. Two of the most remarkable buffalo jumps can be seen at Ulm Pishkun State Park near Great Falls and Madison Buffalo Jump State Park outside Three Forks.

Native Americans

Although the Flathead Indians lived west of the Continental Divide, the Indians that we associate with Montana today did not arrive until the early 1600s, moving westward after European settlement forced them from their traditional homelands. These new migrants—Plains Indians, as we refer to them today—mostly came from the Great Lakes and Mississippi Basin region, where their sedentary life was uprooted by western expansionism. Many Native Americans abandoned their agricultural lifestyle and developed a culture of hunting as they were forced west onto the plains, where the buffalo was plentiful and the newly discovered tipi provided a means to move around and follow the herds.

The Shoshone were among the first Plains Indians to enter Montana, displacing the resident Salish farther north. They brought with them the first horses and were fierce warriors. The Crow Indians followed shortly after, settling in the prairies around the Yellowstone River in eastern Montana. The Blackfeet brought the rifle with them when they settled in Montana during the early 1700s, and together with their allies, the Gros Ventre and Assiniboine, they quickly came to dominate the northern plains. Other groups that came to settle in Montana were the Sioux, Northern Cheyenne, Cree, and Chippewa, causing tensions with so many squeezed into a limited area as white settlers moved farther west.

Lewis and Clark

It was hard to envision what a monumental change would come when President Thomas Jefferson purchased the Louisiana Territory from France in 1803. This large part of the western United States was viewed as an important acquisition, and Jefferson hoped to explore this new territory to find a safe trade route from the Missouri River to the headwaters of the Columbia River and the Pacific. In other words, the West would soon be open for business.

Jefferson charged his personal secretary, Meriwether Lewis, and William Clark with the task of putting together a Corps of Discovery to explore the West, and on May 14, 1804, the two set out from St. Louis with a party of 45 men. Traveling up the Missouri River, the party spent the following winter in a Mandan village in North Dakota. Here they recruited French trader Toussaint Charbonneau, who spoke several Indian languages and had traveled extensively along the Missouri. One of Charbonneau's wives was the young Shoshone Indian named Sacagawea, who accompanied the party as an interpreter and guide.

The Corps entered Montana in April 1805, and followed the Missouri to its headwaters, near the present-day town of Three Forks.

Lewis encountered the expedition's first Native American shortly thereafter, a Shoshone who led them to Sacagawea's brother. The Shoshones led the party down the Bitterroot Valley and over the mountains through Lolo Pass near the Montana-Idaho border. The party then followed the Clearwater, Snake, and Columbia Rivers to the Pacific Ocean, where they built a fort and spent a long cold winter on the coast.

In the spring, the corps backtracked across Oregon and over Lolo Pass and into Montana in June of 1806. The expedition then split into two parties, with Lewis taking the northeast route toward Great Falls and Clark taking the more southern route to explore the Yellowstone River. The two parties met at the confluence of the Yellowstone and Missouri Rivers in August, and they were back in St. Louis by the end of September.

The Fur Trade and the Gold Rush

Although Lewis and Clark's famous expedition failed to find a manageable passage to the Pacific, it opened the door to fur trading, which would come to dominate the first half of the 19th century in the region. Trading posts sprang up along the Missouri and Yellowstone Rivers, and fashionable beaver pelts were soon finding their way to the East and Europe. By 1840, however, the Mountain Man era was over as beavers were trapped nearly to extinction and demand waned.

Catholic missionaries established posts near Stevensville and St. Ignatius and attempted to teach the Native Americans a different way of life. Some of these missions were successful, others were not, but their presence alone signaled that the traditional Native American way of life would soon be changed forever as whites expanded farther into their territory.

If the beaver trade and missionary work marked the initial changes to the Native American way of life, the 1860 discovery of gold in Gold Creek near Deer Lodge signified the end of Native American autonomy. Gold was soon found near Bannack, the first territorial capital, and Virginia City, the second capital, and settlers began flocking to Montana to seek their fortunes. In 1860 there were fewer than 100 whites in the state, but by 1870 that number had jumped to more than 20,000. Soon Montana became a postcard of the Wild West, where miners, settlers, Indians, and thieves interacted to create a dangerous, hostile atmosphere built on greed and fame. The Bozeman Trail, established in the 1860s as an alternate to the more southern Oregon Trail, became known as the "Bloody Bozeman" for its perilous route through Indian country and several famous battles along its path.

By the 1870s, the gold rush was in full swing and the U.S. government was waging a full-on war against the Indians, forcing them onto reservations and land that was not traditionally theirs. Many famous battles were fought in Montana, including General George Custer's infamous "last stand" at the 1876 Battle of the Little Bighorn, where the 7th Cavalry fought several thousand Lakota and Cheyenne warriors and suffered heavy losses.

In 1877 the Nez Perce fled Oregon hoping to settle in Canada. Under the leadership of Chief Joseph, the tribe traveled across Idaho and into Montana, where they engaged with U.S. soldiers near the Big Hole River, a battle that left nearly 90 Indians dead. The Nez Perce continued to flee, passing through Yellowstone National Park and north toward Canada, only to be captured near Chinook just 40 miles from the Canadian border. Even thought they were originally from the Pacific Northwest, they were sent to reservations in Oklahoma.

As gold and other minerals were being plundered, the railroad came to Montana when the Union Pacific built a line from Utah to Butte in 1881. The Northern Pacific linked Chicago with Portland by 1883, opening up Montana's fortunes to the rest of the world. The Great Northern linked Minneapolis to Seattle in 1893, while the Milwaukee Road route across the center part of the state was completed in 1909.

Mining, Agriculture, and the Montana Economy

Fueled by investors from all over the country, the large deposits of gold, copper, and other minerals quickly created vast wealth in Montana. Butte became known as the "richest hill on earth," and its three copper kings—Marcus Daly, William Clark, and Augustus Heinze—were among the richest men in the world. The competition between these men to control Butte's copper mines is worth a book on its own—several have been written—and sounds like something out of a Hollywood movie. Each tried to buy courts, newspapers, politicians, banks, law enforcement, and anything and anyone that could help them or damage their opponents. In 1899, Daly teamed up with Standard Oil to create a behemoth mining company, which soon bought out Heinze's and Clark's interests and became the Anaconda Copper Mining Company. Named after the smelter town to the south, the company would dominate Butte for most of the 20th century.

Copper production in Butte peaked in 1917 and then started to decline, leaving the city in shambles as Anaconda began to shift jobs to places with cheaper labor like Asia and South America. The riches of Butte, once the envy of the West, were leaving town just as fast as the mine workers. Anaconda stopped mining the massive Berkeley pit in 1983, which has since become one of the largest contaminated waste sites in the country.

As the mining industry gained and then lost ground, cattle and sheep ranches continued to take advantage of Montana's abundant grasslands. The passage of the Enlarged Homestead Act in 1909 brought thousands of homesteaders into the state looking for inexpensive land. By the late 1880s there were nearly 700,000 head of cattle in the state. Wheat farming was popular until an extended drought and a drop in market prices after World War I ruined many farmers, who were forced to abandon their land.

Montana's post–World War I depression extended through the 1920s into the Great Depression of the 1930s. President Franklin D. Roosevelt's New Deal then brought relief to the state in the form of various projects and agencies: the building of Fort Peck Dam, the Civilian Conservation Corps (CCC), the Works Projects Administration (WPA), and

© CARTER G. WALKER

Mining has been and continues to be powerful industry in the West.

the Agricultural Adjustment Administration (AAA). These "alphabet agencies" mark the first real dependence of the state on federal spending in the 20th century, a reliance that would build through the rest of the century.

Since World War II, Montana can be characterized by a slow shift from an economy that relied on the extraction of natural resources to one that is service-based. Such traditional industries as copper, petroleum, coal, and timber have suffered wild market fluctuations and unstable employment patterns. Agriculture has remained Montana's primary industry throughout the era. Tourism supplanted mining as the state's second-largest industry in the early 1970s. This era also saw an important shift in the state's transportation system from railroads to cars, trucks, and highways.

Today, Montana's history is what contributes to its current way of life. Gone are the days of the Wild West, but each year thousands of visitors flock to see a real ghost town or an Indian battlefield. Large ranching operations hark back to the days of the cowboy, and the

same rivers Lewis and Clark navigated now take white-water boaters for a thrilling ride. Throughout Montana's history, one thing has remained constant: the appreciation by those who live here for its wide-open spaces, breathtaking scenery, and Western way of life.

WYOMING

Like Montana, Wyoming is a young state with a long history. Both states share many of the same historical traits—cowboys and Indians, cattle barons and miners, railroads and ranching. As the least populous state in the union, Wyoming has remained unchanged since the first settlers came into the area, allowing those who live and visit here today a glimpse into the state's rich and varied past.

Geology and Early Life Forms

Much like Montana, Wyoming's geologic history includes the creation of the Rocky Mountains and the impact of glaciers on the landscape. Of course, Yellowstone National Park is the state's biggest geologic claim to

CLIMBING THE ALPHABET

One of the things you'll notice fairly quickly when driving around Montana is the seemingly endless number of large white letters on the hillsides or mountains. These hillside letters – sometimes called geoglyphs or mountain monograms – are a source of pride for many Montana localities, and in most cases highlight the first letter of the adjacent town, school, or university. Over the years the letters have become not just visible landmarks but cultural ones as well.

Montana has the largest number of hillside letters in the country, with more than 110 that represent everything from Anaconda to White-hall. The most popular hillside letter is the M in Missoula, which sits about halfway up Mount Sentinel overlooking the University of Montana campus. It's a moderate 1.5-mile hike up a well-used trail and provides a panoramic view of the Clark Fork and Bitterroot Rivers and the surrounding mountains. On Saturdays in the fall, the M is often packed with students watching the football game – it offers a great aerial view of the 25,000-seat stadium.

The largest letter is the M in Bozeman, which represents Montana State University and is a popular hike for residents and visitors. The 200-foot letter sits on a steep hillside on the south end of the Bridger Mountains, accessed by a trail that is also the start of the 21-mile Bridger Mountains National Recreational Trail.

The M in Butte is actually electric, and the C near Cut Bank is one of the smallest letters. The town of Anaconda actually has two letters: a C for Central High School and an A for the town's name. Even the tiny towns of Bainville and Froid – population 153 and 195, respectively – in northeastern Montana have letters. The town of Brockton has three letters – BHS – that represent the local high school.

Montana isn't the only state with a plethora of hillside letters. It's a common sight throughout the West, with only a few erected east of the Mississippi River and nearly all of them built in a community-wide effort. Most are made of painted rocks or concrete, some are just painted on existing rock faces, and others are cut out of the vegetation. Wyoming has 16 letters at last count.

The first letter to appear in the West was the C that overlooks the University of California, Berkeley, built in 1905. Missoula's M was built in 1908, originally of rocks, then again with wood in 1912. A blizzard destroyed that one in 1915, and it was replaced by a whitewashed granite letter that lasted until 1968, when the current concrete M was erected. Each fall the letter is lit up at the homecoming football game to welcome former students back to campus.

An interesting read on this subject is Evelyn Corning's *Hillside Letters A to Z: A Guide to Hometown Landmarks*, which explains the history of 60 letters in 14 Western states.

A barely visible A is well tended along the Rocky Mountain Front.

© CARTER G. WALKER

fame, created when a series of three massive volcanic explosions—2.1 million, 1.3 million, and 640,000 years ago—spewed gases and hot ash across North America. Some experts suggest the most recent blast alone was more than 10,000 times larger than the well-known 1980 eruption of Mount St. Helens. Geothermal forces are still at work underneath Yellowstone's surface, giving the park its trademark geysers, hot springs, fumaroles, and mud pots, making it the earth's most active geothermal area.

Wyoming is also a hotbed for dinosaur fossils. A fossil of a giant *Allosaurus*—among the first meat-eating dinosaurs—was found in 1991, providing valuable insight into this carnivore that roamed the earth during the Jurassic Period 130–190 million years ago. The excellent Wyoming Dinosaur Museum (www.wyo.org) in Thermopolis features more than 200 displays and 20 full-size skeletons of various dinosaurs. Fossils of fish, insects, birds, plants, and reptiles are on display at the Fossil Butte National Monument, a 50-million-year-old lake bed near Kemmerer that holds the largest deposit of freshwater fish fossils in the western hemisphere.

By most accounts, humans have inhabited what is now Wyoming for at least 13,000 years. Stone fossils have been found that indicate the presence of early human cultures, including the Plano, a tribe of hunter-gatherers that inhabited the Great Plains 9,000–6,000 B.C. There is also evidence of the Clovis culture, people that lived in the area nearly 13,000 years ago. Their distinctive bone and ivory "Clovis points" have been found in both Wyoming and Montana.

An interesting discovery in Wyoming was the Bighorn Medicine Wheel in the north-central part of the state. This giant stone ring was sacred to indigenous people and is believed to have been used for astronomical, teaching, and healing purposes. Constructed between 900 and 700 years ago, the Bighorn wheel is 80 feet in diameter and is one of the best-preserved stone rings in the world.

Native Americans and Mountain Men

As in Montana, Plains Indians didn't move into the area until the early 1600s, when Native Americans around the Great Lakes and Canadian plains were forced west. The arrival of horses and rifles created nomadic hunters who followed the massive herds of buffalo, and the culture began to change as villages grew larger and tribes had more interaction. Indian society grew more turbulent by the 19th century, and it was soon greeted by early American explorers who sought control of the state's vast geographic and natural resources.

Although French explorers crossed into northern Wyoming in the mid-1700s, two of the most famous names in Wyoming's early history are John Colter and Jim Bridger. Colter, a member of the Lewis and Clark expedition, was most likely the first white American to enter the region in 1807, and he gave birth to the term *mountain man*. He explored what would become Yellowstone National Park and was one of the first nonnatives to see the Grand Tetons, spending a winter alone in the wilderness as he recorded his discoveries. Colter's most legendary story is when he escaped from a group of Blackfeet Indians, running naked and evading capture for 12 days.

Another mountain man, Jim Bridger, had a profound effect on Wyoming's early frontier days in the 19th century. Bridger established the Rocky Mountain Fur Company in 1830 and spent the next 30 years in the West as a fur trader and guide, establishing a trading post on the banks of Wyoming's Green River. Bridger married Indian women—the last being the daughter of Shoshone Chief Washakie—and discovered new trading routes, including shortcuts on the Oregon and Bozeman Trails. He later served as an Army guide and scout in their campaign against the Sioux and Cheyenne, who were attacking parties along the Bozeman Trail.

Blazing Trails Across the State

The famous Oregon Trail passed through central and southern Wyoming on its way from Missouri to the Northwest. Today, Wyoming contains the longest and least-changed stretch of trail—487 miles—that can be recreated by traveling on various state and federal highways. The Oregon Trail was one of the main trading routes for those migrating west and was used by an estimated 400,000 people. Large wagon trains left Missouri as early as 1841, and usage peaked in 1850, but the trail practically disappeared when the first transcontinental railroad was completed in 1869.

With the arrival of the railroad, population gradually began to increase, and the Wyoming Territory was created in 1868. Yellowstone was made the first national park in 1872, and visitors slowly started trickling in from the East. Coal was discovered near Rock Springs in 1885, but no large deposits of minerals like gold or silver were discovered. Wyoming's lack of a gold rush limited its population growth, but in 1890 the territory was officially recognized as the 44th state.

Wyoming played a large role in the women's suffrage movement, being the first to grant women the right to vote in 1869. Wyoming also had the first woman justice of the peace, the first woman court bailiff, and the first woman governor in the country.

Livestock and Energy

The devastation of the West's bison herds and the subsequent placement of Native Americans on reservations led to the development of what would become Wyoming's hallmark industry in the late 19th century: cattle. Millions of cattle were driven into Wyoming in the 1870s and 1880s, and cattle barons soon dominated the natural and political landscape, basically buying off any and all forms of government. Sheep soon followed, taking advantage of vast tracts of grasslands, and by 1902 there were more than 6 million sheep roaming throughout Wyoming. Conflicts between sheepherders and cattlemen often escalated into violence, but these died down as the government enacted policies and divided up the land.

Wyoming's first oil well was drilled in 1884, and by the time of the first oil boom in 1908, the state was pumping out nearly 18,000 barrels per year. Production continued to climb, peaking in 1970, when more than 150 million barrels were

pumped. It has declined since then, leveling off to around 50 million barrels per year. The boom-and-bust oil cycle of the 1970s and 1980s had a profound effect in Wyoming as so-called oil-patch towns like Green River, Rock Springs, and Casper grew rapidly on the promise of high-paying oil jobs, then fell flat as the industry bubble collapsed in the early 1980s. The bust left many of these cities struggling to survive.

The oil industry in Wyoming has been replaced by coal, of which Wyoming is by far the nation's leading producer. Much of the coal is located in the Powder River Basin and is used for coal-fired power plants. The state produced more than 430 million tons of coal in 2009, and still has billions—maybe even trillions—of tons in reserves.

The newest boom is natural gas, and new wells for coal-bed methane are sprouting up in the Powder River and Bighorn Basins. Wyoming is now the second-largest producer of natural gas in the country. Another rapidly growing sector of the economy is wind power. The demand for natural gas and coal has driven Wyoming's population up again and brought the state into a new time of prosperity.

Just as people migrated west and settled in Wyoming hundreds of years ago, people today come to visit Yellowstone National Park, travel the Oregon Trail, or climb one of the majestic peaks of the Teton Mountains. Tourism is now the state's second-largest industry, worth more than $2 billion annually. Towns like Jackson Hole and Cody reap the benefits of being adjacent to Yellowstone, while the park itself attracts more than 3 million visitors annually.

Like Montana, Wyoming's balance among energy development, agriculture, and tourism is the face of the New West, where people move for a better quality of life while still trying to preserve the cultural heritage. Just like the settlers who established trading posts hundreds of years ago, these new immigrants are chasing a dream of living in an unspoiled part of the world and doing anything necessary to pay the bills. As you explore Wyoming, you'll notice that history is never far behind, and that the future holds unlimited possibilities.

Government

MONTANA

Montana became a territory in 1864 and was named the 41st state in 1889. Originally, the state's constitution reflected the mining and timber interests that seemed to run daily life in the early years, but in 1972 Montanans held a second Constitutional Convention, where the earlier, dated document was replaced with a more populist set of laws that placed more responsibility on the individual voter and made significant strides in protecting Montana's environment.

Montana granted women the right to vote in 1916, and the same year elected the first woman representative to the U.S. Congress. Jeannette Rankin, a lifelong pacifist and the only member of Congress to vote against entering World War II, is still the only woman Montana has elected to Congress. She served one term, worked as a lobbyist in Washington, D.C., for 20 years, and then was elected again to Congress in 1940. Her antiwar stance fell out of favor, and she only served one more term before retiring.

The Montana State Legislature is a bicameral body that meets in Helena each odd-numbered year for no longer than 90 days. It consists of a 100-member House and a 50-seat Senate. Montana is often characterized as a swing state, and the legislature has been split along party lines consistently throughout its history, especially since the new state constitution was enacted in 1972. Both parties have enjoyed similar successes over the years, and the legislature often changes hands. Montana's term-limits law survived in 2004 when 70 percent of voters shot down a measure that would have repealed term limits in the state legislature. Originally passed in 1992, the law limits its representatives to four two-year terms and senators to two four-year terms.

Montana's postwar politics have seen some remarkable national politicians, including Mike Mansfield, Lee Metcalf, and Pat Williams. Democrat Mansfield was the longest-serving

majority leader of the U.S. Senate (1961–1977) and was the U.S. ambassador to Japan for more than a decade. Lee Metcalf, another Democrat, was instrumental in creating three new wilderness areas in Montana. The Lee Metcalf Wilderness Area was named for his efforts in 1983, after his death. Williams was yet another Democrat who had a hand in expanding wilderness designation and served in the U.S. House 1979–1997.

Present-day Montana politicians are also gaining notoriety on the national scene. The current governor, Brian Schweitzer, is a Democrat who appeals to members of both parties. In fact, his running mate in 2004 and the current lieutenant governor is Republican John Bohlinger. Schweitzer is known for his down-to-earth persona and in 2008 gave a speech at the Democratic National Convention that was widely acclaimed. Senator Max Baucus, a Democrat, has been

© DONNIE SEXTON

Montana's State Capitol in Helena

CHANGING POLITICS

The political history of Montana and Wyoming is as colorful as the Wild West and has changed over the years to reflect the different population, economy, and culture that exists here.

Wyoming's political history is a study in contrasts. It was the first state to grant women the right to vote and the first state to elect a woman as governor. Yet, the state remains largely conservative and has only voted for one Democratic president since 1960 (Lyndon B. Johnson in 1964). Even though more than half of Wyoming's residents consider themselves Republicans, and Republicans have held a majority in the state senate continuously since 1936 and in the state house since 1964, Democrats have owned the governor's seat for all but eight years since 1975. Democratic governor Dave Freudenthal, in office 2002-2010, had one of the highest approval ratings in the country.

Like many states in the West, Democratic strongholds tend to exist in slightly more urban areas, or areas that have a large number of transplants and a younger population. In Wyoming, Teton County is the only reliably Democratic county, which is no surprise as it includes Jackson Hole. The town's population has boomed over the years, boosted by younger transplants from more liberal parts of the country that come for the skiing, fly fishing, and outdoor lifestyle the town offers.

Montana is a little harder to figure out. At first glance, it may come across as a decidedly Republican state, but its history shows that both parties have had successes. Like Wyoming, it was one of the first states to give

women voting rights, and Montanan Jeannette Rankin became the first woman elected to the U.S. Congress in 1916 as a Republican.

Often characterized as a swing state, Montana has had long-term shifts in party control throughout its history. Five of its first six governors were Democrats, and 1952-1984 it elected only Democratic senators. Republicans held the governorship 1953-1969 and again 1989-2005, with current Democratic governor Brian Schweitzer elected in 2004. In the 2000 election, Judy Martz became the first woman governor of Montana.

The swing-state nature of Montana continues today, and it currently has a Democratic Governor and a Republican Lieutenant Governor. Montana overwhelmingly supported George W. Bush in 2000 and 2004, but both U.S. senators are Democrats. A big change came in 2006 when Democrat John Tester defeated longtime senator Conrad Burns, one of the crucial races that allowed the party to regain control of the U.S. Senate. Montana's lone U.S. representative, Denny Rehberg, is a Republican. Montanans last supported a Democratic president in 1992 (Bill Clinton), although in 2008 the margin was just two percent in favor of Republican John McCain.

As university towns like Bozeman and Missoula gain population and the state's economy shifts toward tourism and the high-tech industry, Montana is becoming a purple state. The lines between political parties are becoming blurred but seem to be shifting slowly toward blue. But then again, as history has proved, it may only last so long.

serving in the U.S. Senate since 1978, and is currently chair of the Senate Committee on Finance, which played a pivotal role in the debate over health care reform.

By most accounts, Montana is a "purple" state on the national scene—once primarily red but slowly turning blue. Montanans have voted for the Republican presidential candidate in every election since 1968, except when they chose Democrat Bill Clinton over Republican

George H. W. Bush in 1992. In 2008, Montana voters gave John McCain a narrow margin—just over 2 percent—over Barack Obama.

An easy characterization of the shift in politics follows the state's population trends. The eastern part of the state—more rural, less industrialized—is more Republican but is losing population. The western part of Montana, from Bozeman west toward Butte and Missoula, is seeing rapid population expansion and more liberal influences taking over. Many observers argue that the younger, more intellectual western part of the state will soon "take over" Montana politics. Only time will tell.

WYOMING

Wyoming Territory was formed in 1869, but the road to statehood did not begin until 1888. After a few statehood bills failed to pass, the House finally passed the bill on March 27, 1890, making Wyoming the 44th state after President Benjamin Harrison signed the bill into law soon after. Its capital is Cheyenne.

During the territorial era, the Wyoming Legislature played a pivotal role in the U.S. suffrage movement. In 1869, just four years after the Civil War and 35 years before women's suffrage became a highly visible political issue in the United States, Wyoming granted all women age 21 and older the right to vote. Democrat Nellie Tayloe Ross became the first female governor in the country when she won a special election in 1924 after then-governor William Ross died in office. She later became the first woman to serve as director of the U.S. Mint, appointed in 1933 by President Franklin D. Roosevelt, a position she held until her retirement in 1953.

Wyoming remains one of the few states that has a true part-time citizen legislature, meaning its members don't enjoy the same accommodations provided to full-time legislators in larger states. There are 60 state representatives elected for two-year terms along with 30 state senators that serve four-year terms. There are no term limits. The state legislature meets in odd-numbered years beginning the second Tuesday in January. The general session is limited to 40 legislative days. The offices of governor, secretary of state, auditor, treasurer, and superintendent of public instruction are all elected every four years.

The Wyoming legislature passed a bill limiting the office of governor to two consecutive terms after Democrat Edgar Herschler served three terms in the mid-1980s. In 1992 voters approved term limits in a ballot initiative, but neither action constituted an amendment to the Wyoming constitution. In 2004 two state legislators challenged the term-limit law in the courts, and the Wyoming Supreme Court subsequently invalidated the limits in a unanimous decision, ruling that a constitutional amendment would be required to establish such a law. Popular Democrat Dave Freudenthal, who served two terms as governor after being elected in 2002 and 2006, did not use the same challenge to seek a third term.

Freudenthal's election and popularity—his approval rating was a staggering 82 percent in the months before the 2010 election—defy Wyoming's Republican nature. In fact, the governorship in general has seen its fair share of Democrats, but Republicans have dominated both houses of the legislature almost since statehood. Wyoming has only voted for one Democratic president in the last half-century (Lyndon B. Johnson in 1964), and Republicans have held a majority in the state senate continuously since 1936 and in the state house since 1964. Despite its tendency to elect Democrats as governor, Wyoming is considered a red state on the national level.

Dick Cheney is Wyoming's best-known political figure. Born in Casper, Cheney was the White House Chief of Staff during the Nixon and Ford administrations and was then elected to the U.S. House of Representatives in 1978. He served five terms and was then selected to be the Secretary of Defense during the first Bush presidency and later served as the Vice President 2001–2009 under George W. Bush.

The Wind River Indian Reservation is home to the Eastern Shoshone Tribal Government, a sovereign government that operates under its own constitution. The Business Council of the Eastern Shoshone Tribe consists of a chair, vice-chair, and four additional council members who are elected by the tribe members. The Tribal Council Chair is the administrative head of the tribe and serves a two-year term with the vice-chairman and the other members of the council. Both the Eastern Shoshone and Northern Arapaho are represented.

INDIAN RESERVATIONS

The Native American population plays an important role in both Montana and Wyoming government and politics. Tribal law prevails within reservation boundaries, and Indian Reservations are federally recognized as independent political units with their own structure and legislation. As sovereign nations, tribes can have their own school systems, constitutions, police and court systems, and legislative councils. They can also regulate transport and trade within reservation boundaries. The state can't tax land or transactions that occur on reservations.

What does this mean to the visitor? Essentially, some state laws may not apply on reservations. Goods and services—mainly gasoline and tobacco—can be much cheaper on the reservations since there are no state taxes enforced. Not all land may be open to the public, and there may be additional fees for recreation, including hunting and fishing. It's best to inquire at a local store or gas station if you are traveling on reservation land in Montana or Wyoming.

Economy

MONTANA

Montana was founded on rural traditions and industries: farming, ranching, mining, and forestry. To a large extent, these industries are still dominant. Agriculture is the state's leading industry, with large-scale farming and ranching operations responsible for about 11 percent of economic output in the state. Top crops include barley, rice, oats, corn, hay, and sugar beets, and Montana is the third-largest wheat-producing state in the country. Beef cattle dominate the ranching sector, although hogs, sheep, dairy cattle, llamas, and horses are also raised. It should be noted that there are about three cows for every person in Montana, and although agriculture is the most prosperous industry in the state, it only accounts for just over 4 percent of total employment.

Cities like Butte and Helena benefited from the mining boom of the late 19th and early 20th centuries. Butte was once one of the richest cities in the country, spurred by the large amount of copper in the area. Today, mining and resource extraction continue to be a large part of Montana's economy. Its coal reserves are the largest in the nation, and the mountain ranges of central, southern, and western Montana hold large ore deposits of copper, gold, lead, silver, and zinc. Montana is the fifth-largest producer of gold and coal in the nation, 11th in crude oil production, and a national leader in talc and vermiculite. The Stillwater Mine in Columbus is the only palladium and platinum producer in the country. In 2008 there were more than 11,000 miners working in Montana.

Tourism is Montana's second-ranked and fastest-growing industry. In 2009 travel spending by nonresident visitors totaled over $2.27 billion, and nearly 10 million people visited the state. The nonresident travel industry in Montana accounts for almost 4 percent of the state's total employment, making it the seventh-largest employer.

The timber industry has played a large and important part in Montana's economic growth but has recently fallen on hard times. Montana lumber production in 2009 was the lowest since the end of World War II. In 2008 there were only an estimated 1,900 people employed in the forestry and logging industries.

Other industries that contribute significantly to Montana's economic output are construction, the retail trade, real estate, health care, education, and government. Montana also has a growing high-tech sector, particularly in Bozeman, Missoula, and Kalispell. The universities in Missoula and Bozeman are two of the state's largest employers, as is Malmstrom Air Force Base in Great Falls. Many of the top 20 employers are in the health care field—including hospitals and clinics in Billings, Great Falls, Kalispell, Missoula, Bozeman, and Helena. There were more than 16,000 state government employees in 2008.

Wind power is increasingly important in Montana and Wyoming.

Since 2001, Montana's economy has out-performed the national economy in real gross domestic product (GDP) statistics: real GDP grew every year 2005–2008. In 2008 Montana had a per capita personal income of $34,622, which is 86 percent of the national average and ranks 39th nationally—up from 47th in 2003. In 2008, Montana was ranked 47th in gross state product (GSP), the state equivalent of the national GDP. Montana typically has a lower unemployment rate than the national average. In 2010, the unemployment rate for Montana was 7.3 percent, compared to the national average of 9.5 percent.

Indeed, when other parts of the country seem to be struggling, Montana's economy keeps chugging along. Real estate has certainly taken a hit since the economic downturn began, but enough people seem to be moving here that home prices have fallen far less than the national average. Resort communities like Big Sky and Whitefish have taken more of a hit, but communities like Missoula, Bozeman, and Helena are still flourishing.

WYOMING

The economy in Wyoming is similar to Montana's in that natural resource extraction, agriculture, and tourism play major roles. Oil production, in which Wyoming ranks eighth in the country, has been eclipsed by coal and natural gas. Wyoming is the leading coal producer and the second-largest natural gas producer in the nation. Eight of the country's largest coal mines are in Wyoming, and the state has billions of tons of coal still below the surface, mainly in the Powder River and Bighorn basins.

Wyoming mines also produce more than 90 percent of the nation's supply of trona, a mineral used to make sodium carbonate, which in turn is used in everything from pool chemicals to glassmaking. The trona deposit in Green River is the largest in the world.

Since most of Wyoming can be classified as rural, it's no surprise that agriculture plays a vital role in the state's economy—more than $1 billion in cash receipts annually. There are more than 9,000 farms and ranches operating in Wyoming, meaning it ranks eighth nationally in total farm and ranch land, and first in average ranch size. The number of ranches and farms peaked at more than 18,000 in the 1930s, then slowly declined, but it has leveled off in the past few decades.

The cattle industry produces the largest agricultural commodity—mainly beef cattle—and it dates back to the mid-1880s, when settlers first came to the West. After the Civil War, cattle ranching became one of the most prominent businesses, and Cheyenne became a world trade center for cattle. For years, Wyoming range cattle have commanded top market value.

The high plains and mountain meadows of Wyoming are renowned for producing some the finest sheep in the world. Wyoming ranks second in the country in stock sheep and the lamb crop, and second in wool production. Wyoming's wool is some of the most desirable in the world. The largest crop produced in Wyoming is hay, followed by sugar beets, barley, corn, wheat, and dry beans. Dryland winter wheat is grown primarily in the eastern part of the state. Other more specialized commodities in the state include oats, hogs, bison, and sunflowers.

More than 7 million people visited Wyoming in 2009, most of them taking advantage of the abundant recreational opportunities. These visitors contributed more than $2.5 billion to the state's economy through tourism, an industry that supports more than 29,000 jobs. Much of the tourism industry is based around Yellowstone and Grand Teton National Parks. More than 3.2 million people visited Yellowstone in 2009, the highest total ever recorded. Excellent skiing gives the Jackson Hole economy a boost each winter, with more than 400,000 skiers visiting during the 2009–2010 ski season. In a booming tourist economy, it's natural for the service industry to be a large sector of the economy, and much of the state's growth over the years can be attributed to it.

The University of Wyoming is the largest employer in the state, followed by the Natrona County school district and the Cheyenne Regional Medical Center. In 2008, Wyoming's per capita personal income was $49,719, well above the national average in large part due to the energy booms across the state. Since 2005, Wyoming's per capita income has risen by more than 28 percent, while income levels in the Rocky Mountain region and the country overall have risen by 12.8 percent and 14.6 percent, respectively. Wyoming's unemployment rate is usually far lower than the national average, and in 2010 it was 6.7 percent compared to 9.5 percent nationally.

People and Culture

Since Montana and Wyoming are two of the newest states in the union (41st and 44th, respectively), it's no surprise that their people and culture are largely tied to the settling of the West and the Native Americans who inhabit the area. It wasn't until the 1860s that settlers started building permanent communities—both were some of the last states to be settled by whites—as the gold rush, the railroad, and the Homestead Act lured those seeking a different and potentially lucrative way of life. Many areas were settled by immigrants and still retain their European heritage.

Both are largely considered conservative states, and both have a population that is more than 90 percent white. More than 8 percent of Wyoming's population is listed as Hispanic or Latino in origin. Like many Western states, both Wyoming and Montana are home to a growing number of Hispanics, many of whom work in the farm, ranch, and construction industry.

NATIVE AMERICANS
Although farming, ranching, and natural resource extraction certainly contributed to the growing cultural landscape, it's the rich Native American history that gives these states a proud and colorful representation of the past that transcends today's modern American culture. Before trappers and settlers came west, Indian people roamed freely across land, following the huge buffalo herds that once covered the plains. Each tribe has unique customs and traditions. While Native Americans have worked to adapt to the changing world around them, they have kept the culture and traditions of their past alive. This rich heritage contributes to the distinct flavor of Montana and Wyoming. Their culture is celebrated through dance, songs, games, language, and religious ceremonies.

There are several museums in each state that pay tribute to the American Indian, and many reservation towns host annual powwows, rodeos, and celebrations. Today just over 6 percent of Montana's population and nearly 3 percent of Wyoming is classified as Native American.

There are 11 different tribes represented in Montana, the majority living on seven different reservations. There is only one reservation in Wyoming, which is home to two different tribes. The following is a list of the Native American groups and the reservations that they inhabit today.

Blackfeet

The 1.5-million-acre Blackfeet Reservation is in northwestern Montana along the eastern slopes of the Rocky Mountains, bordered on the north by Canada and on the west by Glacier National Park. More than 15,000 members make up the tribe, with about 8,500 living on or near the reservation. The Blackfeet are thought to have acquired their name from the characteristic black color of their moccasins, painted or darkened with ashes, and once inhabited land near the Great Lakes before they migrated west. During this migration, the various tribes of the Blackfeet joined together to form the Blackfeet Confederacy, made up of the Piegans, the Bloods, and the Northern Blackfeet. Soon they became one of the largest and most feared Indian tribes, and were great hunters of the buffalo that roamed the northern plains. The Blackfeet were notoriously leery of the settlers moving into their territory.

A worthy detour on the reservation is the Museum of the Plains Indian in Browning, where a permanent exhibit displays artifacts of the northern plains Indians, and two special galleries feature rotating presentations.

Crow

The Crow Indian Reservation is the fifth-largest reservation in the United States, home to nearly 7,500 residents on its 2.3 million acres south of Billings. The tribe originally lived in the Great Lakes region, but was one of the first to enter Montana in the early 1600s. The tribe was called Apsáalooke, which means "children of the large-beaked bird," and are also called Absarokee. Today, nearly 85 percent of the tribe speaks Crow as their first language, and a coal mine on the reservation provides income and employment.

Flathead

The Flathead Indian Reservation is home to the Confederated Salish and Kootenai tribes, a combination of the Salish, Pend d'Oreille, and Kootenai. There are approximately 7,000 registered members, with about 4,500 living on or near the reservation. The 1.2 million-acre piece of land is in Montana between Missoula and Kalispell, north of I-90 among the majestic peaks of the Mission Mountains and along the shores of beautiful Flathead Lake, the largest natural freshwater lake west of the Mississippi.

These Salish-speaking people moved east from Columbia River valleys and adopted a way of life based on hunting buffalo while maintaining the religious and social traditions of the Northwest coast. They were generally friendly to settlers as they entered Montana.

Assiniboine

The Fort Belknap Reservation in north central Montana is home to two tribes: the Assiniboine and the Gros Ventre. There are about 4,000 people in these two tribes spread over the 650,000-acre reservation.

The Assiniboine originated in the Lake of the Woods and the Lake Winnipeg area of Canada and became allied with the Cree. A division between the two tribes happened in 1744, and some bands moved west into the valleys of the Assiniboine and Saskatchewan Rivers in Canada, while others moved south into the Missouri River Valley. The tribes inhabited an area from Minnesota to Montana. The Assiniboine were typically large-game hunters, dependent on bison for a considerable part of their diet, and lived in tipis made from the animal's hide.

The 2-million-acre Fort Peck Reservation is in northeastern Montana, 40 miles west of the North Dakota border and 50 miles south of the Canadian border, with the Missouri River defining its southern perimeter. Nearly 7,000 Assiniboine and Sioux live on the reservation, with another 4,000 living off the reservation. Though separate, both tribes have similar languages that descended from the same language family.

Gros Ventre

The Gros Ventre are closely affiliated with the Algonquin-speaking Arapaho and Cheyenne tribes. All three were among the last to migrate together into Montana, but they soon split up and went their separate ways. The Gros Ventre became allies with the Blackfeet, dominating the northern plains until white settlers moved in and moved the tribe to Fort Belknap in 1878.

Sioux

Nearly 7,000 Assiniboine and Sioux live on the 2-million-acre Fort Peck Reservation in northeastern Montana, with another 4,000 living off the reservation. Though separate, both tribes have similar languages that descended from the same language family.

The Sioux is one of the largest and most famous Indian nations in North America, and its people are divided into three linguistic groups: the Dakota, the Lakota, and the Nakota. All were originally from Canada and didn't arrive in Montana until the beginning of the 19th century, where many settled around the Fort Peck area. Viewed by many as noble yet fearsome, the Sioux were excellent hunters and skilled warriors. The reservation was created in 1888, and today is home to a large industrial park and Fort Peck Community College. The Assiniboine and Sioux Cultural Center and Museum in Poplar features fascinating displays of their history, arts, and crafts.

Northern Cheyenne

This 445,000-acre reservation is located in southeastern Montana. The tribe comes from Algonquin linguistic ancestry and moved west from the Minnesota area under pressure from other tribes. Today there are more than 10,000 members of the Northern Cheyenne, with about half living on the reservation. An interesting stop if you're in the area is the St. Labre Indian School and Museum, established in 1884 by the Franciscan order. The building's visitors center, museum, and Ten Bear Gallery are important showplaces of Cheyenne heritage and art.

Chippewa-Cree

The 130,000-acre Rocky Boy's Reservation near the Canadian border in north central Montana provides a home for about 2,500 members of the Chippewa-Cree tribe. It's Montana's smallest reservation, and in 1916 it was the last to be established in the state. Historically, the Chippewa lived in bands on both sides of what now divides their homelands, the Canadian border and the Great Lakes region. The Cree territory extended from eastern Canada into what are now the provinces of Saskatchewan and Alberta. The tribes began their migrations west in the 1700s, and by the early 1890s they had united in Montana to find a permanent home. The term *Rocky Boy* comes from a misinterpretation of the Chippewa leader's name, Chief Stone Man.

Shoshone

Wyoming's Wind River Reservation, the seventh-largest in the country at more than 2.2 million acres, is home to more than 2,500 Eastern Shoshone and 5,000 Northern Arapaho. The Shoshones have been in Wyoming since the 16th century, and were some of the first Indians to have horses. The eastern part of the tribe was pushed back west of the Laramie Mountains when their enemies—the Sioux, Crow, and Arapaho—invaded their territory.

Fort Washakie is home to the Shoshone Tribal Cultural Center and the cemeteries where both Shoshone Chief Washakie and Lewis and Clark's Shoshone guide, Sacajawea, are buried. Originally called Fort Brown, the name was changed in 1878 to honor the chief, who negotiated the treaty establishing the reservation. Ironically, the Shoshones ended up on the same reservation as their former enemies, the Arapaho, after the U.S. government temporarily placed them together—which soon became a permanent situation, betraying Chief Washakie's wishes to end the arrangement.

Arapaho

The Arapaho ended up on Wyoming's Wind River Reservation along with their former enemies, the Shoshone, after the U.S. government placed them together, supposedly temporarily.

Today Wind River is home to more than 2,500 Eastern Shoshone and 5,000 Northern Arapaho.

Like many tribes, the Arapaho were forced out of Minnesota after the arrival of the settlers and migrated to the Great Plains in the late 18th century. After many years of trying to fight back against the settlers, the tribe was decimated by the late 1800s and ultimately forced onto a reservation with the Shoshones. The Heritage Center at St. Stephens and the Arapaho Cultural Museum in Ethete both provide insight into the tribe and its traditions.

The Arts

Montana and Wyoming are not just filled with cowboys and ungulates; in fact they boast vibrant and varied art scenes with a interesting and colorful history. Towns like Bozeman and Jackson are meccas for Western art, while Missoula and Livingston have a decidedly literary bent. From books and music to landscape painting and sculpture, both states have a remarkable range of fine art to discover.

Montana has an especially long list of literary heroes, both past and present. Andrew Garcia's *Tough Trip Through Paradise* may be the state's first famous export, a gripping first-hand account of the Nez Perce flight in the 1870s. The writing program at the University of Montana in Missoula—established in 1919 by H. G. Merriam—can largely be credited with putting Montana on the map; students and faculty have included A. B. Guthrie Jr., William Kittredge, Annick Smith, Kevin Canty, Judy Blunt, Rick DeMarinis, James Welch, Deirdre McNamer, and poet Richard Hugo. Contemporary authors that call Montana home include Rick Bass (*Winter: Notes From Montana*), Thomas McGuane (*The Bushwhacked Piano*), Richard Ford (*Independence Day*), Walter Kirn (*Up in the Air*), and many more. There are thriving writing communities in Bozeman, Livingston, and Missoula, the latter hosting the annual Montana Festival of the Book every October.

While Wyoming does not have quite the literary lore that Montana has, it has its share of standouts. Platte Valley resident C. J. Box is one of the top-selling mystery writers in the country, and Annie Proulx won a Pulitzer Prize for her novel *The Shipping News*. Other writers that call Wyoming home include Mark Spragg (*Where Rivers Change Direction*), and Kathleen O'Neal Gear (*People of the Longhouse*). In addition, Ernest Hemingway spent a lot of time in Wyoming, where he worked on several novels, including *Death in the Afternoon* and the *Green Hills of Africa*.

Not surprisingly, both Montana and Wyoming are hotbeds for Western art lovers. Two of the West's premier's art events, Jackson's Fall Arts Festival and Cody's Rendezvous Royale, take place each September in Wyoming. Much of the Cody event is centered around the Buffalo Bill Historical Center, which houses the impressive Whitney Gallery of Western Art. Collections here include works from the early 19th century to contemporary times that commemorate the events, people, and landscape of the Rocky Mountain region.

One of the best-known Western artists is Charles M. Russell (1864–1926), who left Missouri for Montana in 1880 at age 16. He soon became a working artist whose colorful and detailed scenes captured the landscape, spirit, and culture of the West during the late 1880s–early 1900s. Russell was also a sculptor and writer, and the excellent C. M. Russell Museum in Great Falls houses five galleries of paintings, sculptures, drawings, and illustrations that Russell created from childhood through the end of his life. His 1918 oil painting, *Piegans,* sold for more than $5 million at auction in 2005, and another sold at auction in 2009 for more than $2 million.

Two particularly art-themed towns are Bozeman, Montana, and Jackson, Wyoming.

Both feature quaint streets lined with galleries and shops, offering everything from locally made stationery to the finest in Western photography, sculpture, and painting. The bustling college town of Bozeman is regionally known for its annual Sweet Pea Festival of the Arts in August, and it also boasts a well-regarded symphony as well as jazz and opera music festivals. The Emerson Center for the Arts and Culture houses studios, galleries, classrooms, and restaurants along with a 700-seat theater in a refurbished two-story elementary school.

Jackson's 10-day Fall Arts Festival is home to one of the region's largest auctions, and the Grand Teton Music Festival hosts some of the world's finest classical musicians each summer in nearby Teton Village. Jackson is also home to the National Museum of Wildlife Art, which boasts more than 5,000 works in its permanent collection, and to the Jackson Hole Center for the Arts, a vibrant community center that offers everything from nationally touring musical and dance acts to educational workshops.

Although both states are well known for historical, landscape, and wildlife art, Montana in particular has its fair share of contemporary art galleries and museums. The Holter Museum in Helena, the Paris Gibson Square Museum in Great Falls, and the Yellowstone Art Museum in Billings have some of Montana's best contemporary works on display. The Archie Bray Foundation in Helena is nationally recognized for modern pottery creations from its resident artists, and the town of Livingston boasts "14 galleries and three stop lights" and is famous for its Friday-night wine-filled art walks.

Montana is home to numerous small town theaters as well as the large theaters associated with the universities in Bozeman and Missoula. The Missoula Children's Theatre is nationally recognized, and year-round theaters can be found in many cities, including Billings, Missoula, Bozeman, and Whitefish. Theaters in West Yellowstone, Fort Peck, and Bigfork offer excellent summer programs,

and the raucous Brewery Follies in historic Virginia City plays to sold-out crowds May–September.

In Wyoming, Jackson's Off Square Theatre Company is a vibrant year-round company founded in 1998, and Casper's Stage III offers six productions each year September–June. In downtown Sheridan, the historic WYO Theater—which opened in 1929 as the Lotus—was saved from demolition and refurbished, opening again in 1989 as a nonprofit organization. Today it offers an array of musical concerts and theater productions that belie its small-town setting. The University of Wyoming is home to one of the most outstanding undergraduate theater programs in the country along with the University of Wyoming Fine Arts Studio, where some of the region's finest facilities are located. Indirectly, Wyoming is probably best-known in the theater world as the setting for *The Laramie Project*, an award-winning play depicting the reaction to the 1998 murder of gay University of Wyoming student Matthew Shepard in Laramie. The play was produced by the New York-based Tectonic Theater Company and was also made into an HBO film of the same name.

Montana Shakespeare in the Parks, a troupe based at the university in Bozeman, takes their show on the road each summer to rural communities in Montana and northern Wyoming. The performances are free and are well regarded for their high quality, drawing actors for the cast from Chicago, Seattle, and Montana. Their plays are often summer highlights in small towns that may not see much cultural infusion the rest of the year.

While towns in Montana and Wyoming certainly don't have the hip music scenes larger cities may offer, there are plenty of tunes around to keep your toes tapping, especially in the summer. Many communities have free music nights, and local bars and taverns are usually good for a fun country band and the occasional touring act. In Montana, Billings and Missoula have the most offerings, including arena shows, nightclubs, and theaters. In Wyoming, Casper and Cheyenne are home to big arenas, while Cheyenne's Frontier Days rodeo offers nightly performances by favorite country music stars each July.

It seems nearly every small town across both states has a bluegrass festival during the summer, and Wyoming's Grand Targhee Bluegrass Festival is one of the nation's best. Other popular music festivals include Montana's Sweet Pea Festival, the Magic City Blues Festival, and Rockin' the Rivers, while Wyoming's Grand Teton Music Festival hosts classical concerts and workshops June–August.

ESSENTIALS

Getting There and Around

Flying into Montana or Wyoming is easier than you think, and it's by far the best way to get here. Flights into the larger airports are becoming increasingly frequent as the region gains ground as an incredible destination for visitors. Although getting here by train or bus is possible, it's not as convenient, and stops can be far from the main travel areas—best left to hardy travelers or those on an extreme budget. If you live in the West, driving to Montana or Wyoming is a great way to get here—major highways will get you into the state, and well-traveled back roads will lead you to your final destination.

By far the best way to get around these large states once you're here is by car. Rental cars are available at the major airports, and you'll see more of each state while driving around. Consider an all-wheel-drive vehicle even if you travel only during the summer, as many of the region's most scenic roads are gravel. In addition to better traction, these vehicles typically offer higher clearance.

BY AIR

In Wyoming, commercial flights are available to and from Casper, Cheyenne, Cody, Gillette, Jackson, Laramie, Riverton, Rock Springs, Sheridan, and Worland. Jackson has the best service, with jet flights from Atlanta,

© DONNIE SEXTON

Salt Lake City, Denver, Dallas, Chicago, Minneapolis, and Los Angeles. Some flights only operate during peak times in the winter and summer, and many people choose to fly into Salt Lake City (275 miles) or Idaho Falls (90 miles) and pick up a rental car for the scenic drive to Jackson. Within Wyoming, Great Lakes Airlines (www.flygreatlakes.com) flies into the smaller cities listed above. Major carriers with service to Wyoming include American, United, Frontier, and Delta. Allegiant Airlines offers direct flights to Las Vegas from Casper twice weekly.

In Montana, the cities of Billings, Bozeman, Kalispell, Helena, Butte, and Missoula are served by major carriers Delta, United, Alaska/Horizon, and Frontier, although some flights may be seasonal. Low-cost Allegiant Airlines offers direct flights to Phoenix or Las Vegas from Billings, Bozeman, Great Falls, Missoula, and Kalispell. Great Lakes Airlines has some flights from Billings on 19- or 32-seat turboprops to the smaller towns of Havre, Lewistown, Glasgow, Wolf Point, Sidney, and Glendive. West Yellowstone's airport is open in the summer only and is served by SkyWest Airlines from Salt Lake City.

If budget is your top priority, be sure to look into flights into nearby airports. For travelers going to Bozeman, for example, sometimes flights in and out of Billings (140 miles) or Butte (85 miles) can be significantly less expensive. That's not always the case; sometimes smaller airports can be even pricier with more limited schedules, but it's worth looking into. Keep in mind that drivers will often encounter wildlife on the roads, particularly late at night. And weather conditions can be sketchy, especially during winter. In other words, make sure the money saved on the flight is worth your time on the road.

BY CAR

Driving around Wyoming and Montana is the most efficient way to experience the scenic grandeur of these two states. In Montana, the I-94–I-90 corridor follows the Yellowstone and Clark Fork Rivers and is the best route across the state. The only major highway running north to south is I-15, which links Great Falls, Helena, and Butte to Canada and Salt Lake City. Some of the state's more famous back roads include U.S. 2, which parallels the Canadian border on Montana's Hi-Line along the old Great Northern rail line, and Highway 200 and U.S. 12, which cut east and west across the central part of the state. U.S. 191 and U.S. 93 are popular north–south routes that connect Montana with Idaho and Canada.

In Wyoming, I-80 runs across the state from Nebraska to Nevada, while I-25 heads north from Colorado up to its intersection with I-90 in Buffalo, then on to Billings, Montana. U.S. 89 is a popular and scenic route to Jackson from Salt Lake City, and then up through Grand Teton and Yellowstone National Parks into Montana.

Highway Safety

A few considerations apply when you are planning a road trip to Montana or Wyoming. In general, interstates and major highways are in good condition across the region, although short summers mean road construction can be expected at any time of the day—or night, in some cases. State highways are often narrow and winding, not compatible with drowsy or inattentive drivers. Wildlife is a concern on any road, particularly at night, and fallen rocks can be a problem in mountainous areas. For Wyoming road conditions, the **Wyoming Department of Transportation** (888/996-7623, www.wyoroad.info) has a wealth of information. Montana information can be found through the **Montana Department of Transportation** (800/226-7623, www.mdt.mt.gov/travinfo).

If you plan on renting a car, it's a good idea to reserve one well in advance. Unless you will be driving entirely on paved roads, which is doubtful, a high-clearance or all-wheel-drive vehicle is a good idea. Many Forest Service campgrounds are located along gravel roads, and any time you venture off the beaten path, you're bound to encounter some type of gravel or dirt road. In the winter, all-wheel drive is

MONTANA LICENSE PLATES

You wouldn't know it just by driving around, but Montana's license plates provide an interesting look at the state's population trends since the first plate was produced in 1914. In the 1930s, the state added a number to the left side of the plate that corresponded to county population – the number 1 was for the county with the highest population, and 56 was for the lowest. If you correlate these with the city that is the county seat, you get a snapshot of the state's population history – and you can tell where people are from just by looking at their plates. A fun game Montanans often play is to see how many plates they can identify while driving around.

When the list for the license plate was created, Silver Bow County was the largest in the state, as Butte – with a population of just under 40,000 people – was a thriving city, booming with the economic flush of mining. Great Falls was number 2, Billings was 3, and Missoula 4. Libby – in northwest Lincoln County – came in last at number 56. In 1930 the total population of the state was just 537,606; the population of Billings was a mere 16,280, and the state capital, Helena, had just under 12,000 residents.

Over the past 80 years, the state motor vehicle department has left the number and corresponding counties the same. That is, a car with a number 1 is still from Butte–Silver Bow County, and a truck with a number 56 is from the Libby area. However, the population snapshot paints a dramatically different picture these days. While Butte has lost about 7,000 people since 1930, other cities have seen significant increases, leaving Butte now the fifth-largest city in Montana. Billings is the largest city, with more than 100,000 residents, and Missoula has moved up to number 2 with nearly 70,000 people.

If they did change the numbers for the license plate, Butte–Silver Bow would now be 8, and the top five counties would be Yellowstone (Billings), Missoula, Gallatin (Bozeman), Flathead (Kalispell), and Cascade (Great Falls). Lincoln County, now with more than 18,000 residents, jumped up more dramatically than any other. It's moved from last place (56) to 10th since 1930. Generally, western Montana is growing in population and eastern Montana is shrinking. Also, transplants tend to settle in the larger, more urban centers where service-related jobs are typically abundant.

Why aren't the numbers on the plates being changed? Montana drivers have a certain amount of pride regarding their heritage, and the numbers hark back to a different era. Newcomers may not pay much attention to it, but old-timers and natives certainly do. The numbers are part of the state's cultural history – something nobody wants to change anytime soon.

---

a must. And be aware that rock chips on the windshield are common occurrences at any time of year. Make sure your insurance will cover it, or consider paying for added insurance from the car-rental agency.

Distances between settlements can be great in Montana and Wyoming, especially in the eastern parts of the states. As a rule of thumb, planning ahead is critical. Don't wait until your gas light is on to fill up your tank, and make sure your spare is inflated. Carrying emergency gear is recommended. Rest areas—even on major highways and interstates—can

be hundreds of miles apart. Most major towns and cities have reliable mechanics and car dealerships, but don't expect to find parts for your old Porsche roadster in very many places.

In general, the speed limit in Montana and Wyoming is 75 mph on interstates and 70 mph on most two-lane highways, although it can vary quite a bit depending on location. Many two-lane roads have numerous turnouts, where slower moving vehicles can pull over and let cars pass. Montana and Wyoming drivers are used to driving faster on these roads, so if you're getting tailgated by a local, just pull over and let them go by. Increasingly, passing lanes are being incorporated into many state highways, particularly on roads over mountain passes.

Winter Travel

Winter driving in Montana and Wyoming takes special care, focus, and—at times—lots of caffeine. Roads can be rendered impassable in a matter of minutes by snow and wind, and mountain passes are especially susceptible to fast-changing conditions. Because of the area covered, it may take a while before snowplows clear the roads. And be extremely cautious when driving behind or toward a snowplow as visibility can be diminished to nothing. Be aware that because of wildlife, salt is rarely used on roads in Montana and Wyoming. Instead, the roads are graveled to provide better traction in icy conditions. Loose gravel often translates into cracked or chipped windshields, so drive with caution, and never get too close to a graveling truck.

Snow tires are a must in many places, and carrying emergency supplies is strongly recommended. A good emergency kit includes a shovel, a first-aid kit, jumper cables, a flashlight, signal flares, extra clothing, some food, water, a tow strap, and a sleeping bag. Don't rely on your cell phone to save you—although service is improving, there are many dead zones across both states.

Both states' transportation websites (www.wyoroad.info, www.mdt.mt.gov/travinfo) have links to current and projected weather patterns, and toll-free information numbers are updated regularly. It's a good idea to carry these numbers in your car. Occasionally weather information can be found on the AM band of your car radio—you'll notice signs along roads indicating when this is possible.

Travel Maps

Free road maps can be found at visitors centers and rest areas in both states, while an excellent supplement is the **Delorme Gazetteer series** (www.delorme.com), available at bookstores and in many gas stations. These oversize companions are a must for those venturing off the beaten path, as they include topographic data, Forest Service roads and trails, camping and hiking information, fishing areas, scenic drives, and more. Sporting goods stores offer more specialized maps, from national forests and wilderness areas to Bureau of Land Management lands and mile-by-mile river guides. The free road maps you get when you enter the national parks are sufficient to use during your stay.

BY TRAIN

For two states that were quite literally built by the railroads, train service today is spotty at best. **Amtrak**'s *Empire Builder,* which travels in both directions daily through Montana between Chicago, Seattle, and Portland, is the only train service in the two states. Most of the stops are in the far northern part of Montana, which can be acceptable if you are going to Glacier National Park, but otherwise the train stops are long distances from the major population centers.

BY BUS

In Montana, **Greyhound** (800/231-2222, www.greyhound.com) buses travel mostly along I-90 and I-94 and north–south on I-15, but service to smaller towns is available on **Rimrock Stages** (800/255-7655, www.rimrocktrailways.com). These routes can also be booked through Greyhound. Greyhound stations are in Basin, Billings, Bozeman, Butte, Dillon, Drummond, Forsyth, Glendive, Great Falls, Helena, Hysham, Kalispell, Livingston, Miles City, Missoula, Polson, Ronan, St. Ignatius, St. Regis, and Wibaux.

Greyhound has service to all major cities and many smaller Wyoming towns, including Basin, Buffalo, Casper Cheyenne, Evanston, Gillette, Laramie, Lovell, Rock Springs, Sheridan, Shoshoni, Thermopolis, Wheatland, and Worland.

Alltrans/Jackson Hole Express (800/652-9510, www.jacksonholealltrans.com) provides daily shuttle service between Salt Lake City, Idaho Falls, Pocatello, and the resort town of Jackson, as well as transfers to and from the Jackson Hole airport.

The Wind River Transportation Authority (800/439-7118, www.wrtabuslines.com) offers on-demand shuttles among Riverton, Jackson, Lander, and Casper.

BY BIKE

Montana and Wyoming have many options for those cycling through. Numerous back roads and accessible campgrounds make for some fun trips, but be prepared for long-distance rides and not much company. Both the Wyoming and Montana transportation websites (www.wyoroad.info, www.mdt.mt.gov/travinfo) offer excellent information for cyclists. You can order a **Montana Bicycle Touring Packet** online, as well as download maps and road grade information from each site.

Recreation

Montana and Wyoming offer some of the premier recreational opportunities in the West, from mountain biking and fishing to boating and horseback riding. Vast areas of untouched land make for scenic beauty that can take a lifetime to explore, luring visitors back time and again to experience the outdoors.

In the summer, rivers come alive with whitewater boaters, and smaller streams entice fly-fishers seeking solitude. Wilderness areas and national forests offer miles of hiking trails, while national parks host visitors from around the world. Surprisingly, excellent golf courses are to be found here and can be relatively uncrowded, even in busy seasons. Look for unusual forms of the sport like the mown-meadow version (www.pasturegolf.com) in Casper, where golfers share the course with pronghorn and prairie dogs for only $2 per round. Lakes buzz with the sound of motorboats, campgrounds

© WYOMING TRAVEL & TOURISM

Montana and Wyoming are havens for skiers and snowboarders.

are full, and everyone seems to be outside doing something. Summers in the West are short, so people take advantage of them.

It's no surprise, then, that winters are particularly long, but those that live and visit Montana and Wyoming take advantage of it by enjoying some of the finest and least-crowded ski slopes in the country. Great snow and majestic mountain trails make snowmobiling extremely popular, and Nordic ski centers and trails can be found in most mountain areas. Ice fishing, dogsledding, and backcountry skiing and snowboarding are other activities that keep folks busy when the snow flies.

NATIONAL PARKS

With three of the country's most popular national parks located in Montana and Wyoming, this is where many visitors begin and end their journey. **Glacier National Park** (www.nps.gov/glac) falls entirely within Montana, and its Canadian counterpart, **Waterton Lakes National Park** (www.pc.gc.ca) is directly across the border and shares some of the same trails. Although most of **Yellowstone National Park** (www.nps.gov/yell) is in Wyoming, three of the park's entrances are located in Montana. Just below Yellowstone is **Grand Teton National Park** (www.nps.gov/grte). Each park offers a different type of beauty, from Glacier's receding namesakes and high alpine scenery to the majestic peaks of the Tetons and Yellowstone's striking geothermal features and abundant wildlife. Visitors will find a variety of accommodations in the parks, including rustic cabins, grand lodges, and tent and RV campgrounds. Popular activities include hiking, boating, fishing, and wildlife viewing. There are informational visitors centers and museums located in each park that offer excellent resources for history buffs.

The entrance fee in the summer for each park is $25 for automobiles, which is valid for seven days. Campground and other lodging fees are extra. Annual passes are available at a discounted rate for frequent park visitors.

Each state also has numerous national monuments, historical sites, trails, and recreation

Old Faithful Geyser at Yellowstone National Park

© DONNIE SEXTON

areas that fall within the national park system. Consult the National Park Service website (www.nps.gov) for more information on these areas. This site also has information on the numerous national monuments, historic sites, and trails in each state.

STATE PARKS

Montana has more than 40 state parks (http://fwp.mt.gov) that focus on both history and recreation. This diverse selection includes historic ghost towns, Native American cultural sites, and lakeside and riverside retreats. Twenty-four of the parks include campgrounds, which are typically open mid-May–mid-September. Camping fees are $15 per site, and many now offer yurts, tipis, and cabins for an additional fee. In late 2010 a measure was introduced to raise the overnight camping fees to $18; despite political wrangling, the increase could take effect as early as summer 2011. Cars with Montana license plates are allowed free admission to all state parks, while nonresidents are charged $5 per vehicle per park.

Wyoming manages more than 30 state parks and historical sites (http://wyoparks. state.wy.us), ranging from battlefields and museums to parks with hot mineral soaking springs. Daily use fees range $2–6, while overnight camping permits range $10–17. Sites can be reserved online no more than 90 days in advance for dates May 15–September 15.

NATIONAL FORESTS

Much of the public land in Montana and Wyoming's mountainous areas is administered by the U.S. Forest Service (www.fs.fed.us), including 17 million acres in Montana and 9 million acres in Wyoming. The Forest Service is a branch of the United States Department of Agriculture (USDA) and manages much of the nation's forest and rangelands. All national forests contain developed hiking and biking trails, and in the winter the roads and trails can often be used for cross-country skiing. Forest Service ranger stations are good places to obtain information on camping and recreation, while most sporting goods stores sell excellent maps that pertain to specific areas. **Beartooth Publishing** (www.beartoothpublishing.com) offers a popular series of waterproof maps that highlight national forest roads, trails, campgrounds, picnic areas, and fishing access sites for specific regions in Montana and Wyoming. For reference, Montana is located in Region 1 (Northern Region) and Wyoming is located in Region 2 (Rocky Mountain Region). You'll notice signs along the highways that indicate when you enter and leave a particular national forest.

Forest Service campgrounds are widespread in Montana and Wyoming and offer some of the finest camping available. Fees range free–$16, depending on the type of site and

---

FOREST SERVICE CABINS AND LOOKOUTS

Imagine waking up in your own rustic cabin, nestled in the woods next to a rambling stream. You stoke the fire, mix up a pot of cowboy coffee, and enjoy a sunny breakfast on the porch with a 10,000-foot peak looming overhead. There is no one else around. Now imagine that you have to pay less than $50 per night for this. Too good to be true? Well, thanks to the U.S. Forest Service cabin rental system, it isn't.

There are literally hundreds of these cabins in Montana and Wyoming, most situated in locations that some people pay millions of dollars to own a piece of. Many are old ranger stations, very few are still used by the Forest Service, and all have their own unique charms. Cabins come in all different shapes and sizes, from extremely remote backcountry sites and mountaintop fire lookouts to larger cabins with electricity and motor vehicle access. Either way, they offer an unparalleled way to enjoy the outdoors.

Each national forest has a number of cabins for rent. You can find a list for Montana at www. fs.fed.us/r1/recreation_r1/cabin_dir.shtml and for Wyoming at www.fs.fed.us/r2/recreation/ rentals. All cabins must be reserved at **www. recreation.gov,** where you can enter when you want to stay, and a list of available cabins will come up. Cabins range from $20 for small, two-room units to upward of $150 for larger rentals that sleep up to 10 people.

Cabins typically have bunk beds (bring your own bedding), wood stoves, wood, and pots and pans. Some have more, some have less. Toilet facilities are usually outside, and potable water is not always available. When you make your reservation, you'll get a list of what to bring as well as detailed directions.

Some of the more interesting rentals are historic fire lookouts, perched high atop a mountain with commanding views of the surrounding peaks. Sitting inside these lookouts, one can imagine backcountry rangers gazing out over the land trying to spot forest fires. These lookouts are especially beautiful at night, when you're out among the stars feeling like you're on top of the world. It's a must-do experience for those who want to get off the beaten path – and one you'll remember for a lifetime.

the amenities offered. Free sites are often very remote and offer limited services. The Forest Service also rents some rustic cabins and lookouts for $20–50 per night. These can be a great way to enjoy the outdoors, as most are in prime locations. These cabins, as well as most campgrounds, can be reserved in advance at www.recreation.gov.

WILDERNESS AREAS

There are 15 federally designated wilderness areas in Wyoming and 15 in Montana. These are roadless and closed to mechanized use, including mountain bikes. Wilderness areas generally offer solitude and amazing scenery, although some areas may be more heavily used than remote nonwilderness areas. Some wilderness areas may fall under Native American jurisdiction, so make sure you have the necessary permits before hiking, hunting, or fishing in these locations.

BLM PUBLIC LAND

The rest of the public land falls under management of the Bureau of Land Management (BLM), which offers everything from camping and boating to caving and backcountry scenic byways. The BLM manages multiple resources and uses, including energy and minerals; timber; forage; recreation; wild horse and burro herds; fish and wildlife habitat; wilderness areas; and archaeological, paleontological, and historical sites. There are 8 million acres of BLM land in Montana and more than 18 million acres in Wyoming. You can find out more about the BLM offerings at www.blm.gov.

HUNTING

Montana and Wyoming are popular destinations for those hunting elk, deer, bears, bighorn sheep, pronghorn, pheasants, and mountain lions. In 2009 both states also implemented a wolf season, but legislation is pending that may or may not allow the hunting of wolves to continue. Montana also has a bison hunt, for which the time, location, and quotas are determined each year.

For more information on hunting in Montana, contact the Montana Department of Fish, Widlife & Parks (http://fwp.mt.gov, 406/444-2535). In Wyoming, contact the Wyoming Game and Fish Department (http://gf.state.wy.us, 307/777-4600). If you would like to enlist a hunting guide, check the websites for recommendations on established outfitters or contact the **Montana Guides and Outfitters Association** (www.montanaoutfitters.org, 406/449-3578), or the **Wyoming Outfitters and Guides Association** (www.wyoga.org, 307/527-7453).

FISHING

Montana and Wyoming are known throughout the world as premier fishing destinations, mainly due to the popularity of fly fishing on beautiful Western rivers that flow throughout the region. Legendary trout streams like the Snake, Yellowstone, Madison, Big Horn, North Platte, Big Hole, and Gallatin lure anglers looking for lunkers, especially June–September. These rivers can be crowded during the summer, but luckily there are literally hundreds of other rivers and smaller streams on which to wet a line. And for diehard anglers, there are plenty of secret spots—think spring creeks—for excellent year-round fishing.

Lake fishing is also popular, with famed walleye fishing in Montana's Canyon Ferry and Fort Peck Reservoirs. In Wyoming, the Flaming Gorge and Buffalo Bill Reservoirs offer lake trout, kokanee salmon, and smallmouth bass. In addition, hundreds of backcountry lakes offer solitude and great fishing in a wilderness setting, and ice fishing is becoming increasingly popular during the winter.

In Wyoming, nonresident fishing permits cost $14 for one day or $92 for a full season. Resident fishing licenses cost $24 per year. With the exception of a one-day license, you'll also need to purchase a Wyoming Conservation Stamp for $12.50, which is good for one calendar year. Youth under 14 do not need a license if fishing with an adult who has a valid fishing license. Annual Montana fishing licenses cost $60 for nonresidents, or $15 for two consecutive days, plus a $10 Conservation License.

fishing one of the West's fabled waters from a float tube

Residents pay $18 for the season. Nonresidents under 15 do not need a license if accompanied by an adult who has a valid license. Check the websites for each state (http://fwp.mt.gov, http://gf.state.wy.us) for specific stamps you may need when fishing in certain waters. Fishing outfitters and stores sell licenses, as do many gas stations.

It's important to remember that you need a separate license to fish in Yellowstone National Park. Anglers 16 years of age and older are required to purchase either a $15 three-day, $20 seven-day, or $35 season permit. Permits are available at park ranger stations, stores, and many businesses in the Greater Yellowstone area.

Outfitters and guide services are abundant in Montana and Wyoming. Although it's not necessary, using one of these outfitters is a good idea if you're new to angling or want to hone your fly-fishing skills. Guides also know the hot spots on the rivers, can tell you what is hatching on any given day, and may have access to private sites along various streams.

Two excellent private websites for general fishing information and a good overview of the region are **Big Sky Fishing** (www.bigsky-fishing.com) and **Wyoming Fishing Network** (www.wyomingfishing.net).

For detailed fishing information, contact the **Montana Department of Fish, Widlife & Parks** (http://fwp.mt.gov, 406/444-2535) or the **Wyoming Game and Fish Department** (http://gf.state.wy.us, 307/777-4600).

TOUR OPERATORS

Wyoming and Montana cover a large geographic area, so it can be difficult to choose what to see in the time you have. There are many tour operators with well-researched itineraries that can cater to your specific needs and wishes. Many of these tours cater to families or a particular interest: biking, cultural and history tours, wildlife, and more. **Austin-Lehman Adventures** (800/575-1540, www.austinlehman.com), for whom this writer used to guide, offers numerous multiple-sport trips (think biking, hiking, horseback riding, and rafting on one trip) in the region, including Yellowstone and Grand Teton National Parks and Glacier National Park. The Montana-based **Adventure Cycling Association** (800/755-2453, www.adventurecycling.org) offers self-contained and supported bicycle tours in Montana and in Yellowstone and Grand Teton National Parks. **Backroads** (800/462-2848, www.backroads.com) offers multiple-sport tours throughout Greater Yellowstone and in Glacier National Park. **Big Wild Adventures** (406/848-7000, www.bigwildadventures.com) offers backpacking and canoeing trips in Montana, Wyoming, and in Yellowstone and Grand Teton National Parks. **Yellow Dog Fly-fishing Adventures** (888/777-5060, www.yellowdogflyfishing.com) offers custom trips around the area. In addition, there are operators in nearly every town that offer specific adventures, such as white-water rafting, horseback riding, fly fishing, hiking, biking and more.

SPECTATOR SPORTS
Rodeo

Most communities in Montana and Wyoming have rodeos at least once during the summer, and some of the larger towns like Jackson,

West Yellowstone also hosts a rodeo during each weekend in the summer June–August, and the **Professional Bull Riders** tour (719/242-2800, www.pbrnow.com) stops in Montana at Billings, Livingston, Helena, and Sidney, and in Wyoming at Cheyenne, Casper, and Afton.

Minor League Baseball

A popular spectator sport in Montana and Wyoming is professional minor league baseball. The **Pioneer League** (www.pioneer-league.com) has teams in Missoula (Arizona Diamondbacks), Helena (Milwaukee Brewers), Great Falls (Chicago White Sox), Billings (Cincinnati Reds), and Casper (Colorado Rockies). This rookie league plays about 70 games June–September, and most players are recent draft picks. Games often draw good crowds and are enjoyed by baseball aficionados who live in these states that have no major league sports teams.

College Football

Both the **Montana State University Bobcats** (www.msubobcats.com) and the **University of Montana Grizzlies** (www.montanagrizzlies.com) compete in the Football Championship Subdivision (formerly Division 1-AA) of college football. Both teams have won national championships, and there has been a fierce rivalry between the two teams since the first game was played in 1897. The Grizzlies have been one of the top teams in the country for the past two decades, and their games often draw crowds of more than 20,000 rowdy fans.

With only one university in the state, it's no great surprise that the NCAA Division I **University of Wyoming Cowboys** (www.wyomingathletics.com) draw rabid fans to their home games in Laramie. The annual "border war" match between Colorado State and Wyoming has been going on since 1899 and is considered the oldest (and probably among the fiercest) interstate rivalries west of the Mississippi River. Since 1968, the winner of that game takes home the Bronze Boot, one of the best-known and highly sought-after traveling trophies in college football.

rodeo at Crow Fair near Crow Agency, Montana

© DONNIE SEXTON

Cody, and West Yellowstone have nightly or weekly rodeos that showcase the sport's nonstop action. Some of the best rodeos are the smaller ones, often called "ranch rodeos," that feature real cowboys and cowgirls from area ranches competing against each other in real-life ranch activities. Many rodeos offer events for kids, such as greased-pig contests or wild-sheep riding. Generally speaking, rodeos are great family-oriented events.

Frontier Days (800/227-6336, www.cfdrodeo.com) in Cheyenne is the country's largest outdoor rodeo, with attendance of nearly 200,000 people each summer for the 10-day festival. The **Buffalo Bill Cody Stampede Rodeo** (307/587-5155, www.codystampederodeo.com) in Cody has had bucking broncs for more than 90 years, and the family-friendly **Cody Nite Rodeo** runs nightly June–August. Jackson Hole offers rodeos twice weekly, on Wednesday and Saturday nights, Memorial Day–Labor Day. The small town of Buffalo offers two weekly rodeos, including an all-women rodeo, **The Cowgirl Rodeo** on Tuesday nights.

Tips for Travelers

ACCOMMODATIONS

Since Montana and Wyoming are both big destinations for visitors, it's no surprise that there are a wide variety of lodging options available, from standard hotels and motels to luxury resorts and guest ranches. Generally speaking, all lodging is more expensive in the summer, and rooms fill rapidly—advance reservations are a must, especially around special events like Cheyenne's Frontier Days or Bozeman's Sweet Pea Festival. Rooms, cabins, and even campgrounds in the national parks fill up several months—if not longer—in advance. Shoulder seasons (spring and fall) offer reduced rates and thin crowds, while rooms at the ski resort lodges fill up fast in the winter but may be wide open during the summer.

Most larger towns have numerous choices for chain motels, which are typically clustered around the interstate exits. Gateway towns to Yellowstone and Grand Teton National Parks also have chain hotels, as well as a number of mom-and-pop motels sprinkled around town. Travelers used to standard hotels will be happy with these choices, but those that seek a more unique experience will want to try some of the smaller boutique hotels located in towns around the West. It just depends on whether you would rather stay in the usual Super 8 or sleep in a room that once accommodated Ernest Hemingway or Annie Oakley. An excellent resource is **Historic Hotels of the Rockies** (www.historic-hotels.com).

There are a number of bed-and-breakfasts in Montana and Wyoming, most of which are located in the higher-traffic tourist areas. Many are located on the banks of a river or nestled in the pine trees and are often great escapes from the busier hotel atmosphere. A fairly comprehensive listing can be found at **BnBFinder** (www.bnbfinder.com). Very few hostels exist in Montana and Wyoming, but

There are a variety of rustic accommodations throughout the region.

© XANTERRA PARKS & RESORT

LAWS OF THE WILD WEST

Both Montana and Wyoming were born of the Wild West, and in many cases there still exists a hands-off, "we don't need no government" mentality. While this may work in some areas, some outdated laws and rules are being updated or eliminated. First of all, there *is* a speed limit in Montana. While the limit used to be listed as "reasonable and prudent," it was changed in 1999 after the Montana Supreme Court deemed the law too vague. Currently, the speed limit for automobiles is 75 mph on Interstates, 70 mph on most two-lane highways, usually with lower speeds for night driving. Wyoming's laws are similar.

Believe it or not, it used to be legal to operate a vehicle in Montana and Wyoming with an open container of alcohol, whether you were driving or were just along for the ride. In states where distances are often measured in "six-packs," this was a big deal. After much public debate, the Montana law was finally changed in 2005, making it illegal for drivers and passengers to have any amount of open alcohol. Montana had the highest rate of alcohol-related fatalities per vehicle-mile traveled in the nation in 2002-2003, as reported by the National Highway Traffic Safety Administration, and the rates are still high. However, if you're taking a cab, bus, or limo, or riding in the back of a traveling motor home, you can still drink legally. Bottoms up!

Wyoming passed a weak open-container law in 2002, which became known as the "Here, hold my beer while I talk to this officer" law, but passed a stricter version, similar to Montana's, in 2007. It is taken much more seriously these days.

Speaking of alcohol, Wyoming is one of the few states where you can still buy a bottle from a drive-through liquor store – just don't open it in the car. And they no longer serve "to go" cocktails.

In case you're wondering, it's also illegal in Montana to have a sheep in the cab or your truck without a proper "chaperone," and certain animals caught running at large can be castrated if not claimed within five days – at the owner's expense. Montana is still open range country, so if you hit a black cow standing in the middle of the highway in the middle of the night, it's your responsibility to reimburse the rancher. And in Wyoming, make sure you close the gate if you cross a river or onto private land; otherwise it could cost you $750.

Hostels.com (www.hostels.com) has a list of what may be available.

Guest ranches range from traditional horse-and-cowboy dude ranches to luxury "glamping" (a portmanteau of *glamorous* and *camping*) resorts that offer spa services and high-end cuisine. Two excellent resources for those seeking a real Western working vacation are the **Montana Dude Ranchers' Association** (www.montanadra.com) and the **Wyoming Dude Ranchers' Association** (www.wyomingdra.com). Many of these are focused around horseback riding, fly fishing, and family activities and are often booked in weeklong blocks. In the winter, many of these ranches offer cross-country skiing, snowshoeing, or dogsledding.

Higher-end guest ranches are becoming very popular in Montana and Wyoming, offering guests a chance to experience a more rustic atmosphere with upscale amenities. These are typically set in remote locations with beautiful surroundings and are private, in some cases gated from public access. Typically these are the priciest accommodations, ranging from several hundred to $1,000 per night.

Cabins and other vacation rentals are becoming increasingly popular, as many travelers are looking for that Western cabin experience. These can range from rustic—just beds, no plumbing—to luxurious—down linens, a rock fireplace—and are perhaps the best way to stay. Sites like **VRBO** (www.vrbo.com) offer private homes and cabins for rent while many resorts offer nightly cabin rentals.

There are plenty of RV and tent camping

sites in Montana and Wyoming for those on the road. From national forest campgrounds to large private RV resorts, there is something for everyone. RV campers will find private campgrounds in most towns, and most national forest campgrounds have room for all but the longest RVs. It's generally legal to camp on national forest land, unless you see a sign indicating that overnight camping isn't allowed. For a real backcountry experience, drive on a Forest Service road until you find a nice campsite, pull over, and set up camp. Not only is it often scenic, it's free.

FOOD

One thing is certain: This is meat-and-potatoes country, which can be great for those craving a good steak, as you can find one in almost every town. Locally raised beef can be found on the menus of many restaurants, and bison is becoming increasingly popular as well. If you haven't had it, it's highly recommended, and beef lovers will generally enjoy bison as well. A good bison burger or tenderloin is hard to

beat. Wild-game dishes, mostly elk and venison, are also found at finer establishments, with pheasant occasionally on the menu. If you enjoy trying new fare, this could be an exciting option.

With all the meat on the menu, you would think that vegetarians would be out of luck when dining out, but surprisingly, options abound, especially at higher-end restaurants. The "eat local" campaigns are in full swing out West, and many of the best restaurants get as much of their food as possible from local and regional growers. Despite being seriously landlocked, seafood is no longer a bad idea in either state. Fresh seafood is flown in from Hawaii or Seattle daily in many places, and it is generally pretty good. Yes, there are even fresh sushi bars in Montana and Wyoming, and some are darn tasty. Innovative cuisine can be found in every major town, but certainly Jackson, Bozeman, Bigfork, Whitefish, Missoula, Billings, and Cheyenne stand out.

Does either state have a standout meal? Well, not really. Montana is famous for its

Hamburger lovers will have much to sample in Montana and Wyoming.

huckleberries and Flathead cherries, so a good pie or milk shake is a must. Pasties in Butte are considered indispensable regional cuisine, and Rocky Mountain oysters (calf testicles) are usually breaded and fried—not exactly gourmet, and not exactly popular or necessarily worth trying. Delicious Indian tacos load the ingredients onto fry bread, and good Mexican and Chinese restaurants can be found throughout the region.

You'll also see the standard fast-food establishments, especially near the interstates, but avoid these and try a local restaurant instead. You'll find the best food at the most random of places—and it will certainly be a more culinary and cultural experience. And remember, folks out here are friendly—if you stop and ask someone about the best place in town, they will happily point you in the right direction and will probably know the owner.

If you are traveling the back roads and small towns and get tired of ordinary bar-type food (burgers, burgers, and more burgers), consider a quest to find the best chicken-fried steak or the best piece of pie. Sometimes a personal challenge can relieve the boredom of limited options. Plus, who doesn't want an excuse to eat homemade pie at every opportunity?

CANADIAN CROSSINGS AND CUSTOMS

Of the many roads that cross into Canada from Montana, only three border crossings are open 24 hours. U.S. 93 (Roosville) and I-15 (Sweet Grass) are the busiest, while the remote crossing near Raymond on Highway 16 sees much less traffic. U.S. citizens are now required to carry passports when crossing into Canada; Canadians entering the United States must have a passport, a NEXUS card, or a birth certificate with a driver's license. Citizens of other countries must show their passports and appropriate visas, and may be asked to prove that they have sufficient funds for their length of stay. U.S. citizens returning to the United States by air must present a U.S. passport.

When heading north into Canada, travelers age 21 and older can import, duty free, a maximum of 40 ounces of liquor or 24 twelve-ounce cans of beer or ale into the country as personal luggage. Up to 50 cigars and 200 cigarettes may be allowed entry duty-free for those age 18 or over. U.S. visitors spending more than 48 hours in Canada may bring $400 worth of duty-free goods back with them, or $200 if staying less than 48 hours. If you're carrying more than $10,000, you'll need to declare the amount. Handguns can't be taken into Canada, although hunting rifles are allowed.

TRAVELERS WITH DISABILITIES

For the most part, Montana and Wyoming comply with state and federal guidelines for handicapped access. Most hotels offer accessible rooms, and the national parks and even some state parks feature accessible trails. However, it's important to remember that many parts of both states are rural, and some features may be outdated, less accessible, or nonexistent.

WOMEN TRAVELERS

Overall, Montana and Wyoming can be exciting for a woman traveling alone. For the most part, the West is full of independent and strong women, and you won't seem out of place in most areas. Outgoing and talkative women—as well as men—will feel right at home. Folks are pretty friendly and accommodating around these parts, and in general they like to meet people from other places. Of course, there is always the occasional weirdo, so if a place or a person makes you uncomfortable, the best thing to do is just leave. Use the same precautions and common sense that you would at home.

GAY AND LESBIAN TRAVELERS

It's safe to say that many people in Montana and Wyoming are socially conservative, and same-sex public displays of affection will be less than welcome. You shouldn't necessarily anticipate discrimination or hostility if you are gay, but you'll want to be aware of your surroundings. You might not think much of expressing yourself at a back-road Montana or Wyoming bar, but you never know what the group of cowboys in the corner is thinking. Sadly, this is where Matthew Shepard was brutally murdered in 1998 for no other reason than that he was gay. Montana and Wyoming still have a long way to go in terms of recognizing and celebrating alternative lifestyles. In general, "don't ask, don't tell" is the safest policy to assume when traveling here.

That being said, there are thriving—although often underground—gay communities in many Montana and Wyoming towns, particularly college towns like Missoula, Bozeman, and Laramie. Two excellent resources for gay and lesbian travelers are the **Western Montana Gay and Lesbian Community Center** (406/543-2224, www.gaymontana.org) and the **University of Wyoming's Rainbow Resource Center** (307/766-3478, http://uwadmnweb.uwyo.edu/RRC).

Health and Safety

While medical services and health care in many of the larger Montana and Wyoming towns are excellent—and in some cases on par with bigger cities—it's important to remember that when traveling around, you'll mostly likely be far away from emergency medical services. Rural and mountainous highways are especially troublesome, as cell-phone coverage can be spotty. Most small towns have a local clinic, and there are services in the national parks. Refer to specific areas of the text for emergency numbers, and remember that calling 911 doesn't always work in many rural areas.

In general, **weather, altitude,** and **insect bites** pose the greatest risk traveling here. The summer sun can get extremely hot, and it is easy to get dehydrated, so make sure to drink plenty of water during the day. Hiking—and just walking, for some people—can be a strenuous activity as the altitude increases. It's best to carry plenty of food and water, and take your time getting to your destination. The earliest and most obvious sign of altitude-related health problems is a headache, and the best remedy is drinking water and moving to a lower elevation if possible.

The common insect nuisances are mosquitoes and ticks. While Montana and Wyoming mosquitoes rarely carry any diseases, they can be annoying at certain times during the summer. So far, West Nile virus has shown up only in a few nonhuman cases in Wyoming. Carry bug repellent with DEET, especially when hiking or camping near water. Ticks can pose a small threat of Rocky Mountain fever or Lyme disease, and they seem to have become more pervasive in the last 10 years or so. It's a good idea to check every part of your skin after a day of hiking or fishing outdoors—places where you might encounter underbrush, dense trees, and grassy meadows. If you find a tick with its head stuck in your skin, pull gently with tweezers or your fingers until the tick works its way out. Don't forget to check your pets too.

A common backcountry ill is **giardia,** sometimes called "beaver fever," a microscopic parasite that lives in mountain streams and can wreak havoc in your intestinal tract. Avoid drinking unfiltered or untreated water directly from streams, rivers, springs, or lakes. Carry a water filter or water-purifying tablets (iodine or similar products), and you'll have nothing to worry about.

If you're camping or staying in a cabin, **hantavirus** can be a concern. Hantavirus is a potentially fatal disease caused by contact with rodent droppings, particularly those of deer mice. Symptoms include fever, muscle aches, coughing, and difficulty breathing. Campers should avoid sleeping on bare ground, and avoid cabins if you see signs of rodents. For more information visit the Centers for Disease Control and Prevention (www.cdc.gov).

Winter poses different types of health concerns, namely **hypothermia and frostbite.**

If you or someone in your party shows any signs of hypothermia—uncontrollable shivering, slurred speech, loss of coordination—get them out of the wind and inside immediately. If you're camping, a dry sleeping bag is your best bet. It's a good idea to dress in layers, avoid cotton clothing, always bring a hat, and—most important—make good decisions before you put yourself in a situation where you could be stranded in the wind and cold. If you're outside in the winter, a sign of frostbite is the whitening and hardening of the skin. The best way to warm the affected area is with other skin, but avoid warming it too quickly because thawing can be quite painful.

WEATHER

The old saying is a tad cliché but nonetheless often true: If you don't like the weather in Montana or Wyoming, just wait five minutes. What this means to the traveler is that weather in this part of the West can change dramatically in an unbelievably short time. In the summer, extreme heat can dehydrate the human body rapidly, and in the winter, extreme cold can render your body useless in a matter of minutes. Sudden changes in the weather can happen at any time of the year in mountainous areas. It can snow, sleet, hail, and rain at a moment's notice. If you're heading into the backcountry or getting ready for a three-day river float, check the forecast, but don't rely on it; plan for the worst with extra gear and plenty of food and water.

In general, Montana and Wyoming have a semiarid climate. There is enough moisture at certain times of the year, but summers are typically dry and warm, with July–August being the hottest. Mountainous areas see heavy snowfall during the winter (to the delight of skiers), while the eastern part of each state can seem downright desertlike much of the year.

WILDLIFE

Although many people visit Montana and Wyoming for the abundant wildlife, with so much human interaction, safety is a real concern. A general rule of thumb is *never* to approach wildlife, no matter what the situation is. It's just a bad idea, and each year people are hurt or killed because they ignore this basic rule. Not only are they putting themselves in harm's way, they are often precipitating imminent doom for the animal as well. The old adage, "A fed bear is a dead bear," can be applied universally to wildlife.

SAFETY IN BEAR COUNTRY

Grizzly bears and black bears live in many parts of Montana and Wyoming, and although encounters are rare, it is necessary to learn what to do in case it happens to you. It is also important to know how to avoid the situation in the first place. No method is absolutely foolproof, but with caution and attentiveness you can avoid most of the common mistakes that lead to bear encounters.

When out in the backcountry, it's the unexpected bear encounter you really want to avoid. The best way to do this is to let them know you are present. Make noise in areas of dense cover and blind spots on hiking or biking trails. Immediately move away from any animal carcass you come across, as there may be a bear nearby protecting it. Avoid hiking or biking in the early morning or at dusk, and travel in larger groups; the more of you there are hiking together, the more likely the bear will sense you and move away. Making noise is a great way to let bears know you are near, and in most cases they will be long gone before you have the chance to get a glimpse of them. Dogs can provoke bears, so it's best to leave them at home, and never leave food out.

If you're camping in an area frequented by bears, look for bear signs (waste, overturned rocks, decimated fallen timber, claw marks and hair on trees) around the campsite. Since bears are attracted to all kinds of odors—food, toothpaste, soap, deodorant—your cooking, eating, and food storage area should be at least 50 yards from your tent. It's tempting to bring tasty items like sausage, ham, tuna, and bacon with you, but these smell good to bears too. Freeze-dried foods are your best bet. Store foods in airtight bags, and be sure to hang

Ursus horribilus, grizzly bear

all food at least 12–15 feet off the ground and away from tree trunks. Some designated campsites have bear storage containers or food storage poles.

Carrying **pepper spray** (sold in most sporting goods stores) is a must in bear country, and it has been proven useful in fending off bear attacks. These sprays only work at close range (10–30 feet) and can be quickly dissipated in the wind or sometimes blow back in your face. Carry the spray in a holster or on a belt across your chest for easy access. It's important to note that these spray canisters are not allowed on commercial airplanes, they expire after a certain date, and they should not be left in a very hot place like a closed car. Also, test your container every now and then in light or no wind to make sure it works.

If you happen to encounter a bear, and it notices you, try not to panic or make any sudden moves. Do not run—bears can run more than 40 mph in short bursts—or try to climb a tree. Make yourself visible by moving out into the open so the bear can identify you. Don't

stare directly at the bear, but talking in a low voice may convince the bear you are human. If the bear is sniffing the air or standing on its hind legs, it's most likely trying to identify you. If it's woofing and posturing, this could be a challenge. Stand your ground if the bear charges; most charges are bluffs, where the bear will stop short and wander away.

If a grizzly does charge and knocks you to the ground, curl up in the fetal position with your hands wrapped behind your neck and your elbows tucked over your face. Keeping your backpack on may protect you somewhat. Remain as still as possible, as bears will often only sniff or nip you and leave. Remain on the ground until you know the bear has vacated the area.

In general, black bears are more common and seem to have more interaction with people. In many places they can be a nuisance—getting into garbage, breaking into homes—but don't think that they are not dangerous. Black bears will generally try to avoid you and are easily scared away, but if you encounter an attacking or aggressive bear, this usually means it views you as food. In this case, most experts recommend fighting back with whatever means possible: large rocks or sticks, yelling, and shouting.

In the rare event that a bear attacks sleeping campers in tents at night, as tragically happened at the Soda Butte campground near Cooke City in July 2010, defend yourself as aggressively as you can. In these circumstances, bears are viewing you as prey and may give up if you fight back. Never play dead, and keep pepper spray and a flashlight handy.

Before you go into the backcountry, brush up on your **bear identification.** You can't tell what kind of bear you see by its color alone. Grizzlies are often larger and have a trademark hump at the top of their neck. Grizzlies have more of a dish-shaped face profile, compared to a straighter profile of black bears.

OTHER WILDLIFE

Although bears get the majority of the press, there are other animals that you need to be aware of when traveling around Montana and Wyoming. **Moose** are huge animals that are prone to sudden charges when surprised, especially females traveling with young. If you travel through Yellowstone National Park, you'll encounter numerous **bison,** large animals with sharp horns. Although it may be tempting to walk up to them, avoid doing so. While they are not vicious, bison can charge if provoked and have maimed and even killed visitors in the past. Be aware that these lumbering beasts can sprint the length of a football field in six seconds and can leap a six-foot fence. Likewise, elk in the park can seem downright docile, but it's important to remember not to approach them.

Mountain lions generally keep a low profile, but as humans encroach on their habitat, encounters are becoming more frequent in the West. Most attacks have been on unattended children, and they rarely provoke adults. If you happen to find yourself in a situation with a mountain lion, be aggressive and fight back if necessary, or throw rocks and sticks to try to make it go away.

Rattlesnakes can be found in the central and eastern parts of Montana and Wyoming, especially in the drier prairies. Rattlesnake bites are rarely fatal (less than 4 percent when antivenin is used in time), and they generally avoid humans. Be careful where you step when hiking around these areas, and pay attention if children are with you. If you surprise or step on a rattlesnake—chances are you'll hear its trademark rattle before you do—it may coil and strike. Any bite from a rattlesnake should be regarded as a life-threatening medical emergency that requires immediate hospital treatment by trained professionals.

With all of the incredible wildlife viewing opportunities around Montana and Wyoming, it can be easy for some people to get complacent when taking pictures or hiking around. Treat all wildlife with respect and care, and never feed or approach any type of wild animal. If you are lucky enough to see many of these critters, observe them in their natural habitat and then carry on. The last thing you want is to become a statistic.

Information and Services

TOURIST INFORMATION

Both states have excellent information available for those interested in traveling to the region. Most chambers of commerce and visitors centers (listed for each town in this book) are good sources when driving around, but the online sites are where you should start your research. For Wyoming, visit **Wyoming Tourism** (307/777-7777, www.wyomingtourism.org) for the latest information. You can check out the various towns, attractions, and events, as well as order a **free vacation guide.**

For Montana, **Travel Montana** (800/847-4868, www.visitmt.com) is the state's official tourism organization for vacation information and to order the annual free **Montana Vacation Planner.** Montana has divided the state into six different tourism regions, and specific booklets are available for each one.

In truth, having spent a great deal of time on both websites, I can say with confidence that the Montana site is beautifully organized and easy to follow. You can easily find subjects as vast as "accommodations" and as narrow as "fishing" broken down by region. The Wyoming site is much harder to navigate as you cannot often refine categories beyond such broad strokes as "Things to Do." Instead, many of the cities, counties, and regions of Wyoming have well-organized comprehensive sites, making them an excellent place to start.

COMMUNICATIONS AND MEDIA

Although Montana and Wyoming may be remote, cell-phone coverage is overall very good and getting better each year. That being said, rural and mountainous areas may have spotty coverage. Indeed, check the storefronts in some of the smaller towns in the region (I'm looking at you, Augusta) and you'll see that cellphone service is just being brought to the area. Verizon is the main carrier, although AT&T plans to move into these states soon. Many coffee shops and public libraries have computers available for Internet use, and most larger towns have business centers with computers and fax machines.

High-speed Internet connections are generally available, but the service is often slower and more problematic compared to larger metropolitan areas. Wireless Internet is frequently offered at coffee shops, libraries, hotels, and other public places.

Media

USA Today is the one national newspaper that can be found throughout the region, and **The Wall Street Journal** is also popular. If you want a national newspaper like **The New York Times** or **The Washington Post,** many towns still have smaller newspaper and magazine stores, but you may get a copy that is a few days old at best. Large grocery stores typically have regional dailies. In Montana, the larger dailies are the **Missoulian,** the **Great Falls Tribune,** and the **Billings Gazette,** although every small town seems to have at least a weekly newspaper, which can be a great source of information on local events and attractions. Other Montana publications to look out for include the **Lively Times,** a monthly statewide guide to entertainment, and **Montana Magazine,** a good roundup of life in Montana. The **Montana Quarterly** and **Big Sky Journal** are excellent literary reads and feature well-written articles about the Treasure State and the Greater Yellowstone area.

In Wyoming, the larger daily newspapers include the **Casper Star-Tribune** (the only statewide newspaper), the **Wyoming Tribune Eagle** in Cheyenne, and the **Laramie Boomerang.** Other popular papers include the **Jackson Hole News & Guide** and Worland's **Northern Wyoming Daily News.**

One of best sources of local and national news is **National Public Radio,** which can be heard in even the smallest of towns in both states. **Montana Public Radio** covers Western Montana (www.mtpr.org), while **Yellowstone Public Radio** (www.ypr.org) covers the rest of the state as well as northern Wyoming. **Wyoming Public Radio** (www.wyomingpublicradio.net) also covers about 80 percent of the state.

RESOURCES

Suggested Reading

MONTANA

Information and Travel

Davis, Seabring. *Food Lovers' Guide to Montana.* Guilford, CT: Globe Pequot Press, 2010. Beautifully written and broken down into the state's six regions, this smart little book guides foodies to the state's best restaurants, farmers markets and stands, specialty stores, local producers, and food-related events.

Fifer, Barbara, and Vicky Soderberg. *Along the Trail with Lewis and Clark,* second edition. Helena: Farcountry Press and *Montana Magazine,* 2001. Full of colorful maps, this is the most in-depth guide to the Lewis and Clark Trail.

Green, Stewart M. *Scenic Driving: Back Country Byways.* Helena: Falcon Press, 2001. This book covers 45 jaw-droppingly beautiful drives around the West.

Merrill, Andrea, and Judy Jacobson. *Montana Almanac.* Helena: Falcon Publishing, 1997. Written by a former legislative researcher and a former state senator, this tome compiles thousands of interesting facts about Big Sky Country.

Montanans Inc. *Montana: A Profile in Pictures.* New York: Fleming Publishing, 1941. What I love about this tiny little picture book is that so little has changed in more than 70 years. Swap out newer cars, modern fashions, and perhaps some racier skis, and nearly every one of these photographs could have been taken in the last decade.

Spencer, Janet. *Montana Trivia.* Helena: Riverbend Publishing, 2005. A quirky and fascinating compendium of factoids about Montana, this book covers geography, history, entertainment, sports, arts, science, and nature.

History and Culture

Ambrose, Stephen E. *Undaunted Courage.* New York: Simon & Schuster, 1996. This has long been considered the definitive account of Lewis and Clark's extraordinary expedition.

Cheney, Roberta Carkeek. *Names on the Face of Montana.* Missoula: Mountain Press Publishing, 2003. In its eight printing, this is a classic for anyone who wants to know the stories behind names like Freeze Out Lake, Ekalaka, Deadman's Basin, and more than 1,000 others.

Fritz, Harry, Mary Murphy, and Robert Swartout. *Montana Legacy: Essays on History, People and Place.* Helena: Montana Historical Society Press, 2002. A wonderful collection of essays reflecting the state's surprising diversity.

Horner, John R. (Jack), and James Gorman. *Digging Dinosaurs.* New York: Harper Collins, 1990. A popular science book for good reason, it redefined the way we think of dinosaurs as parents.

Howard, Joseph Kinsey. *Montana: High, Wide and Handsome.* Lincoln, NE: University of Nebraska Press, 1943. Before Big Sky, this compelling text was the source of one of Montana's earliest tag lines.

Hungry Wolf, Adolf, and Beverly Hungry Wolf, compilers. *Indian Tribes of the Northern Rockies.* Skookumchuck, Canada: Good Medicine Books, 1989. With historic photos and copies of treaties, this volume offers a well-rounded cultural and historic overview of numerous tribes.

MacGregor, Carol Lynn, editor. *The Journals of Patrick Gass.* Missoula: Mountain Press Publishing, 1997. A well-edited and annotated version of the journals of Patrick Gass, a member of the Lewis and Clark expedition, this work focuses on the day-to-day activities of the Corps of Discovery.

Malone, Michael P., editor. *Montana Century: 100 Years in Pictures and Words.* Helena: Falcon Publishing, 1999. This gorgeous coffee-table book look at the faces, places, and events that shaped Montana in the 20th century.

Malone, Michael P., Richard B. Roeder, and William L. Lang. *Montana: A History of Two Centuries.* Seattle and London: University of Washington Press, 1991. First written in 1976, this authoritative history of Montana deals with prehistory, Native American studies, ethnic history, women's studies, oral history, and contemporary political history.

Munn, Debra D. *Big Sky Ghosts: Eerie True Tales of Montana,* volume 2. Boulder, CO: Pruett Publishing, 1994. A fun read for ghost lovers, this short volume spins tales of 16 favorite Montana ghosts.

Spritzer, Don. *Roadside History of Montana.* Missoula: Mountain Press Publishing, 1999. Organized insightfully by natural travel routes, this book is filled with nice overviews of towns and regions as well as interesting little anecdotes.

Literature

Bass, Rick. *Winter: Notes from Montana.* Boston: Houghton Mifflin, 1991. Written by one of the region's great nature writers, this lovely book celebrates the quietude of Montana's longest season.

Blew, Mary Clearman. *All But the Waltz.* Norman, OK: University of Oklahoma Press, 2001. Clearman Blew is a strong voice for central Montana in this hauntingly beautiful collection of essays spanning five generations of her family in the state.

Fromm, Pete. *Indian Creek Chronicles: A Winter in the Bitterroot.* New York: Picador, 2003. Hired to tend salmon eggs during winter in Montana 40 miles from the nearest road, this memoir is an exquisite introduction to the icy solitude of a Montana winter.

Guthrie, A. B. Jr. *The Big Sky.* Boston: Houghton Mifflin, 1947. This timeless novel about three frontiersmen gave the state its well-known moniker.

Hugo, Richard. *Making Certain It Goes On.* New York: W. W. Norton, 1984. A collection of Hugo's poems, this is an absolute classic.

Kittredge, William, and Annick Smith. *The Last Best Place: A Montana Anthology.* Helena: The Montana Historical Society Press, 1988. This is the ultimate reader's guide to Montana literature, with nearly 1,200 pages of literary selections spanning Native American stories and myths to contemporary fiction and poetry with everything in between.

Maclean, Norman. *A River Runs Through It.* Chicago: University of Chicago Press, 1976. The book that launched a thousand drift boats.

Maclean, Norman. *Young Men and Fire.* Chicago and London: University of Chicago Press, 1992. The posthumously published work by the author of *A River Runs Through It,* this nonfiction work about the fire that claimed 12 airborne firefighters is considered a modern tragedy and a magnificent piece of literature.

McMurtry, Larry. *Lonesome Dove.* New York: Pocket Books, 1985. Another can't-miss classic about the legendary Texas Cattle drives.

Stegner, Wallace. *Collected Stories of Wallace Stegner.* New York: Random House, 1990. A wonderful collection of Stegner's masterful fiction.

Stegner, Wallace. *Where the Bluebird Sings to the Lemonade Springs.* New York: Penguin Books, 1992. A classic and luminous Western writer, Wallace Stegner writes about the land and the human condition in these 16 brilliant essays.

Recreation

Fischer, Hank, and Carol Fischer. *Paddling Montana.* Billings and Helena: Falcon Press, 2008. Detailed paddling info for 32 rivers.

Grossenbacher, Brian, and Jenny Grossenbacher. *Fly Fishing Montana: A No Nonsense Guide to Top Waters.* Tucson: No Nonsense Fly Fishing Guidebooks, 2007. A great guide covering the entire state.

Lomax, Becky. *Moon Montana, Wyoming & Idaho Camping.* Berkeley, CA: Avalon Travel, 2010. Hands down the best guide for camping in the region.

Schneider, Bill, and Russ Schneider. *Hiking Montana.* Helena and Guilford, CT: Falcon Publishing and Globe Pequot Press, 2004. The 25th anniversary edition, this hiking guide offers excellent advice, clear directions, and descriptive details, plus great maps for hiking trails across the state.

Sedlack, Elaine. *The Nordic Skier's Guide to Montana.* Billings and Helena: Falcon Press Publishing, 1980. A little outdated in terms of specific trail information, this book, which has since been updated several times, gives readers a great launching point for Nordic adventures in Montana.

Straub, Patrick (Paddy). *Montana on the Fly: An Angler's Guide.* Woodstock, VT: Countryman Press, 2008. A comprehensive guide to waters and outfitters.

Magazines

A longtime literary publication for Montana and the Northern Rockies, including Wyoming and Idaho, *Big Sky Journal* (subscriptions 800/731-1227, www.bigskyjournal.com) is published six times annually and includes special issues devoted to fly fishing and the arts. Regular features by well-known writers focus on ranching and rodeo, hunting, fishing, art, and architecture. Also published six times annually, *Montana Magazine* (subscriptions 888/666-8624, www.montanamagazine.com) approaches life in Montana with broad strokes.

Montana Outdoors (subscriptions 800/678-6668, www.fwp.mt.gov/mtoutdoors) is an excellent publication produced by Montana Fish, Wildlife & Parks, focusing on the state's natural resources, including fishing and hunting. The magazine has won countless awards and is a fantastic resource for natural historians. You can read the current issue online.

A publication of Bozeman's local paper, *Montana Quarterly* (subscriptions 800/275-0401, www.themontanaquarterly.com) is a beautiful magazine that tackles the issues of the state—politics, science, arts, and culture—head on.

For history buffs, there is no better publication than *Montana: The Magazine of Western History* (subscriptions 800/243-9900, www.mhs.mt.gov/pub/magazine), produced quarterly by the Montana Historical Society.

Maps

Montana Atlas & Gazetteer. Yarmouth, ME: Delorme Publishing, 2004. The most indispensable map book you'll find, these topographic maps cover roads and trails all over the state.

THE NATIONAL PARKS: GRAND TETON, YELLOWSTONE, AND GLACIER
History

Guthrie, C. W. *Glacier National Park, The First 100 Years*. Helena: Farcountry Press, 2008. A marvelous volume compiled to celebrate the park's centennial in 2010, this book features exquisite photos and artwork in addition to compelling history.

Haines, Aubrey. *The Yellowstone Story: A History of Our First National Park*. Yellowstone National Park, WY, and Niwot, CO: The Yellowstone Association for Natural Science, History, and Education and The University Press of Colorado, 1996. This comprehensive volume tackles the park's early years, from primitive exploration to early development.

Righter, Robert W. *Crucible for Conservation: The Struggle for Grand Teton National Park*. Moose, WY: Grand Teton Natural History Association, 1982. This gripping history makes one grateful that things worked out the way they did.

Saunders, Richard L., editor. *A Yellowstone Reader: The National Park in Folklore, Popular Fiction, and Verse*. Salt Lake City: University of Utah Press, 2003. A core sample of historical literature that spans the late nineteenth century through the 1980s.

Whittlesey, Lee H. *Death in Yellowstone: Accidents and Foolhardiness in the First National Park*. Lanham, MD: Roberts Rinehart Publishers, 1995. Who doesn't love reading about a little gore and some good old-fashioned stupidity when traveling through Yellowstone?

Natural History

Murie, Margaret, and Olaus Johan Murie. *Wapiti Wilderness*. Boulder, CO: University of Colorado Press, 1985. A magnificent read by two of the region's now deceased but beloved conservationists, the chapters alternate between his work studying elk and her descriptions of their fascinating life together.

Phillips, Michael K., and Douglas W. Smith. *The Wolves of Yellowstone*. Stillwater, MN: Voyageur Press, 1996. Told with fabulous color photos and intimate details by the two men who oversaw the project, this book tells the story of the wolves' reintroduction to Yellowstone in 1995.

Schreier, Carl. *A Field Guide to Yellowstone's Geysers, Hot Springs and Fumaroles*. Moose, WY: Homestead Publishing, 1999. This slightly larger-than-your-pocket book is the authoritative guide to Yellowstone's best-known thermal features, with information about the origin of their names, regular and irregular activity, statistics, and anecdotal histories.

Schullery, Paul. *Searching for Yellowstone: Ecology and Wonder in the Last Wilderness*. Helena: Montana Historical Society Press, 2004. A fascinating and compelling environmental history of the world's first national park.

Schullery, Paul. *Yellowstone Bear Tales*. Boulder, CO: Roberts Rinehart Publishers, 1991. Hair-raising accounts of bear encounters by one of the park's most respected natural historians.

Wilkinson, Todd. *Yellowstone Wildlife: A Watcher's Guide*. Minocqua, WI: NorthWord Press, 1992. An excellent guide for where to see wildlife, with fascinating must-know information about each creature.

Recreation

Henry, Jeff. *Yellowstone Winter Guide*. Boulder, CO: Roberts Rinehart Publishers, 1998. This full-color guide is a must for travelers seeing Yellowstone in its quietest and arguably most magical season.

Lilly, Bud, and Paul Schullery. *Bud Lilly's Guide to Fly Fishing the New West.* Portland, OR: Frank Amato Publications, 2000. Written by the father of Western trout fishing and one of the West's most respected natural historians, this book weaves Lilly's personal history as an angler, guide, and conservationist with the history of fly fishing in the region along with sage advice.

Lomax, Becky. *Moon Glacier National Park.* Berkeley, CA: Avalon Travel, 2011. The best resource for visitors to this phenomenal park.

Marschall, Mark C. *Yellowstone Trails: A Hiking Guide.* Yellowstone National Park, WY: Yellowstone National Park Association, 1999. Another great hiking guide, this one includes descriptions of more than 100 trails ranging from day hikes to backpack trips.

Nystrom, Andrew Dean, and Morgan Konn. *Top Trails Yellowstone & Grand Tetons: Must-do Hikes for Everyone.* Berkeley, CA: Wilderness Press, 2009. This book covers 45 wonderful hikes from half-mile jaunts to 30-mile treks.

Pitcher, Don. *Moon Yellowstone & Grand Teton.* Berkeley, CA: Avalon Travel, 2011. The ultimate guide to what to see and how to see it in these two national parks.

Schneider, Bill. *Hiking Yellowstone National Park.* Helena: Falcon Publishing and Globe Pequot Press, 1997. This excellent hiking guide offers short, moderate, and long hikes throughout Yellowstone.

Watters, Ron. *Winter Tales and Trails: Skiing, Snowshoeing and Snowboarding in Idaho, the Grand Tetons and Yellowstone National Park.* Pocatello, ID: Great Rift Press, 1997. Intertwining guide advice with great stories, you'll wish Ron was along for the trip.

WYOMING
Description and Travel

Kilgore, Gene. *Gene Kilgore's Ranch Vacations.* Berkeley, CA: Avalon Travel, 2005. The best resource for finding a ranch vacation perfectly suited to you and your family.

Pitcher, Don. *Moon Wyoming.* Berkeley, CA: Avalon Travel, 2006. The best guide to the state, bar none.

Roberts, Stephen L., David L. Roberts, and Phil Roberts. *Wyoming Almanac.* Laramie: Skyline West Press, 1997. Every factoid you could ever want to know about Wyoming.

History

Ehrlich, Gretel. *Heart Mountain.* New York: Penguin, 1989. A historical novel by one of Wyoming's best-loved writers, set in the Heart Mountain Relocation Camp.

Haines, Aubrey L. *Historic Sites Along the Oregon Trail.* St. Louis: Patrice Press, 1994. A nice look at the historic sites along the trail written by a well-respected historian.

Harris, Burton. *John Colter: His Years in the Rockies.* Lincoln, NE: University of Nebraska Press, 1993. This book, first published in 1952, provides the best look at early explorer and legendary figure John Colter, considered the first nonnative to lay eyes on Yellowstone.

Larson, T. A. *History of Wyoming.* Lincoln, NE: University of Nebraska Press, 1990. This massive volume covers it all and is considered the best single-volume history of the state in print.

McPhee, John. *Rising from the Plains.* New York: Farrar, Straus and Giroux, 1987. McPhee masterfully parallels Wyoming's geology with frontier history.

Moulton, Candy. *Roadside History of Wyoming.* Missoula: Mountain Press Publishing, 1995. An excellent guide organized by driving routes across the state.

Munn, Debra D. *Ghosts on the Range: Eerie True Tales of Wyoming.* Boulder, CO: Pruett Publishing, 1991. A fun read for ghost lovers, this short volume rounds up ghost stories from across the state.

Murray, Robert A. *The Bozeman Trail: Highway of History.* Boulder, CO: Pruett Publishing, 1989. A short but meaty volume on the bloodiest settler route of them all.

Russell, Don. *The Lives and Legends of Buffalo Bill.* Norman, OK: University of Oklahoma Press, 1979. When it comes to biographies of the legendary figure, this is the bible.

Trenholm, Virginia Cole. *The Arapahoes, Our People.* Norman, OK: The University of Oklahoma Press, 1970. This compelling history of the Arapaho tribe follows their ways of life from prehistoric Minnesota and Canada through the 20th century in Montana, Wyoming, and Oklahoma.

Urbanek, Mae Bobb. *Wyoming Place Names.* Missoula: Mountain Press Publishing, 1988. The best guide for those who want to know the stories behind names like Bessemer Bend and Tensleep Canyon.

Literature

Ehrlich, Gretel. *A Match to the Heart: One Woman's Story of Being Struck by Lightning.* New York: Penguin, 1995. Another masterpiece from Ehrlich, this one a memoir about her near death and subsequent reawakening.

Ehrlich, Gretel. *The Solace of Open Spaces.* New York: Viking Penguin, 1985. Arriving in Wyoming to work on a PBS film in 1976, Gretel Ehrlich could barely extricate herself from the independent and hard-won life she created for herself there. This collection of essays is one of the best ever written about Wyoming's landscape, people, and culture.

Proulx, E. Annie. *Close Range: Wyoming Stories.* New York: Scribner, 2000. Pulitzer Prize–winning Proulx is among the state's best-known writers, and for good reason. The tales are dark and the landscape unforgiving, but the characters in this collection are sublime.

Twain, Mark. *Roughing It.* Mineola, NY: Dover, 2007. Published originally in 1872, this nearly 900-page work is an account of Twain's six years in the wild, wooly West.

Wister, Owen. *The Virginian.* Mineola, NY: Dover, 2006. This classic 1902 novel put Wyoming on the map.

Recreation

Birkby, Jeff. *Touring Montana and Wyoming Hot Springs.* Helena: Falcon Publishing, 1999. A comprehensive guide to public and private springs across the region.

Graham, Kenneth Lee. *Fishing Wyoming.* Helena: Falcon, 1998. This comprehensive guide offers advice on where to fish and what to use, and includes waters in Yellowstone and Grand Teton.

Hunger, Bill. *Hiking Wyoming.* Helena and Guilford, CT: Falcon Publishing and Globe Pequot Press, 2008. This guide carefully outlines 110 of Wyoming's best hiking trails.

Lewis, Dan. *Paddle and Portage: The Floater's Guide to Wyoming Rivers.* Douglas, WY: Wyoming Naturalist, 1991. Intended more for less experienced boaters, this book gives an overview of various waters around the state.

Lomax, Becky. *Moon Montana, Wyoming & Idaho Camping.* Berkeley, CA: Avalon Travel, 2010. Hands down the best guide for camping in the region.

Magazines
Wyoming Wildlife (subscriptions 800/710-8345) is an award-winning publication of the Wyoming Game and Fish Department.

Maps
Wyoming Atlas & Gazetteer. Yarmouth, ME: Delorme Publishing, 1998. The most indispensable map book you'll find, these topographic maps cover roads and trails all over the state.

Internet Resources

MONTANA
Travel Montana
www.visitmt.com
Searchable by region and town, places to go, things to do, and a variety of other user-friendly options, the website is superbly organized and easy to navigate.

Travel Montana for Kids
www.montanakids.com
The kids' version of the Travel Montana site is loaded with fun facts, games, and information on the state.

Montana Travel and Tourism Information
www.travelmt.com
Searchable by region, this website provides hotel, restaurant, shopping, recreation, and business information for each city and town in the state.

Winter Montana
www.wintermt.com
Another product of the State of Montana, this site is invaluable for visitors during Montana's longest season.

National Park Service
www.nps.gov
The NPS website is helpful for making plans to visit any of the national parks.

Montana Fish, Wildlife & Parks
www.fwp.mt.gov
This official state site is useful for finding state parks, fishing and hunting information, and other recreational opportunities.

U.S. Forest Service
www.fs.fed.us/r1
The Forest Service's website is helpful for pursuing recreational opportunities—including multiuse trails, campgrounds, and cabin rentals—throughout Montana.

Recreation.gov
www.recreation.gov
This government-run site allows visitors to make reservations at public campgrounds.

Montana Outfitters & Guides Association
www.montanaoutfitters.org
An ideal source for visitors looking for a professionally guided hunting, fishing, or other types of outdoors experiences.

Museums Association of Montana
www.montanamuseums.org
A great database of museums across the state.

Montana Bed-and-Breakfast Association
www.mtbba.com
A useful resource for visitors looking for a B&B experience.

Traveler Updates
www.mdt.mt.gov/travinfo
The best resource for up-to-date road information comes courtesy of the Montana Department of Transportation.

WYOMING
State of Wyoming
www.wyoming.gov
Wyoming's official website offers a wealth of information about the state and its government.

Wyoming Travel and Tourism
www.wyomingtourism.org
The state's comprehensive offering for visitors. I found it difficult to navigate, but most of the major cities in Wyoming also have websites that are more user-friendly.

Wyoming State Parks, Historic Sites, and Trails
www.wyoparks.state.wy.us
Useful information on parks, recreation, and historic preservation.

Wyoming Travel Information
www.wyoroad.info
Up-to-date road information provided by the Wyoming Department of Transportation.

Park Camper
www.parkcamper.com
This site provides interactive camping maps for Grand Teton and Yellowstone National Parks.

National Park Service
www.nps.gov
The NPS website is helpful for making plans to visit any of the national parks.

Recreation.gov
www.recreation.gov
This government-run site allows visitors to make reservations at public campgrounds.

Wyoming Game and Fish Department
www.gf.state.wy.us
The website offers much of what visitors need to know about fishing and hunting in the state.

U.S. Forest Service
www.fs.fed.us
The Forest Service website is helpful for pursuing recreational opportunities—including multiuse trails, campgrounds, and cabin rentals—throughout the eight national forests, recreation areas, and grasslands in Wyoming.

Wyoming Outfitters and Guides Association
www.wyoga.com
A fantastic resource for planning guided outdoor adventures.

Wyoming Dude Ranchers Association
www.wyomingdra.com
An excellent place to look for dude ranch vacations.

Index

arts, the: 443–445
Arts in the Park: 160
Assiniboine tribe: 441
Atlas Bar: 236
Aunt Dofe's Hall of Recent Memory: 225
authors, Montana: 136
auto travel: 447–449
Avalanche Creek Trail: 106
Ayres Natural Bridge: 397

XYZ

List of Maps

Acknowledgments

There is a bottle-top African proverb affixed to my computer screen. It reads, "If you want to go quickly, go alone. If you want to go far, go together." During my two-plus-year-journey to create this book, I have never wanted for company. There are many people to whom I owe an enormous debt of gratitude.

First and foremost, thanks to the indefatigable Aparna Sundaram, my co-everything for as long as I can remember. Without her—and her patient and amazing family—this book would be a mountain of notes and a bowl of salty tears at the edge of my cluttered desk. There simply aren't words enough to praise her diligent efforts. Thanks also to Brian Hurlbut, whose natural talent and invaluable insight pushed the project forward when I needed it most, and to my steadfast and generous editors, Tiffany Watson and Kevin McLain, and the whole team at Avalon Travel for taking the leap and working so hard to make me look good.

I am forever grateful to the talented Donnie Sexton for the use of her gorgeous images. And thanks to Lori Hogan from Wyoming Travel and Tourism, who was instrumental in getting some wonderful photos into the book.

I am profoundly grateful to those who have shared the trail with me the last 19 years as a Westerner, and longer. My dear friend and colleague, Seabring Davis was always lighting the way, and helping me to laugh in the murkiest parts. The phenomenally talented Annie Sherwood's own spirit of adventure fueled countless unforgettable exploits. Dr. Jon Awerbuck endured my most misguided efforts at guiding with tremendous grace and humor. My wonderful Norwegian family—the Sæterens and Stensruds—offered their love, support, and constant willingness to hit the open road. I have to thank my mom for seeing the cowgirl in me at 8, and supporting my dreams at every turn. Dad and Carol were my constant champions, understanding wholeheartedly why I love the West. Mary, Wendy, and Isabelle pledged their unflagging love and encouragement. And thanks to Chip, the world's greatest brother and my hero, for boiling life's most serious questions down to this: "Would you rather date a cowboy or a hippie?" I love you all.

And last but certainly not least, I am grateful to the most precious little family on the planet, and all that matters: Bjørn, Sissel, and Siri. You are what I love most about this spectacular place. Sharing the adventure and bliss with the three of you is, and forever will be, my life's greatest blessing.

www.moon.com

DESTINATIONS | ACTIVITIES | BLOGS | MAPS | BOOKS

MOON.COM is ready to help plan your next trip! Filled with fresh trip ideas and strategies, author interviews, informative travel blogs, a detailed map library, and descriptions of all the Moon guidebooks, Moon.com is all you need to get out and explore the world—or even places in your own backyard. While at Moon.com, sign up for our monthly e-newsletter for updates on new releases, travel tips, and expert advice from our on-the-go Moon authors. As always, when you travel with Moon, expect an experience that is uncommon and truly unique.

MOON IS ON FACEBOOK—BECOME A FAN!
JOIN THE MOON PHOTO GROUP ON FLICKR

MAP SYMBOLS

▬▬▬	Expressway	【	Highlight	✗	Airfield	⚑	Golf Course
▬▬▬	Primary Road	○	City/Town	✈	Airport	🅿	Parking Area
▬▬▬	Secondary Road	◉	State Capital	▲	Mountain	⬟	Archaeological Site
▬▬▬	Unpaved Road	⊛	National Capital	✛	Unique Natural Feature	⬗	Church
------	Trail	★	Point of Interest			⬛	Gas Station
··········	Ferry	•	Accommodation	🕊	Waterfall	◌	Glacier
▬▬▬	Railroad	▼	Restaurant/Bar	▲	Park		Mangrove
▬▬▬	Pedestrian Walkway	■	Other Location	🚩	Trailhead		Reef
⊞⊞⊞	Stairs	Λ	Campground	🎿	Skiing Area		Swamp

CONVERSION TABLES

°C = (°F − 32) / 1.8
°F = (°C x 1.8) + 32
1 inch = 2.54 centimeters (cm)
1 foot = 0.304 meters (m)
1 yard = 0.914 meters
1 mile = 1.6093 kilometers (km)
1 km = 0.6214 miles
1 fathom = 1.8288 m
1 chain = 20.1168 m
1 furlong = 201.168 m
1 acre = 0.4047 hectares
1 sq km = 100 hectares
1 sq mile = 2.59 square km
1 ounce = 28.35 grams
1 pound = 0.4536 kilograms
1 short ton = 0.90718 metric ton
1 short ton = 2,000 pounds
1 long ton = 1.016 metric tons
1 long ton = 2,240 pounds
1 metric ton = 1,000 kilograms
1 quart = 0.94635 liters
1 US gallon = 3.7854 liters
1 Imperial gallon = 4.5459 liters
1 nautical mile = 1.852 km

°FAHRENHEIT | °CELSIUS

230 — — 110
220 — — 100 WATER BOILS
210 —
200 — — 90
190 —
180 — — 80
170 —
160 — — 70
150 —
140 — — 60
130 —
120 — — 50
110 —
100 — — 40
90 —
80 — — 30
70 — — 20
60 —
50 — — 10
40 —
30 — — 0 WATER FREEZES
20 —
10 — — -10
0 —
-10 — — -20
-20 — — -30
-30 —
-40 — — -40

INCH: 0 1 2 3 4

CM: 0 1 2 3 4 5 6 7 8 9 10

MOON MONTANA & WYOMING

Avalon Travel
a member of the Perseus Books Group
1700 Fourth Street
Berkeley, CA 94710, USA
www.moon.com

Editors: Tiffany Watson, Kevin McLain
Series Manager: Kathryn Ettinger
Copy Editor: Christopher Church
Graphics and Production Coordinator: Darren Alessi
Cover Designer: Darren Alessi
Map Editor: Brice Ticen
Cartographers: Chris Henrick, Kat Bennett,
  Chris Markiewicz
Proofreader: Kia Wang Nevarez
Indexer: Rachel Kuhn

ISBN: 978-1-59880-352-5
ISSN: 2159-8517

Printing History
1st Edition – May 2011
5 4 3 2 1

Front cover photo: © Reflex Stock
Title page photo: © Donnie Sexton
Interior color photos: Page 10, 11 © Donnie Sexton; page 12 (inset) © Donnie Sexton, (bottom) © Osamu Hoshino/Wyoming Travel & Tourism; page 13 (upper left, upper right, and lower right) © Donnie Sexton, (lower left) © Carter G. Walker; page 14 © Donnie Sexton; page 16 © Wyoming Travel & Tourism; page 18 © Carter G. Walker; page 21 © Osamu Hoshino/Wyoming Travel & Tourism; page 22 © Carter G. Walker; page 26, 28 © Wyoming Travel & Tourism

Printed in Canada by Friesens

KEEPING CURRENT

If you have a favorite gem you'd like to see included in the next edition, or see anything that needs updating, clarification, or correction, please drop us a line. Send your comments via email to feedback@moon.com, or use the address above.